M

D0516045

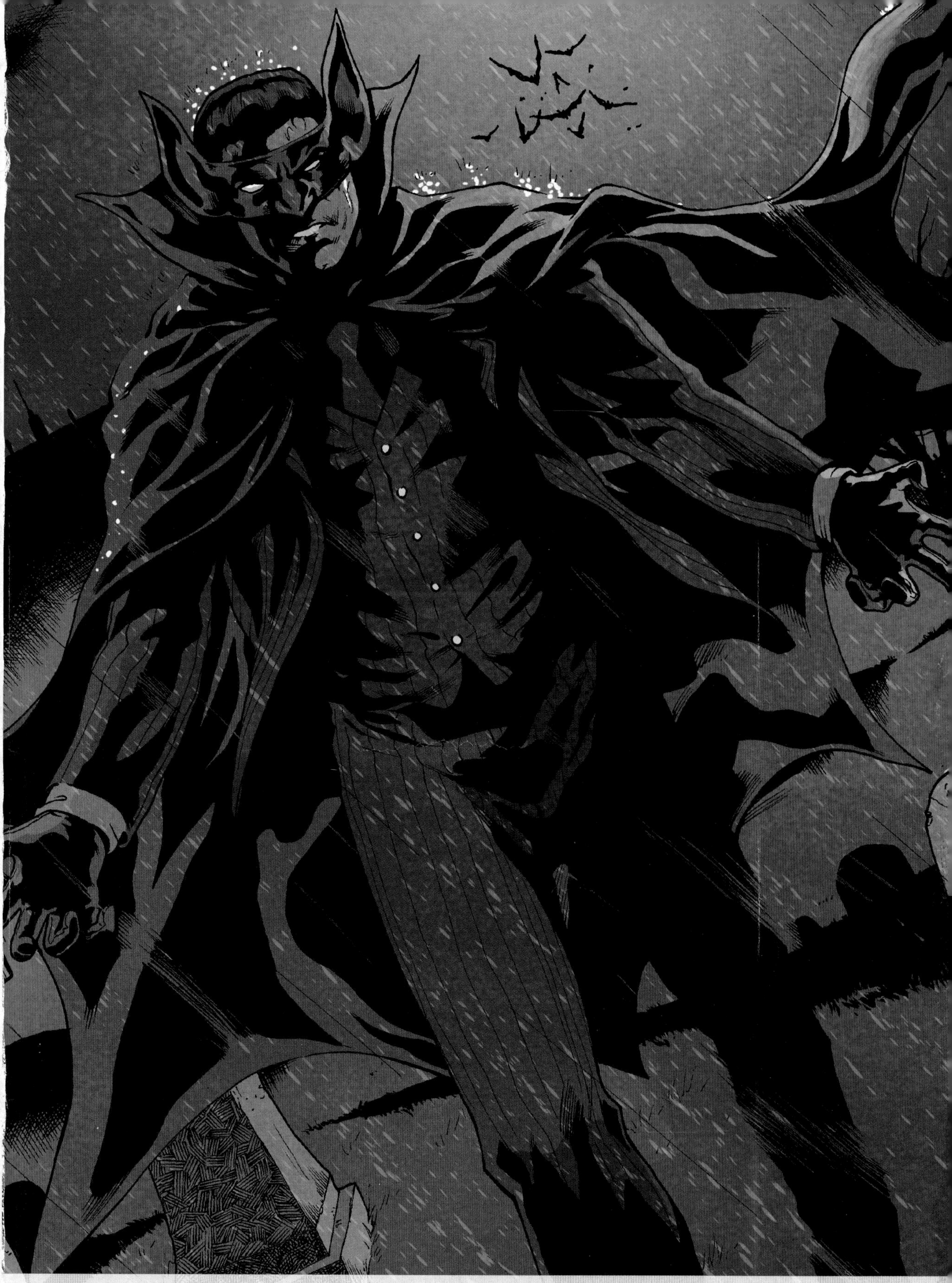

BATMAN THE RETURN OF BRUCE WAYNE

THE DELUXE EDITION

Written by
Grant Morrison

Art by
Chris Sprouse
Frazer Irving
Yanick Paquette
Georges Jeanty
Ryan Sook
Lee Garbett
Karl Story
Michel Lacombe
Waldon Wong
Mick Gray
Pere Perez
Alejandro Sicat

Colored by
Guy Major
Nathan Fairbairn
Tony Aviña
José Villarrubia

Lettered by
Jared K. Fletcher
Travis Lanham

Cover Art by
Andy Kubert

Original Series Covers by
Andy Kubert
Chris Sprouse
Frazer Irving
Yanick Paquette
Cameron Stewart
Ryan Sook
Lee Garbett
Bill Sienkiewicz

Batman created by
Bob Kane

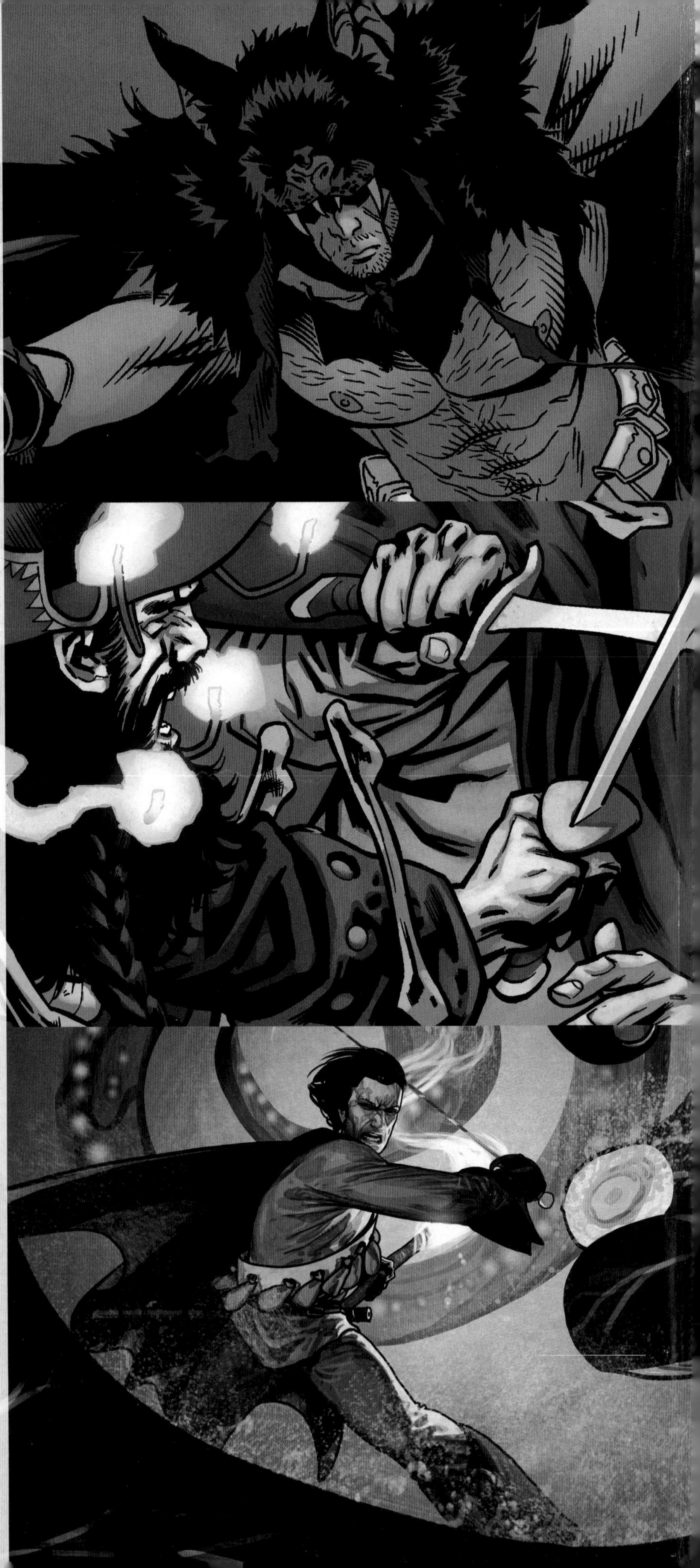

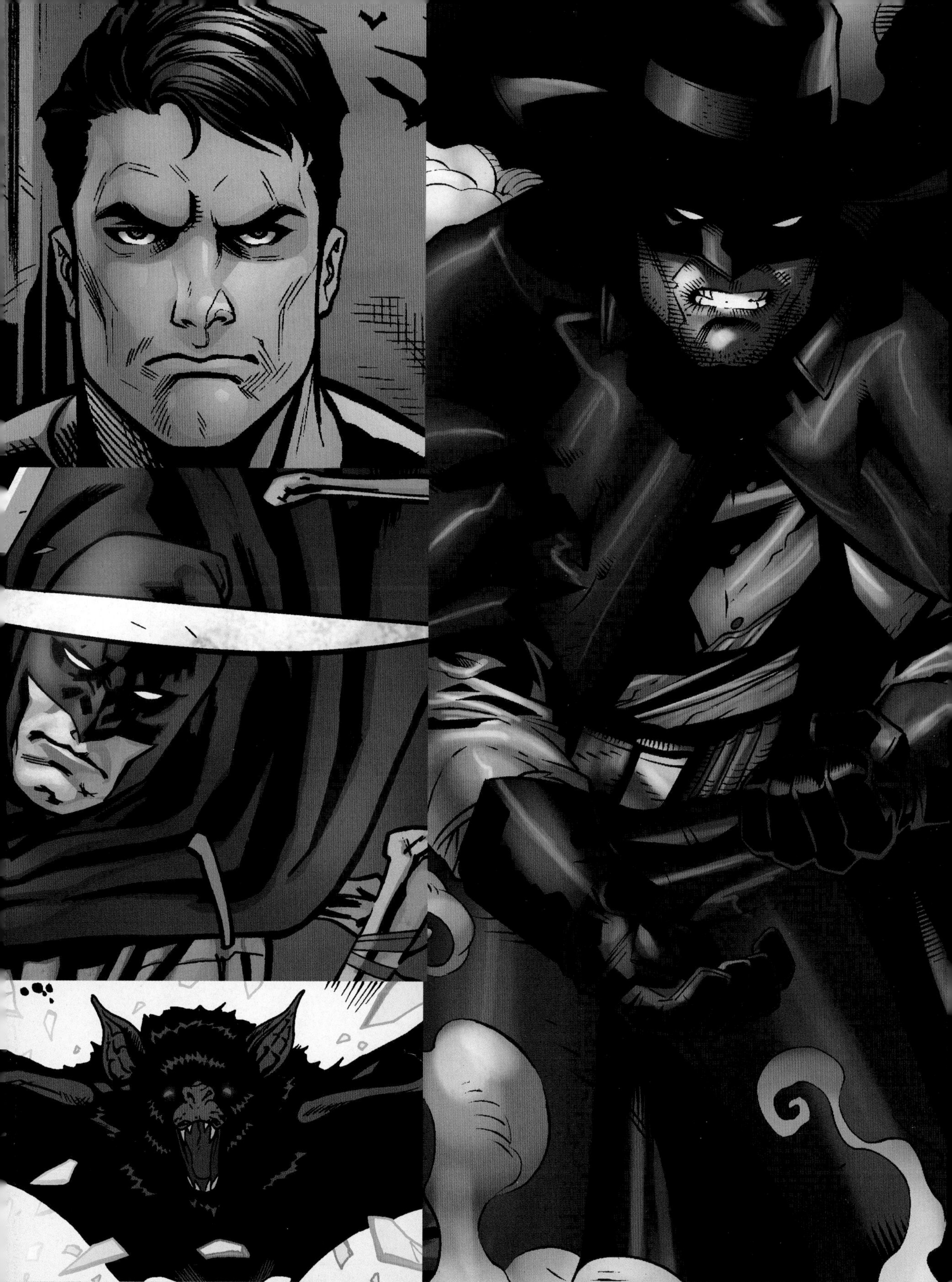

BATMAN THE RETURN OF BRUCE WAYNE

THE DELUXE EDITION

Mike Marts   Editor — Original Series

Janelle Siegel   Associate Editor — Original Series

Bob Harras   Group Editor — Collected Editions

Scott Nybakken   Editor

Robbin Brosterman   Design Director — Books

Louis Prandi   Art Director

DC COMICS

Diane Nelson   President

Dan DiDio and Jim Lee   Co-Publishers

Geoff Johns   Chief Creative Officer

Patrick Caldon   EVP — Finance and Administration

John Rood   EVP — Sales, Marketing and Business Development

Amy Genkins   SVP — Business and Legal Affairs

Steve Rotterdam   SVP — Sales and Marketing

John Cunningham   VP — Marketing

Terri Cunningham   VP — Managing Editor

Alison Gill   VP — Manufacturing

David Hyde   VP — Publicity

Sue Pohja   VP — Book Trade Sales

Alysse Soll   VP — Advertising and Custom Publishing

Bob Wayne   VP — Sales

Mark Chiarello   Art Director

Cover color by Brad Anderson.

BATMAN: THE RETURN OF BRUCE WAYNE — THE DELUXE EDITION

DC Comics
1700 Broadway, New York, NY 10019
A Warner Bros. Entertainment Company.
Printed by RR Donnelley, Salem, VA, USA 1/5/11. First Printing.
ISBN: 978-1-4012-2968-9

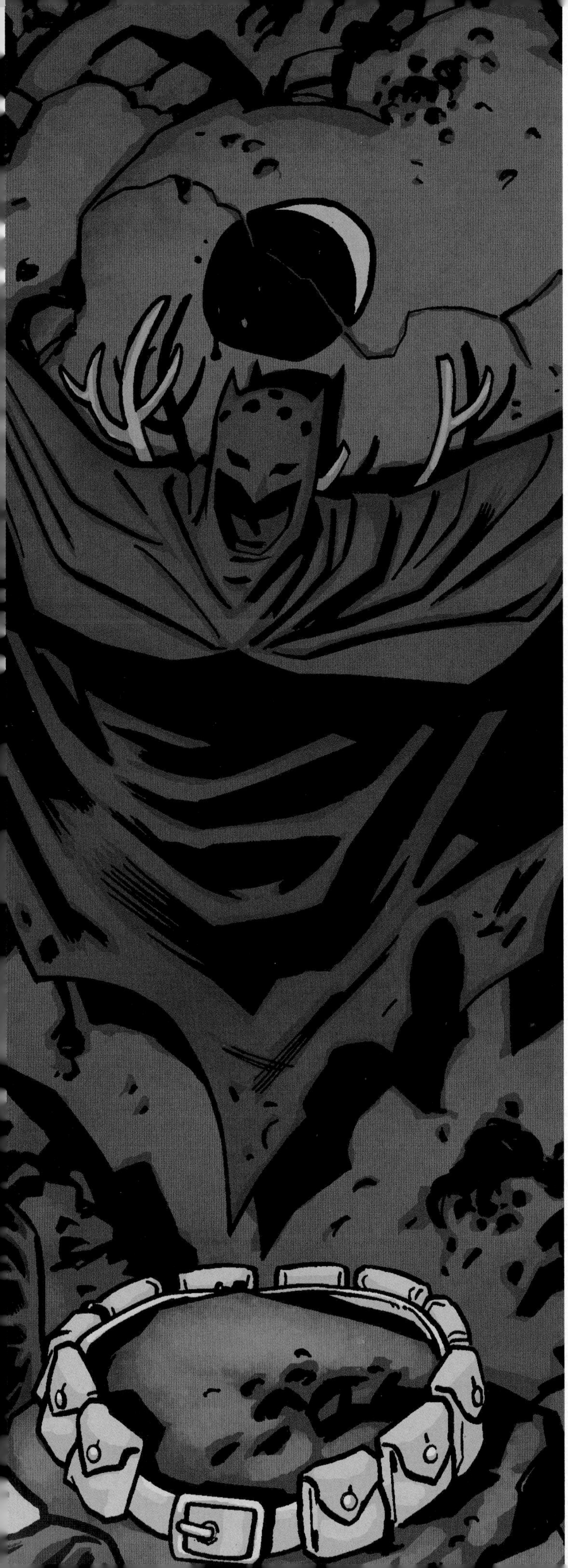

THE RETURN OF BRUCE WAYNE

"GOD BE GOOD TO THE MAN iN BLACK
WHO GUARDS THE DOOR AND KEEPS THAT KEY.

"BUT SPARE ME HiS DREAD RETURN
AND WHAT MUST COME NEXT..."

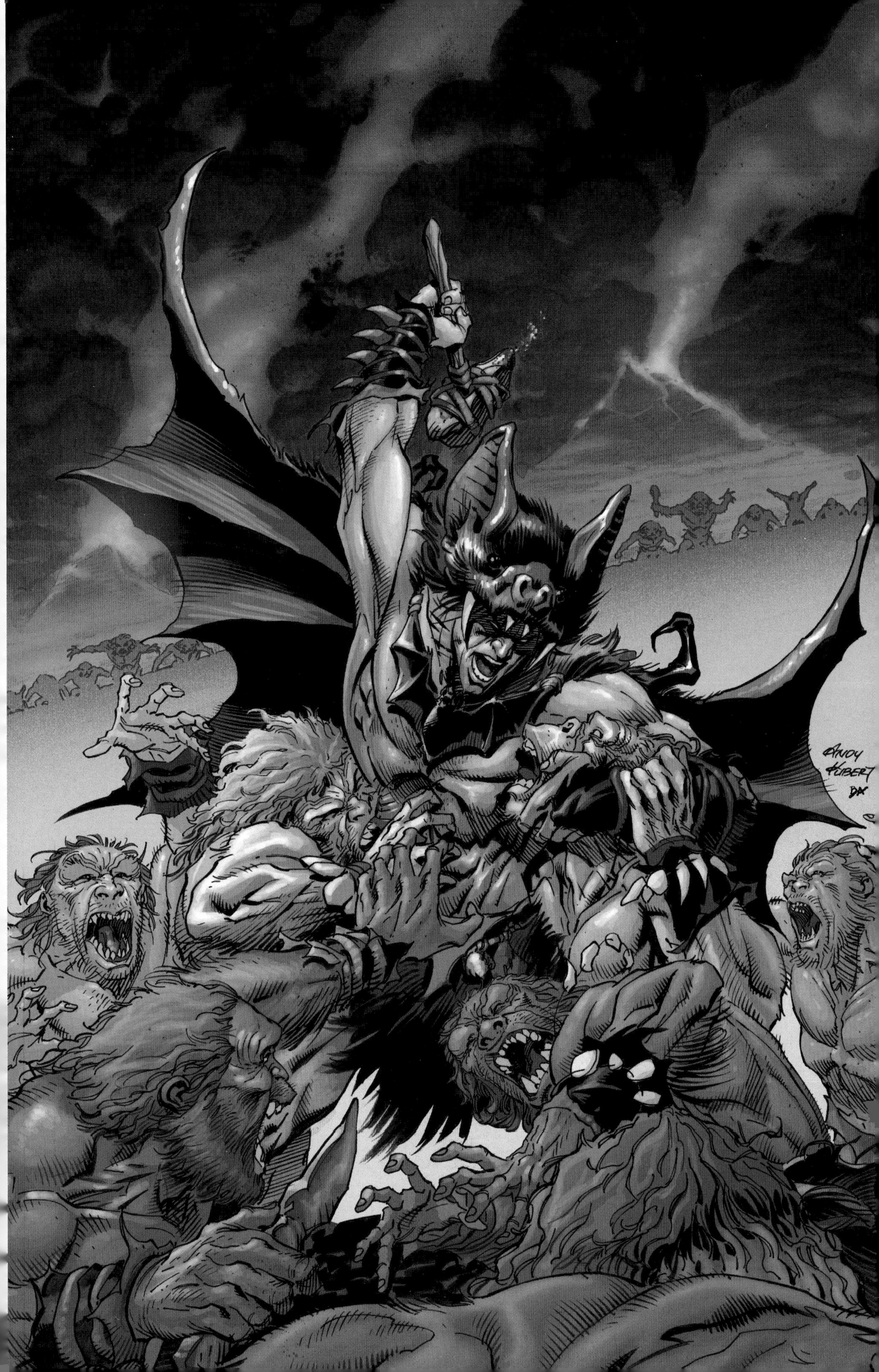
ANDY
KUBERT
DAX

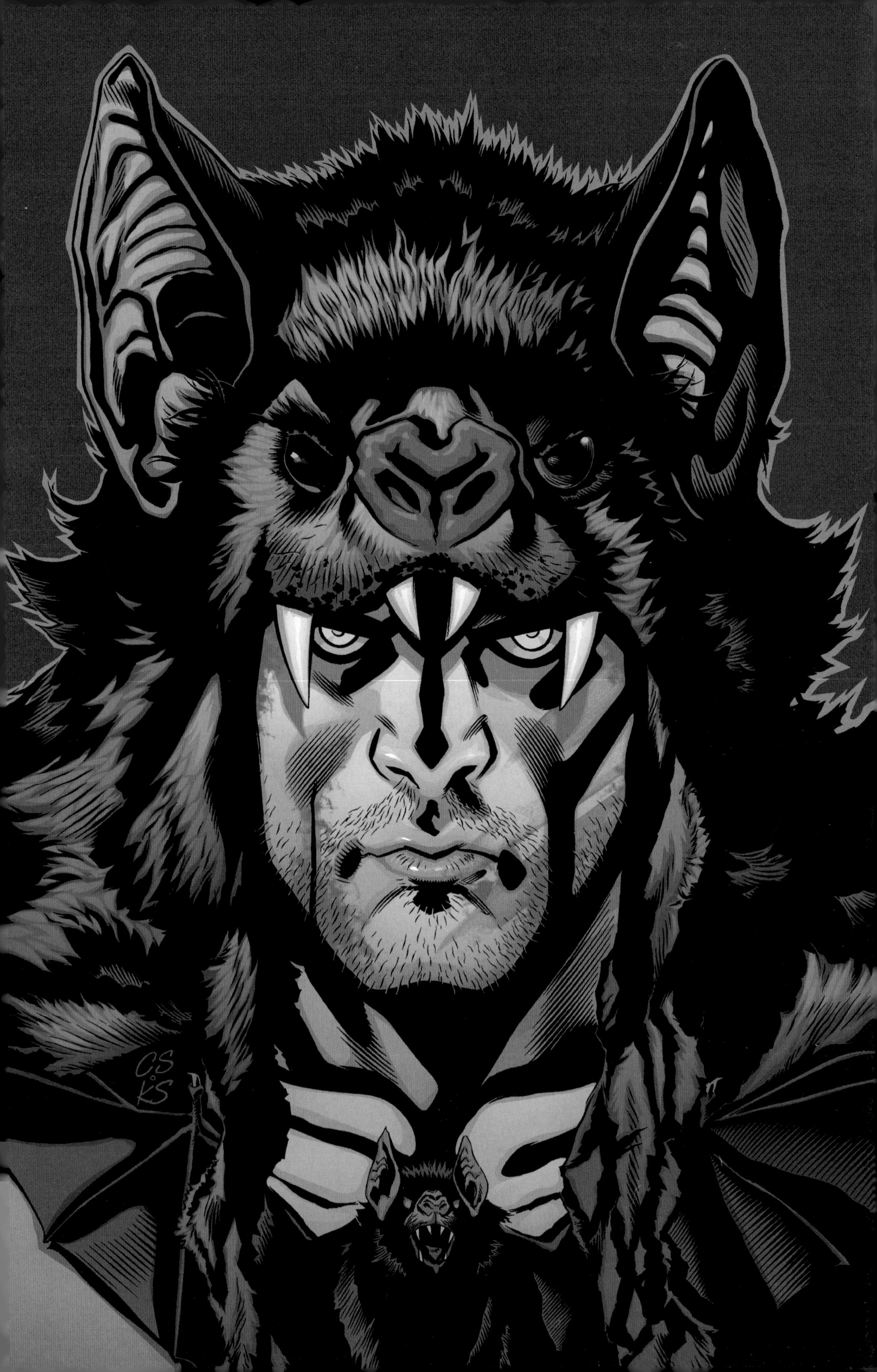

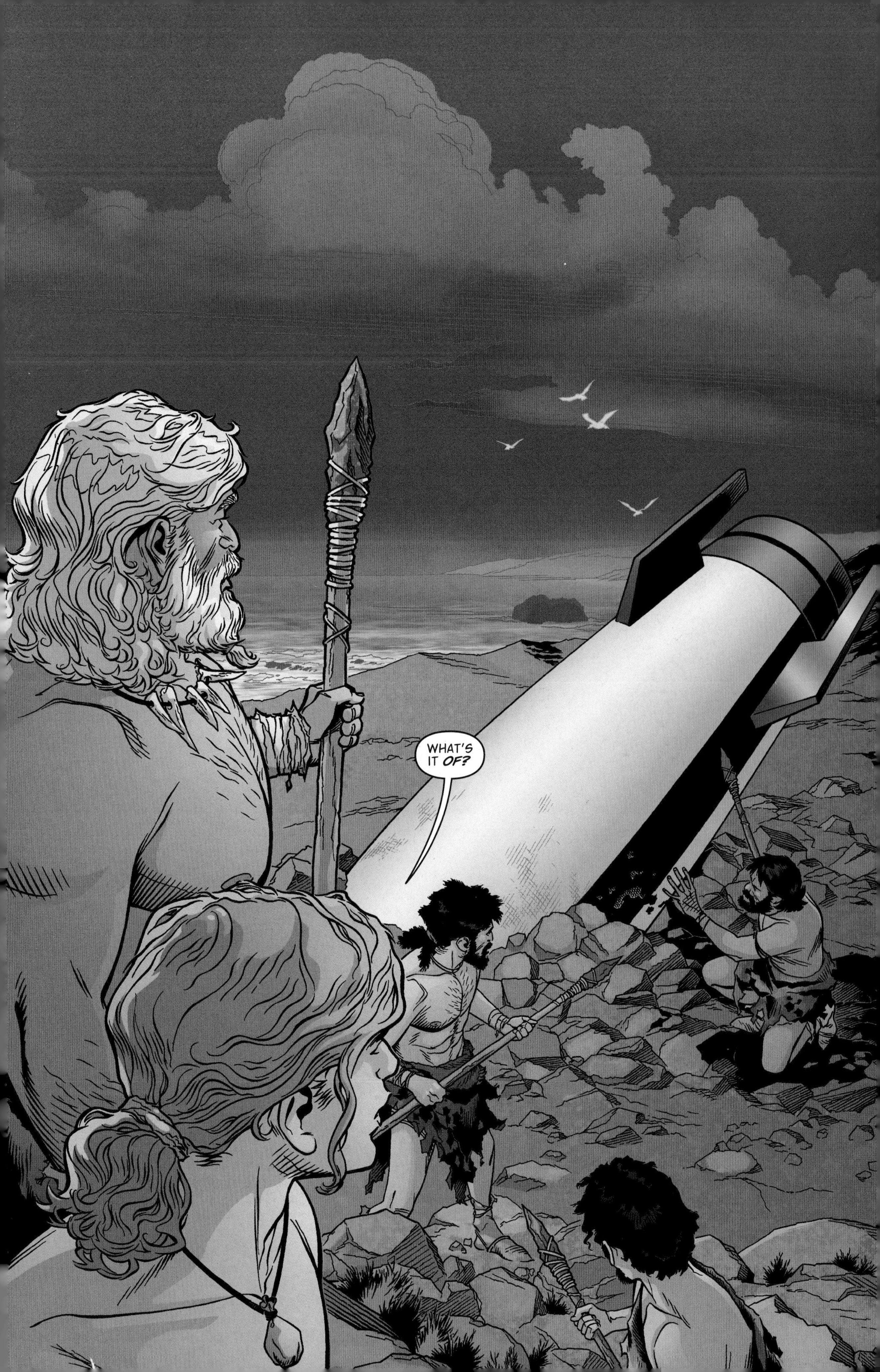
WHAT'S IT OF?

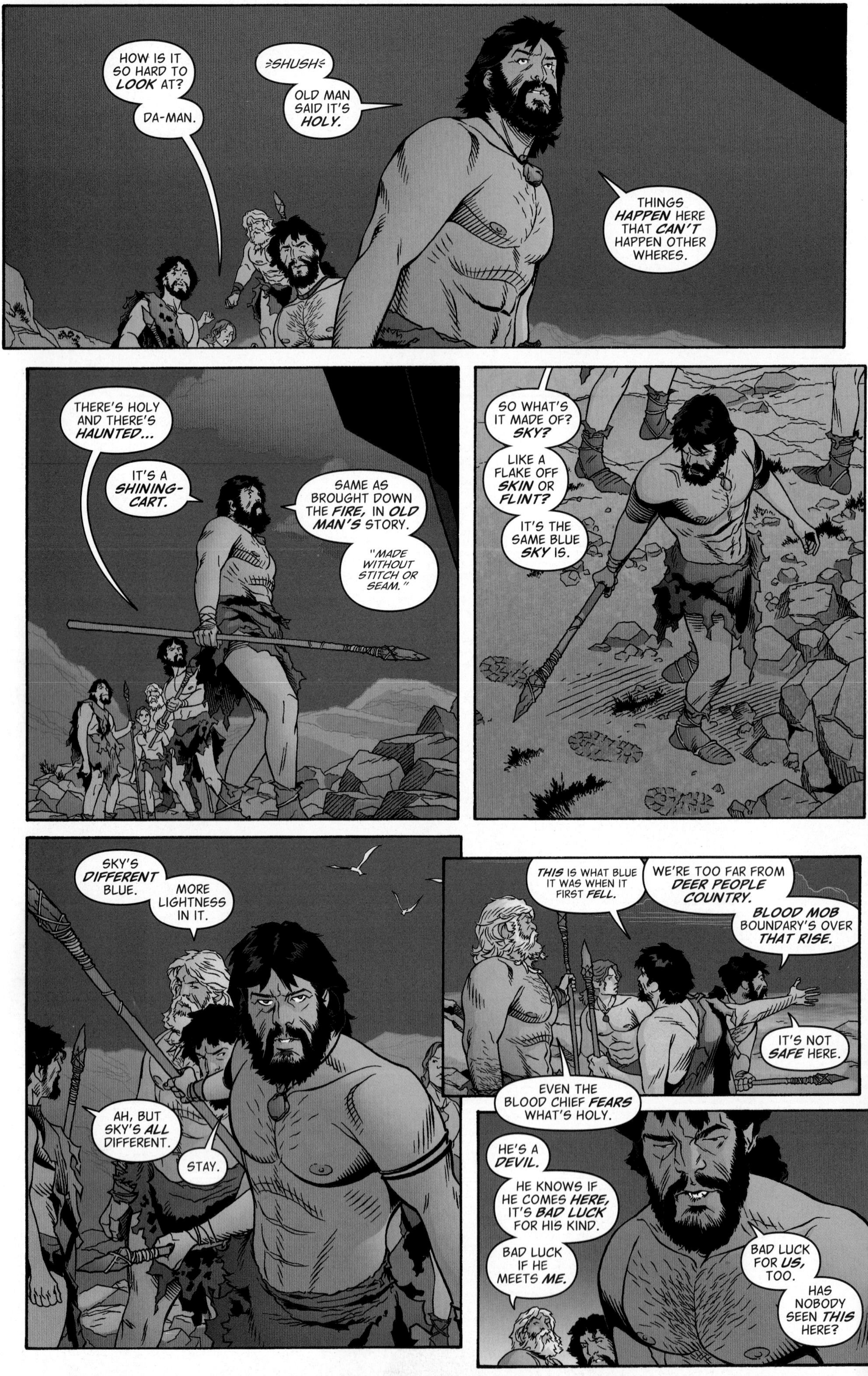

HOW IS IT SO HARD TO LOOK AT?
DA-MAN.
SHUSH
OLD MAN SAID IT'S HOLY.
THINGS HAPPEN HERE THAT CAN'T HAPPEN OTHER WHERES.
THERE'S HOLY AND THERE'S HAUNTED...
IT'S A SHINING-CART.
SAME AS BROUGHT DOWN THE FIRE, IN OLD MAN'S STORY.
"MADE WITHOUT STITCH OR SEAM."
SO WHAT'S IT MADE OF? SKY?
LIKE A FLAKE OFF SKIN OR FLINT?
IT'S THE SAME BLUE SKY IS.
SKY'S DIFFERENT BLUE.
MORE LIGHTNESS IN IT.
AH, BUT SKY'S ALL DIFFERENT.
STAY.
THIS IS WHAT BLUE IT WAS WHEN IT FIRST FELL.
WE'RE TOO FAR FROM DEER PEOPLE COUNTRY.
BLOOD MOB BOUNDARY'S OVER THAT RISE.
IT'S NOT SAFE HERE.
EVEN THE BLOOD CHIEF FEARS WHAT'S HOLY.
HE'S A DEVIL.
HE KNOWS IF HE COMES HERE, IT'S BAD LUCK FOR HIS KIND.
BAD LUCK IF HE MEETS ME.
BAD LUCK FOR US, TOO.
HAS NOBODY SEEN THIS HERE?

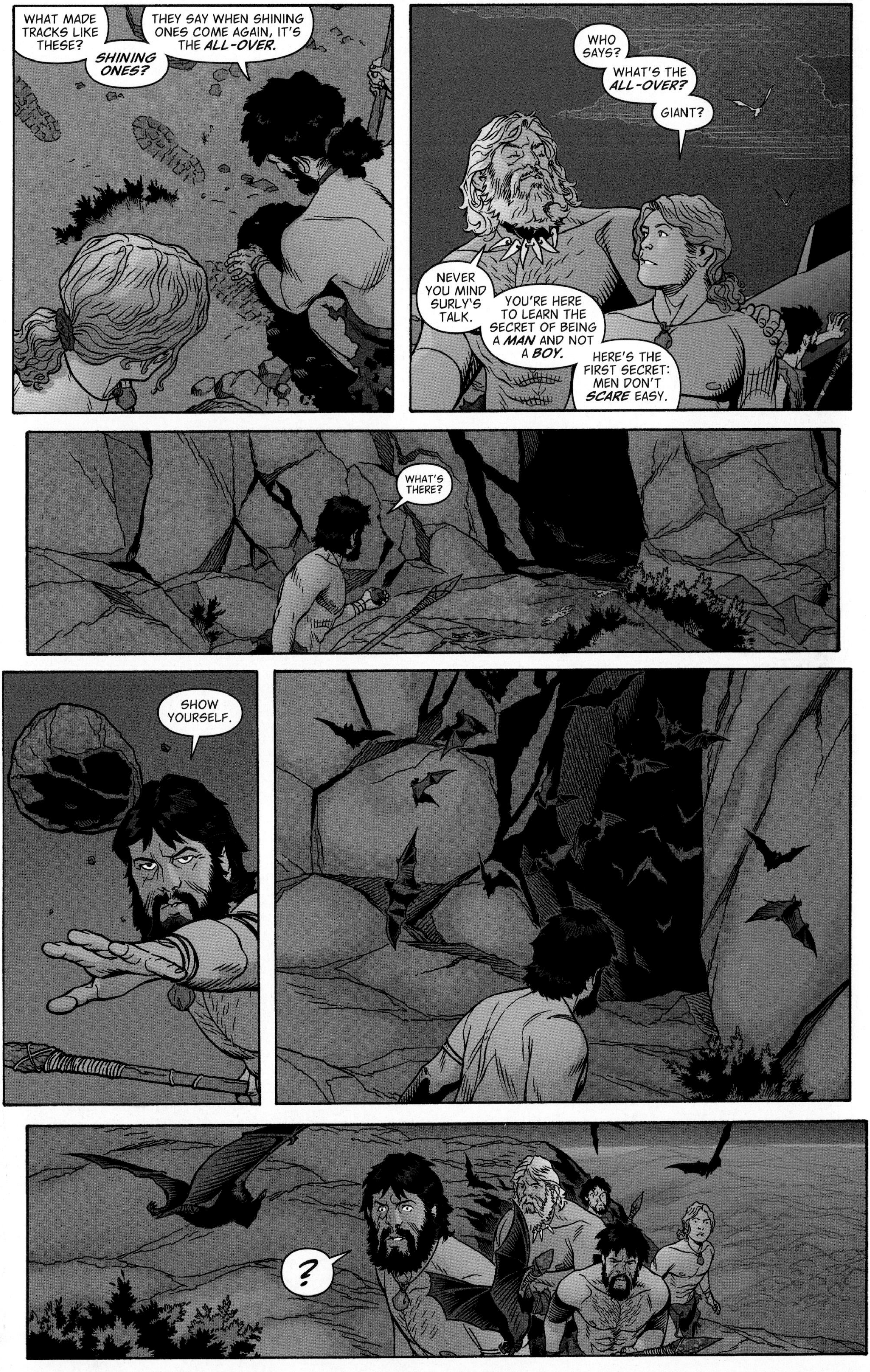
WHAT MADE TRACKS LIKE THESE?
THEY SAY WHEN SHINING ONES COME AGAIN, IT'S THE ALL-OVER.
SHINING ONES?
WHO SAYS?
WHAT'S THE ALL-OVER?
GIANT?
NEVER YOU MIND SURLY'S TALK.
YOU'RE HERE TO LEARN THE SECRET OF BEING A MAN AND NOT A BOY.
HERE'S THE FIRST SECRET: MEN DON'T SCARE EASY.
WHAT'S THERE?
SHOW YOURSELF.
?

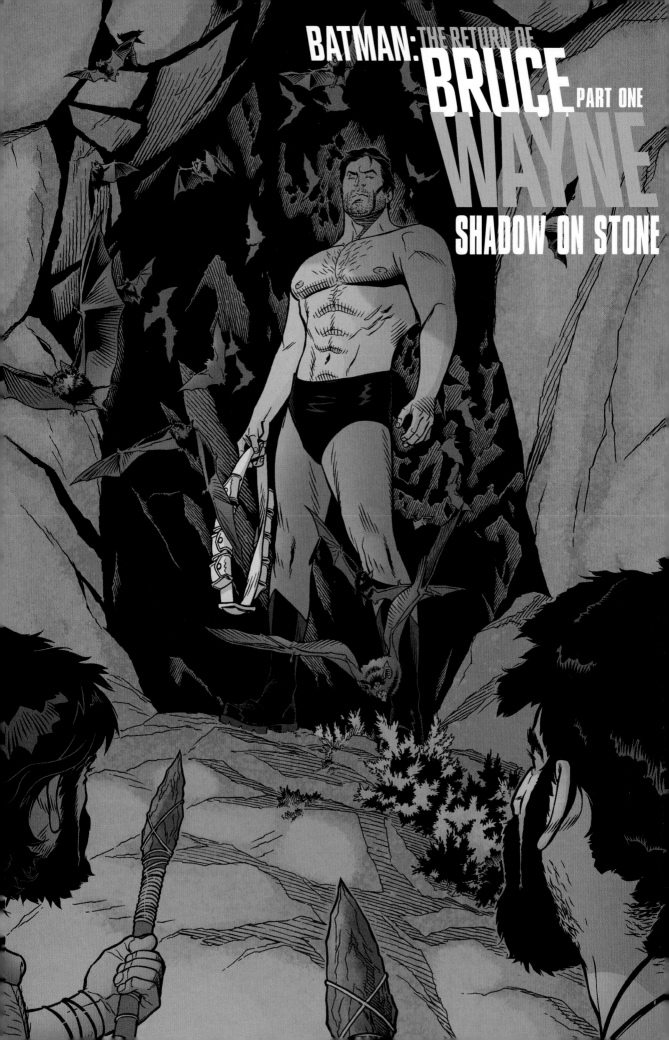

BATMAN: THE RETURN OF BRUCE WAYNE PART ONE

SHADOW ON STONE

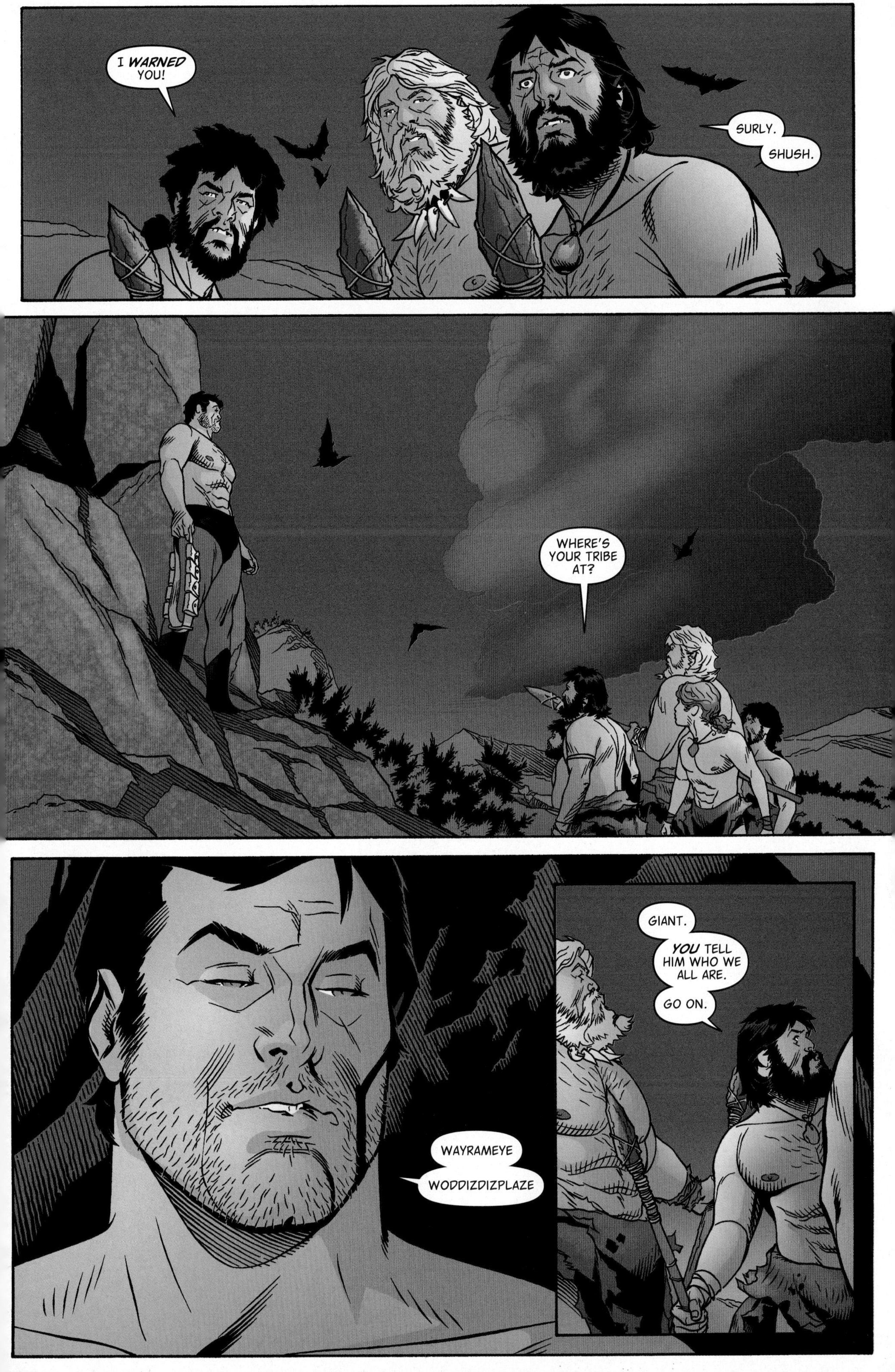
I *WARNED* YOU!
SURLY.
SHUSH.
WHERE'S YOUR TRIBE AT?
WAYRAMEYE
WODDIZDIZPLAZE
GIANT.
YOU TELL HIM WHO WE ALL ARE.
GO ON.

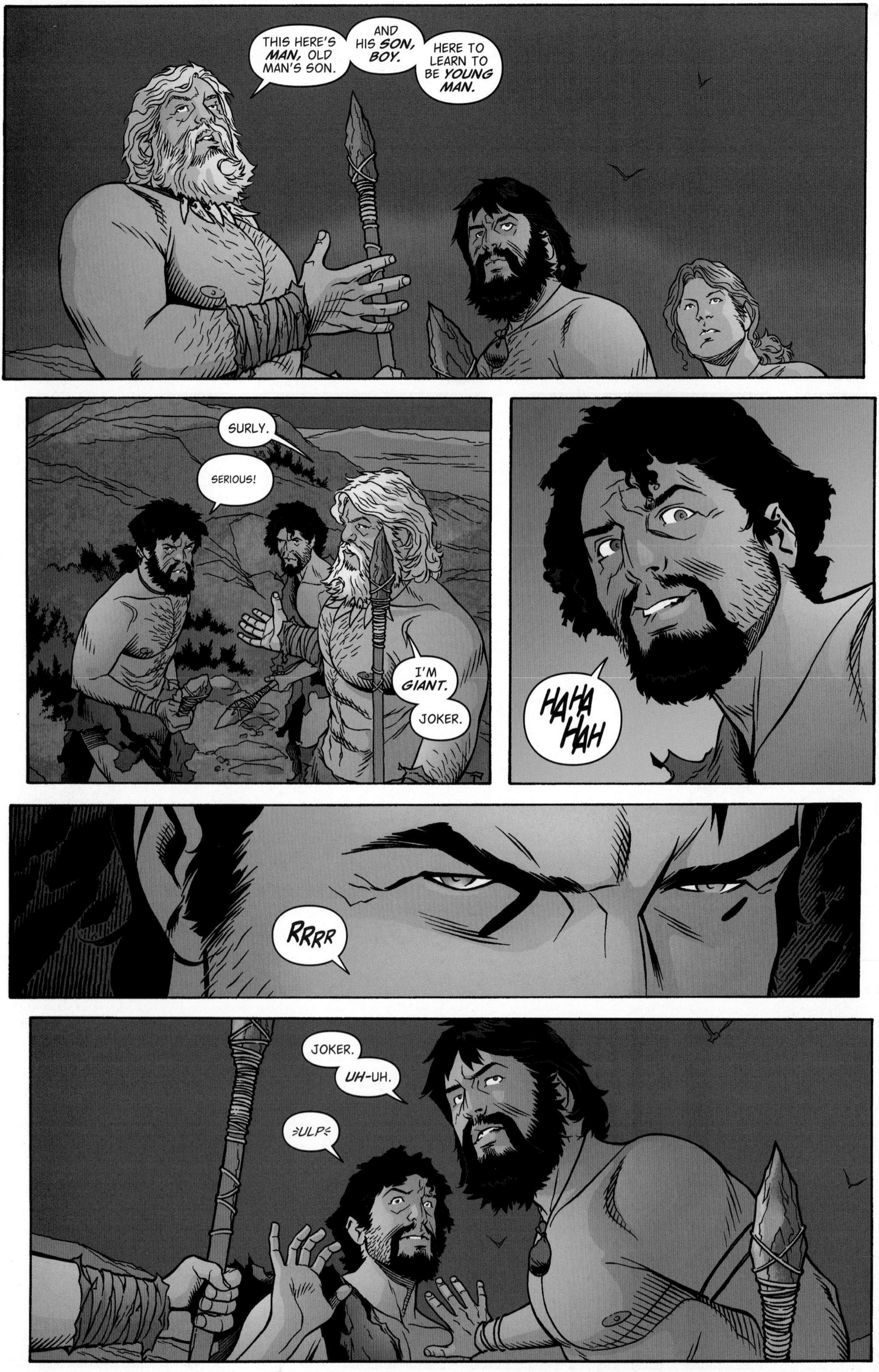
THIS HERE'S *MAN,* OLD MAN'S SON.
AND HIS *SON, BOY.*
HERE TO LEARN TO BE *YOUNG MAN.*
SURLY.
SERIOUS!
I'M *GIANT.*
JOKER.
HAHAHAH
RRRR
JOKER.
UH-UH.
ULP

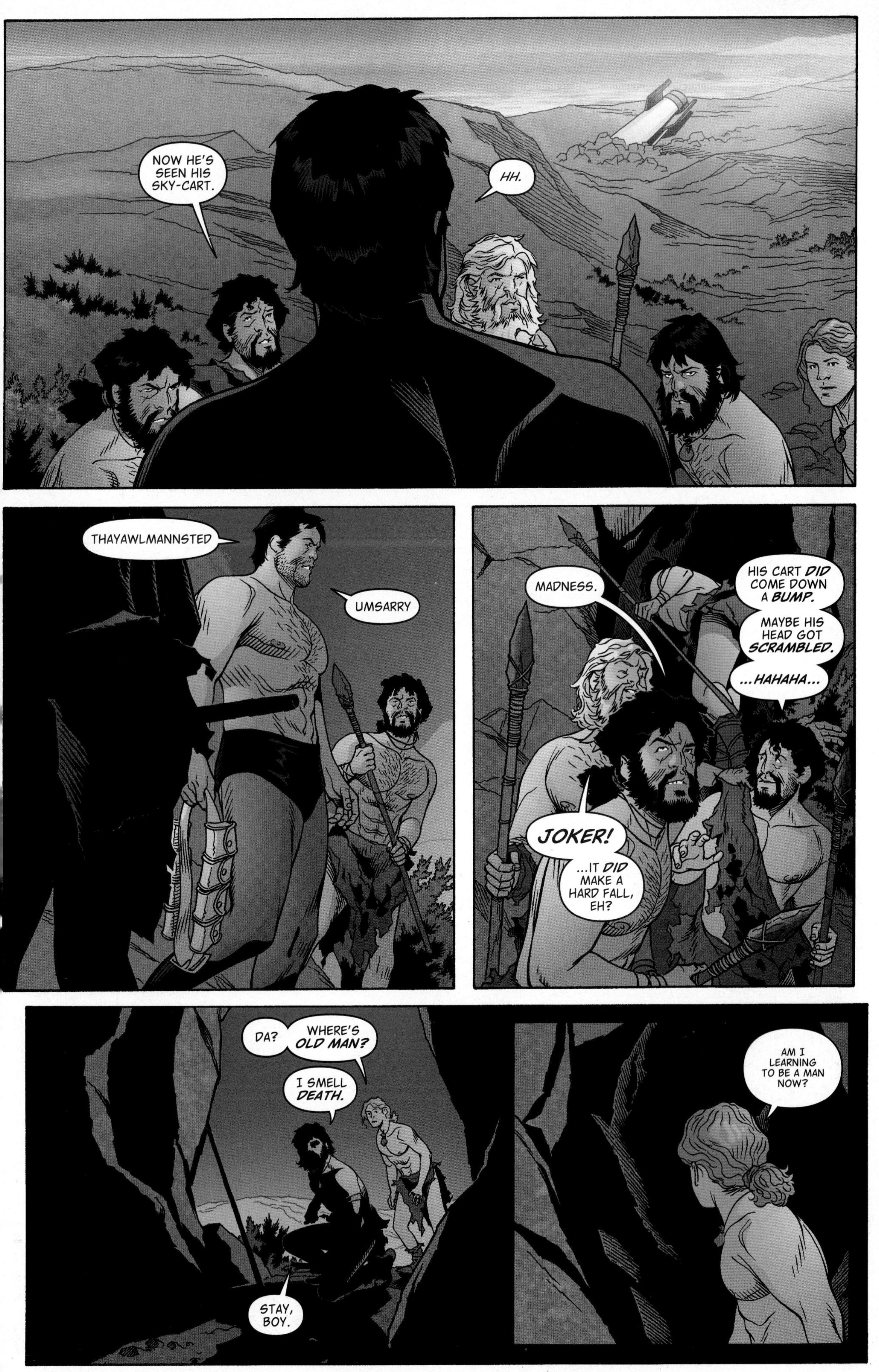
NOW HE'S SEEN HIS SKY-CART.
HH.
THAYAWLMANNSTED
UMSARRY
MADNESS.
HIS CART DID COME DOWN A BUMP.
MAYBE HIS HEAD GOT SCRAMBLED.
...HAHAHA...
JOKER!
...IT DID MAKE A HARD FALL, EH?
DA?
WHERE'S OLD MAN?
I SMELL DEATH.
STAY, BOY.
AM I LEARNING TO BE A MAN NOW?

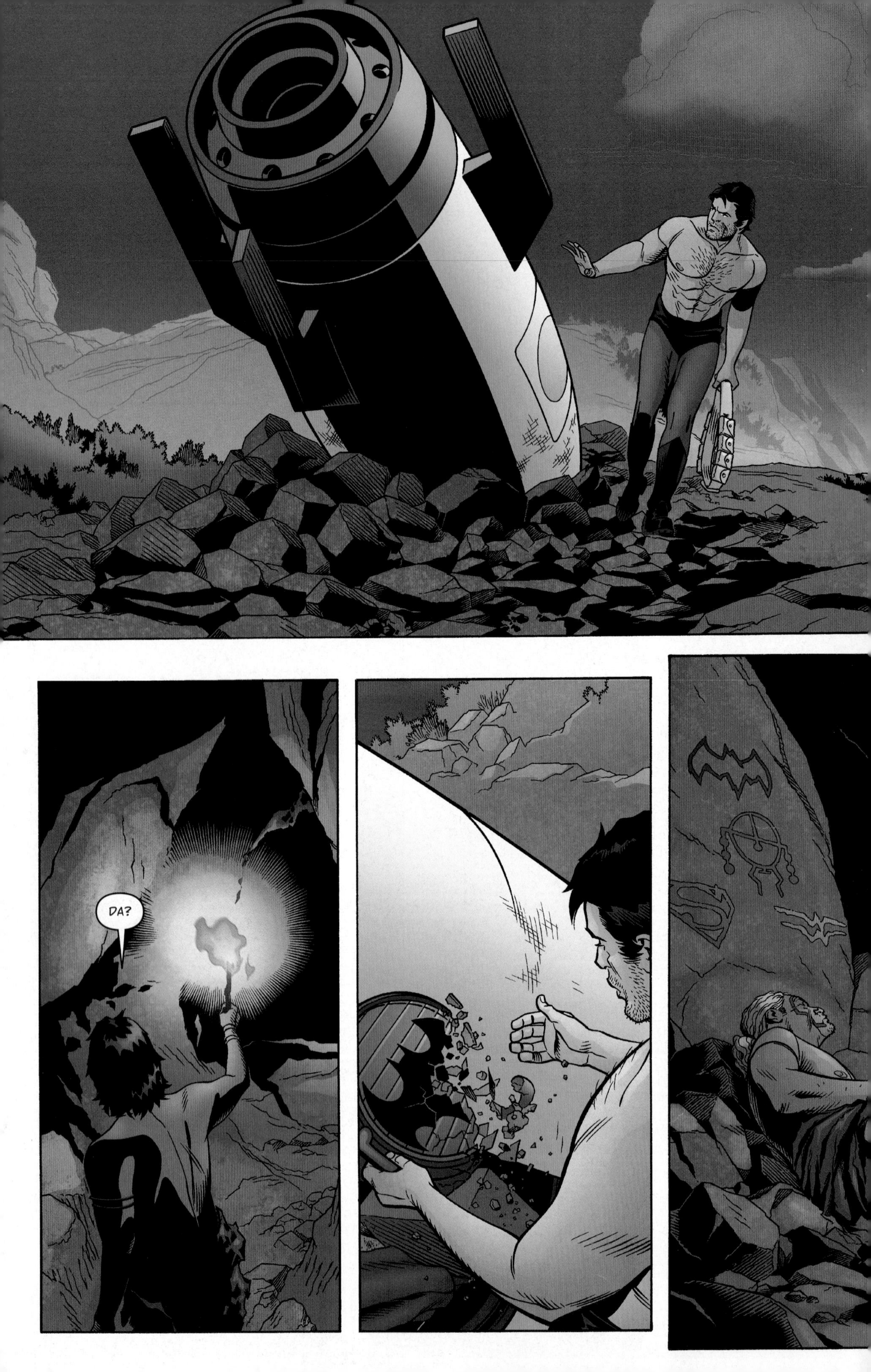
DA?

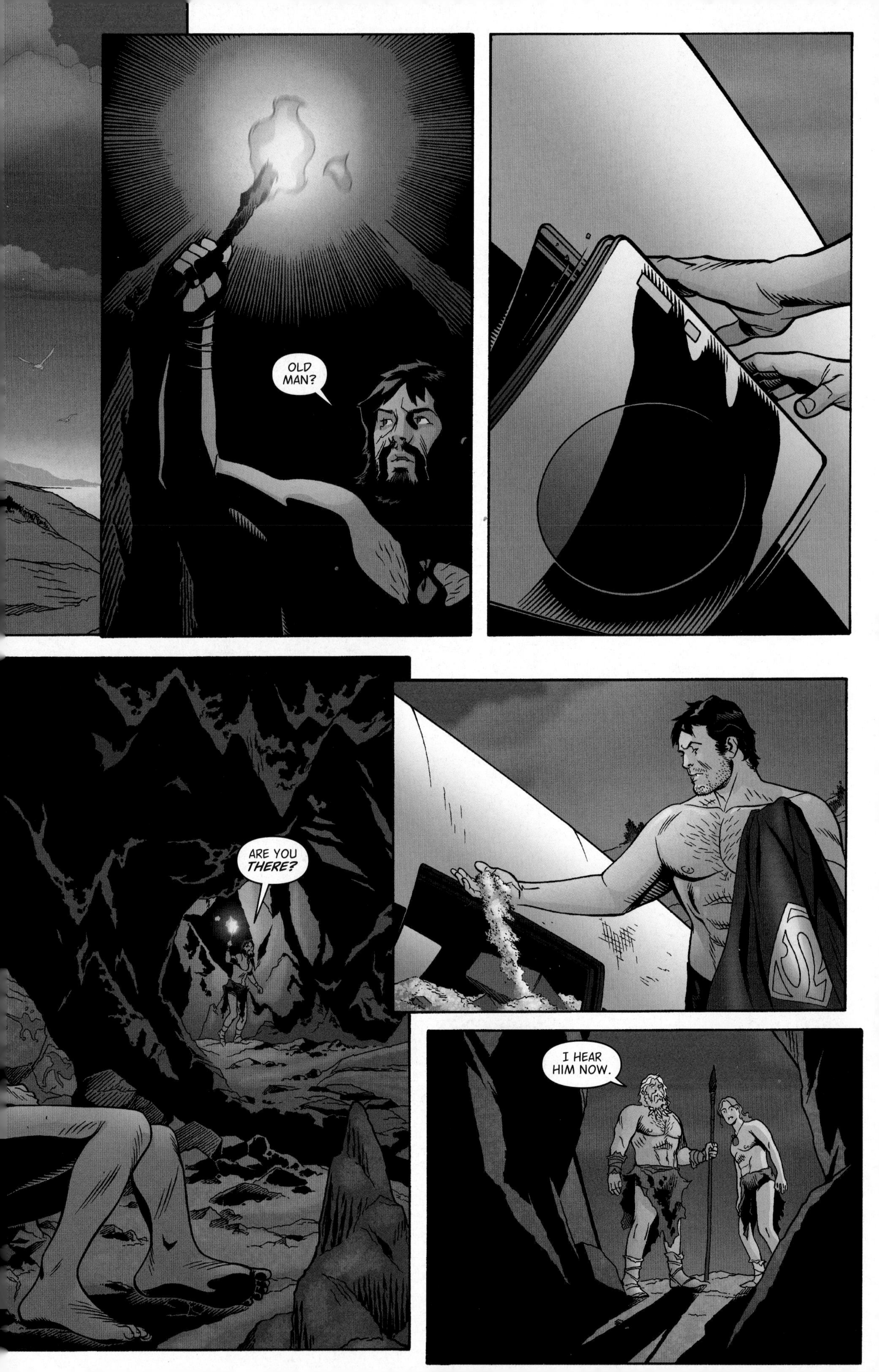
OLD MAN?
ARE YOU THERE?
I HEAR HIM NOW.

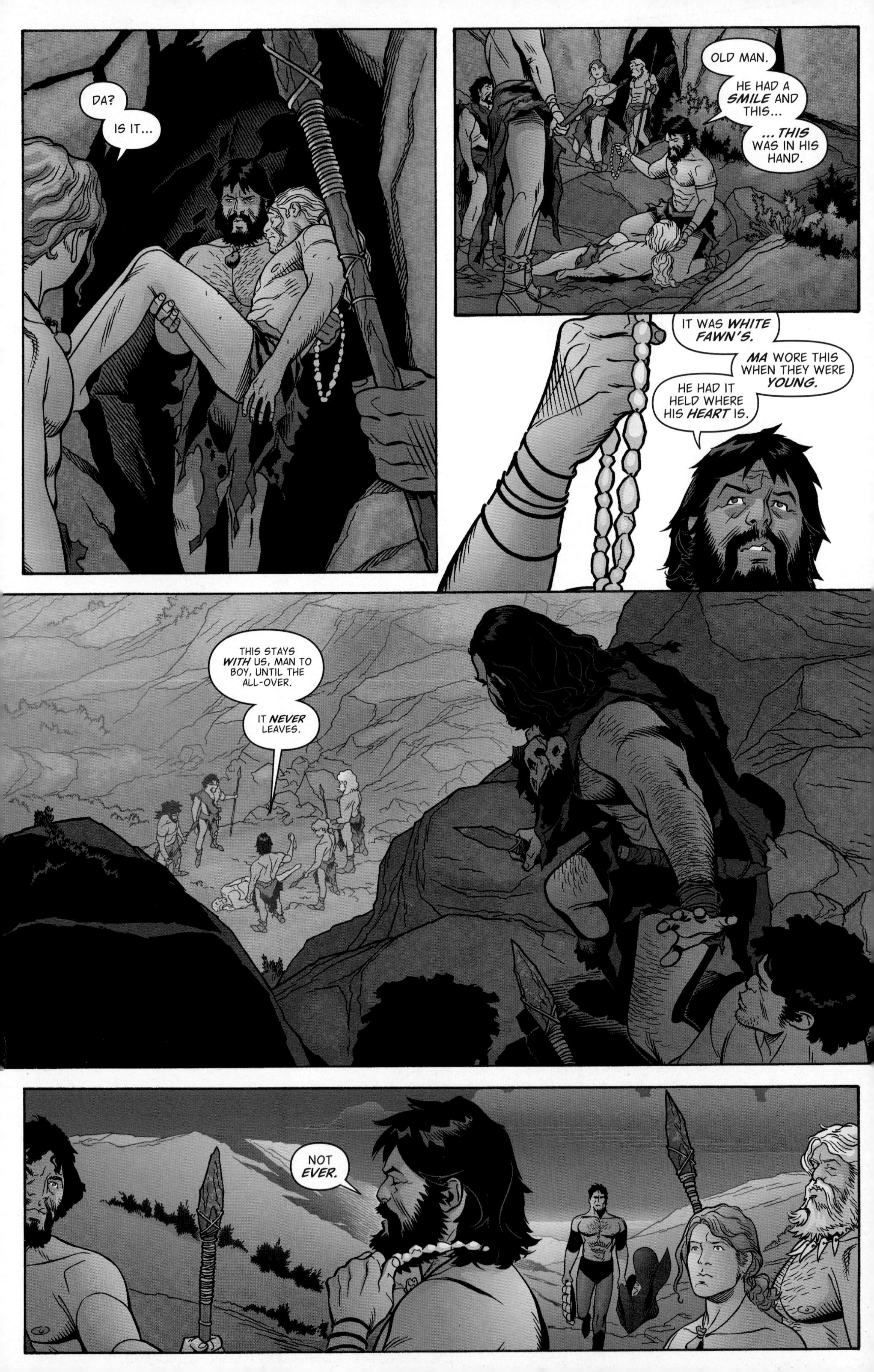
DA?
IS IT...
OLD MAN.
HE HAD A SMILE AND THIS...
...THIS WAS IN HIS HAND.
IT WAS WHITE FAWN'S.
MA WORE THIS WHEN THEY WERE YOUNG.
HE HAD IT HELD WHERE HIS HEART IS.
THIS STAYS WITH US, MAN TO BOY, UNTIL THE ALL-OVER.
IT NEVER LEAVES.
NOT EVER.

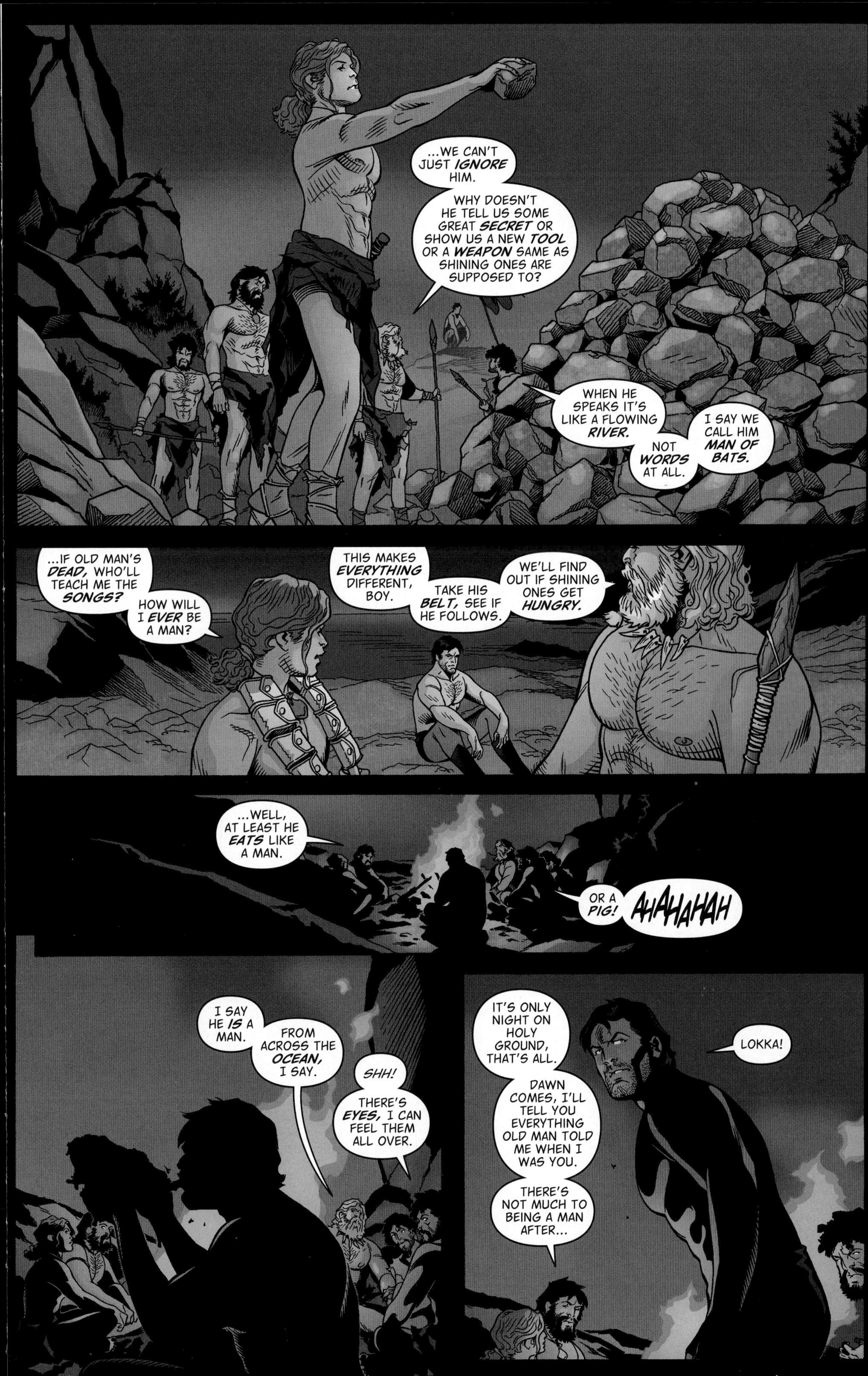
...WE CAN'T JUST IGNORE HIM.
WHY DOESN'T HE TELL US SOME GREAT SECRET OR SHOW US A NEW TOOL OR A WEAPON SAME AS SHINING ONES ARE SUPPOSED TO?
WHEN HE SPEAKS IT'S LIKE A FLOWING RIVER.
NOT WORDS AT ALL.
I SAY WE CALL HIM MAN OF BATS.
...IF OLD MAN'S DEAD, WHO'LL TEACH ME THE SONGS?
HOW WILL I EVER BE A MAN?
THIS MAKES EVERYTHING DIFFERENT, BOY.
TAKE HIS BELT, SEE IF HE FOLLOWS.
WE'LL FIND OUT IF SHINING ONES GET HUNGRY.
...WELL, AT LEAST HE EATS LIKE A MAN.
OR A PIG!
AHAHAHAH
I SAY HE IS A MAN.
FROM ACROSS THE OCEAN, I SAY.
SHH!
THERE'S EYES, I CAN FEEL THEM ALL OVER.
IT'S ONLY NIGHT ON HOLY GROUND, THAT'S ALL.
DAWN COMES, I'LL TELL YOU EVERYTHING OLD MAN TOLD ME WHEN I WAS YOU.
THERE'S NOT MUCH TO BEING A MAN AFTER...
LOKKA!

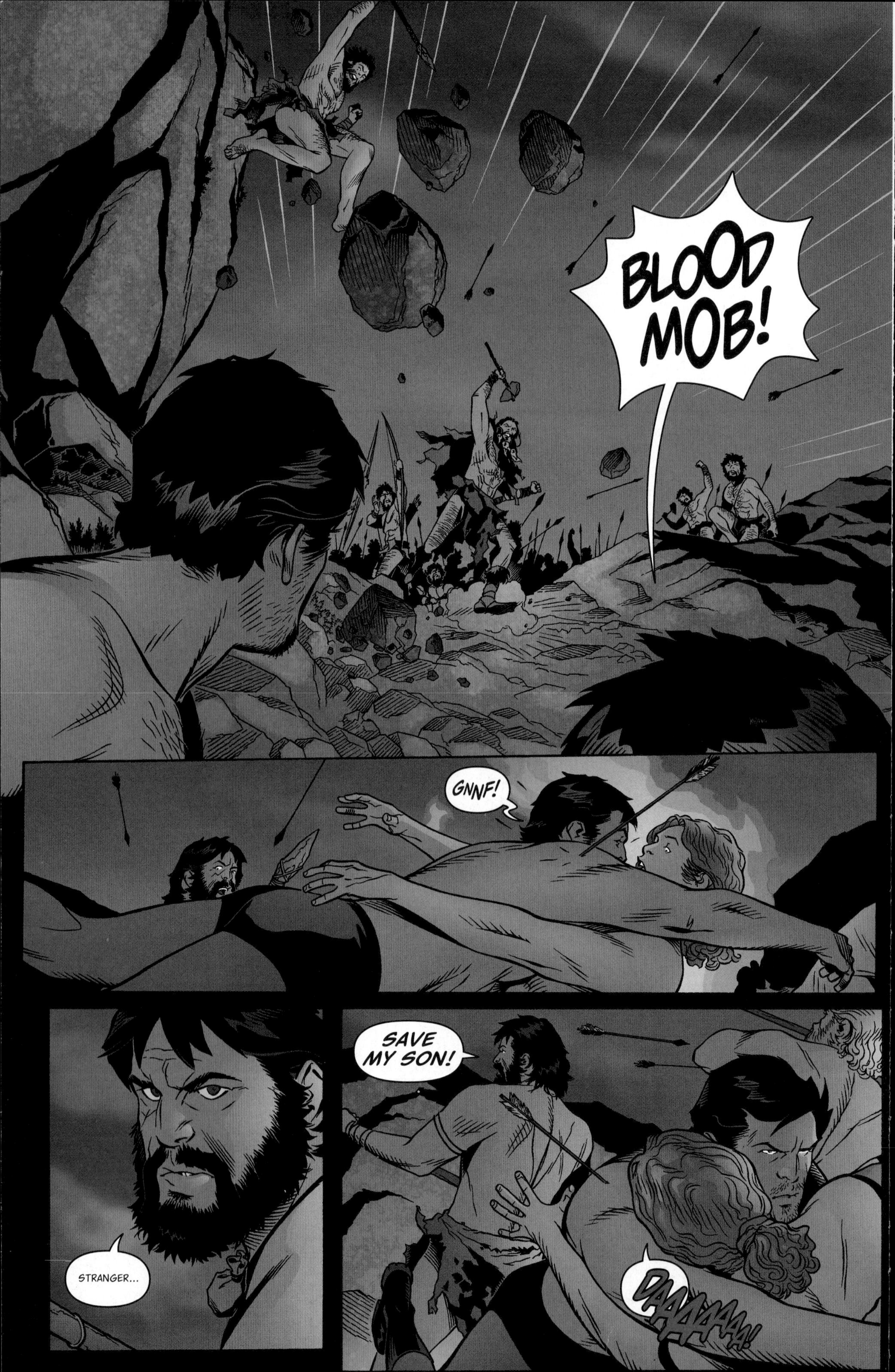
BLOOD MOB!
GNNF!
STRANGER...
SAVE MY SON!
DAAAAAAA!

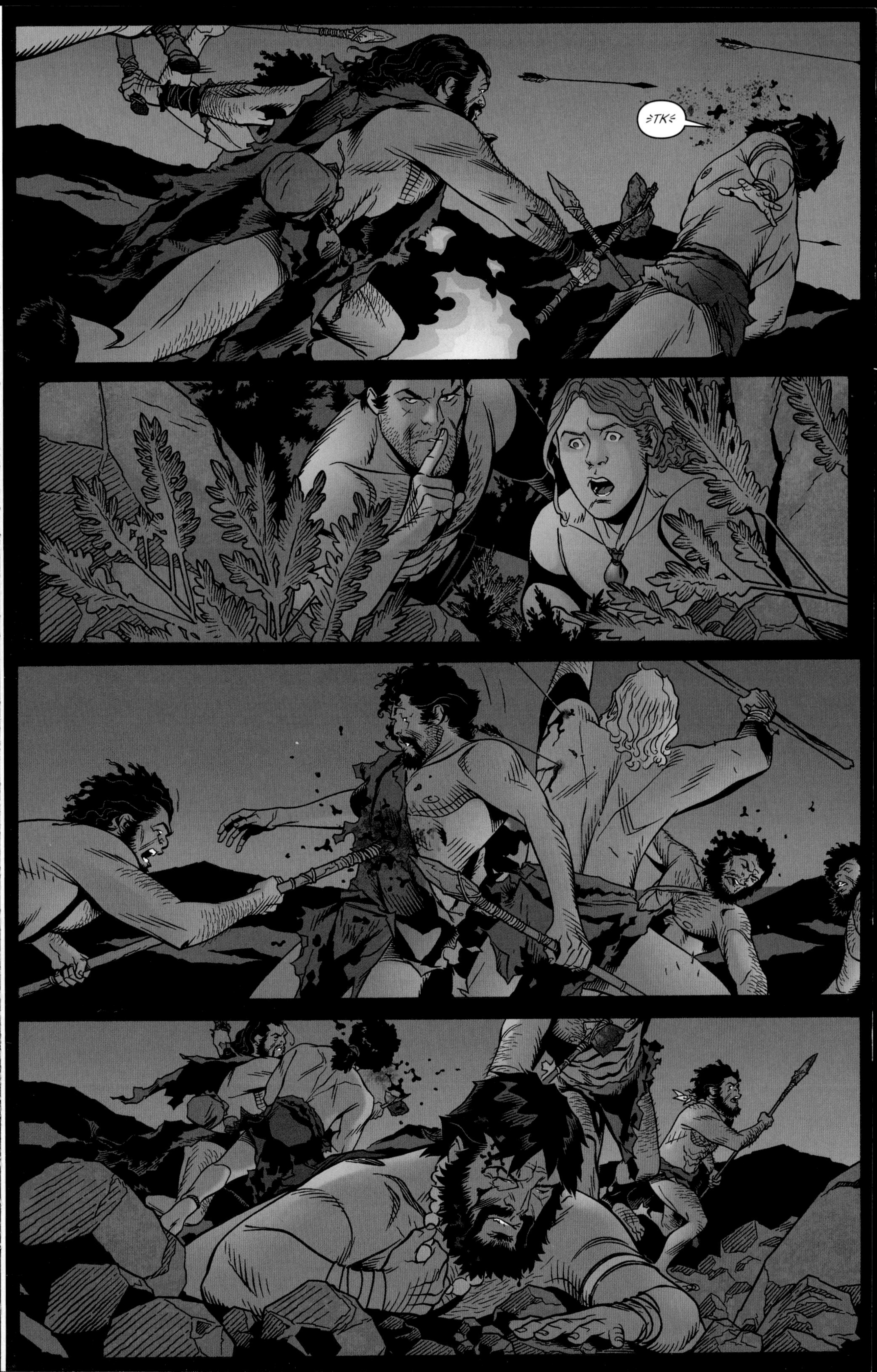
TK

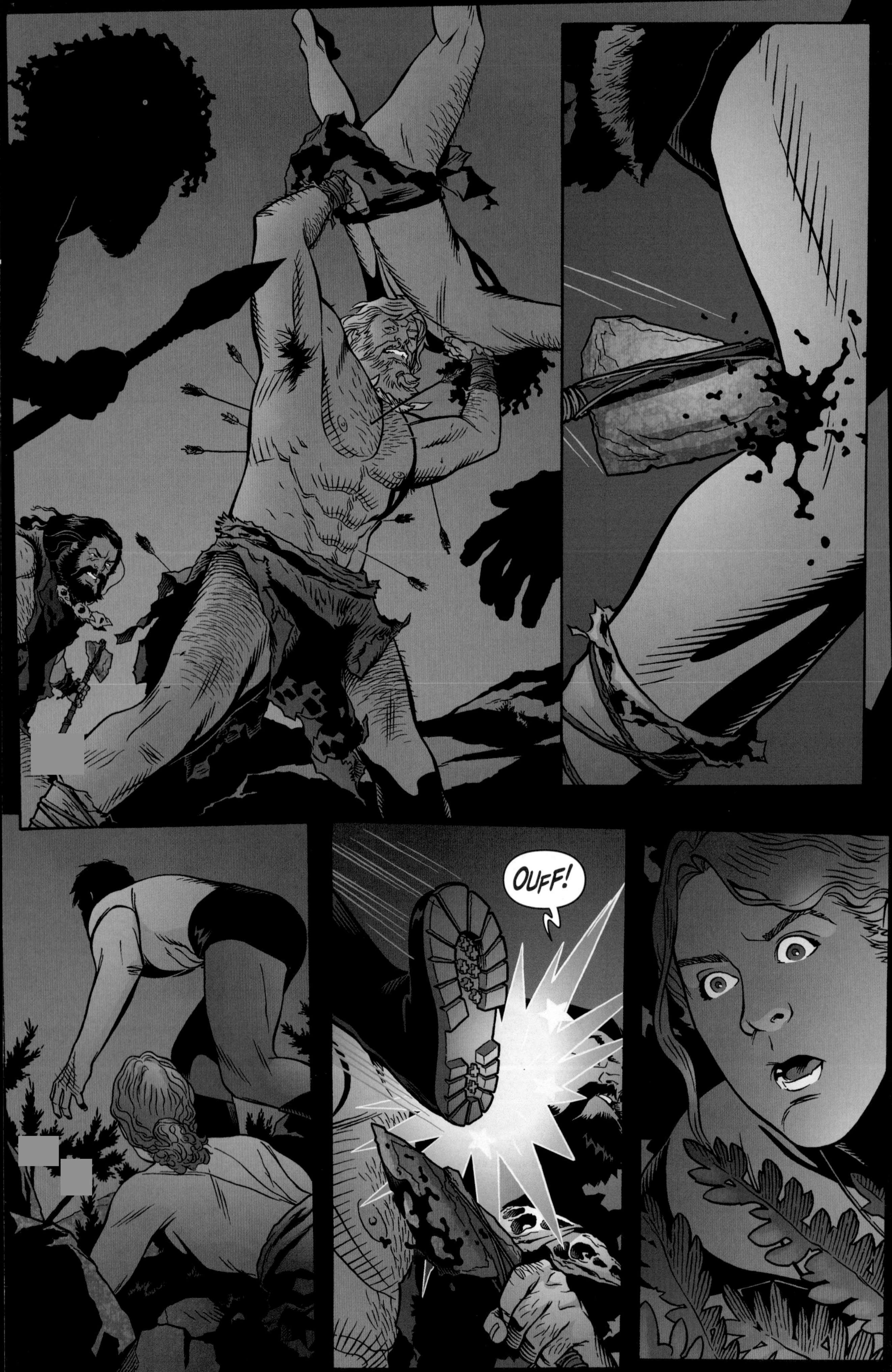
OUFF!

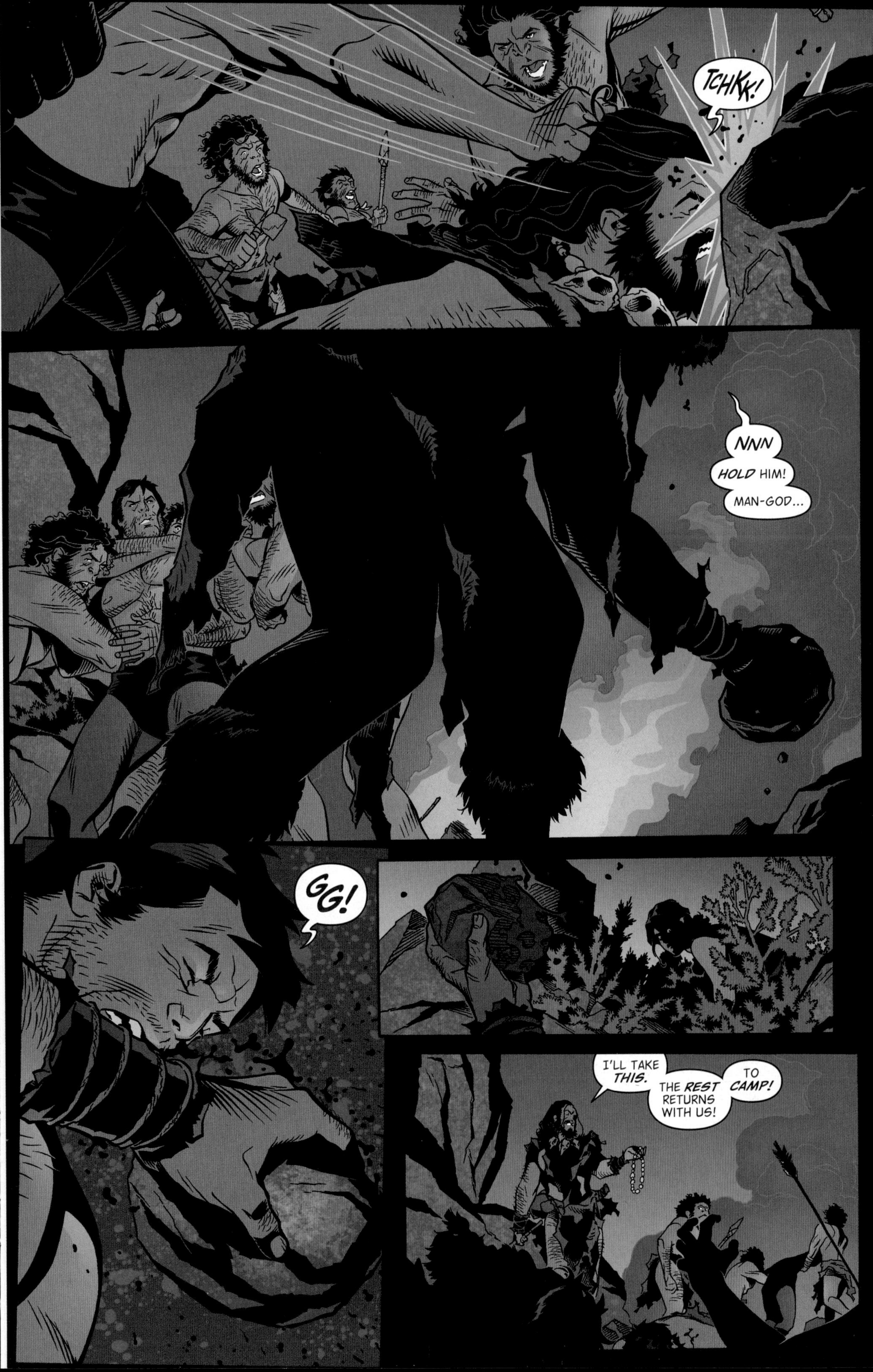
TCHKK!
NNN
HOLD HIM!
MAN-GOD...
GG!
I'LL TAKE THIS.
THE REST RETURNS WITH US!
TO CAMP!

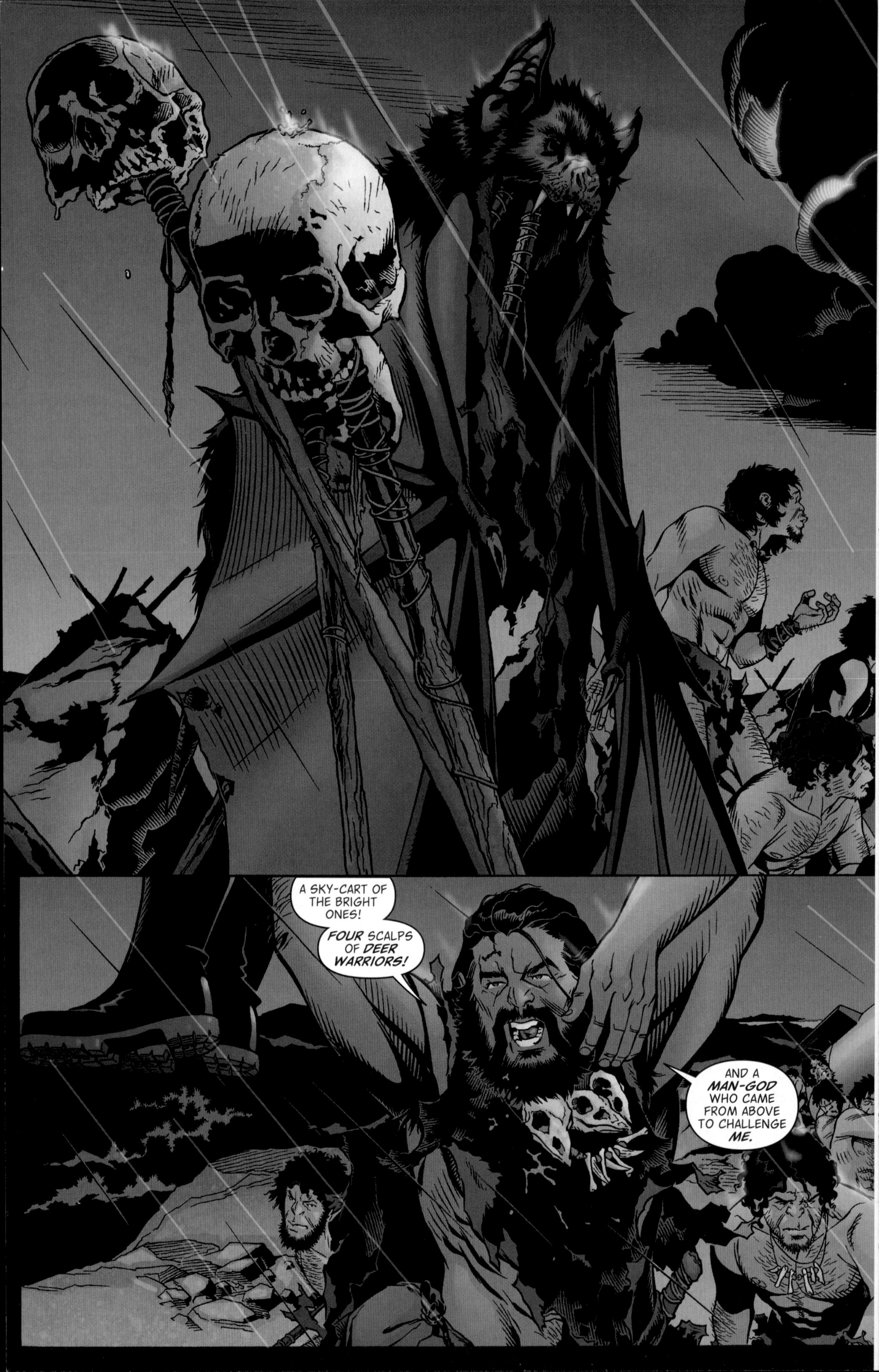
A SKY-CART OF THE BRIGHT ONES!
FOUR SCALPS OF DEER WARRIORS!
AND A MAN-GOD WHO CAME FROM ABOVE TO CHALLENGE ME.

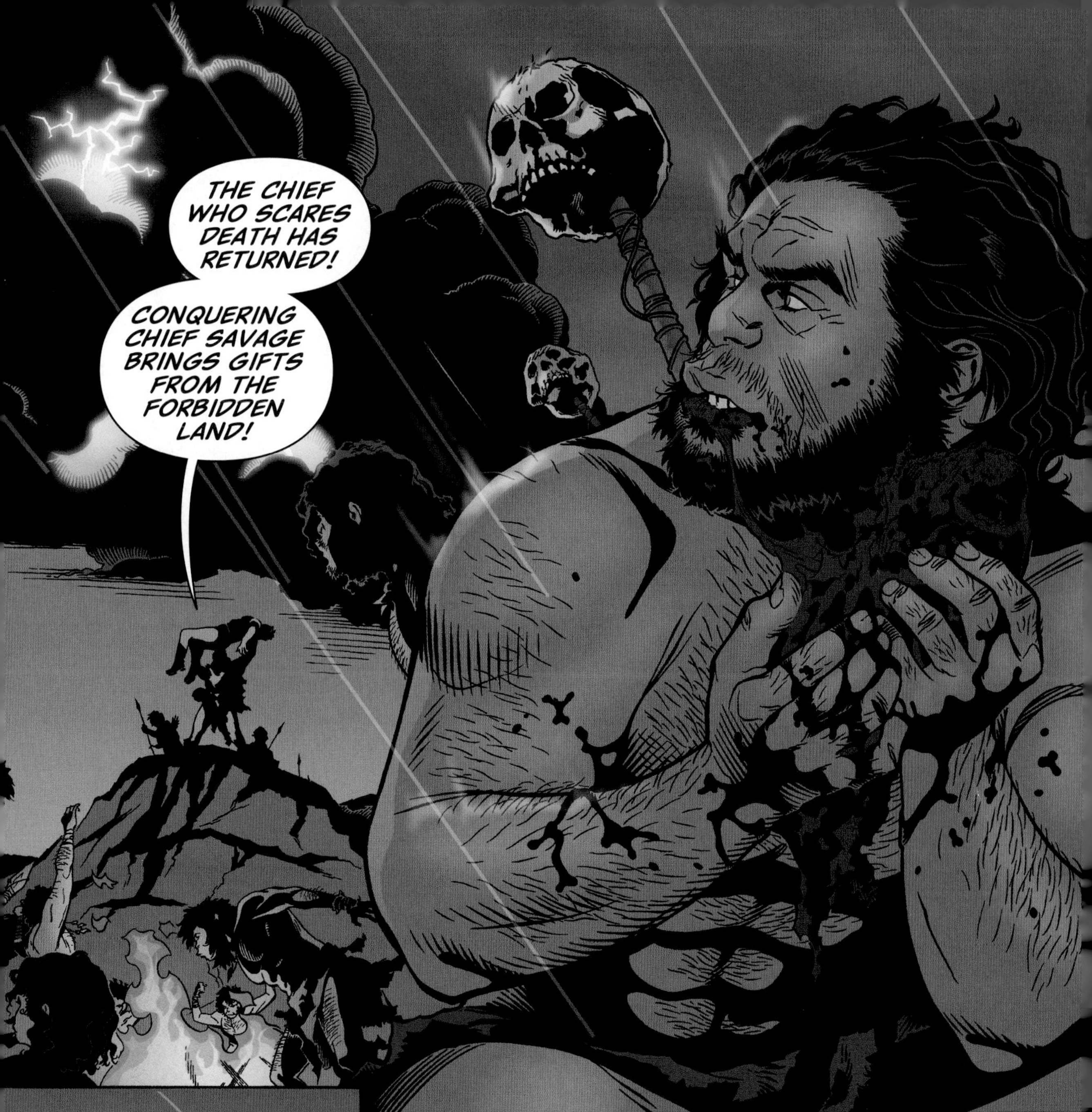
THE CHIEF WHO SCARES DEATH HAS RETURNED!
CONQUERING CHIEF SAVAGE BRINGS GIFTS FROM THE FORBIDDEN LAND!

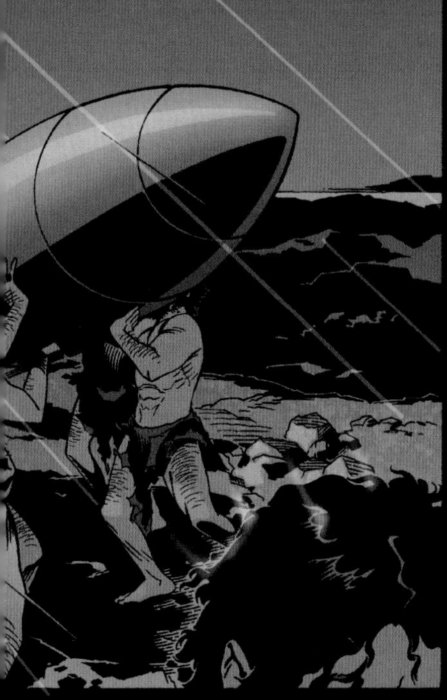

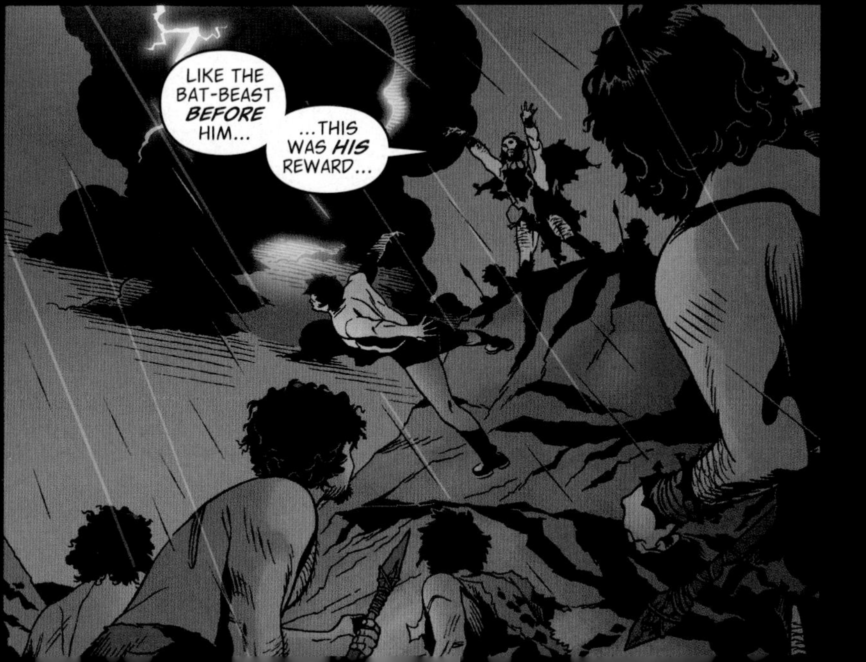
LIKE THE BAT-BEAST *BEFORE* HIM...
...THIS WAS *HIS* REWARD...

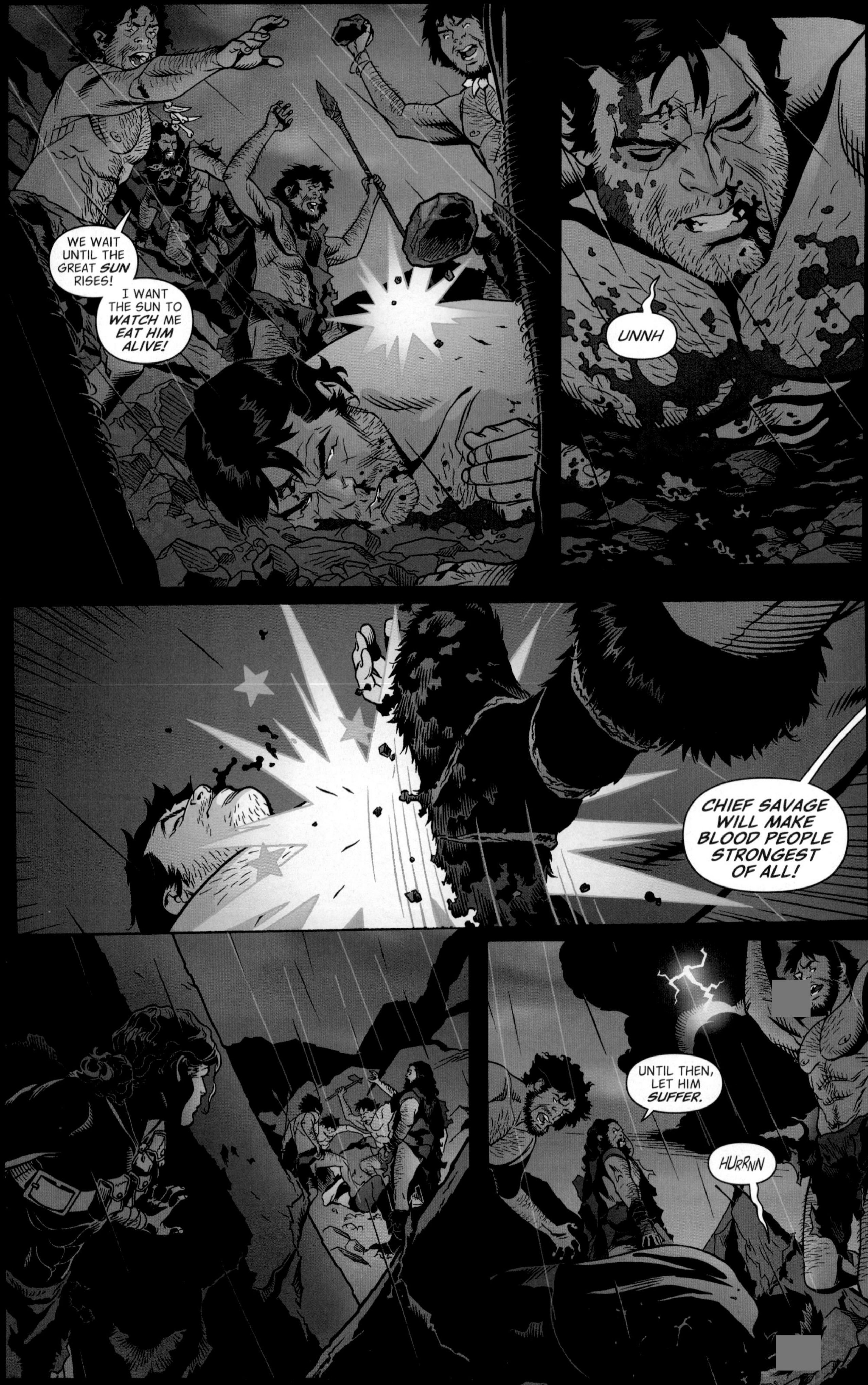
WE WAIT UNTIL THE GREAT SUN RISES!
I WANT THE SUN TO WATCH ME EAT HIM ALIVE!
UNNH
CHIEF SAVAGE WILL MAKE BLOOD PEOPLE STRONGEST OF ALL!
UNTIL THEN, LET HIM SUFFER.
HURRNN

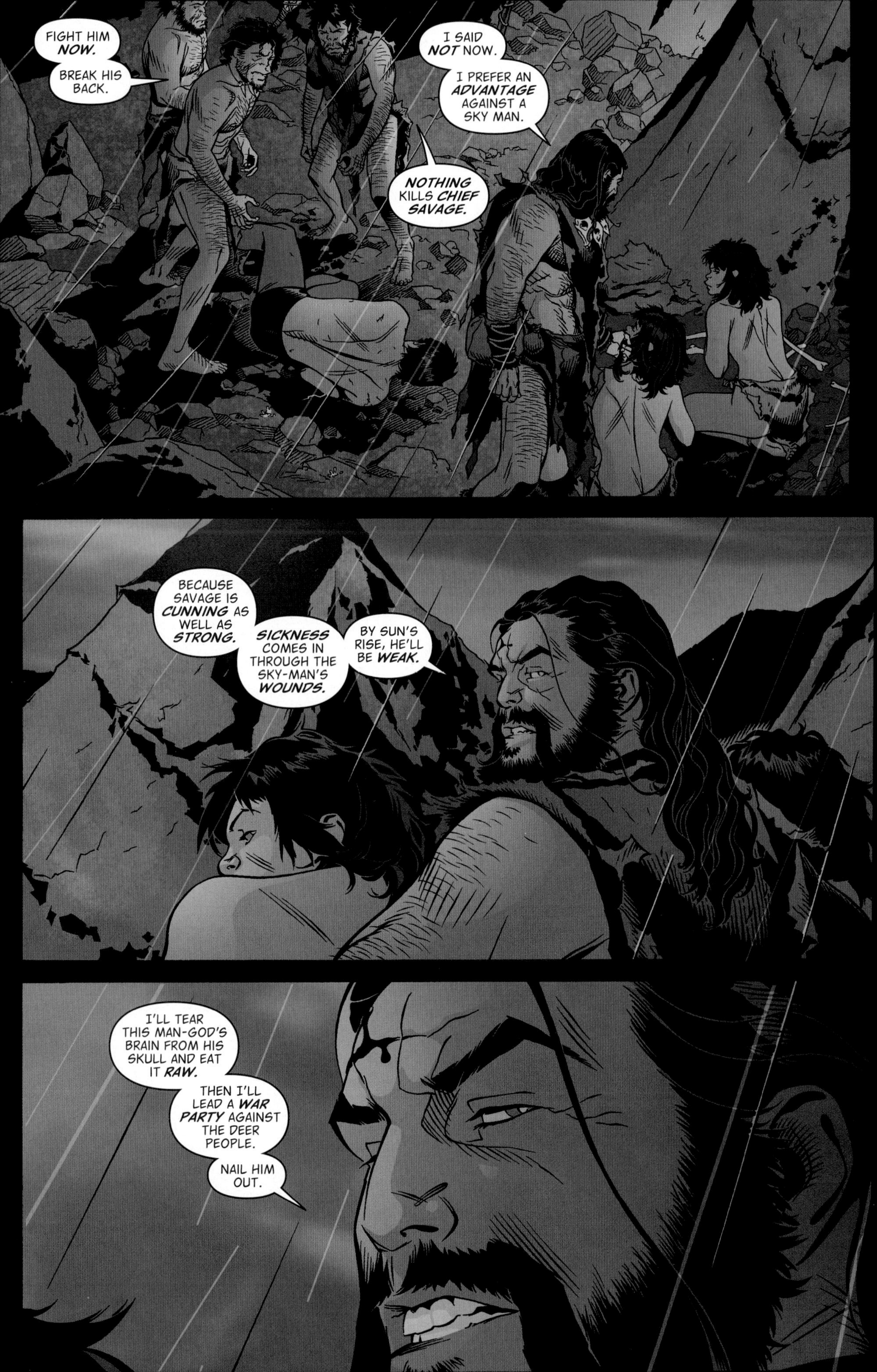
FIGHT HIM NOW.
BREAK HIS BACK.
I SAID NOT NOW.
I PREFER AN ADVANTAGE AGAINST A SKY MAN.
NOTHING KILLS CHIEF SAVAGE.
BECAUSE SAVAGE IS CUNNING AS WELL AS STRONG.
SICKNESS COMES IN THROUGH THE SKY-MAN'S WOUNDS.
BY SUN'S RISE, HE'LL BE WEAK.
I'LL TEAR THIS MAN-GOD'S BRAIN FROM HIS SKULL AND EAT IT RAW.
THEN I'LL LEAD A WAR PARTY AGAINST THE DEER PEOPLE.
NAIL HIM OUT.

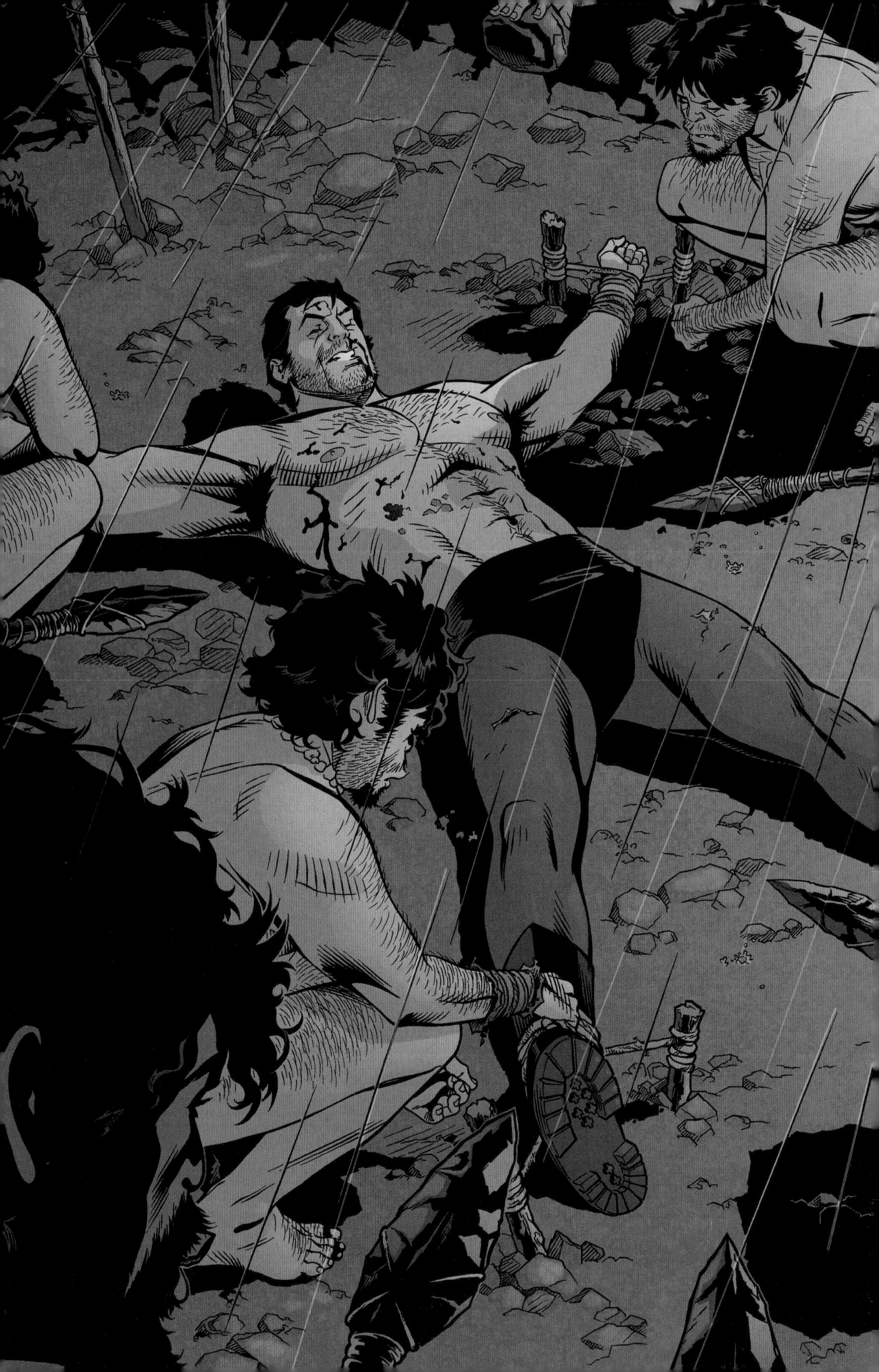

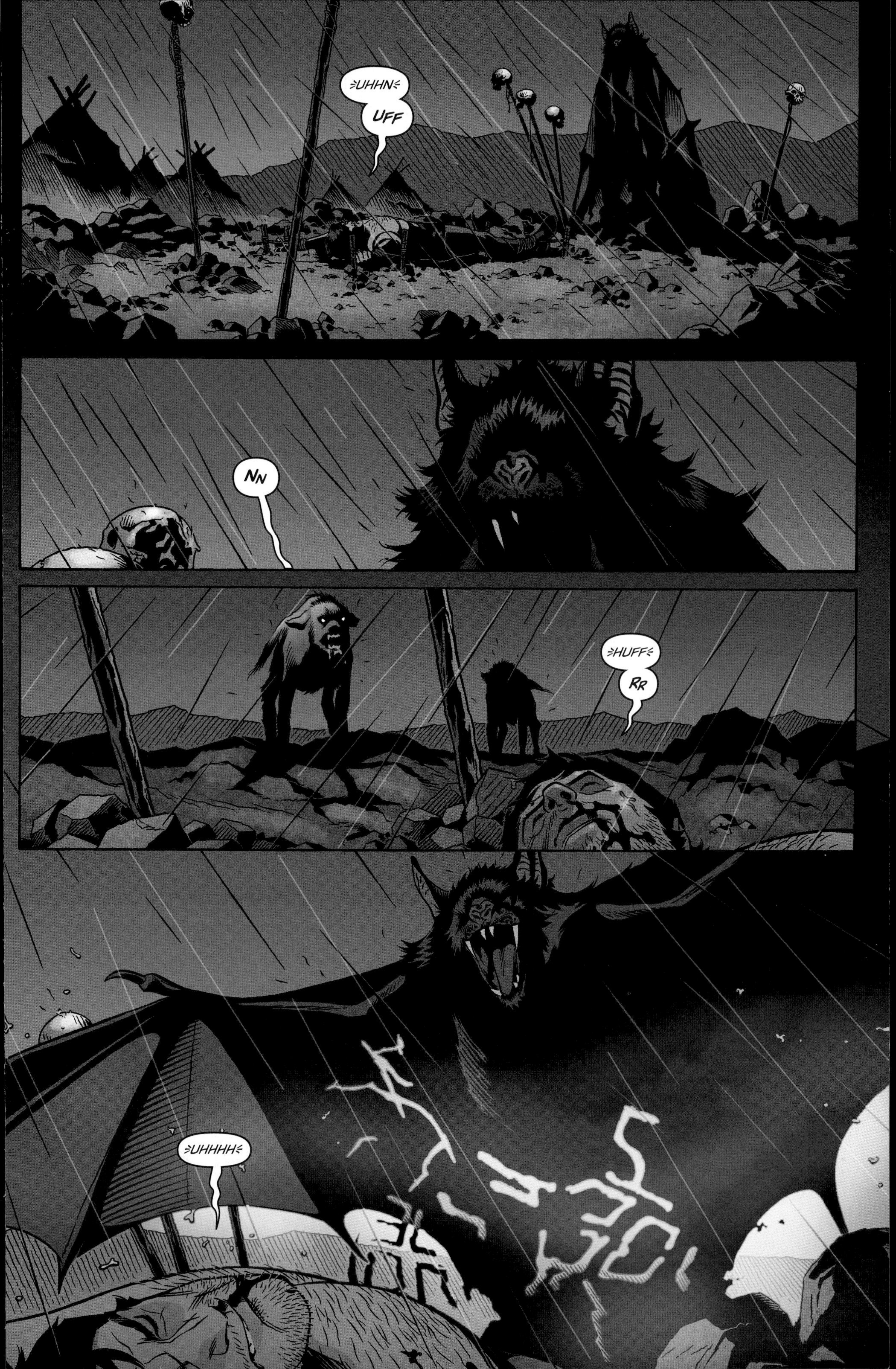

UHHN
UFF
NN
HUFF
RR
UHHHH

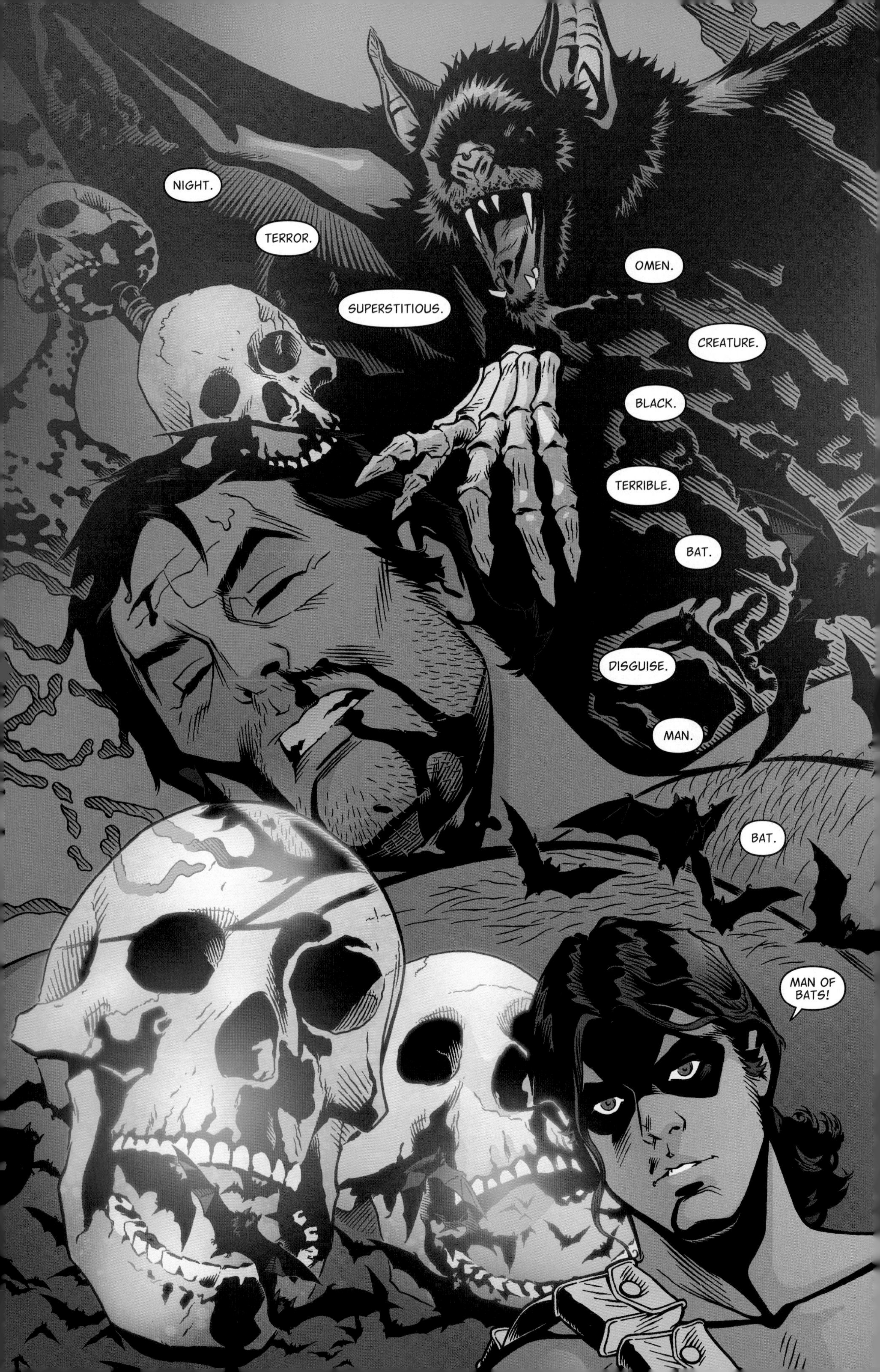
NIGHT.
TERROR.
SUPERSTITIOUS.
OMEN.
CREATURE.
BLACK.
TERRIBLE.
BAT.
DISGUISE.
MAN.
BAT.
MAN OF BATS!

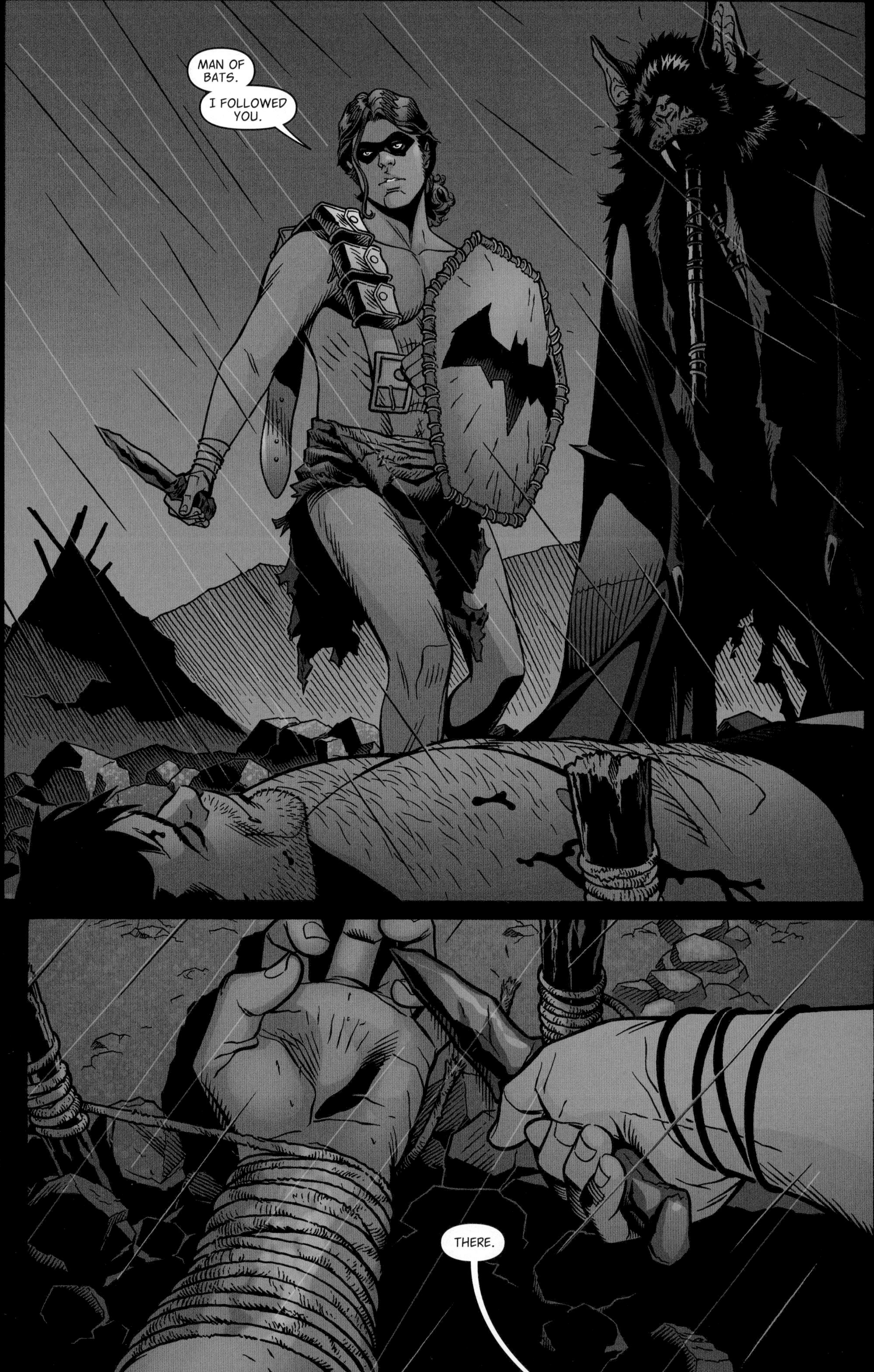
MAN OF BATS.
I FOLLOWED YOU.
THERE.

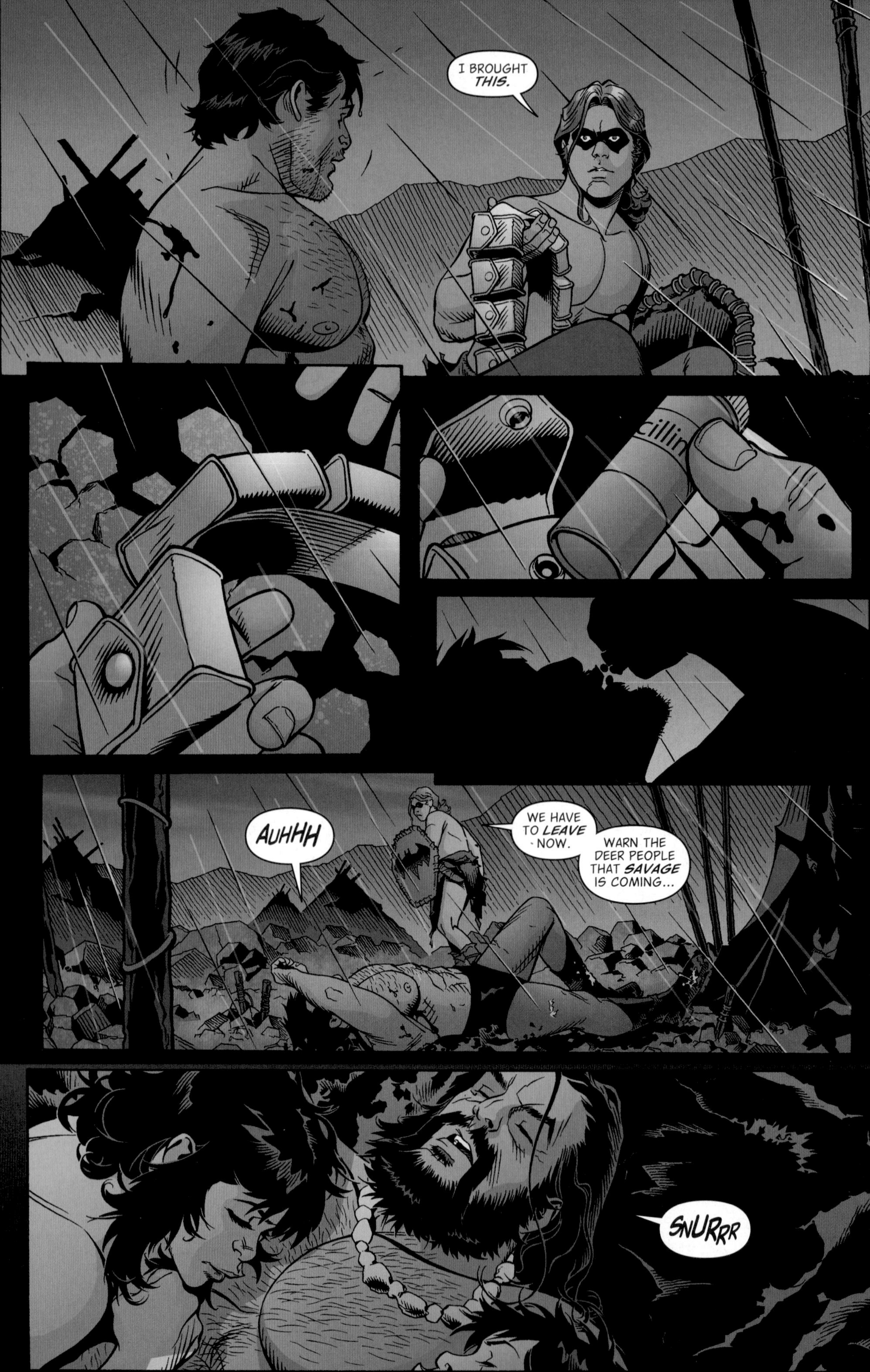
I BROUGHT THIS.
AUHHH
WE HAVE TO LEAVE NOW.
WARN THE DEER PEOPLE THAT SAVAGE IS COMING...
SNURRR

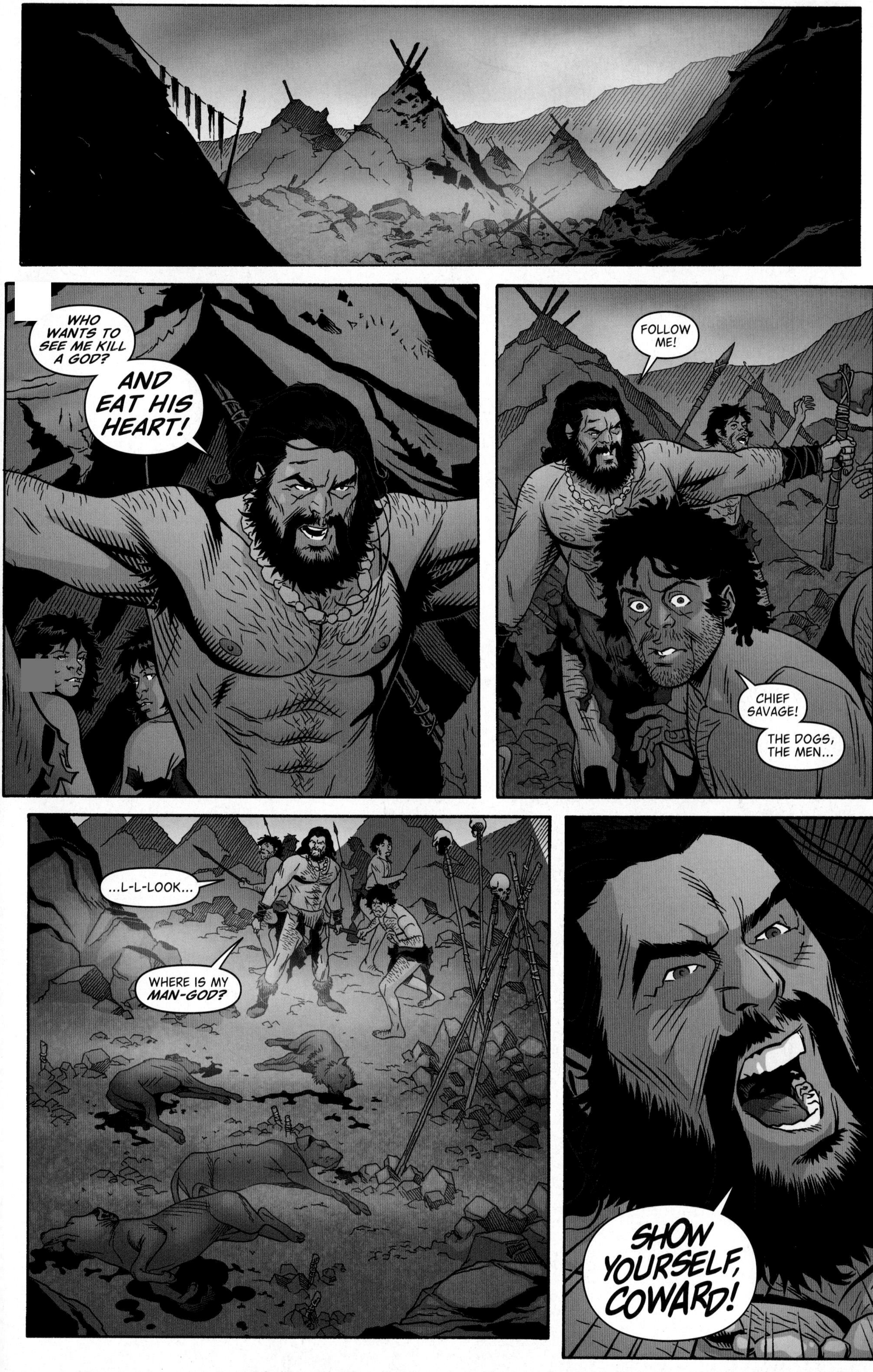
WHO WANTS TO SEE ME KILL A GOD?
AND EAT HIS HEART!
FOLLOW ME!
CHIEF SAVAGE!
THE DOGS, THE MEN...
...L-L-LOOK...
WHERE IS MY *MAN-GOD?*
SHOW YOURSELF, COWARD!

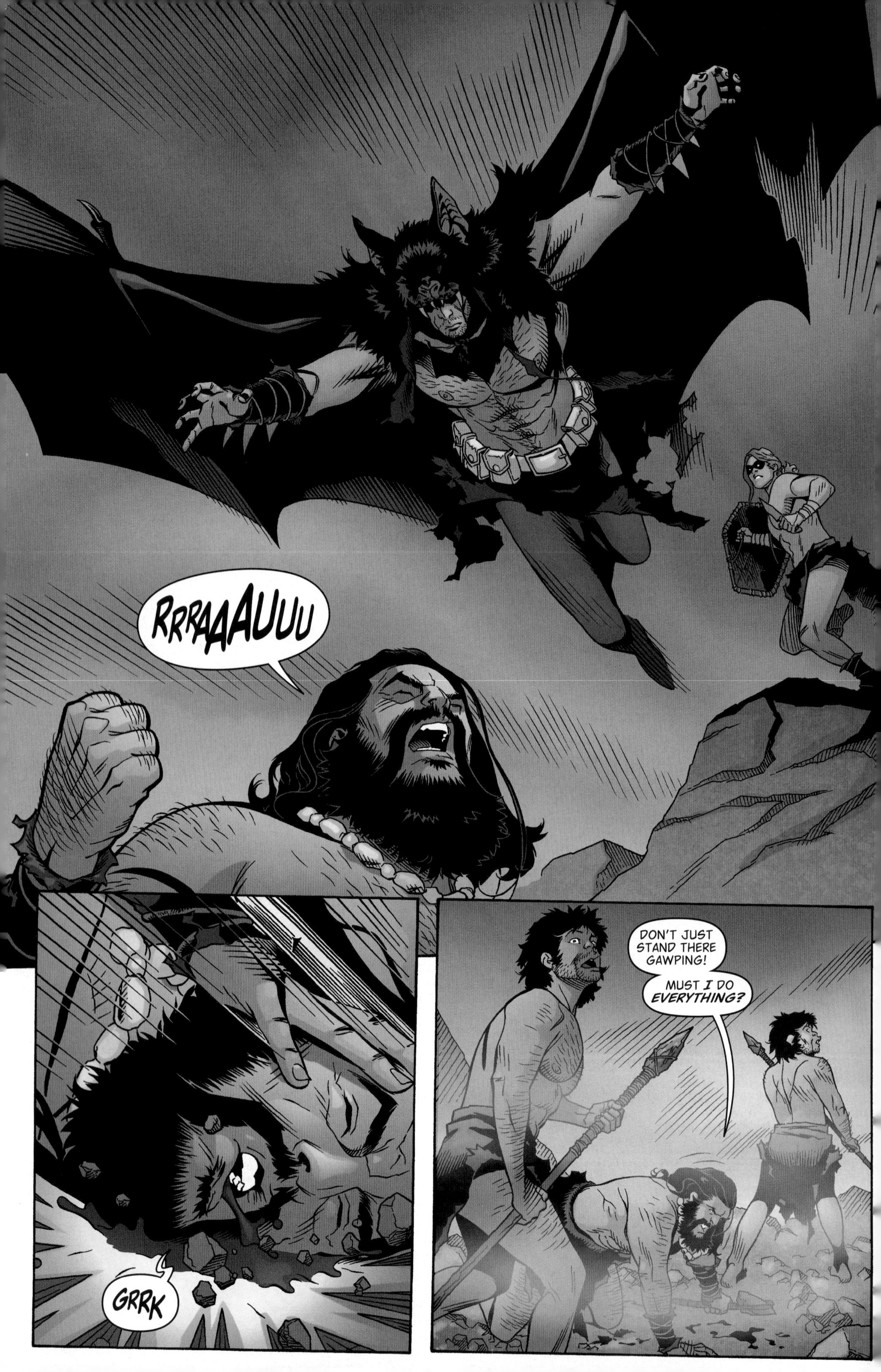
RRRAAAUUU
GRRK
DON'T JUST STAND THERE GAWPING!
MUST I DO EVERYTHING?

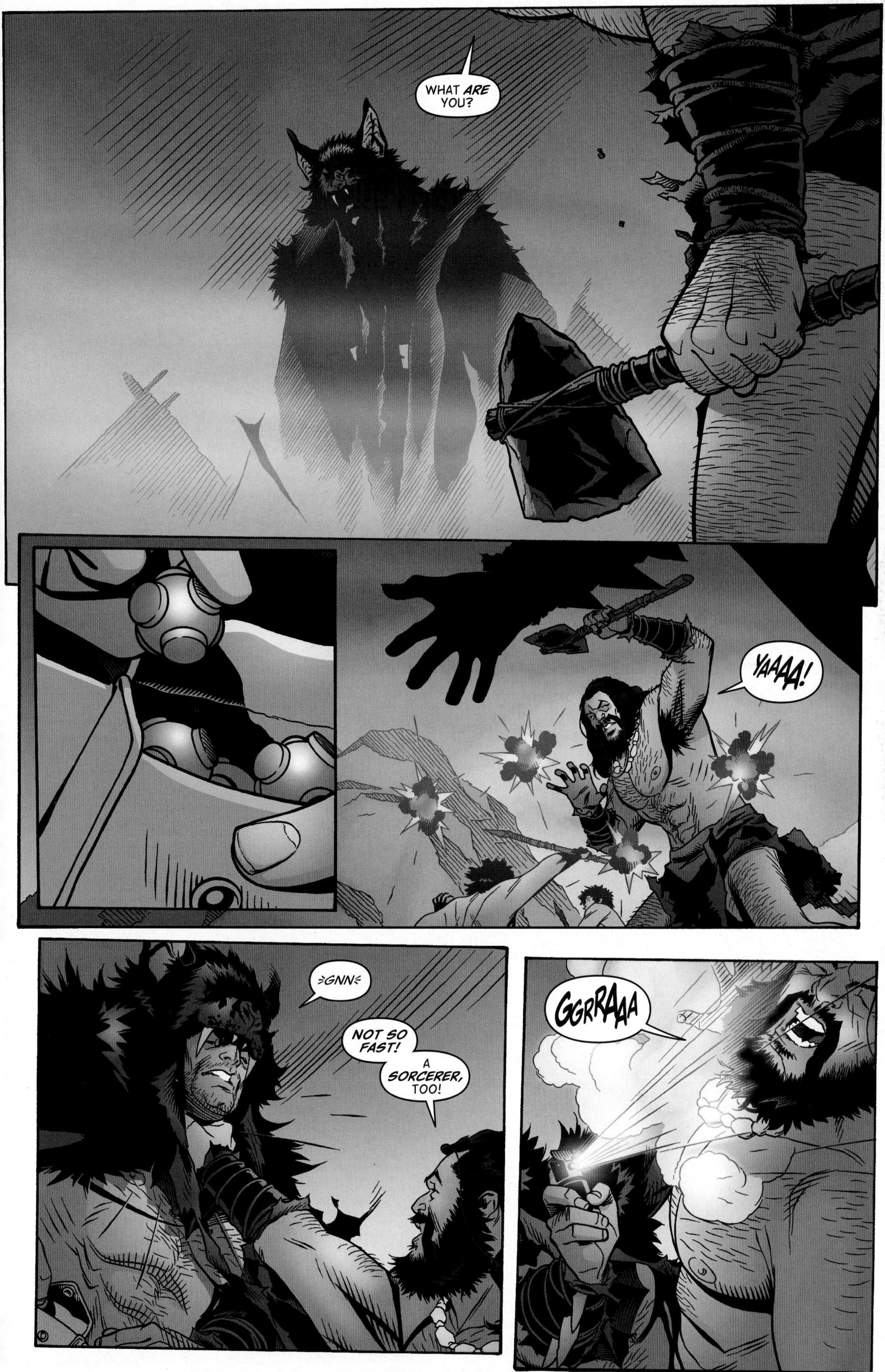
WHAT ARE YOU?
YAAAA!
GNN
NOT SO FAST!
A SORCERER, TOO!
GGRRAAA

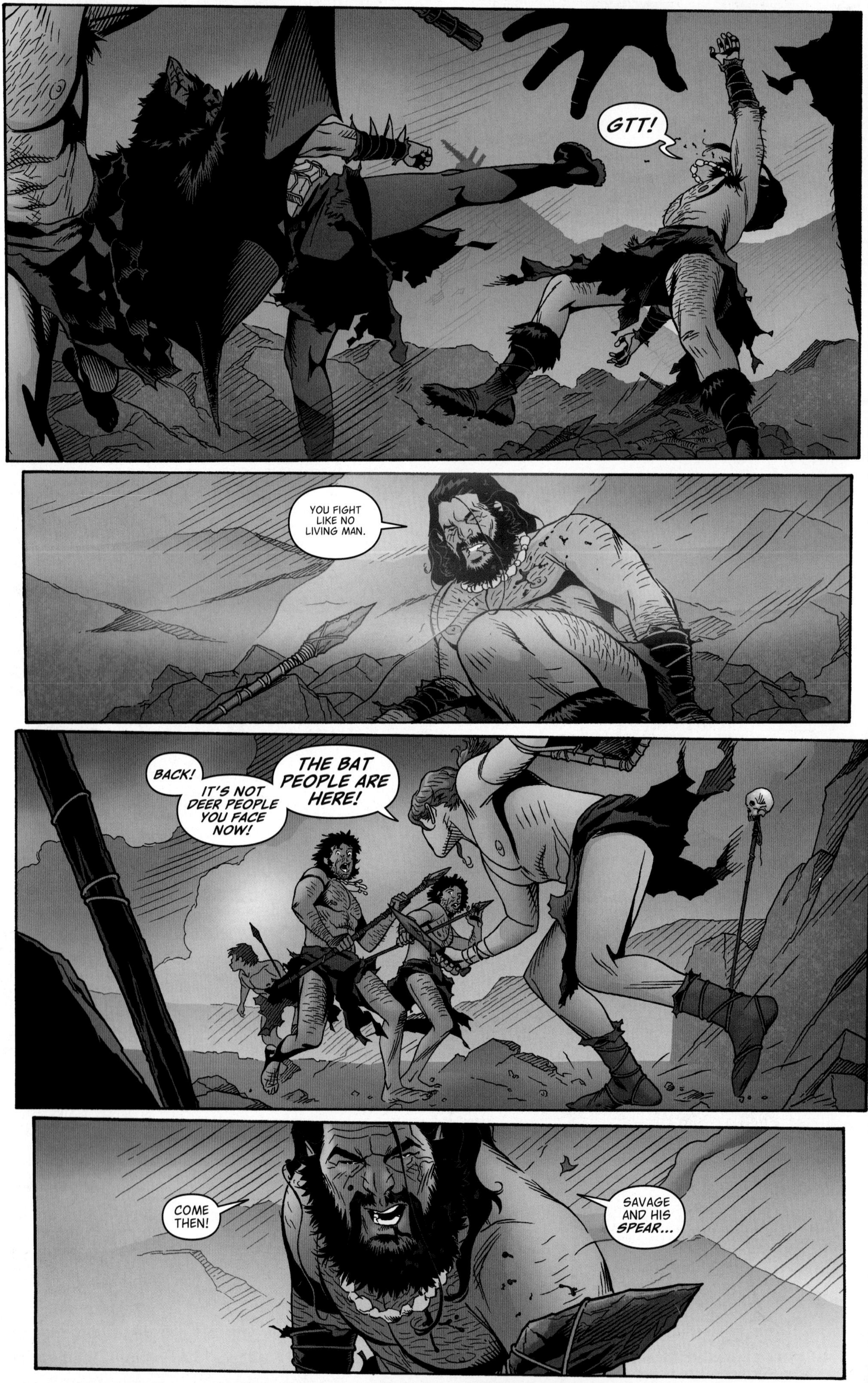
GTT!
YOU FIGHT LIKE NO LIVING MAN.
BACK!
IT'S NOT DEER PEOPLE YOU FACE NOW!
THE BAT PEOPLE ARE HERE!
COME THEN!
SAVAGE AND HIS SPEAR...

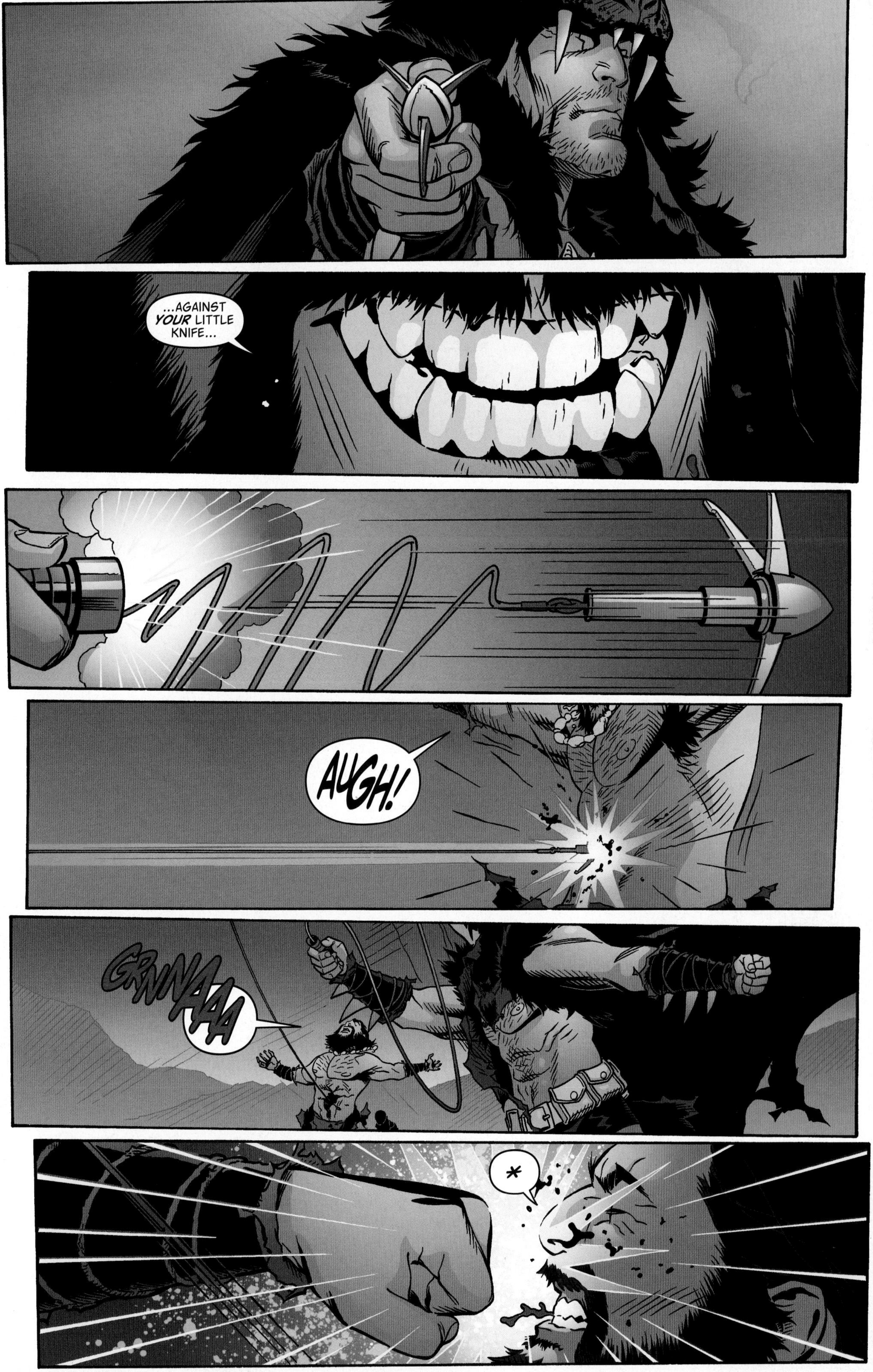
...AGAINST YOUR LITTLE KNIFE...
AUGH!
GRNNAAA
*

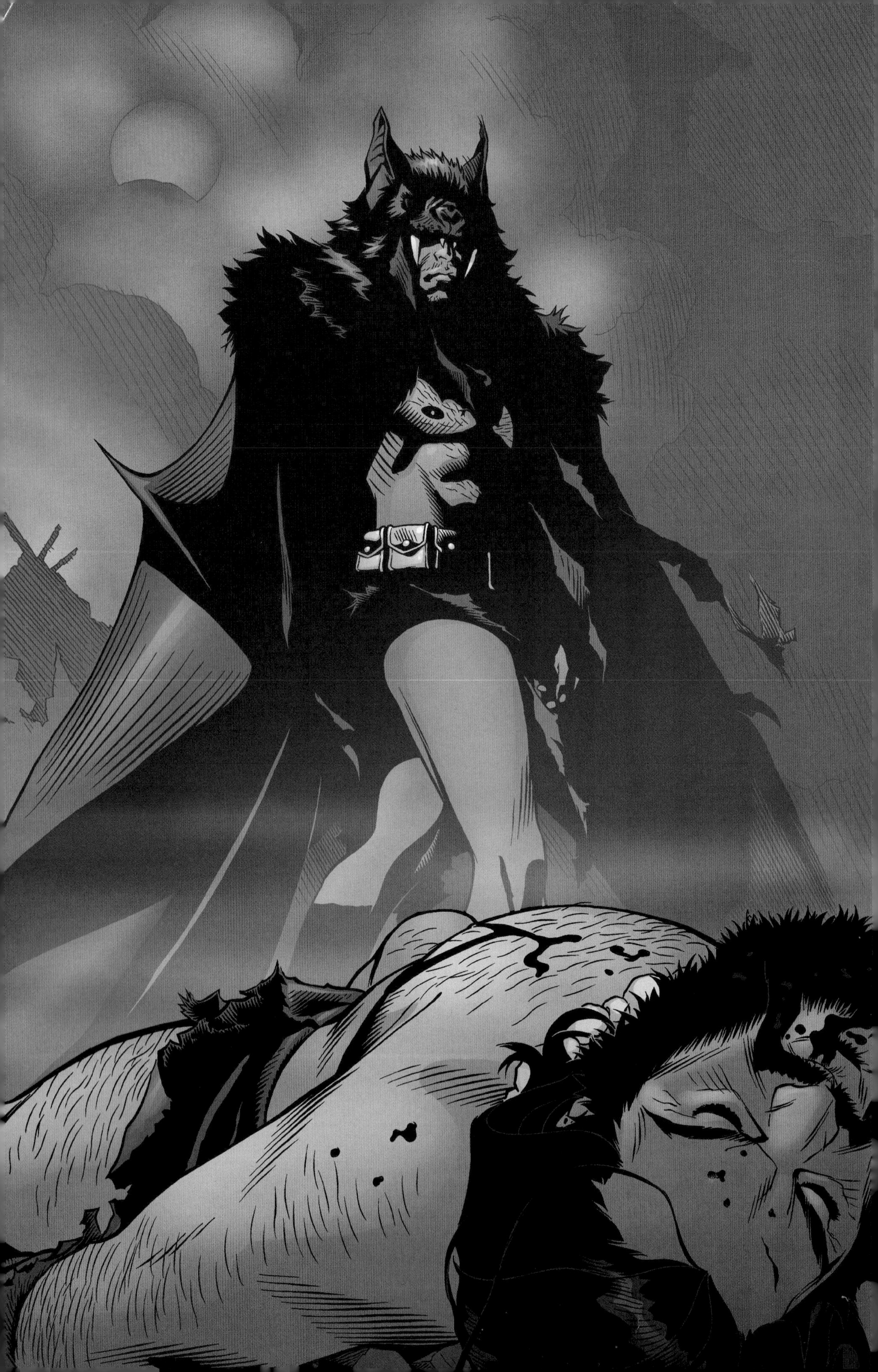

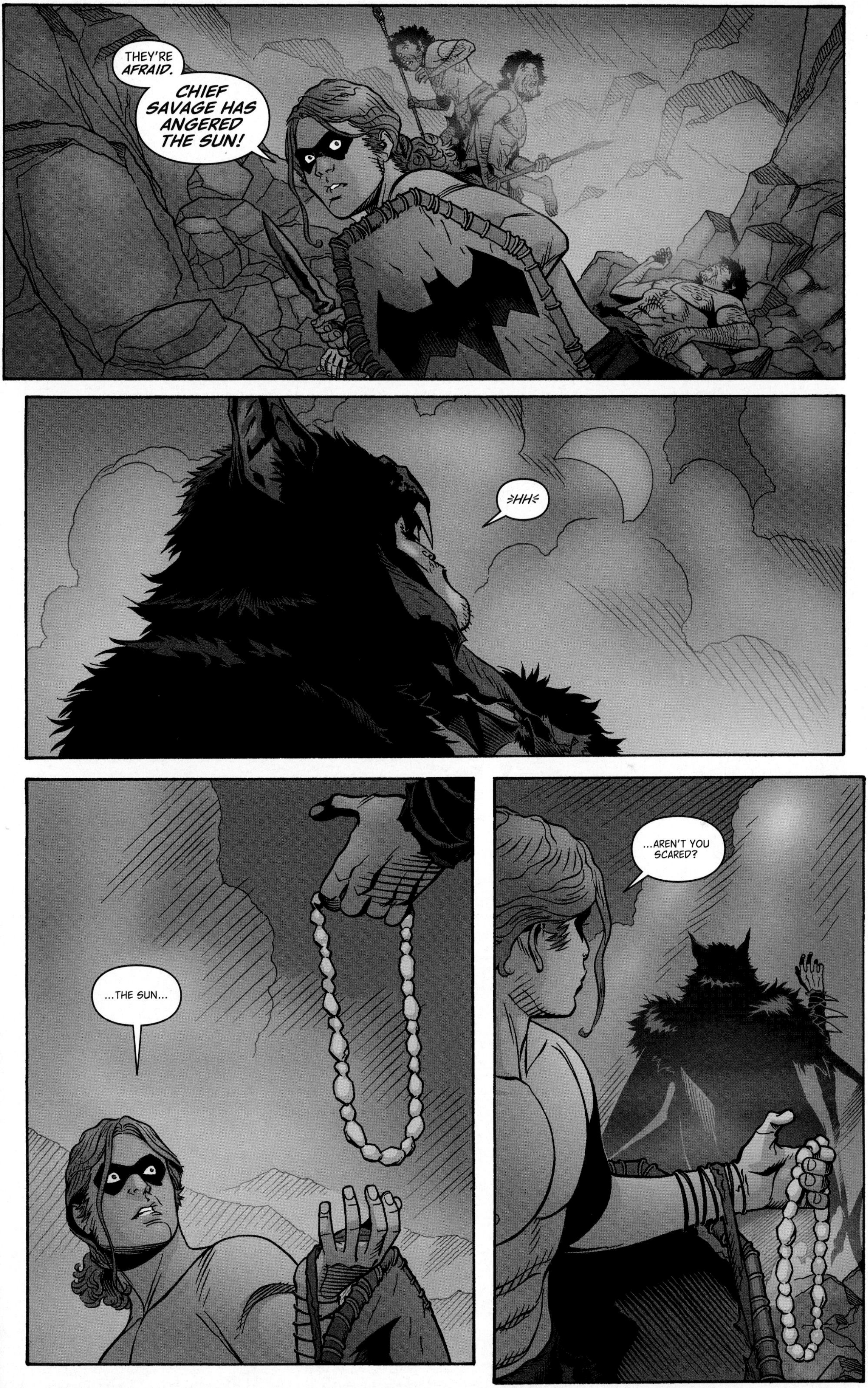
THEY'RE *AFRAID.*
CHIEF SAVAGE HAS ANGERED THE SUN!
HH
...THE SUN...
...AREN'T YOU SCARED?

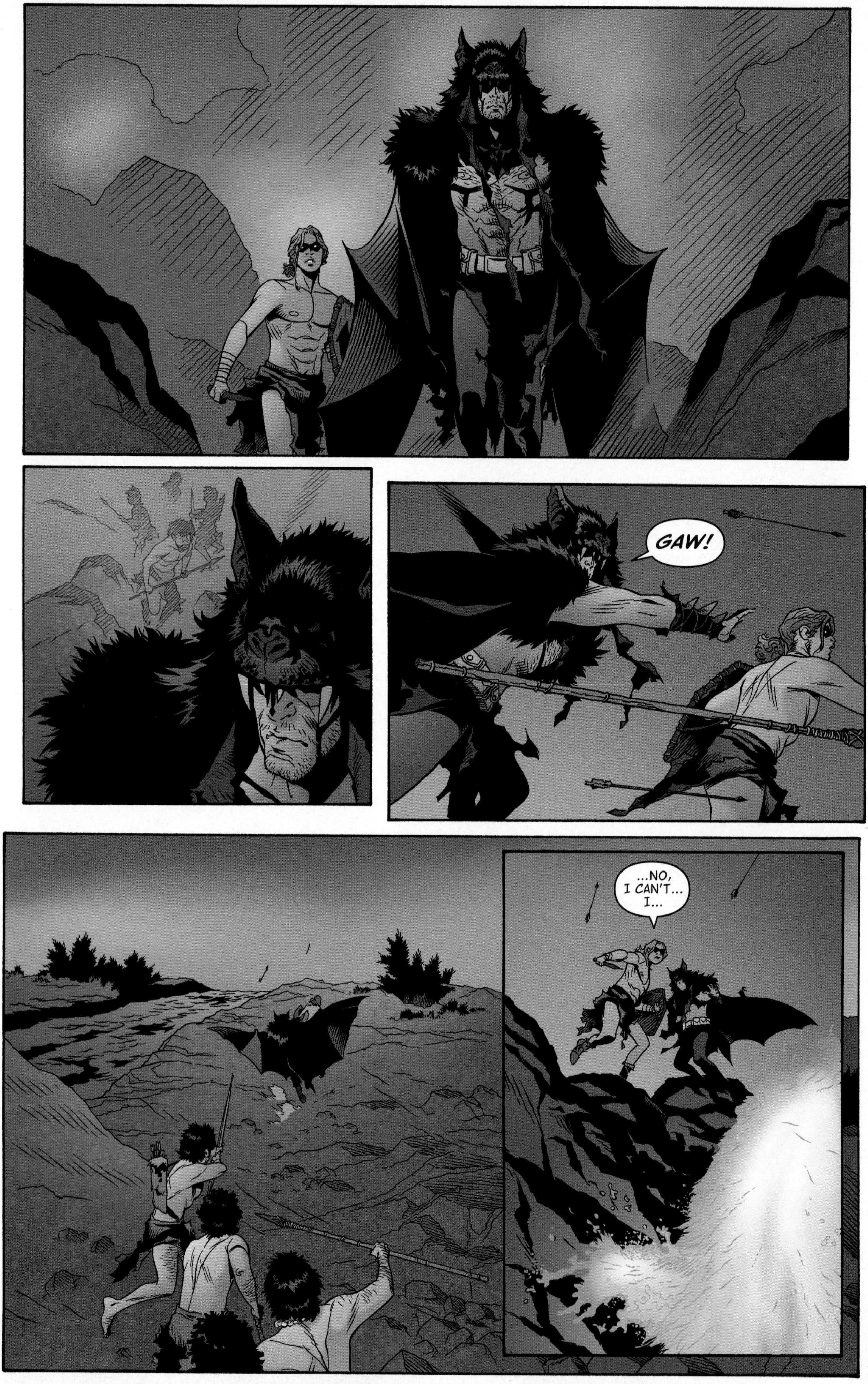
GAW!
...NO, I CAN'T... I...

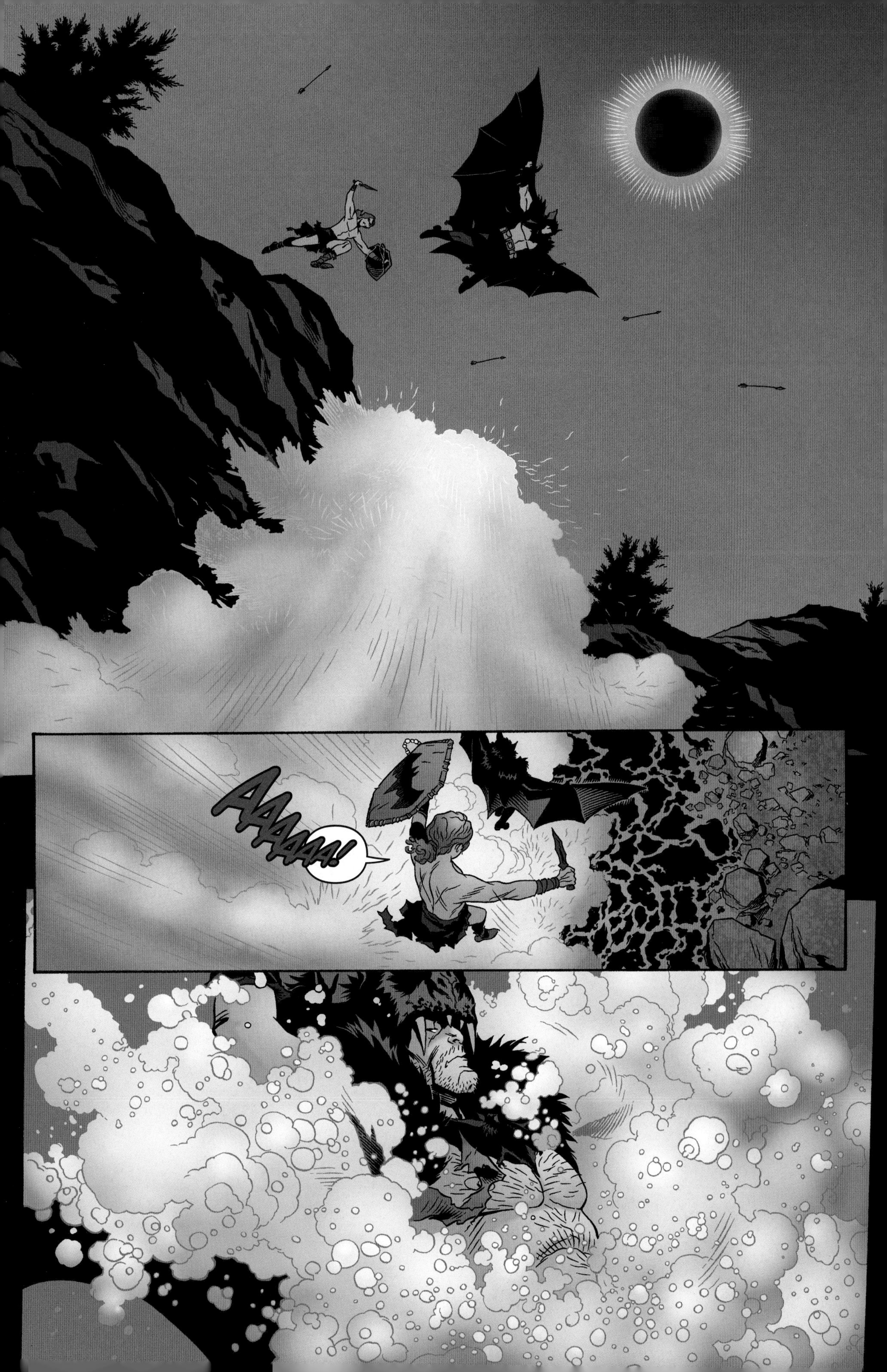
AAAAAA!

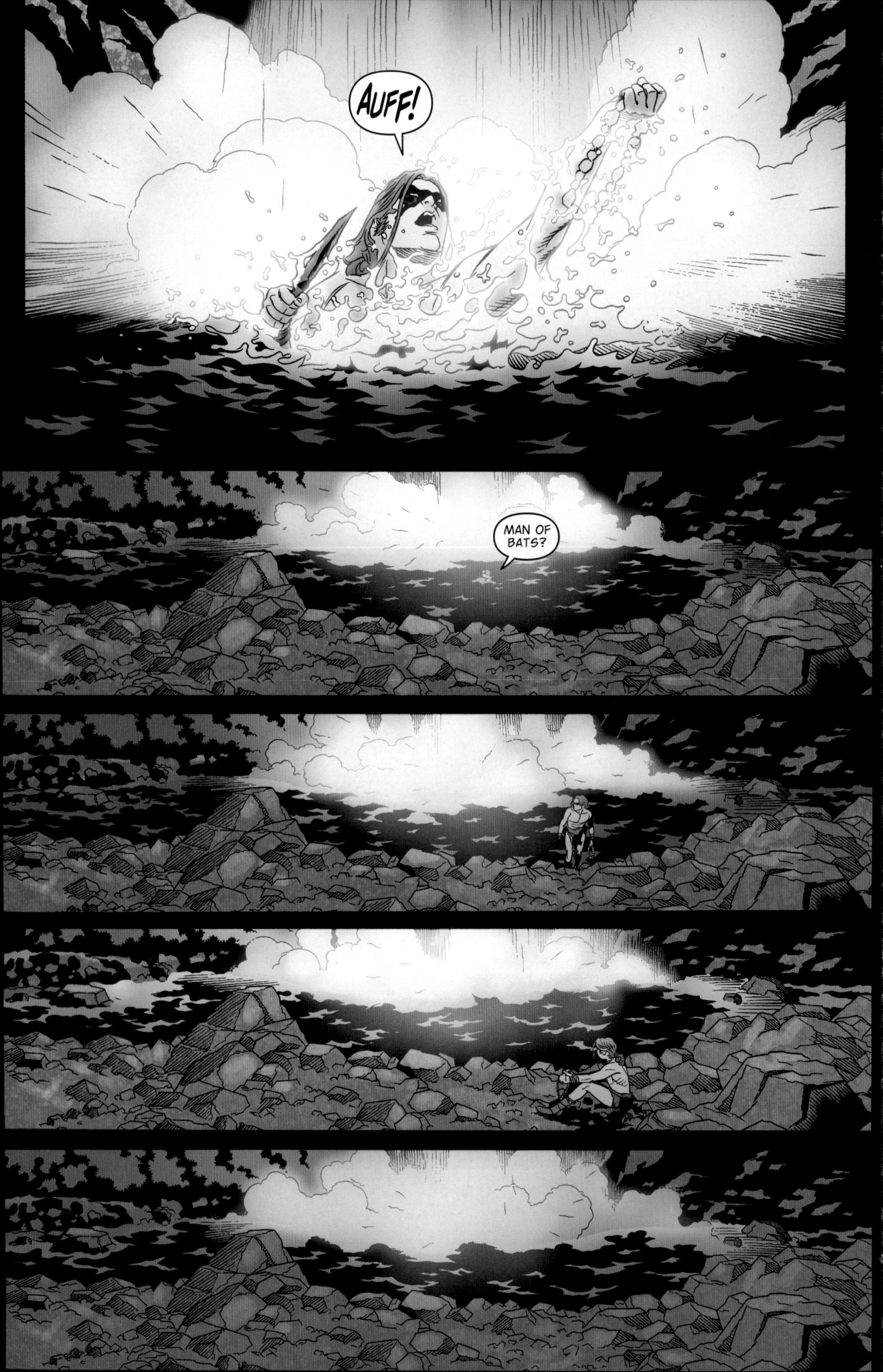
AUFF!
MAN OF BATS?

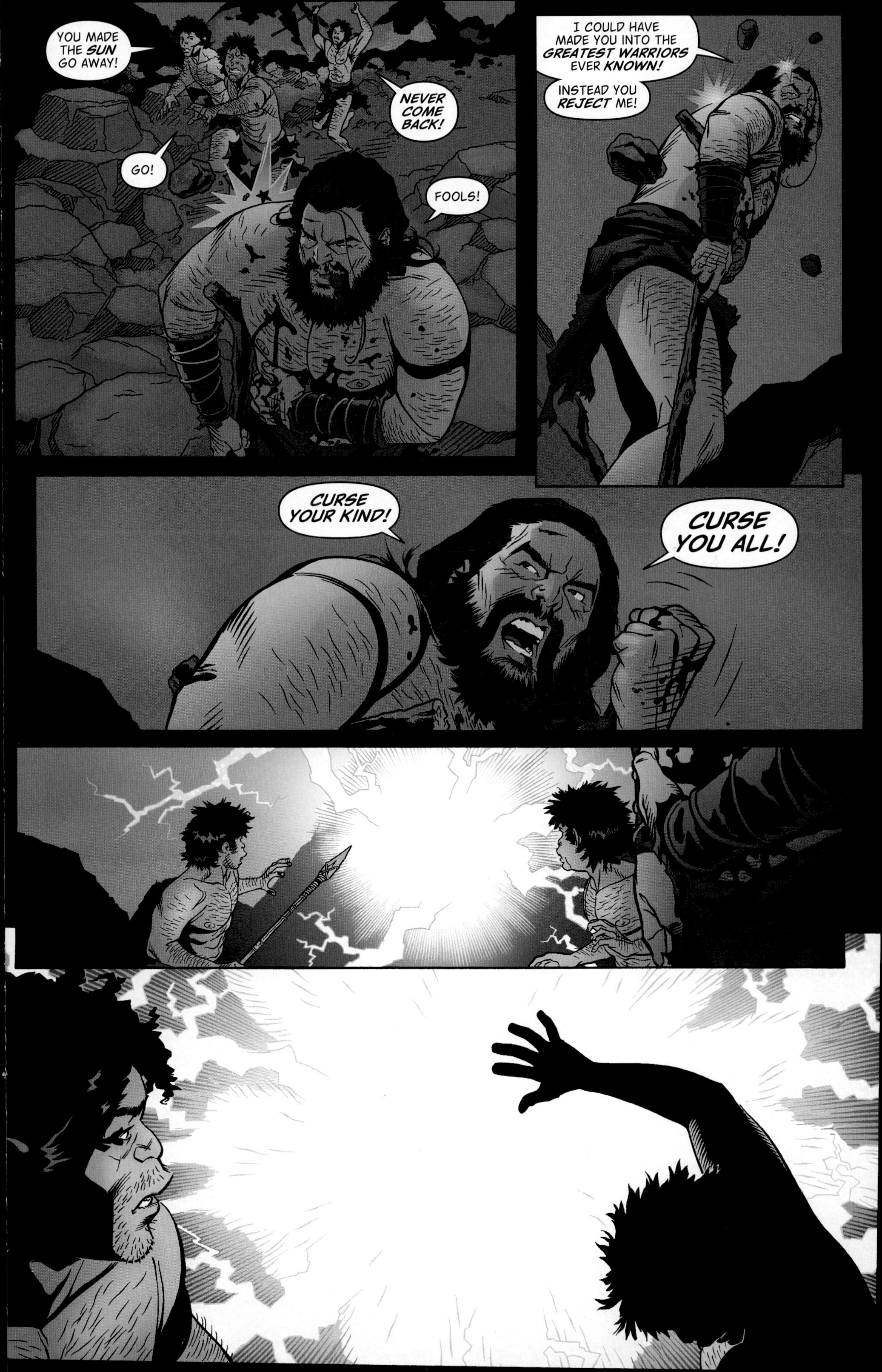
YOU MADE THE SUN GO AWAY!
NEVER COME BACK!
GO!
FOOLS!
I COULD HAVE MADE YOU INTO THE GREATEST WARRIORS EVER KNOWN!
INSTEAD YOU REJECT ME!
CURSE YOUR KIND!
CURSE YOU ALL!

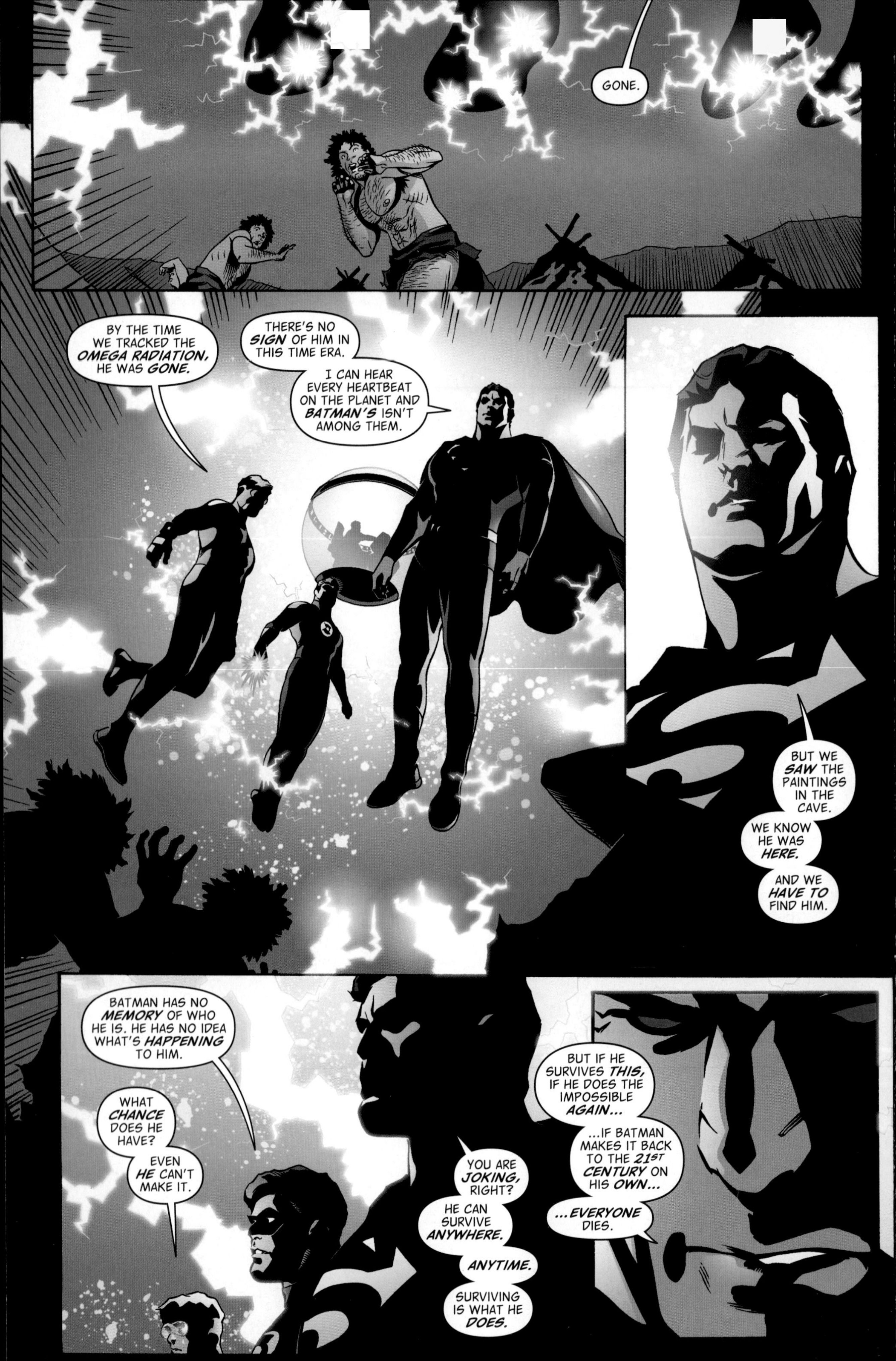
GONE.
BY THE TIME WE TRACKED THE OMEGA RADIATION, HE WAS GONE.
THERE'S NO SIGN OF HIM IN THIS TIME ERA.
I CAN HEAR EVERY HEARTBEAT ON THE PLANET AND BATMAN'S ISN'T AMONG THEM.
BUT WE SAW THE PAINTINGS IN THE CAVE.
WE KNOW HE WAS HERE.
AND WE HAVE TO FIND HIM.
BATMAN HAS NO MEMORY OF WHO HE IS. HE HAS NO IDEA WHAT'S HAPPENING TO HIM.
WHAT CHANCE DOES HE HAVE?
EVEN HE CAN'T MAKE IT.
YOU ARE JOKING, RIGHT?
HE CAN SURVIVE ANYWHERE.
ANYTIME.
SURVIVING IS WHAT HE DOES.
BUT IF HE SURVIVES THIS, IF HE DOES THE IMPOSSIBLE AGAIN...
...IF BATMAN MAKES IT BACK TO THE 21ST CENTURY ON HIS OWN...
...EVERYONE DIES.

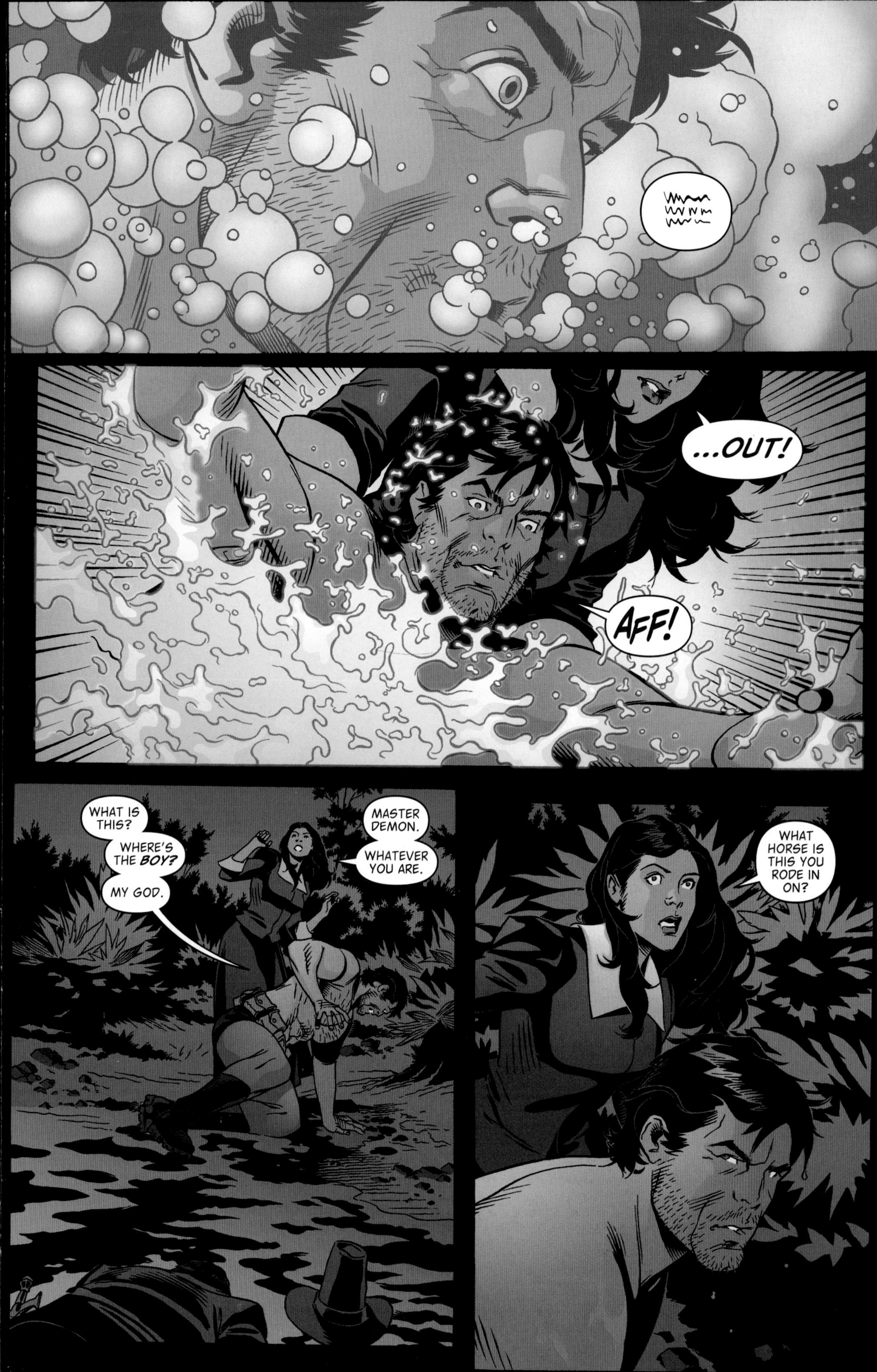

...OUT!
AFF!
WHAT IS THIS?
WHERE'S THE *BOY?*
MY GOD.
MASTER DEMON.
WHATEVER YOU ARE.
WHAT HORSE IS THIS YOU RODE IN ON?

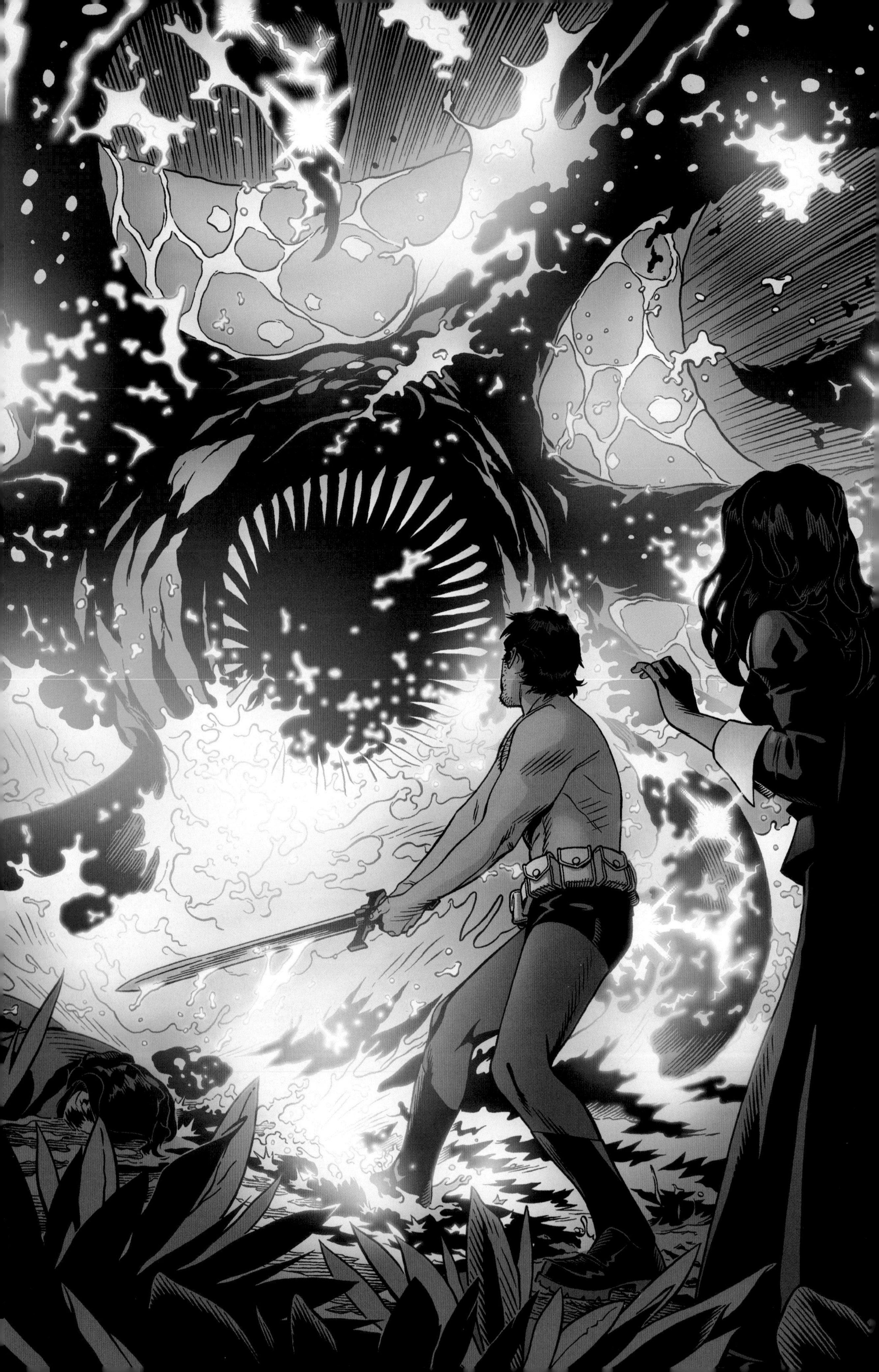

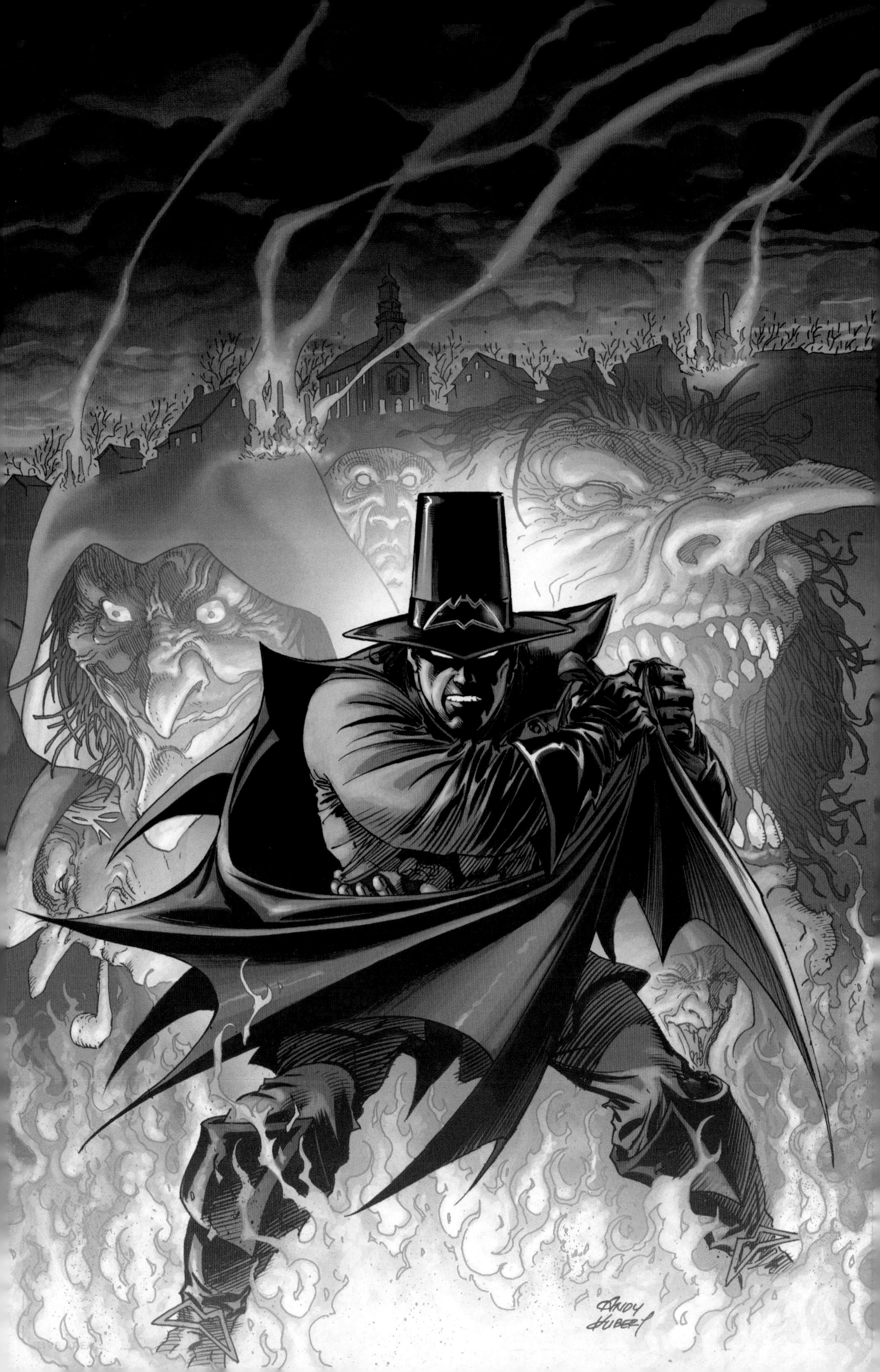
ANDY KUBERT

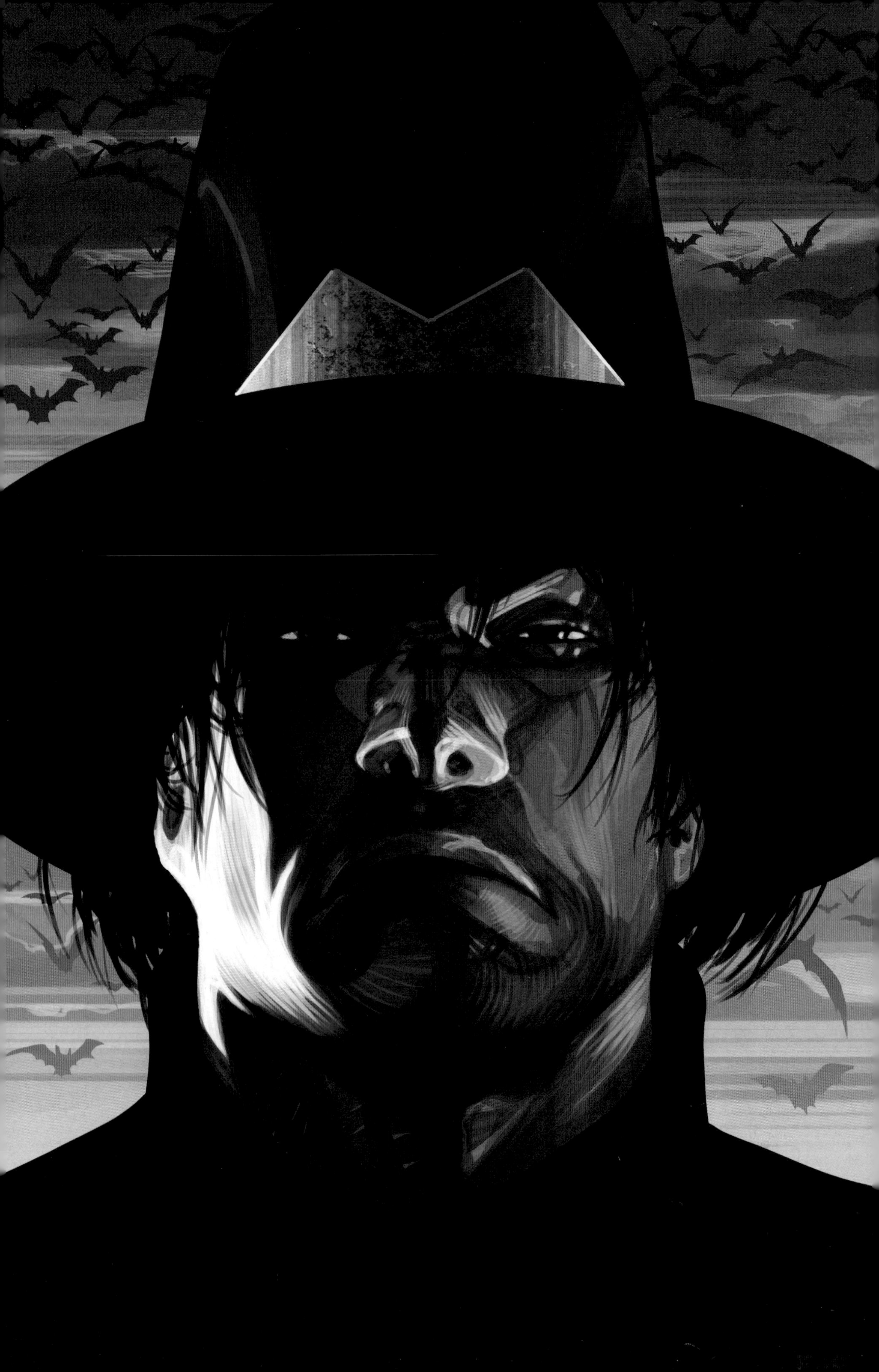

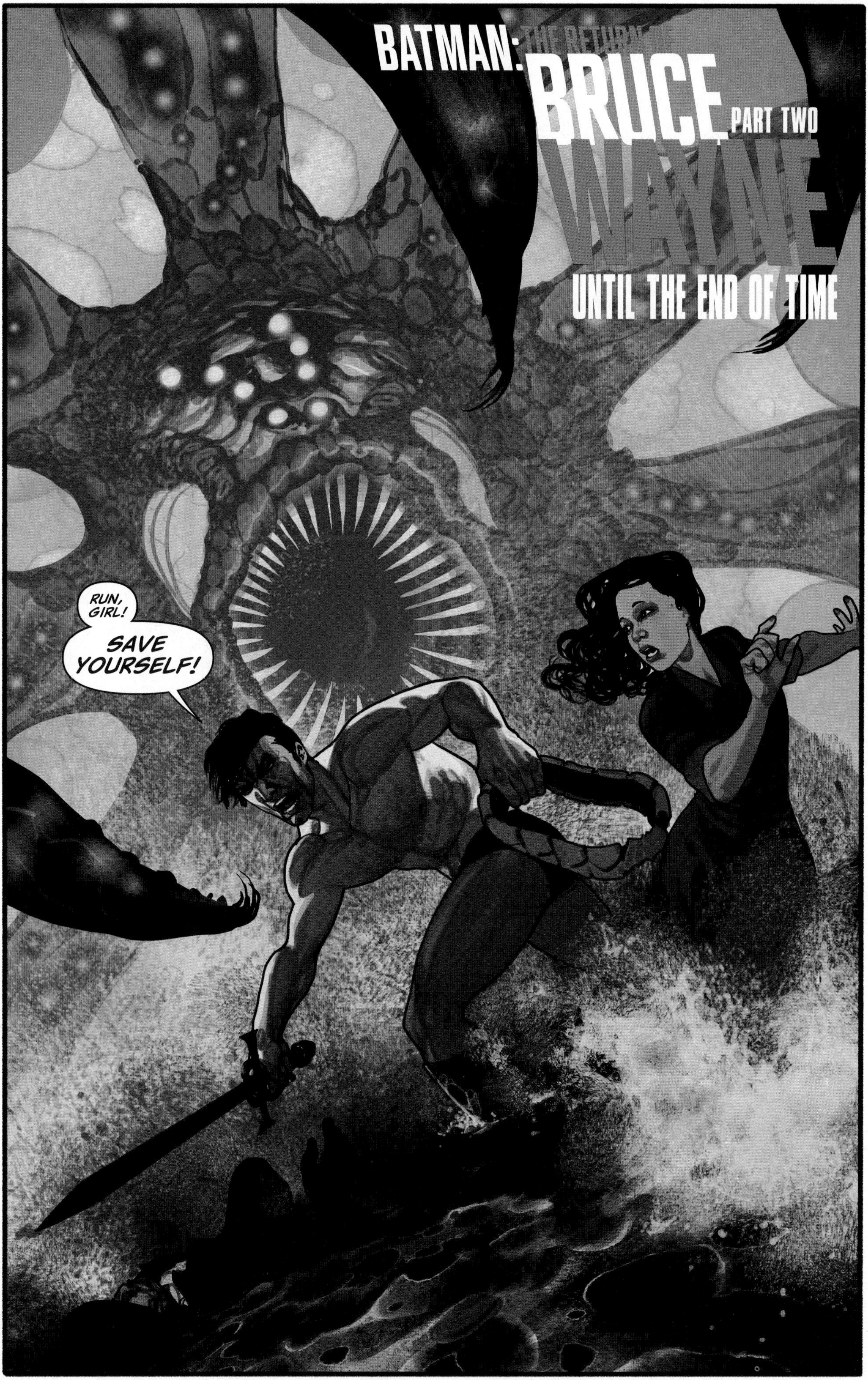
BATMAN: THE RETURN OF BRUCE WAYNE PART TWO
UNTIL THE END OF TIME
RUN, GIRL!
SAVE YOURSELF!

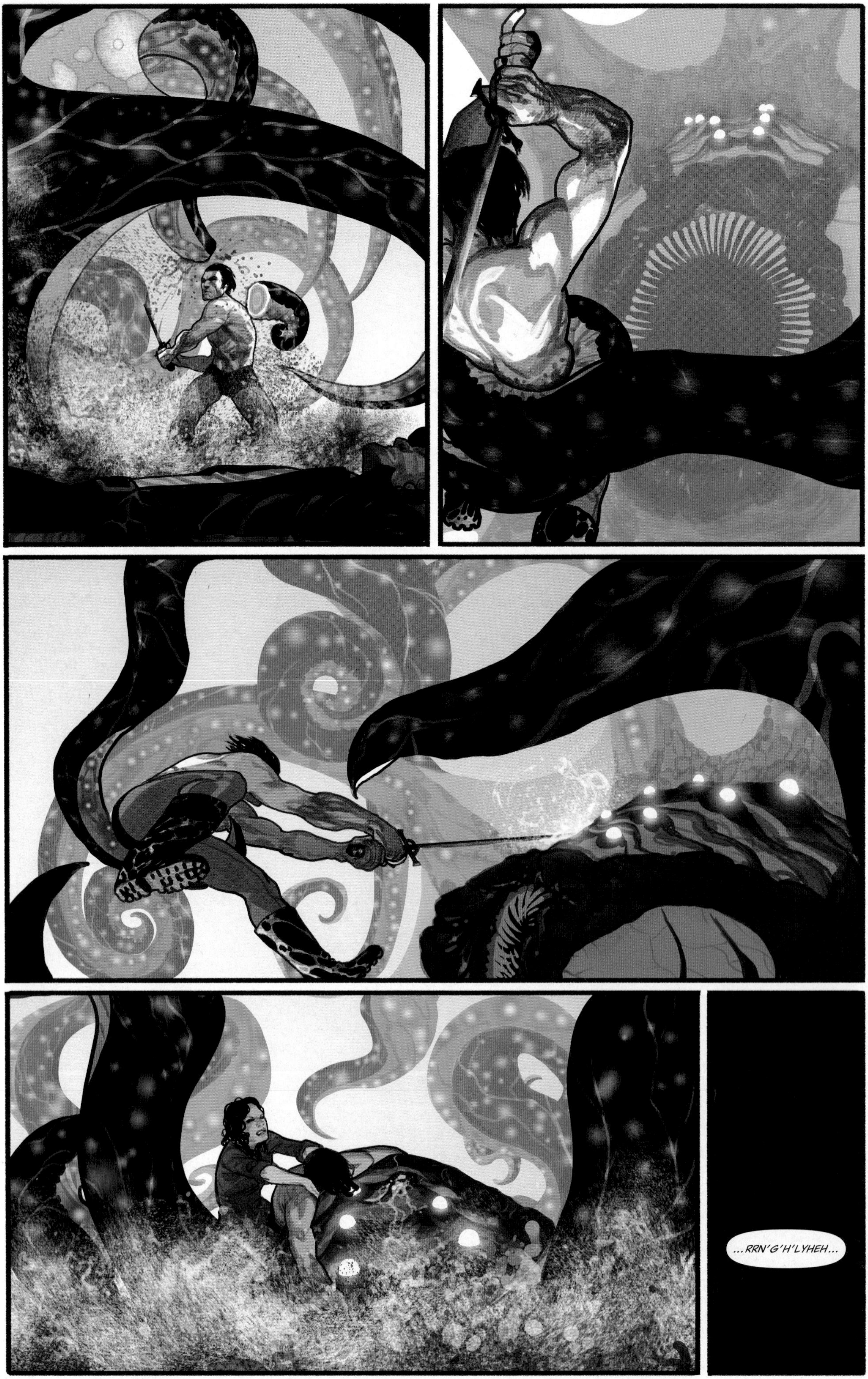
...RRN'G'H'LYHEH...

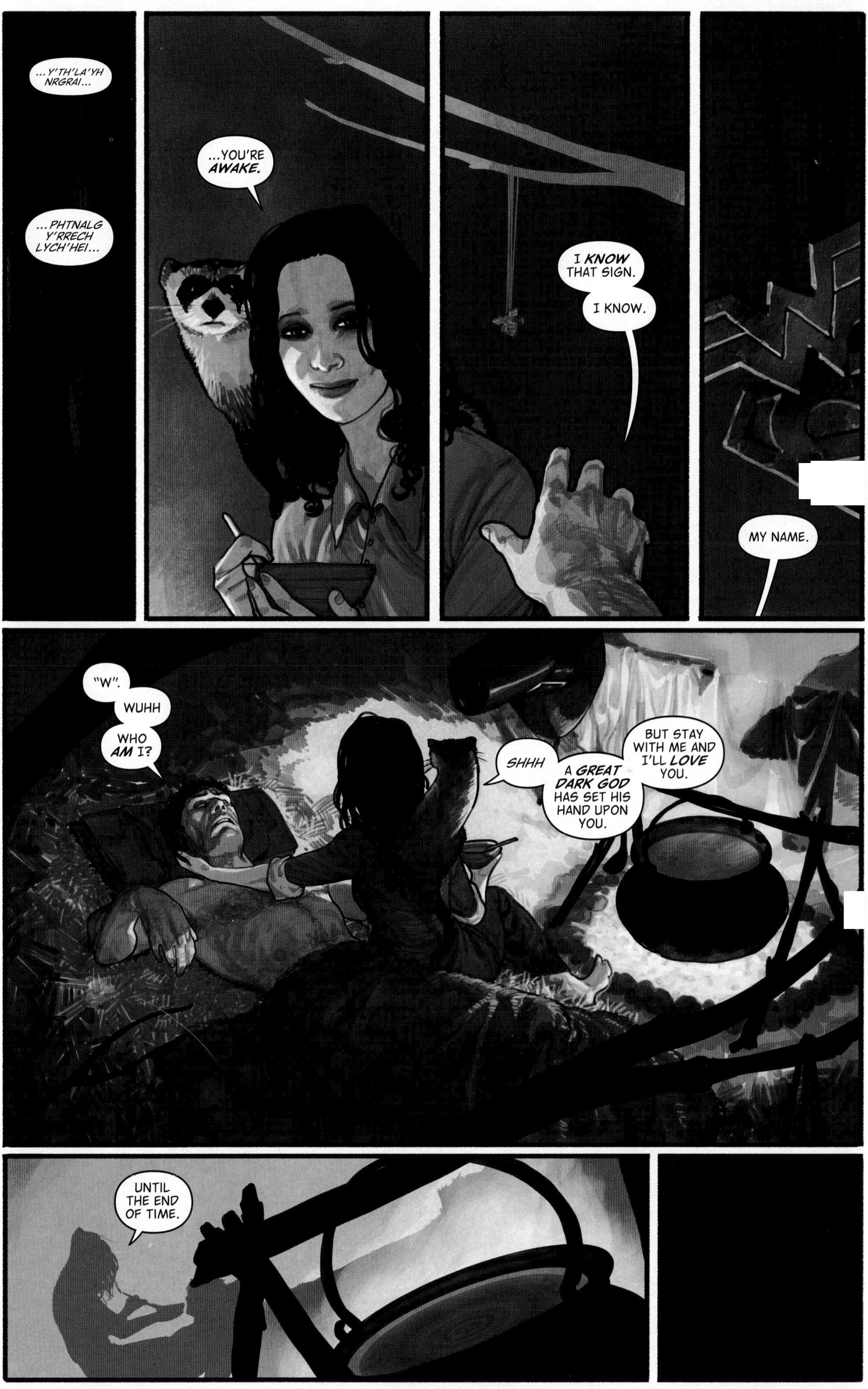
...Y'TH'LA'YH NRGRAI...
...PHTNALG Y'RRECH LYCH'HEI...
...YOU'RE AWAKE.
I KNOW THAT SIGN.
I KNOW.
MY NAME.
"W".
WUHH
WHO AM I?
SHHH
A GREAT DARK GOD HAS SET HIS HAND UPON YOU.
BUT STAY WITH ME AND I'LL LOVE YOU.
UNTIL THE END OF TIME.

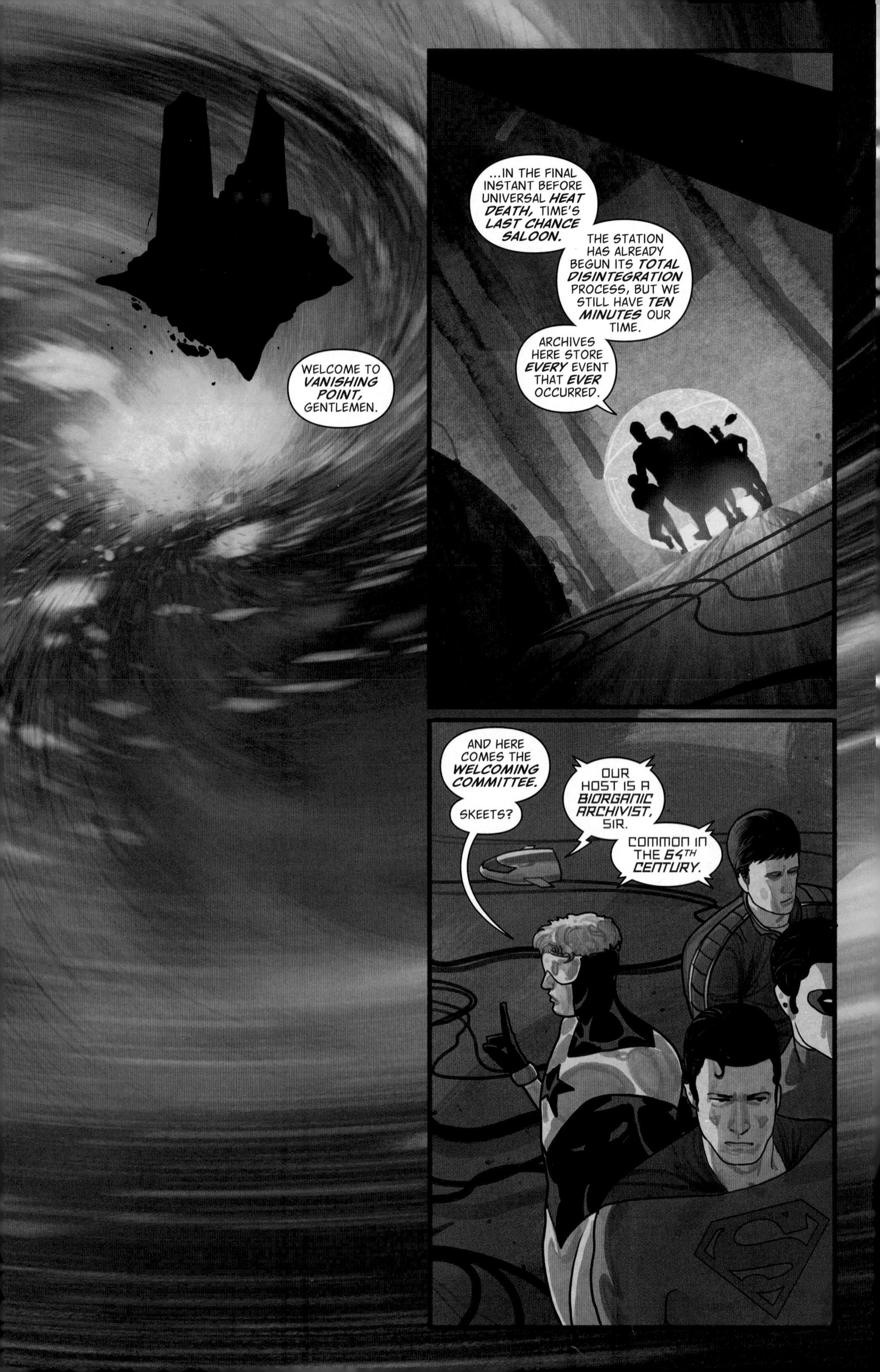
WELCOME TO VANISHING POINT, GENTLEMEN.
...IN THE FINAL INSTANT BEFORE UNIVERSAL HEAT DEATH, TIME'S LAST CHANCE SALOON.
THE STATION HAS ALREADY BEGUN ITS TOTAL DISINTEGRATION PROCESS, BUT WE STILL HAVE TEN MINUTES OUR TIME.
ARCHIVES HERE STORE EVERY EVENT THAT EVER OCCURRED.
AND HERE COMES THE WELCOMING COMMITTEE.
SKEETS?
OUR HOST IS A BIORGANIC ARCHIVIST, SIR.
COMMON IN THE 64TH CENTURY.

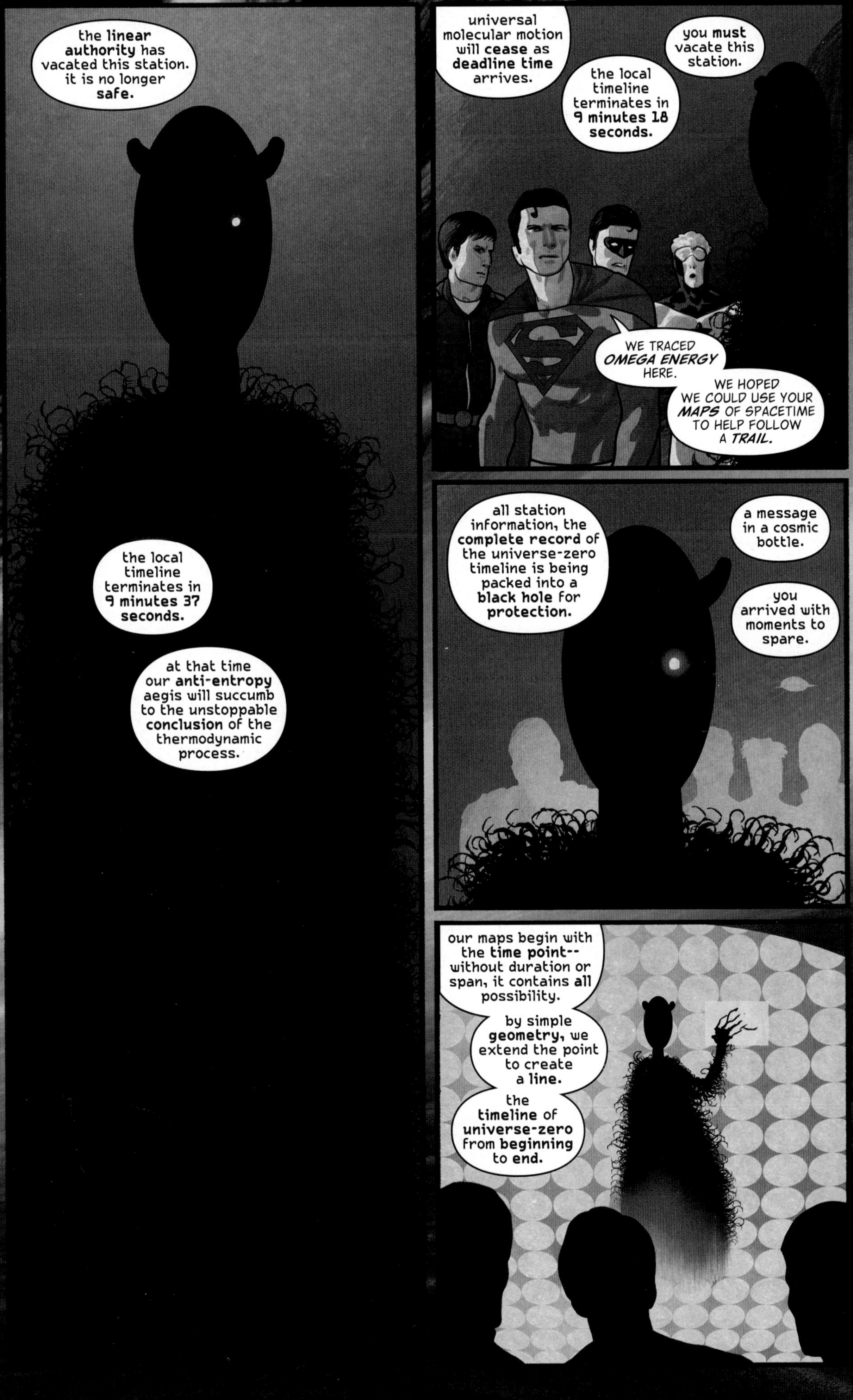
the linear authority has vacated this station. it is no longer safe.
the local timeline terminates in 9 minutes 37 seconds.
at that time our anti-entropy aegis will succumb to the unstoppable conclusion of the thermodynamic process.
universal molecular motion will cease as deadline time arrives.
the local timeline terminates in 9 minutes 18 seconds.
you must vacate this station.
WE TRACED OMEGA ENERGY HERE.
WE HOPED WE COULD USE YOUR MAPS OF SPACETIME TO HELP FOLLOW A TRAIL.
all station information, the complete record of the universe-zero timeline is being packed into a black hole for protection.
a message in a cosmic bottle.
you arrived with moments to spare.
our maps begin with the time point-- without duration or span, it contains all possibility.
by simple geometry, we extend the point to create a line.
the timeline of universe-zero from beginning to end.

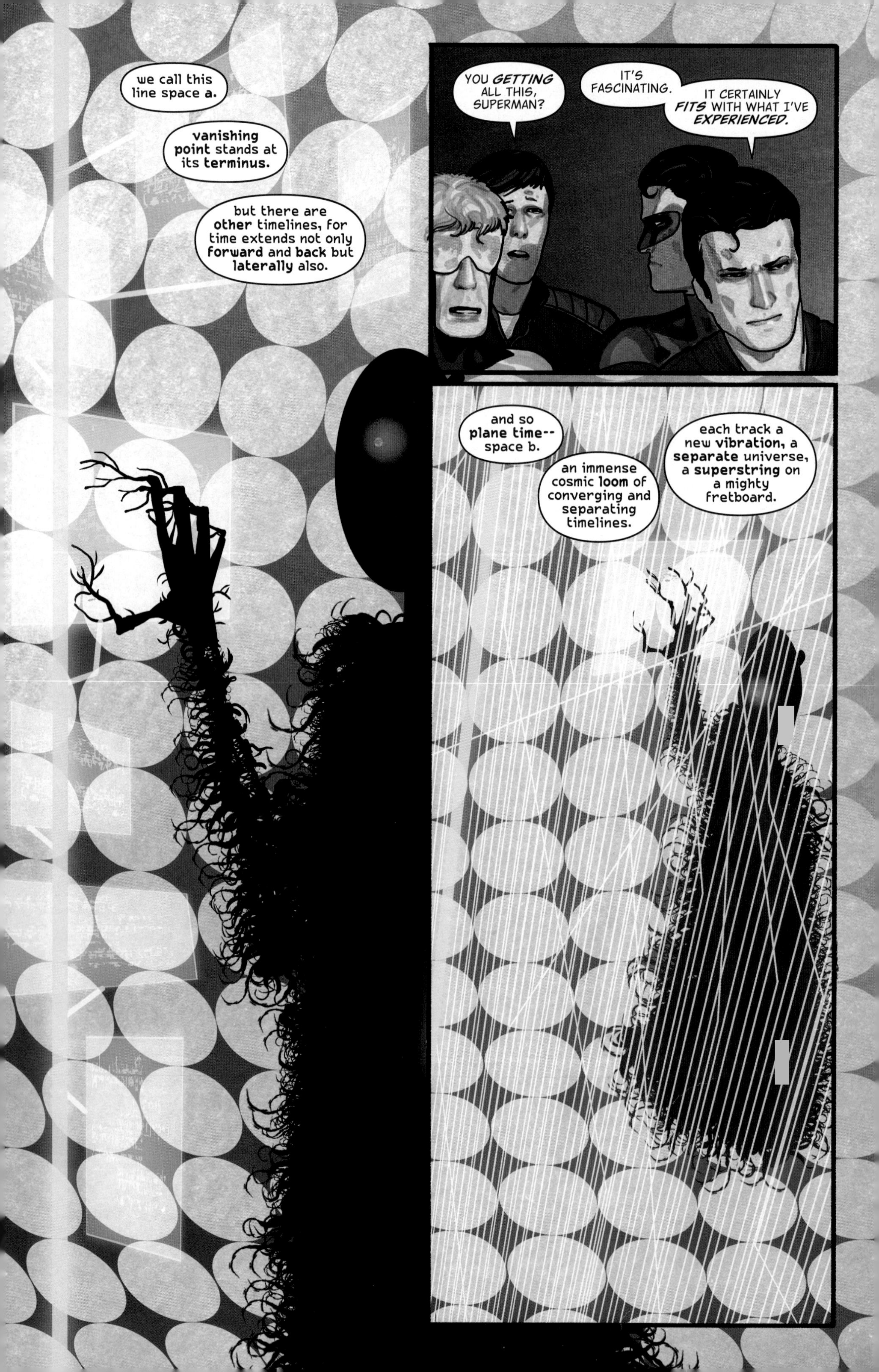
we call this line space a.
vanishing point stands at its terminus.
but there are other timelines, for time extends not only forward and back but laterally also.
YOU GETTING ALL THIS, SUPERMAN?
IT'S FASCINATING.
IT CERTAINLY FITS WITH WHAT I'VE EXPERIENCED.
and so plane time--space b.
an immense cosmic loom of converging and separating timelines.
each track a new vibration, a separate universe, a superstring on a mighty fretboard.

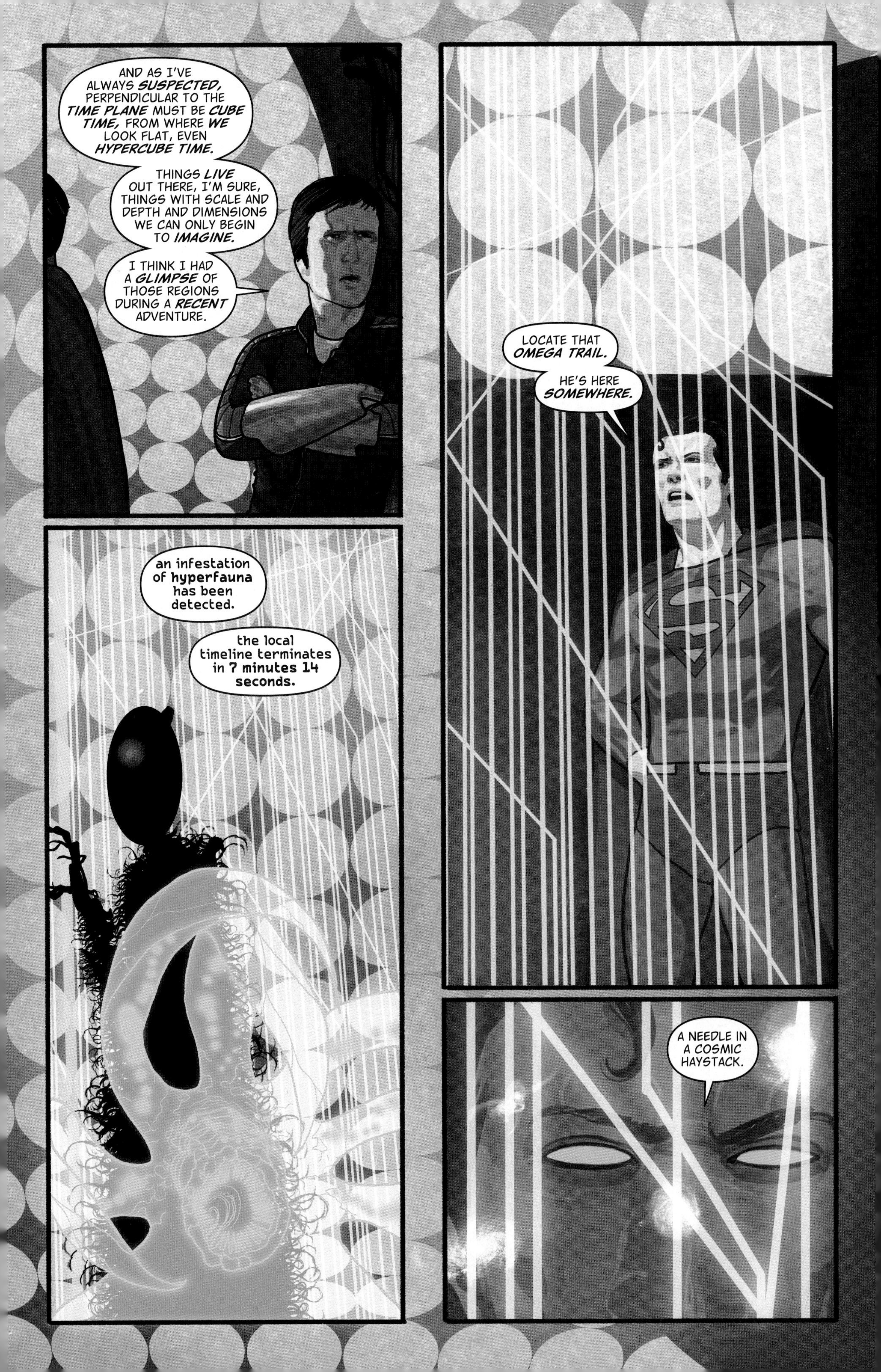
AND AS I'VE ALWAYS SUSPECTED, PERPENDICULAR TO THE TIME PLANE MUST BE CUBE TIME, FROM WHERE WE LOOK FLAT, EVEN HYPERCUBE TIME.
THINGS LIVE OUT THERE, I'M SURE, THINGS WITH SCALE AND DEPTH AND DIMENSIONS WE CAN ONLY BEGIN TO IMAGINE.
I THINK I HAD A GLIMPSE OF THOSE REGIONS DURING A RECENT ADVENTURE.
LOCATE THAT OMEGA TRAIL.
HE'S HERE SOMEWHERE.
an infestation of hyperfauna has been detected.
the local timeline terminates in 7 minutes 14 seconds.
A NEEDLE IN A COSMIC HAYSTACK.

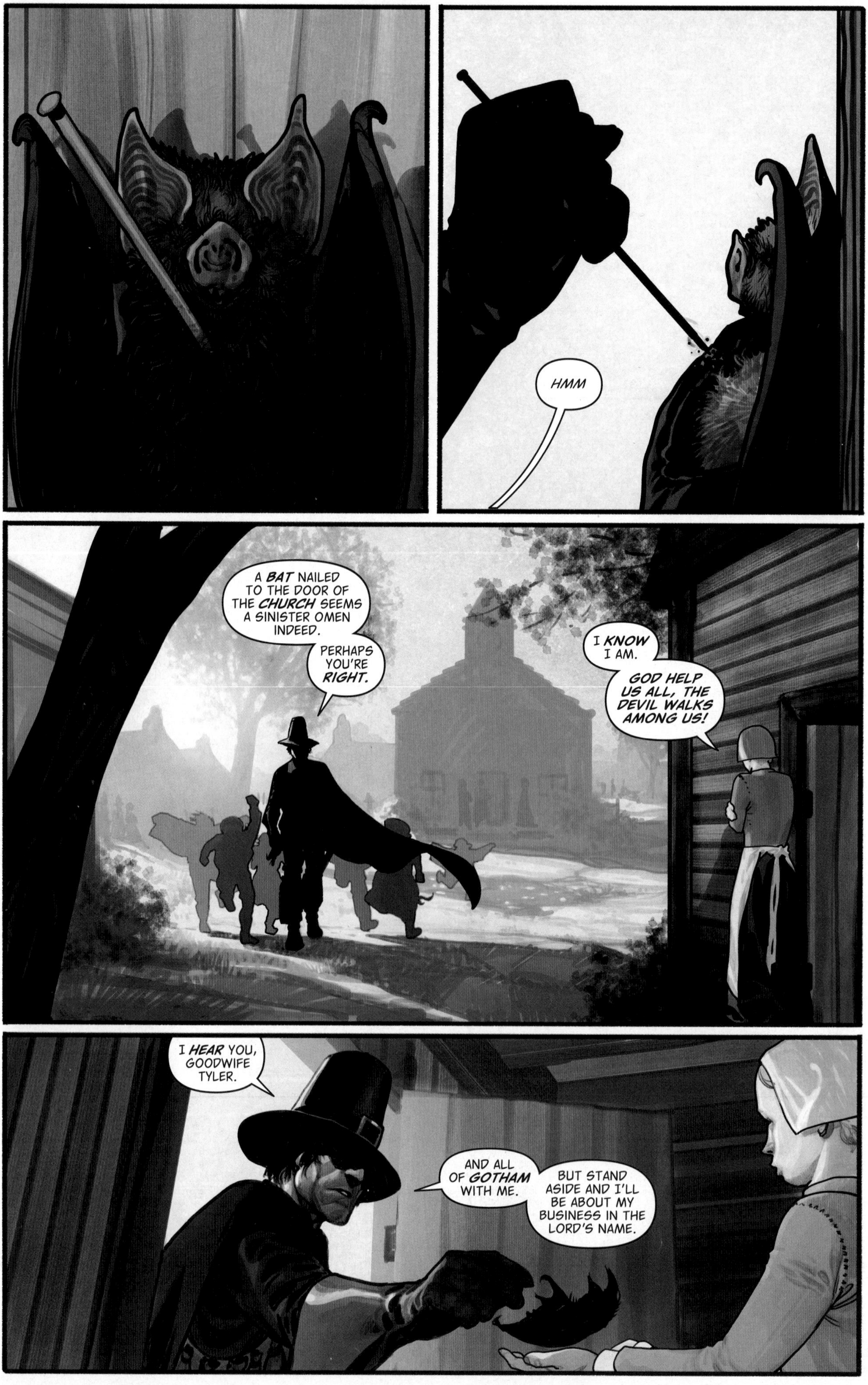
HMM
A BAT NAILED TO THE DOOR OF THE CHURCH SEEMS A SINISTER OMEN INDEED.
PERHAPS YOU'RE RIGHT.
I KNOW I AM.
GOD HELP US ALL, THE DEVIL WALKS AMONG US!
I HEAR YOU, GOODWIFE TYLER.
AND ALL OF GOTHAM WITH ME.
BUT STAND ASIDE AND I'LL BE ABOUT MY BUSINESS IN THE LORD'S NAME.

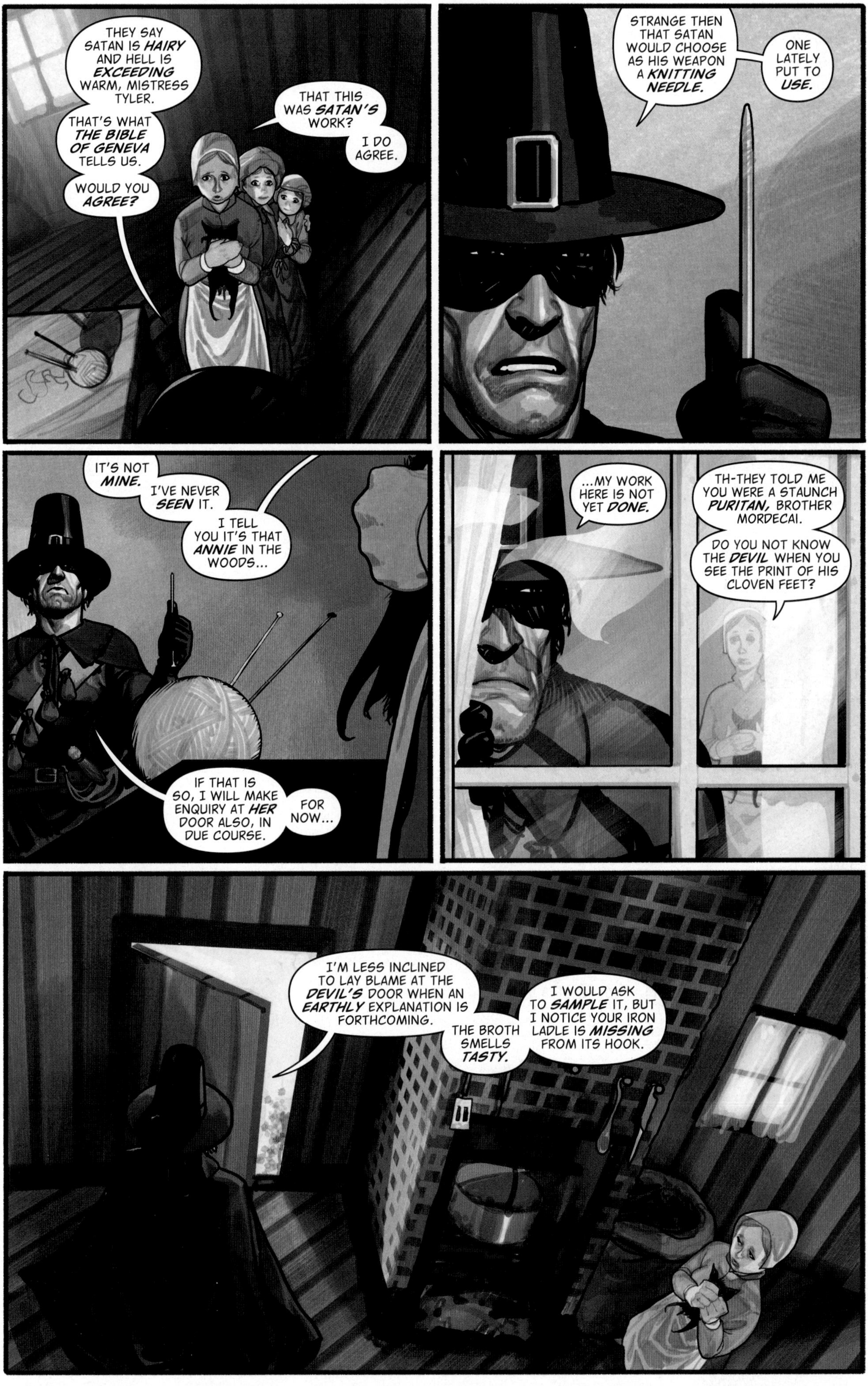
THEY SAY SATAN IS HAIRY AND HELL IS EXCEEDING WARM, MISTRESS TYLER.
THAT'S WHAT THE BIBLE OF GENEVA TELLS US.
WOULD YOU AGREE?
THAT THIS WAS SATAN'S WORK?
I DO AGREE.
STRANGE THEN THAT SATAN WOULD CHOOSE AS HIS WEAPON A KNITTING NEEDLE.
ONE LATELY PUT TO USE.
IT'S NOT MINE.
I'VE NEVER SEEN IT.
I TELL YOU IT'S THAT ANNIE IN THE WOODS...
IF THAT IS SO, I WILL MAKE ENQUIRY AT HER DOOR ALSO, IN DUE COURSE.
FOR NOW...
...MY WORK HERE IS NOT YET DONE.
TH-THEY TOLD ME YOU WERE A STAUNCH PURITAN, BROTHER MORDECAI.
DO YOU NOT KNOW THE DEVIL WHEN YOU SEE THE PRINT OF HIS CLOVEN FEET?
I'M LESS INCLINED TO LAY BLAME AT THE DEVIL'S DOOR WHEN AN EARTHLY EXPLANATION IS FORTHCOMING.
THE BROTH SMELLS TASTY.
I WOULD ASK TO SAMPLE IT, BUT I NOTICE YOUR IRON LADLE IS MISSING FROM ITS HOOK.

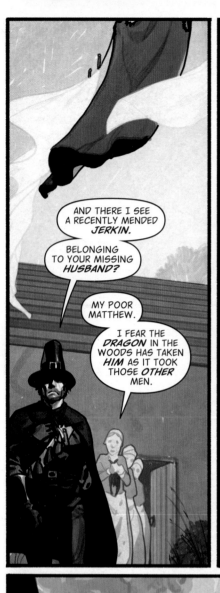

AND THERE I SEE A RECENTLY MENDED *JERKIN*.

BELONGING TO YOUR MISSING *HUSBAND?*

MY POOR MATTHEW.

I FEAR THE *DRAGON* IN THE WOODS HAS TAKEN *HIM* AS IT TOOK THOSE *OTHER* MEN.

JUDGING BY THE *YARN,* I'D SAY THE DEVIL'S BEEN HARD AT WORK *HERE,* TOO.

AN EXCELLENT *REPAIR.*

ALTHO' I IMAGINE MATTHEW TYLER WILL HAVE NO MORE NEED OF *THIS.*

EXCEPT AS A *SHROUD* TO WARM HIS SWIFTLY COOLING BONES.

IT SEEMS THE INNOCENT *BAT* WAS THE REAL VICTIM HERE.

BUT... BUT...

THE DEVIL.

TAKE HER AWAY!

AND AS FOR *THIS* MAN!

THIS FLEMISH *PAINTER,* VAN DERM.

IT'S MY JOB TO MAINTAIN THE *REGISTER* HERE IN GOTHAM COLONY, BROTHER *MALLEUS.*

DRAGONS OR NO DRAGONS.

WITCHES OR NO WITCHES.

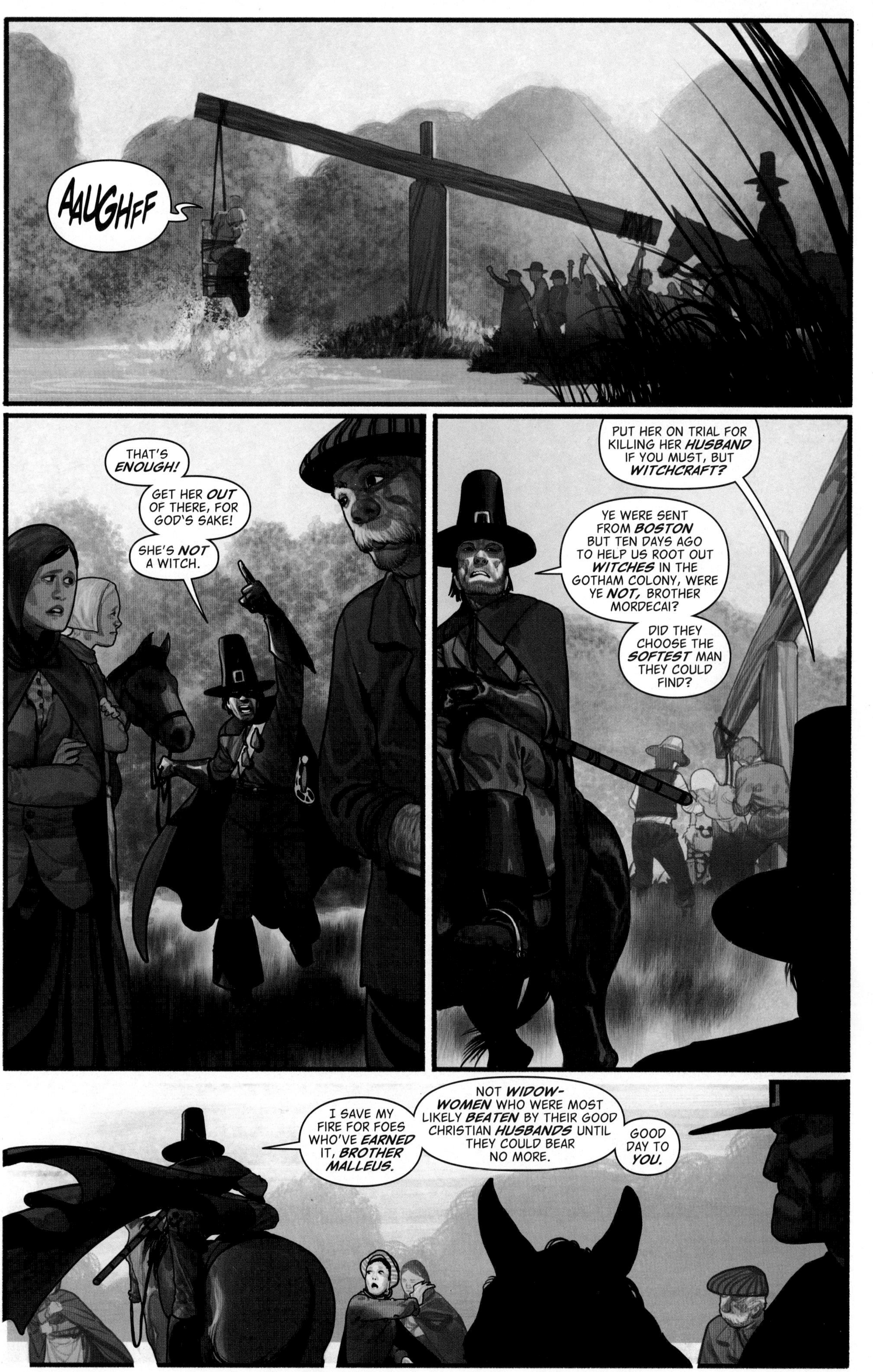
AAUGHFF
THAT'S ENOUGH!
GET HER OUT OF THERE, FOR GOD'S SAKE!
SHE'S NOT A WITCH.
PUT HER ON TRIAL FOR KILLING HER HUSBAND IF YOU MUST, BUT WITCHCRAFT?
YE WERE SENT FROM BOSTON BUT TEN DAYS AGO TO HELP US ROOT OUT WITCHES IN THE GOTHAM COLONY, WERE YE NOT, BROTHER MORDECAI?
DID THEY CHOOSE THE SOFTEST MAN THEY COULD FIND?
I SAVE MY FIRE FOR FOES WHO'VE EARNED IT, BROTHER MALLEUS.
NOT WIDOW-WOMEN WHO WERE MOST LIKELY BEATEN BY THEIR GOOD CHRISTIAN HUSBANDS UNTIL THEY COULD BEAR NO MORE.
GOOD DAY TO YOU.

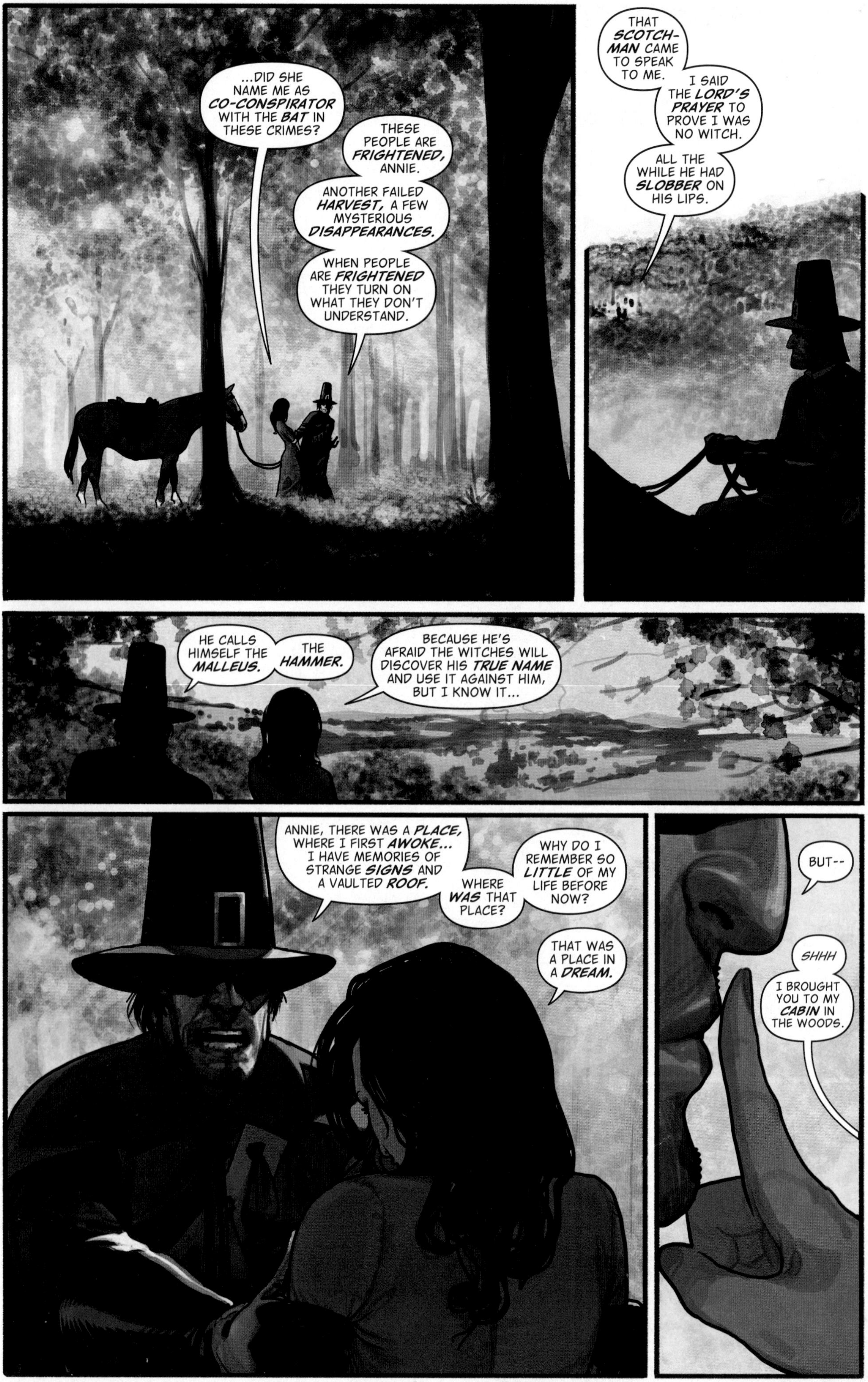

...DID SHE NAME ME AS CO-CONSPIRATOR WITH THE BAT IN THESE CRIMES?
THESE PEOPLE ARE FRIGHTENED, ANNIE.
ANOTHER FAILED HARVEST, A FEW MYSTERIOUS DISAPPEARANCES.
WHEN PEOPLE ARE FRIGHTENED THEY TURN ON WHAT THEY DON'T UNDERSTAND.
THAT SCOTCHMAN CAME TO SPEAK TO ME.
I SAID THE LORD'S PRAYER TO PROVE I WAS NO WITCH.
ALL THE WHILE HE HAD SLOBBER ON HIS LIPS.
HE CALLS HIMSELF THE MALLEUS.
THE HAMMER.
BECAUSE HE'S AFRAID THE WITCHES WILL DISCOVER HIS TRUE NAME AND USE IT AGAINST HIM, BUT I KNOW IT...
ANNIE, THERE WAS A PLACE, WHERE I FIRST AWOKE... I HAVE MEMORIES OF STRANGE SIGNS AND A VAULTED ROOF.
WHERE WAS THAT PLACE?
WHY DO I REMEMBER SO LITTLE OF MY LIFE BEFORE NOW?
THAT WAS A PLACE IN A DREAM.
BUT--
SHHH
I BROUGHT YOU TO MY CABIN IN THE WOODS.

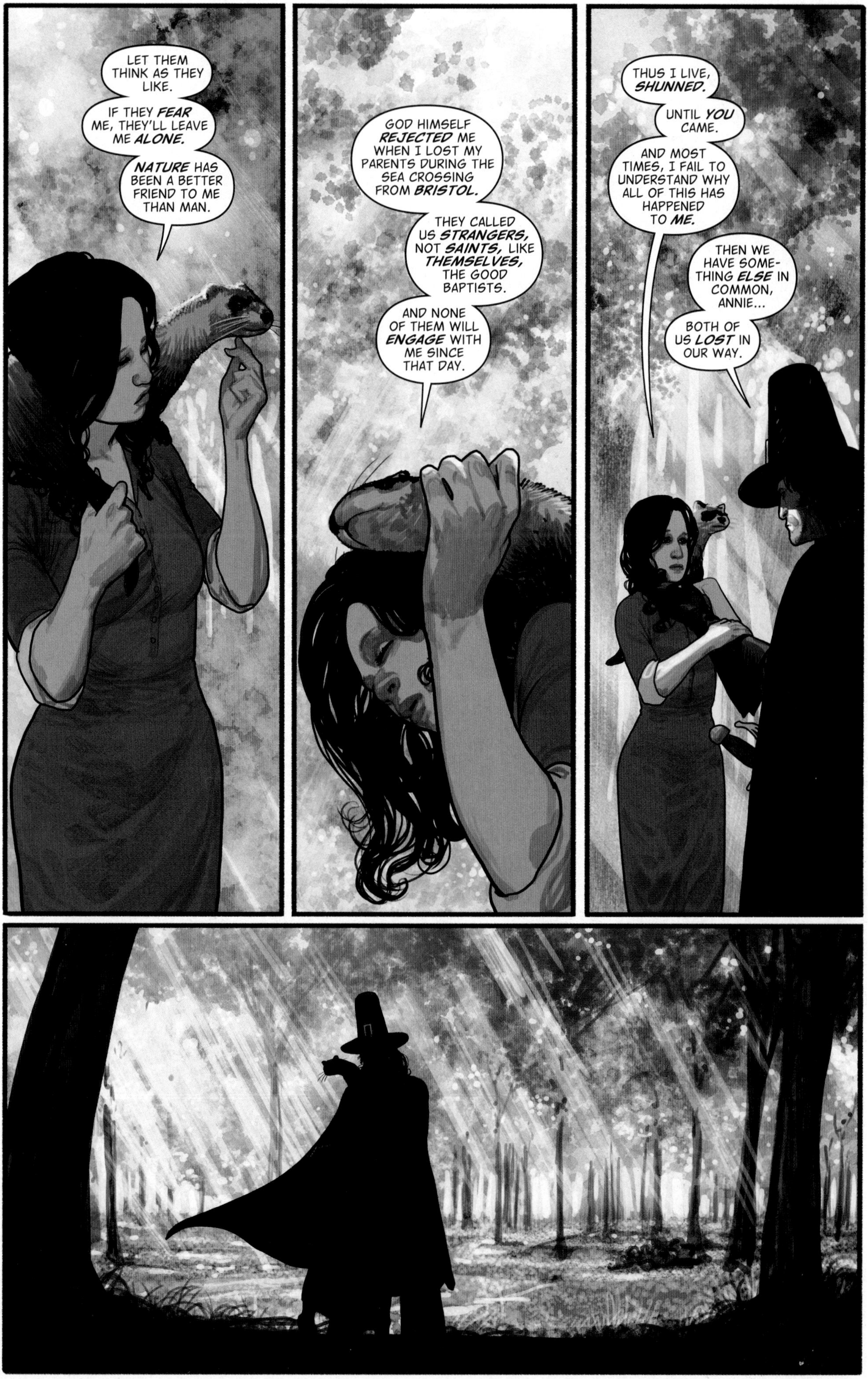

LET THEM THINK AS THEY LIKE.
IF THEY FEAR ME, THEY'LL LEAVE ME ALONE.
NATURE HAS BEEN A BETTER FRIEND TO ME THAN MAN.
GOD HIMSELF REJECTED ME WHEN I LOST MY PARENTS DURING THE SEA CROSSING FROM BRISTOL.
THEY CALLED US STRANGERS, NOT SAINTS, LIKE THEMSELVES, THE GOOD BAPTISTS.
AND NONE OF THEM WILL ENGAGE WITH ME SINCE THAT DAY.
THUS I LIVE, SHUNNED.
UNTIL YOU CAME.
AND MOST TIMES, I FAIL TO UNDERSTAND WHY ALL OF THIS HAS HAPPENED TO ME.
THEN WE HAVE SOMETHING ELSE IN COMMON, ANNIE...
BOTH OF US LOST IN OUR WAY.

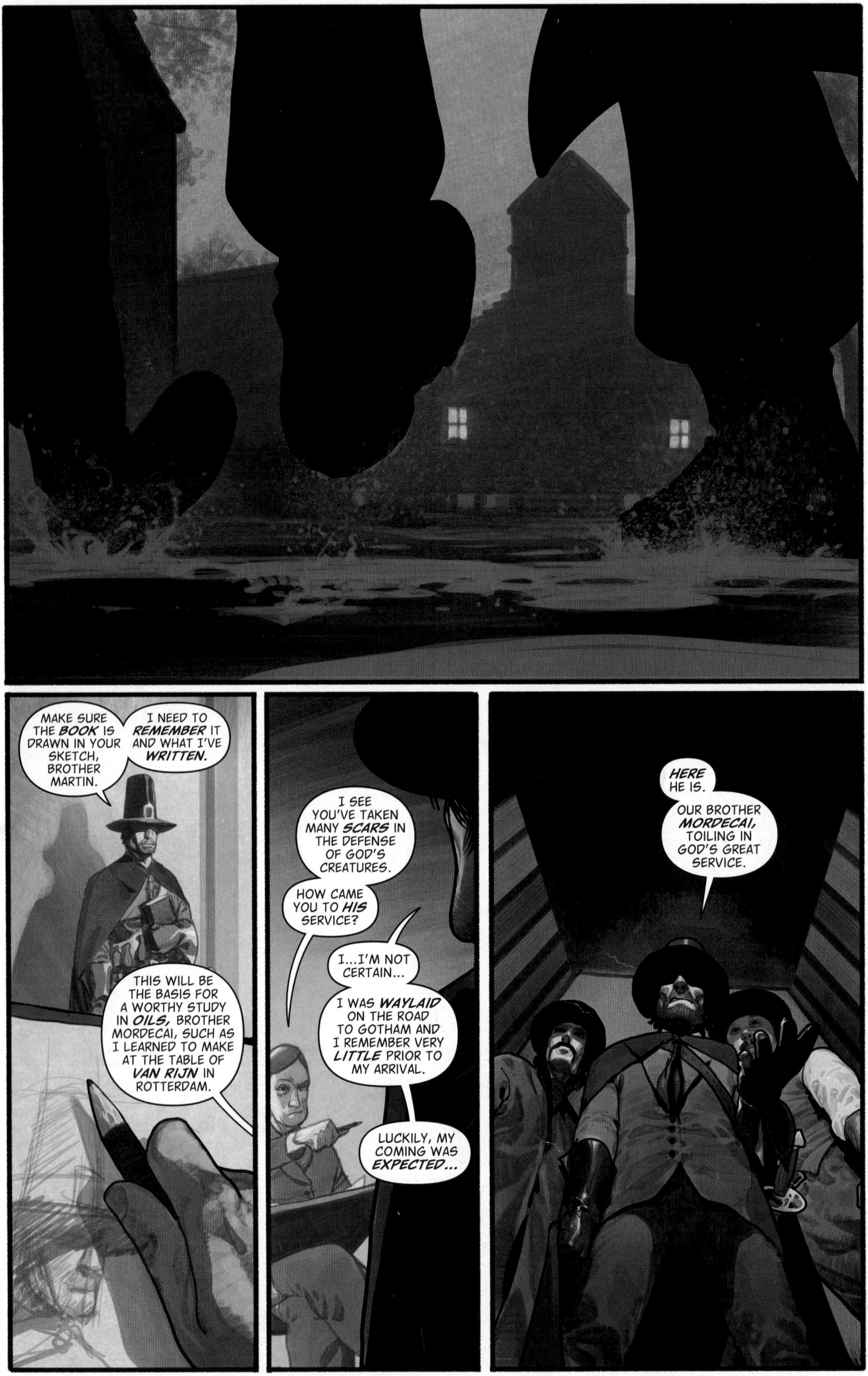
MAKE SURE THE BOOK IS DRAWN IN YOUR SKETCH, BROTHER MARTIN.
I NEED TO REMEMBER IT AND WHAT I'VE WRITTEN.
THIS WILL BE THE BASIS FOR A WORTHY STUDY IN OILS, BROTHER MORDECAI, SUCH AS I LEARNED TO MAKE AT THE TABLE OF VAN RIJN IN ROTTERDAM.
I SEE YOU'VE TAKEN MANY SCARS IN THE DEFENSE OF GOD'S CREATURES.
HOW CAME YOU TO HIS SERVICE?
I...I'M NOT CERTAIN...
I WAS WAYLAID ON THE ROAD TO GOTHAM AND I REMEMBER VERY LITTLE PRIOR TO MY ARRIVAL.
LUCKILY, MY COMING WAS EXPECTED...
HERE HE IS.
OUR BROTHER MORDECAI, TOILING IN GOD'S GREAT SERVICE.

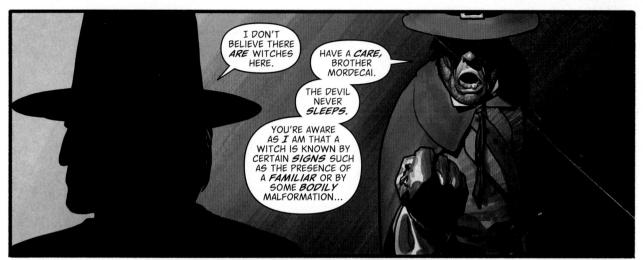

I DON'T BELIEVE THERE *ARE* WITCHES HERE.

HAVE A *CARE,* BROTHER MORDECAI.

THE DEVIL NEVER *SLEEPS.*

YOU'RE AWARE AS *I* AM THAT A WITCH IS KNOWN BY CERTAIN *SIGNS* SUCH AS THE PRESENCE OF A *FAMILIAR* OR BY SOME *BODILY* MALFORMATION...

ALL AGREE THY SPEECH IS *STRANGER* EVEN THAN THE DUTCHMAN'S HERE.

AS IF THE *KING'S ENGLISH* WERE NOT THY *NATIVE* TONGUE.

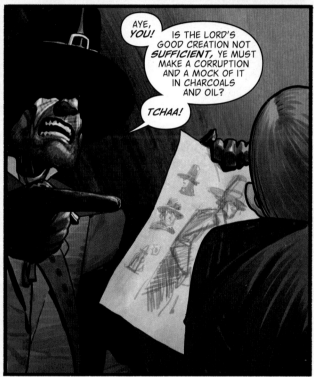

AYE, *YOU!* IS THE LORD'S GOOD CREATION NOT *SUFFICIENT,* YE MUST MAKE A CORRUPTION AND A MOCK OF IT IN CHARCOALS AND OIL?

TCHAA!

ATTEND TO THY VANITY IF IT SO PLEASES YE, BROTHER MORDECAI.

THE *DRAGON* HAS BEEN SIGHTED IN THE FOREST WEST OF *BRISTOL BAY.*

I HAVE WHAT I NEED TO CONTINUE.

I MUST GO *WITH* THEM, BROTHER MARTIN.

IF THERE *IS* A DRAGON, I OWE IT AN *APOLOGY.*

KEEP MY BOOK SAFE.

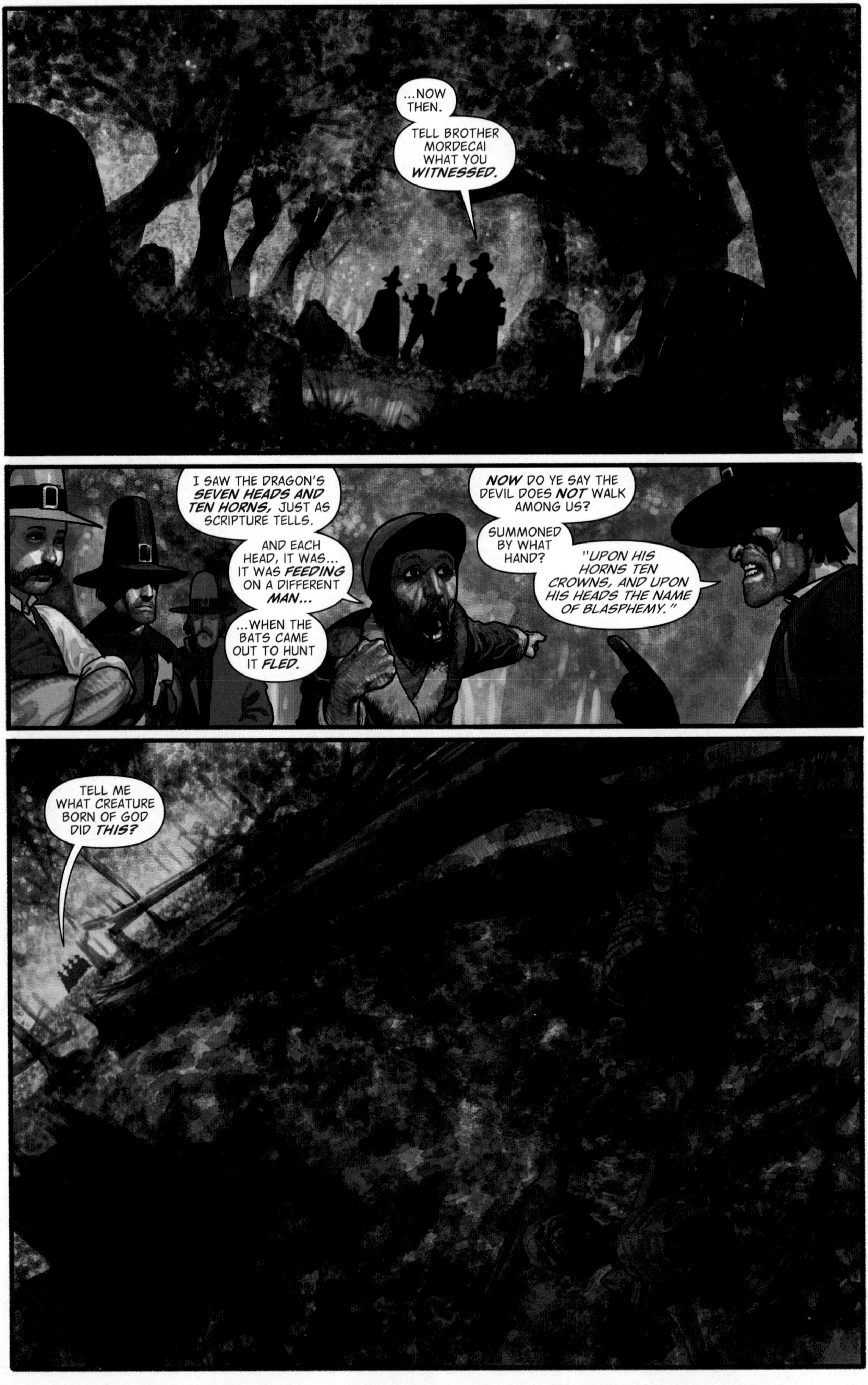
...NOW THEN.
TELL BROTHER MORDECAI WHAT YOU WITNESSED.
I SAW THE DRAGON'S SEVEN HEADS AND TEN HORNS, JUST AS SCRIPTURE TELLS.
AND EACH HEAD, IT WAS... IT WAS FEEDING ON A DIFFERENT MAN...
...WHEN THE BATS CAME OUT TO HUNT IT FLED.
NOW DO YE SAY THE DEVIL DOES NOT WALK AMONG US?
SUMMONED BY WHAT HAND?
"UPON HIS HORNS TEN CROWNS, AND UPON HIS HEADS THE NAME OF BLASPHEMY."
TELL ME WHAT CREATURE BORN OF GOD DID THIS?

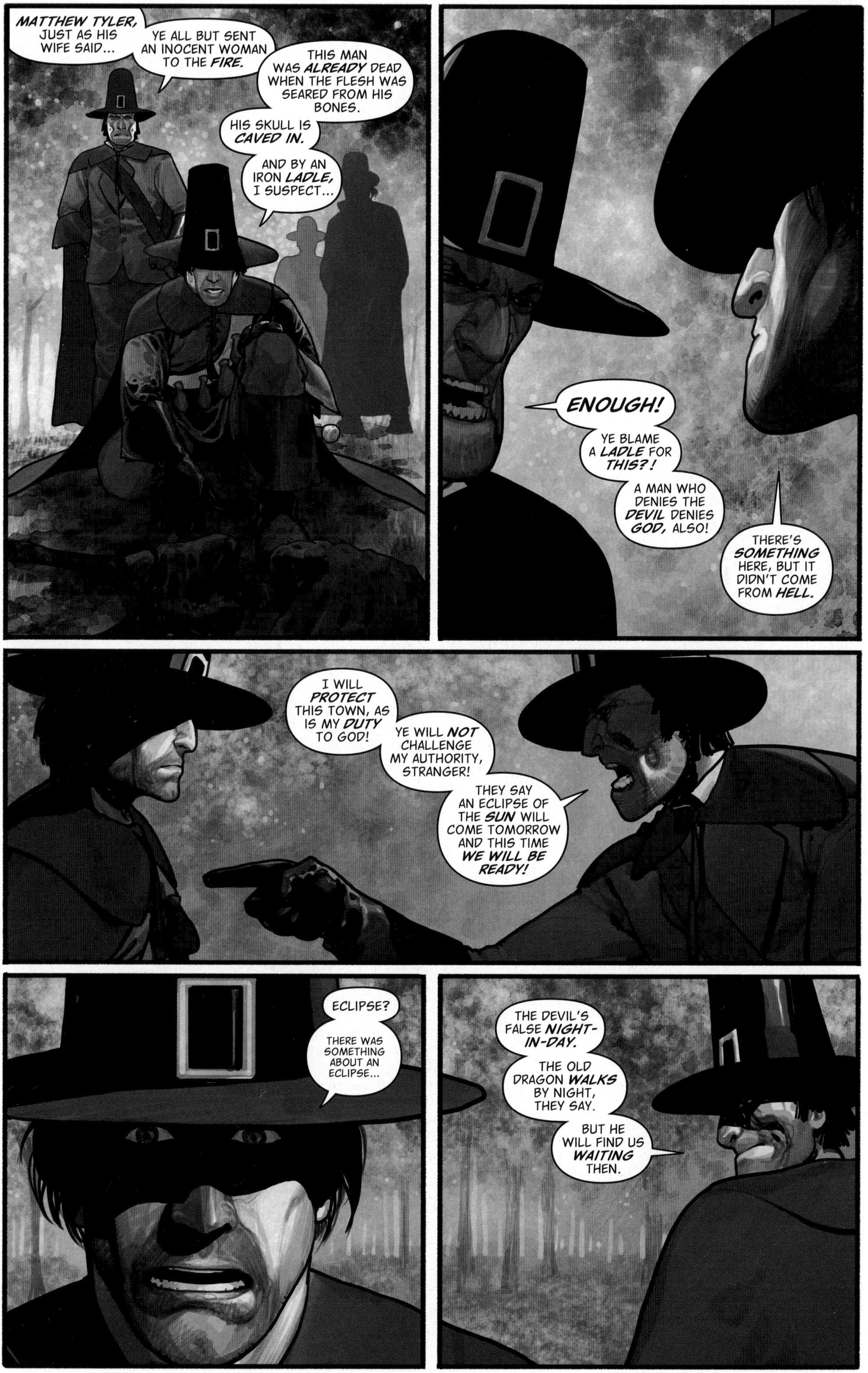
MATTHEW TYLER, JUST AS HIS WIFE SAID...
YE ALL BUT SENT AN INOCENT WOMAN TO THE FIRE.
THIS MAN WAS ALREADY DEAD WHEN THE FLESH WAS SEARED FROM HIS BONES.
HIS SKULL IS CAVED IN.
AND BY AN IRON LADLE, I SUSPECT...
ENOUGH!
YE BLAME A LADLE FOR THIS?!
A MAN WHO DENIES THE DEVIL DENIES GOD, ALSO!
THERE'S SOMETHING HERE, BUT IT DIDN'T COME FROM HELL.
I WILL PROTECT THIS TOWN, AS IS MY DUTY TO GOD!
YE WILL NOT CHALLENGE MY AUTHORITY, STRANGER!
THEY SAY AN ECLIPSE OF THE SUN WILL COME TOMORROW AND THIS TIME WE WILL BE READY!
ECLIPSE?
THERE WAS SOMETHING ABOUT AN ECLIPSE...
THE DEVIL'S FALSE NIGHT-IN-DAY.
THE OLD DRAGON WALKS BY NIGHT, THEY SAY.
BUT HE WILL FIND US WAITING THEN.

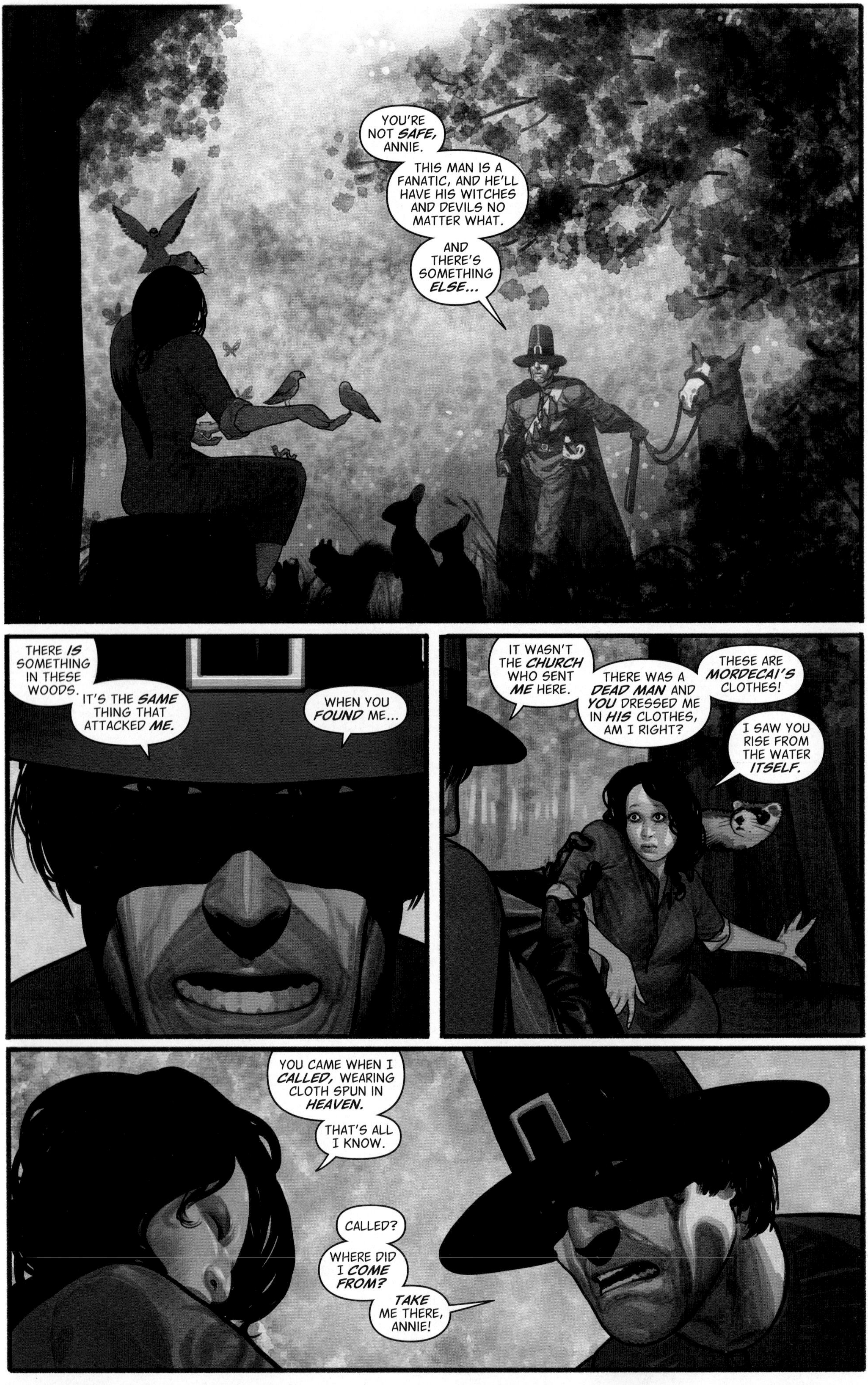
YOU'RE NOT SAFE, ANNIE.
THIS MAN IS A FANATIC, AND HE'LL HAVE HIS WITCHES AND DEVILS NO MATTER WHAT.
AND THERE'S SOMETHING ELSE...
THERE IS SOMETHING IN THESE WOODS.
IT'S THE SAME THING THAT ATTACKED ME.
WHEN YOU FOUND ME...
IT WASN'T THE CHURCH WHO SENT ME HERE.
THERE WAS A DEAD MAN AND YOU DRESSED ME IN HIS CLOTHES, AM I RIGHT?
THESE ARE MORDECAI'S CLOTHES!
I SAW YOU RISE FROM THE WATER ITSELF.
YOU CAME WHEN I CALLED, WEARING CLOTH SPUN IN HEAVEN.
THAT'S ALL I KNOW.
CALLED?
WHERE DID I COME FROM?
TAKE ME THERE, ANNIE!

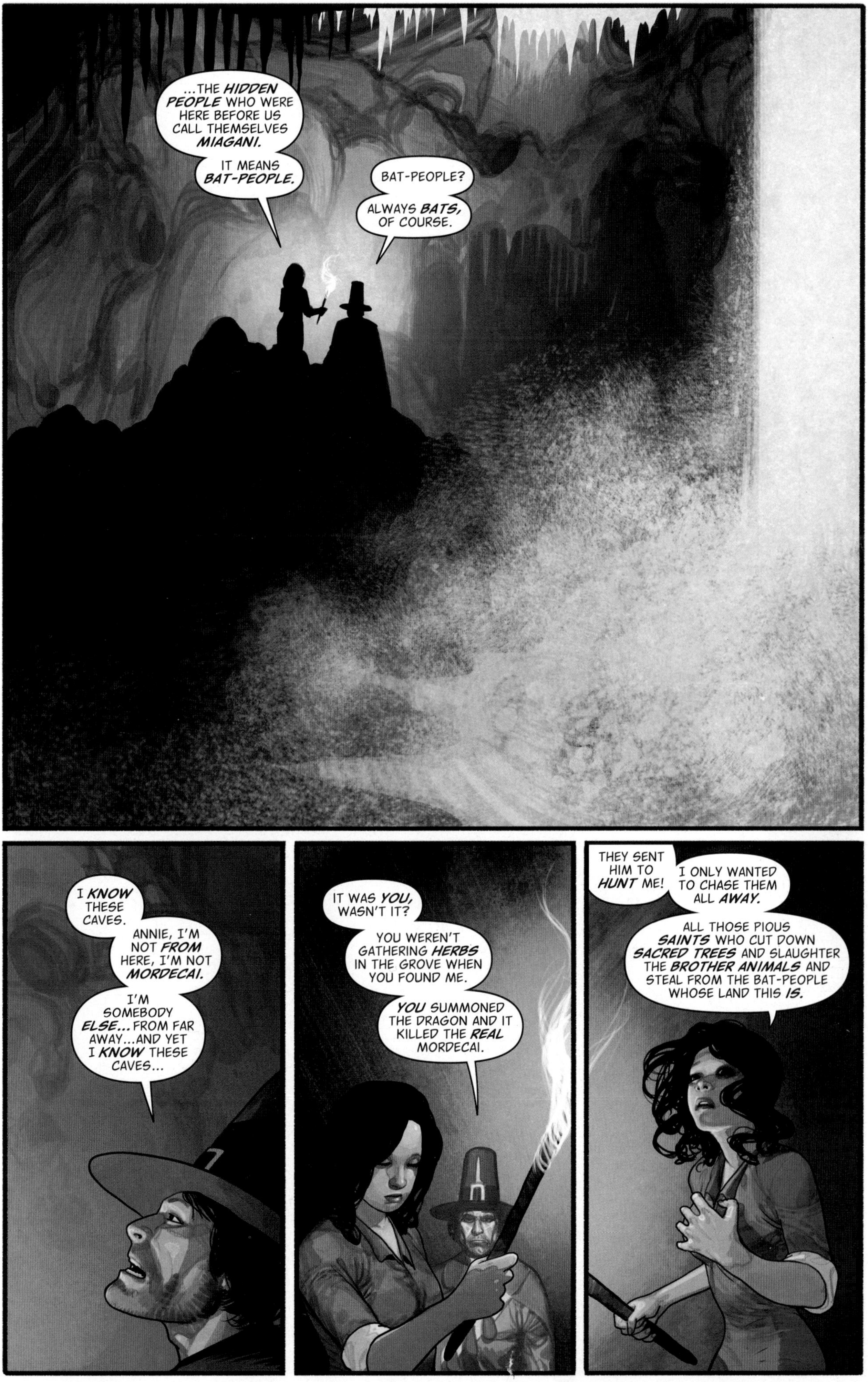
...THE HIDDEN PEOPLE WHO WERE HERE BEFORE US CALL THEMSELVES MIAGANI.
IT MEANS BAT-PEOPLE.
BAT-PEOPLE?
ALWAYS BATS, OF COURSE.
I KNOW THESE CAVES.
ANNIE, I'M NOT FROM HERE, I'M NOT MORDECAI.
I'M SOMEBODY ELSE... FROM FAR AWAY...AND YET I KNOW THESE CAVES...
IT WAS YOU, WASN'T IT?
YOU WEREN'T GATHERING HERBS IN THE GROVE WHEN YOU FOUND ME.
YOU SUMMONED THE DRAGON AND IT KILLED THE REAL MORDECAI.
THEY SENT HIM TO HUNT ME!
I ONLY WANTED TO CHASE THEM ALL AWAY.
ALL THOSE PIOUS SAINTS WHO CUT DOWN SACRED TREES AND SLAUGHTER THE BROTHER ANIMALS AND STEAL FROM THE BAT-PEOPLE WHOSE LAND THIS IS.

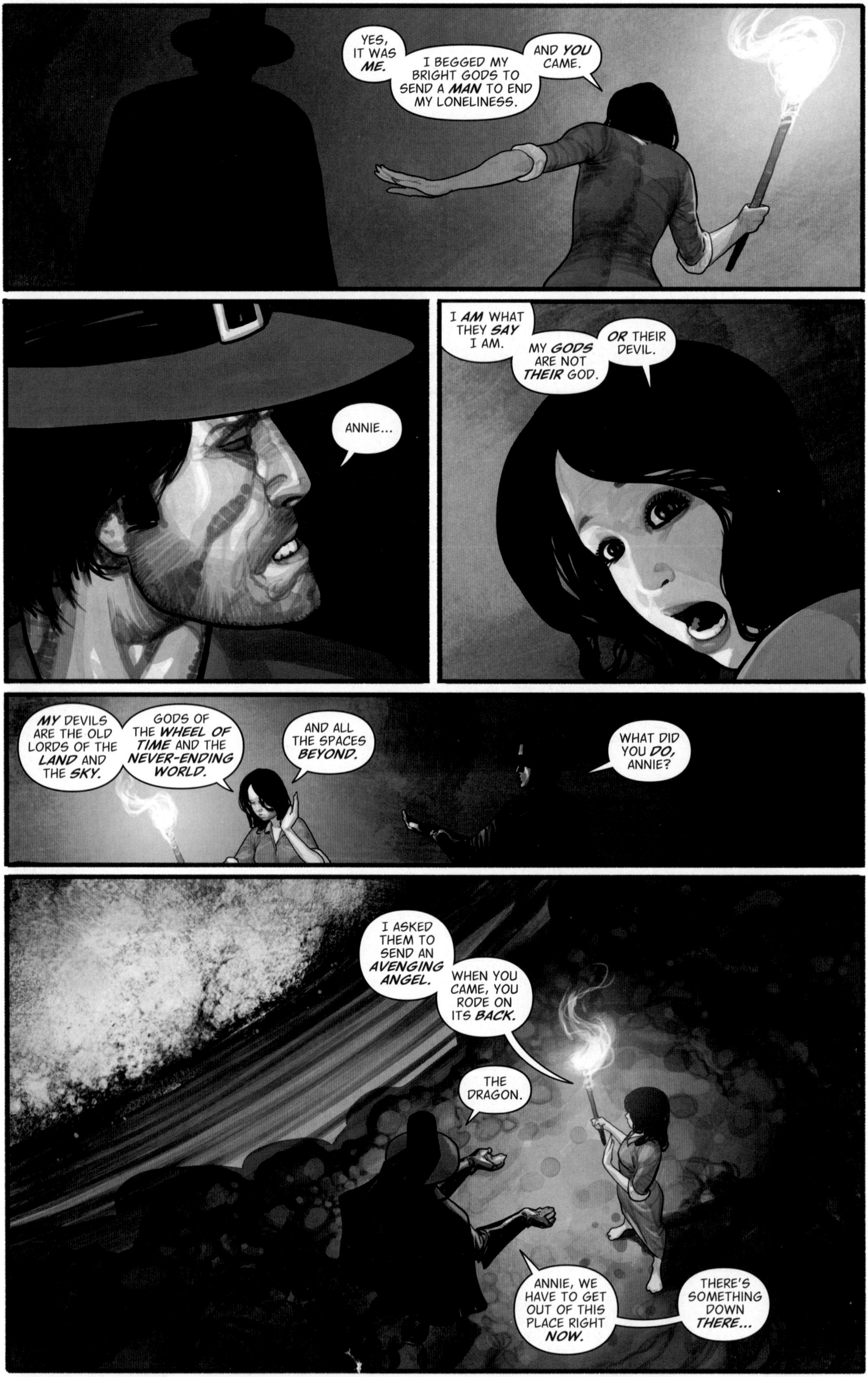
YES, IT WAS ME.
I BEGGED MY BRIGHT GODS TO SEND A MAN TO END MY LONELINESS.
AND YOU CAME.
ANNIE...
I AM WHAT THEY SAY I AM.
MY GODS ARE NOT THEIR GOD.
OR THEIR DEVIL.
MY DEVILS ARE THE OLD LORDS OF THE LAND AND THE SKY.
GODS OF THE WHEEL OF TIME AND THE NEVER-ENDING WORLD.
AND ALL THE SPACES BEYOND.
WHAT DID YOU DO, ANNIE?
I ASKED THEM TO SEND AN AVENGING ANGEL.
WHEN YOU CAME, YOU RODE ON ITS BACK.
THE DRAGON.
ANNIE, WE HAVE TO GET OUT OF THIS PLACE RIGHT NOW.
THERE'S SOMETHING DOWN THERE...

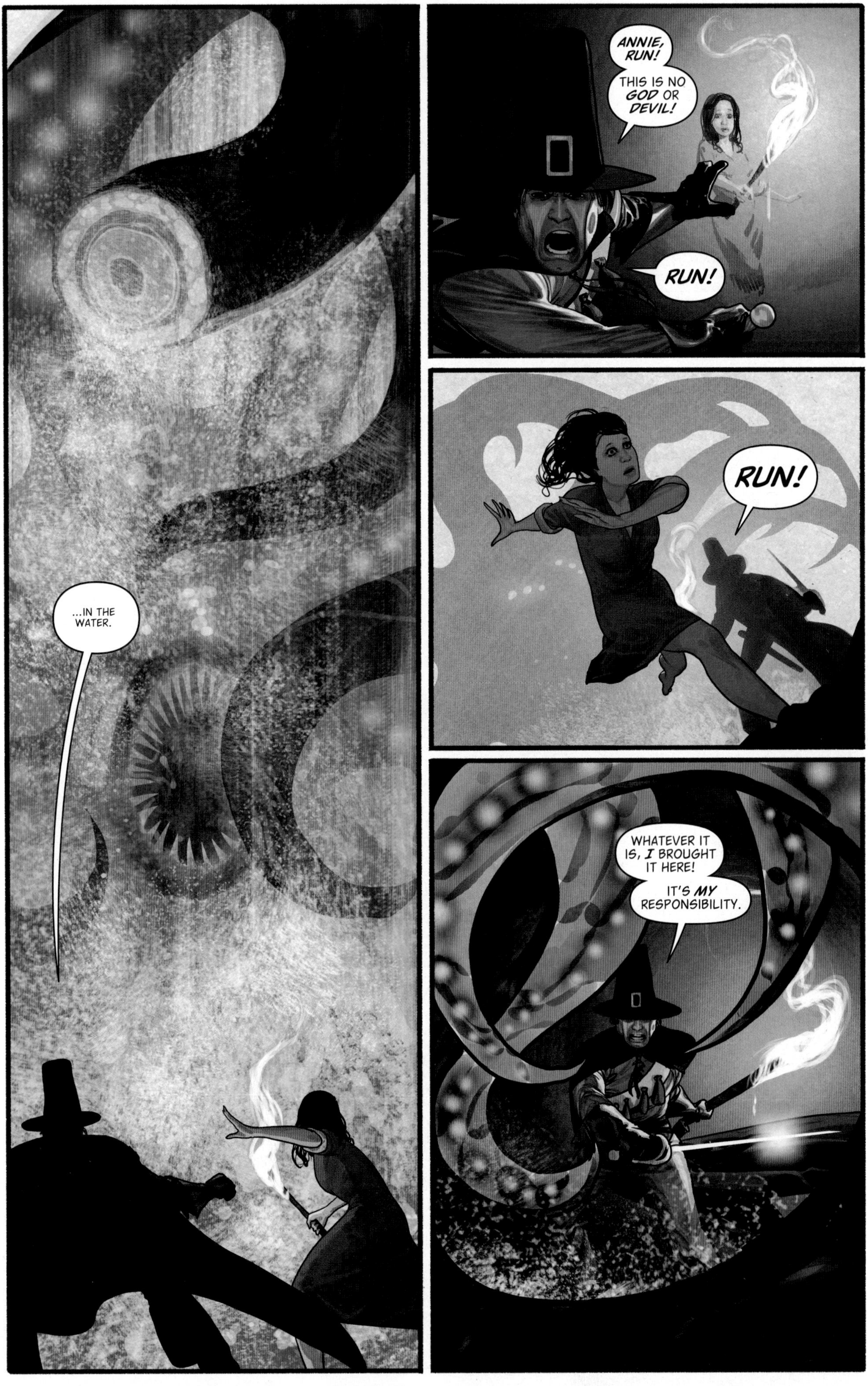
...IN THE WATER.
ANNIE, RUN!
THIS IS NO GOD OR DEVIL!
RUN!
RUN!
WHATEVER IT IS, I BROUGHT IT HERE!
IT'S MY RESPONSIBILITY.

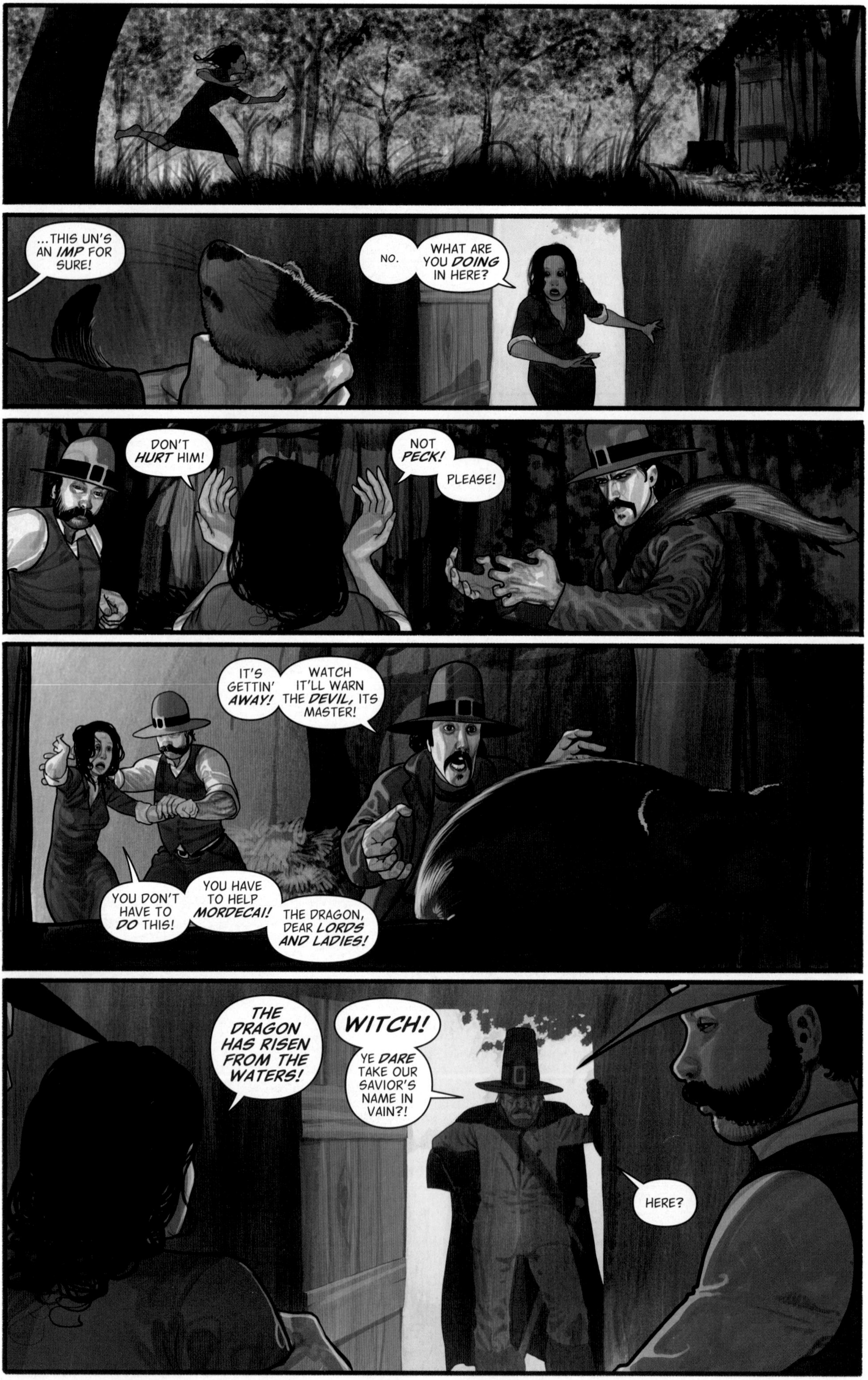
...THIS UN'S AN IMP FOR SURE!
NO.
WHAT ARE YOU DOING IN HERE?
DON'T HURT HIM!
NOT PECK!
PLEASE!
IT'S GETTIN' AWAY!
WATCH IT'LL WARN THE DEVIL, ITS MASTER!
YOU DON'T HAVE TO DO THIS!
YOU HAVE TO HELP MORDECAI!
THE DRAGON, DEAR LORDS AND LADIES!
THE DRAGON HAS RISEN FROM THE WATERS!
WITCH!
YE DARE TAKE OUR SAVIOR'S NAME IN VAIN?!
HERE?

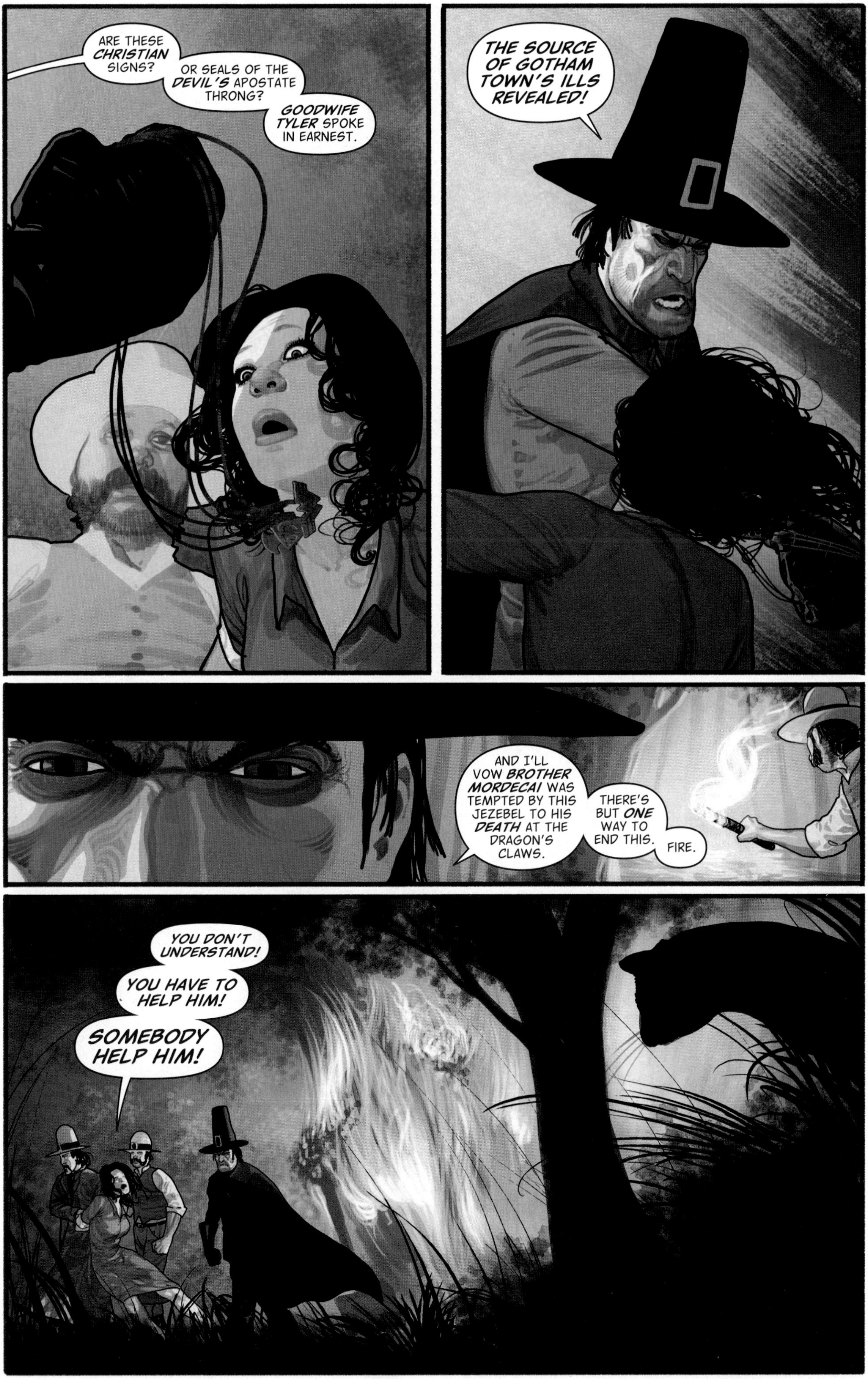
ARE THESE *CHRISTIAN* SIGNS?
OR SEALS OF THE *DEVIL'S* APOSTATE THRONG?
GOODWIFE TYLER SPOKE IN EARNEST.
THE SOURCE OF GOTHAM TOWN'S ILLS REVEALED!
AND I'LL VOW *BROTHER MORDECAI* WAS TEMPTED BY THIS JEZEBEL TO HIS *DEATH* AT THE DRAGON'S CLAWS.
THERE'S BUT *ONE* WAY TO END THIS.
FIRE.
YOU DON'T UNDERSTAND!
YOU HAVE TO HELP HIM!
SOMEBODY HELP HIM!

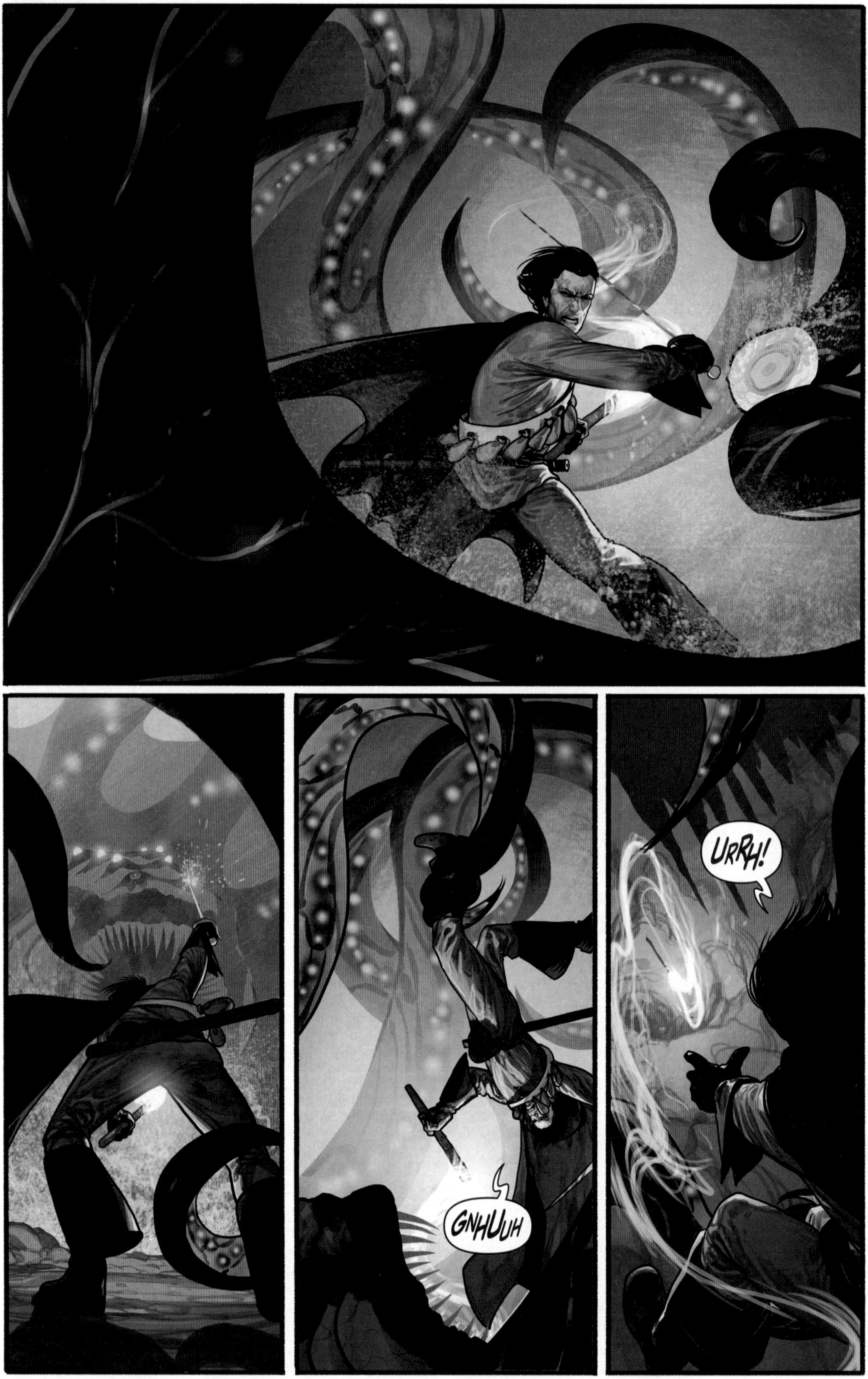
GNHUUH
URRH!

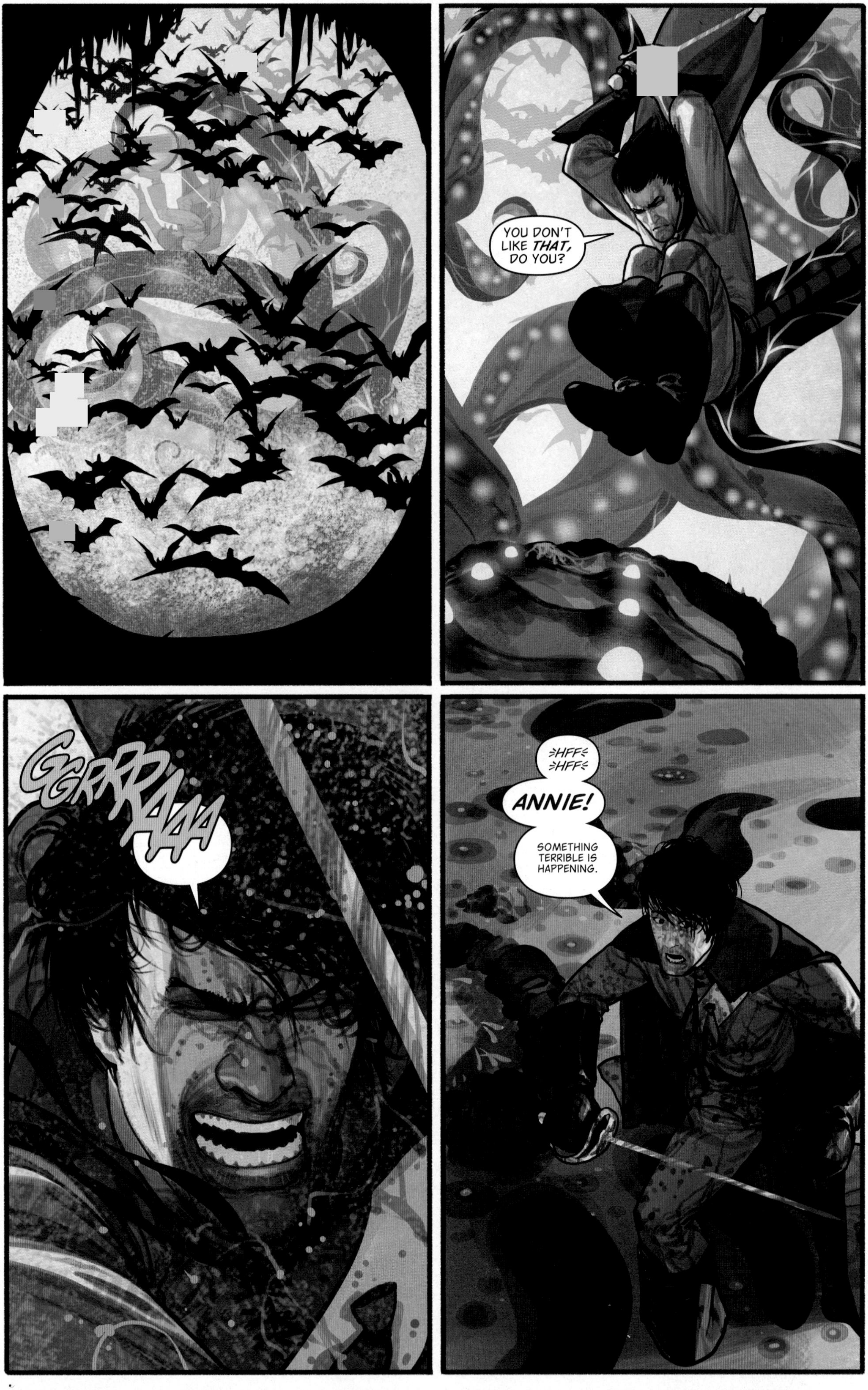
YOU DON'T LIKE *THAT,* DO YOU?
GGRRRAAAA
HFF
HFF
ANNIE!
SOMETHING TERRIBLE IS HAPPENING.

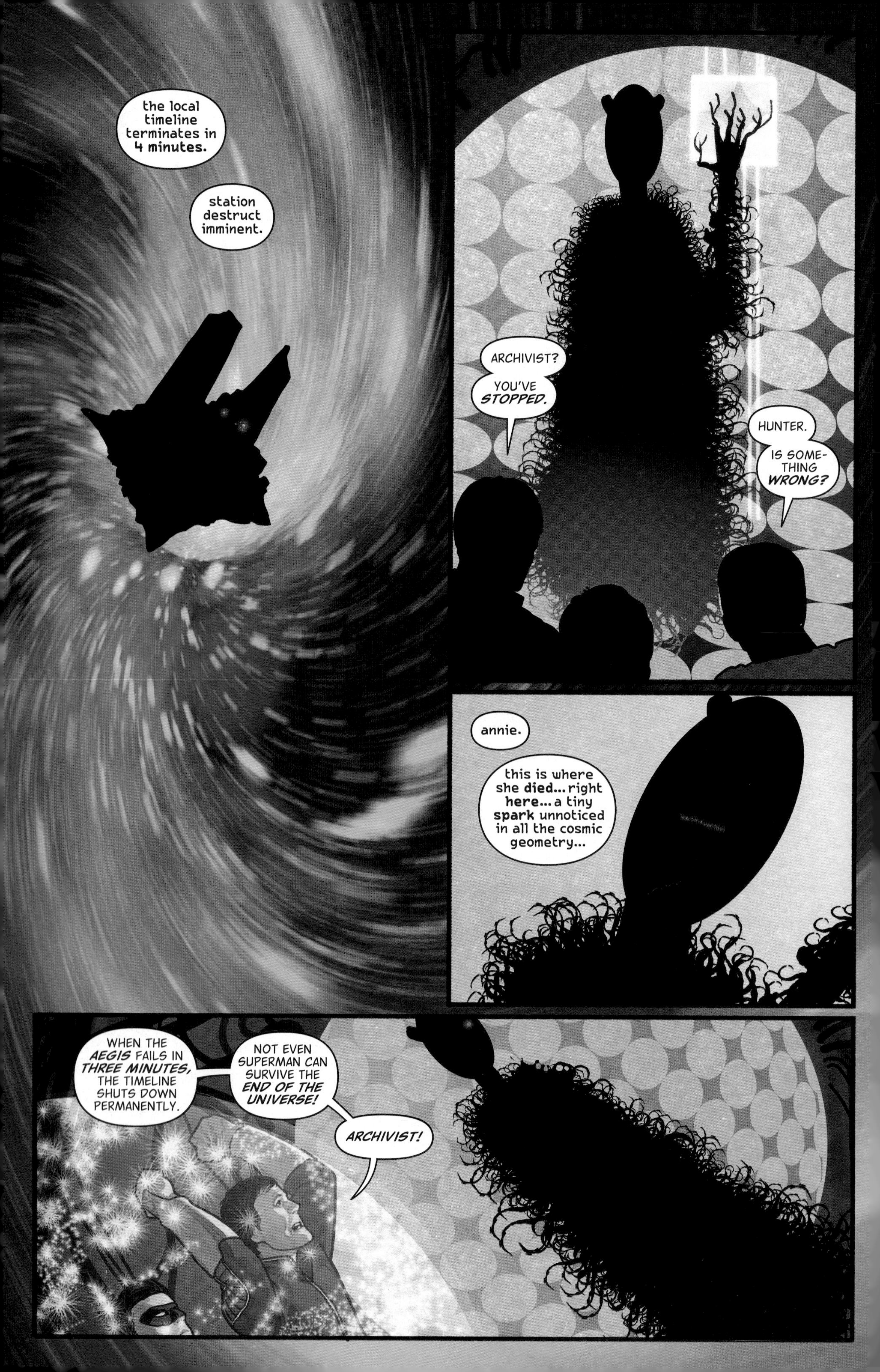

the local timeline terminates in 4 minutes.
station destruct imminent.
ARCHIVIST?
YOU'VE STOPPED.
HUNTER.
IS SOMETHING WRONG?
annie.
this is where she died... right here... a tiny spark unnoticed in all the cosmic geometry...
WHEN THE AEGIS FAILS IN THREE MINUTES, THE TIMELINE SHUTS DOWN PERMANENTLY.
NOT EVEN SUPERMAN CAN SURVIVE THE END OF THE UNIVERSE!
ARCHIVIST!

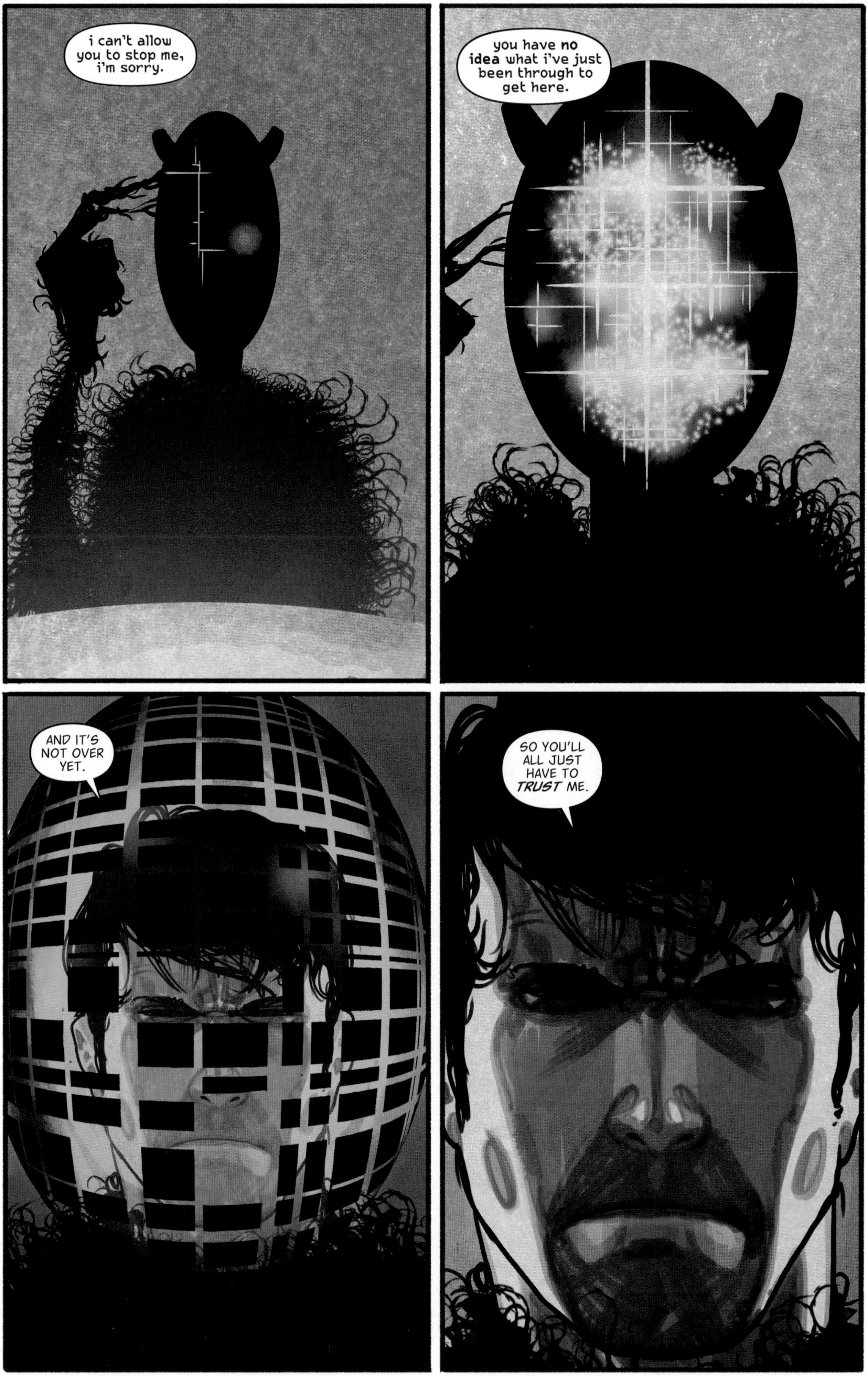
i can't allow you to stop me, i'm sorry.
you have **no idea** what i've just been through to get here.
AND IT'S NOT OVER YET.
SO YOU'LL ALL JUST HAVE TO *TRUST* ME.

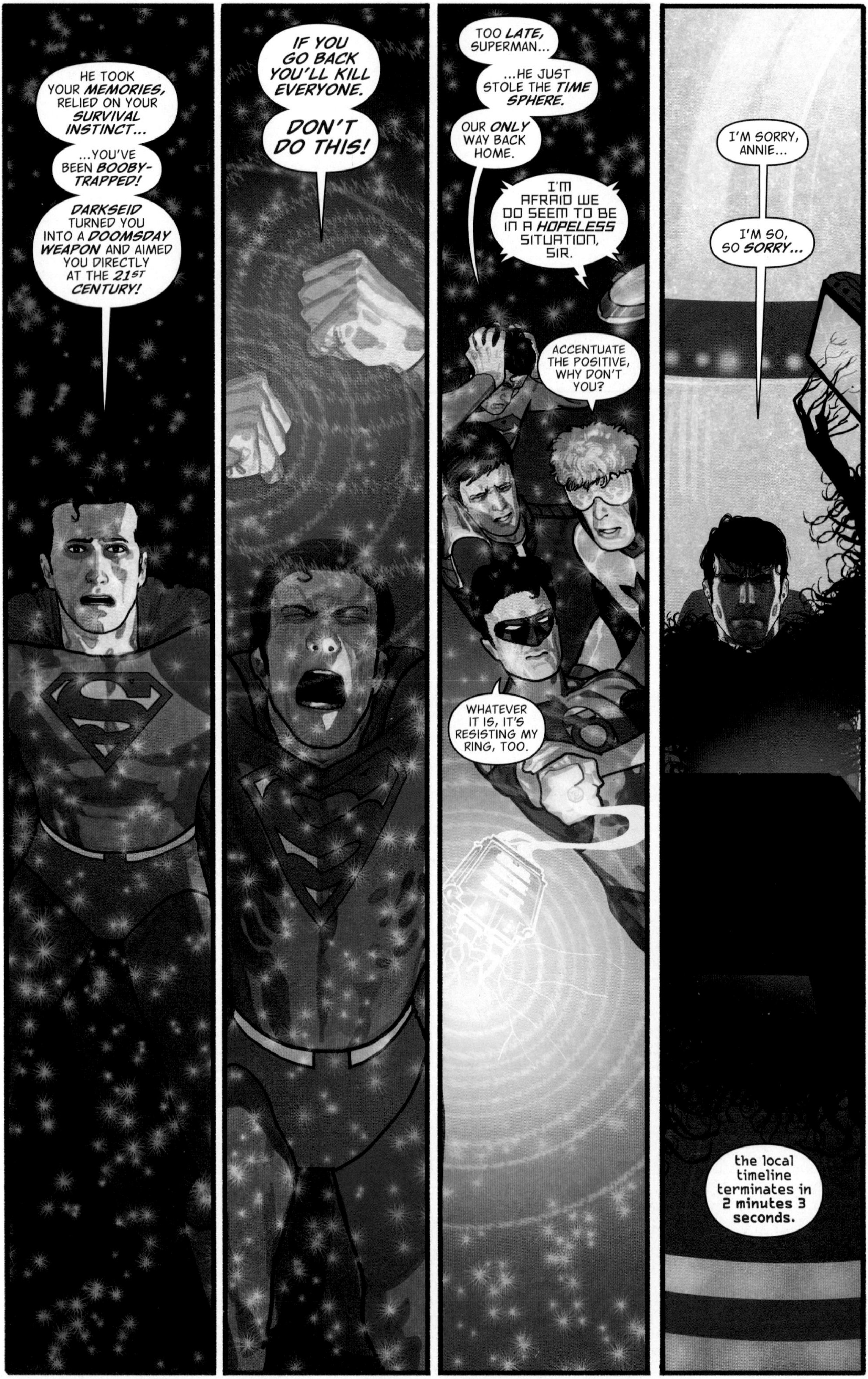
HE TOOK YOUR MEMORIES, RELIED ON YOUR SURVIVAL INSTINCT...
...YOU'VE BEEN BOOBY-TRAPPED!
DARKSEID TURNED YOU INTO A DOOMSDAY WEAPON AND AIMED YOU DIRECTLY AT THE 21ST CENTURY!
IF YOU GO BACK YOU'LL KILL EVERYONE.
DON'T DO THIS!
TOO LATE, SUPERMAN...
...HE JUST STOLE THE TIME SPHERE.
OUR ONLY WAY BACK HOME.
I'M AFRAID WE DO SEEM TO BE IN A HOPELESS SITUATION, SIR.
ACCENTUATE THE POSITIVE, WHY DON'T YOU?
WHATEVER IT IS, IT'S RESISTING MY RING, TOO.
I'M SORRY, ANNIE...
I'M SO, SO SORRY...
the local timeline terminates in 2 minutes 3 seconds.

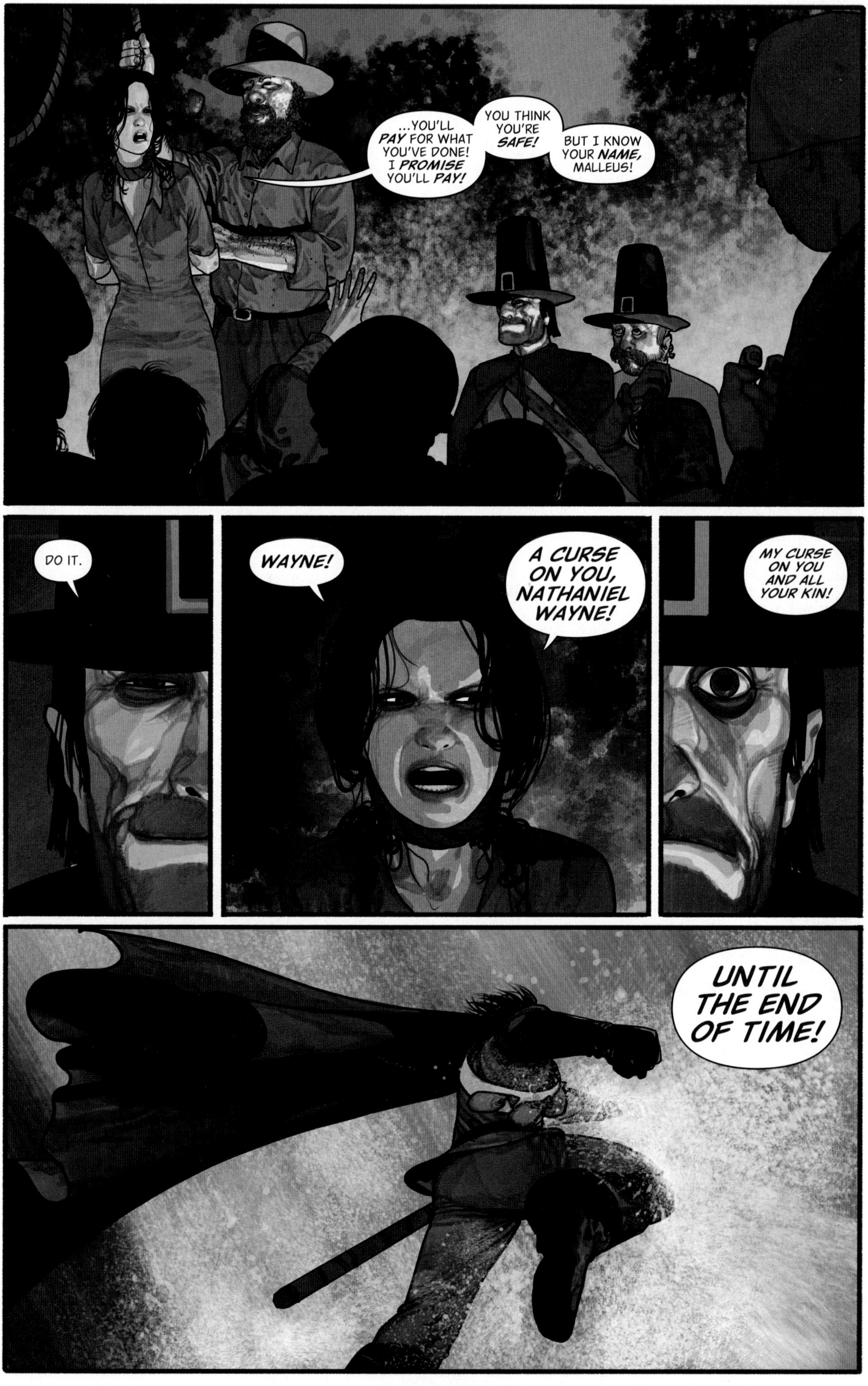
...YOU'LL PAY FOR WHAT YOU'VE DONE! I PROMISE YOU'LL PAY!
YOU THINK YOU'RE SAFE!
BUT I KNOW YOUR NAME, MALLEUS!
DO IT.
WAYNE!
A CURSE ON YOU, NATHANIEL WAYNE!
MY CURSE ON YOU AND ALL YOUR KIN!
UNTIL THE END OF TIME!

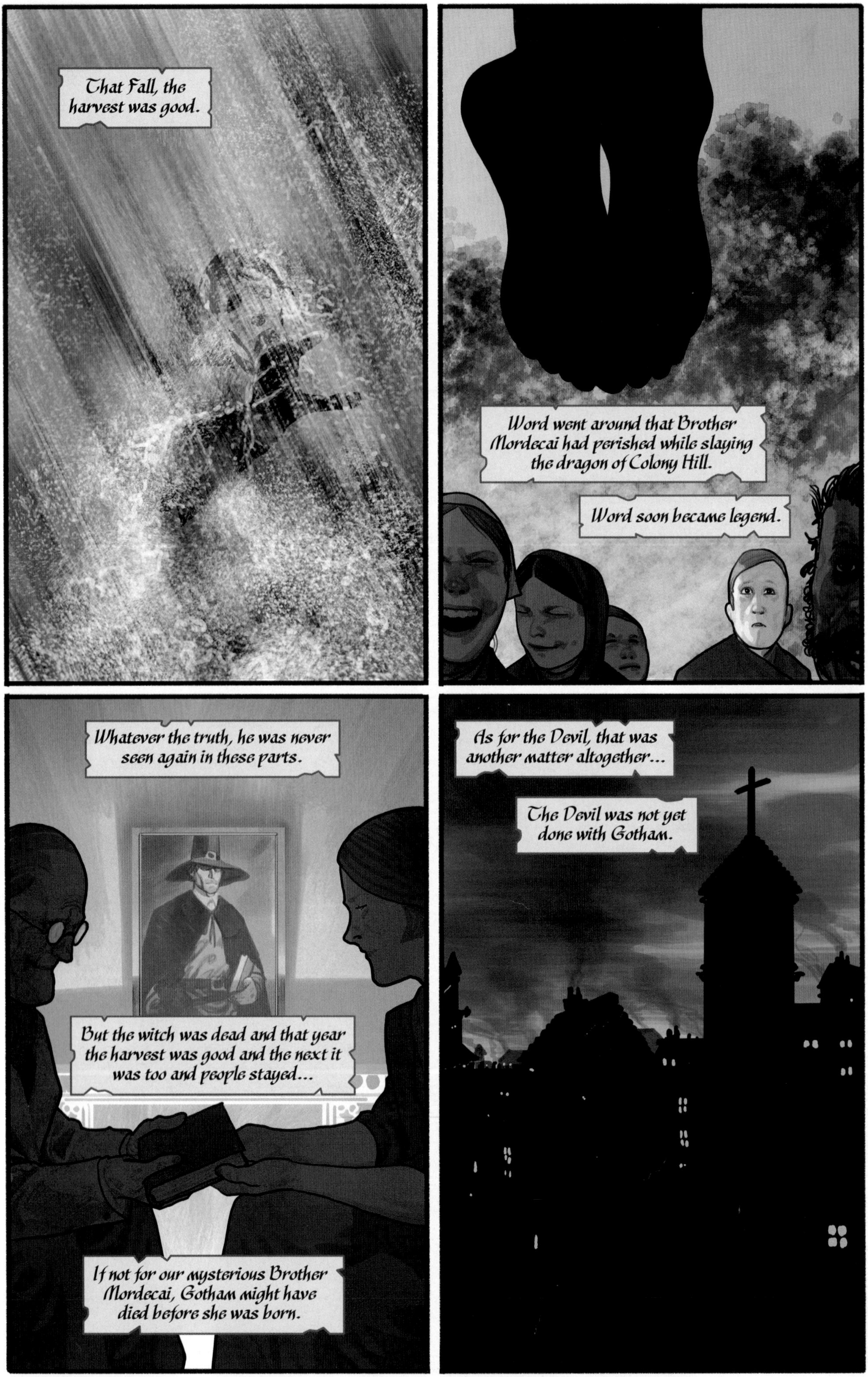
That Fall, the harvest was good.
Word went around that Brother Mordecai had perished while slaying the dragon of Colony Hill.
Word soon became legend.
Whatever the truth, he was never seen again in these parts.
But the witch was dead and that year the harvest was good and the next it was too and people stayed...
If not for our mysterious Brother Mordecai, Gotham might have died before she was born.
As for the Devil, that was another matter altogether...
The Devil was not yet done with Gotham.

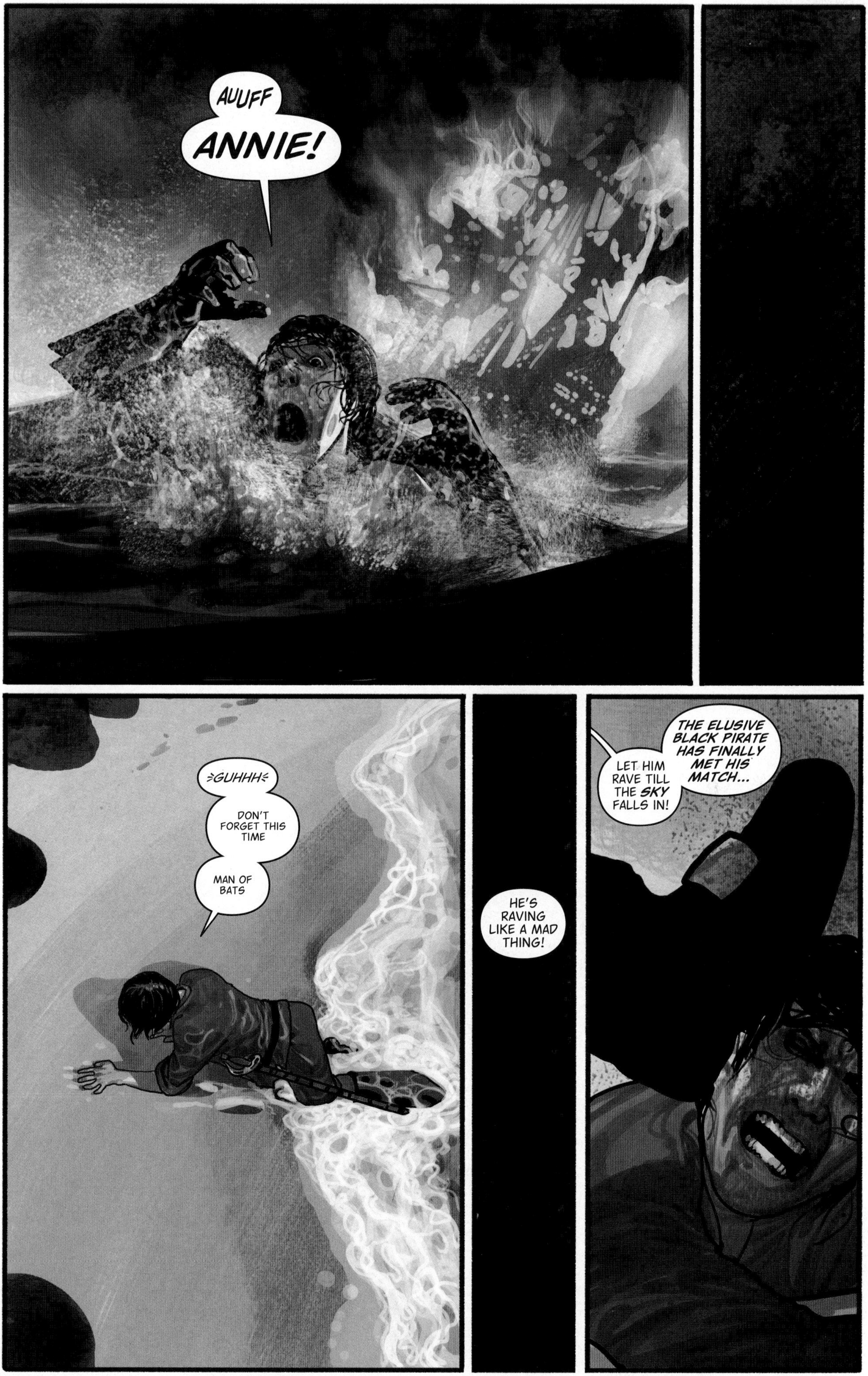
AUUFF
ANNIE!
≈GUHHH≈
DON'T FORGET THIS TIME
MAN OF BATS
HE'S RAVING LIKE A MAD THING!
THE ELUSIVE BLACK PIRATE HAS FINALLY MET HIS MATCH...
LET HIM RAVE TILL THE SKY FALLS IN!

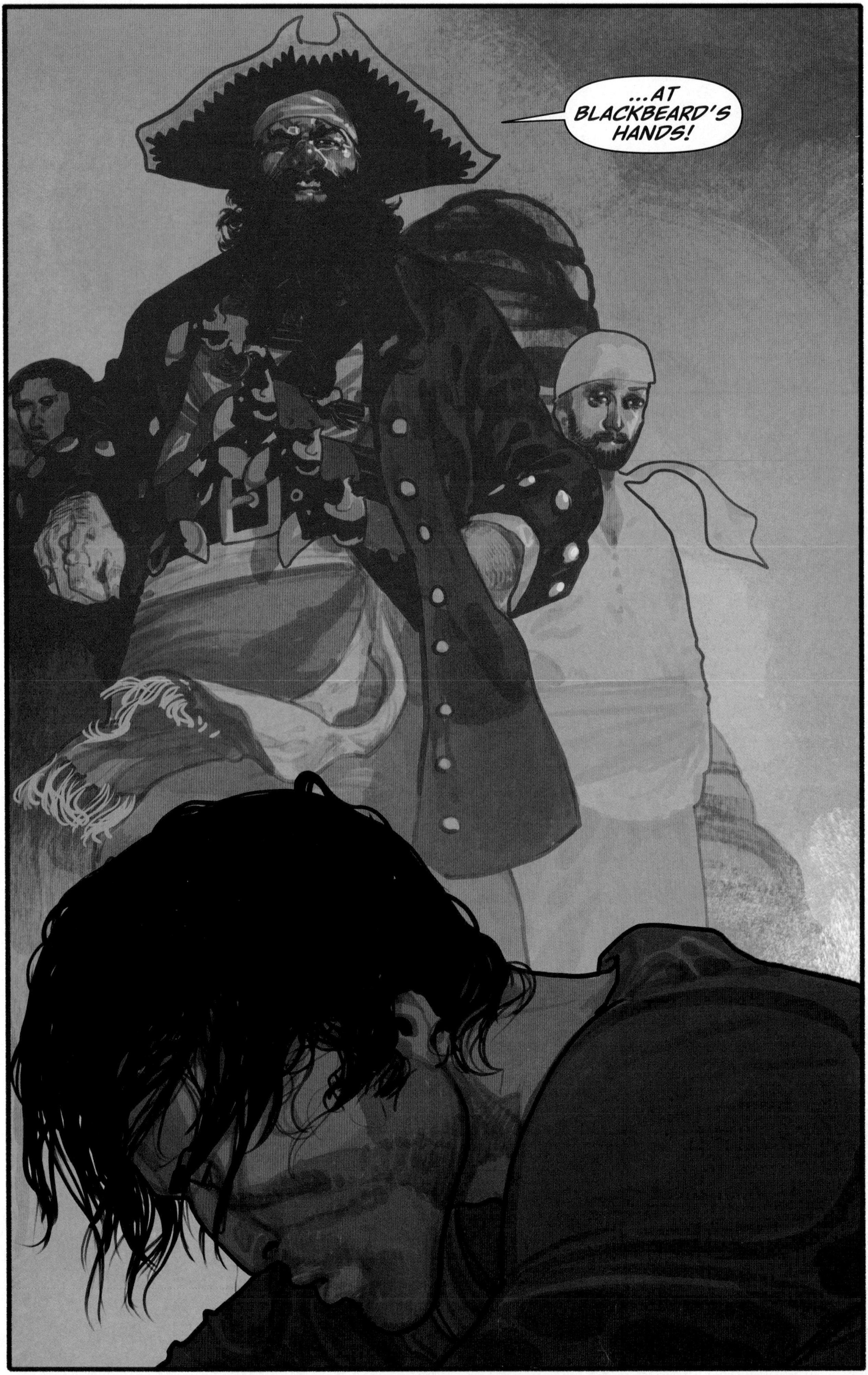
...AT BLACKBEARD'S HANDS!

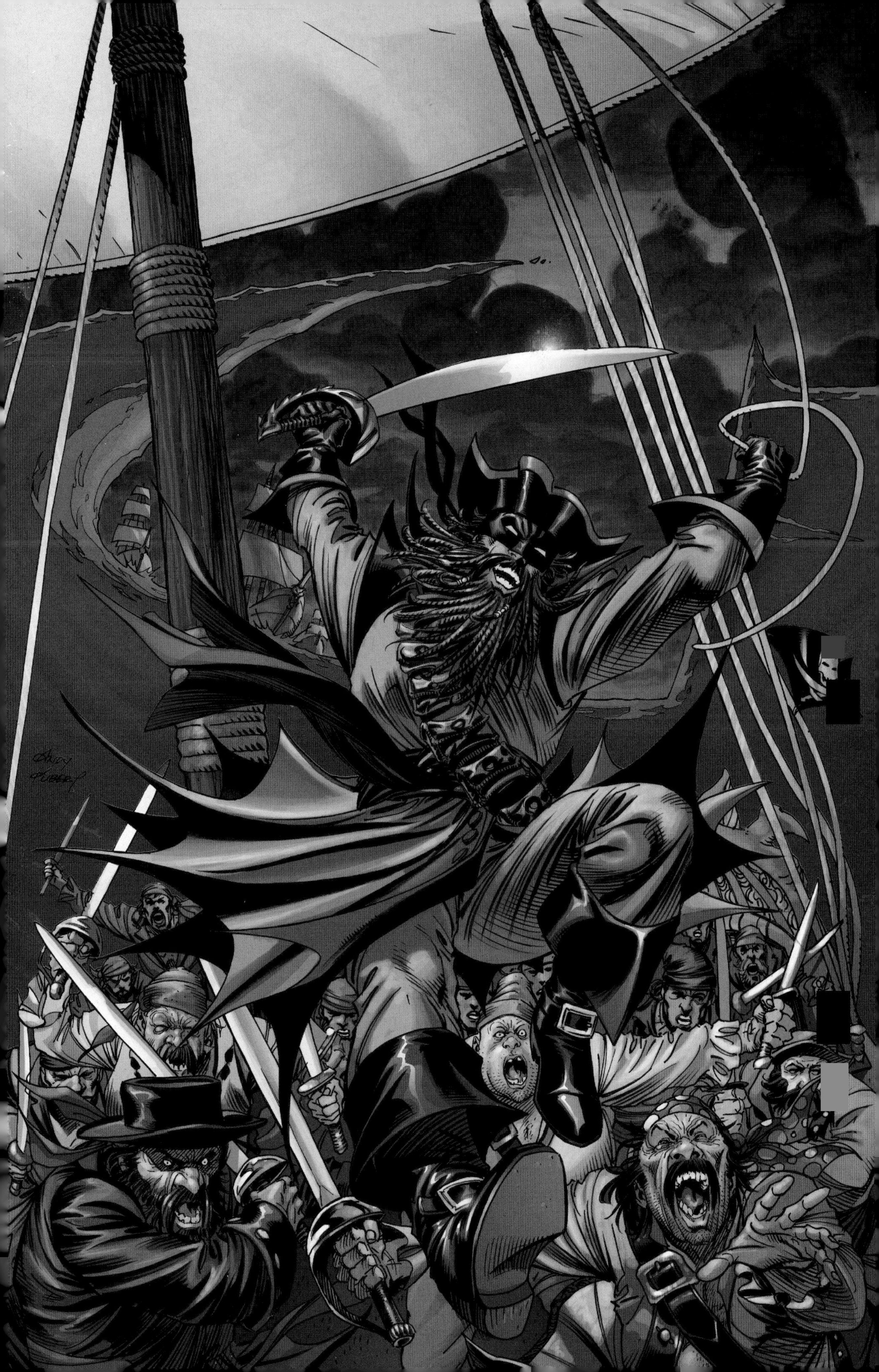

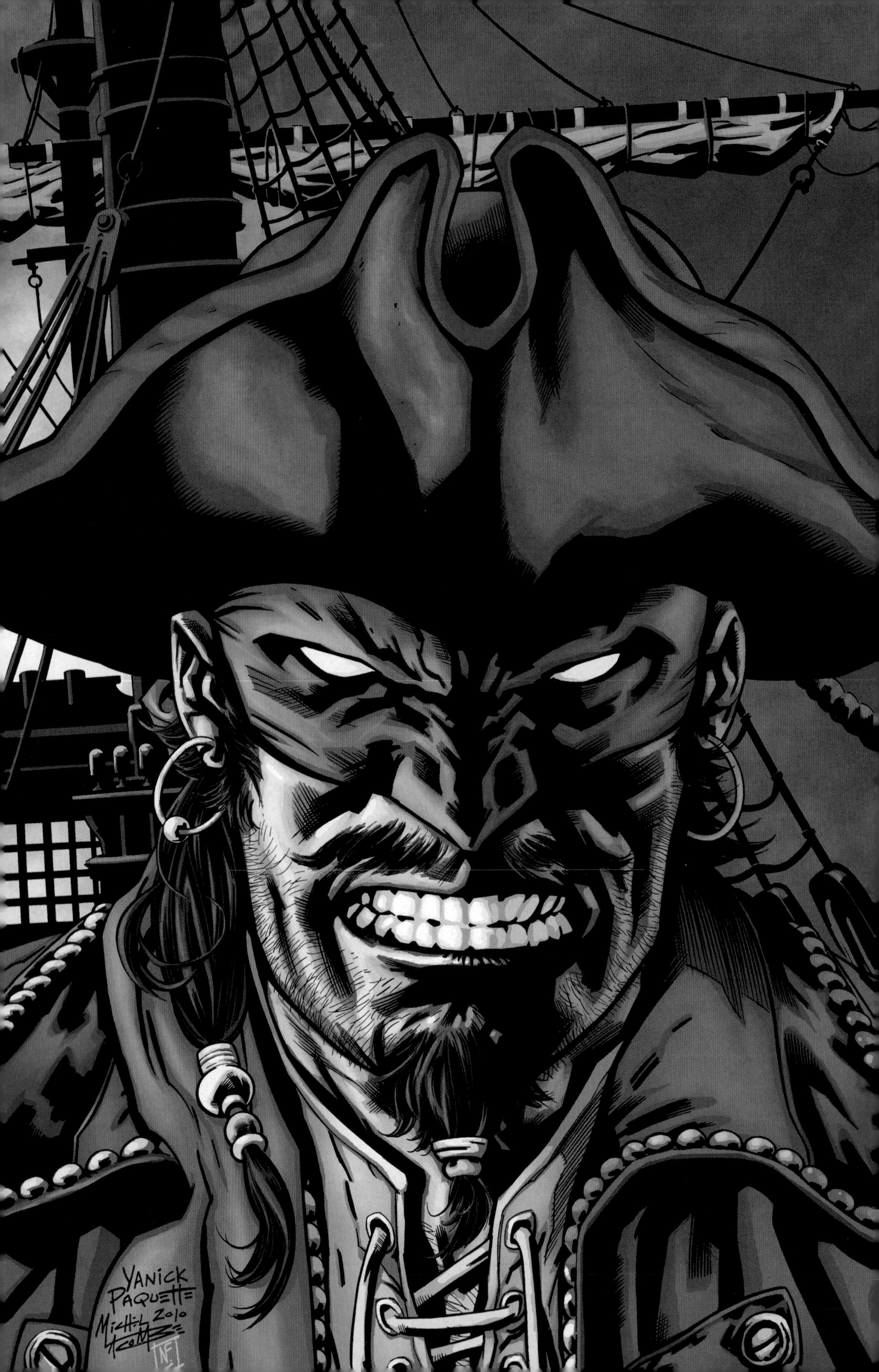
YANICK PAQUETTE 2010
MICHEL LACOMBE

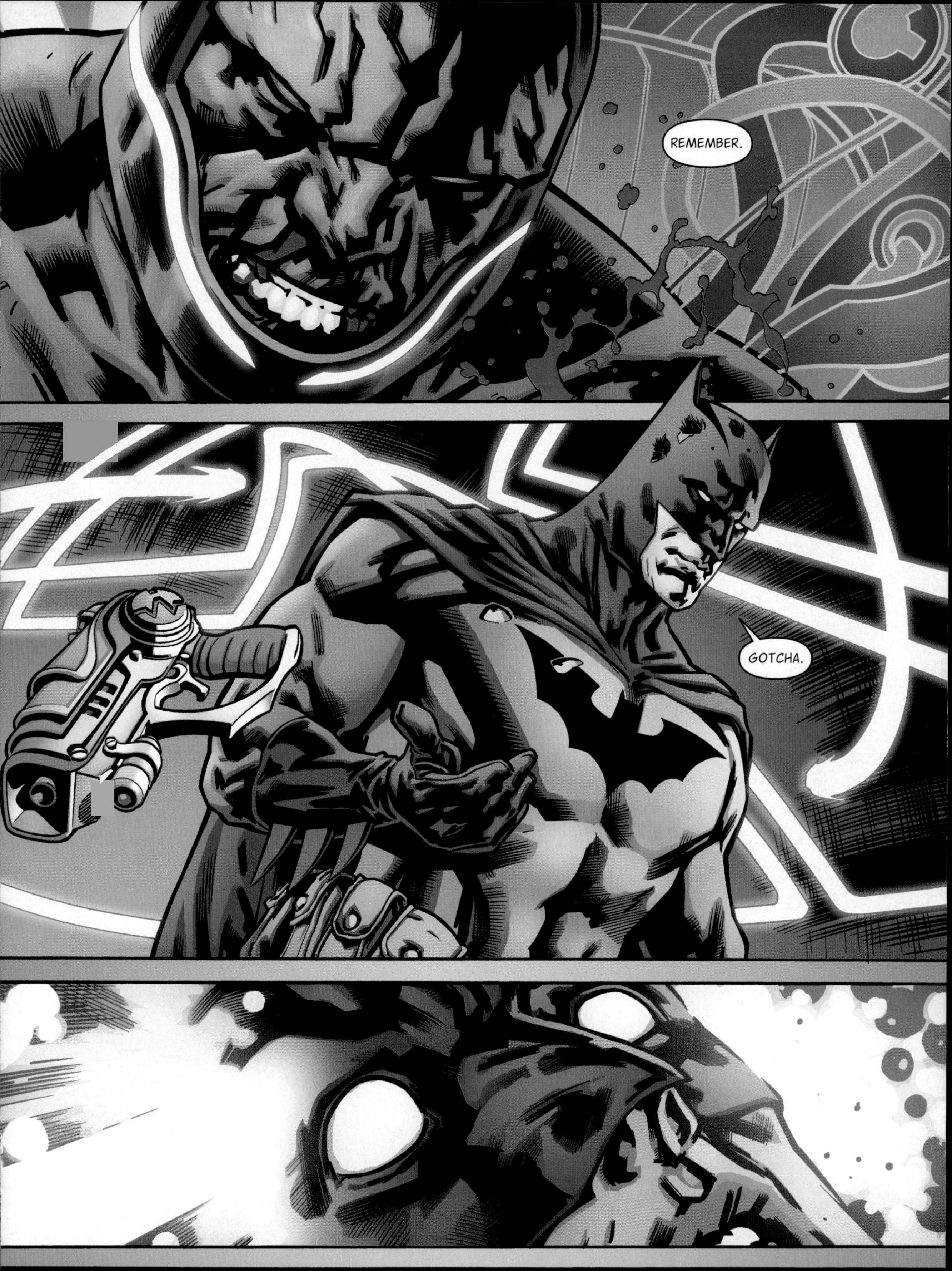
REMEMBER.
GOTCHA.

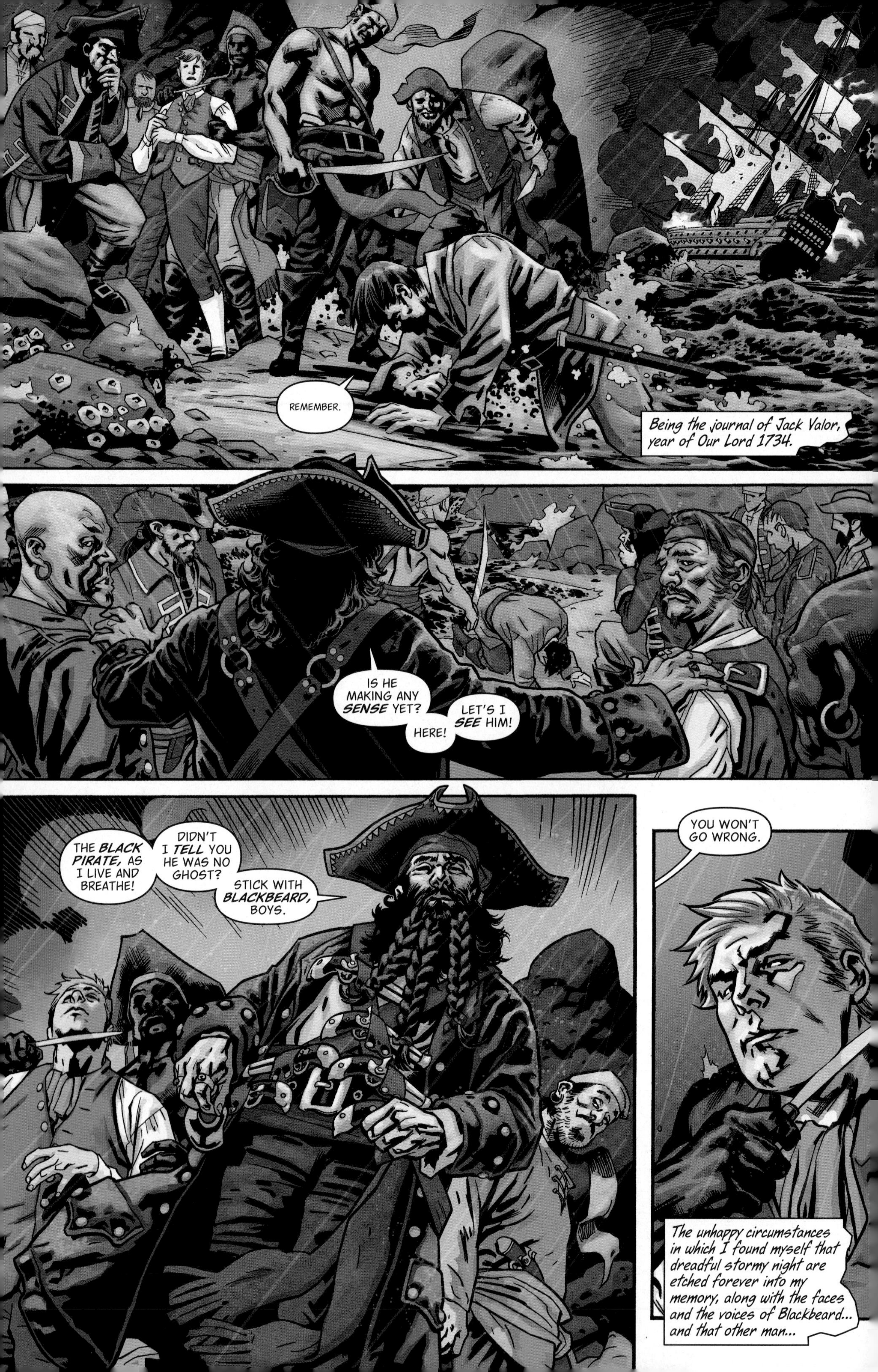
REMEMBER.
Being the journal of Jack Valor, year of Our Lord 1734.
IS HE MAKING ANY SENSE YET?
HERE!
LET'S I SEE HIM!
THE BLACK PIRATE, AS I LIVE AND BREATHE!
DIDN'T I TELL YOU HE WAS NO GHOST?
STICK WITH BLACKBEARD, BOYS.
YOU WON'T GO WRONG.
The unhappy circumstances in which I found myself that dreadful stormy night are etched forever into my memory, along with the faces and the voices of Blackbeard... and that other man...

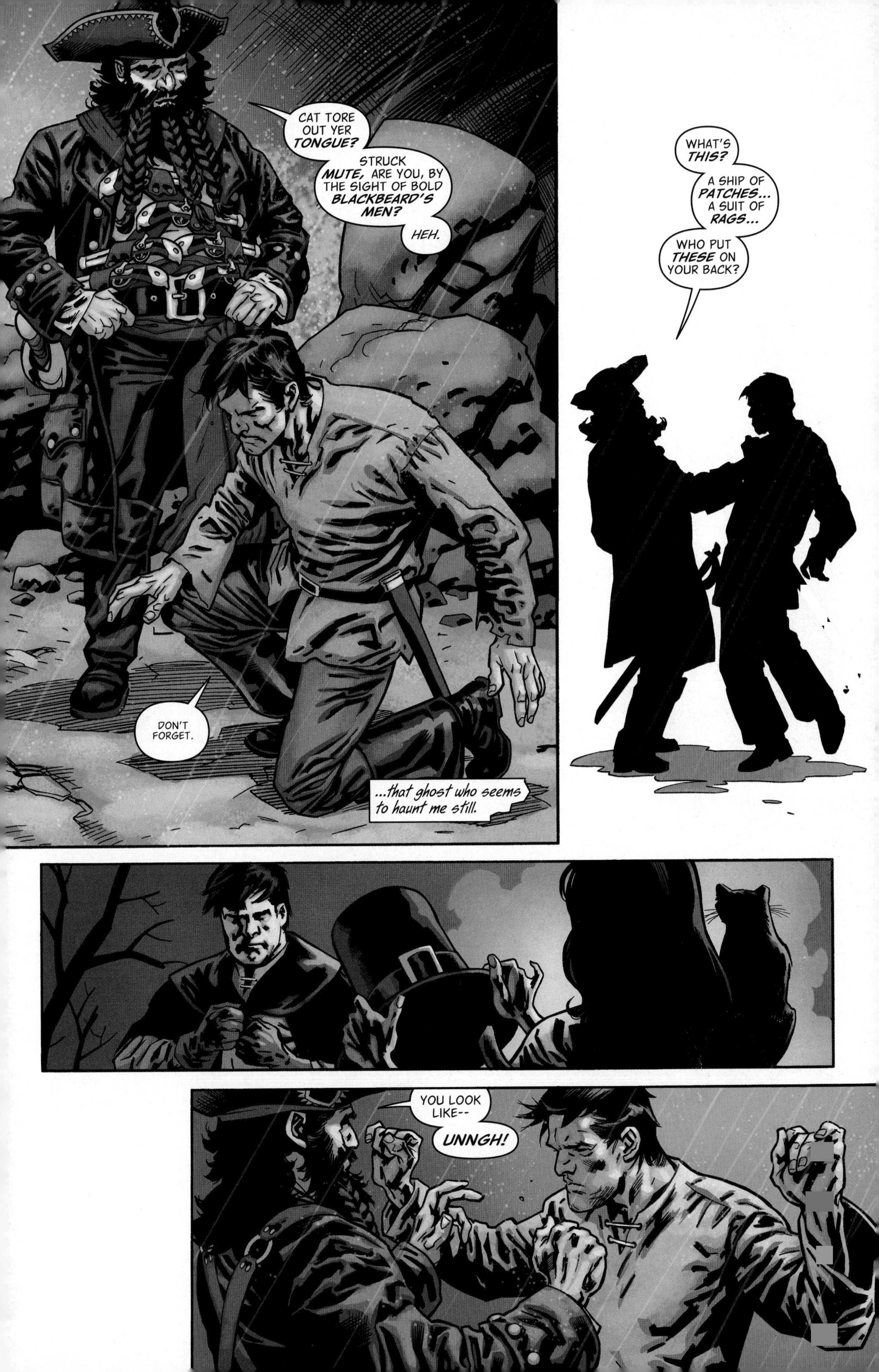
CAT TORE OUT YER TONGUE?
STRUCK MUTE, ARE YOU, BY THE SIGHT OF BOLD BLACKBEARD'S MEN?
HEH.
DON'T FORGET.
...that ghost who seems to haunt me still.
WHAT'S THIS?
A SHIP OF PATCHES... A SUIT OF RAGS...
WHO PUT THESE ON YOUR BACK?
YOU LOOK LIKE--
UNNGH!

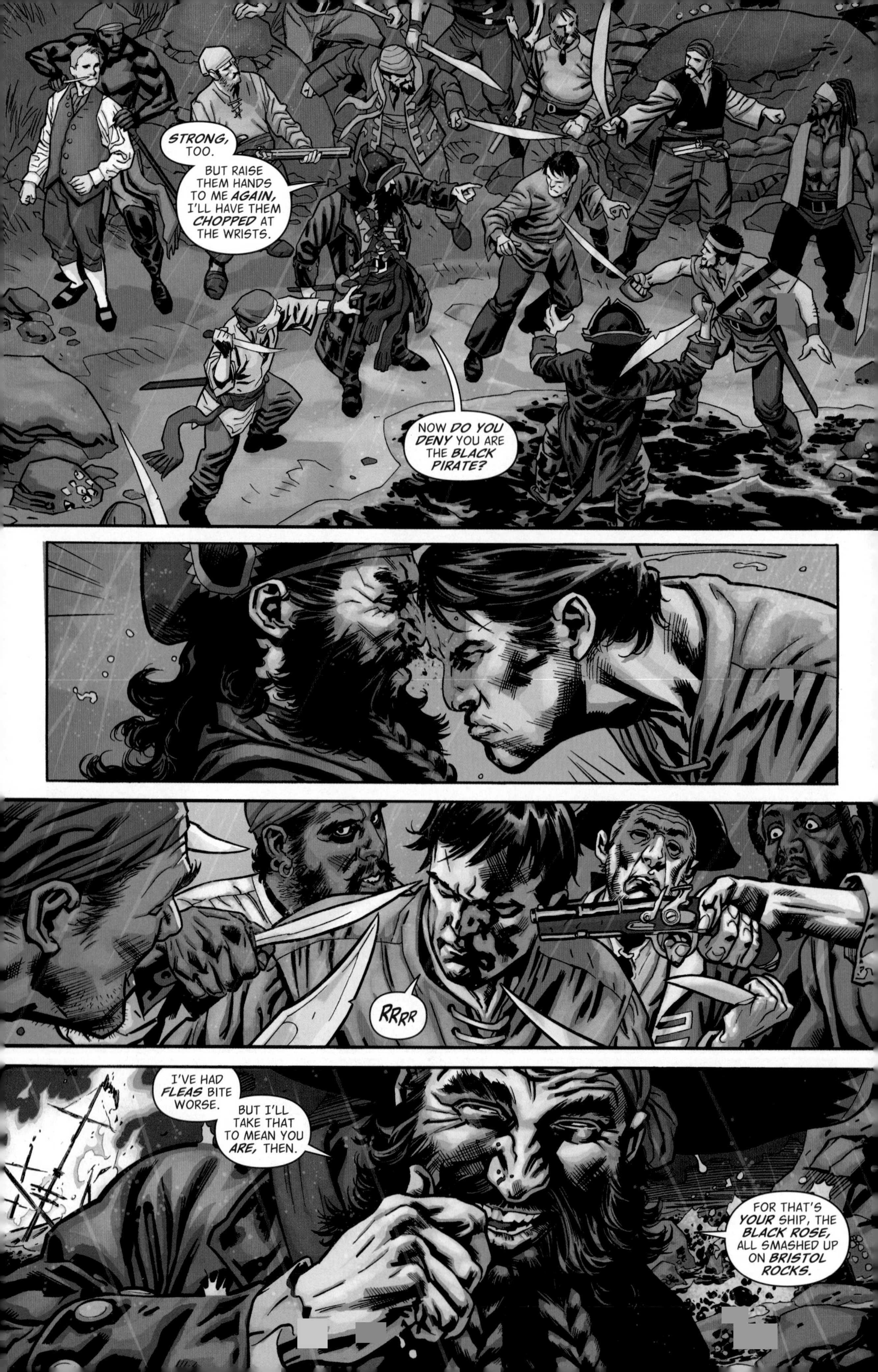
STRONG, TOO.
BUT RAISE THEM HANDS TO ME AGAIN, I'LL HAVE THEM CHOPPED AT THE WRISTS.
NOW DO YOU DENY YOU ARE THE BLACK PIRATE?
RRRR
I'VE HAD FLEAS BITE WORSE.
BUT I'LL TAKE THAT TO MEAN YOU ARE, THEN.
FOR THAT'S YOUR SHIP, THE BLACK ROSE, ALL SMASHED UP ON BRISTOL ROCKS.

AND THERE'S *MINE,* THE *REVENGE,* SAFE ON THE EDGE OF THE STORM.

NOW I DIDN'T COME *ALL THAT WAY* AND WASTE ALL THAT *SHOT* ON YE FOR NAUGHT, DID I?

THEY SAID YOU WAS A *GHOST,* AND I THINK I'VE SET 'EM RIGHT ON *THAT* SCORE.

BLACK PIRATE, SPIRIT OF THE SEAS--*HAH!*

AND NOW IF THE BLACK PIRATE'S *REAL...*

THEN SO'S THAT FABLED INDIAN *TREASURE HOARD* THEY SAY HE KEEPS TO *HIMSELF.*

SOMEWHERE HIDDEN IN THE *GOTHAM COUNTY CATACOMBS,* THEY SAY.

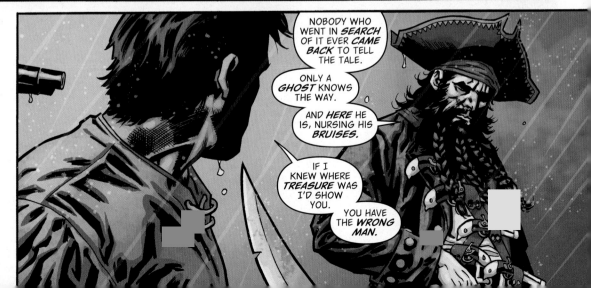

NOBODY WHO WENT IN *SEARCH* OF IT EVER *CAME BACK* TO TELL THE TALE.

ONLY A *GHOST* KNOWS THE WAY.

AND *HERE* HE IS, NURSING HIS *BRUISES.*

IF I KNEW WHERE *TREASURE* WAS I'D SHOW YOU.

YOU HAVE THE *WRONG MAN.*

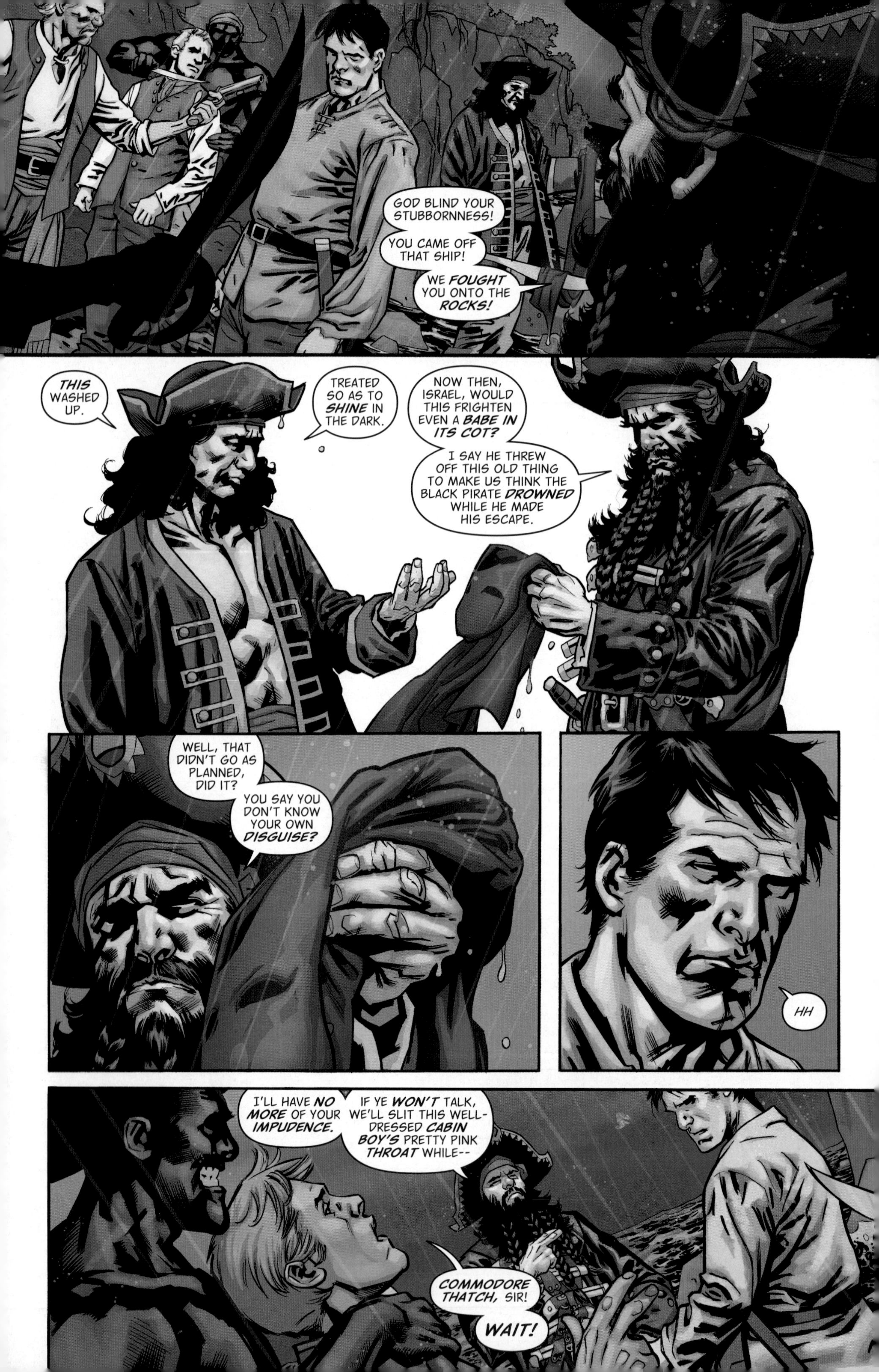
GOD BLIND YOUR STUBBORNNESS!
YOU CAME OFF THAT SHIP!
WE FOUGHT YOU ONTO THE ROCKS!
THIS WASHED UP.
TREATED SO AS TO SHINE IN THE DARK.
NOW THEN, ISRAEL, WOULD THIS FRIGHTEN EVEN A BABE IN ITS COT?
I SAY HE THREW OFF THIS OLD THING TO MAKE US THINK THE BLACK PIRATE DROWNED WHILE HE MADE HIS ESCAPE.
WELL, THAT DIDN'T GO AS PLANNED, DID IT?
YOU SAY YOU DON'T KNOW YOUR OWN DISGUISE?
HH
I'LL HAVE NO MORE OF YOUR IMPUDENCE.
IF YE WON'T TALK, WE'LL SLIT THIS WELL-DRESSED CABIN BOY'S PRETTY PINK THROAT WHILE--
COMMODORE THATCH, SIR!
WAIT!

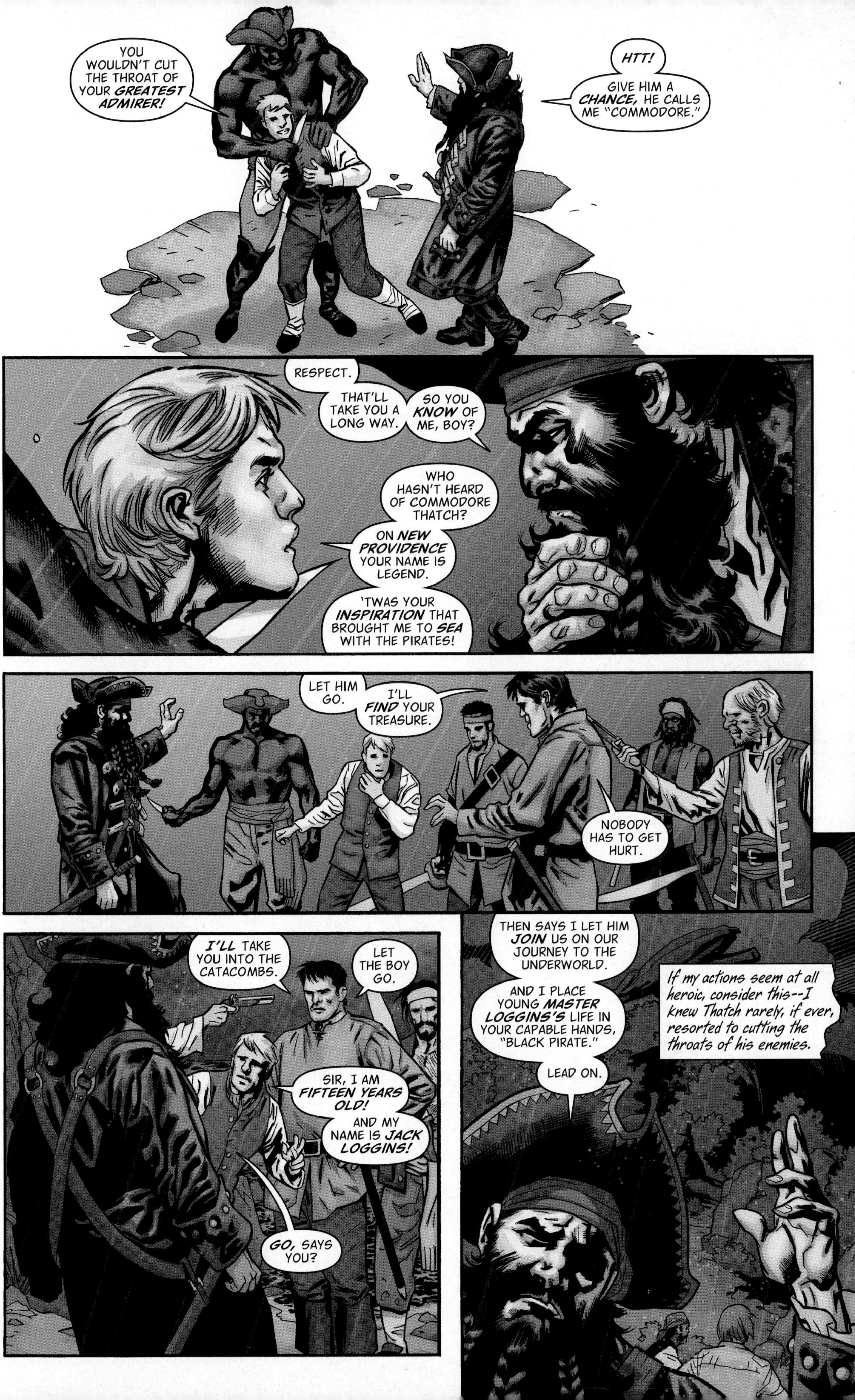
YOU WOULDN'T CUT THE THROAT OF YOUR GREATEST ADMIRER!
HTT!
GIVE HIM A CHANCE, HE CALLS ME "COMMODORE."
RESPECT.
THAT'LL TAKE YOU A LONG WAY.
SO YOU KNOW OF ME, BOY?
WHO HASN'T HEARD OF COMMODORE THATCH?
ON NEW PROVIDENCE YOUR NAME IS LEGEND.
'TWAS YOUR INSPIRATION THAT BROUGHT ME TO SEA WITH THE PIRATES!
LET HIM GO.
I'LL FIND YOUR TREASURE.
NOBODY HAS TO GET HURT.
I'LL TAKE YOU INTO THE CATACOMBS.
LET THE BOY GO.
SIR, I AM FIFTEEN YEARS OLD!
AND MY NAME IS JACK LOGGINS!
GO, SAYS YOU?
THEN SAYS I LET HIM JOIN US ON OUR JOURNEY TO THE UNDERWORLD.
AND I PLACE YOUNG MASTER LOGGINS'S LIFE IN YOUR CAPABLE HANDS, "BLACK PIRATE."
LEAD ON.
If my actions seem at all heroic, consider this--I knew Thatch rarely, if ever, resorted to cutting the throats of his enemies.

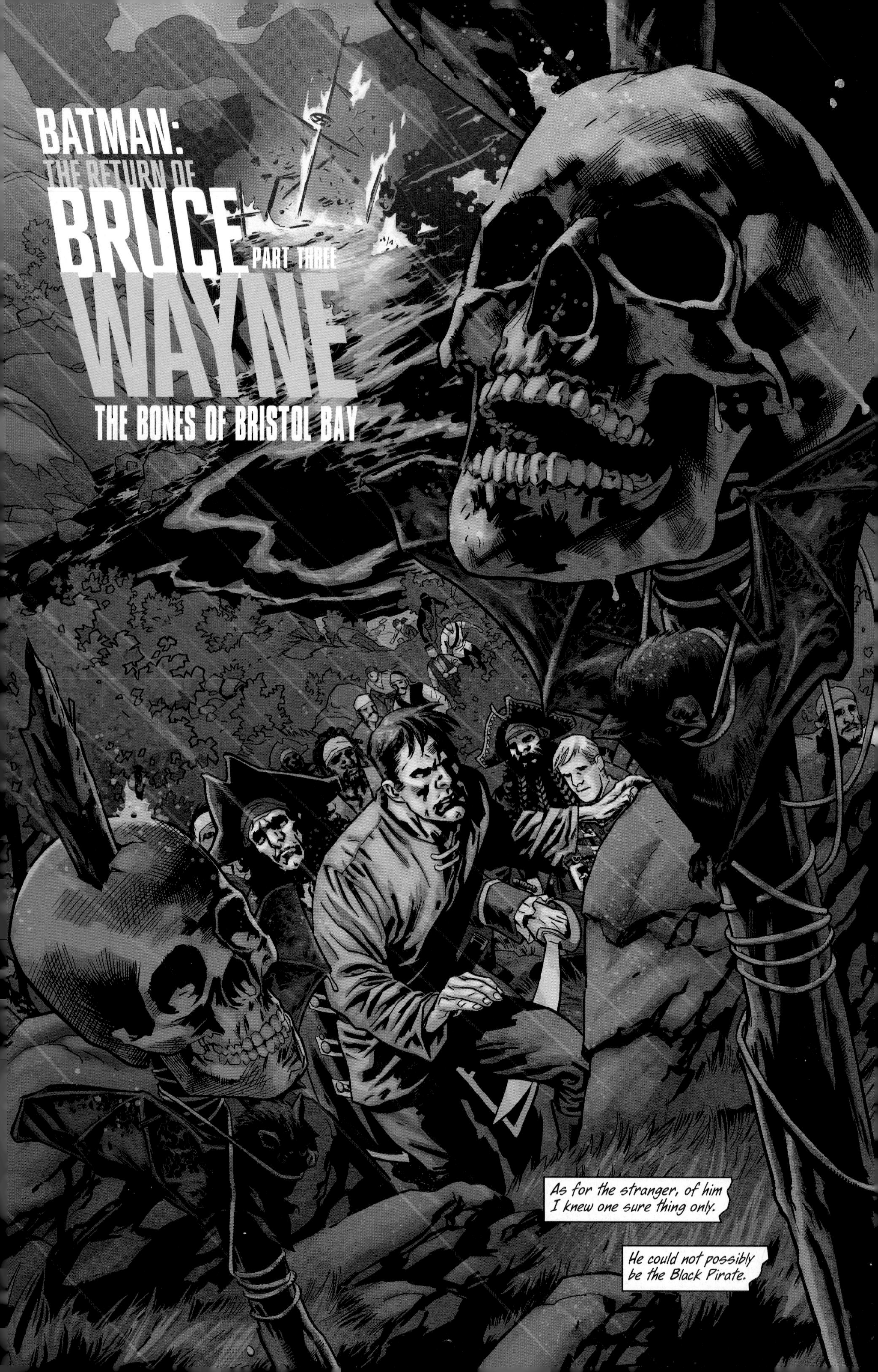
BATMAN:
THE RETURN OF
BRUCE WAYNE
PART THREE
THE BONES OF BRISTOL BAY
As for the stranger, of him I knew one sure thing only.
He could not possibly be the Black Pirate.

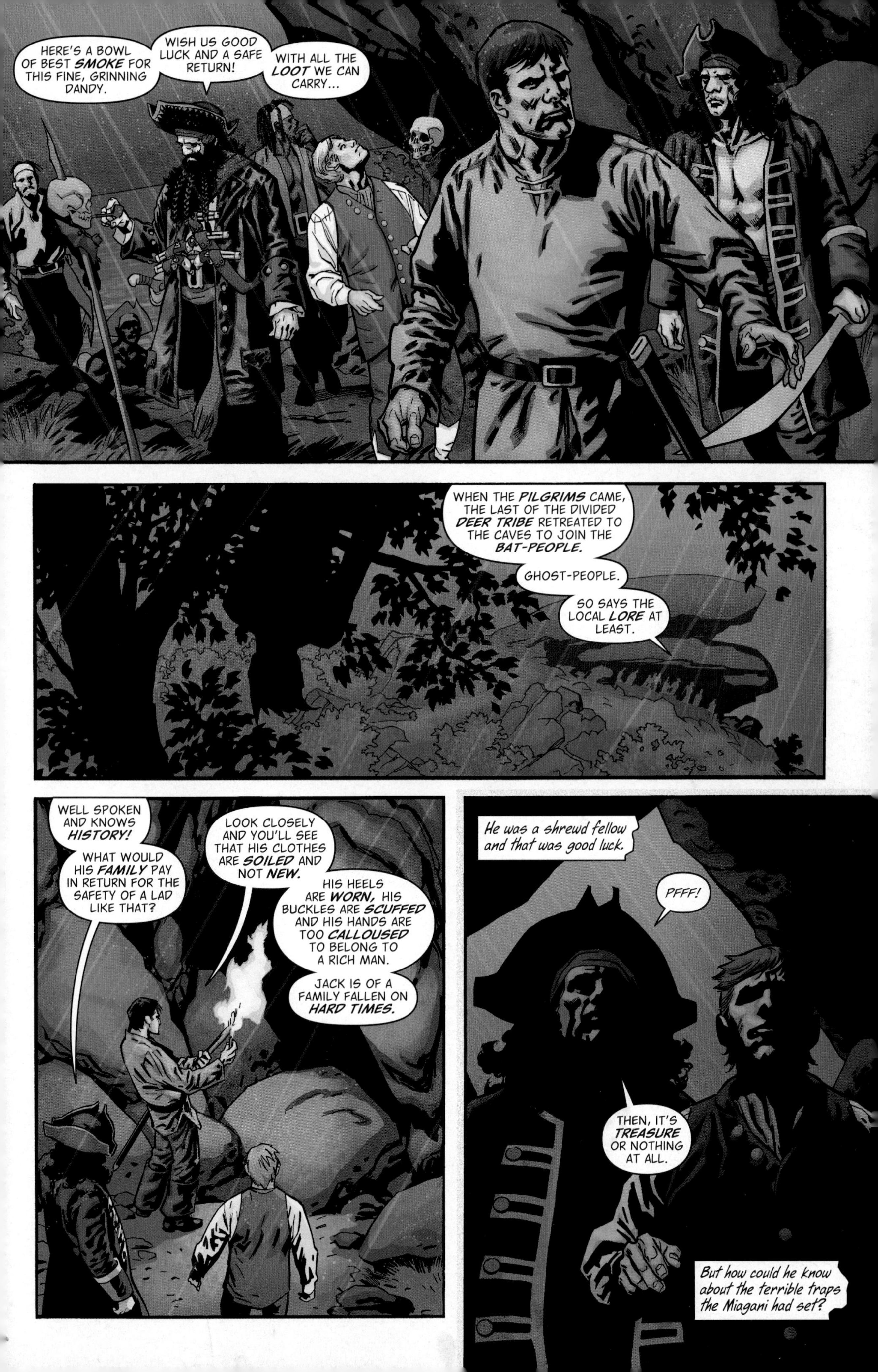
HERE'S A BOWL OF BEST SMOKE FOR THIS FINE, GRINNING DANDY.
WISH US GOOD LUCK AND A SAFE RETURN!
WITH ALL THE LOOT WE CAN CARRY...
WHEN THE PILGRIMS CAME, THE LAST OF THE DIVIDED DEER TRIBE RETREATED TO THE CAVES TO JOIN THE BAT-PEOPLE.
GHOST-PEOPLE.
SO SAYS THE LOCAL LORE AT LEAST.
WELL SPOKEN AND KNOWS HISTORY!
WHAT WOULD HIS FAMILY PAY IN RETURN FOR THE SAFETY OF A LAD LIKE THAT?
LOOK CLOSELY AND YOU'LL SEE THAT HIS CLOTHES ARE SOILED AND NOT NEW.
HIS HEELS ARE WORN, HIS BUCKLES ARE SCUFFED AND HIS HANDS ARE TOO CALLOUSED TO BELONG TO A RICH MAN.
JACK IS OF A FAMILY FALLEN ON HARD TIMES.
He was a shrewd fellow and that was good luck.
PFFF!
THEN, IT'S TREASURE OR NOTHING AT ALL.
But how could he know about the terrible traps the Miagani had set?

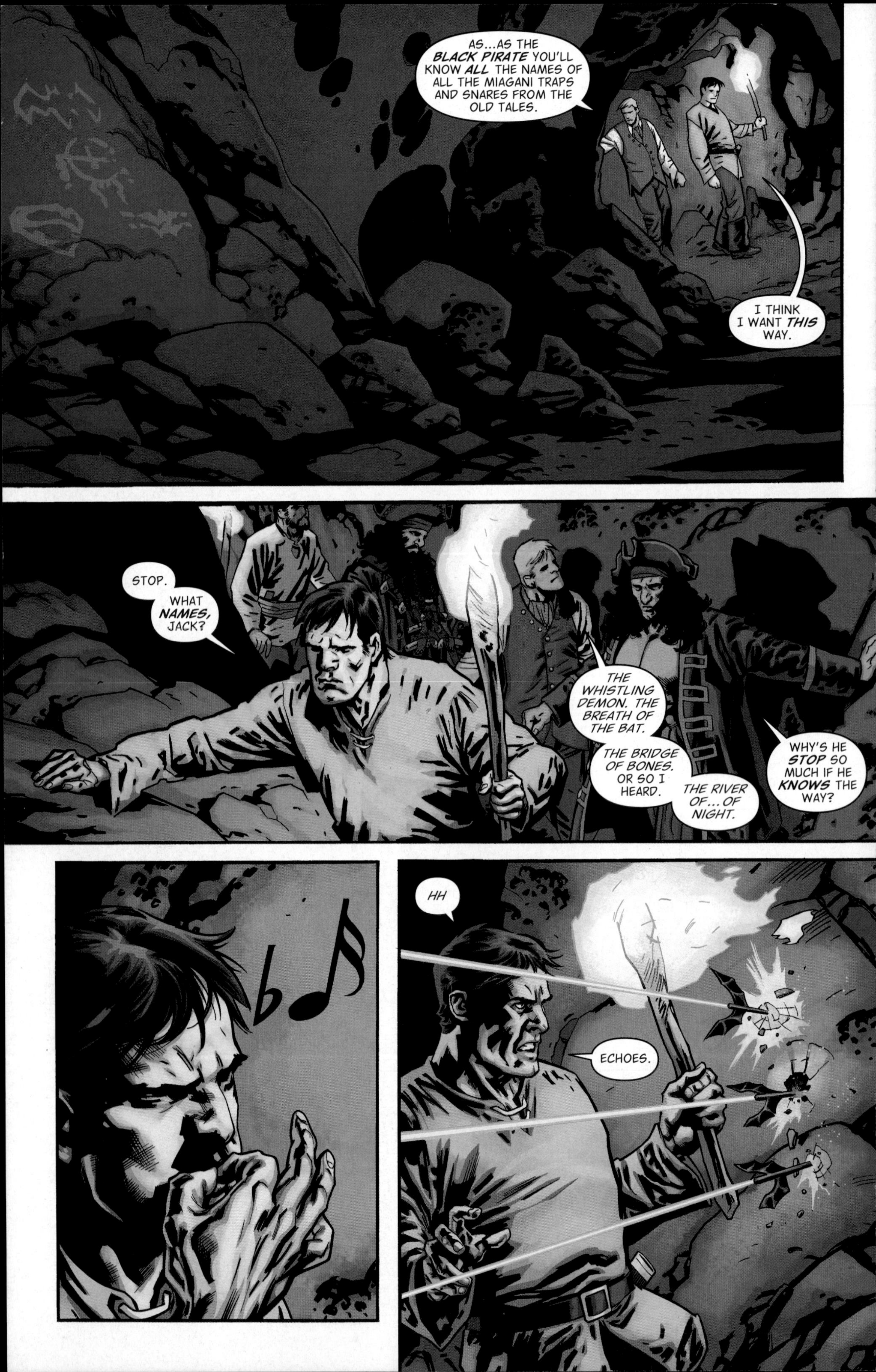
AS...AS THE BLACK PIRATE YOU'LL KNOW ALL THE NAMES OF ALL THE MIAGANI TRAPS AND SNARES FROM THE OLD TALES.
I THINK I WANT THIS WAY.
STOP.
WHAT NAMES, JACK?
THE WHISTLING DEMON. THE BREATH OF THE BAT.
THE BRIDGE OF BONES. OR SO I HEARD.
THE RIVER OF... OF NIGHT.
WHY'S HE STOP SO MUCH IF HE KNOWS THE WAY?
HH
ECHOES.

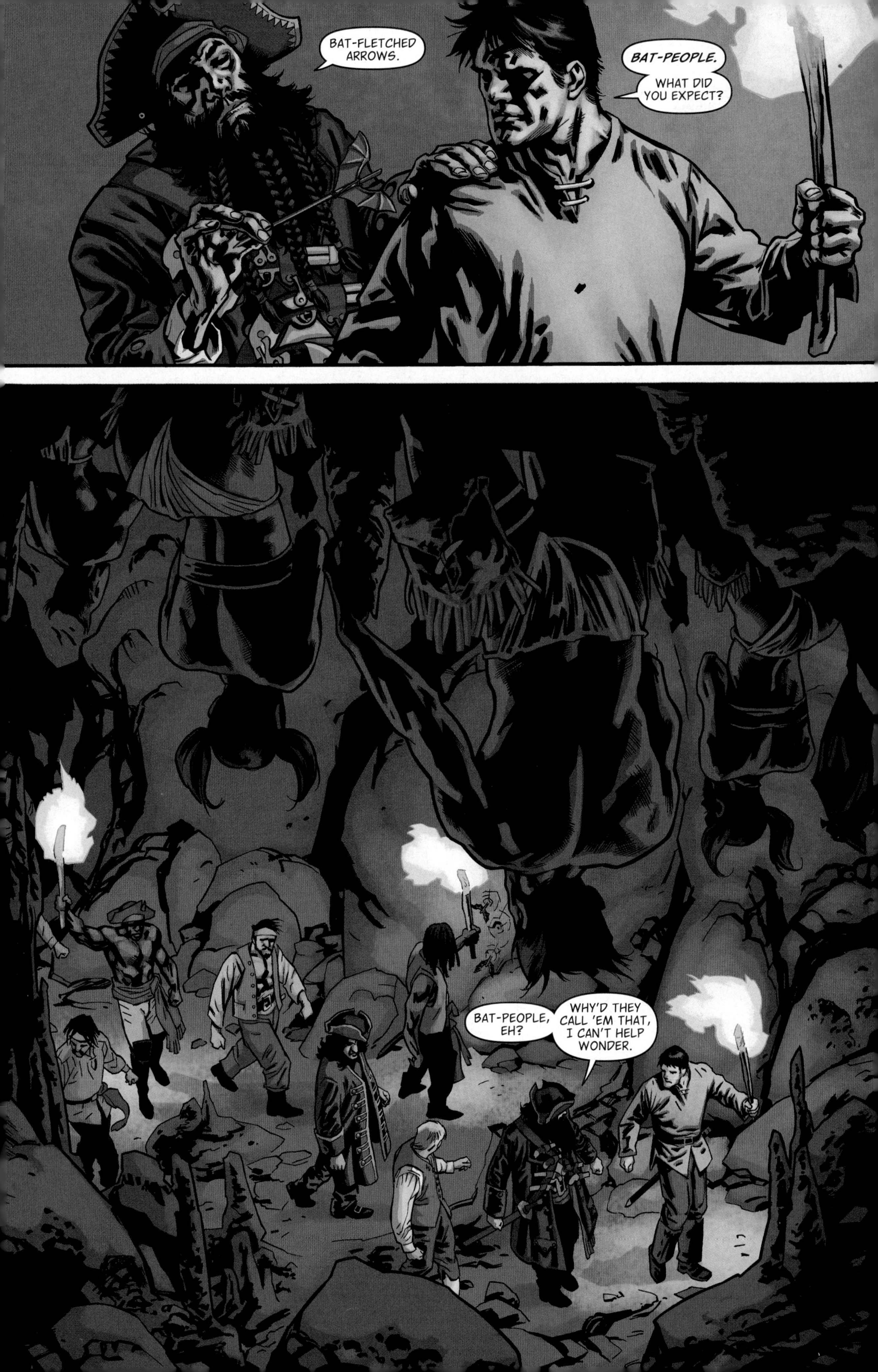
BAT-FLETCHED ARROWS.
BAT-PEOPLE. WHAT DID YOU EXPECT?
BAT-PEOPLE, EH?
WHY'D THEY CALL 'EM THAT, I CAN'T HELP WONDER.

DEAD MEN AHEAD.

AND THE TORCH IS *FLARING*...

WHO RESETS THE SNARES IF NOT *YOU?*

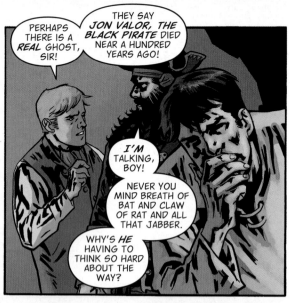

PERHAPS THERE IS A *REAL* GHOST, SIR!

THEY SAY *JON VALOR, THE BLACK PIRATE* DIED NEAR A HUNDRED YEARS AGO!

I'M TALKING, BOY!

NEVER YOU MIND BREATH OF BAT AND CLAW OF RAT AND ALL THAT JABBER.

WHY'S *HE* HAVING TO THINK SO HARD ABOUT THE WAY?

THOSE ARE BAT-DROPPINGS.

THE METHANE WILL *ASPHYXIATE* US...

THAT'S WHAT KILLED THESE MEN, NOT GHOSTS.

AND...AND CERTAIN STONES ARE NOT *LEVEL.*

METHANE IS HIGHLY FLAMMABLE SO PUT OUT YOUR TORCHES, TAKE AS DEEP A BREATH AS YOU'RE ABLE TO AND MOVE VERY, VERY *CAREFULLY.*

IF YOU VALUE YOUR LIVES, DO *EXACTLY* AS I DO.

AND DON'T STEP ON ANY *RAISED* STONES.

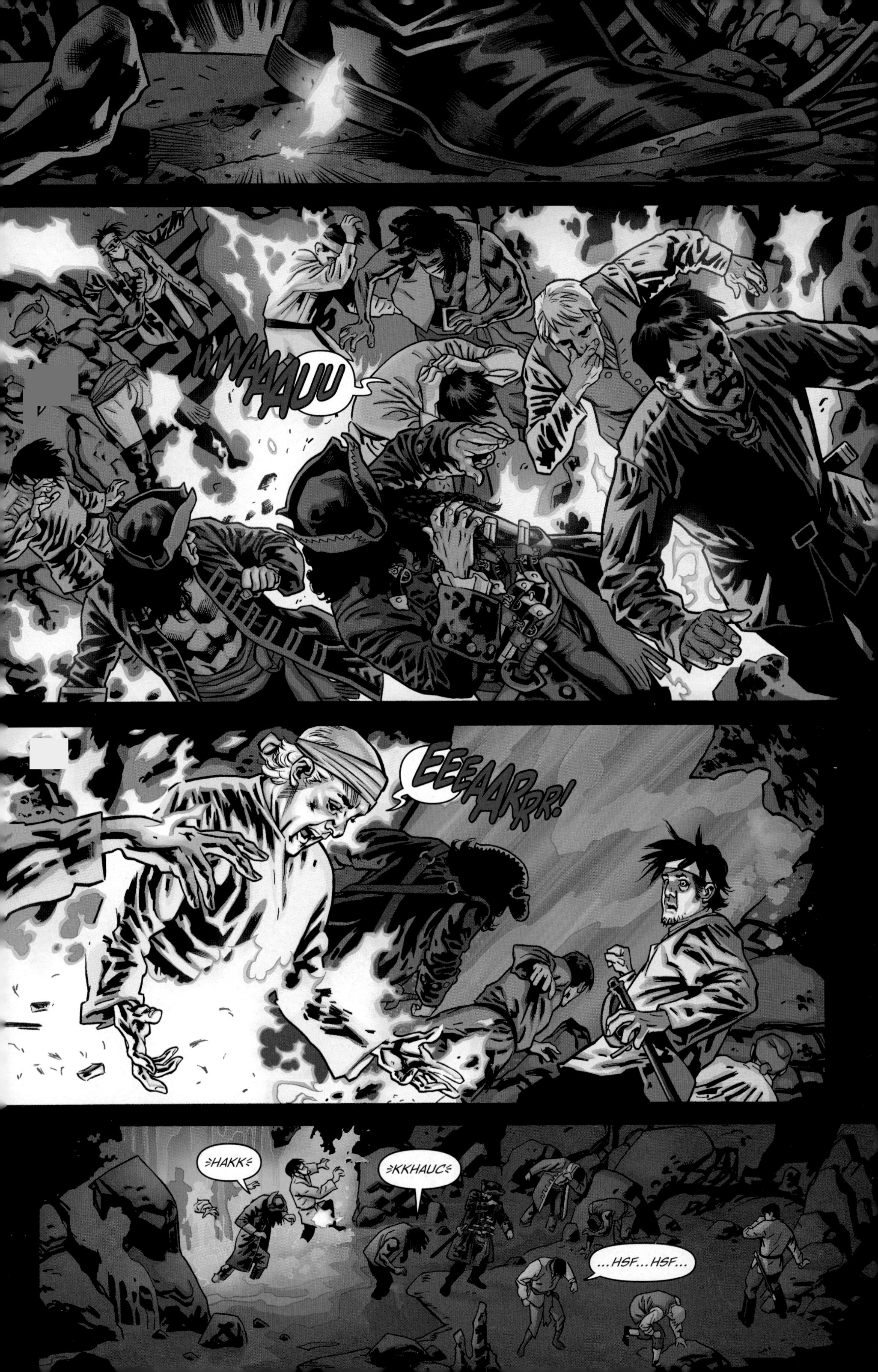
WNAAAUU
EEEAARRRR!
HAKK
KKHAUC
...HSF...HSF...

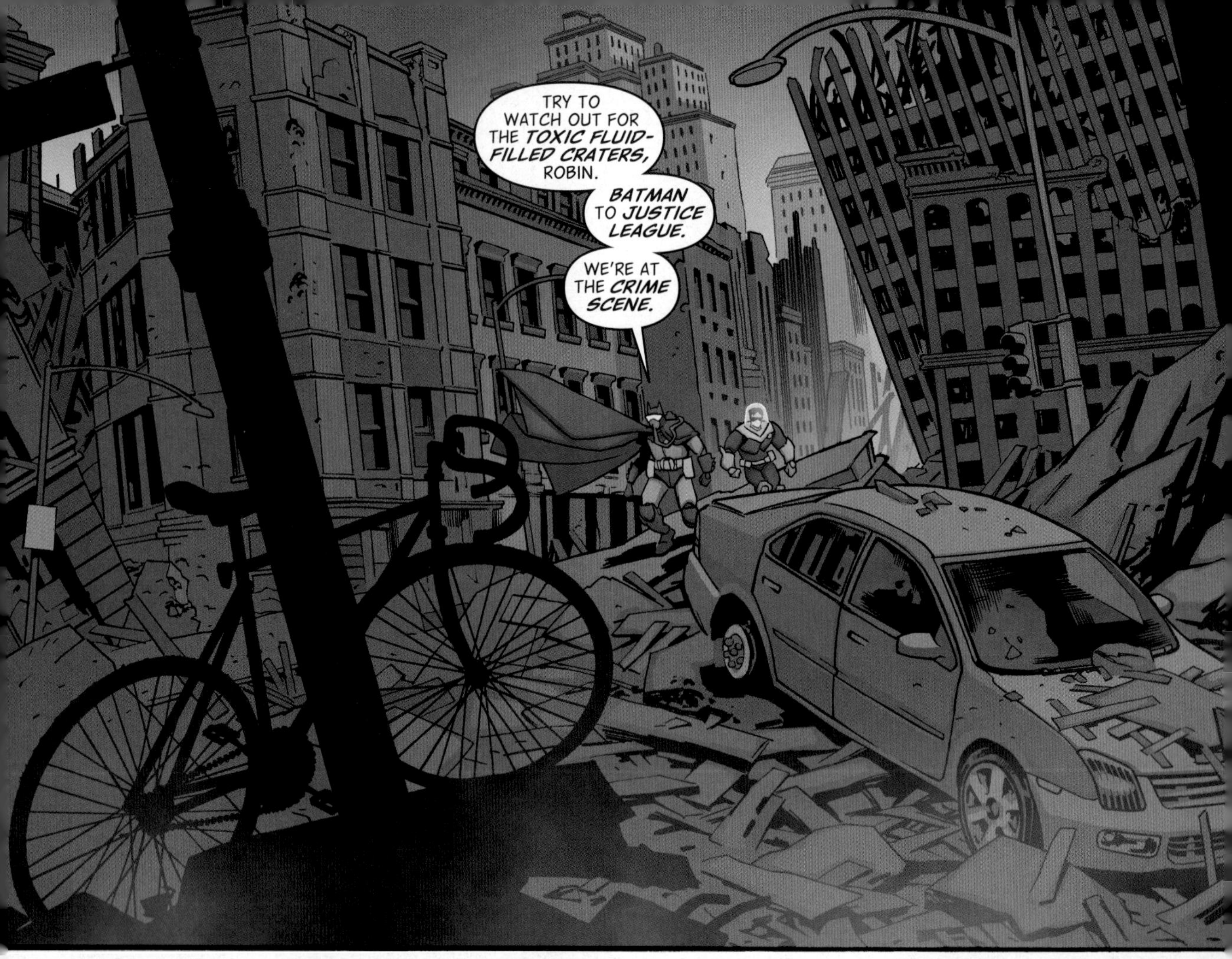
TRY TO WATCH OUT FOR THE TOXIC FLUID-FILLED CRATERS, ROBIN.
BATMAN TO JUSTICE LEAGUE.
WE'RE AT THE CRIME SCENE.

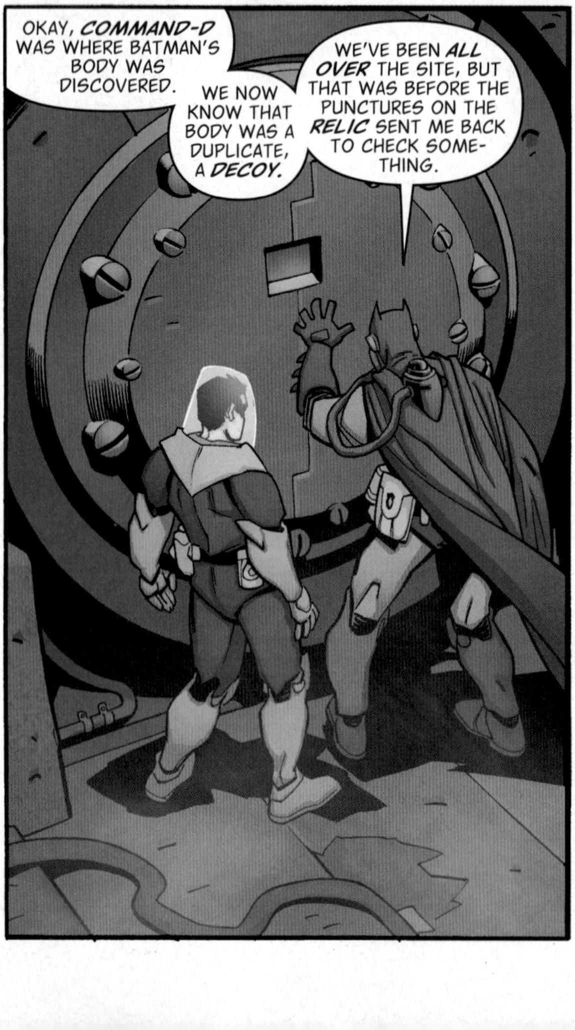
OKAY, COMMAND-D WAS WHERE BATMAN'S BODY WAS DISCOVERED.
WE NOW KNOW THAT BODY WAS A DUPLICATE, A DECOY.
WE'VE BEEN ALL OVER THE SITE, BUT THAT WAS BEFORE THE PUNCTURES ON THE RELIC SENT ME BACK TO CHECK SOME-THING.

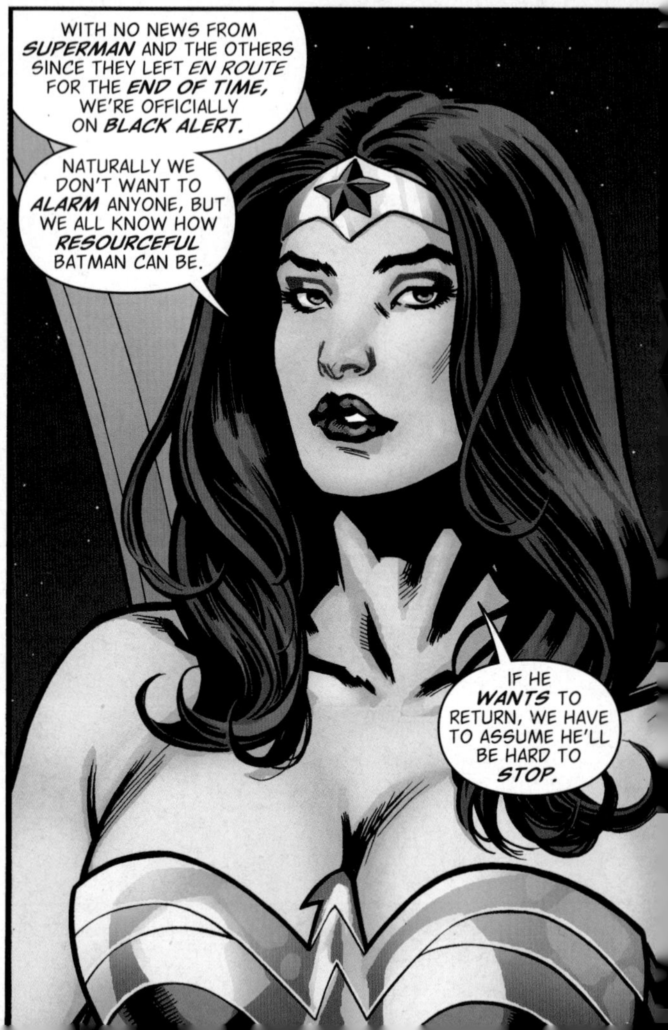
WITH NO NEWS FROM SUPERMAN AND THE OTHERS SINCE THEY LEFT EN ROUTE FOR THE END OF TIME, WE'RE OFFICIALLY ON BLACK ALERT.
NATURALLY WE DON'T WANT TO ALARM ANYONE, BUT WE ALL KNOW HOW RESOURCEFUL BATMAN CAN BE.
IF HE WANTS TO RETURN, WE HAVE TO ASSUME HE'LL BE HARD TO STOP.

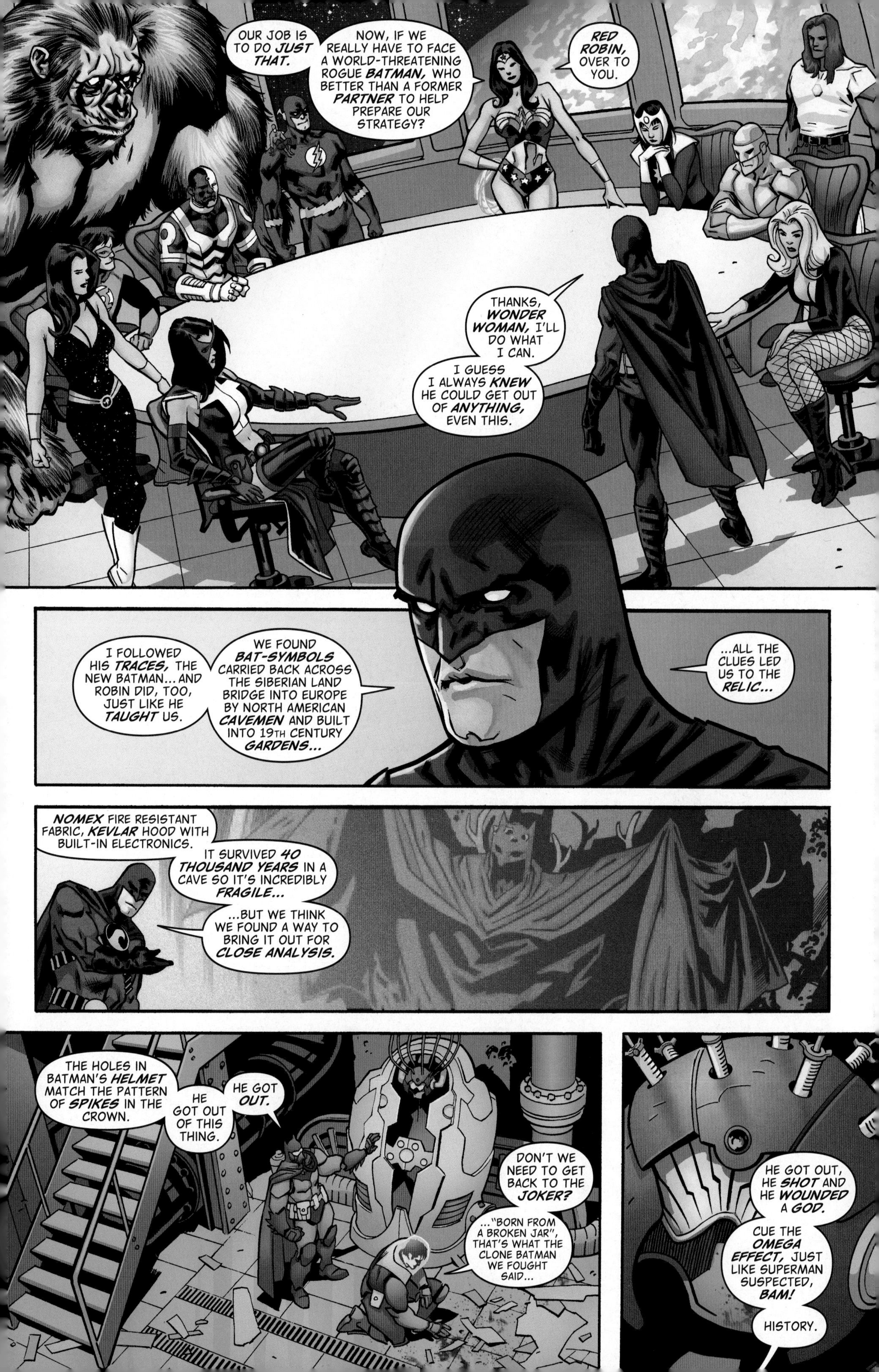
OUR JOB IS TO DO JUST THAT.
NOW, IF WE REALLY HAVE TO FACE A WORLD-THREATENING ROGUE BATMAN, WHO BETTER THAN A FORMER PARTNER TO HELP PREPARE OUR STRATEGY?
RED ROBIN, OVER TO YOU.
THANKS, WONDER WOMAN, I'LL DO WHAT I CAN.
I GUESS I ALWAYS KNEW HE COULD GET OUT OF ANYTHING, EVEN THIS.
I FOLLOWED HIS TRACES, THE NEW BATMAN... AND ROBIN DID, TOO, JUST LIKE HE TAUGHT US.
WE FOUND BAT-SYMBOLS CARRIED BACK ACROSS THE SIBERIAN LAND BRIDGE INTO EUROPE BY NORTH AMERICAN CAVEMEN AND BUILT INTO 19TH CENTURY GARDENS...
...ALL THE CLUES LED US TO THE RELIC...
NOMEX FIRE RESISTANT FABRIC, KEVLAR HOOD WITH BUILT-IN ELECTRONICS.
IT SURVIVED 40 THOUSAND YEARS IN A CAVE SO IT'S INCREDIBLY FRAGILE...
...BUT WE THINK WE FOUND A WAY TO BRING IT OUT FOR CLOSE ANALYSIS.
THE HOLES IN BATMAN'S HELMET MATCH THE PATTERN OF SPIKES IN THE CROWN.
HE GOT OUT OF THIS THING.
HE GOT OUT.
DON'T WE NEED TO GET BACK TO THE JOKER?
..."BORN FROM A BROKEN JAR", THAT'S WHAT THE CLONE BATMAN WE FOUGHT SAID...
HE GOT OUT, HE SHOT AND HE WOUNDED A GOD.
CUE THE OMEGA EFFECT, JUST LIKE SUPERMAN SUSPECTED, BAM!
HISTORY.

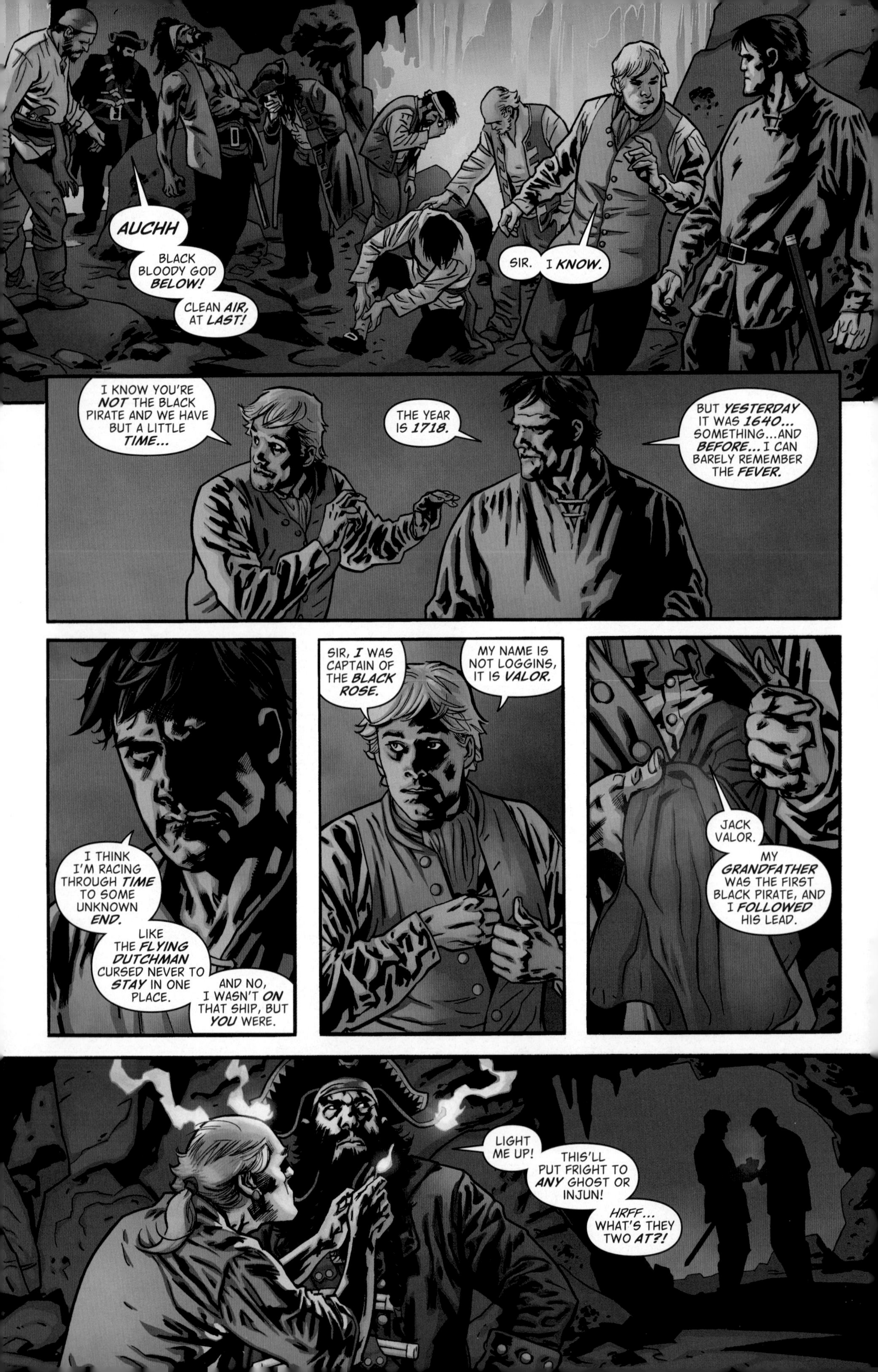
AUCHH
BLACK BLOODY GOD BELOW!
CLEAN AIR, AT LAST!
SIR.
I KNOW.
I KNOW YOU'RE NOT THE BLACK PIRATE AND WE HAVE BUT A LITTLE TIME...
THE YEAR IS 1718.
BUT YESTERDAY IT WAS 1640... SOMETHING...AND BEFORE... I CAN BARELY REMEMBER THE FEVER.
I THINK I'M RACING THROUGH TIME TO SOME UNKNOWN END.
LIKE THE FLYING DUTCHMAN CURSED NEVER TO STAY IN ONE PLACE.
AND NO, I WASN'T ON THAT SHIP, BUT YOU WERE.
SIR, I WAS CAPTAIN OF THE BLACK ROSE.
MY NAME IS NOT LOGGINS, IT IS VALOR.
JACK VALOR.
MY GRANDFATHER WAS THE FIRST BLACK PIRATE, AND I FOLLOWED HIS LEAD.
LIGHT ME UP!
THIS'LL PUT FRIGHT TO ANY GHOST OR INJUN!
HRFF... WHAT'S THEY TWO AT?!

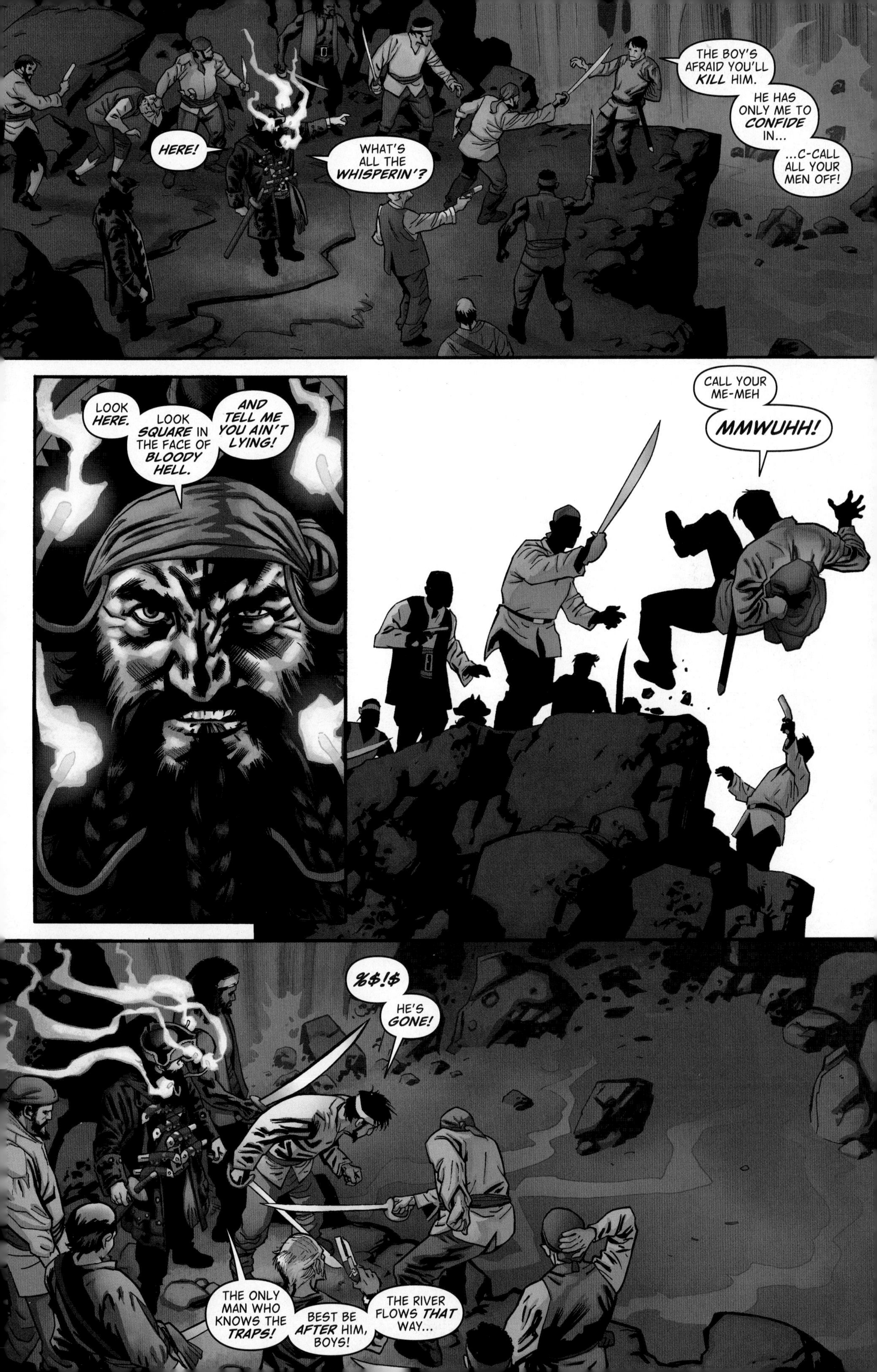
HERE!
WHAT'S ALL THE WHISPERIN'?
THE BOY'S AFRAID YOU'LL KILL HIM.
HE HAS ONLY ME TO CONFIDE IN...
...C-CALL ALL YOUR MEN OFF!
LOOK HERE.
LOOK SQUARE IN THE FACE OF BLOODY HELL.
AND TELL ME YOU AIN'T LYING!
CALL YOUR ME-MEH
MMWUHH!
%$!$
HE'S GONE!
THE ONLY MAN WHO KNOWS THE TRAPS!
BEST BE AFTER HIM, BOYS!
THE RIVER FLOWS THAT WAY...

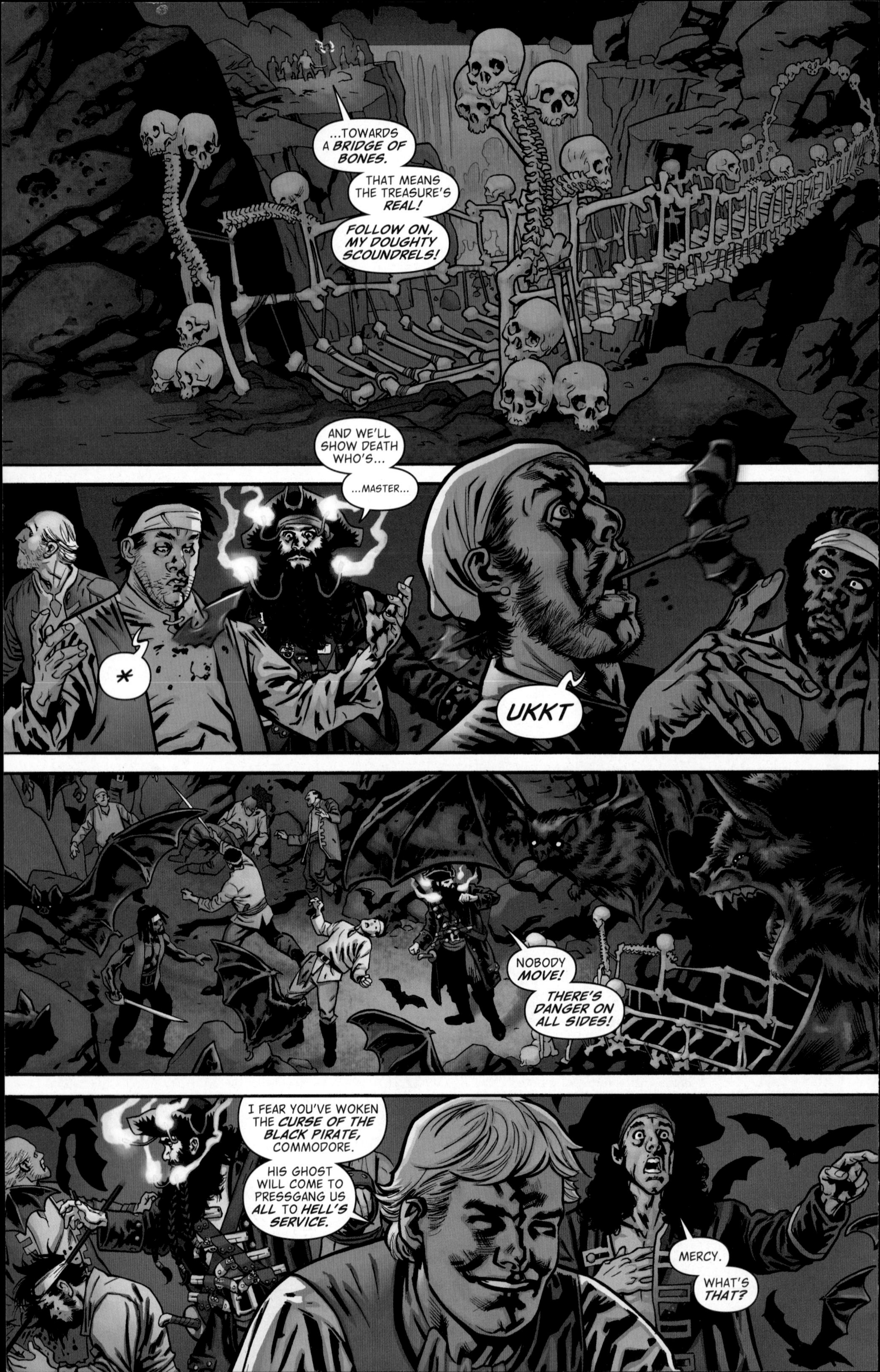
...TOWARDS A BRIDGE OF BONES.
THAT MEANS THE TREASURE'S REAL!
FOLLOW ON, MY DOUGHTY SCOUNDRELS!
AND WE'LL SHOW DEATH WHO'S...
...MASTER...
*
UKKT
NOBODY MOVE!
THERE'S DANGER ON ALL SIDES!
I FEAR YOU'VE WOKEN THE CURSE OF THE BLACK PIRATE, COMMODORE.
HIS GHOST WILL COME TO PRESSGANG US ALL TO HELL'S SERVICE.
MERCY.
WHAT'S THAT?

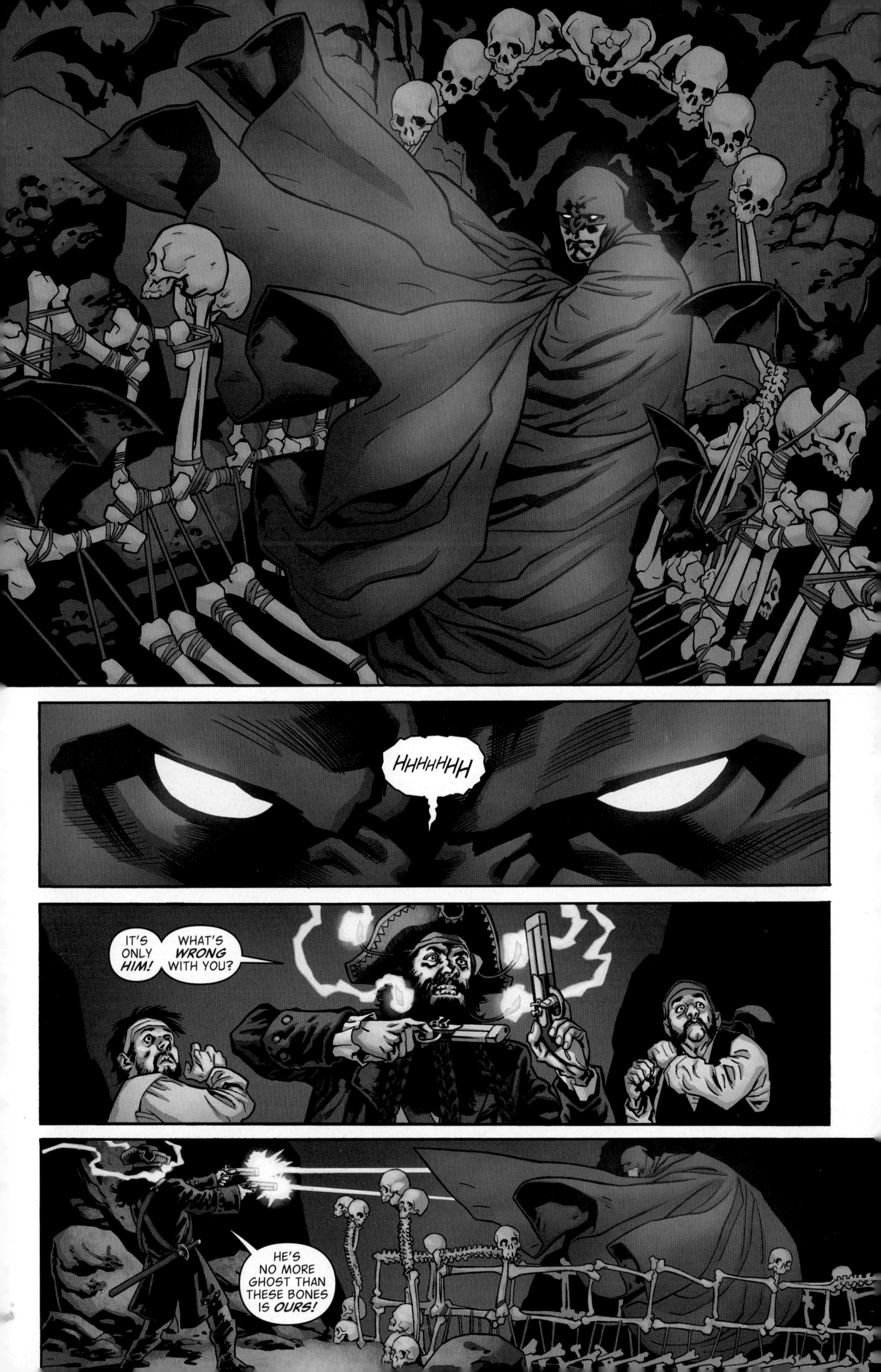
HHHHHHH
IT'S ONLY HIM!
WHAT'S WRONG WITH YOU?
HE'S NO MORE GHOST THAN THESE BONES IS OURS!

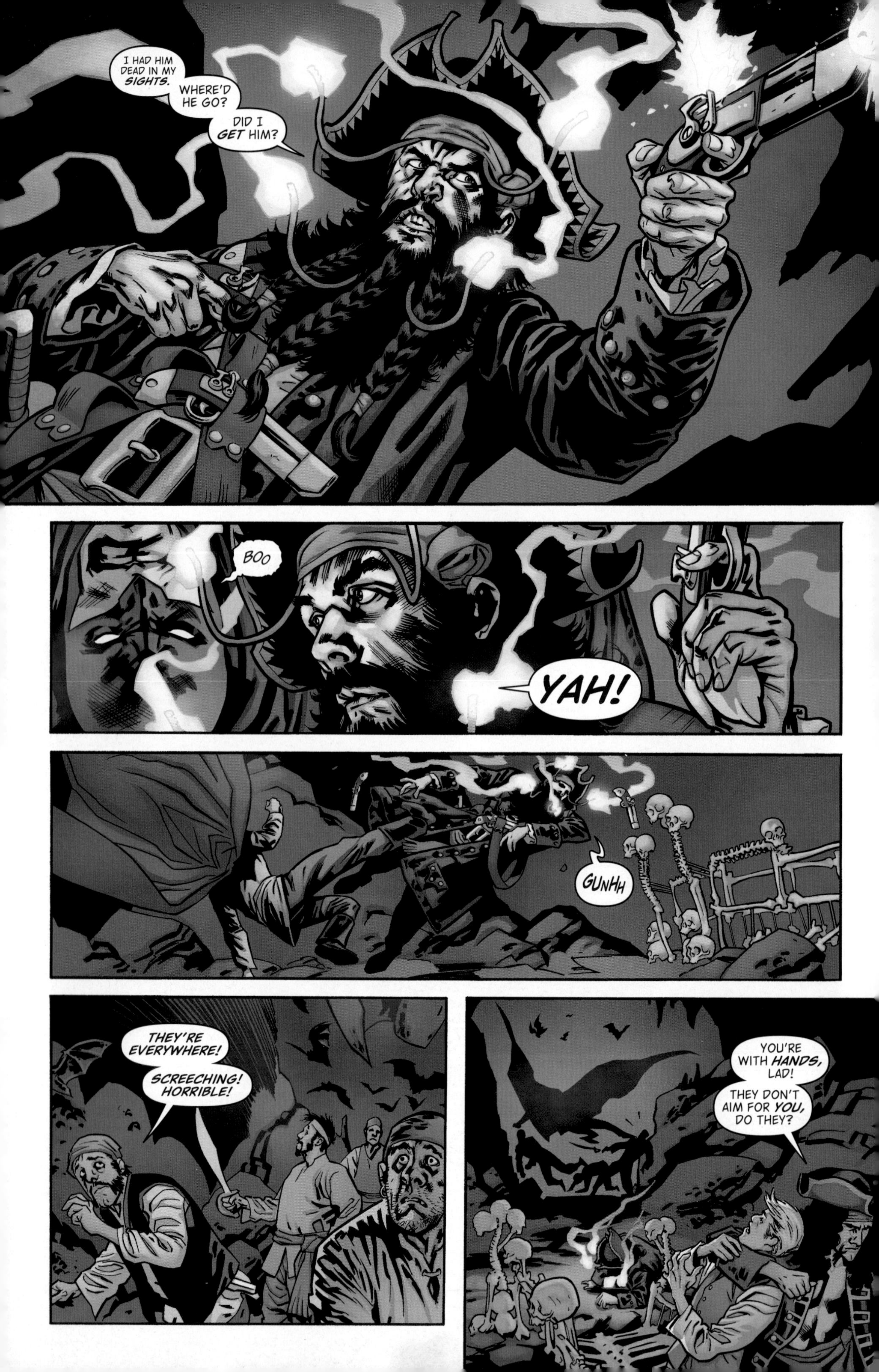
I HAD HIM DEAD IN MY SIGHTS.
WHERE'D HE GO?
DID I GET HIM?
BOO
YAH!
GUNHH
THEY'RE EVERYWHERE!
SCREECHING! HORRIBLE!
YOU'RE WITH HANDS, LAD!
THEY DON'T AIM FOR YOU, DO THEY?

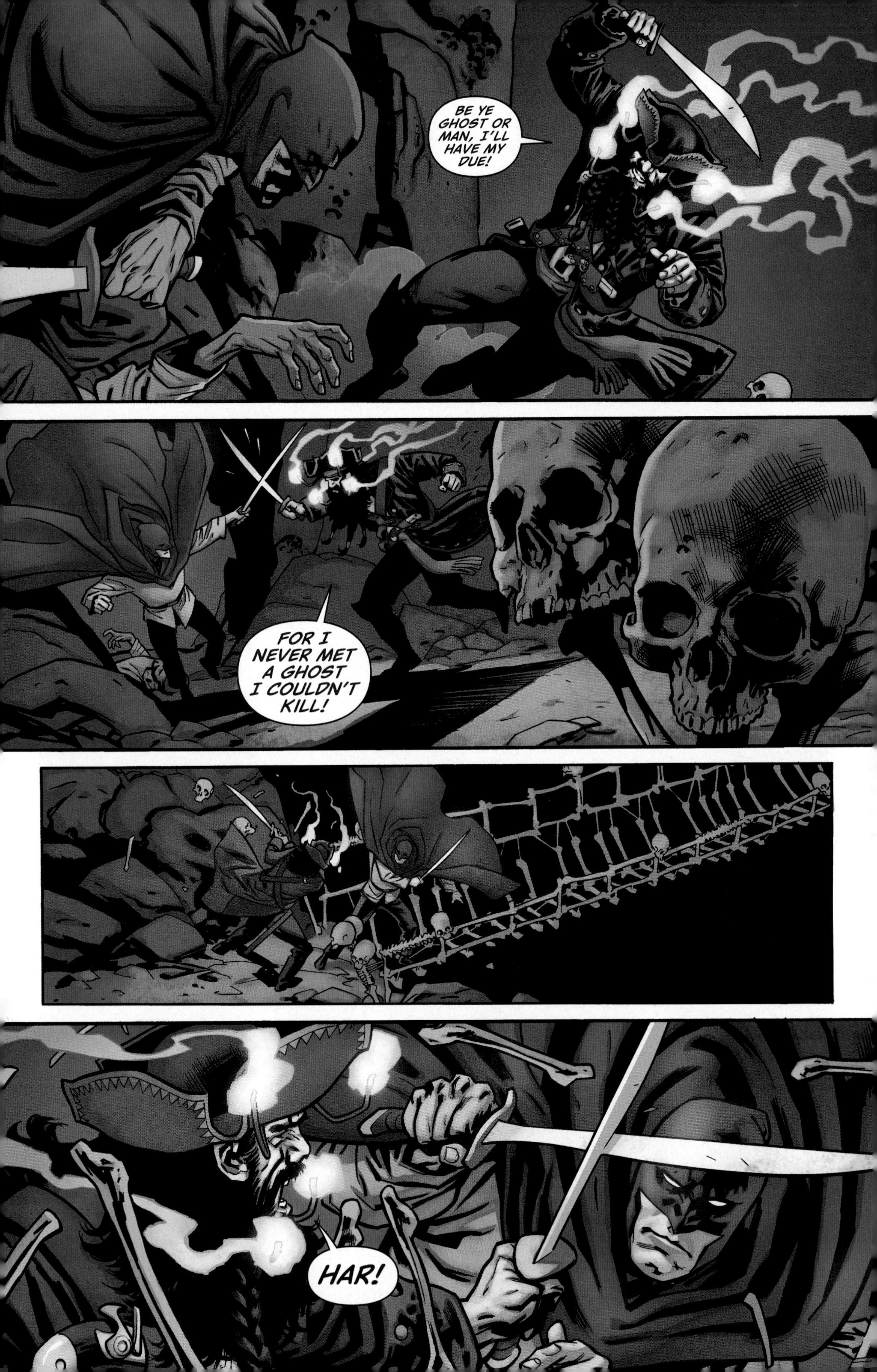
BE YE GHOST OR MAN, I'LL HAVE MY DUE!
FOR I NEVER MET A GHOST I COULDN'T KILL!
HAR!

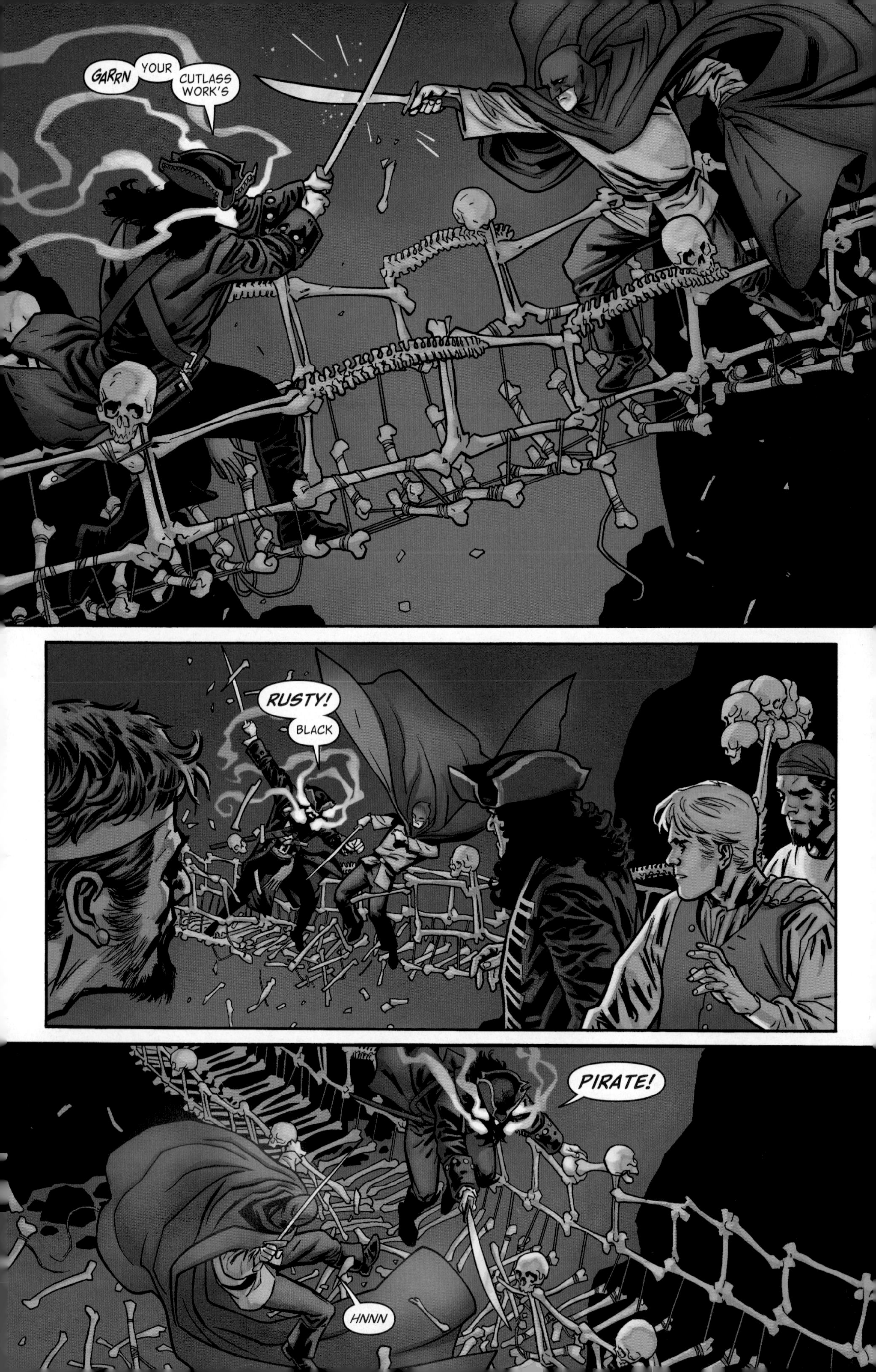
GARRN
YOUR
CUTLASS WORK'S
RUSTY!
BLACK
PIRATE!
HNNN

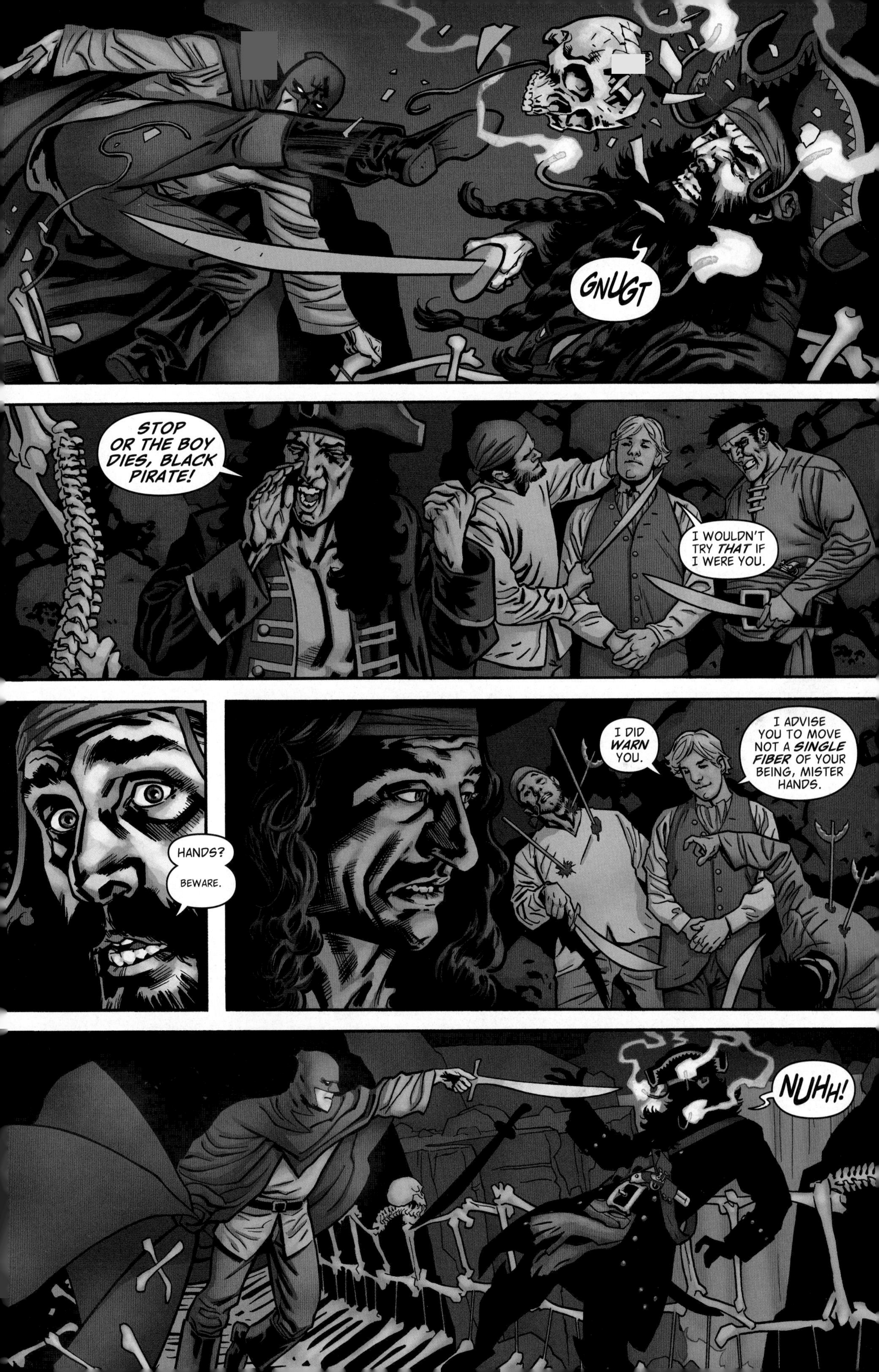
GNUGT
STOP OR THE BOY DIES, BLACK PIRATE!
I WOULDN'T TRY THAT IF I WERE YOU.
HANDS?
BEWARE.
I DID WARN YOU.
I ADVISE YOU TO MOVE NOT A SINGLE FIBER OF YOUR BEING, MISTER HANDS.
NUHH!

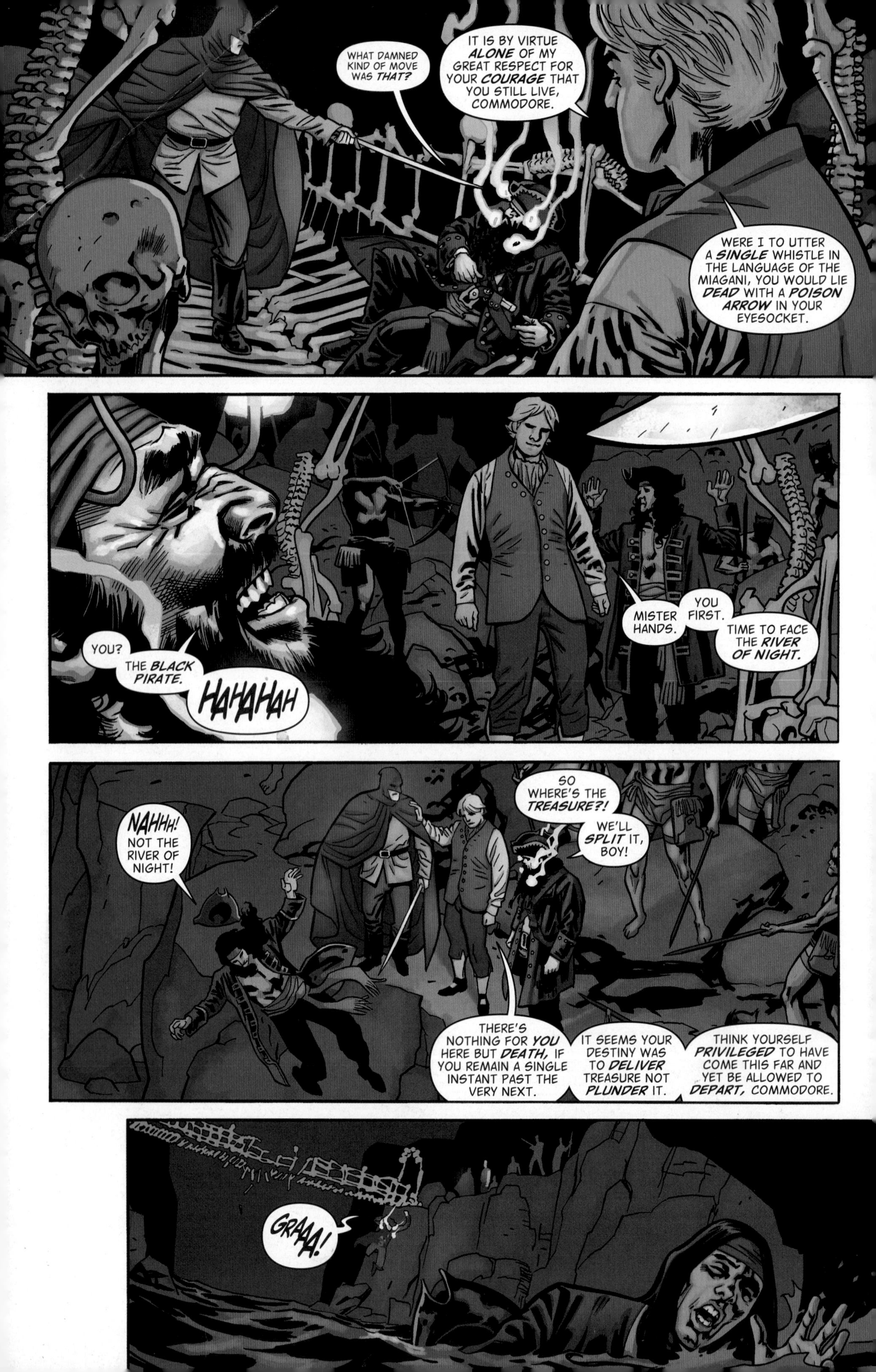
WHAT DAMNED KIND OF MOVE WAS THAT?
IT IS BY VIRTUE ALONE OF MY GREAT RESPECT FOR YOUR COURAGE THAT YOU STILL LIVE, COMMODORE.
WERE I TO UTTER A SINGLE WHISTLE IN THE LANGUAGE OF THE MIAGANI, YOU WOULD LIE DEAD WITH A POISON ARROW IN YOUR EYESOCKET.
YOU?
THE BLACK PIRATE.
HAHAHAH
MISTER HANDS.
YOU FIRST.
TIME TO FACE THE RIVER OF NIGHT.
NAHHH! NOT THE RIVER OF NIGHT!
SO WHERE'S THE TREASURE?!
WE'LL SPLIT IT, BOY!
THERE'S NOTHING FOR YOU HERE BUT DEATH, IF YOU REMAIN A SINGLE INSTANT PAST THE VERY NEXT.
IT SEEMS YOUR DESTINY WAS TO DELIVER TREASURE NOT PLUNDER IT.
THINK YOURSELF PRIVILEGED TO HAVE COME THIS FAR AND YET BE ALLOWED TO DEPART, COMMODORE.
GRAAA!

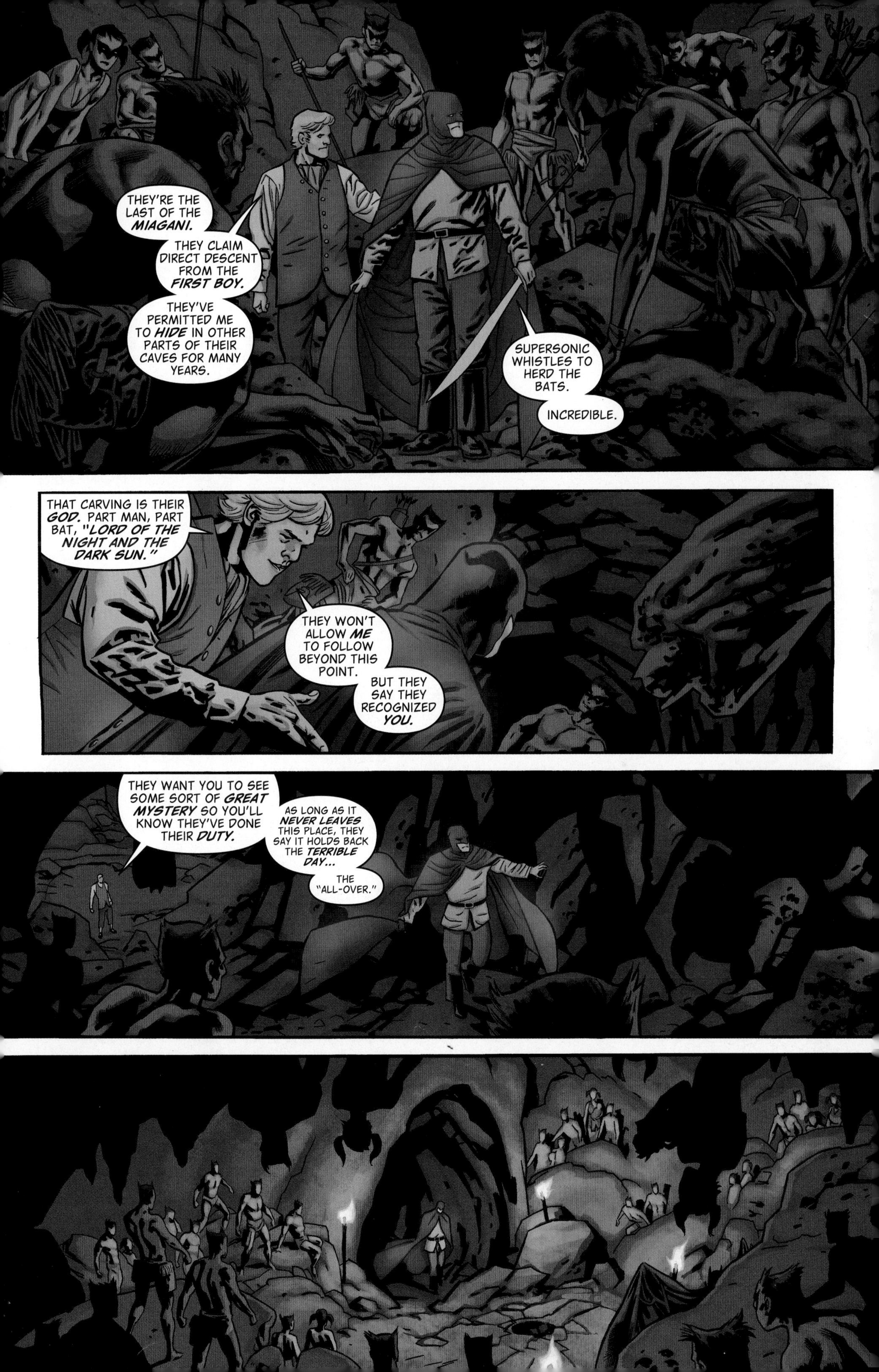
THEY'RE THE LAST OF THE MIAGANI.
THEY CLAIM DIRECT DESCENT FROM THE FIRST BOY.
THEY'VE PERMITTED ME TO HIDE IN OTHER PARTS OF THEIR CAVES FOR MANY YEARS.
SUPERSONIC WHISTLES TO HERD THE BATS.
INCREDIBLE.
THAT CARVING IS THEIR GOD. PART MAN, PART BAT, "LORD OF THE NIGHT AND THE DARK SUN."
THEY WON'T ALLOW ME TO FOLLOW BEYOND THIS POINT.
BUT THEY SAY THEY RECOGNIZED YOU.
THEY WANT YOU TO SEE SOME SORT OF GREAT MYSTERY SO YOU'LL KNOW THEY'VE DONE THEIR DUTY.
AS LONG AS IT NEVER LEAVES THIS PLACE, THEY SAY IT HOLDS BACK THE TERRIBLE DAY...
THE "ALL-OVER."

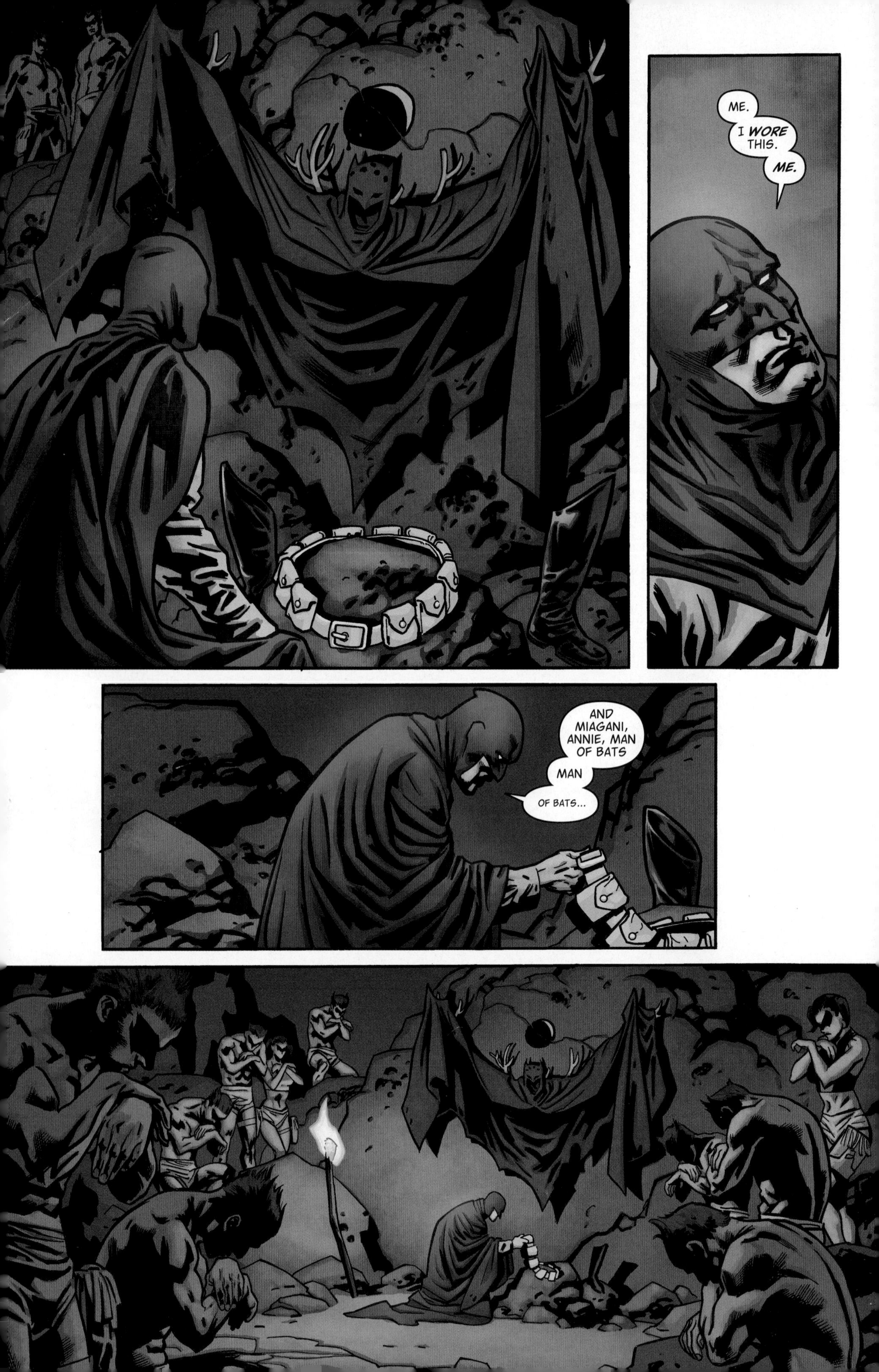
ME.
I WORE THIS.
ME.
AND MIAGANI, ANNIE, MAN OF BATS
MAN
OF BATS...

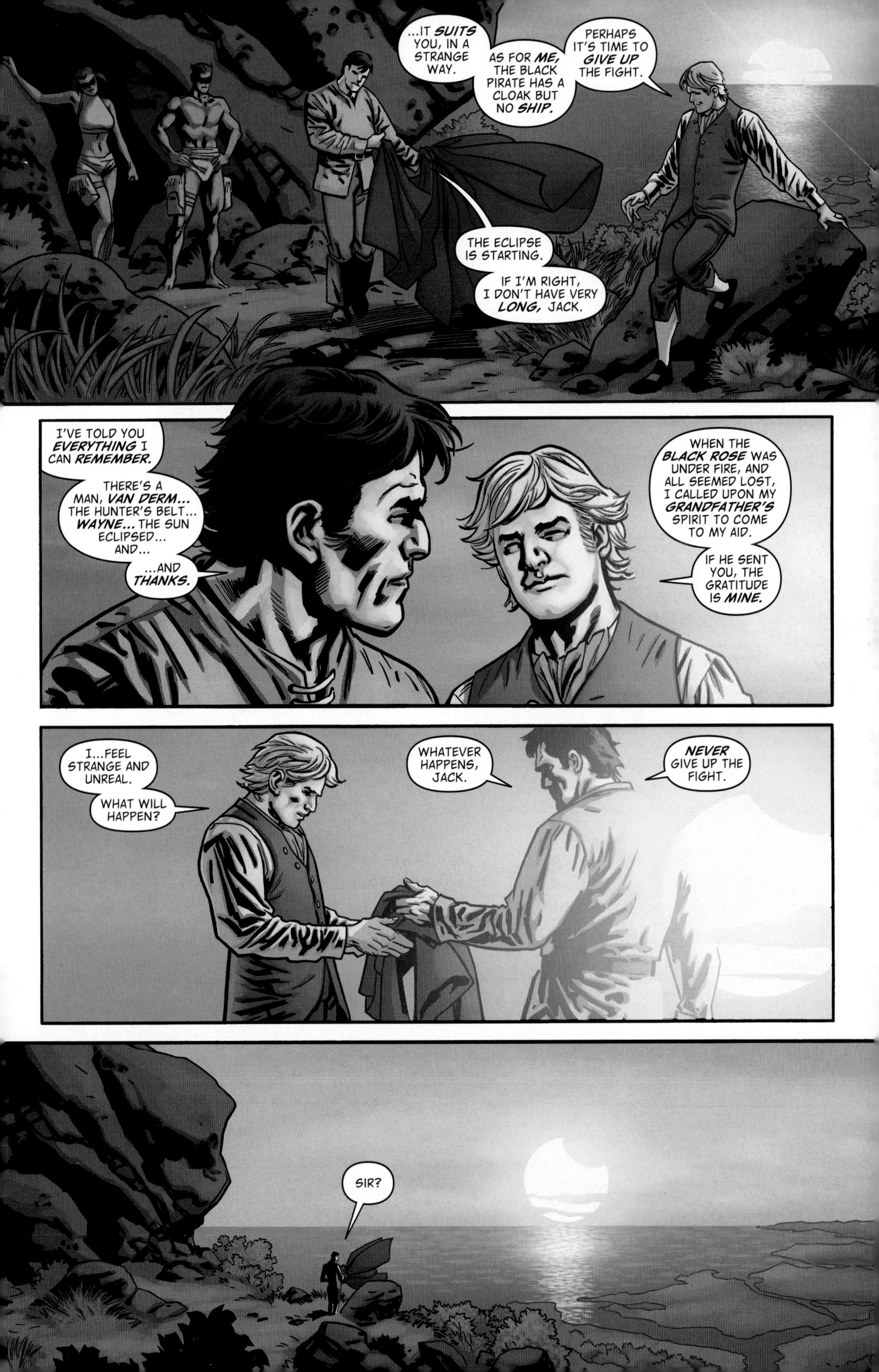
...IT SUITS YOU, IN A STRANGE WAY.
AS FOR ME, THE BLACK PIRATE HAS A CLOAK BUT NO SHIP.
PERHAPS IT'S TIME TO GIVE UP THE FIGHT.
THE ECLIPSE IS STARTING.
IF I'M RIGHT, I DON'T HAVE VERY LONG, JACK.
I'VE TOLD YOU EVERYTHING I CAN REMEMBER.
THERE'S A MAN, VAN DERM... THE HUNTER'S BELT... WAYNE... THE SUN ECLIPSED... AND...
...AND THANKS.
WHEN THE BLACK ROSE WAS UNDER FIRE, AND ALL SEEMED LOST, I CALLED UPON MY GRANDFATHER'S SPIRIT TO COME TO MY AID.
IF HE SENT YOU, THE GRATITUDE IS MINE.
I...FEEL STRANGE AND UNREAL.
WHAT WILL HAPPEN?
WHATEVER HAPPENS, JACK.
NEVER GIVE UP THE FIGHT.
SIR?

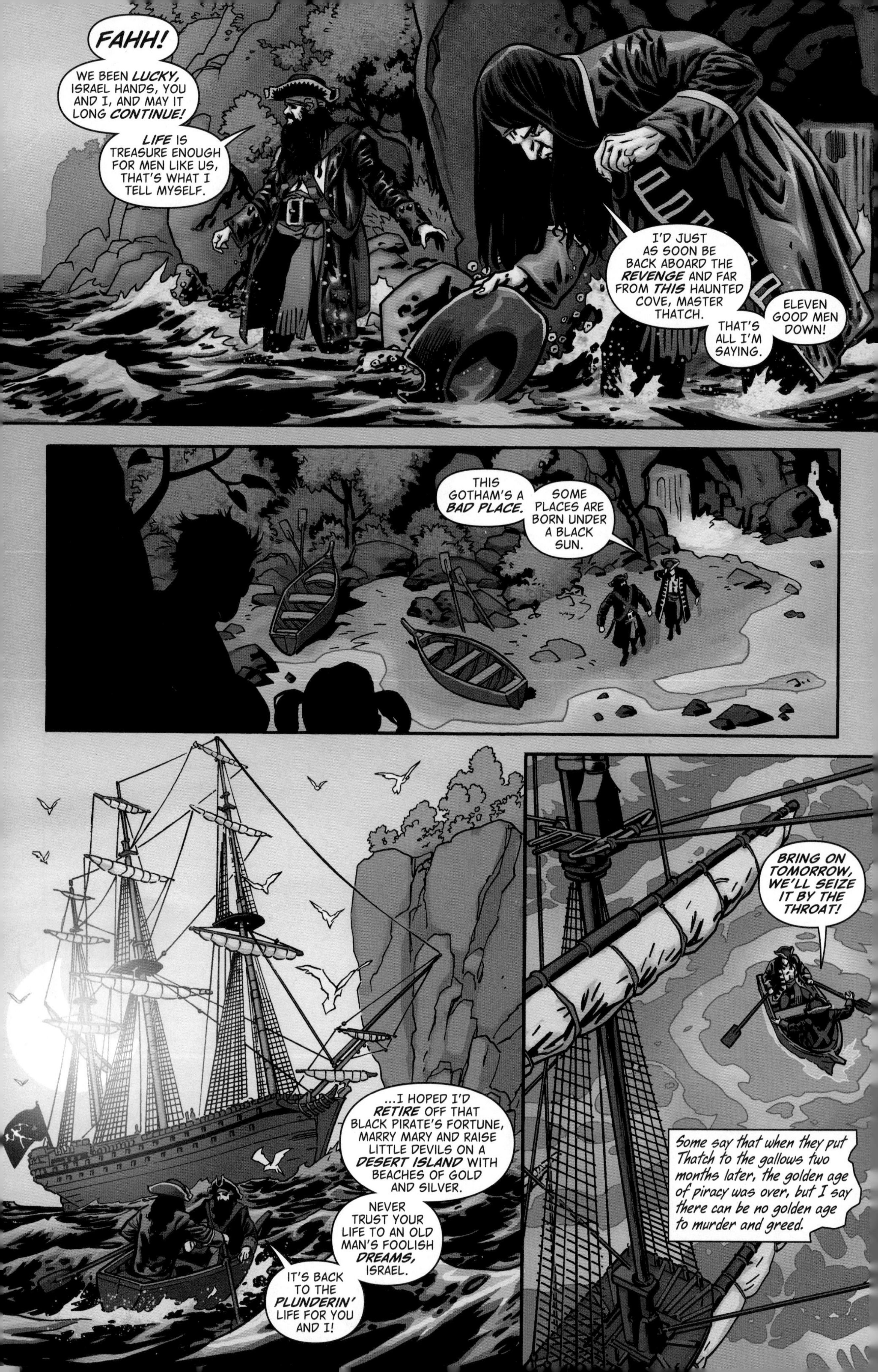
FAHH!
WE BEEN LUCKY, ISRAEL HANDS, YOU AND I, AND MAY IT LONG CONTINUE!
LIFE IS TREASURE ENOUGH FOR MEN LIKE US, THAT'S WHAT I TELL MYSELF.
I'D JUST AS SOON BE BACK ABOARD THE REVENGE AND FAR FROM THIS HAUNTED COVE, MASTER THATCH.
THAT'S ALL I'M SAYING.
ELEVEN GOOD MEN DOWN!
THIS GOTHAM'S A BAD PLACE.
SOME PLACES ARE BORN UNDER A BLACK SUN.
...I HOPED I'D RETIRE OFF THAT BLACK PIRATE'S FORTUNE, MARRY MARY AND RAISE LITTLE DEVILS ON A DESERT ISLAND WITH BEACHES OF GOLD AND SILVER.
NEVER TRUST YOUR LIFE TO AN OLD MAN'S FOOLISH DREAMS, ISRAEL.
IT'S BACK TO THE PLUNDERIN' LIFE FOR YOU AND I!
BRING ON TOMORROW, WE'LL SEIZE IT BY THE THROAT!
Some say that when they put Thatch to the gallows two months later, the golden age of piracy was over, but I say there can be no golden age to murder and greed.

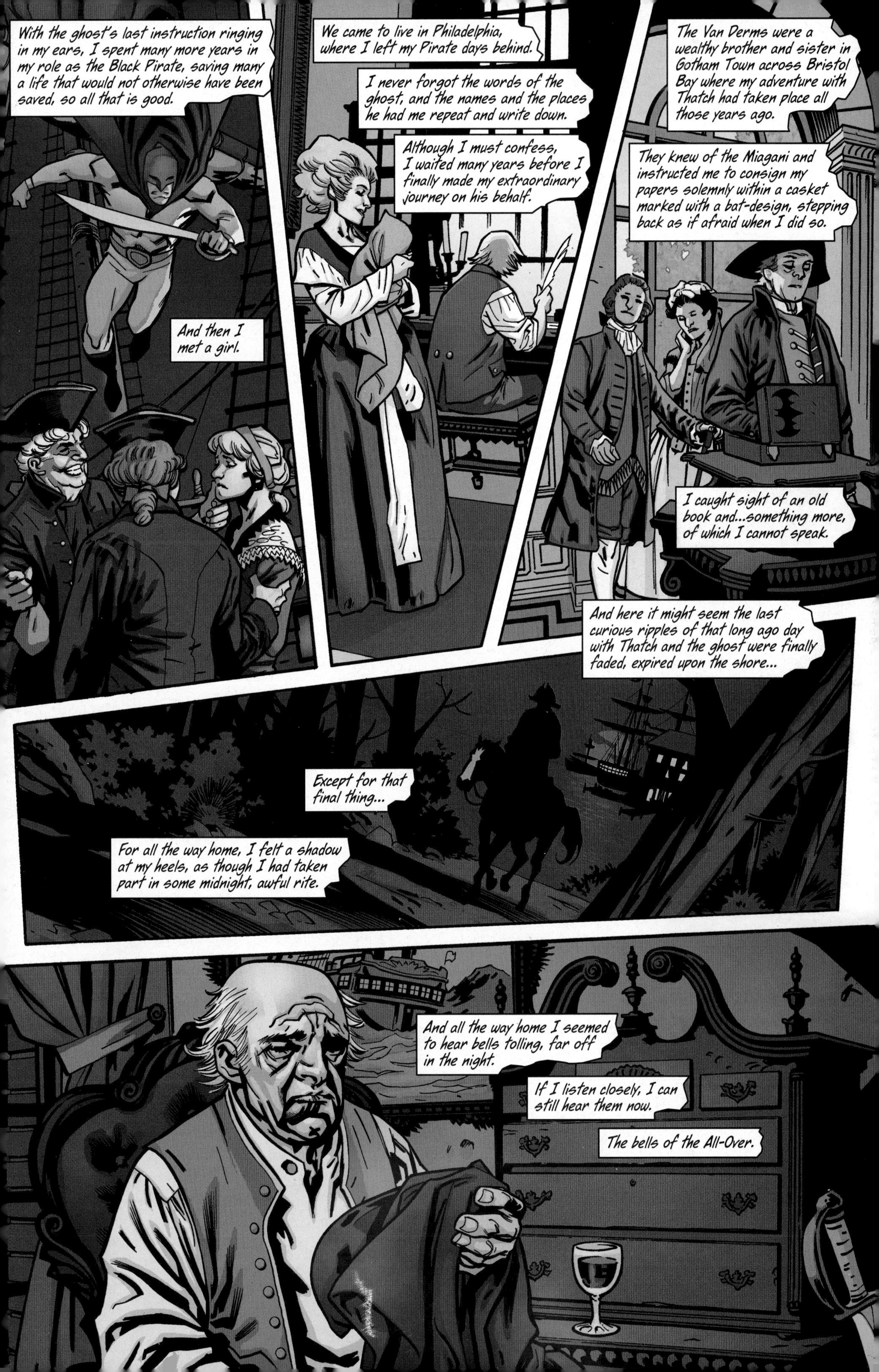
With the ghost's last instruction ringing in my ears, I spent many more years in my role as the Black Pirate, saving many a life that would not otherwise have been saved, so all that is good.
And then I met a girl.
We came to live in Philadelphia, where I left my Pirate days behind.
I never forgot the words of the ghost, and the names and the places he had me repeat and write down.
Although I must confess, I waited many years before I finally made my extraordinary journey on his behalf.
The Van Derms were a wealthy brother and sister in Gotham Town across Bristol Bay where my adventure with Thatch had taken place all those years ago.
They knew of the Miagani and instructed me to consign my papers solemnly within a casket marked with a bat-design, stepping back as if afraid when I did so.
I caught sight of an old book and...something more, of which I cannot speak.
And here it might seem the last curious ripples of that long ago day with Thatch and the ghost were finally faded, expired upon the shore...
Except for that final thing...
For all the way home, I felt a shadow at my heels, as though I had taken part in some midnight, awful rite.
And all the way home I seemed to hear bells tolling, far off in the night.
If I listen closely, I can still hear them now.
The bells of the All-Over.

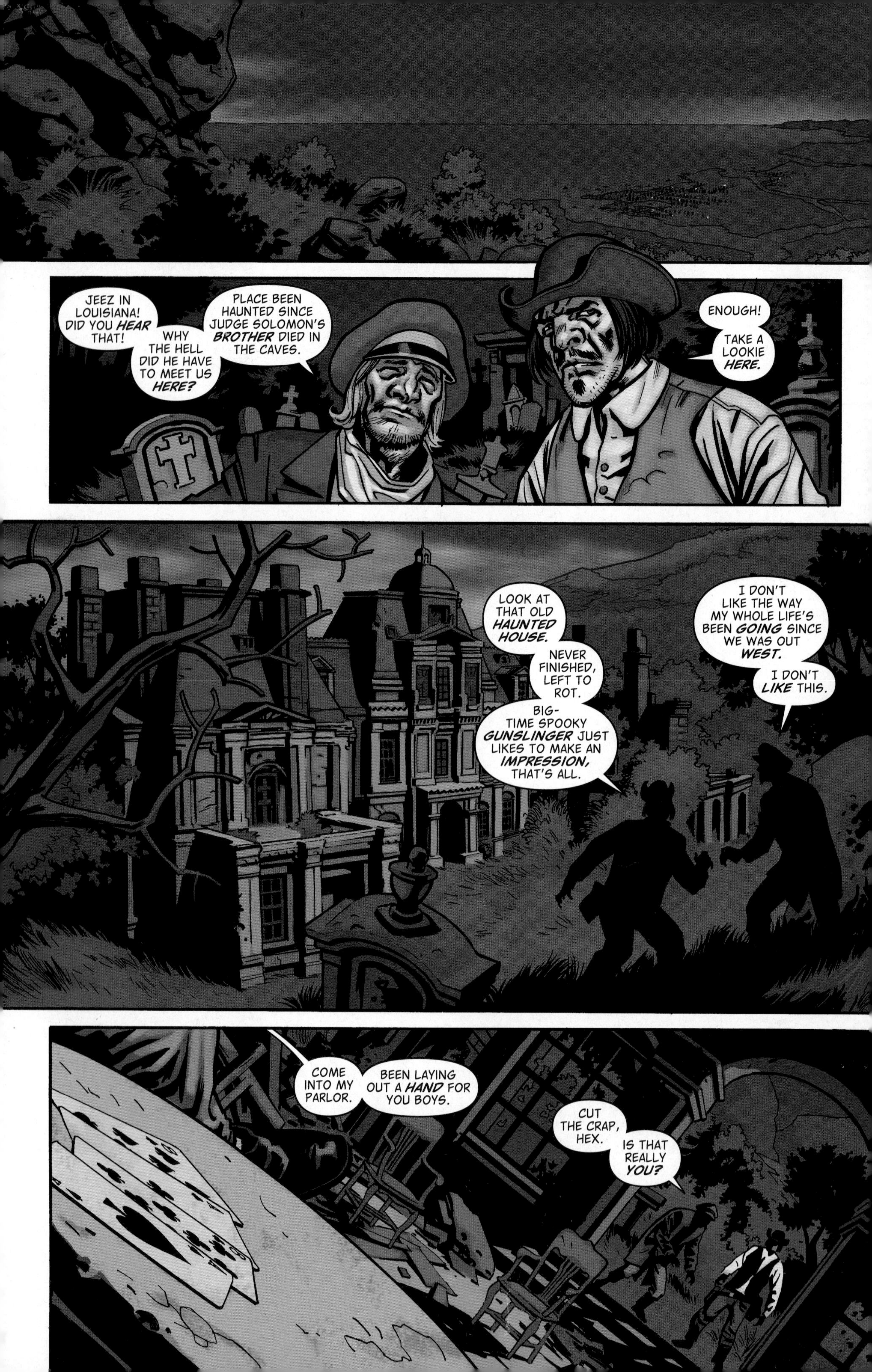
JEEZ IN LOUISIANA! DID YOU HEAR THAT!
WHY THE HELL DID HE HAVE TO MEET US HERE?
PLACE BEEN HAUNTED SINCE JUDGE SOLOMON'S BROTHER DIED IN THE CAVES.
ENOUGH!
TAKE A LOOKIE HERE.
LOOK AT THAT OLD HAUNTED HOUSE.
NEVER FINISHED, LEFT TO ROT.
BIG-TIME SPOOKY GUNSLINGER JUST LIKES TO MAKE AN IMPRESSION, THAT'S ALL.
I DON'T LIKE THE WAY MY WHOLE LIFE'S BEEN GOING SINCE WE WAS OUT WEST.
I DON'T LIKE THIS.
COME INTO MY PARLOR.
BEEN LAYING OUT A HAND FOR YOU BOYS.
CUT THE CRAP, HEX.
IS THAT REALLY YOU?

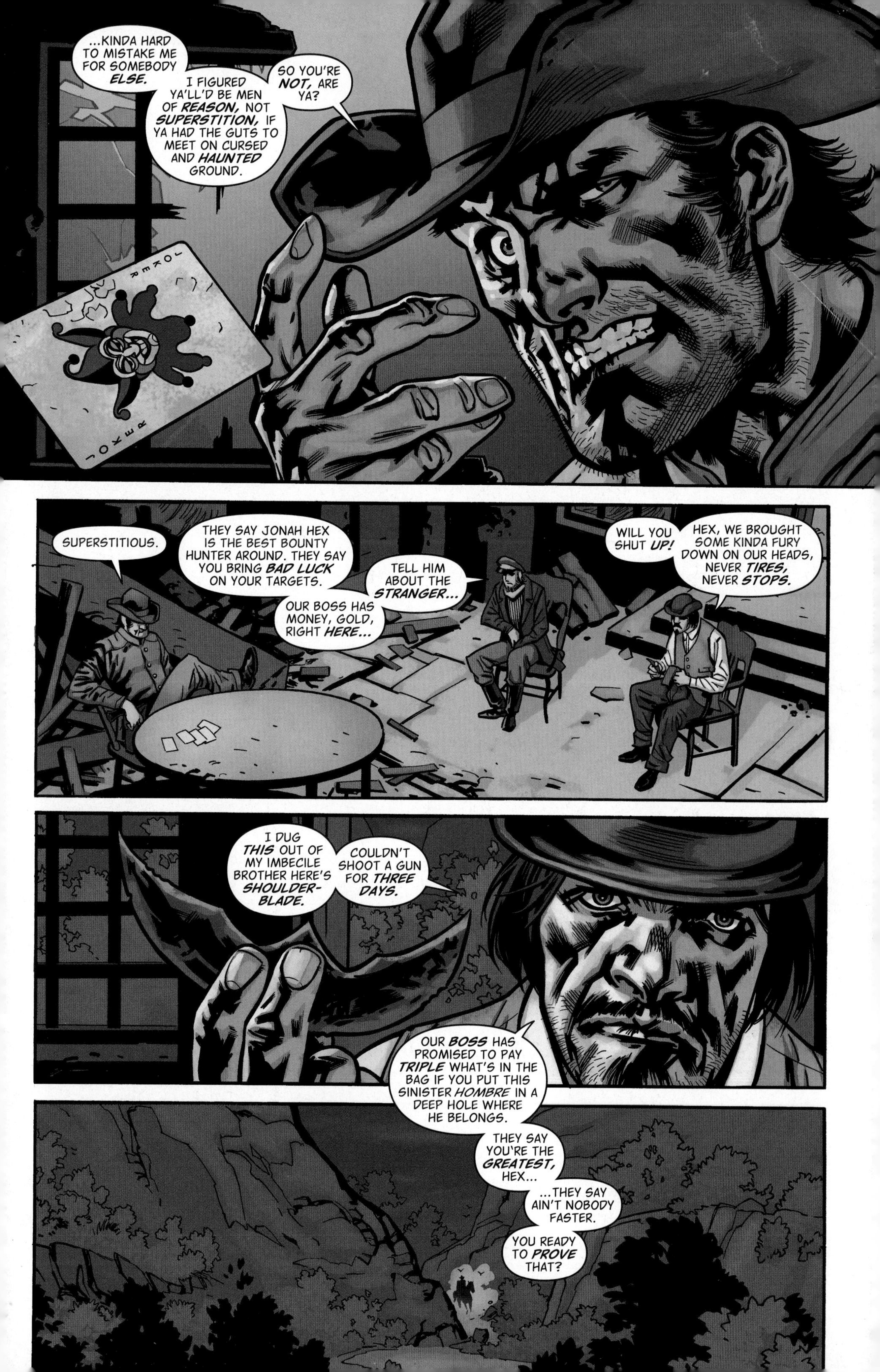
...KINDA HARD TO MISTAKE ME FOR SOMEBODY ELSE.
I FIGURED YA'LL'D BE MEN OF REASON, NOT SUPERSTITION, IF YA HAD THE GUTS TO MEET ON CURSED AND HAUNTED GROUND.
SO YOU'RE NOT, ARE YA?
JOKER
JOKER
SUPERSTITIOUS.
THEY SAY JONAH HEX IS THE BEST BOUNTY HUNTER AROUND. THEY SAY YOU BRING BAD LUCK ON YOUR TARGETS.
OUR BOSS HAS MONEY, GOLD, RIGHT HERE...
TELL HIM ABOUT THE STRANGER...
WILL YOU SHUT UP!
HEX, WE BROUGHT SOME KINDA FURY DOWN ON OUR HEADS, NEVER TIRES, NEVER STOPS.
I DUG THIS OUT OF MY IMBECILE BROTHER HERE'S SHOULDER-BLADE.
COULDN'T SHOOT A GUN FOR THREE DAYS.
OUR BOSS HAS PROMISED TO PAY TRIPLE WHAT'S IN THE BAG IF YOU PUT THIS SINISTER HOMBRE IN A DEEP HOLE WHERE HE BELONGS.
THEY SAY YOU'RE THE GREATEST, HEX...
...THEY SAY AIN'T NOBODY FASTER.
YOU READY TO PROVE THAT?

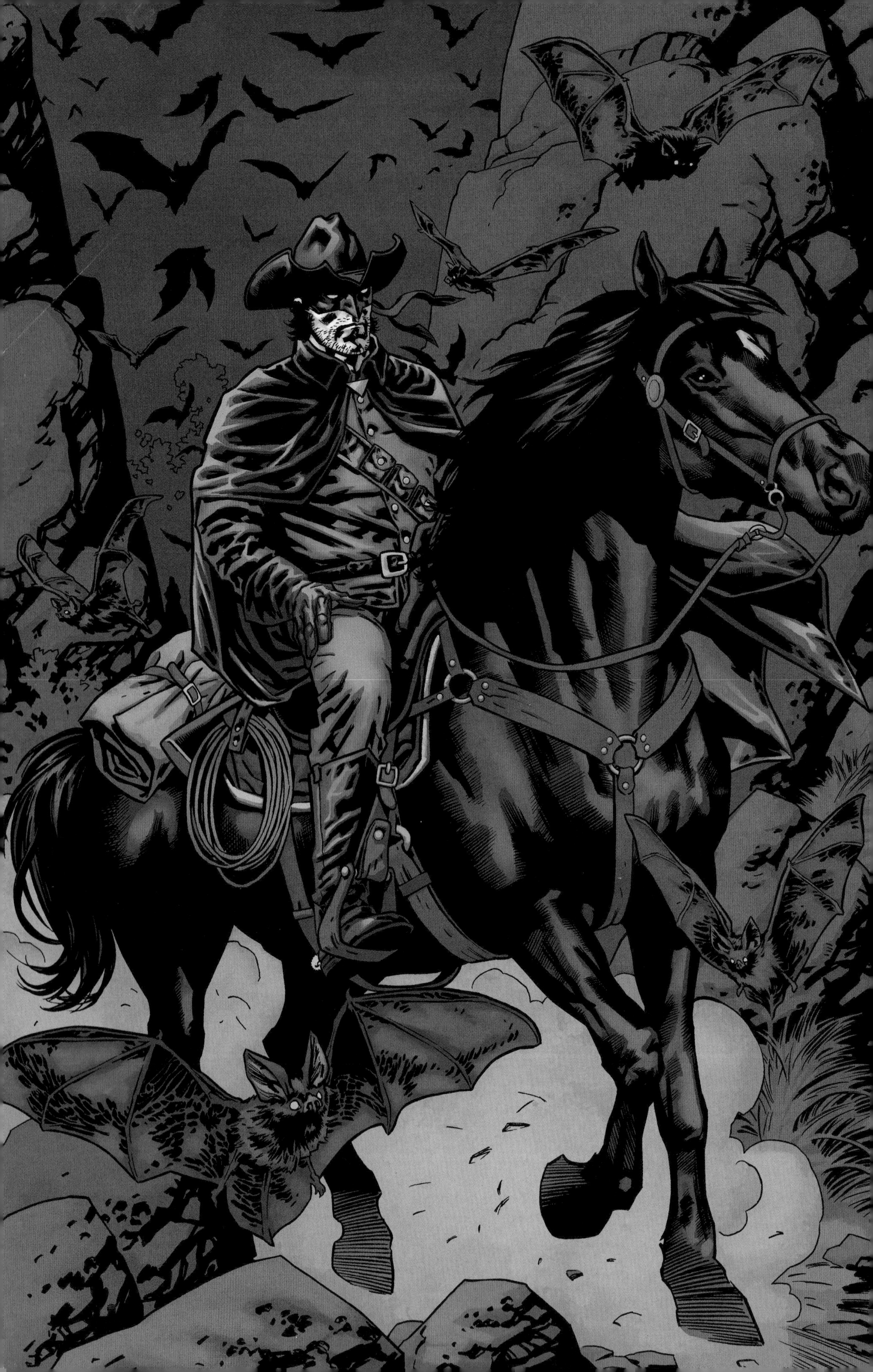

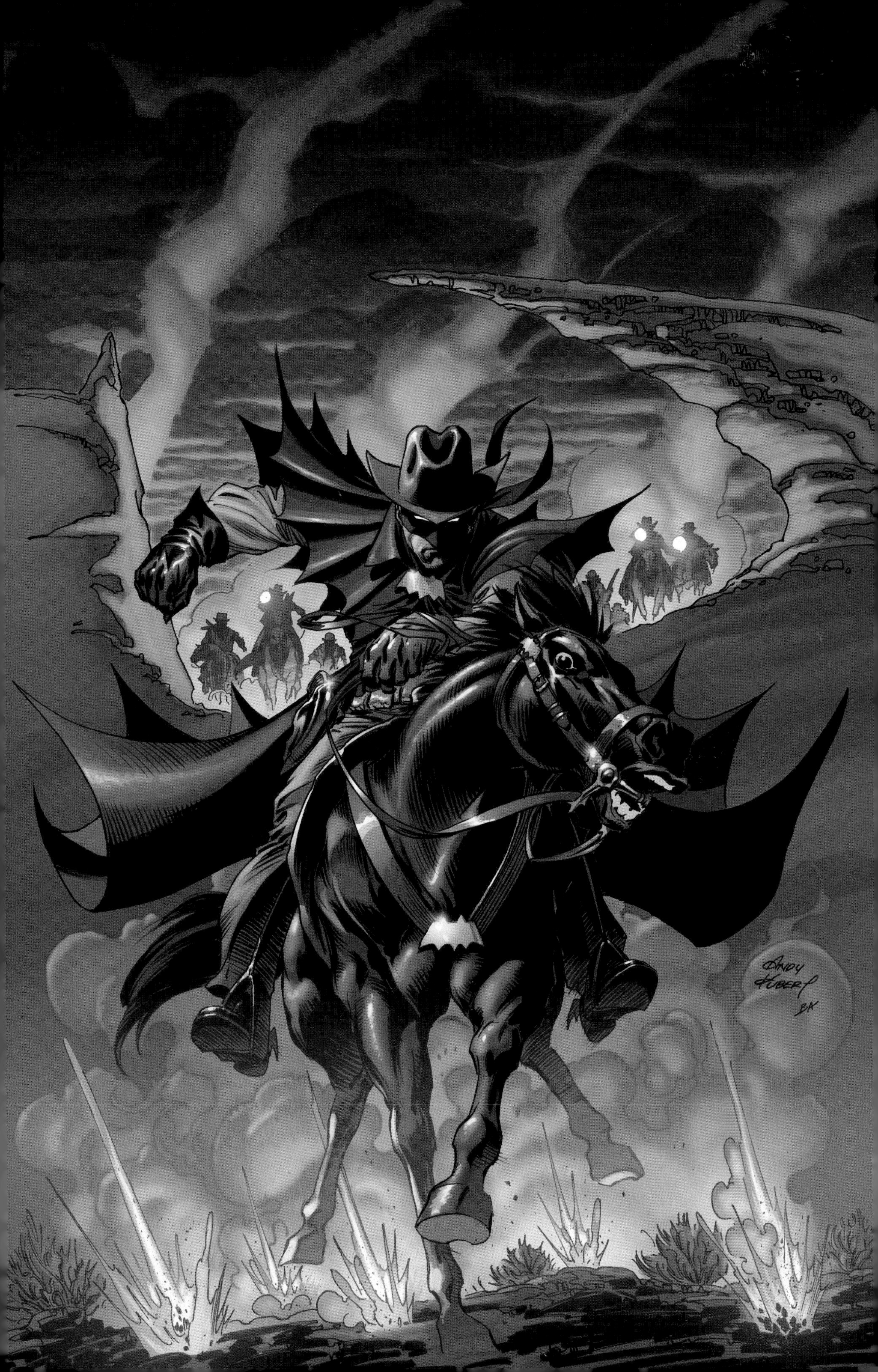
ANDY KUBERT
BA

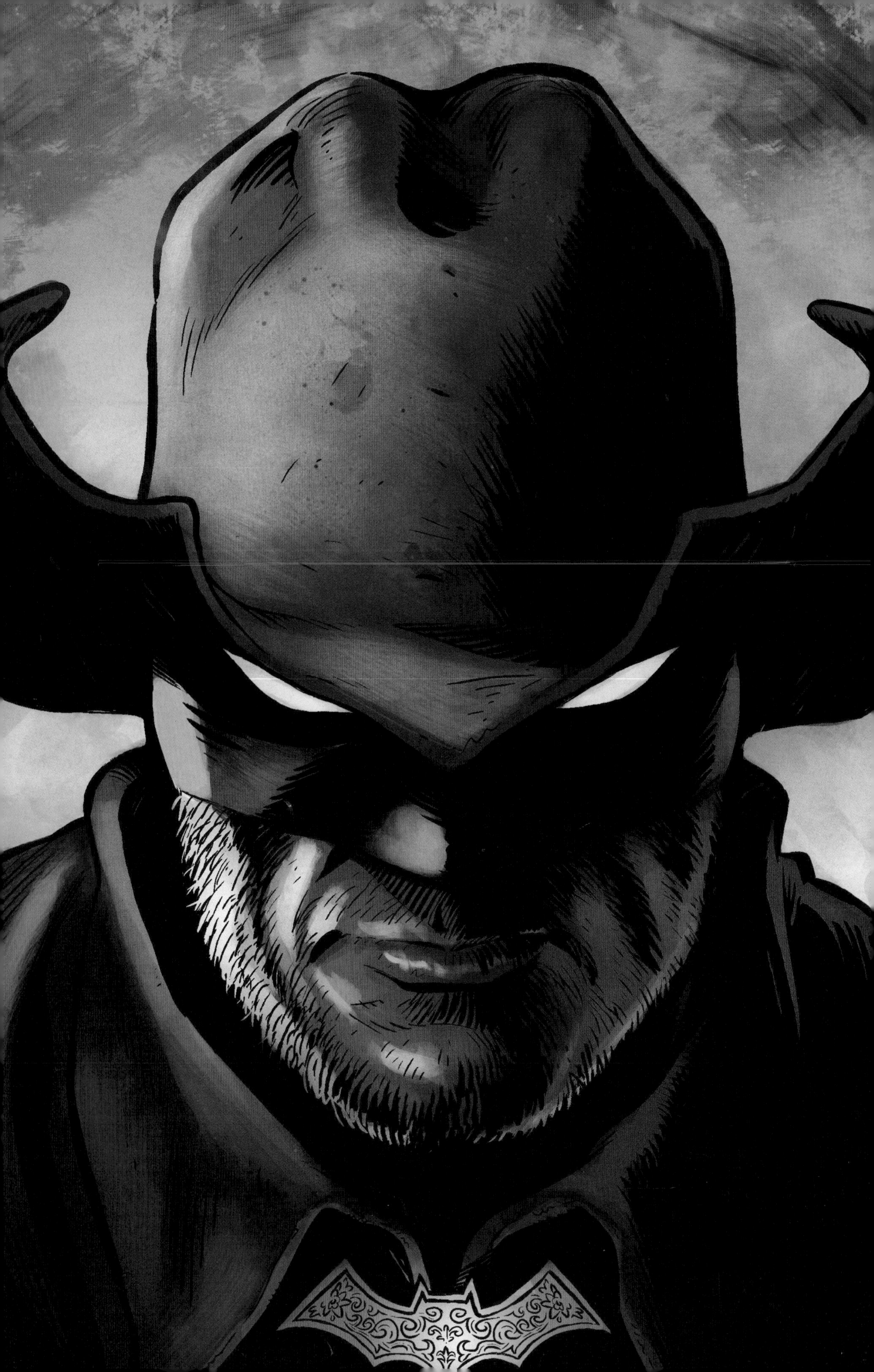

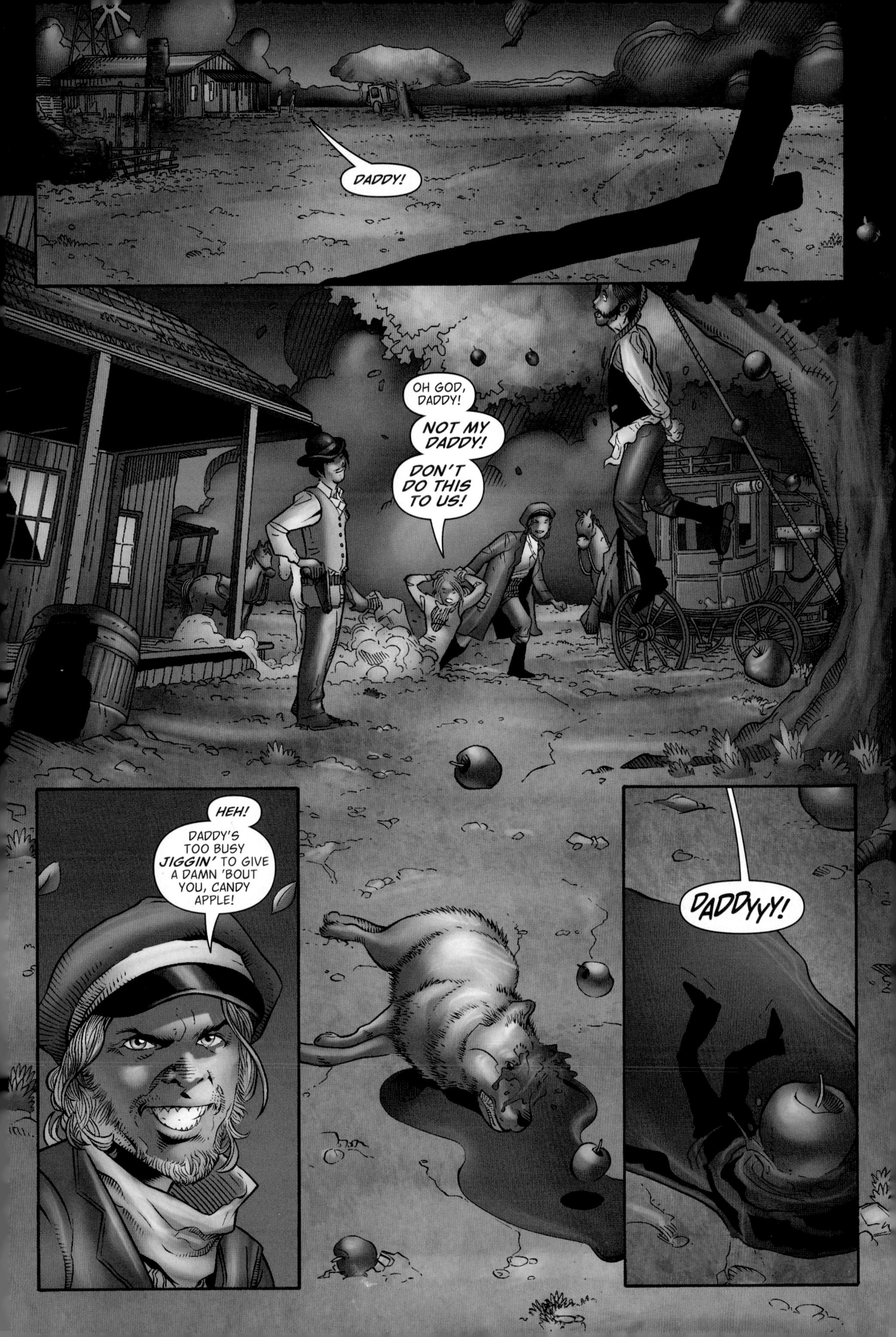
DADDY!
OH GOD, DADDY!
NOT MY DADDY!
DON'T DO THIS TO US!
HEH!
DADDY'S TOO BUSY JIGGIN' TO GIVE A DAMN 'BOUT YOU, CANDY APPLE!
DADDYYY!

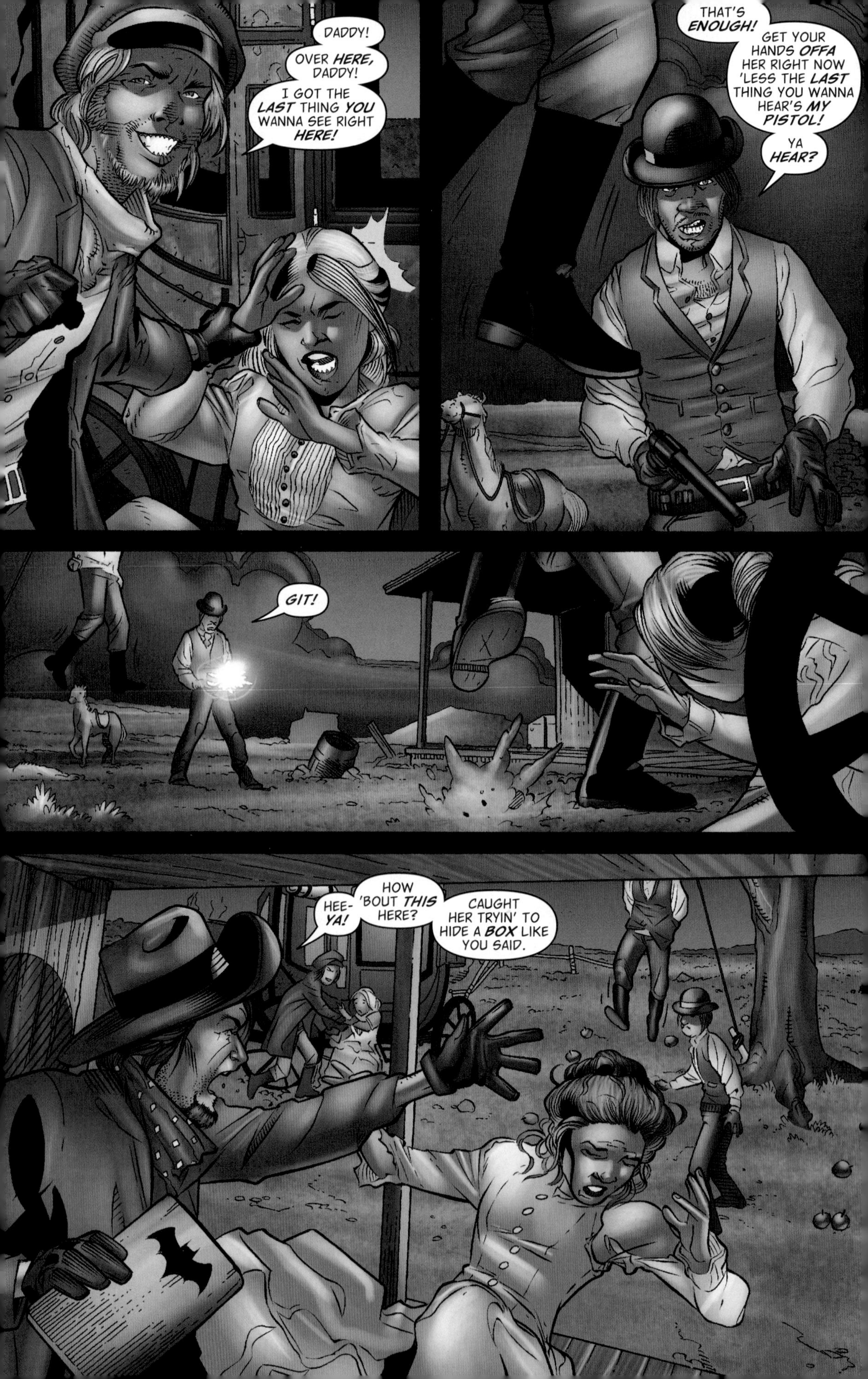
DADDY!
OVER HERE, DADDY!
I GOT THE LAST THING YOU WANNA SEE RIGHT HERE!
THAT'S ENOUGH!
GET YOUR HANDS OFFA HER RIGHT NOW 'LESS THE LAST THING YOU WANNA HEAR'S MY PISTOL!
YA HEAR?
GIT!
HEE-YA!
HOW 'BOUT THIS HERE?
CAUGHT HER TRYIN' TO HIDE A BOX LIKE YOU SAID.

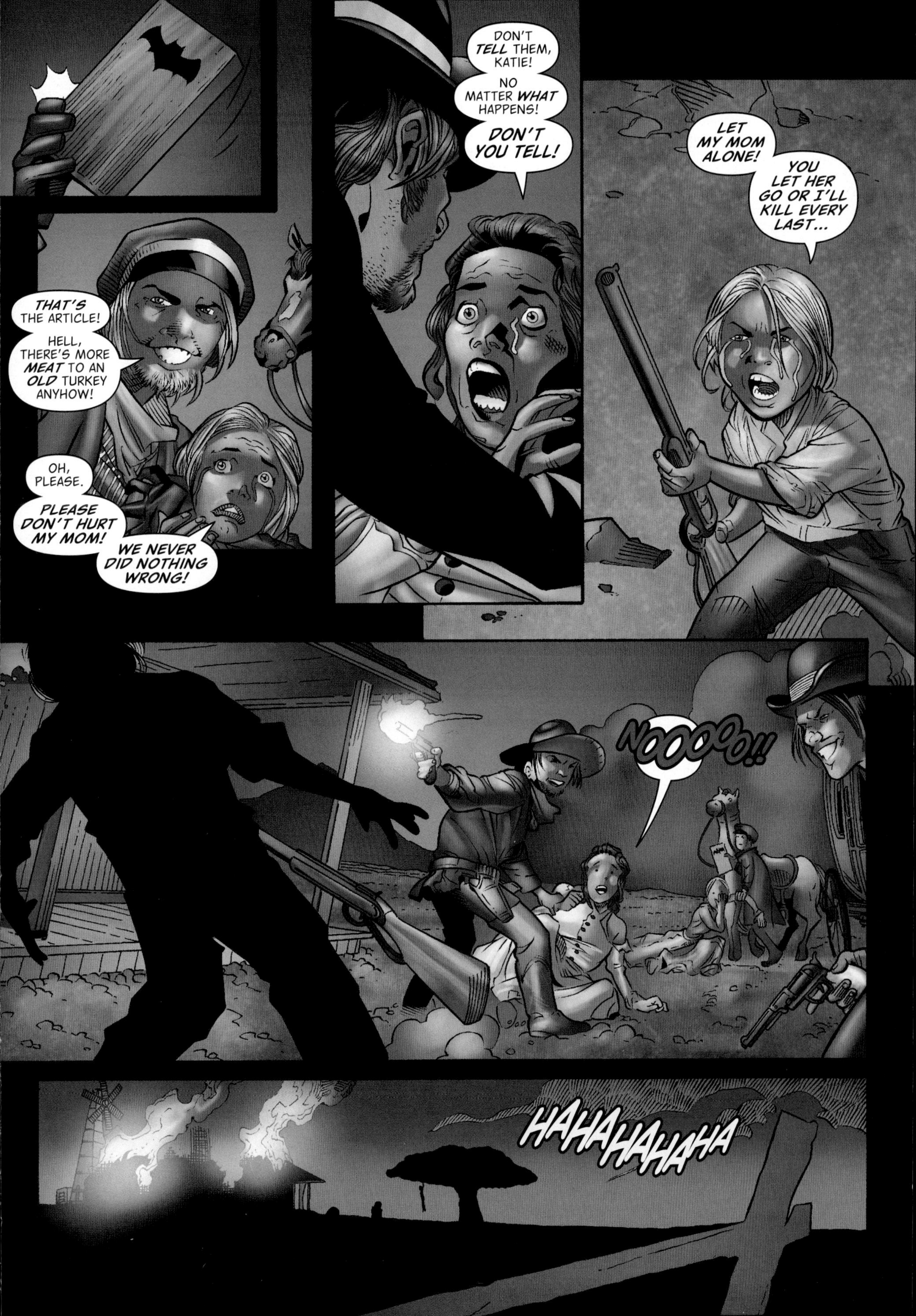
THAT'S THE ARTICLE!
HELL, THERE'S MORE MEAT TO AN OLD TURKEY ANYHOW!
OH, PLEASE.
PLEASE DON'T HURT MY MOM!
WE NEVER DID NOTHING WRONG!
DON'T TELL THEM, KATIE!
NO MATTER WHAT HAPPENS!
DON'T YOU TELL!
LET MY MOM ALONE!
YOU LET HER GO OR I'LL KILL EVERY LAST...
NOOOOO!!
HAHAHAHAHAHA

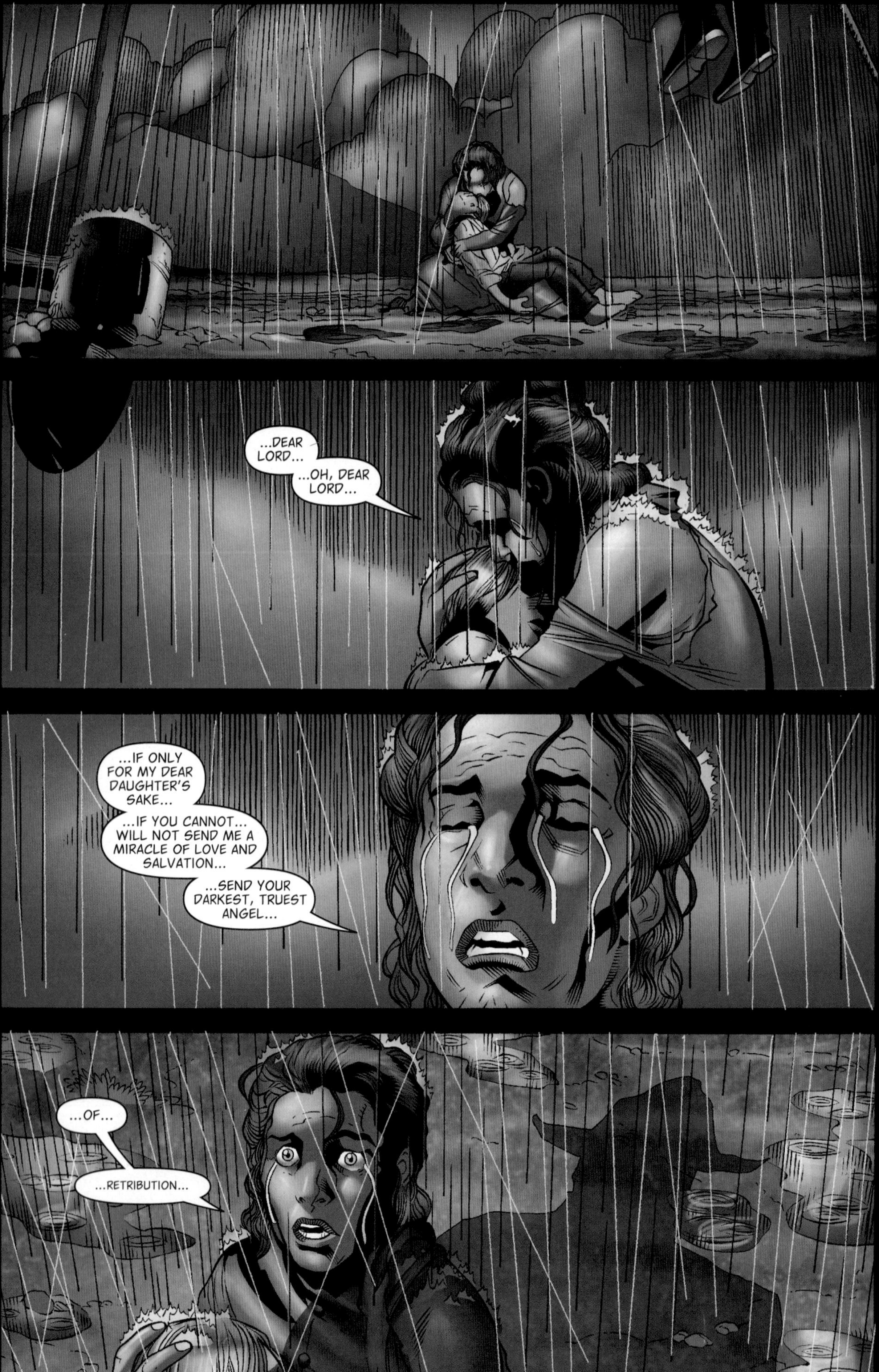
...DEAR LORD...
...OH, DEAR LORD...
...IF ONLY FOR MY DEAR DAUGHTER'S SAKE...
...IF YOU CANNOT... WILL NOT SEND ME A MIRACLE OF LOVE AND SALVATION...
...SEND YOUR DARKEST, TRUEST ANGEL...
...OF...
...RETRIBUTION...

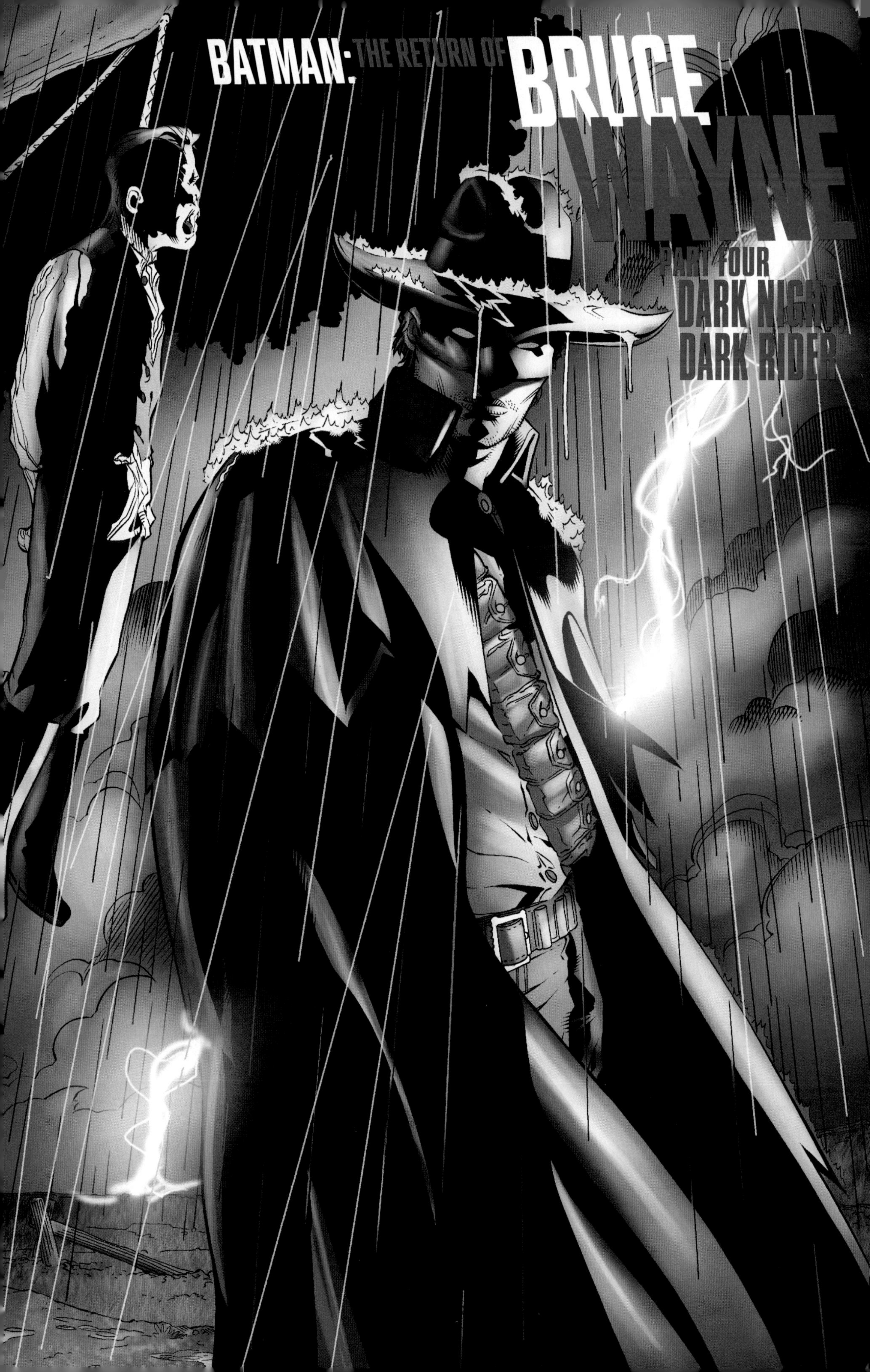
BATMAN: THE RETURN OF BRUCE WAYNE
PART FOUR
DARK NIGHT, DARK RIDER

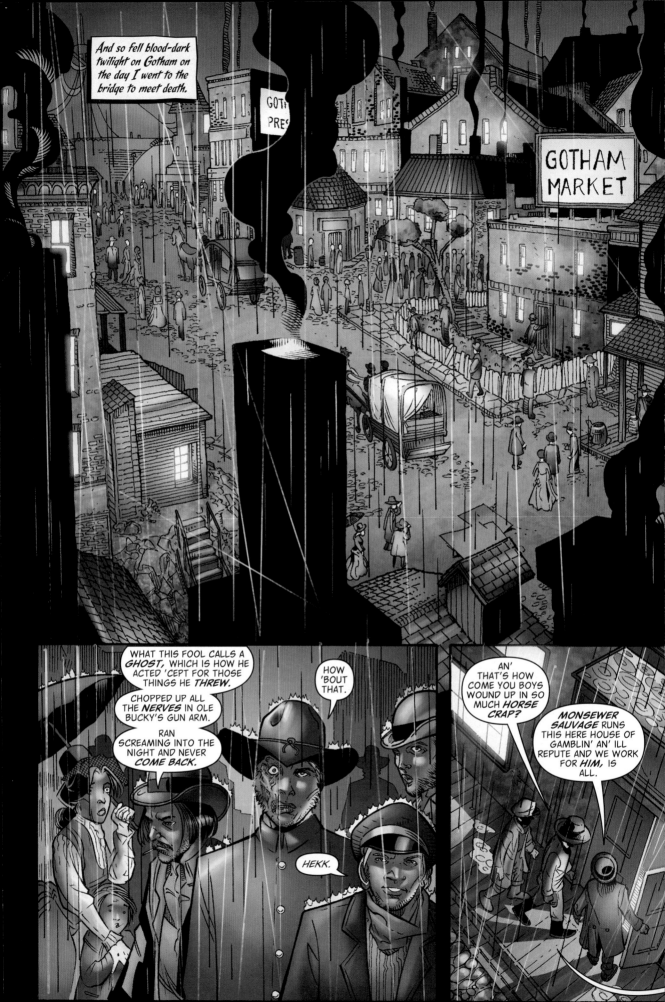

And so fell blood-dark twilight on Gotham on the day *I* went to the bridge to meet death.

GOT...
PRE...

GOTHAM MARKET

WHAT THIS FOOL CALLS A *GHOST,* WHICH IS HOW HE ACTED 'CEPT FOR THOSE THINGS HE *THREW.*

CHOPPED UP ALL THE *NERVES* IN OLE BUCKY'S GUN ARM.

RAN SCREAMING INTO THE NIGHT AND NEVER *COME BACK.*

HOW 'BOUT THAT.

HEKK.

AN' THAT'S HOW COME YOU BOYS WOUND UP IN SO MUCH *HORSE CRAP?*

MONSEWER SAUVAGE RUNS THIS HERE HOUSE OF GAMBLIN' AN' ILL REPUTE AND WE WORK FOR *HIM,* IS ALL.

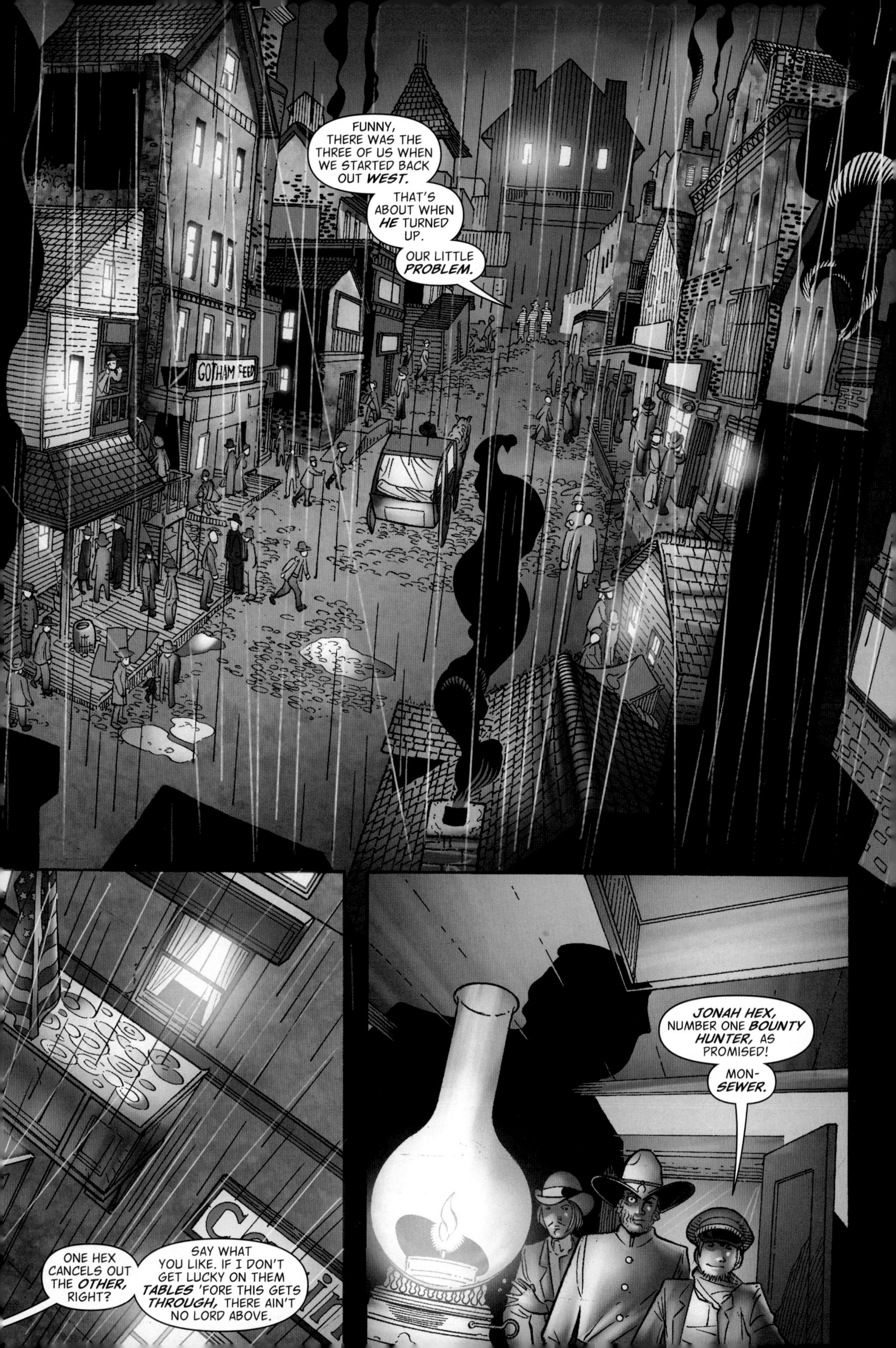
FUNNY, THERE WAS THE THREE OF US WHEN WE STARTED BACK OUT *WEST.*
THAT'S ABOUT WHEN *HE* TURNED UP.
OUR LITTLE *PROBLEM.*
GOTHAM FEED
ONE HEX CANCELS OUT THE *OTHER,* RIGHT?
SAY WHAT YOU LIKE. IF I DON'T GET LUCKY ON THEM *TABLES* 'FORE THIS GETS *THROUGH,* THERE AIN'T NO LORD ABOVE.
JONAH HEX, NUMBER ONE *BOUNTY HUNTER,* AS PROMISED!
MON-*SEWER.*

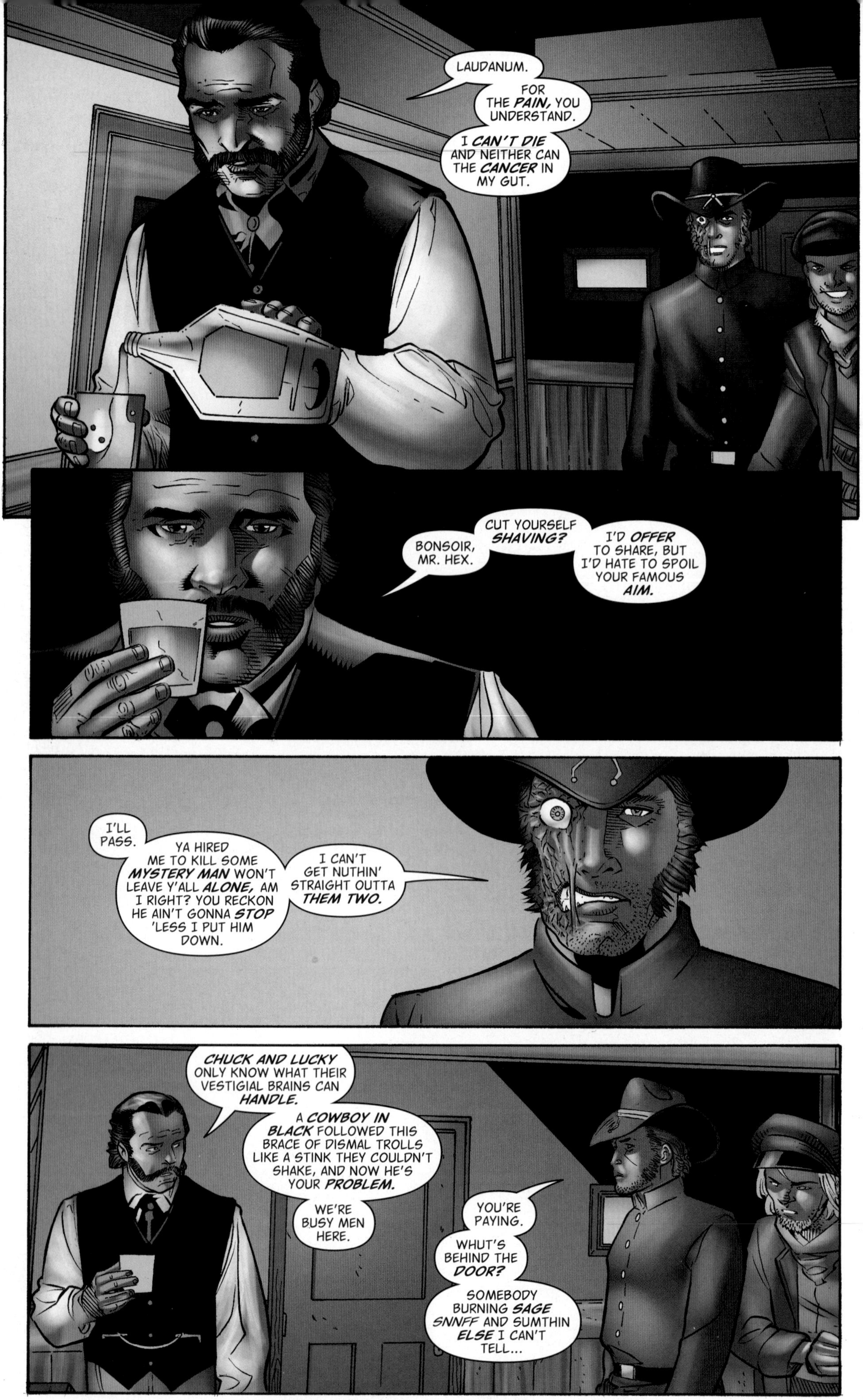
LAUDANUM.
FOR THE PAIN, YOU UNDERSTAND.
I CAN'T DIE AND NEITHER CAN THE CANCER IN MY GUT.
BONSOIR, MR. HEX.
CUT YOURSELF SHAVING?
I'D OFFER TO SHARE, BUT I'D HATE TO SPOIL YOUR FAMOUS AIM.
I'LL PASS.
YA HIRED ME TO KILL SOME MYSTERY MAN WON'T LEAVE Y'ALL ALONE, AM I RIGHT? YOU RECKON HE AIN'T GONNA STOP 'LESS I PUT HIM DOWN.
I CAN'T GET NUTHIN' STRAIGHT OUTTA THEM TWO.
CHUCK AND LUCKY ONLY KNOW WHAT THEIR VESTIGIAL BRAINS CAN HANDLE.
A COWBOY IN BLACK FOLLOWED THIS BRACE OF DISMAL TROLLS LIKE A STINK THEY COULDN'T SHAKE, AND NOW HE'S YOUR PROBLEM.
WE'RE BUSY MEN HERE.
YOU'RE PAYING.
WHUT'S BEHIND THE DOOR?
SOMEBODY BURNING SAGE SNNFF AND SUMTHIN ELSE I CAN'T TELL...

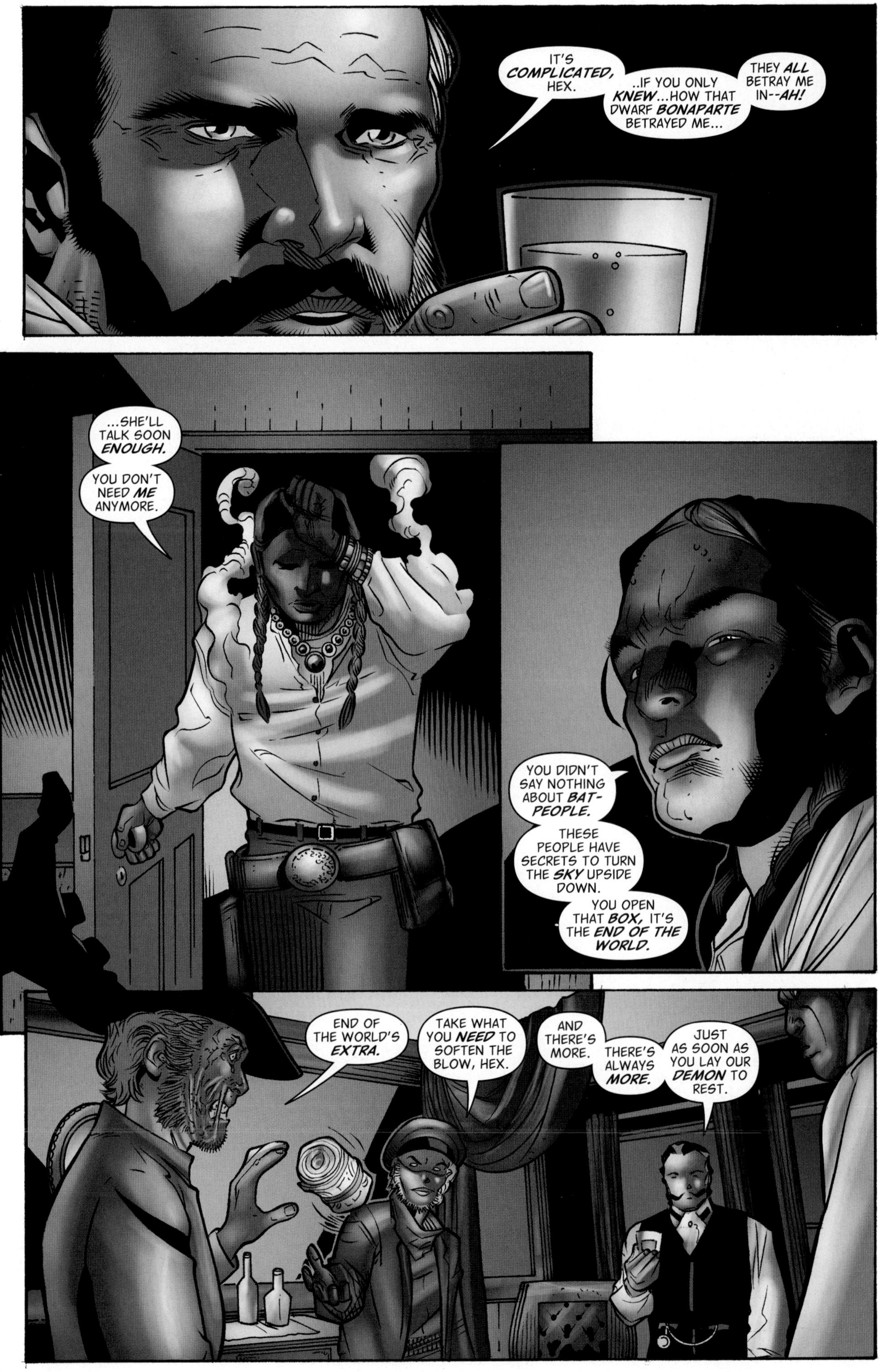
IT'S COMPLICATED, HEX.
..IF YOU ONLY KNEW...HOW THAT DWARF BONAPARTE BETRAYED ME...
THEY ALL BETRAY ME IN--AH!
...SHE'LL TALK SOON ENOUGH.
YOU DON'T NEED ME ANYMORE.
YOU DIDN'T SAY NOTHING ABOUT BAT-PEOPLE.
THESE PEOPLE HAVE SECRETS TO TURN THE SKY UPSIDE DOWN.
YOU OPEN THAT BOX, IT'S THE END OF THE WORLD.
END OF THE WORLD'S EXTRA.
TAKE WHAT YOU NEED TO SOFTEN THE BLOW, HEX.
AND THERE'S MORE.
THERE'S ALWAYS MORE.
JUST AS SOON AS YOU LAY OUR DEMON TO REST.

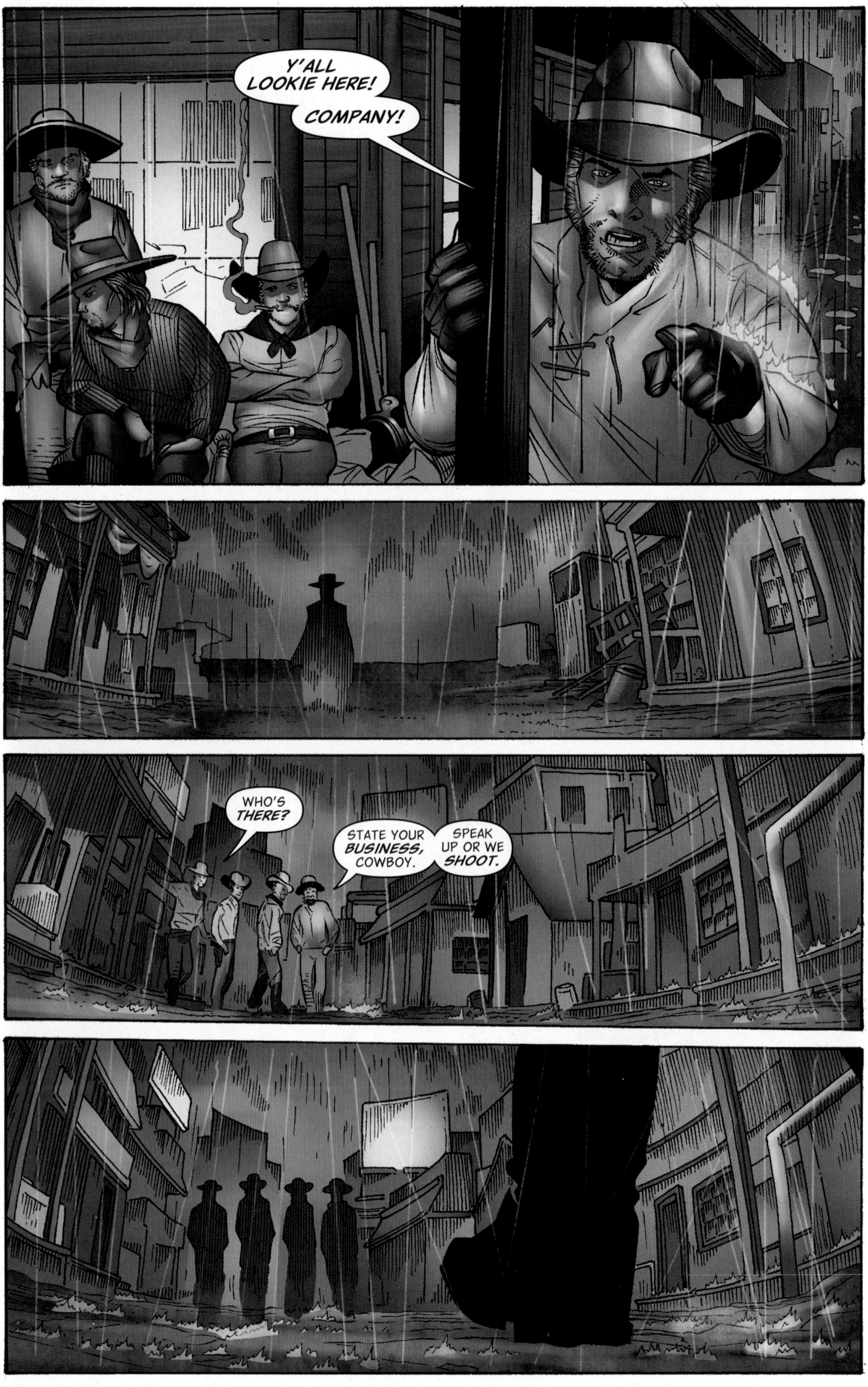
Y'ALL LOOKIE HERE!
COMPANY!
WHO'S THERE?
STATE YOUR BUSINESS, COWBOY.
SPEAK UP OR WE SHOOT.

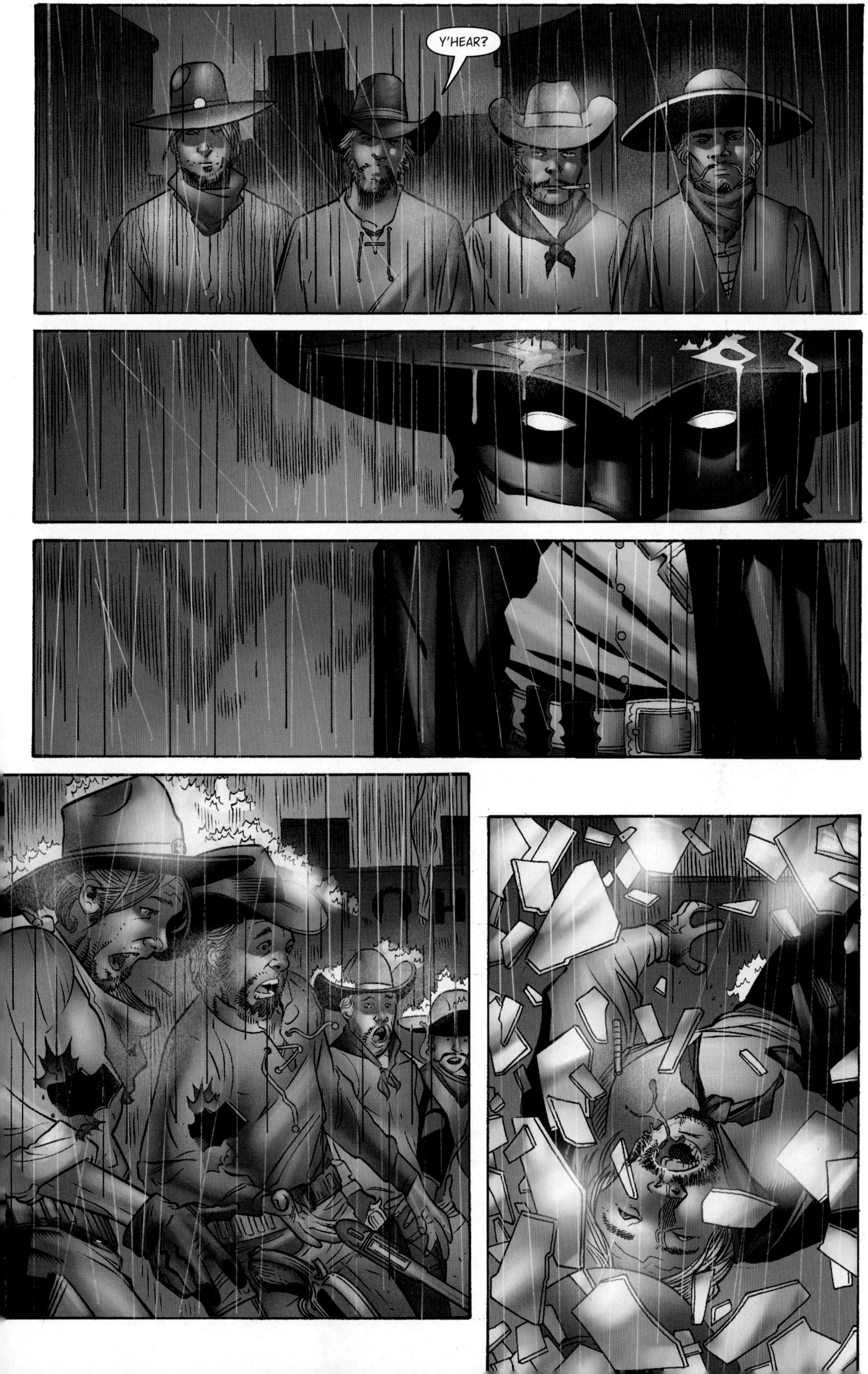
Y'HEAR?

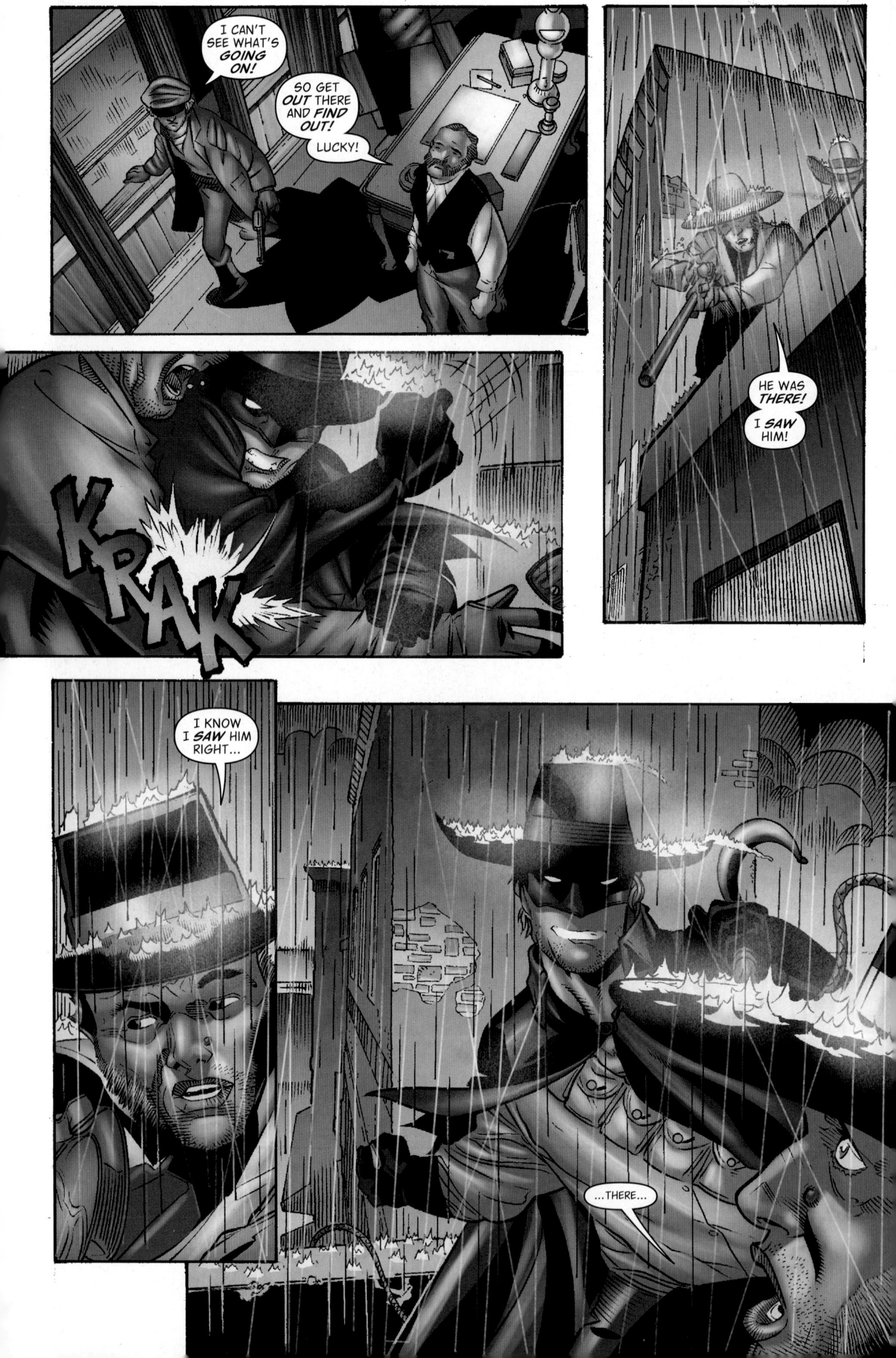
I CAN'T SEE WHAT'S GOING ON!
SO GET OUT THERE AND FIND OUT!
LUCKY!
HE WAS THERE!
I SAW HIM!
KRAK
I KNOW I SAW HIM RIGHT...
...THERE...

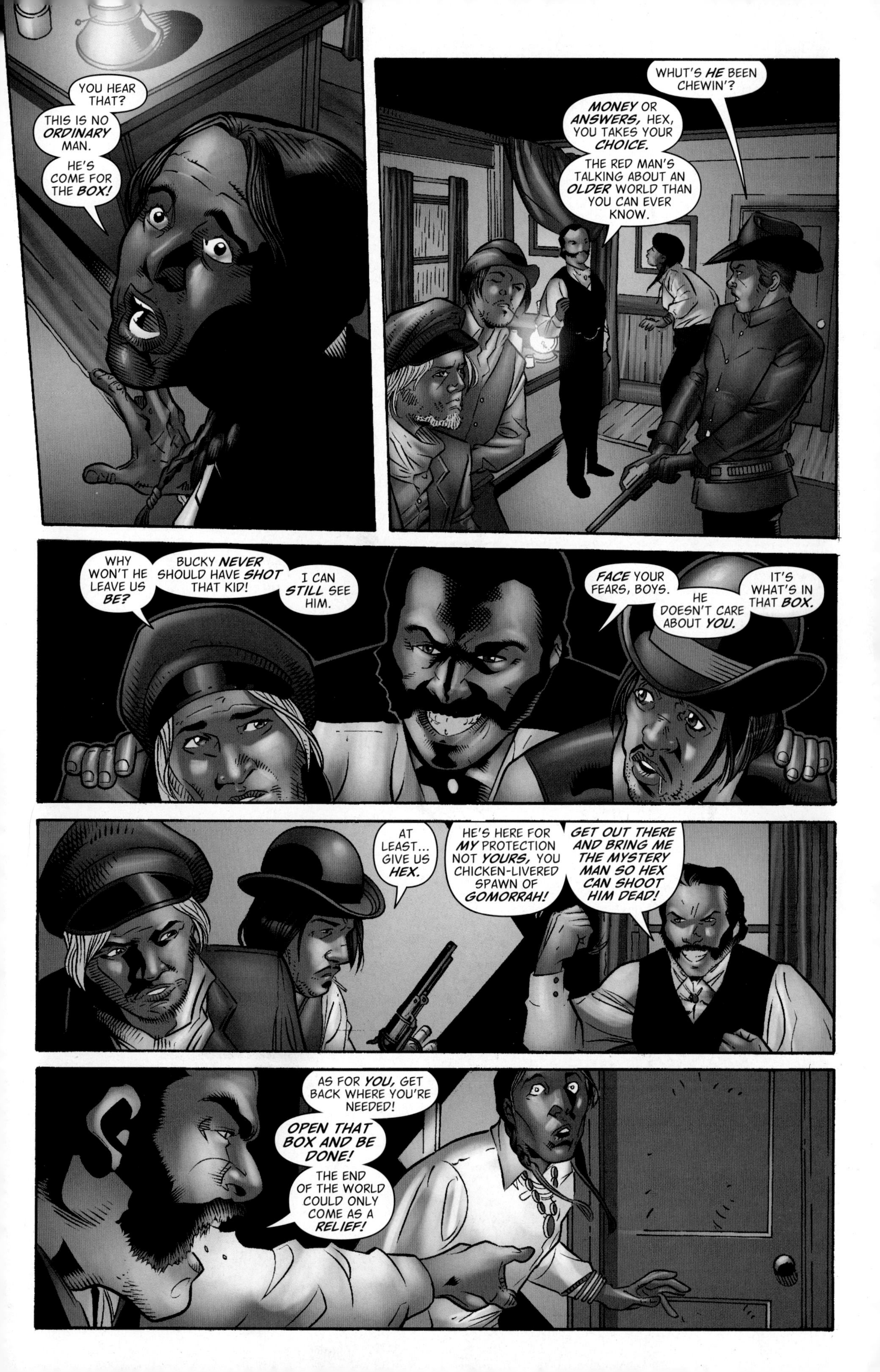
YOU HEAR THAT?
THIS IS NO ORDINARY MAN.
HE'S COME FOR THE BOX!
WHUT'S HE BEEN CHEWIN'?
MONEY OR ANSWERS, HEX, YOU TAKES YOUR CHOICE.
THE RED MAN'S TALKING ABOUT AN OLDER WORLD THAN YOU CAN EVER KNOW.
WHY WON'T HE LEAVE US BE?
BUCKY NEVER SHOULD HAVE SHOT THAT KID!
I CAN STILL SEE HIM.
FACE YOUR FEARS, BOYS.
HE DOESN'T CARE ABOUT YOU.
IT'S WHAT'S IN THAT BOX.
AT LEAST... GIVE US HEX.
HE'S HERE FOR MY PROTECTION NOT YOURS, YOU CHICKEN-LIVERED SPAWN OF GOMORRAH!
GET OUT THERE AND BRING ME THE MYSTERY MAN SO HEX CAN SHOOT HIM DEAD!
AS FOR YOU, GET BACK WHERE YOU'RE NEEDED!
OPEN THAT BOX AND BE DONE!
THE END OF THE WORLD COULD ONLY COME AS A RELIEF!

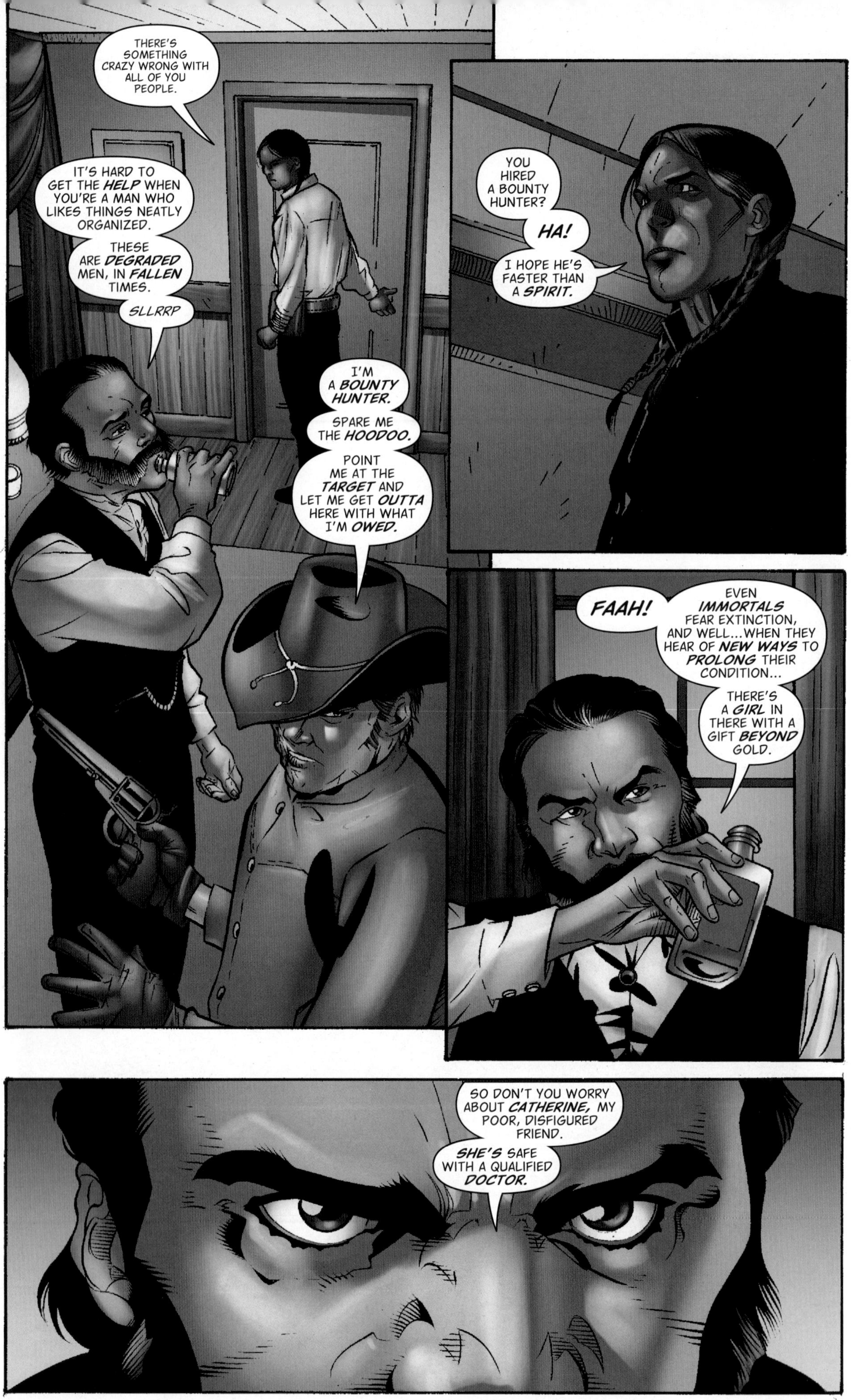
THERE'S SOMETHING CRAZY WRONG WITH ALL OF YOU PEOPLE.
IT'S HARD TO GET THE HELP WHEN YOU'RE A MAN WHO LIKES THINGS NEATLY ORGANIZED.
THESE ARE DEGRADED MEN, IN FALLEN TIMES.
SLLRRP
I'M A BOUNTY HUNTER.
SPARE ME THE HOODOO.
POINT ME AT THE TARGET AND LET ME GET OUTTA HERE WITH WHAT I'M OWED.
YOU HIRED A BOUNTY HUNTER?
HA!
I HOPE HE'S FASTER THAN A SPIRIT.
FAAH!
EVEN IMMORTALS FEAR EXTINCTION, AND WELL...WHEN THEY HEAR OF NEW WAYS TO PROLONG THEIR CONDITION...
THERE'S A GIRL IN THERE WITH A GIFT BEYOND GOLD.
SO DON'T YOU WORRY ABOUT CATHERINE, MY POOR, DISFIGURED FRIEND.
SHE'S SAFE WITH A QUALIFIED DOCTOR.

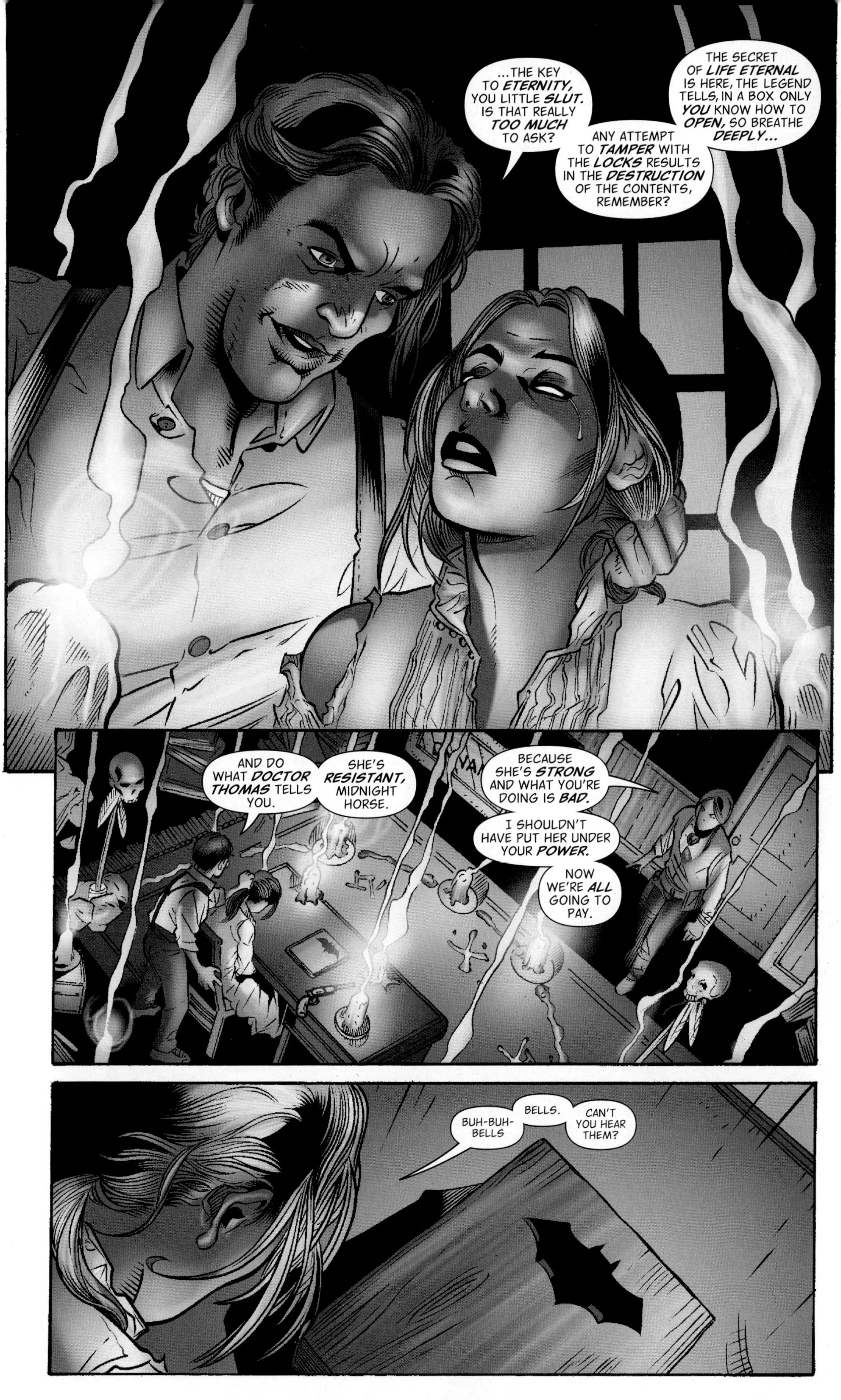
...THE KEY TO ETERNITY, YOU LITTLE SLUT. IS THAT REALLY TOO MUCH TO ASK?
ANY ATTEMPT TO TAMPER WITH THE LOCKS RESULTS IN THE DESTRUCTION OF THE CONTENTS, REMEMBER?
THE SECRET OF LIFE ETERNAL IS HERE, THE LEGEND TELLS, IN A BOX ONLY YOU KNOW HOW TO OPEN, SO BREATHE DEEPLY...
AND DO WHAT DOCTOR THOMAS TELLS YOU.
SHE'S RESISTANT, MIDNIGHT HORSE.
BECAUSE SHE'S STRONG AND WHAT YOU'RE DOING IS BAD.
I SHOULDN'T HAVE PUT HER UNDER YOUR POWER.
NOW WE'RE ALL GOING TO PAY.
BUH-BUH-BELLS
BELLS.
CAN'T YOU HEAR THEM?

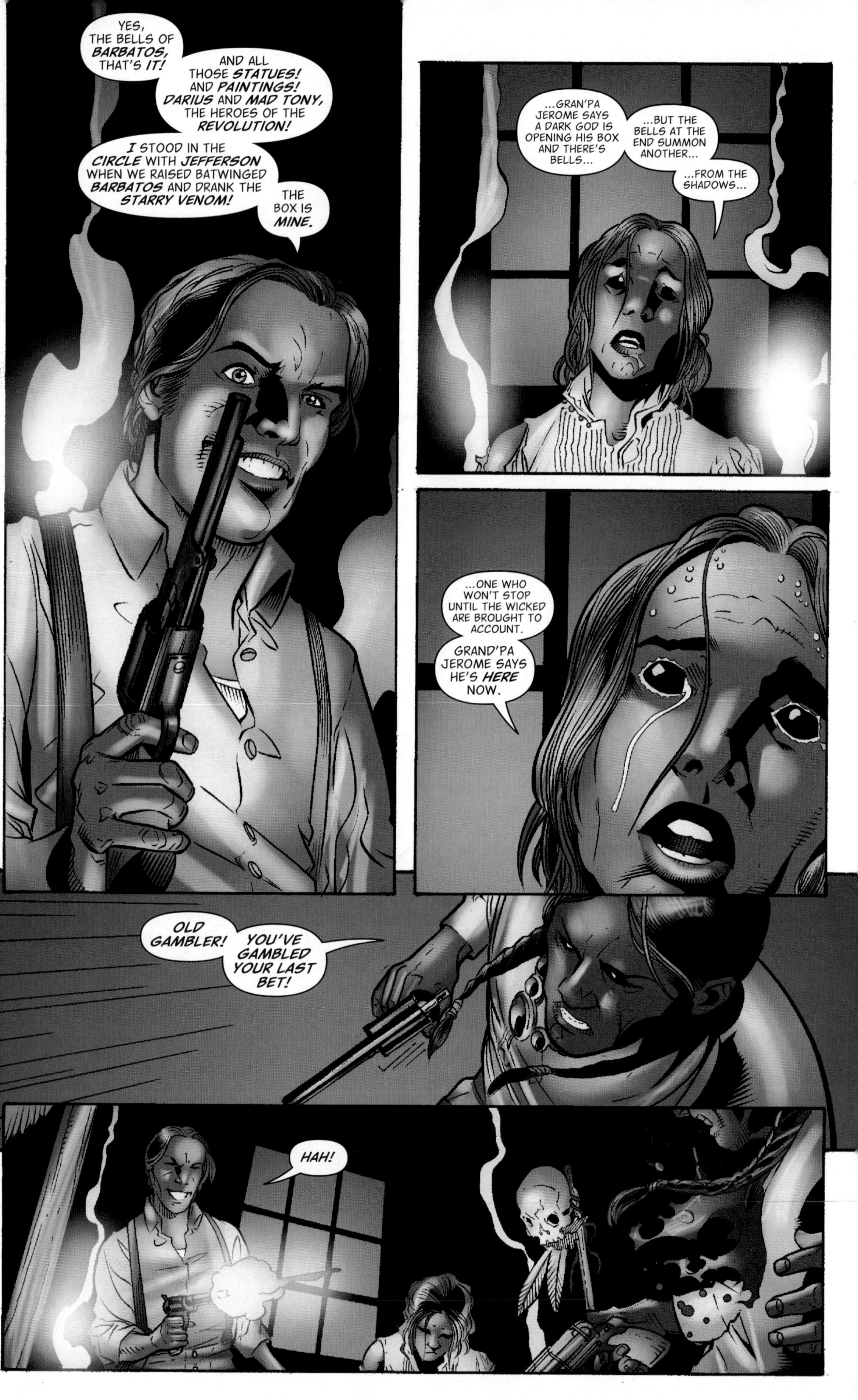

YES, THE BELLS OF *BARBATOS,* THAT'S *IT!*
AND ALL THOSE *STATUES!* AND *PAINTINGS! DARIUS* AND *MAD TONY,* THE HEROES OF THE *REVOLUTION!*
I STOOD IN THE *CIRCLE* WITH *JEFFERSON* WHEN WE RAISED BATWINGED *BARBATOS* AND DRANK THE *STARRY VENOM!*
THE BOX IS *MINE.*
...GRAN'PA JEROME SAYS A DARK GOD IS OPENING HIS BOX AND THERE'S BELLS...
...BUT THE BELLS AT THE END SUMMON ANOTHER...
...FROM THE SHADOWS...
...ONE WHO WON'T STOP UNTIL THE WICKED ARE BROUGHT TO ACCOUNT.
GRAND'PA JEROME SAYS HE'S *HERE* NOW.
OLD GAMBLER!
YOU'VE GAMBLED YOUR LAST BET!
HAH!

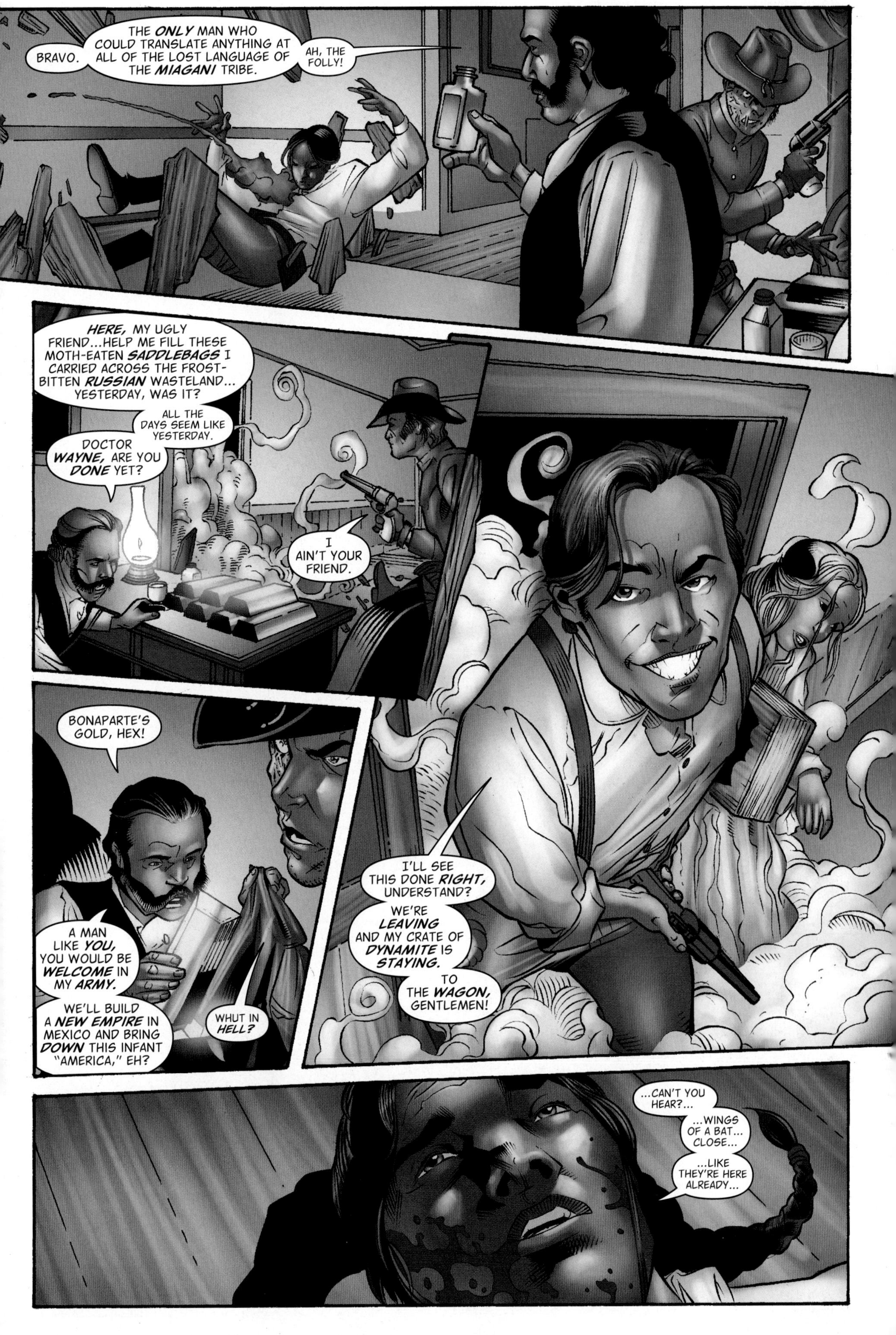
BRAVO.
THE ONLY MAN WHO COULD TRANSLATE ANYTHING AT ALL OF THE LOST LANGUAGE OF THE MIAGANI TRIBE.
AH, THE FOLLY!
HERE, MY UGLY FRIEND...HELP ME FILL THESE MOTH-EATEN SADDLEBAGS I CARRIED ACROSS THE FROST-BITTEN RUSSIAN WASTELAND... YESTERDAY, WAS IT?
ALL THE DAYS SEEM LIKE YESTERDAY.
DOCTOR WAYNE, ARE YOU DONE YET?
I AIN'T YOUR FRIEND.
BONAPARTE'S GOLD, HEX!
A MAN LIKE YOU, YOU WOULD BE WELCOME IN MY ARMY.
WE'LL BUILD A NEW EMPIRE IN MEXICO AND BRING DOWN THIS INFANT "AMERICA," EH?
WHUT IN HELL?
I'LL SEE THIS DONE RIGHT, UNDERSTAND?
WE'RE LEAVING AND MY CRATE OF DYNAMITE IS STAYING.
TO THE WAGON, GENTLEMEN!
...CAN'T YOU HEAR?...
...WINGS OF A BAT... CLOSE...
...LIKE THEY'RE HERE ALREADY...

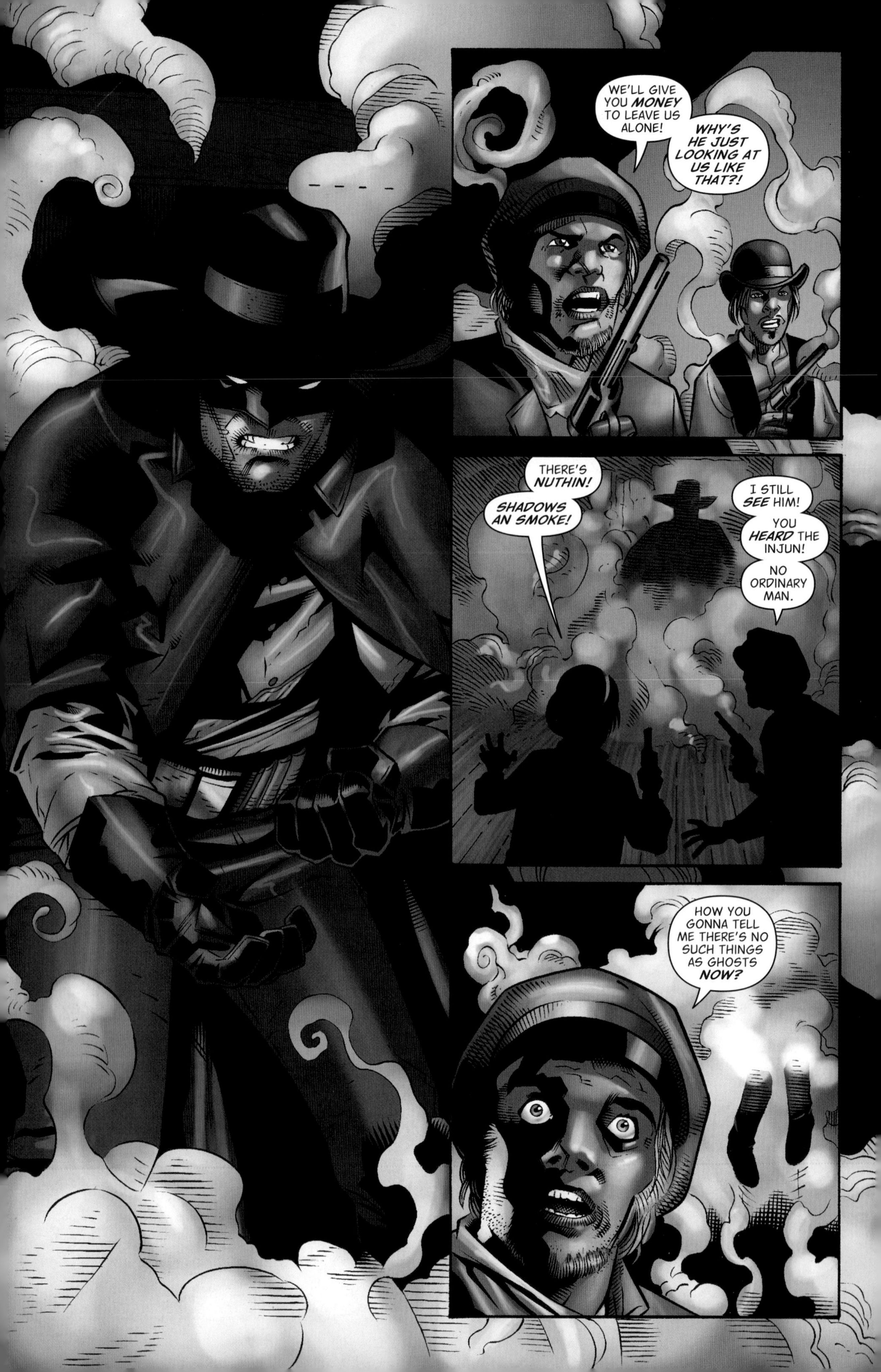
WE'LL GIVE YOU MONEY TO LEAVE US ALONE!
WHY'S HE JUST LOOKING AT US LIKE THAT?!
THERE'S NUTHIN!
SHADOWS AN SMOKE!
I STILL SEE HIM!
YOU HEARD THE INJUN!
NO ORDINARY MAN.
HOW YOU GONNA TELL ME THERE'S NO SUCH THINGS AS GHOSTS NOW?

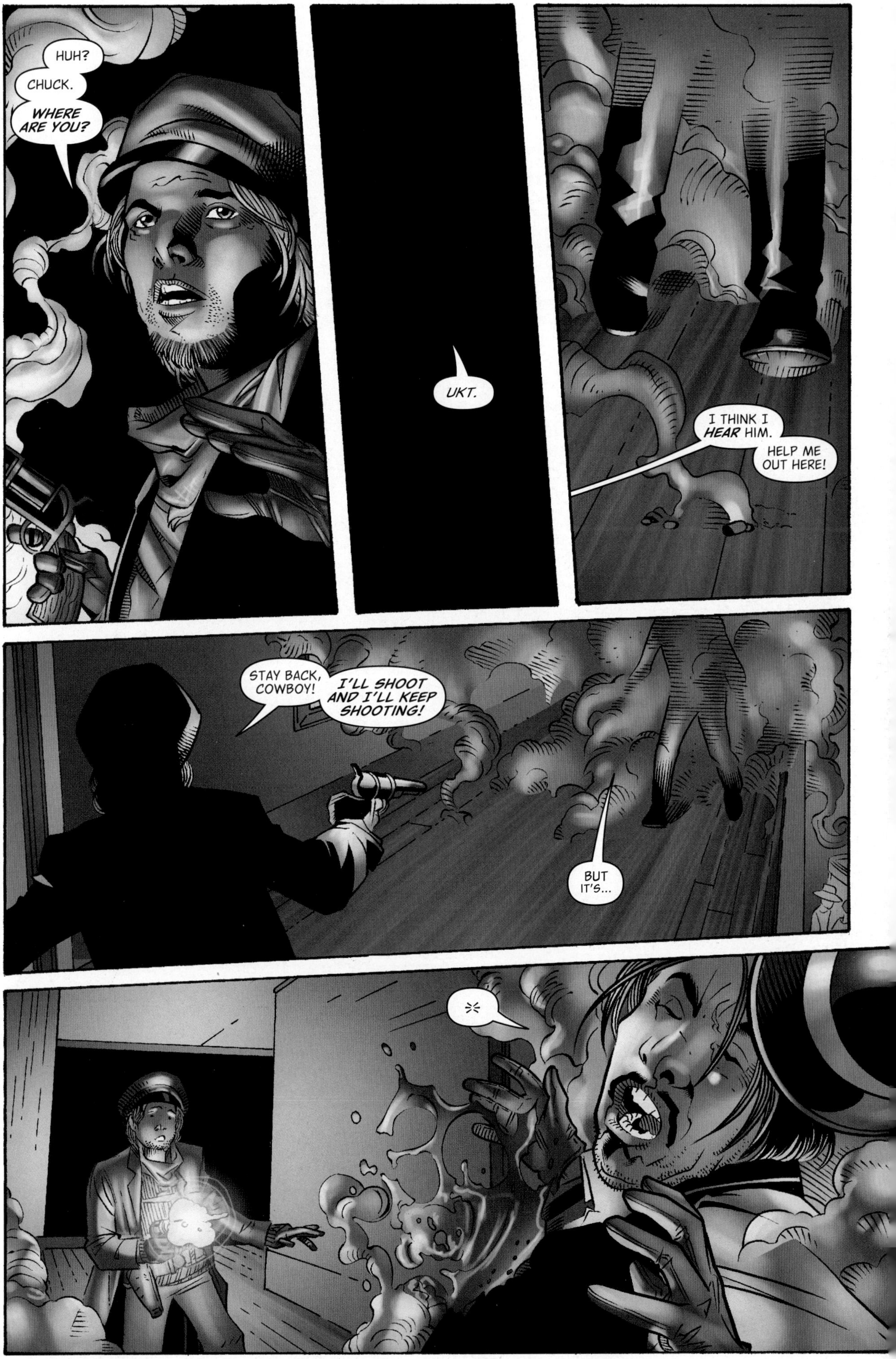
HUH?
CHUCK.
WHERE ARE YOU?
UKT.
I THINK I HEAR HIM.
HELP ME OUT HERE!
STAY BACK, COWBOY!
I'LL SHOOT AND I'LL KEEP SHOOTING!
BUT IT'S...

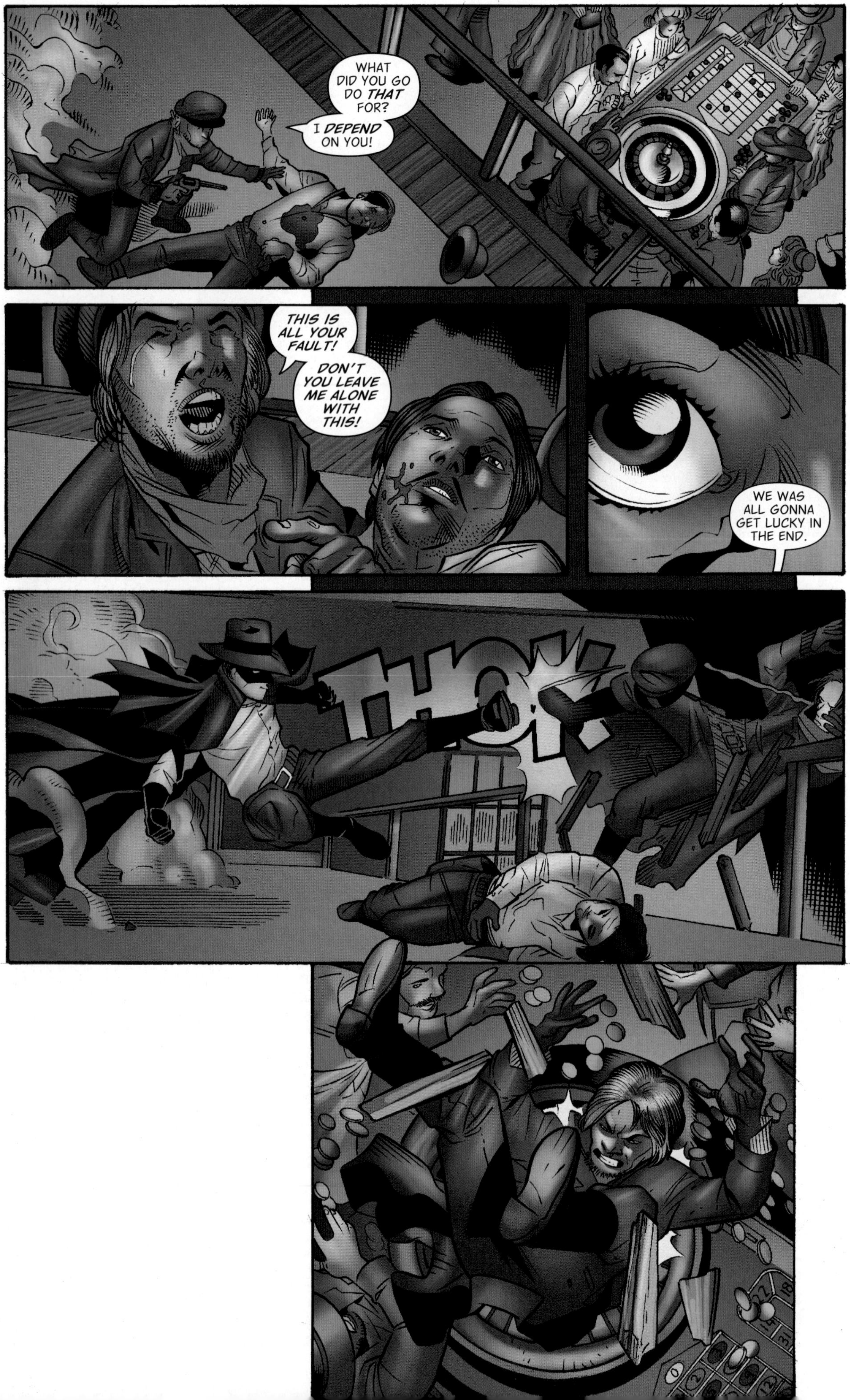
WHAT DID YOU GO DO *THAT* FOR?
I *DEPEND* ON YOU!
THIS IS ALL YOUR FAULT!
DON'T YOU LEAVE ME ALONE WITH THIS!
WE WAS ALL GONNA GET LUCKY IN THE END.
THOK!

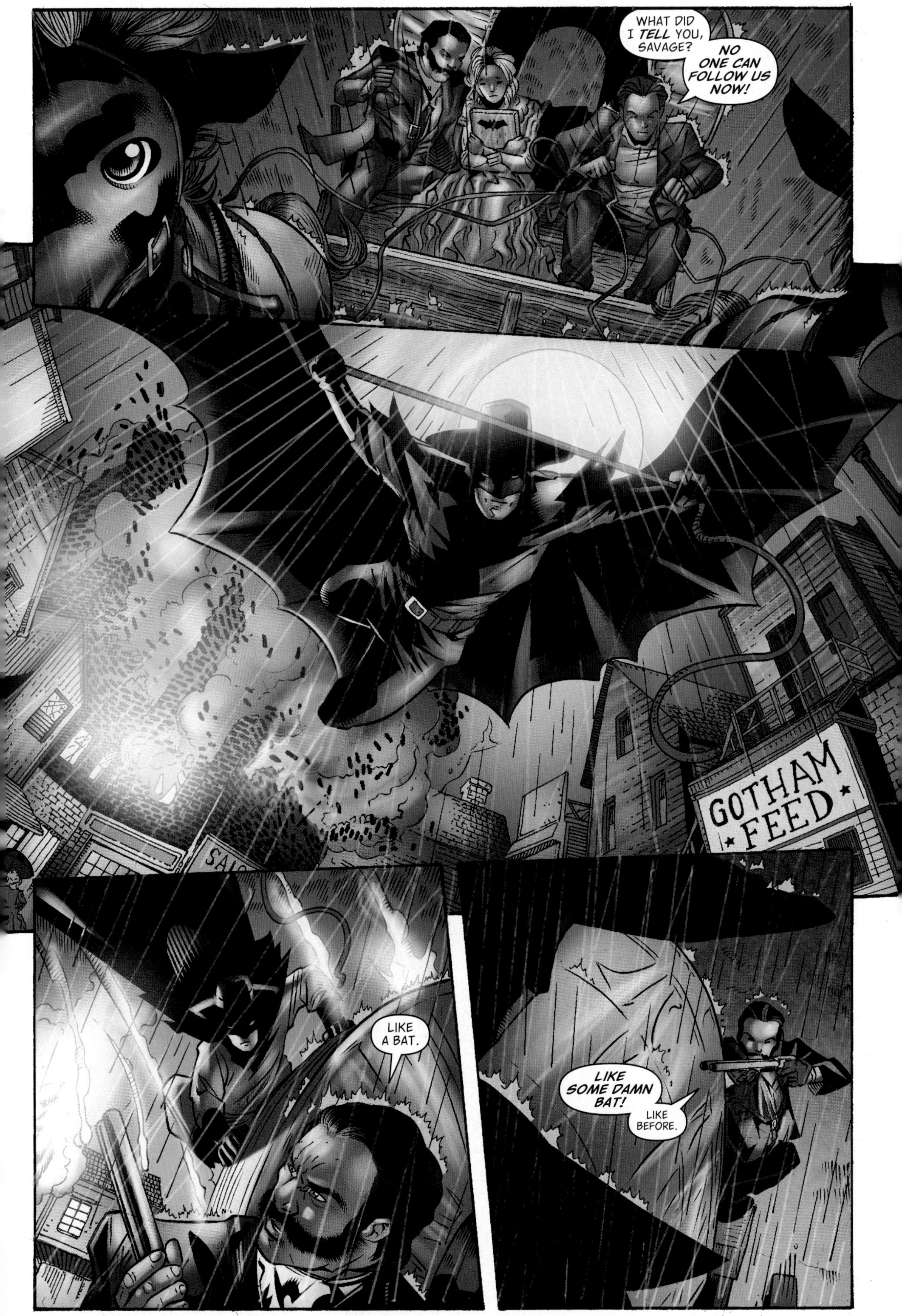
WHAT DID I TELL YOU, SAVAGE?
NO ONE CAN FOLLOW US NOW!
GOTHAM FEED
LIKE A BAT.
LIKE SOME DAMN BAT!
LIKE BEFORE.

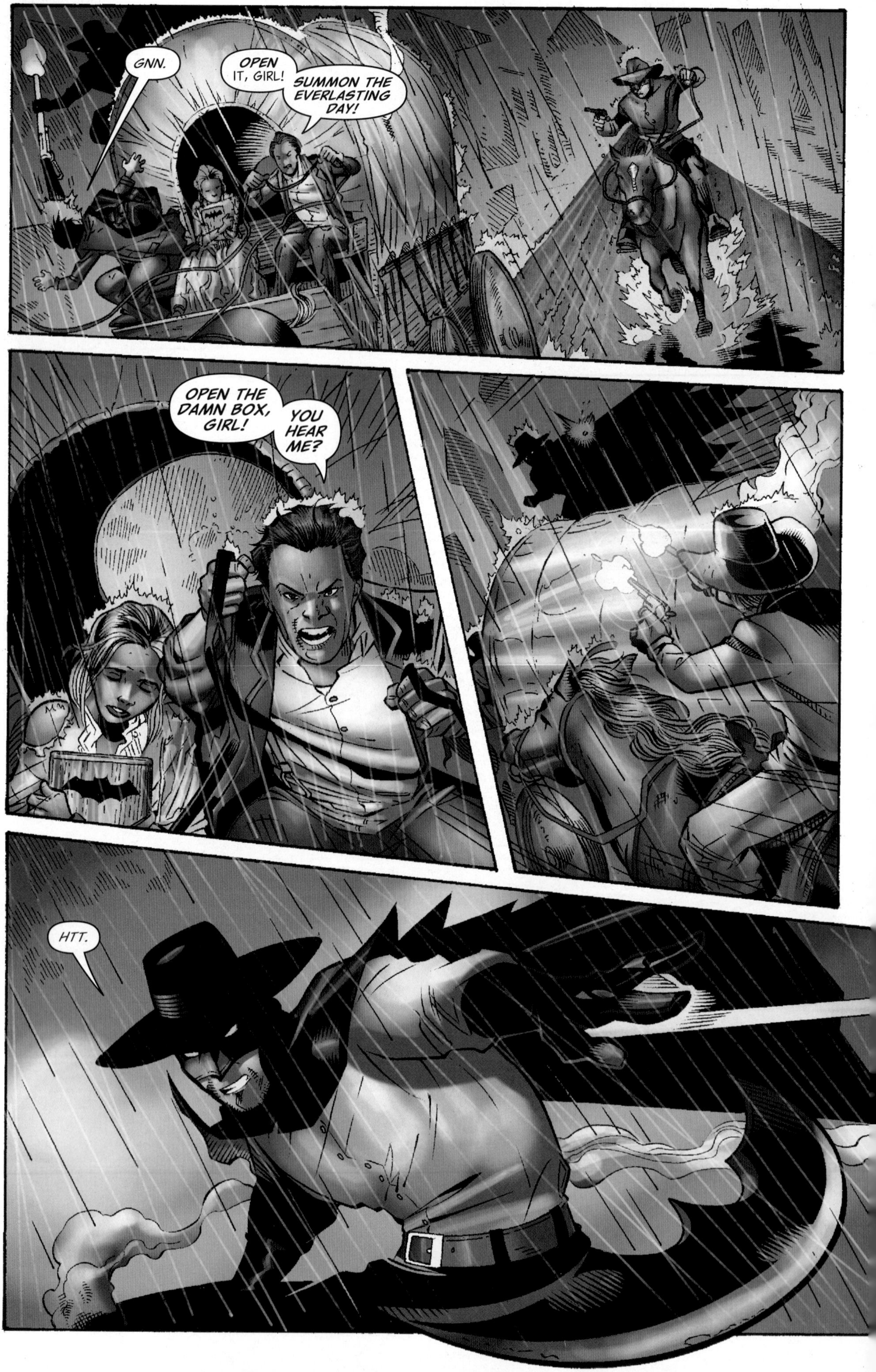
GNN.
OPEN IT, GIRL!
SUMMON THE EVERLASTING DAY!
OPEN THE DAMN BOX, GIRL!
YOU HEAR ME?
HTT.

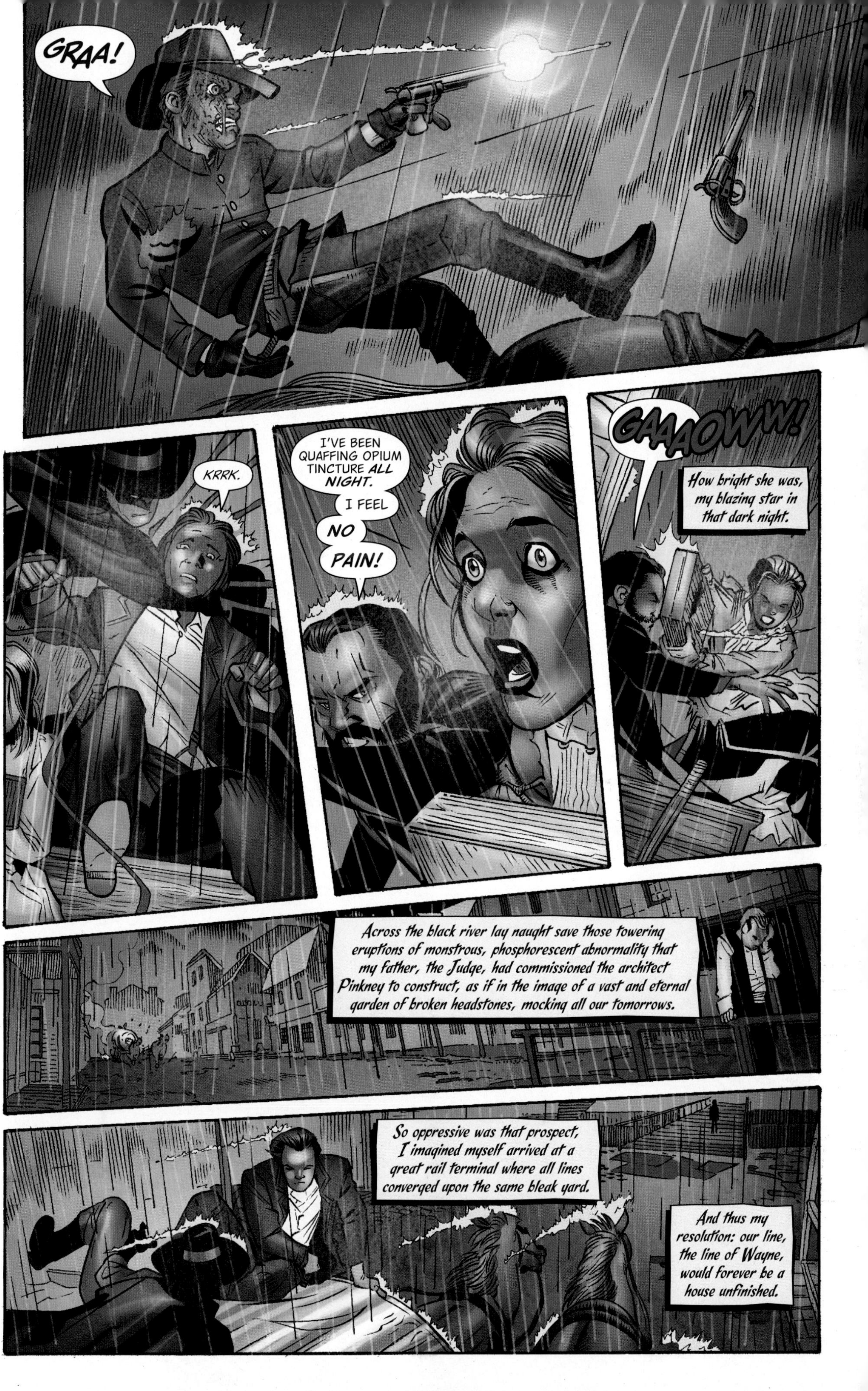
GRAA!
KRRK.
I'VE BEEN QUAFFING OPIUM TINCTURE ALL NIGHT.
I FEEL
NO
PAIN!
GAAAOWW!
How bright she was, my blazing star in that dark night.
Across the black river lay naught save those towering eruptions of monstrous, phosphorescent abnormality that my father, the Judge, had commissioned the architect Pinkney to construct, as if in the image of a vast and eternal garden of broken headstones, mocking all our tomorrows.
So oppressive was that prospect, I imagined myself arrived at a great rail terminal where all lines converged upon the same bleak yard.
And thus my resolution: our line, the line of Wayne, would forever be a house unfinished.

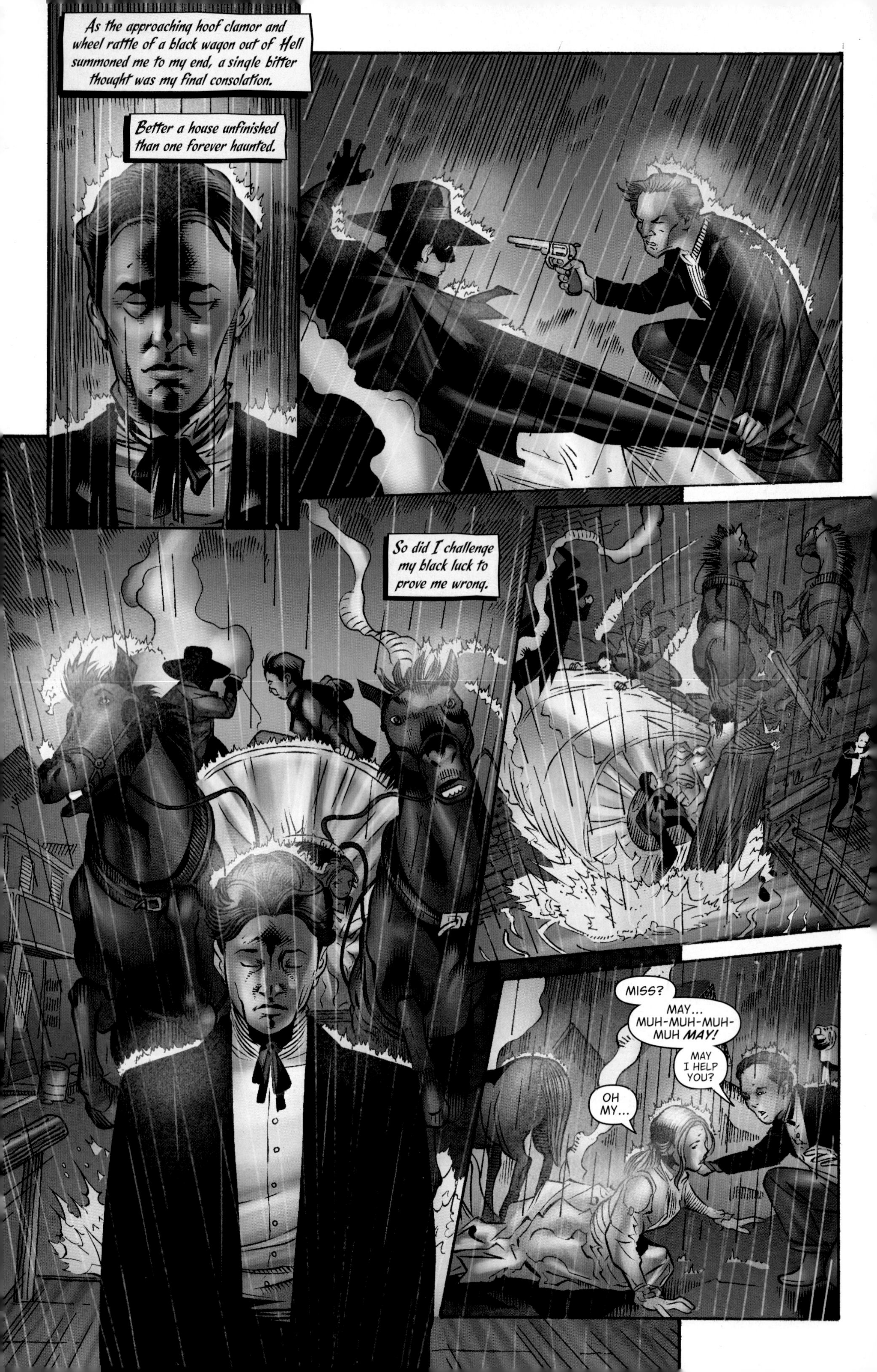
As the approaching hoof clamor and wheel rattle of a black wagon out of Hell summoned me to my end, a single bitter thought was my final consolation.
Better a house unfinished than one forever haunted.
So did I challenge my black luck to prove me wrong.
MISS?
MAY... MUH-MUH-MUH-MUH MAY!
MAY I HELP YOU?
OH MY...

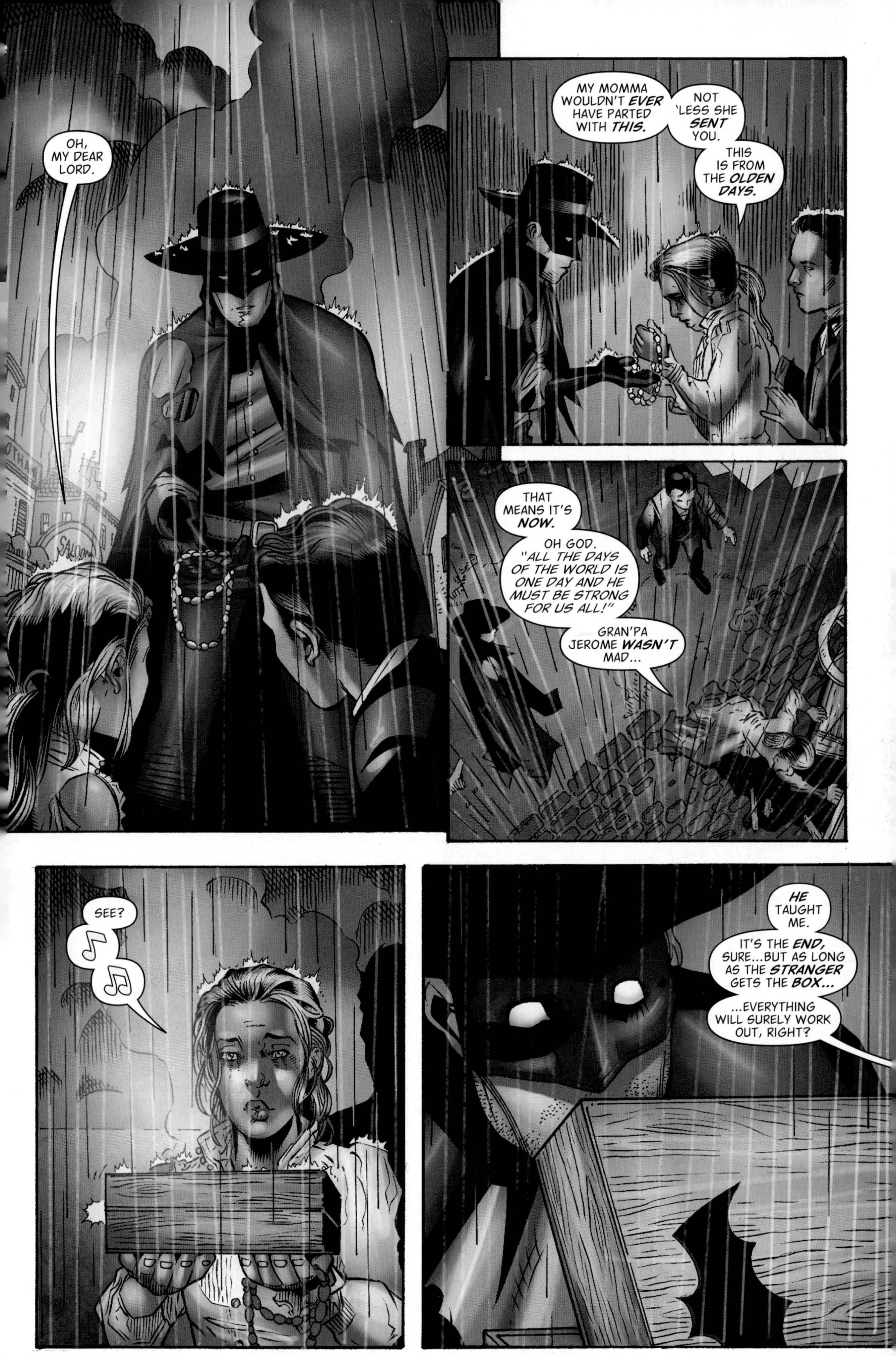
OH, MY DEAR LORD.
MY MOMMA WOULDN'T EVER HAVE PARTED WITH THIS.
NOT 'LESS SHE SENT YOU.
THIS IS FROM THE OLDEN DAYS.
THAT MEANS IT'S NOW.
OH GOD. "ALL THE DAYS OF THE WORLD IS ONE DAY AND HE MUST BE STRONG FOR US ALL!"
GRAN'PA JEROME WASN'T MAD...
SEE?
HE TAUGHT ME.
IT'S THE END, SURE...BUT AS LONG AS THE STRANGER GETS THE BOX...
...EVERYTHING WILL SURELY WORK OUT, RIGHT?

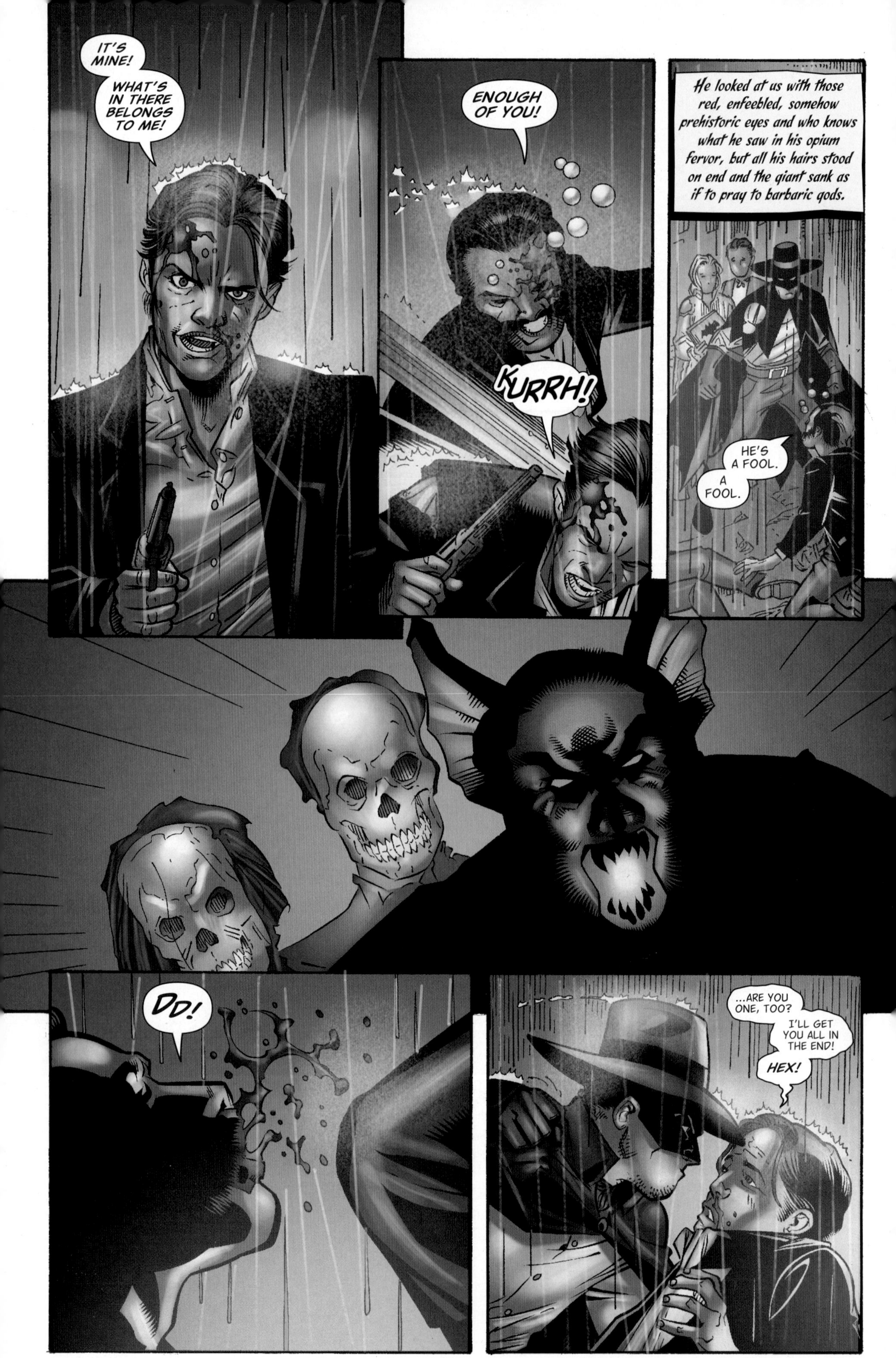
IT'S MINE!
WHAT'S IN THERE BELONGS TO ME!
ENOUGH OF YOU!
KURRH!
He looked at us with those red, enfeebled, somehow prehistoric eyes and who knows what he saw in his opium fervor, but all his hairs stood on end and the giant sank as if to pray to barbaric gods.
HE'S A FOOL.
A FOOL.
DD!
...ARE YOU ONE, TOO?
I'LL GET YOU ALL IN THE END!
HEX!

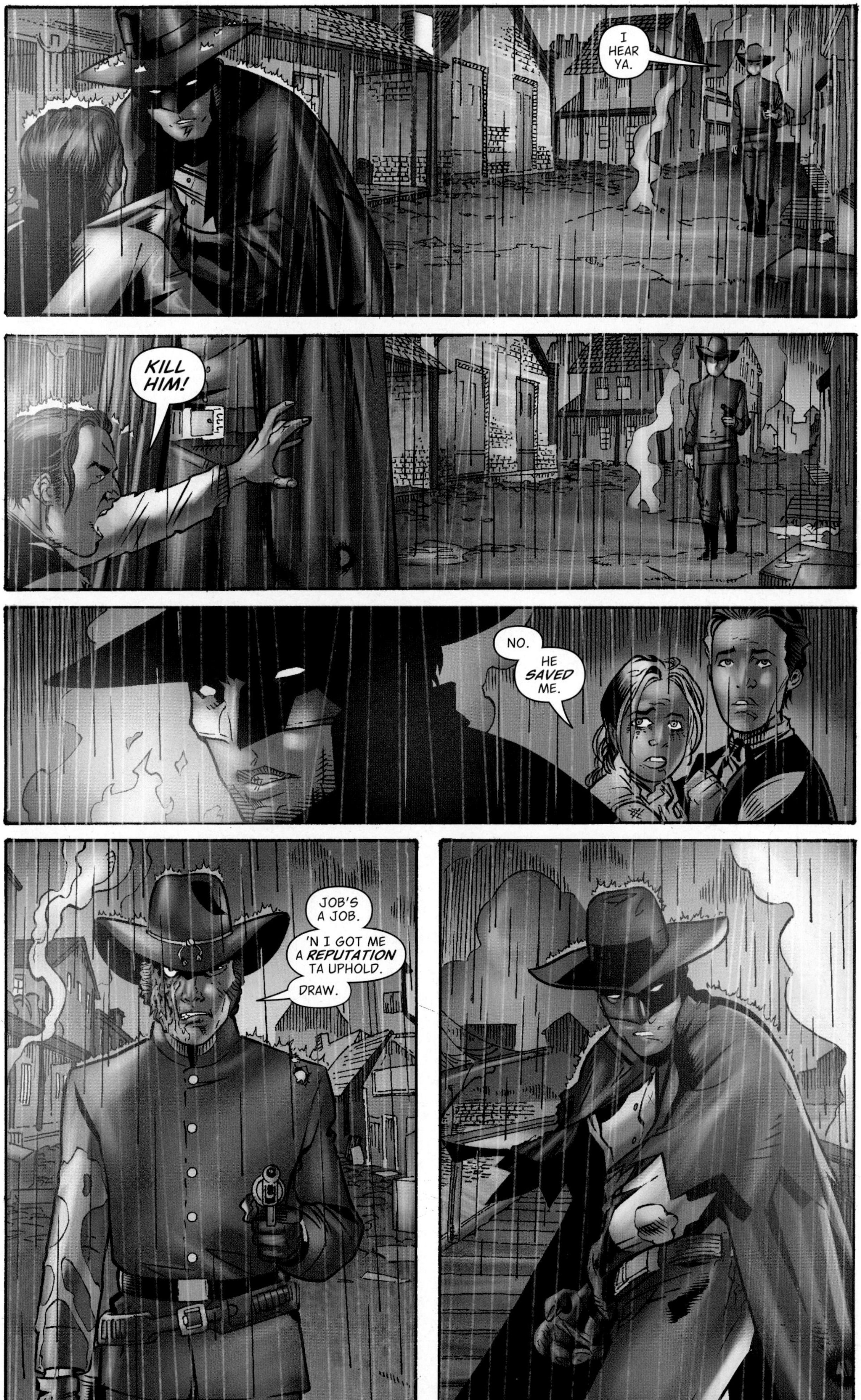
I HEAR YA.
KILL HIM!
NO. HE SAVED ME.
JOB'S A JOB.
'N I GOT ME A REPUTATION TA UPHOLD.
DRAW.

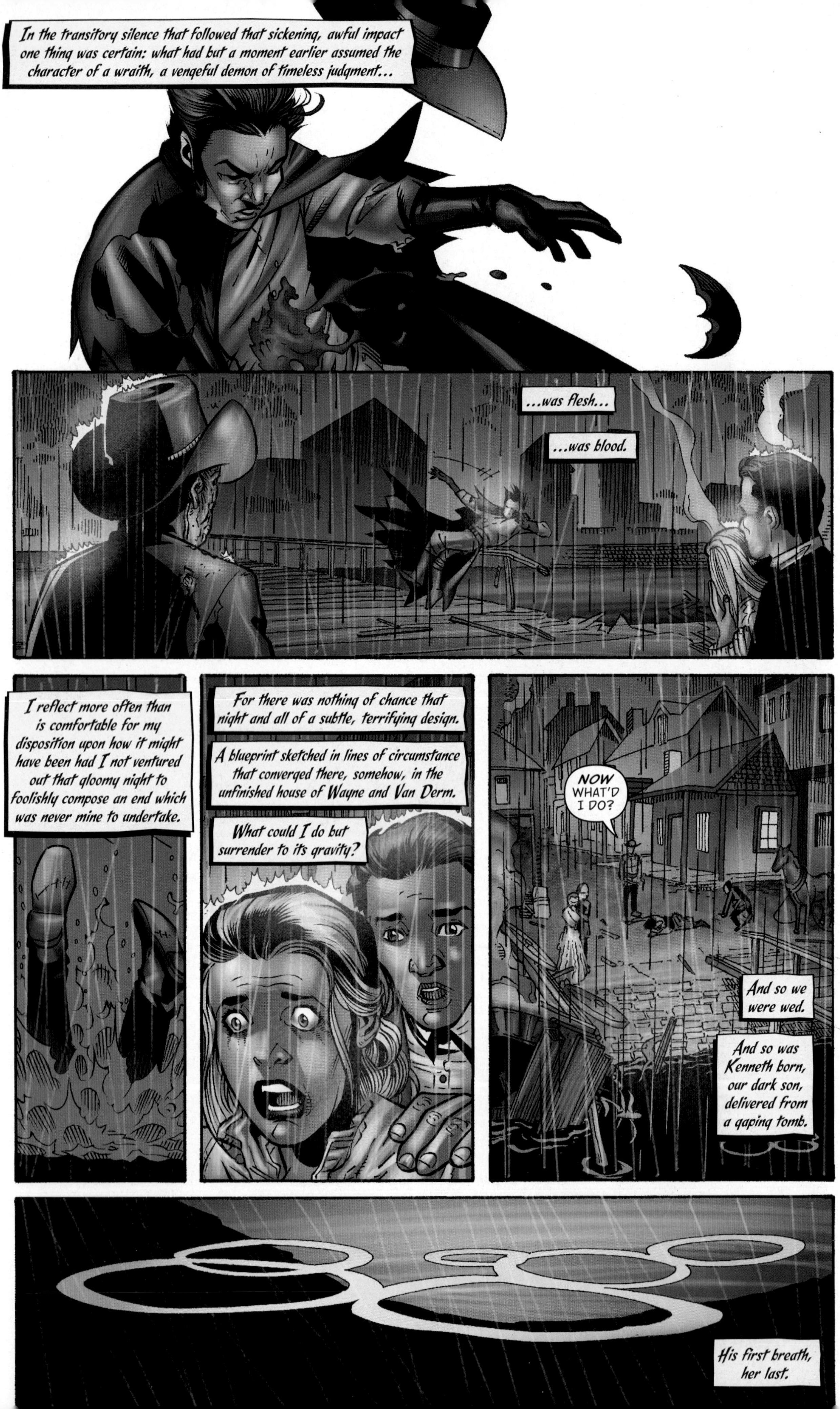

In the transitory silence that followed that sickening, awful impact one thing was certain: what had but a moment earlier assumed the character of a wraith, a vengeful demon of timeless judgment...
...was flesh...
...was blood.
I reflect more often than is comfortable for my disposition upon how it might have been had I not ventured out that gloomy night to foolishly compose an end which was never mine to undertake.
For there was nothing of chance that night and all of a subtle, terrifying design.
A blueprint sketched in lines of circumstance that converged there, somehow, in the unfinished house of Wayne and Van Derm.
What could I do but surrender to its gravity?
NOW WHAT'D I DO?
And so we were wed.
And so was Kenneth born, our dark son, delivered from a gaping tomb.
His first breath, her last.

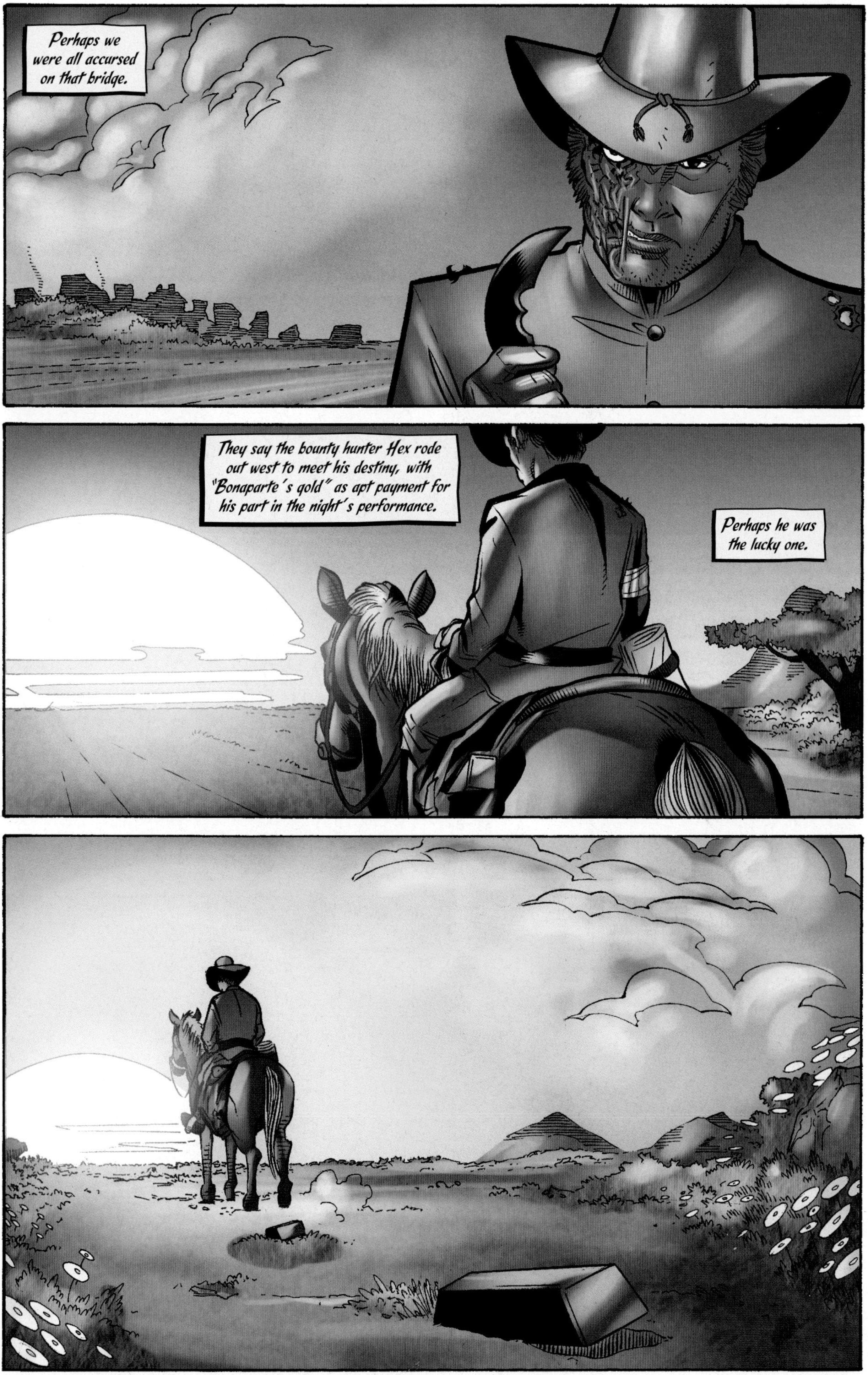
Perhaps we were all accursed on that bridge.
They say the bounty hunter Hex rode out west to meet his destiny, with "Bonaparte's gold" as apt payment for his part in the night's performance.
Perhaps he was the lucky one.

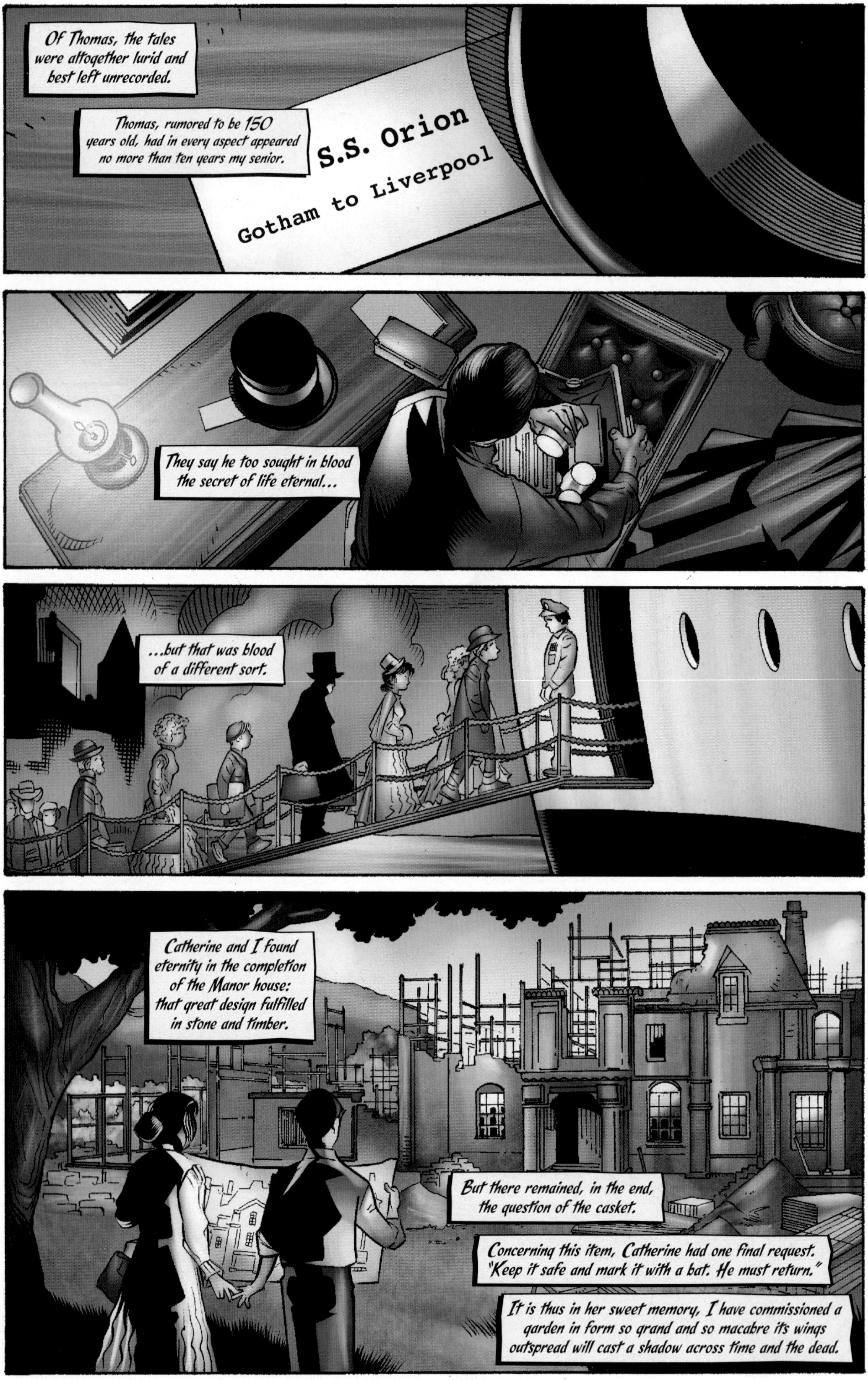

Of Thomas, the tales were altogether lurid and best left unrecorded.
Thomas, rumored to be 150 years old, had in every aspect appeared no more than ten years my senior.
S.S. Orion
Gotham to Liverpool
They say he too sought in blood the secret of life eternal...
...but that was blood of a different sort.
Catherine and I found eternity in the completion of the Manor house: that great design fulfilled in stone and timber.
But there remained, in the end, the question of the casket.
Concerning this item, Catherine had one final request. "Keep it safe and mark it with a bat. He must return."
It is thus in her sweet memory, I have commissioned a garden in form so grand and so macabre its wings outspread will cast a shadow across time and the dead.

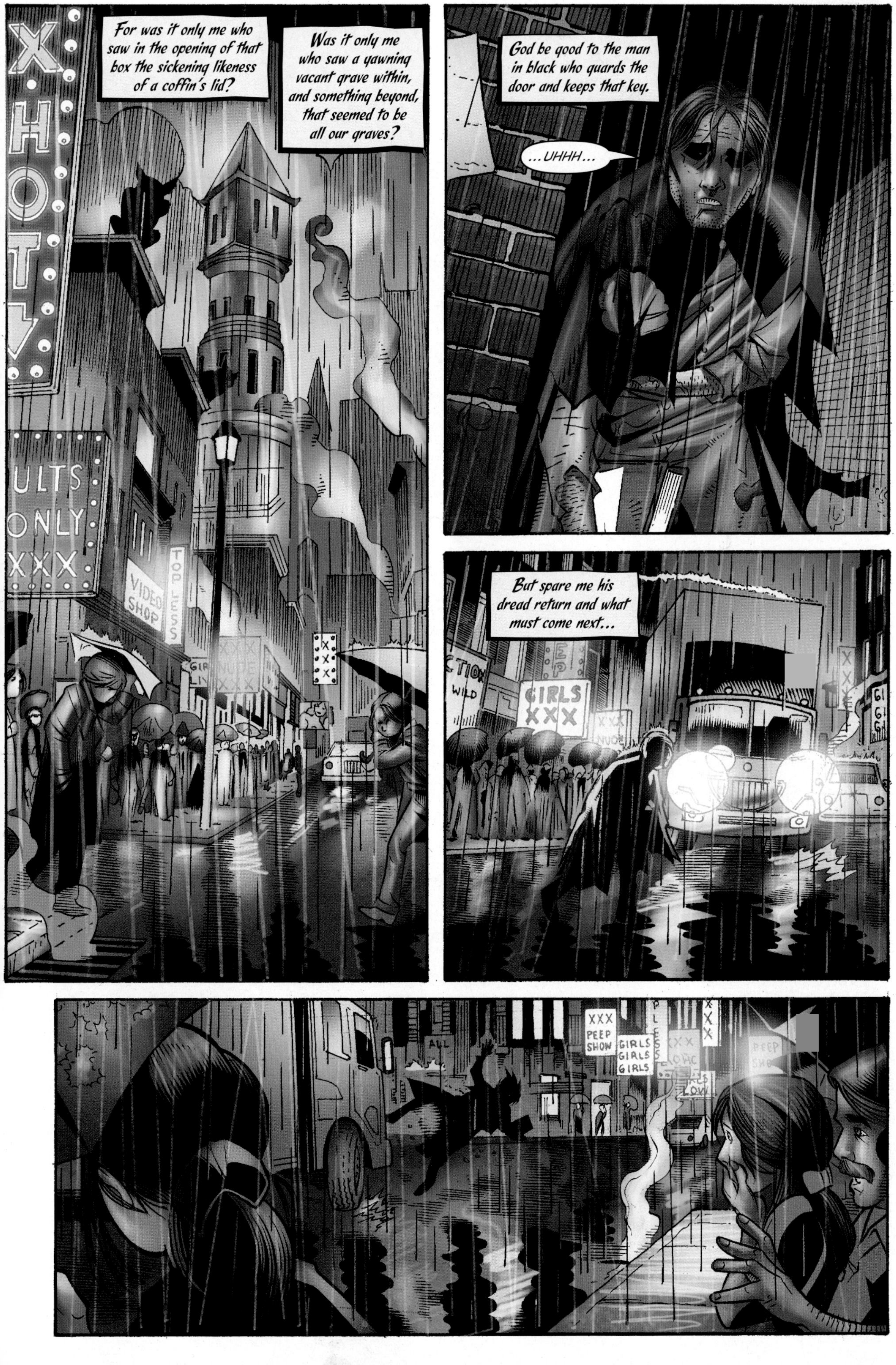
For was it only me who saw in the opening of that box the sickening likeness of a coffin's lid?
Was it only me who saw a yawning vacant grave within, and something beyond, that seemed to be all our graves?
HOT
ULTS ONLY XXX
VIDEO SHOP
TOP LESS
XXX NUDE XXX
God be good to the man in black who guards the door and keeps that key.
...UHHH...
But spare me his dread return and what must come next...
GIRLS XXX
XXX NUDE
XXX PEEP SHOW
GIRLS GIRLS GIRLS
PEEP SHO

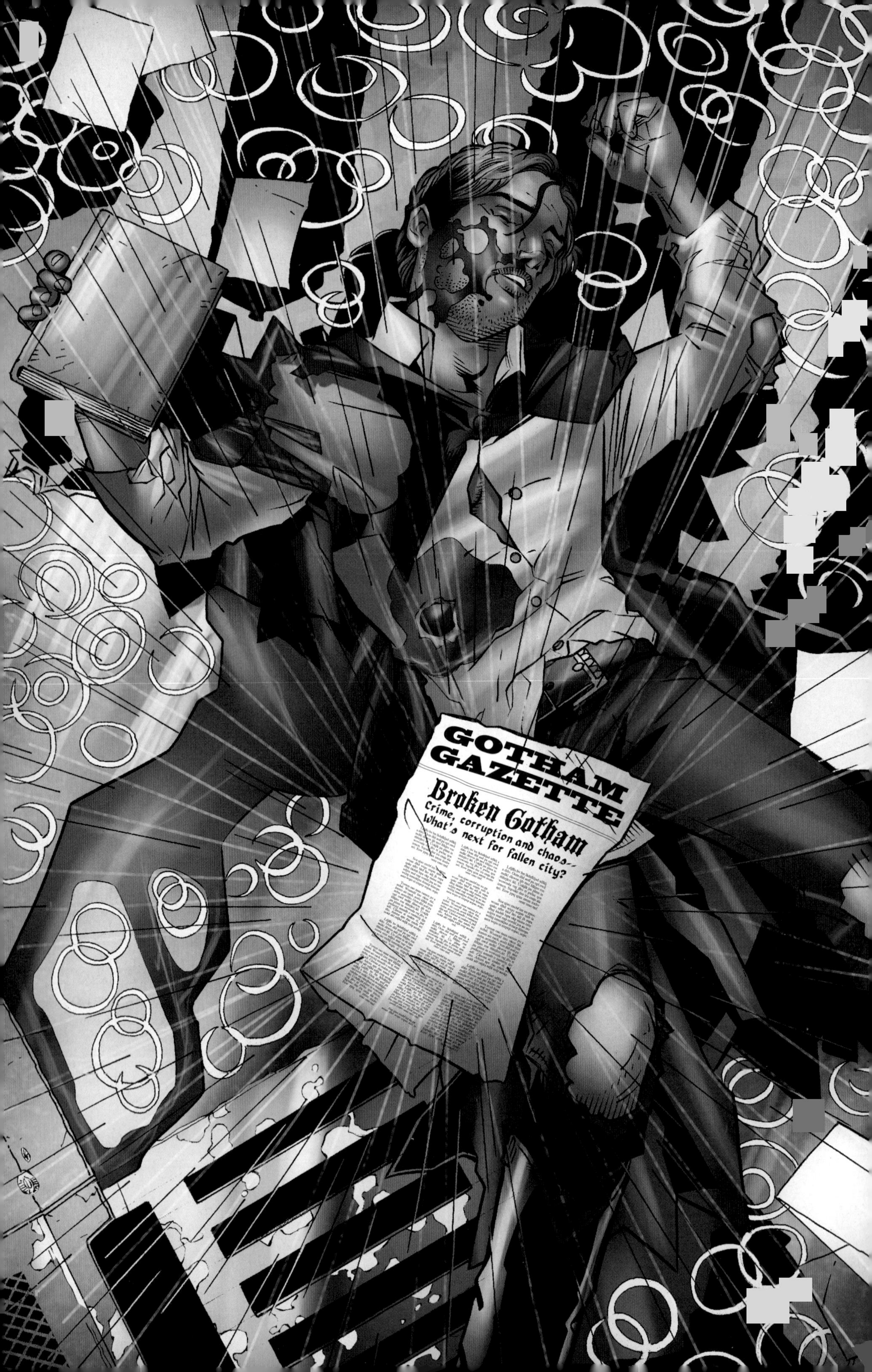
GOTHAM GAZETTE
Broken Gotham
Crime, corruption and chaos--
What's next for fallen city?

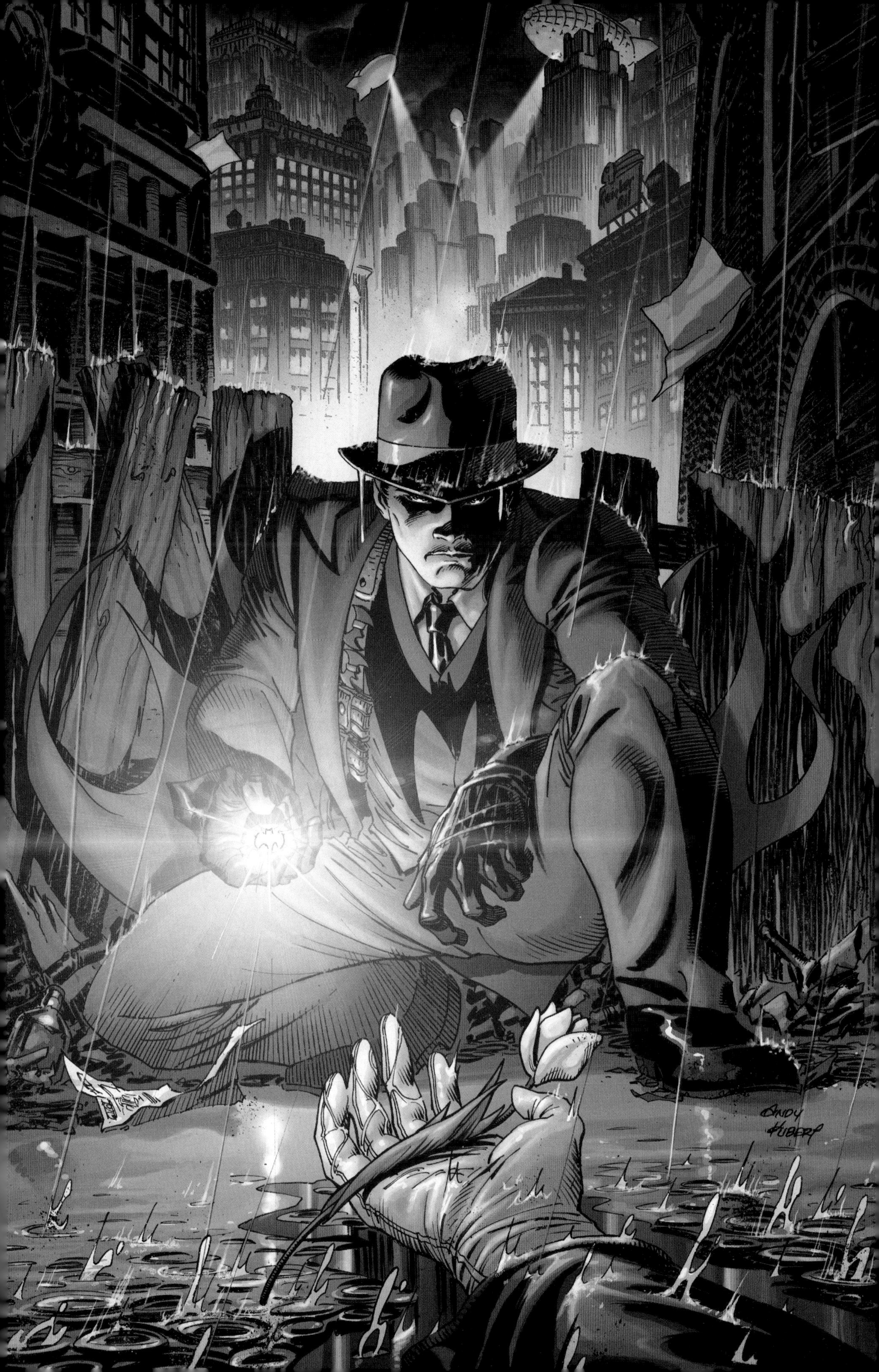
ANDY KUBERT

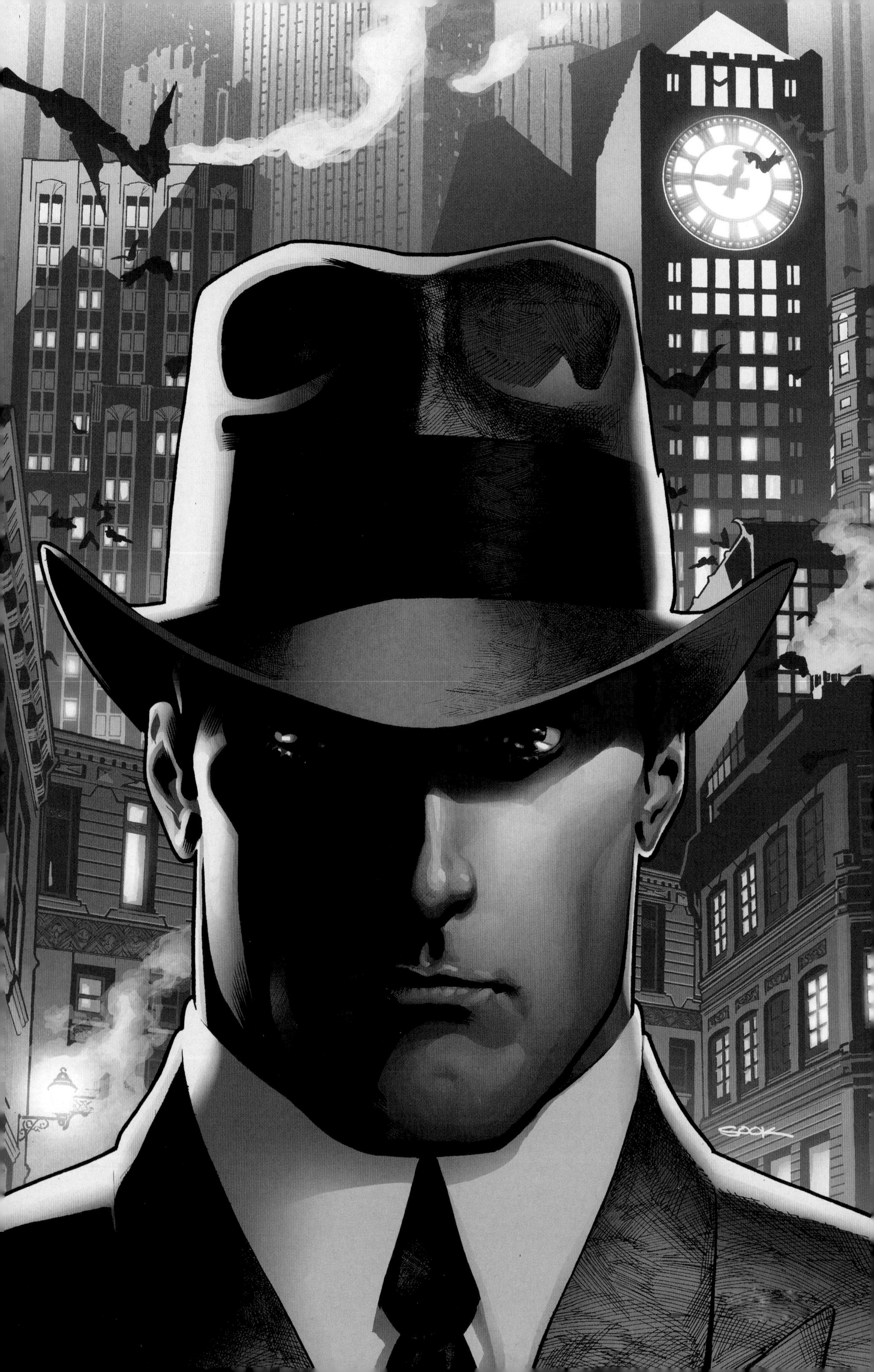

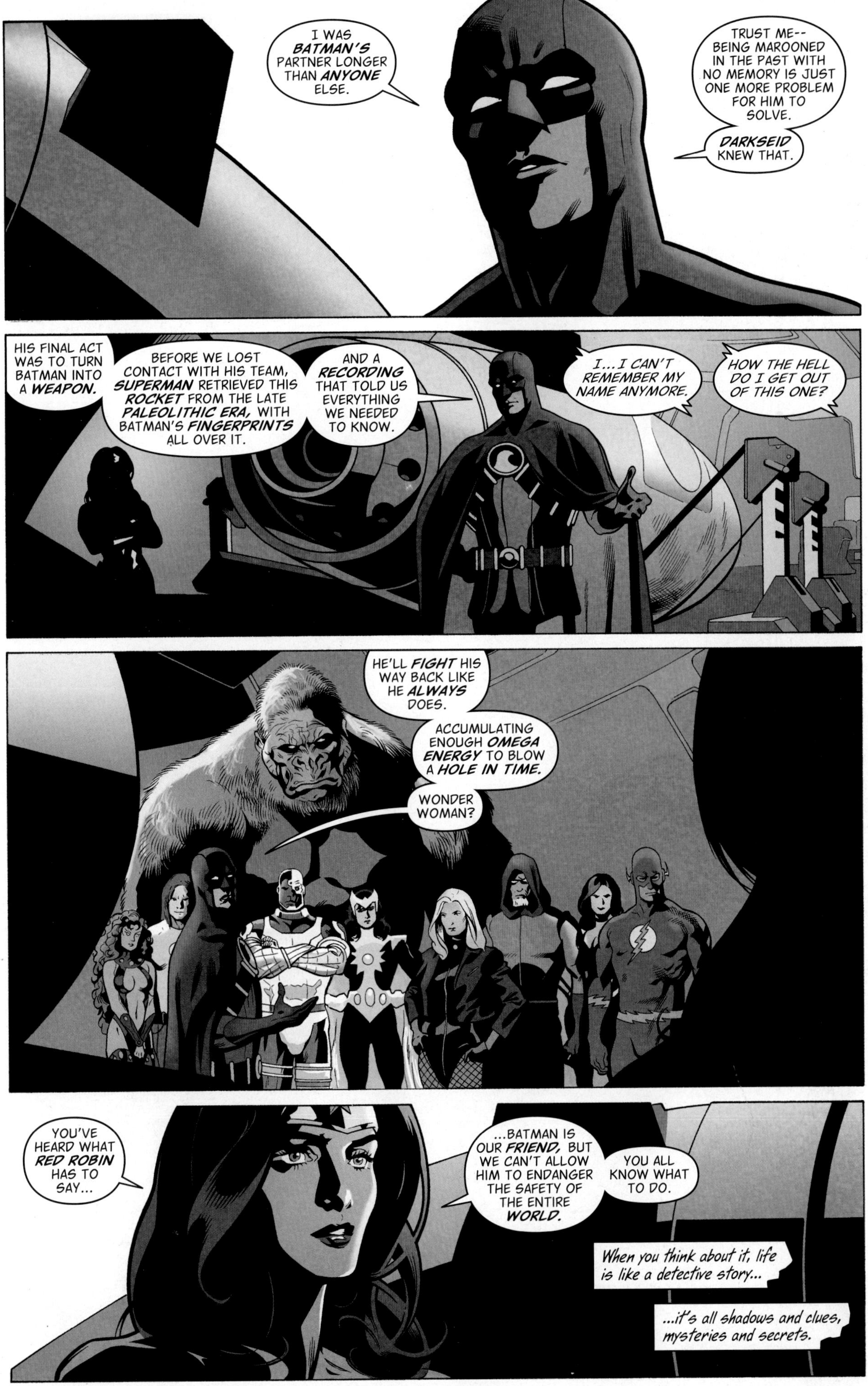
I WAS BATMAN'S PARTNER LONGER THAN ANYONE ELSE.
TRUST ME-- BEING MAROONED IN THE PAST WITH NO MEMORY IS JUST ONE MORE PROBLEM FOR HIM TO SOLVE.
DARKSEID KNEW THAT.
HIS FINAL ACT WAS TO TURN BATMAN INTO A WEAPON.
BEFORE WE LOST CONTACT WITH HIS TEAM, SUPERMAN RETRIEVED THIS ROCKET FROM THE LATE PALEOLITHIC ERA, WITH BATMAN'S FINGERPRINTS ALL OVER IT.
AND A RECORDING THAT TOLD US EVERYTHING WE NEEDED TO KNOW.
I...I CAN'T REMEMBER MY NAME ANYMORE.
HOW THE HELL DO I GET OUT OF THIS ONE?
HE'LL FIGHT HIS WAY BACK LIKE HE ALWAYS DOES.
ACCUMULATING ENOUGH OMEGA ENERGY TO BLOW A HOLE IN TIME.
WONDER WOMAN?
YOU'VE HEARD WHAT RED ROBIN HAS TO SAY...
...BATMAN IS OUR FRIEND, BUT WE CAN'T ALLOW HIM TO ENDANGER THE SAFETY OF THE ENTIRE WORLD.
YOU ALL KNOW WHAT TO DO.
When you think about it, life is like a detective story...
...it's all shadows and clues, mysteries and secrets.

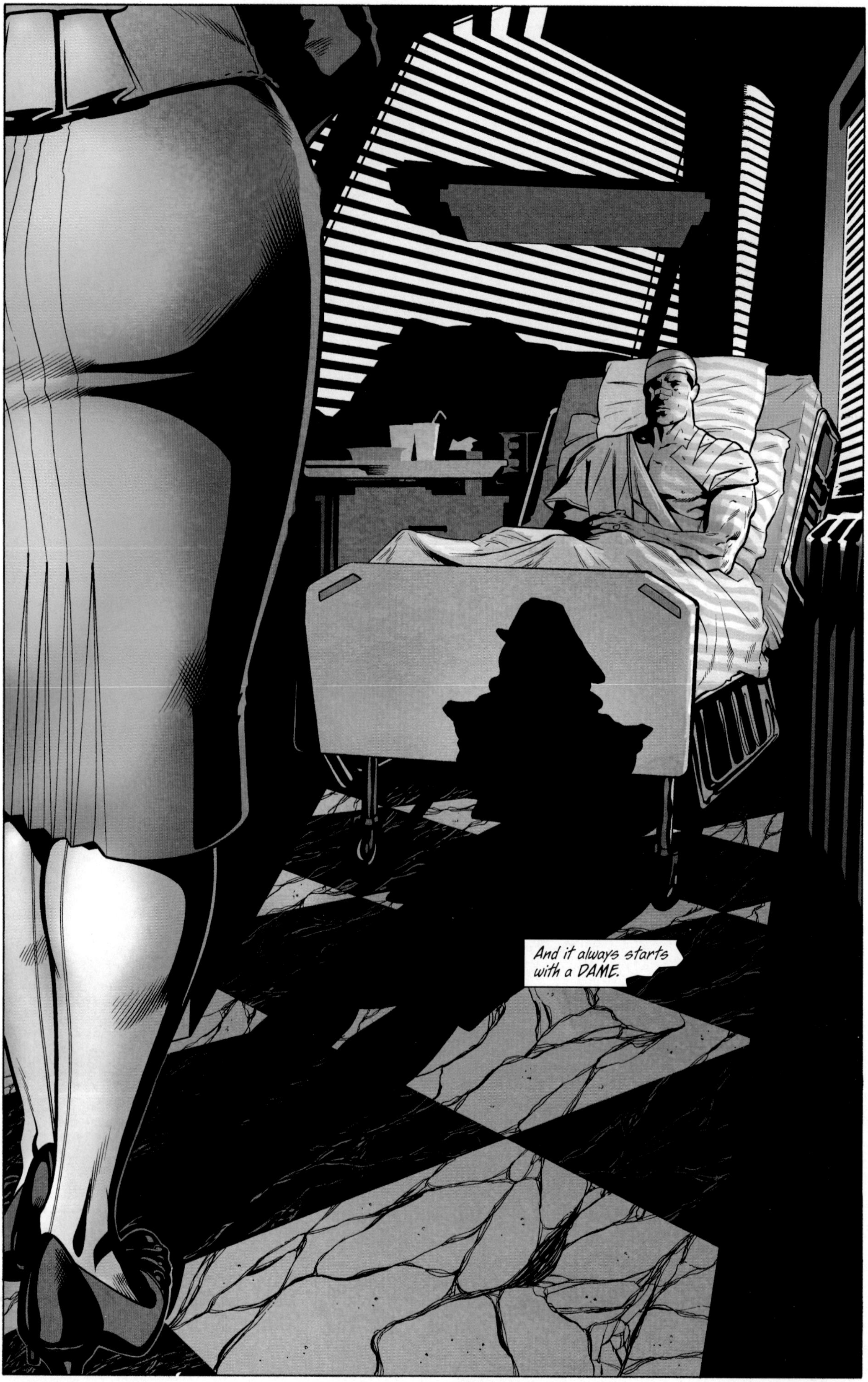
And it always starts with a DAME.

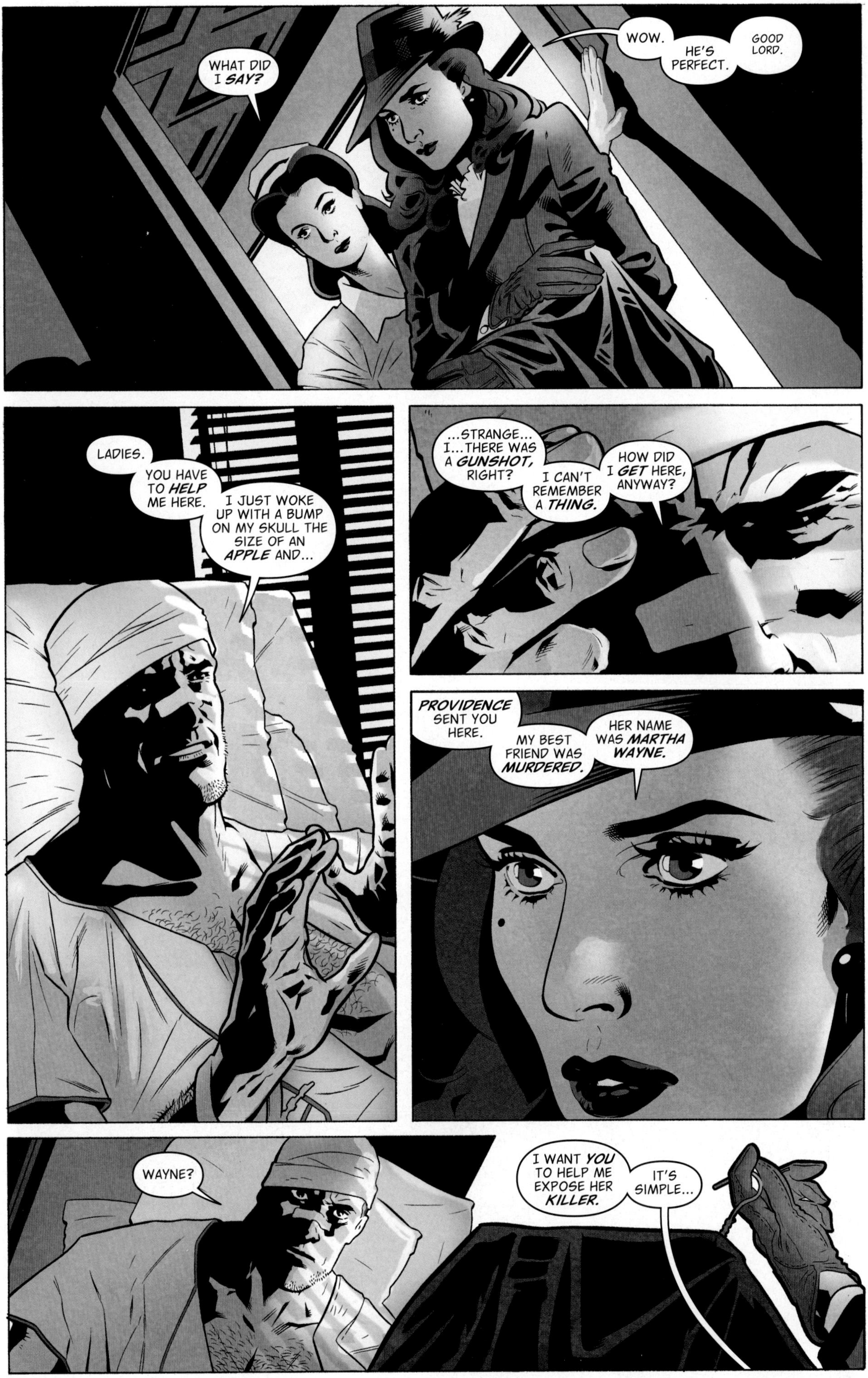
WHAT DID I *SAY?*
WOW.
HE'S PERFECT.
GOOD LORD.
LADIES.
YOU HAVE TO *HELP* ME HERE.
I JUST WOKE UP WITH A BUMP ON MY SKULL THE SIZE OF AN *APPLE* AND...
...STRANGE... I...THERE WAS A *GUNSHOT,* RIGHT?
I CAN'T REMEMBER A *THING.*
HOW DID I *GET* HERE, ANYWAY?
PROVIDENCE SENT YOU HERE.
MY BEST FRIEND WAS *MURDERED.*
HER NAME WAS *MARTHA WAYNE.*
WAYNE?
I WANT *YOU* TO HELP ME EXPOSE HER *KILLER.*
IT'S SIMPLE...

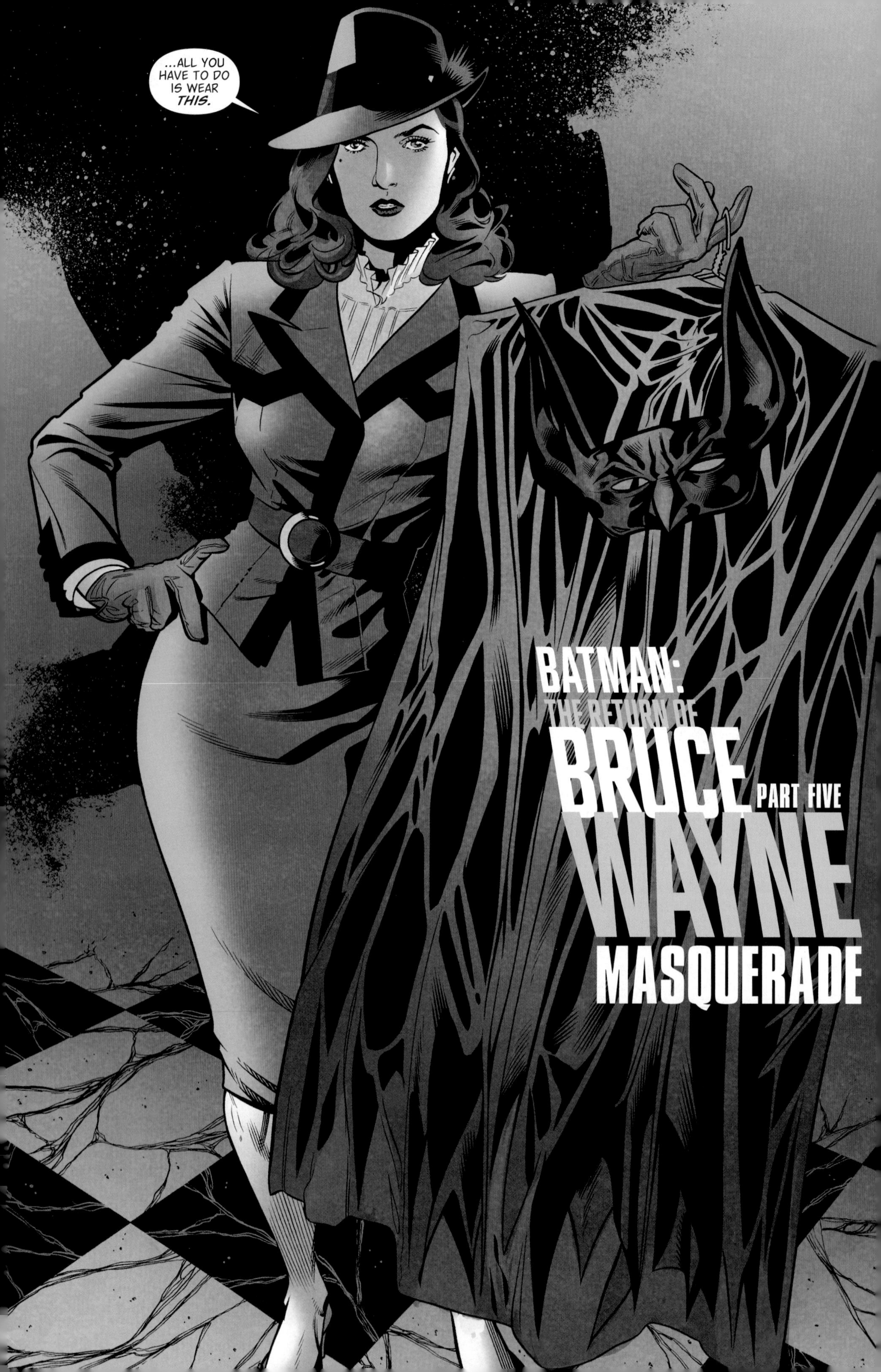
...ALL YOU HAVE TO DO IS WEAR *THIS.*
BATMAN: THE RETURN OF BRUCE WAYNE
PART FIVE
MASQUERADE

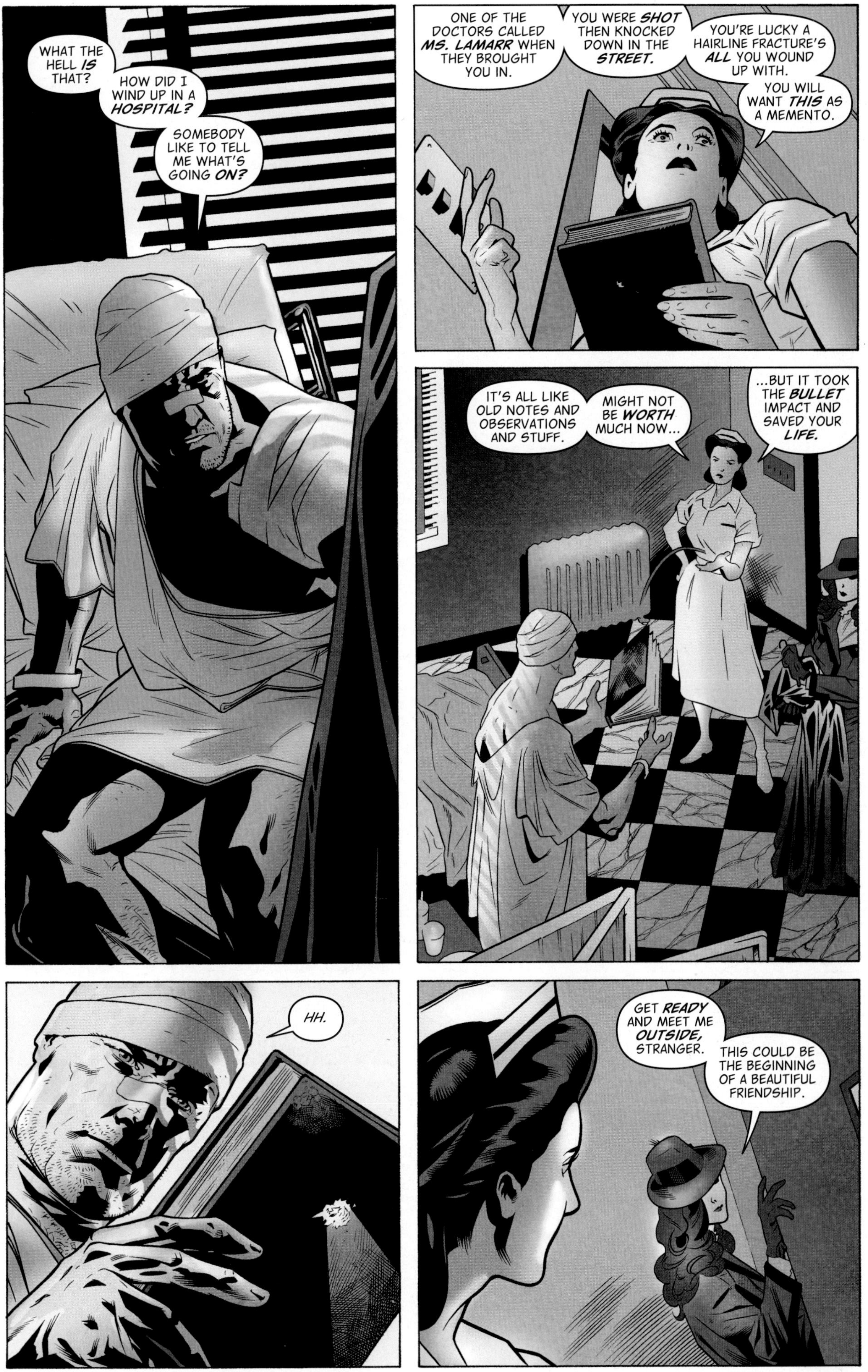
WHAT THE HELL IS THAT?
HOW DID I WIND UP IN A HOSPITAL?
SOMEBODY LIKE TO TELL ME WHAT'S GOING ON?
ONE OF THE DOCTORS CALLED MS. LAMARR WHEN THEY BROUGHT YOU IN.
YOU WERE SHOT THEN KNOCKED DOWN IN THE STREET.
YOU'RE LUCKY A HAIRLINE FRACTURE'S ALL YOU WOUND UP WITH.
YOU WILL WANT THIS AS A MEMENTO.
IT'S ALL LIKE OLD NOTES AND OBSERVATIONS AND STUFF.
MIGHT NOT BE WORTH MUCH NOW...
...BUT IT TOOK THE BULLET IMPACT AND SAVED YOUR LIFE.
HH.
GET READY AND MEET ME OUTSIDE, STRANGER.
THIS COULD BE THE BEGINNING OF A BEAUTIFUL FRIENDSHIP.

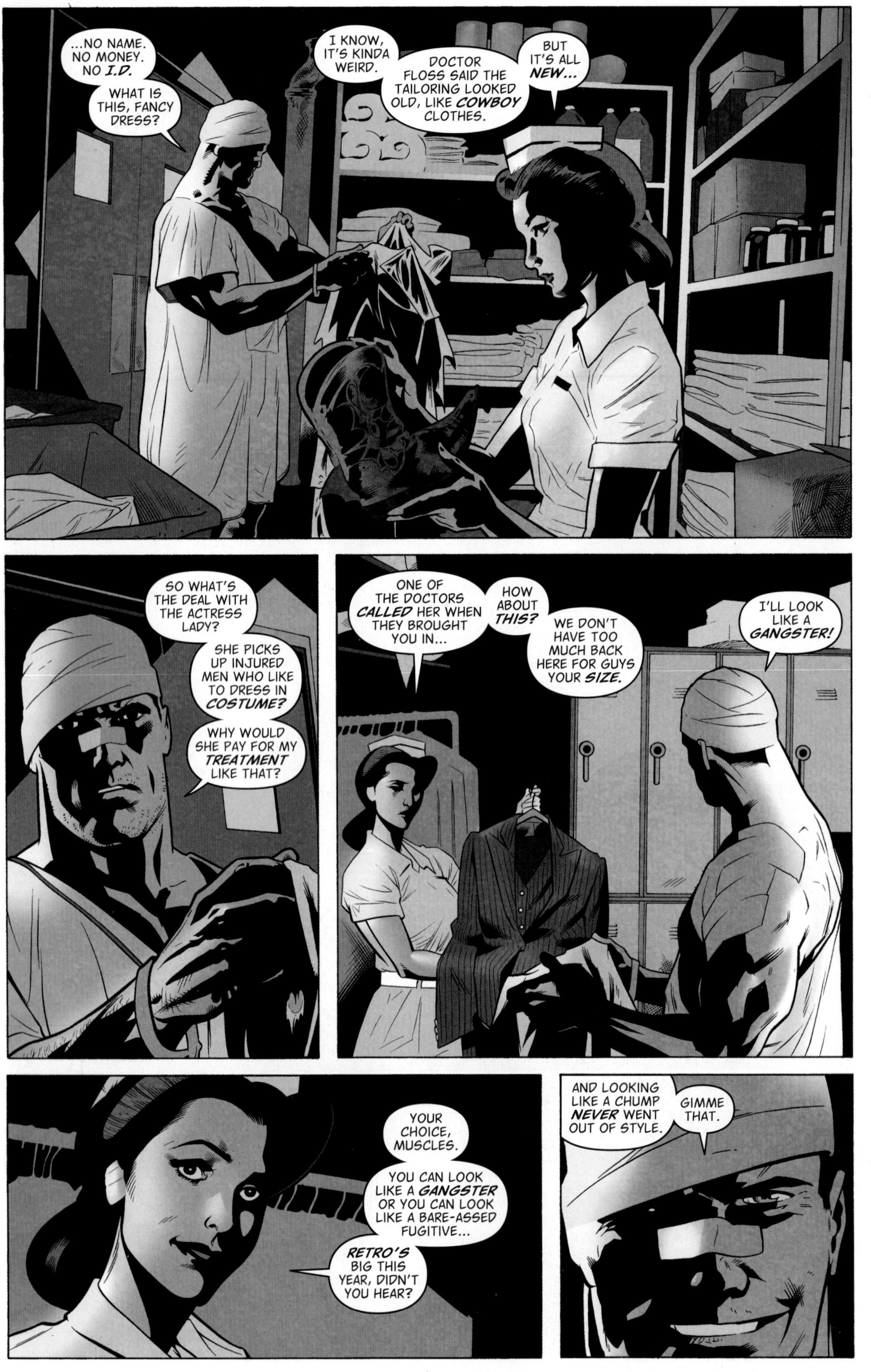
...NO NAME. NO MONEY. NO I.D.
WHAT IS THIS, FANCY DRESS?
I KNOW, IT'S KINDA WEIRD.
DOCTOR FLOSS SAID THE TAILORING LOOKED OLD, LIKE COWBOY CLOTHES.
BUT IT'S ALL NEW...
SO WHAT'S THE DEAL WITH THE ACTRESS LADY?
SHE PICKS UP INJURED MEN WHO LIKE TO DRESS IN COSTUME?
WHY WOULD SHE PAY FOR MY TREATMENT LIKE THAT?
ONE OF THE DOCTORS CALLED HER WHEN THEY BROUGHT YOU IN...
HOW ABOUT THIS?
WE DON'T HAVE TOO MUCH BACK HERE FOR GUYS YOUR SIZE.
I'LL LOOK LIKE A GANGSTER!
YOUR CHOICE, MUSCLES.
YOU CAN LOOK LIKE A GANGSTER OR YOU CAN LOOK LIKE A BARE-ASSED FUGITIVE...
RETRO'S BIG THIS YEAR, DIDN'T YOU HEAR?
AND LOOKING LIKE A CHUMP NEVER WENT OUT OF STYLE.
GIMME THAT.

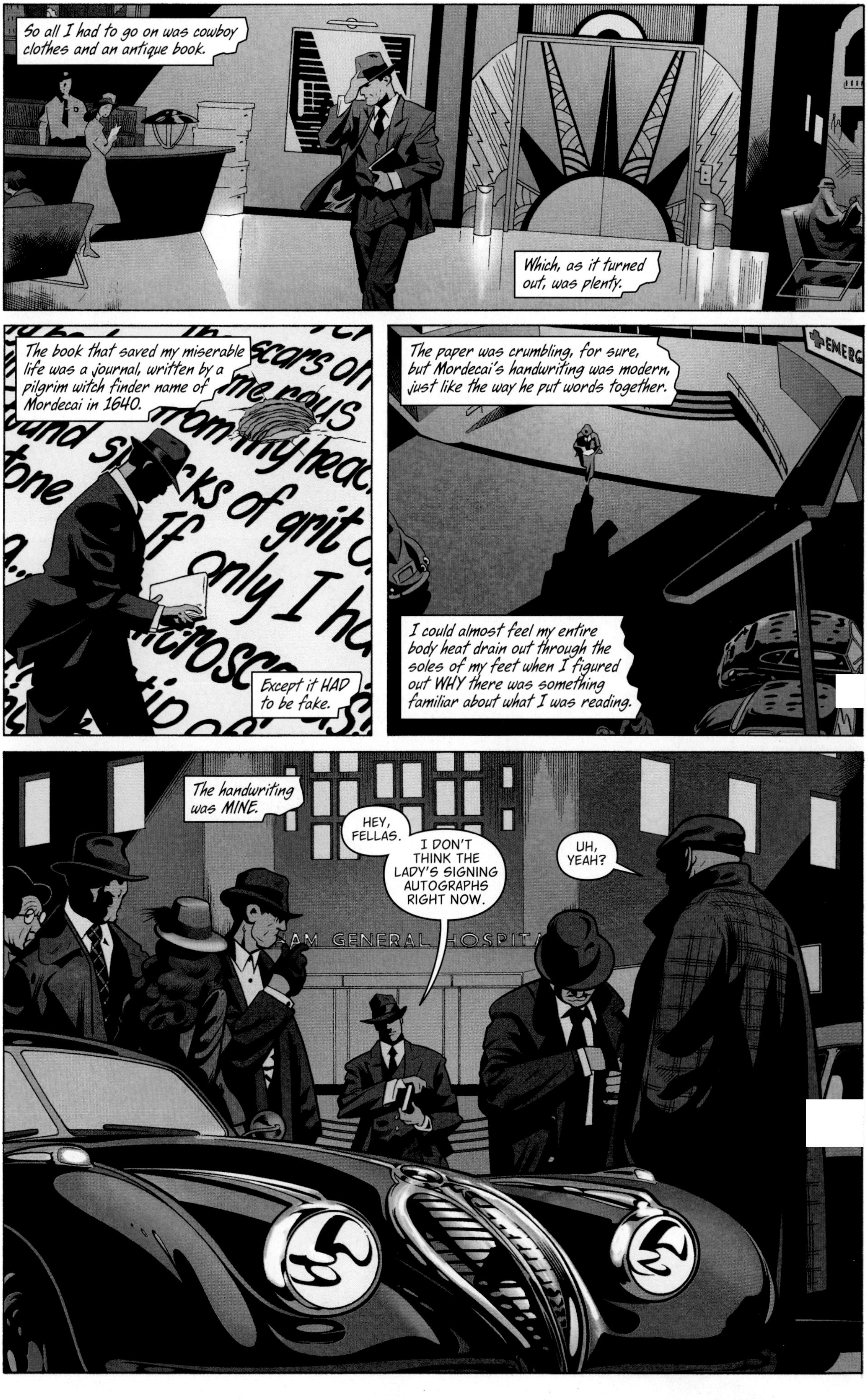
So all I had to go on was cowboy clothes and an antique book.
Which, as it turned out, was plenty.
The book that saved my miserable life was a journal, written by a pilgrim witch finder name of Mordecai in 1640.
Except it HAD to be fake.
The paper was crumbling, for sure, but Mordecai's handwriting was modern, just like the way he put words together.
I could almost feel my entire body heat drain out through the soles of my feet when I figured out WHY there was something familiar about what I was reading.
The handwriting was MINE.
HEY, FELLAS.
I DON'T THINK THE LADY'S SIGNING AUTOGRAPHS RIGHT NOW.
UH, YEAH?

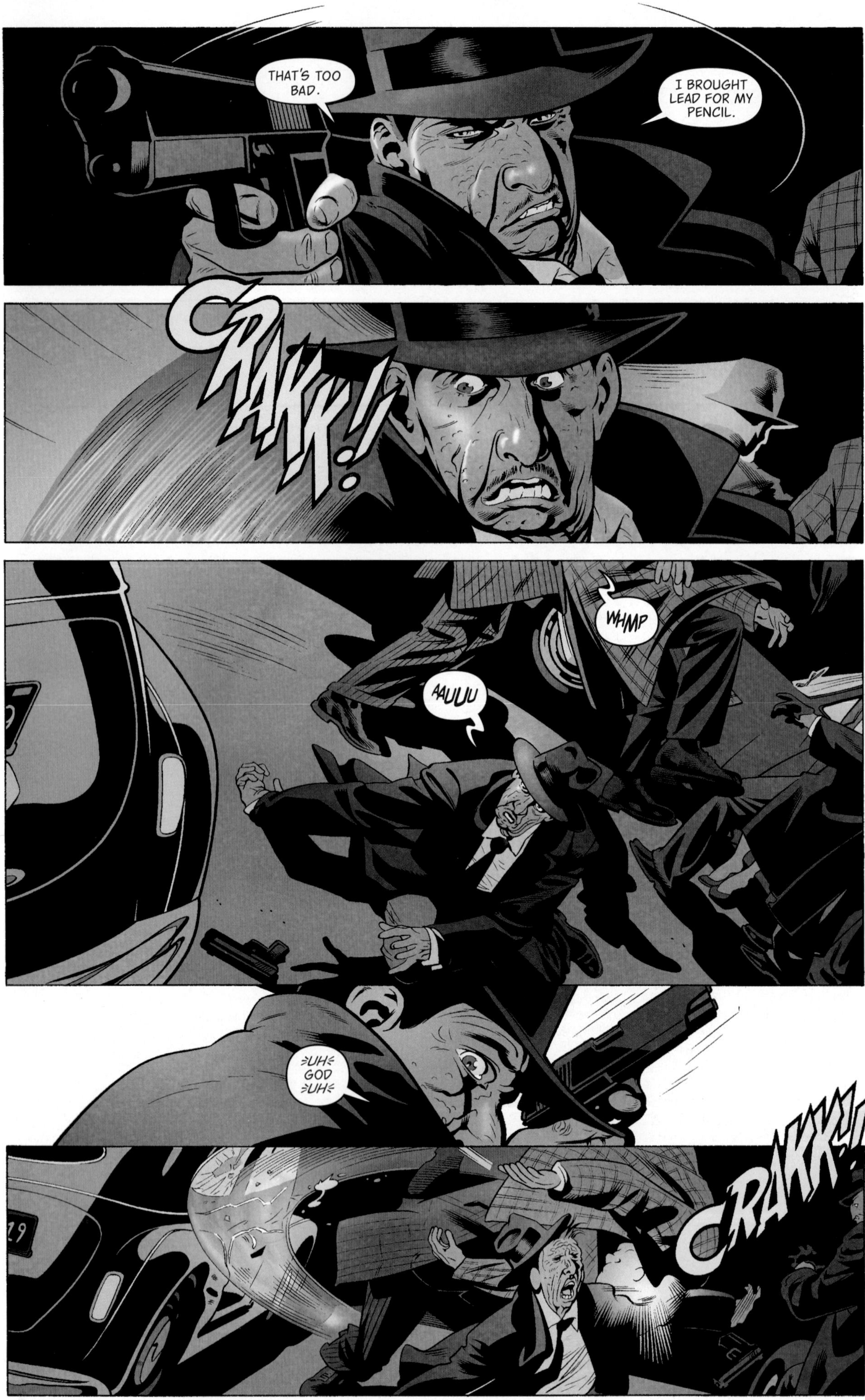
THAT'S TOO BAD.
I BROUGHT LEAD FOR MY PENCIL.
CRAKK!!
WHMP
AAUUU
UH GOD UH
CRAKK!!

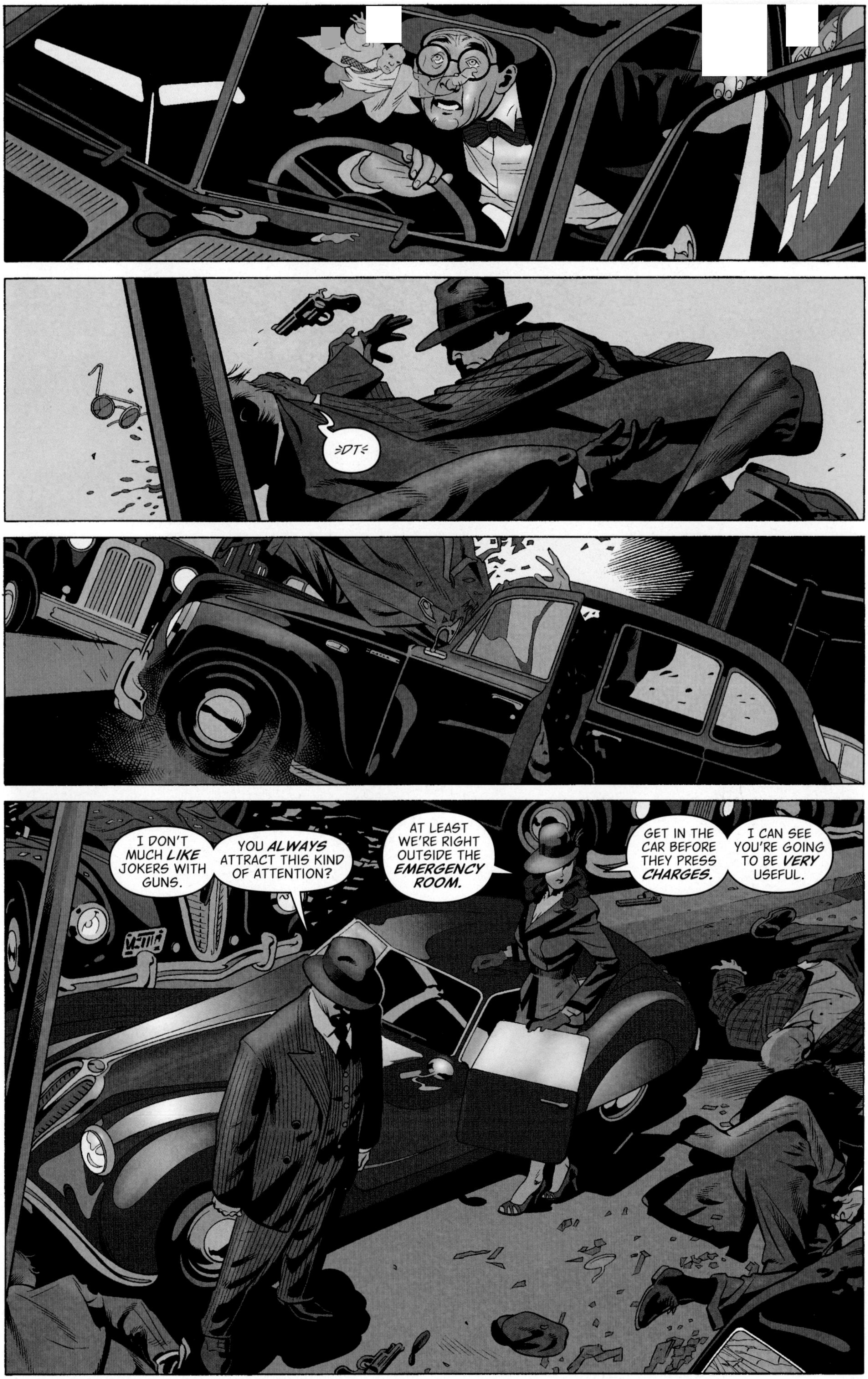
DT
I DON'T MUCH LIKE JOKERS WITH GUNS.
YOU ALWAYS ATTRACT THIS KIND OF ATTENTION?
AT LEAST WE'RE RIGHT OUTSIDE THE EMERGENCY ROOM.
GET IN THE CAR BEFORE THEY PRESS CHARGES.
I CAN SEE YOU'RE GOING TO BE VERY USEFUL.

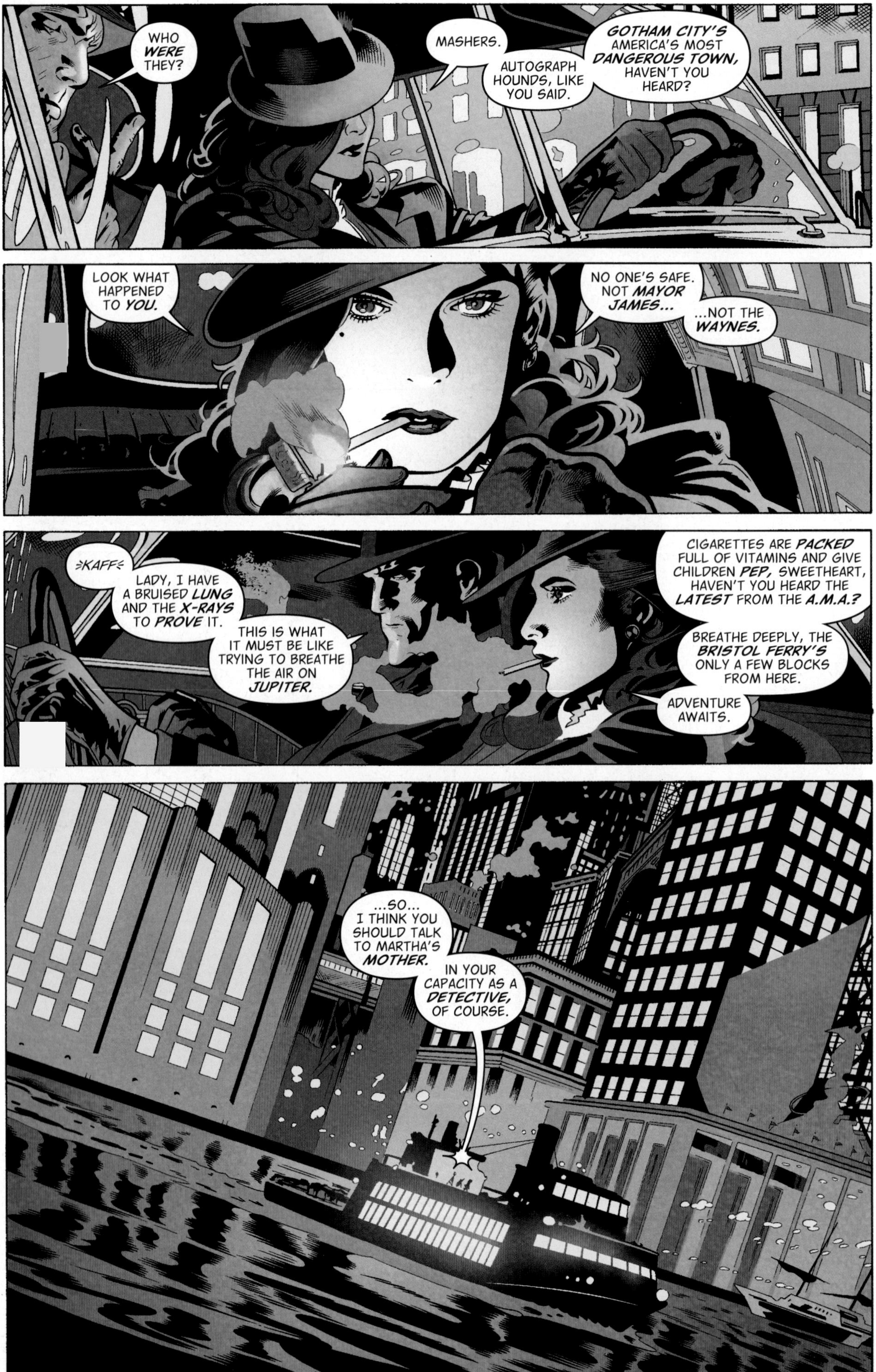
WHO WERE THEY?
MASHERS.
AUTOGRAPH HOUNDS, LIKE YOU SAID.
GOTHAM CITY'S AMERICA'S MOST DANGEROUS TOWN, HAVEN'T YOU HEARD?
LOOK WHAT HAPPENED TO YOU.
NO ONE'S SAFE. NOT MAYOR JAMES...
...NOT THE WAYNES.
KAFF
LADY, I HAVE A BRUISED LUNG AND THE X-RAYS TO PROVE IT.
THIS IS WHAT IT MUST BE LIKE TRYING TO BREATHE THE AIR ON JUPITER.
CIGARETTES ARE PACKED FULL OF VITAMINS AND GIVE CHILDREN PEP, SWEETHEART, HAVEN'T YOU HEARD THE LATEST FROM THE A.M.A.?
BREATHE DEEPLY, THE BRISTOL FERRY'S ONLY A FEW BLOCKS FROM HERE.
ADVENTURE AWAITS.
...SO... I THINK YOU SHOULD TALK TO MARTHA'S MOTHER.
IN YOUR CAPACITY AS A DETECTIVE, OF COURSE.

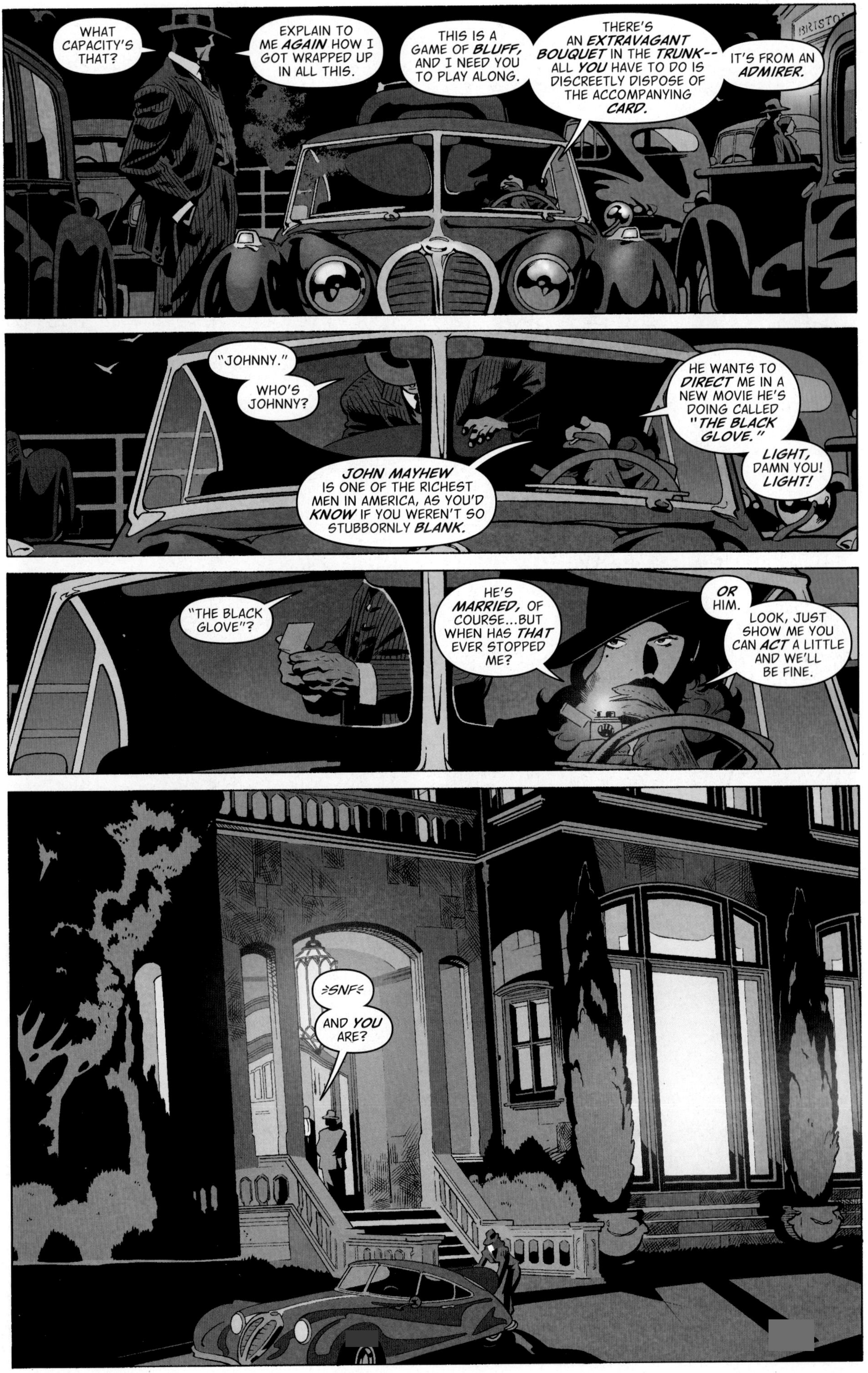
WHAT CAPACITY'S THAT?
EXPLAIN TO ME AGAIN HOW I GOT WRAPPED UP IN ALL THIS.
THIS IS A GAME OF BLUFF, AND I NEED YOU TO PLAY ALONG.
THERE'S AN EXTRAVAGANT BOUQUET IN THE TRUNK-- ALL YOU HAVE TO DO IS DISCREETLY DISPOSE OF THE ACCOMPANYING CARD.
IT'S FROM AN ADMIRER.
BRISTO
"JOHNNY."
WHO'S JOHNNY?
JOHN MAYHEW IS ONE OF THE RICHEST MEN IN AMERICA, AS YOU'D KNOW IF YOU WEREN'T SO STUBBORNLY BLANK.
HE WANTS TO DIRECT ME IN A NEW MOVIE HE'S DOING CALLED "THE BLACK GLOVE."
LIGHT, DAMN YOU! LIGHT!
"THE BLACK GLOVE"?
HE'S MARRIED, OF COURSE...BUT WHEN HAS THAT EVER STOPPED ME?
OR HIM.
LOOK, JUST SHOW ME YOU CAN ACT A LITTLE AND WE'LL BE FINE.
≈SNF≈
AND YOU ARE?

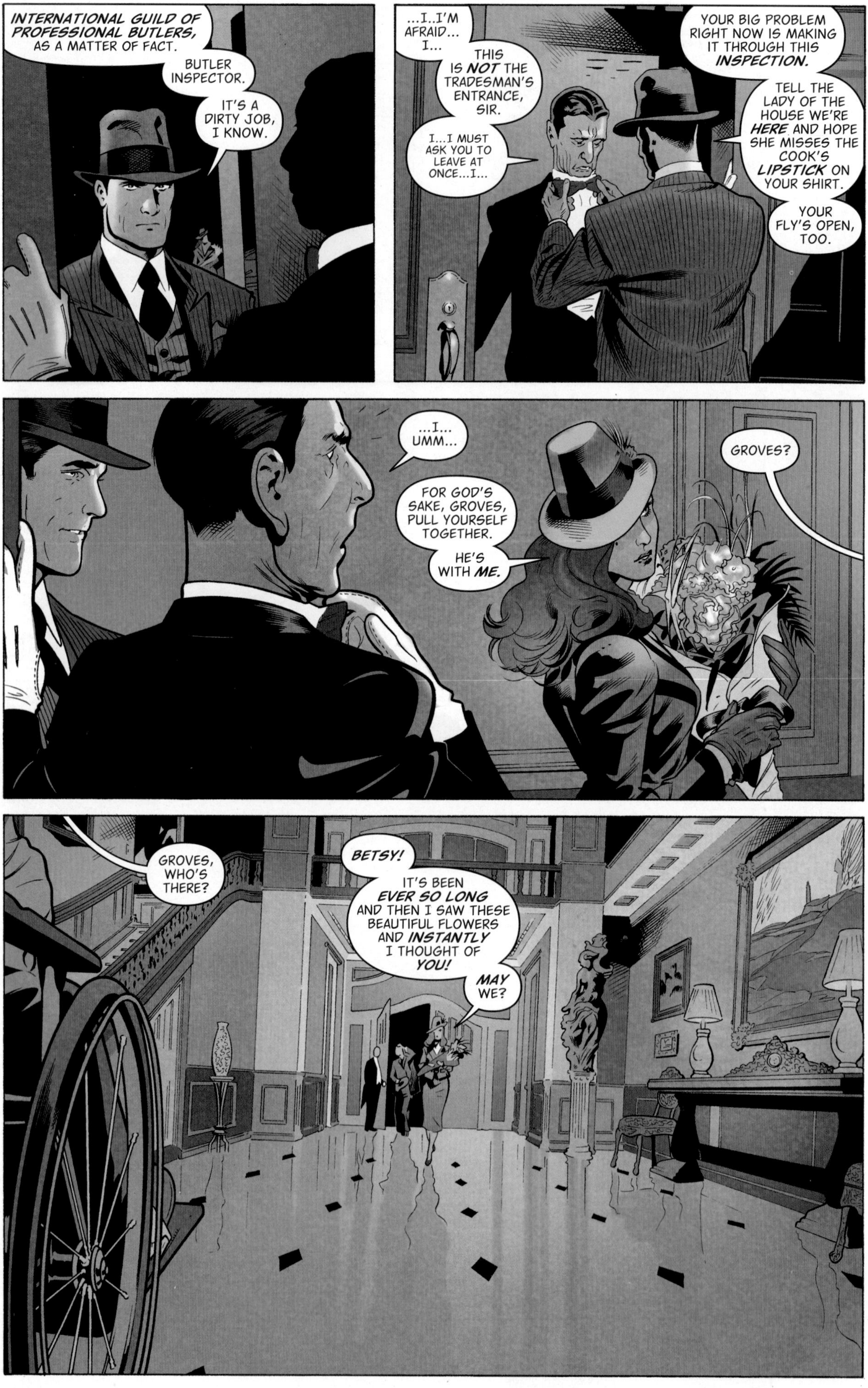
INTERNATIONAL GUILD OF PROFESSIONAL BUTLERS, AS A MATTER OF FACT.
BUTLER INSPECTOR.
IT'S A DIRTY JOB, I KNOW.
...I..I'M AFRAID... I...
THIS IS NOT THE TRADESMAN'S ENTRANCE, SIR.
I...I MUST ASK YOU TO LEAVE AT ONCE...I...
YOUR BIG PROBLEM RIGHT NOW IS MAKING IT THROUGH THIS INSPECTION.
TELL THE LADY OF THE HOUSE WE'RE HERE AND HOPE SHE MISSES THE COOK'S LIPSTICK ON YOUR SHIRT.
YOUR FLY'S OPEN, TOO.
...I... UMM...
FOR GOD'S SAKE, GROVES, PULL YOURSELF TOGETHER.
HE'S WITH ME.
GROVES?
GROVES, WHO'S THERE?
BETSY!
IT'S BEEN EVER SO LONG AND THEN I SAW THESE BEAUTIFUL FLOWERS AND INSTANTLY I THOUGHT OF YOU!
MAY WE?

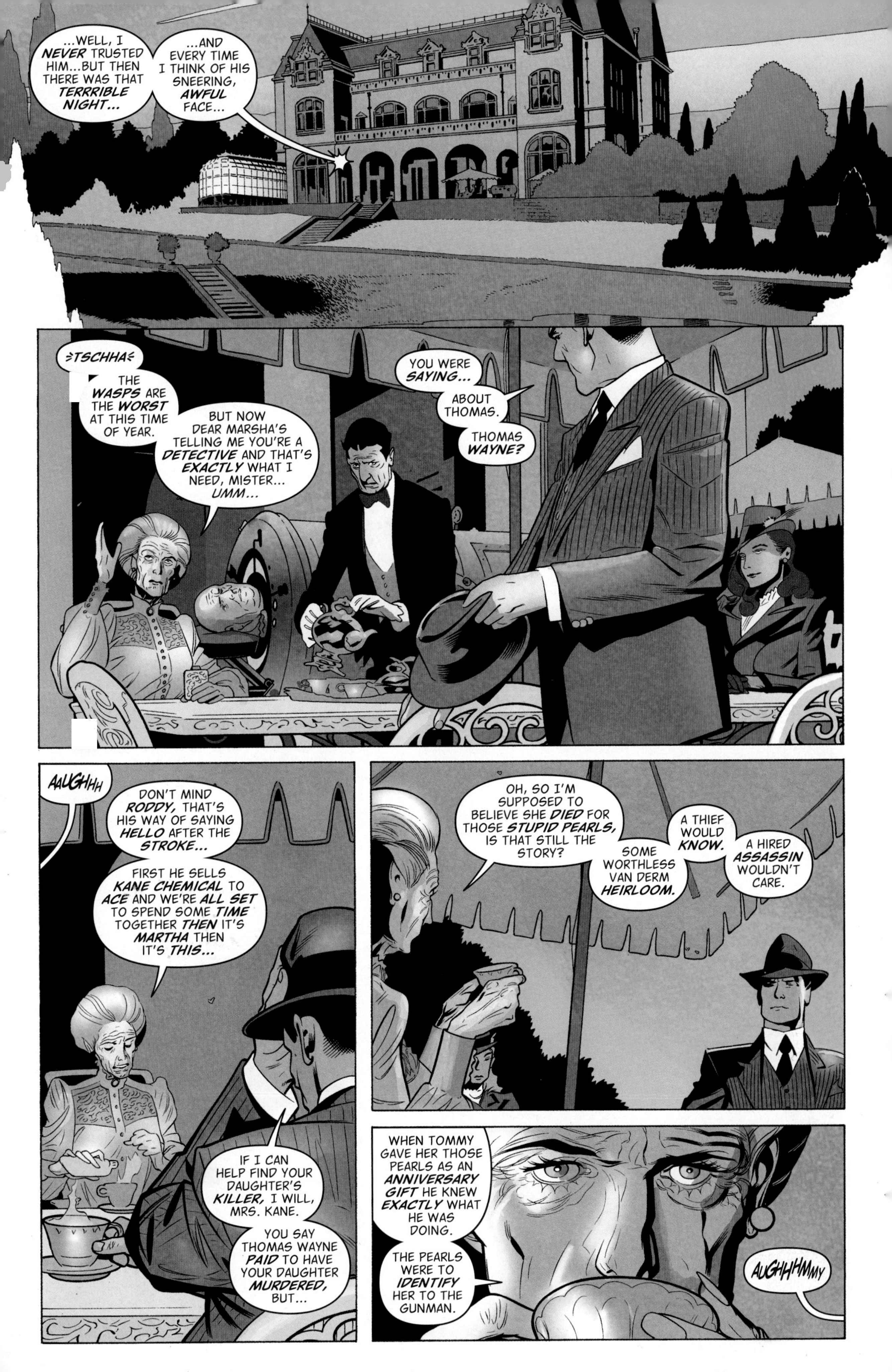
...WELL, I NEVER TRUSTED HIM...BUT THEN THERE WAS THAT TERRRIBLE NIGHT...
...AND EVERY TIME I THINK OF HIS SNEERING, AWFUL FACE...
TSCHHA
THE WASPS ARE THE WORST AT THIS TIME OF YEAR.
BUT NOW DEAR MARSHA'S TELLING ME YOU'RE A DETECTIVE AND THAT'S EXACTLY WHAT I NEED, MISTER... UMM...
YOU WERE SAYING...
ABOUT THOMAS.
THOMAS WAYNE?
AAUGHHH
DON'T MIND RODDY, THAT'S HIS WAY OF SAYING HELLO AFTER THE STROKE...
FIRST HE SELLS KANE CHEMICAL TO ACE AND WE'RE ALL SET TO SPEND SOME TIME TOGETHER THEN IT'S MARTHA THEN IT'S THIS...
IF I CAN HELP FIND YOUR DAUGHTER'S KILLER, I WILL, MRS. KANE.
YOU SAY THOMAS WAYNE PAID TO HAVE YOUR DAUGHTER MURDERED, BUT...
OH, SO I'M SUPPOSED TO BELIEVE SHE DIED FOR THOSE STUPID PEARLS, IS THAT STILL THE STORY?
SOME WORTHLESS VAN DERM HEIRLOOM.
A THIEF WOULD KNOW.
A HIRED ASSASSIN WOULDN'T CARE.
WHEN TOMMY GAVE HER THOSE PEARLS AS AN ANNIVERSARY GIFT HE KNEW EXACTLY WHAT HE WAS DOING.
THE PEARLS WERE TO IDENTIFY HER TO THE GUNMAN.
AUGHHHMMY

RODDY, *PLEASE!*

YOUR HACKING AND CHOKING AND ROARING IS ADDING *NOTHING* TO THE CONVERSATION.

CHAUCHH

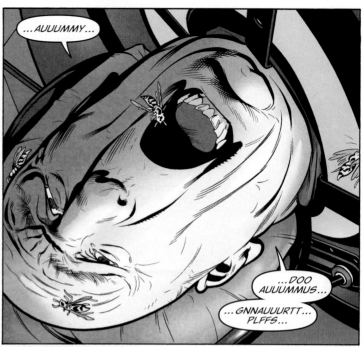

...AUUUMMY...

...DOO AUUUMMUS...

...GNNAUUURTT... PLFFS...

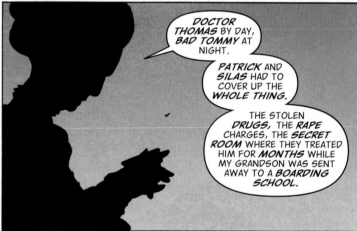

DOCTOR *THOMAS* BY DAY, *BAD TOMMY* AT NIGHT.

PATRICK AND *SILAS* HAD TO COVER UP THE *WHOLE THING.*

THE STOLEN *DRUGS,* THE *RAPE* CHARGES, THE *SECRET ROOM* WHERE THEY TREATED HIM FOR *MONTHS* WHILE MY GRANDSON WAS SENT AWAY TO A *BOARDING SCHOOL.*

HE *KILLED* MY DAUGHTER, OF THAT I HAVE NO DOUBT.

THEN HE *STOOD* THERE AND *ADMITTED* HE'D TURNED HER INTO A *DRUG ADDICT* AND... AND *WORSE...*

MAAUTHH

THOMAS WAYNE *TOLD* YOU THIS?

AFTER HIS ALLEGED DEATH?

SO WHO WAS WITH YOUR DAUGHTER OUTSIDE THE THEATER ON *PARK ROW* WHEN SHE WAS MURDERED?

WHOEVER *THAT* MAN WAS, IT WASN'T *TOM WAYNE!*

THOMAS WAYNE IS *ALIVE!*

LAUGHING AT ALL OF US!

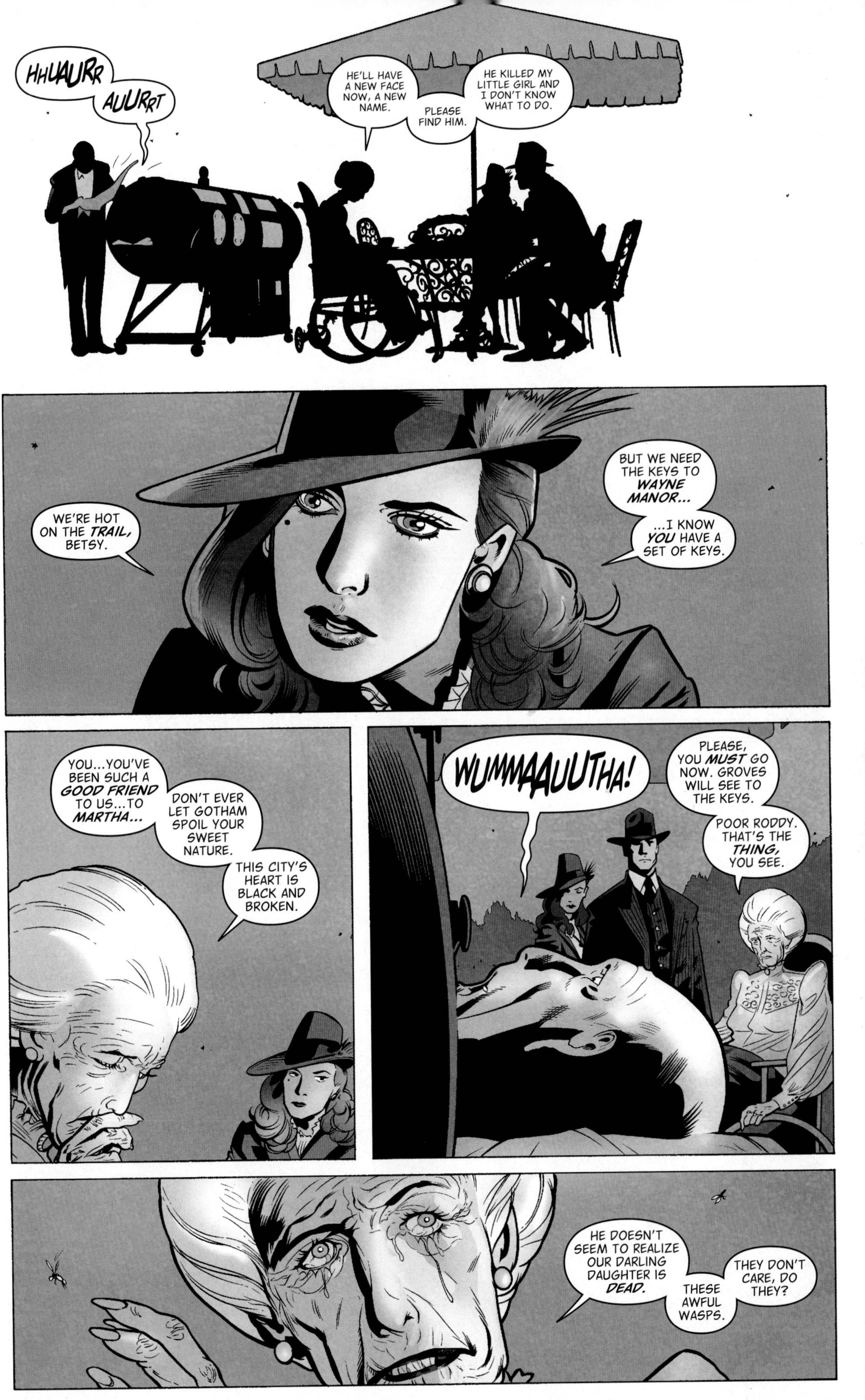

HHUAURR
AUURRT
HE'LL HAVE A NEW FACE NOW, A NEW NAME.
PLEASE FIND HIM.
HE KILLED MY LITTLE GIRL AND I DON'T KNOW WHAT TO DO.
WE'RE HOT ON THE TRAIL, BETSY.
BUT WE NEED THE KEYS TO WAYNE MANOR...
...I KNOW YOU HAVE A SET OF KEYS.
YOU...YOU'VE BEEN SUCH A GOOD FRIEND TO US...TO MARTHA...
DON'T EVER LET GOTHAM SPOIL YOUR SWEET NATURE.
THIS CITY'S HEART IS BLACK AND BROKEN.
WUMMAAUUTHA!
PLEASE, YOU MUST GO NOW. GROVES WILL SEE TO THE KEYS.
POOR RODDY. THAT'S THE THING, YOU SEE.
HE DOESN'T SEEM TO REALIZE OUR DARLING DAUGHTER IS DEAD.
THESE AWFUL WASPS.
THEY DON'T CARE, DO THEY?

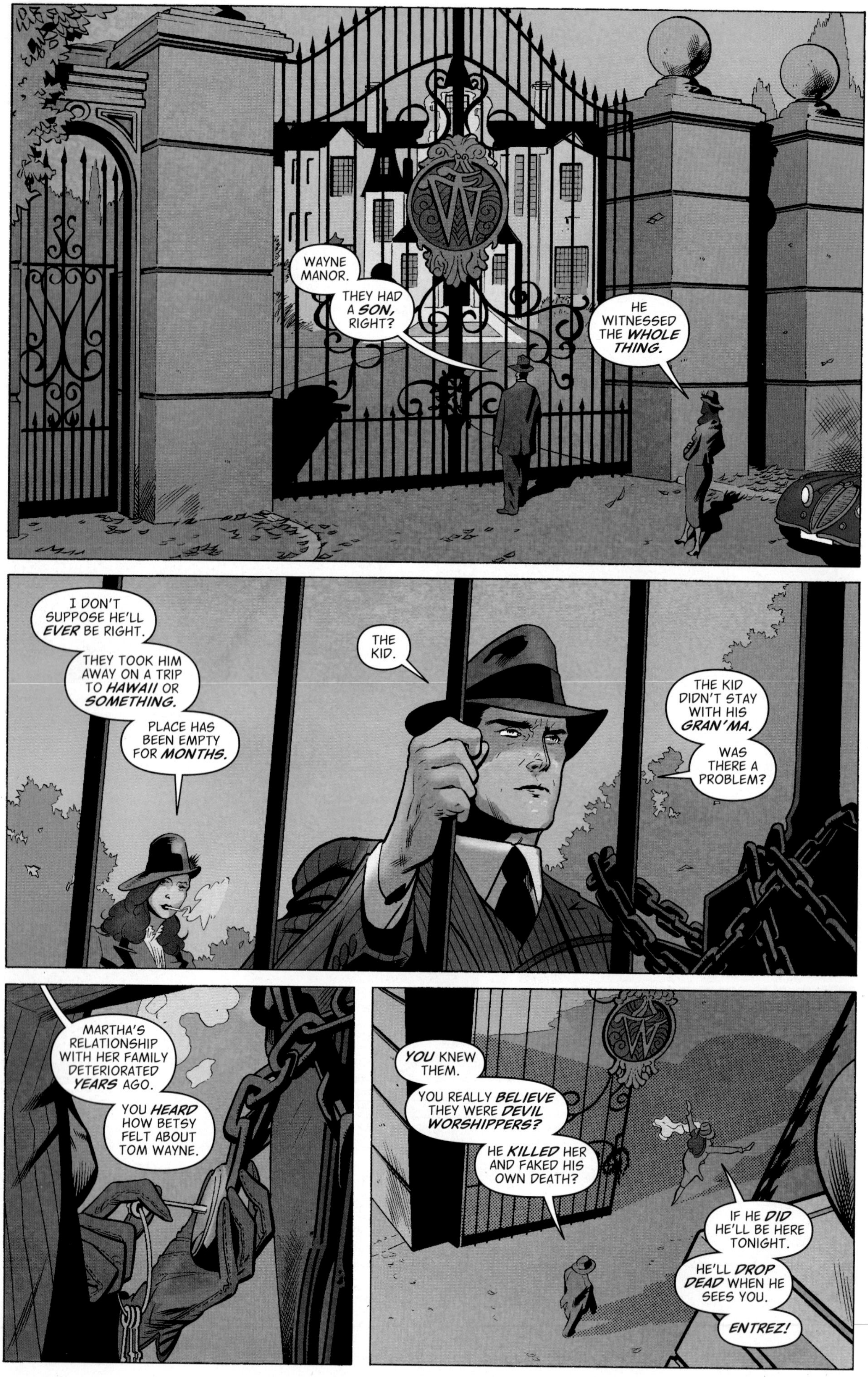
WAYNE MANOR.
THEY HAD A SON, RIGHT?
HE WITNESSED THE WHOLE THING.
I DON'T SUPPOSE HE'LL EVER BE RIGHT.
THEY TOOK HIM AWAY ON A TRIP TO HAWAII OR SOMETHING.
PLACE HAS BEEN EMPTY FOR MONTHS.
THE KID.
THE KID DIDN'T STAY WITH HIS GRAN'MA.
WAS THERE A PROBLEM?
MARTHA'S RELATIONSHIP WITH HER FAMILY DETERIORATED YEARS AGO.
YOU HEARD HOW BETSY FELT ABOUT TOM WAYNE.
YOU KNEW THEM.
YOU REALLY BELIEVE THEY WERE DEVIL WORSHIPPERS?
HE KILLED HER AND FAKED HIS OWN DEATH?
IF HE DID HE'LL BE HERE TONIGHT.
HE'LL DROP DEAD WHEN HE SEES YOU.
ENTREZ!

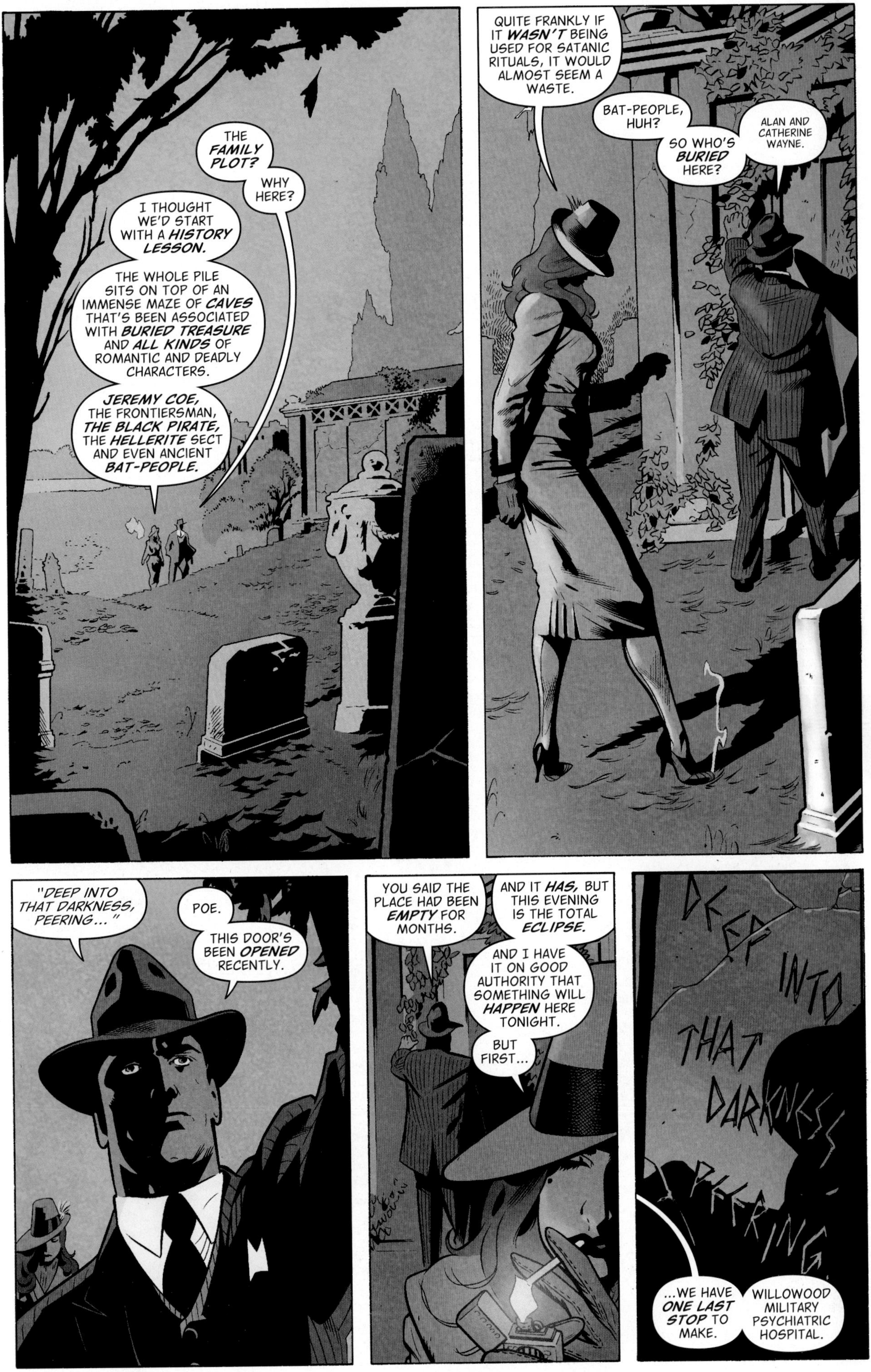

THE FAMILY PLOT?
WHY HERE?
I THOUGHT WE'D START WITH A HISTORY LESSON.
THE WHOLE PILE SITS ON TOP OF AN IMMENSE MAZE OF CAVES THAT'S BEEN ASSOCIATED WITH BURIED TREASURE AND ALL KINDS OF ROMANTIC AND DEADLY CHARACTERS.
JEREMY COE, THE FRONTIERSMAN, THE BLACK PIRATE, THE HELLERITE SECT AND EVEN ANCIENT BAT-PEOPLE.
QUITE FRANKLY IF IT WASN'T BEING USED FOR SATANIC RITUALS, IT WOULD ALMOST SEEM A WASTE.
BAT-PEOPLE, HUH?
SO WHO'S BURIED HERE?
ALAN AND CATHERINE WAYNE.
"DEEP INTO THAT DARKNESS, PEERING..."
POE.
THIS DOOR'S BEEN OPENED RECENTLY.
YOU SAID THE PLACE HAD BEEN EMPTY FOR MONTHS.
AND IT HAS, BUT THIS EVENING IS THE TOTAL ECLIPSE.
AND I HAVE IT ON GOOD AUTHORITY THAT SOMETHING WILL HAPPEN HERE TONIGHT.
BUT FIRST...
DEEP INTO THAT DARKNESS PEERING.
...WE HAVE ONE LAST STOP TO MAKE.
WILLOWOOD MILITARY PSYCHIATRIC HOSPITAL.

...MY METHODS ARE ABOUT *HELPING* SERVICEMEN AND WOMEN TO *RELIVE* THOSE TRAUMATIC MOMENTS AND...AND...FIND *HEALING*...

...I CAME TO WILLOWOOD TO HELP PEOPLE.

THE *TIME HYPNOSIS* TECHNIQUE IS THE *LEAST* OF WHAT YOU HAVE TO OFFER YOUR COUNTRY, CARTER.

WHAT ABOUT YOUR PATENT APPLICATIONS FOR *PROBABILITY VIEWERS*, PORTABLE *TIME TRAVEL FIELD GENERATORS*?

YOU COULD BE THE *RICHEST MAN ON EARTH.*

YOU *KNOW* WHO I AM.

I'M OFFERING *YOU* THE SAME DEAL I OFFERED THE *OTHERS*.

AND I BET YOU *EVERYTHING* YOU CAN'T REFUSE.

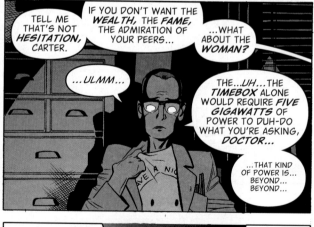

TELL ME THAT'S NOT *HESITATION*, CARTER.

IF YOU DON'T WANT THE *WEALTH,* THE *FAME,* THE ADMIRATION OF YOUR PEERS...

...WHAT ABOUT THE *WOMAN?*

...ULMM...

THE...UH...THE *TIMEBOX* ALONE WOULD REQUIRE *FIVE GIGAWATTS* OF POWER TO DUH-DO WHAT YOU'RE ASKING, *DOCTOR*...

...THAT KIND OF POWER IS... BEYOND... BEYOND...

THINK ABOUT WHAT HAPPENED WHEN *RODERICK KANE* CHOSE NOT TO PLAY.

BUT DON'T THINK *TOO* LONG.

YOUR *VISITOR* WON'T KEEP FOREVER.

BATMAN BEWARE

THE HOLE IN THINGS

EXCUSE ME?

HE...ER...YOU MUST HAVE MISHEARD...

...HE *CAN'T* ACTUALLY SPEAK...

...THE WAR.

CARTER, YOU *MUST* MEET MY NEW FRIEND.

HE'S HELPING ME UNRAVEL ALL *KINDS* OF MYSTERIES.

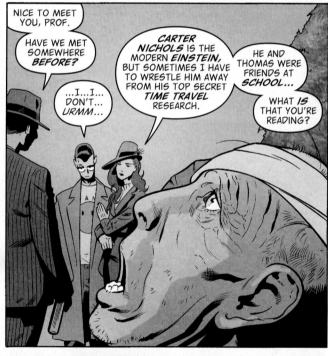

NICE TO MEET YOU, PROF.

HAVE WE MET SOMEWHERE *BEFORE?*

...I...I... DON'T... URMM...

CARTER NICHOLS IS THE MODERN *EINSTEIN,* BUT SOMETIMES I HAVE TO WRESTLE HIM AWAY FROM HIS TOP SECRET *TIME TRAVEL* RESEARCH.

HE AND THOMAS WERE FRIENDS AT *SCHOOL...*

WHAT *IS* THAT YOU'RE READING?

A STORY CLOSE TO MY *HEART,* YOU COULD SAY.

THE PLOT'S GOT A FEW *HOLES,* BUT I THINK IT'S STARTING TO MAKE SENSE.

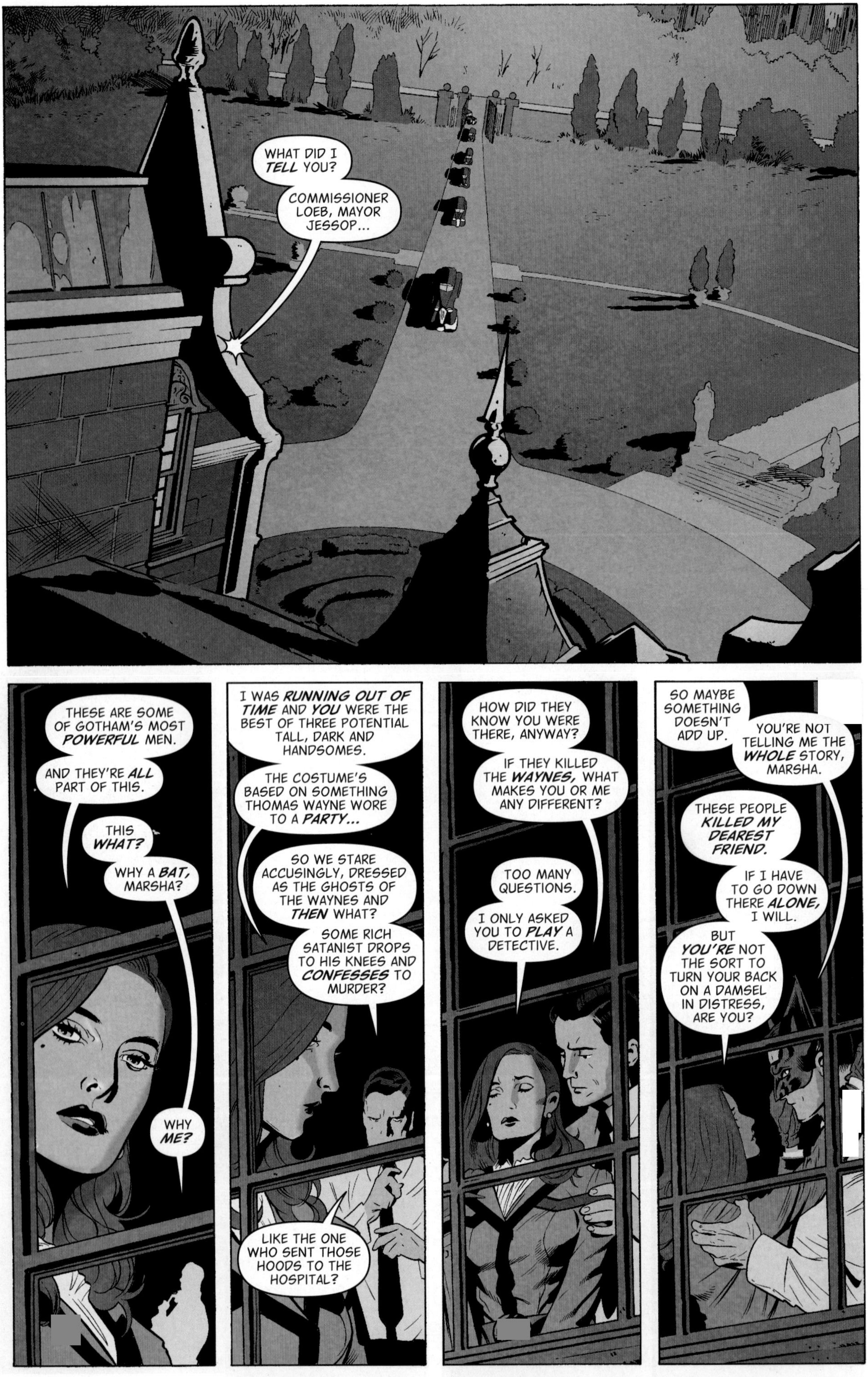

WHAT DID I TELL YOU?
COMMISSIONER LOEB, MAYOR JESSOP...
THESE ARE SOME OF GOTHAM'S MOST POWERFUL MEN.
AND THEY'RE ALL PART OF THIS.
THIS WHAT?
WHY A BAT, MARSHA?
WHY ME?
I WAS RUNNING OUT OF TIME AND YOU WERE THE BEST OF THREE POTENTIAL TALL, DARK AND HANDSOMES.
THE COSTUME'S BASED ON SOMETHING THOMAS WAYNE WORE TO A PARTY...
SO WE STARE ACCUSINGLY, DRESSED AS THE GHOSTS OF THE WAYNES AND THEN WHAT?
SOME RICH SATANIST DROPS TO HIS KNEES AND CONFESSES TO MURDER?
LIKE THE ONE WHO SENT THOSE HOODS TO THE HOSPITAL?
HOW DID THEY KNOW YOU WERE THERE, ANYWAY?
IF THEY KILLED THE WAYNES, WHAT MAKES YOU OR ME ANY DIFFERENT?
TOO MANY QUESTIONS.
I ONLY ASKED YOU TO PLAY A DETECTIVE.
SO MAYBE SOMETHING DOESN'T ADD UP.
YOU'RE NOT TELLING ME THE WHOLE STORY, MARSHA.
THESE PEOPLE KILLED MY DEAREST FRIEND.
IF I HAVE TO GO DOWN THERE ALONE, I WILL.
BUT YOU'RE NOT THE SORT TO TURN YOUR BACK ON A DAMSEL IN DISTRESS, ARE YOU?

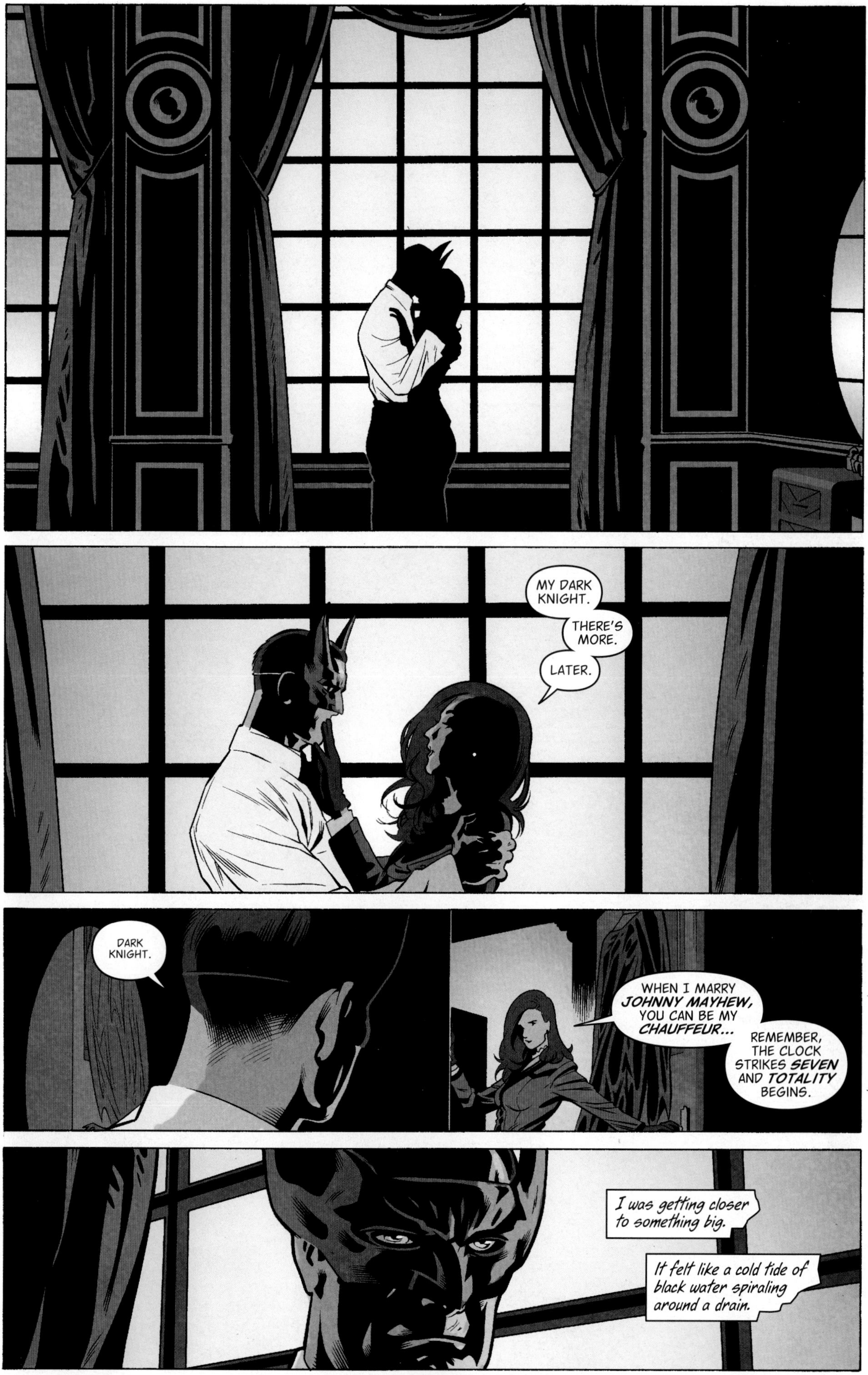
MY DARK KNIGHT.
THERE'S MORE.
LATER.
DARK KNIGHT.
WHEN I MARRY JOHNNY MAYHEW, YOU CAN BE MY CHAUFFEUR...
REMEMBER, THE CLOCK STRIKES SEVEN AND TOTALITY BEGINS.
I was getting closer to something big.
It felt like a cold tide of black water spiraling around a drain.

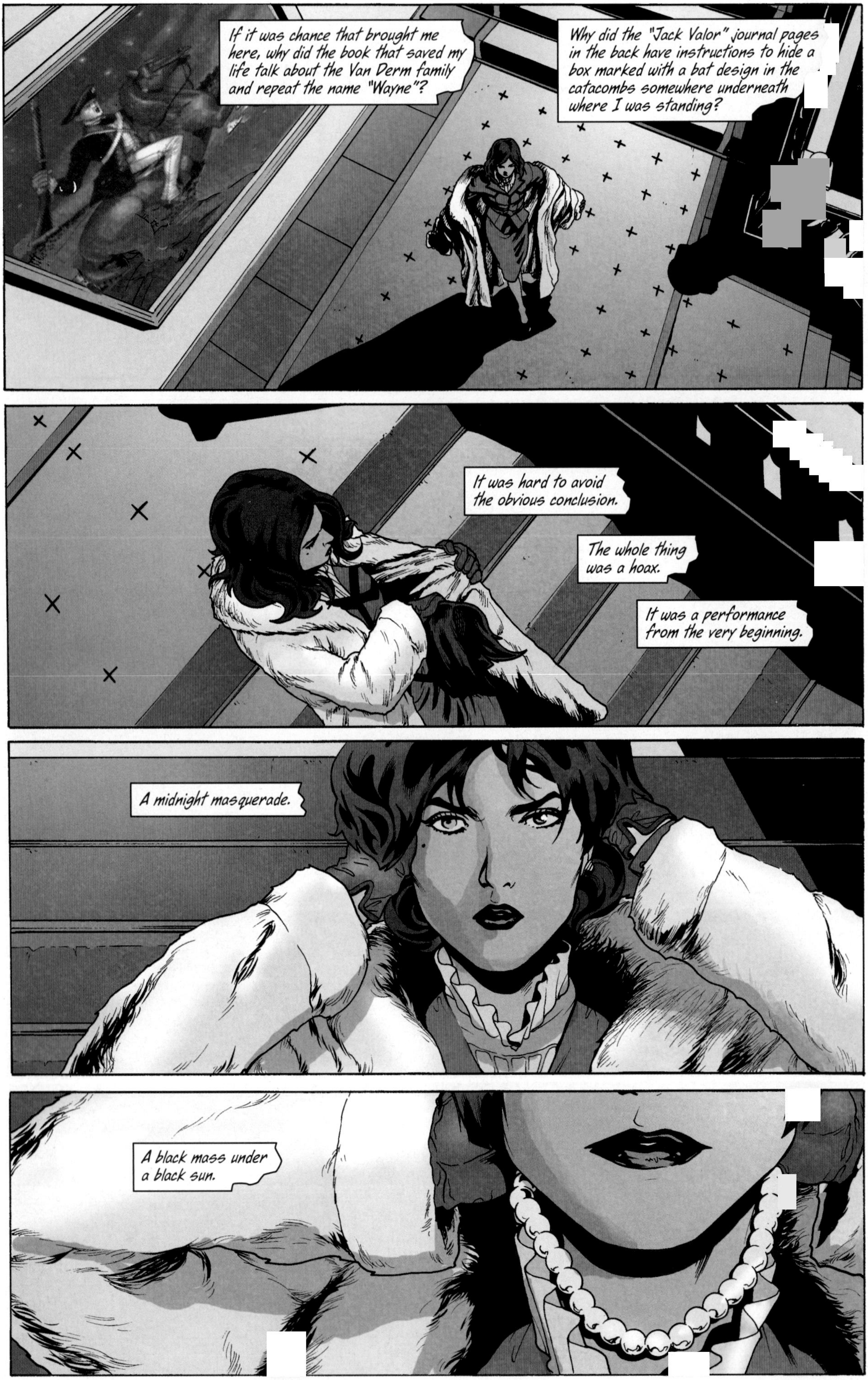
If it was chance that brought me here, why did the book that saved my life talk about the Van Derm family and repeat the name "Wayne"?
Why did the "Jack Valor" journal pages in the back have instructions to hide a box marked with a bat design in the catacombs somewhere underneath where I was standing?
It was hard to avoid the obvious conclusion.
The whole thing was a hoax.
It was a performance from the very beginning.
A midnight masquerade.
A black mass under a black sun.

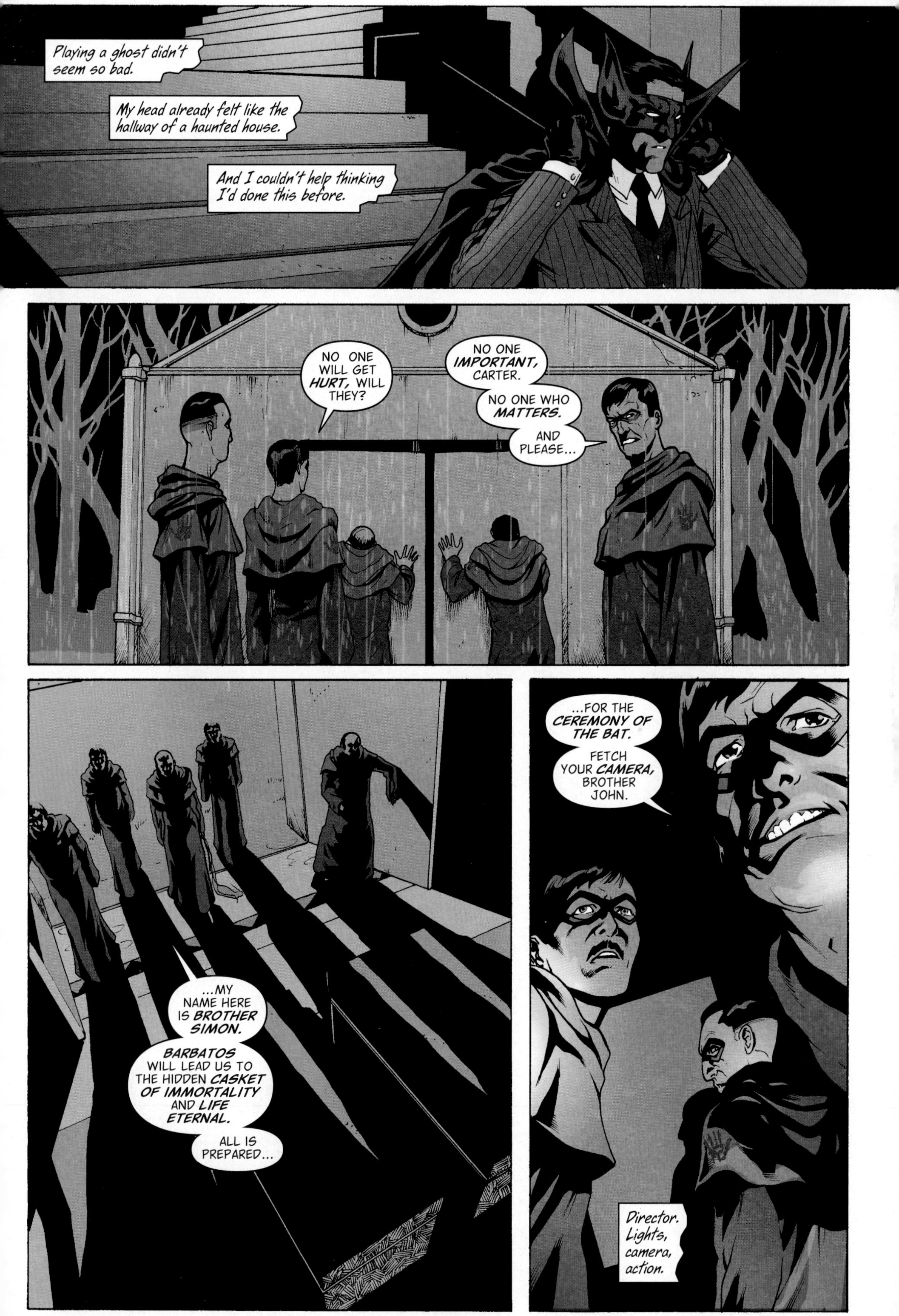
Playing a ghost didn't seem so bad.
My head already felt like the hallway of a haunted house.
And I couldn't help thinking I'd done this before.
NO ONE WILL GET HURT, WILL THEY?
NO ONE IMPORTANT, CARTER.
NO ONE WHO MATTERS.
AND PLEASE...
...MY NAME HERE IS BROTHER SIMON.
BARBATOS WILL LEAD US TO THE HIDDEN CASKET OF IMMORTALITY AND LIFE ETERNAL.
ALL IS PREPARED...
...FOR THE CEREMONY OF THE BAT.
FETCH YOUR CAMERA, BROTHER JOHN.
Director. Lights, camera, action.

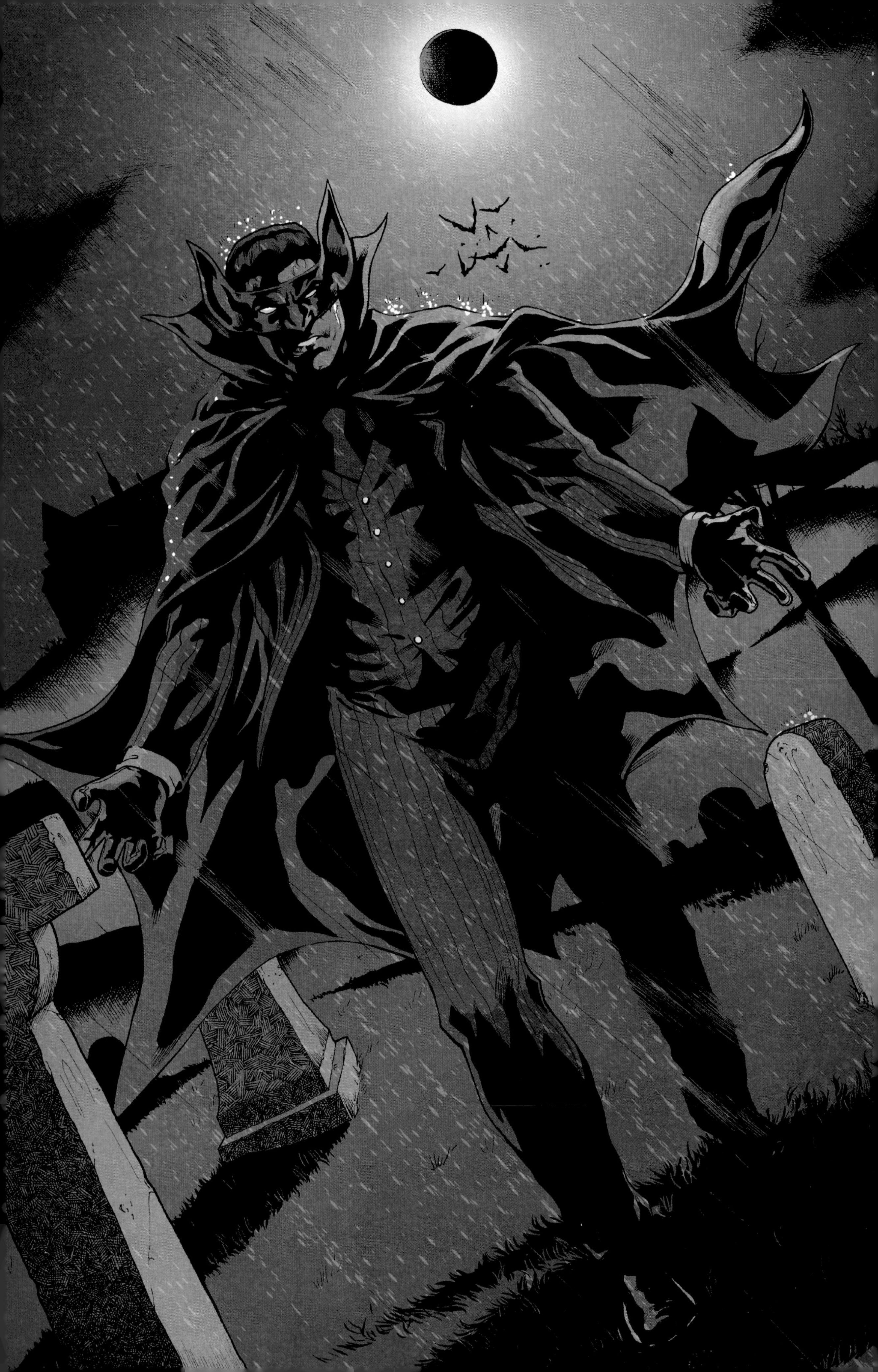

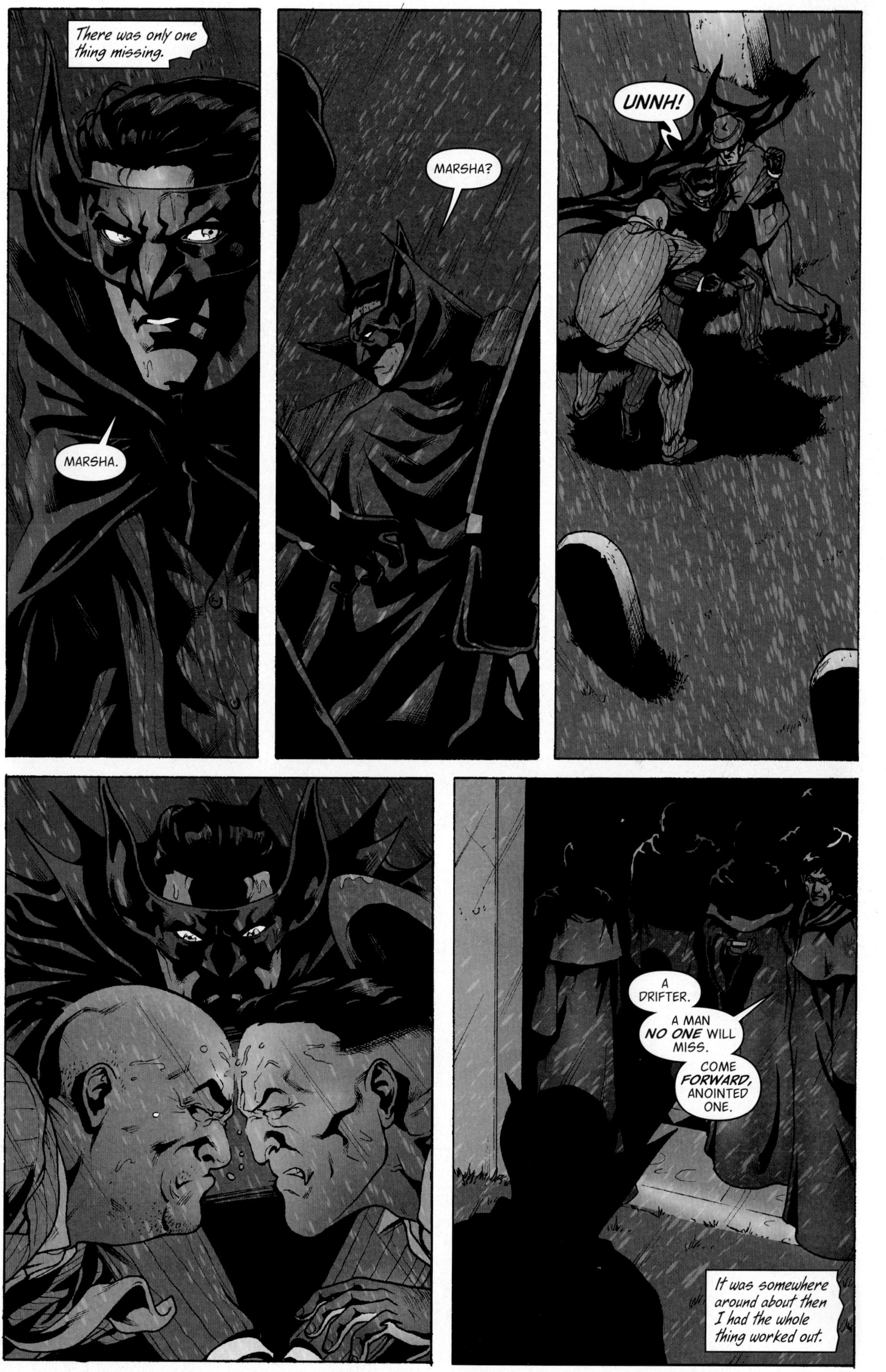
There was only one thing missing.
MARSHA.
MARSHA?
UNNH!
A DRIFTER.
A MAN NO ONE WILL MISS.
COME FORWARD, ANOINTED ONE.
It was somewhere around about then I had the whole thing worked out.

But that didn't make it hurt any less.

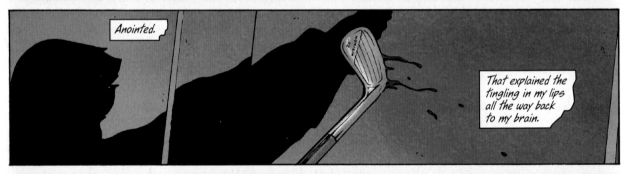

Anointed.

That explained the tingling in my lips all the way back to my brain.

A poison kiss.

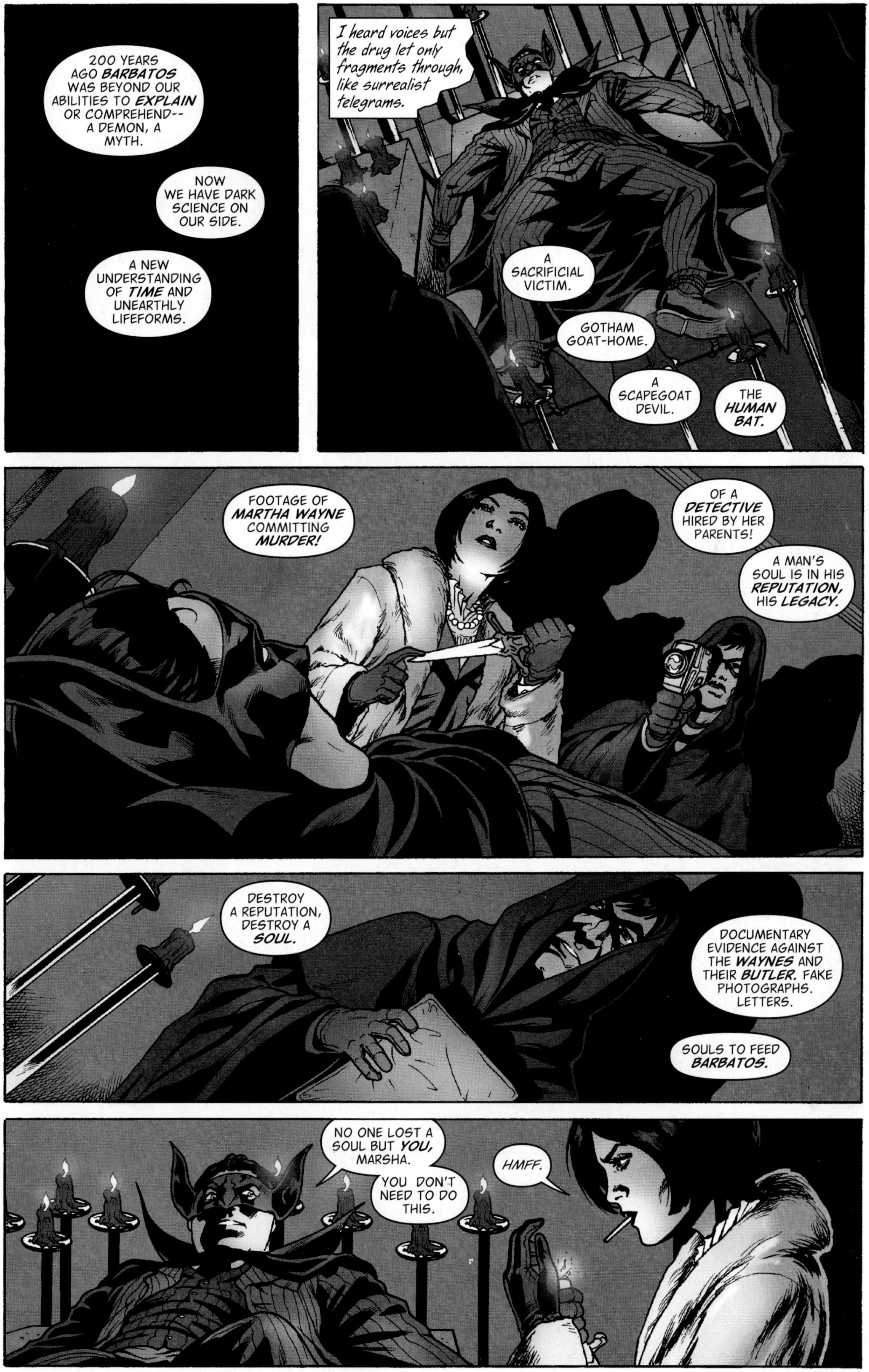
200 YEARS AGO BARBATOS WAS BEYOND OUR ABILITIES TO EXPLAIN OR COMPREHEND-- A DEMON, A MYTH.
NOW WE HAVE DARK SCIENCE ON OUR SIDE.
A NEW UNDERSTANDING OF TIME AND UNEARTHLY LIFEFORMS.
I heard voices but the drug let only fragments through, like surrealist telegrams.
A SACRIFICIAL VICTIM.
GOTHAM GOAT-HOME.
A SCAPEGOAT DEVIL.
THE HUMAN BAT.
FOOTAGE OF MARTHA WAYNE COMMITTING MURDER!
OF A DETECTIVE HIRED BY HER PARENTS!
A MAN'S SOUL IS IN HIS REPUTATION, HIS LEGACY.
DESTROY A REPUTATION, DESTROY A SOUL.
DOCUMENTARY EVIDENCE AGAINST THE WAYNES AND THEIR BUTLER. FAKE PHOTOGRAPHS. LETTERS.
SOULS TO FEED BARBATOS.
NO ONE LOST A SOUL BUT YOU, MARSHA.
YOU DON'T NEED TO DO THIS.
HMFF.

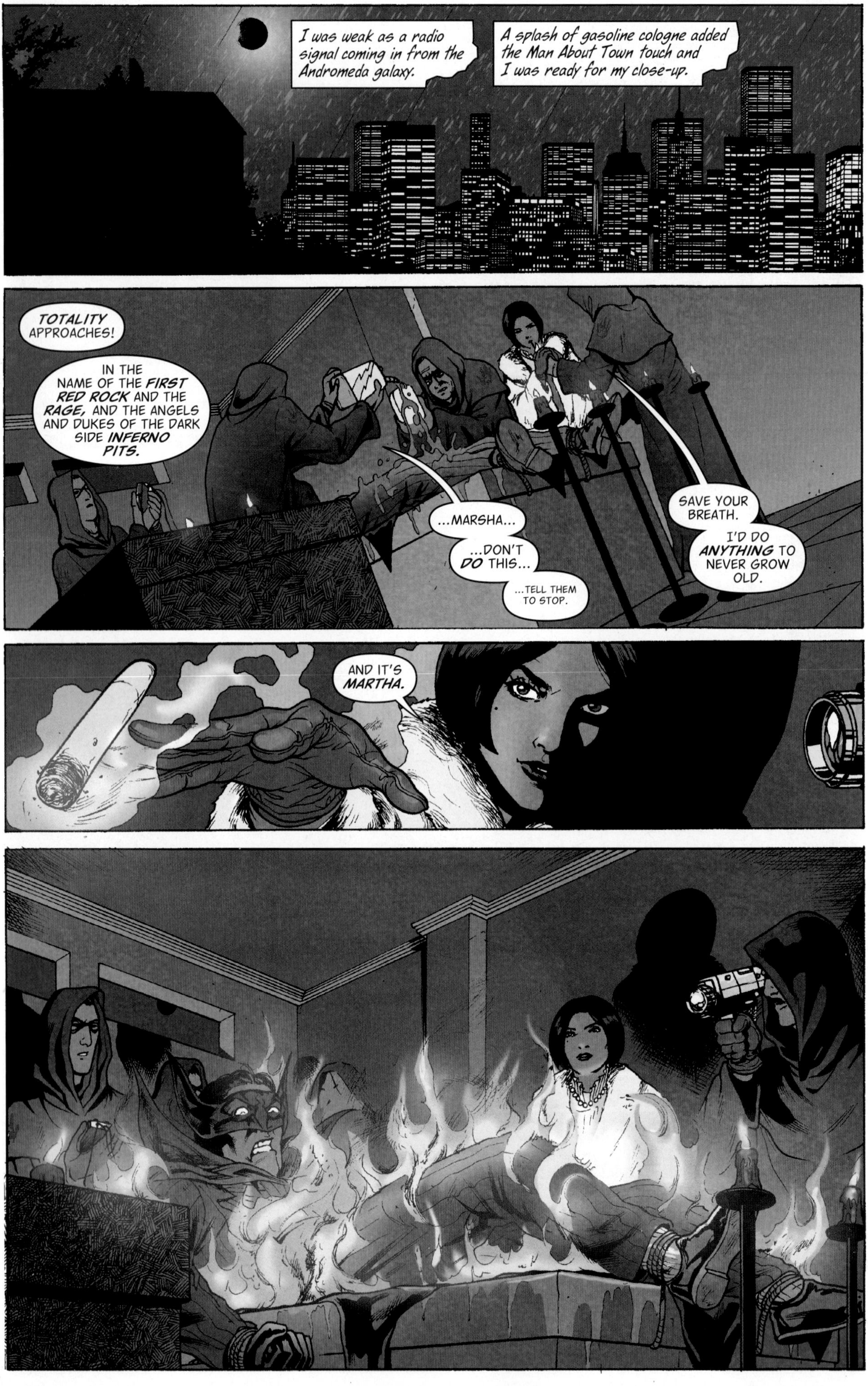

I was weak as a radio signal coming in from the Andromeda galaxy.
A splash of gasoline cologne added the Man About Town touch and I was ready for my close-up.
TOTALITY APPROACHES!
IN THE NAME OF THE FIRST RED ROCK AND THE RAGE, AND THE ANGELS AND DUKES OF THE DARK SIDE INFERNO PITS.
...MARSHA...
...DON'T DO THIS...
...TELL THEM TO STOP.
SAVE YOUR BREATH.
I'D DO ANYTHING TO NEVER GROW OLD.
AND IT'S MARTHA.

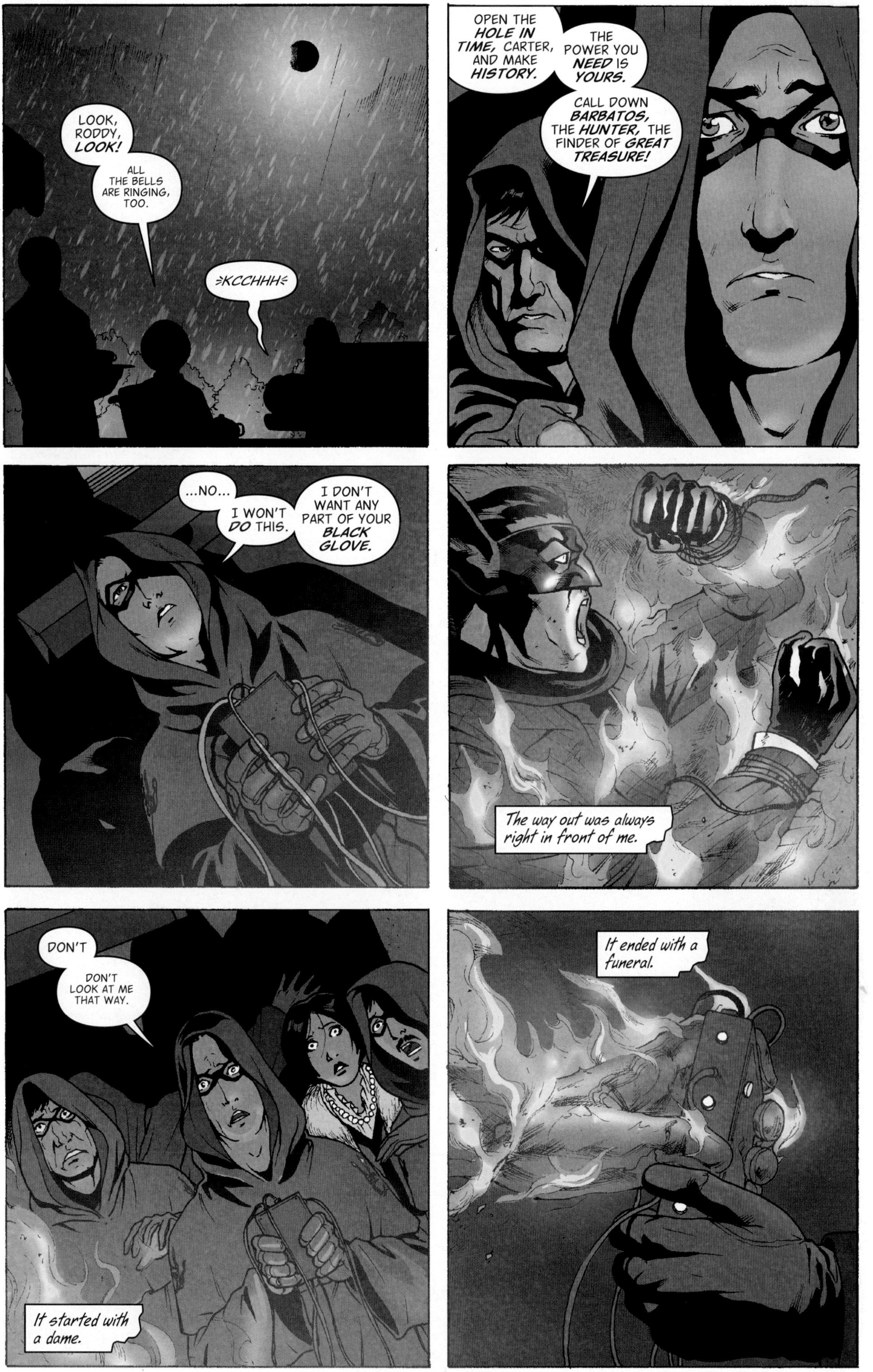
LOOK, RODDY, LOOK!
ALL THE BELLS ARE RINGING, TOO.
KCCHHH
OPEN THE HOLE IN TIME, CARTER, AND MAKE HISTORY.
THE POWER YOU NEED IS YOURS.
CALL DOWN BARBATOS, THE HUNTER, THE FINDER OF GREAT TREASURE!
...NO...
I WON'T DO THIS.
I DON'T WANT ANY PART OF YOUR BLACK GLOVE.
The way out was always right in front of me.
DON'T
DON'T LOOK AT ME THAT WAY.
It started with a dame.
It ended with a funeral.

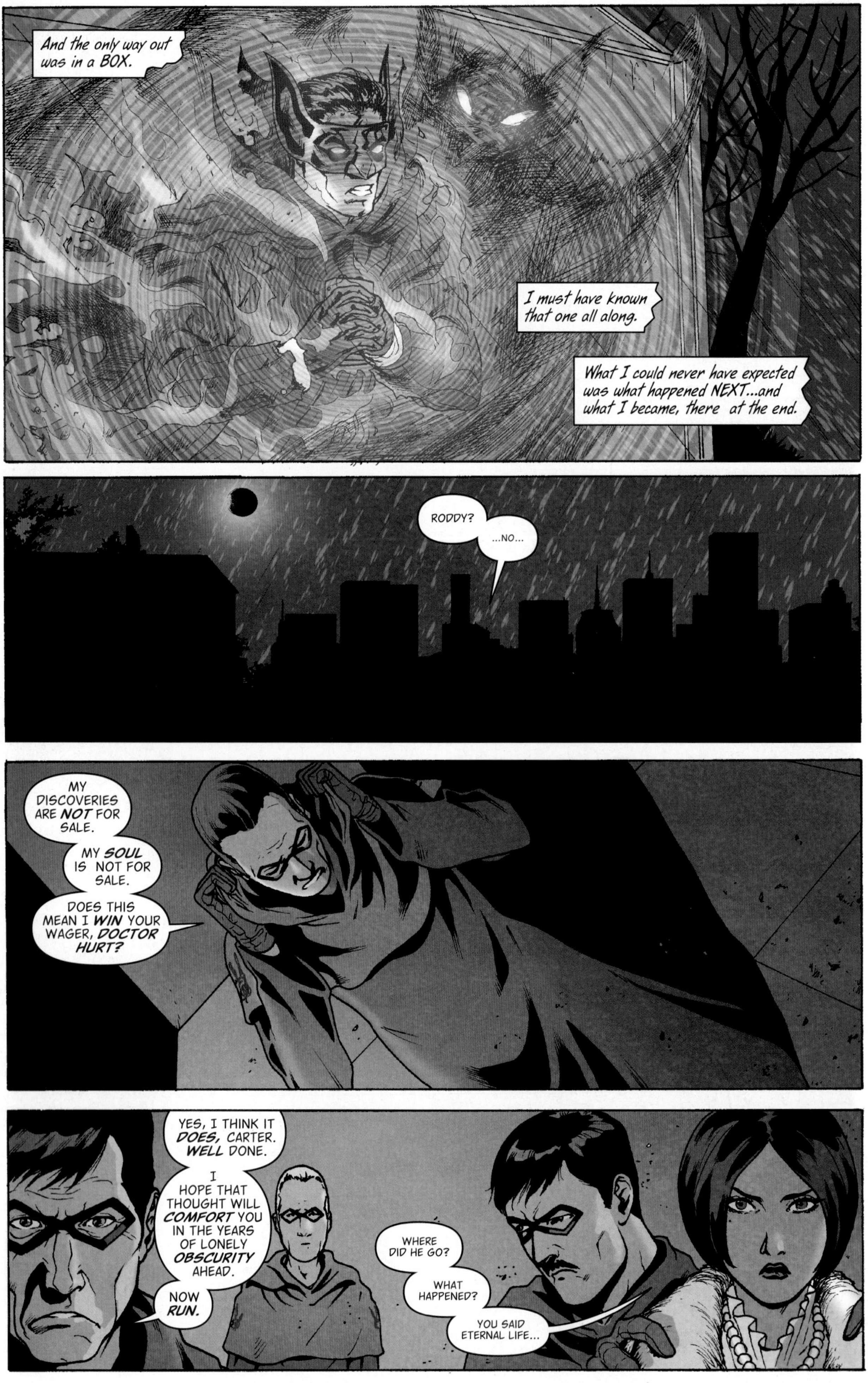
And the only way out was in a BOX.
I must have known that one all along.
What I could never have expected was what happened NEXT...and what I became, there at the end.
RODDY?
...NO...
MY DISCOVERIES ARE NOT FOR SALE.
MY SOUL IS NOT FOR SALE.
DOES THIS MEAN I WIN YOUR WAGER, DOCTOR HURT?
YES, I THINK IT DOES, CARTER. WELL DONE.
I HOPE THAT THOUGHT WILL COMFORT YOU IN THE YEARS OF LONELY OBSCURITY AHEAD.
NOW RUN.
WHERE DID HE GO?
WHAT HAPPENED?
YOU SAID ETERNAL LIFE...

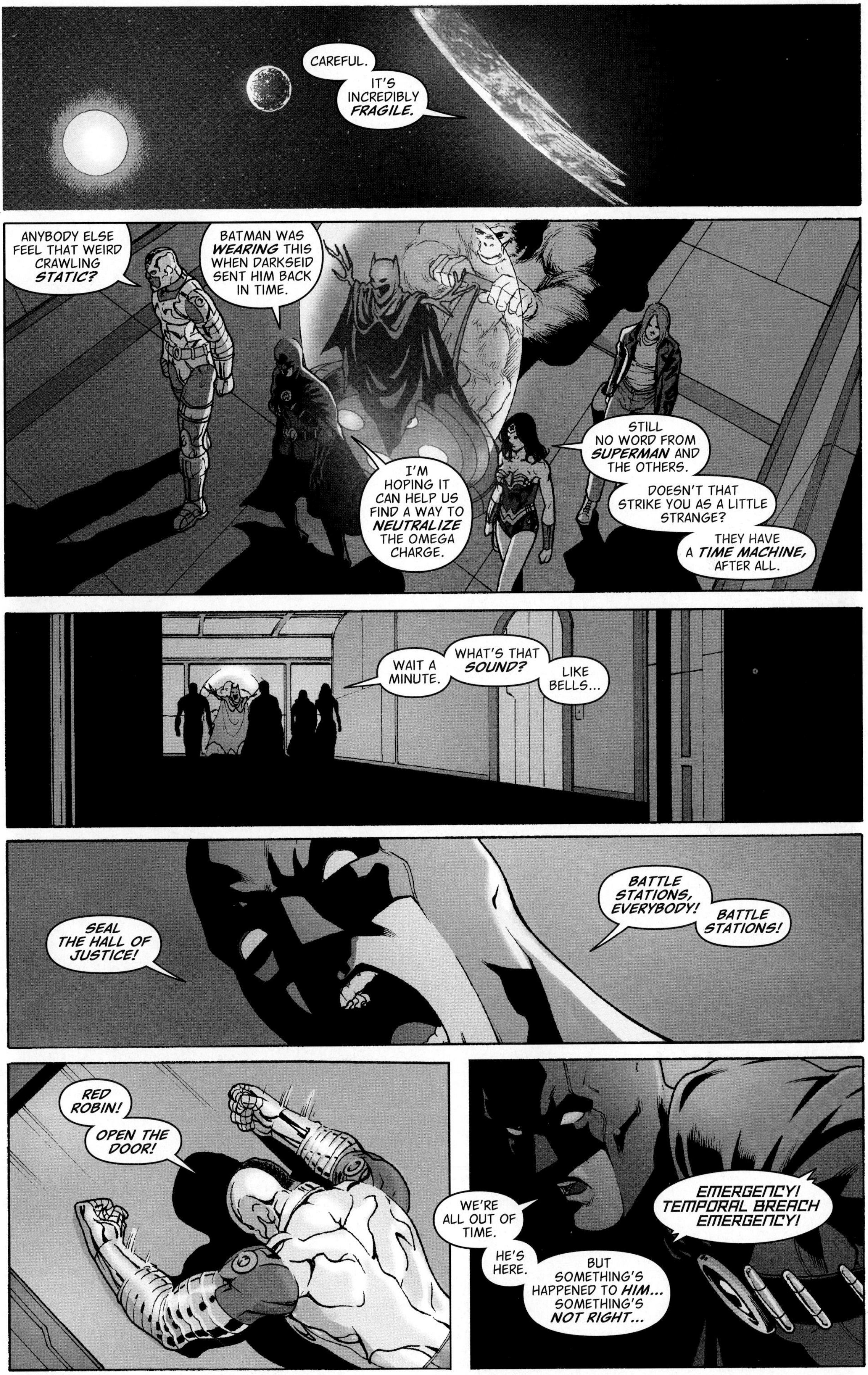
CAREFUL.
IT'S INCREDIBLY FRAGILE.
ANYBODY ELSE FEEL THAT WEIRD CRAWLING STATIC?
BATMAN WAS WEARING THIS WHEN DARKSEID SENT HIM BACK IN TIME.
I'M HOPING IT CAN HELP US FIND A WAY TO NEUTRALIZE THE OMEGA CHARGE.
STILL NO WORD FROM SUPERMAN AND THE OTHERS.
DOESN'T THAT STRIKE YOU AS A LITTLE STRANGE?
THEY HAVE A TIME MACHINE, AFTER ALL.
WAIT A MINUTE.
WHAT'S THAT SOUND?
LIKE BELLS...
SEAL THE HALL OF JUSTICE!
BATTLE STATIONS, EVERYBODY!
BATTLE STATIONS!
RED ROBIN!
OPEN THE DOOR!
WE'RE ALL OUT OF TIME.
HE'S HERE.
BUT SOMETHING'S HAPPENED TO HIM... SOMETHING'S NOT RIGHT...
EMERGENCY! TEMPORAL BREACH EMERGENCY!

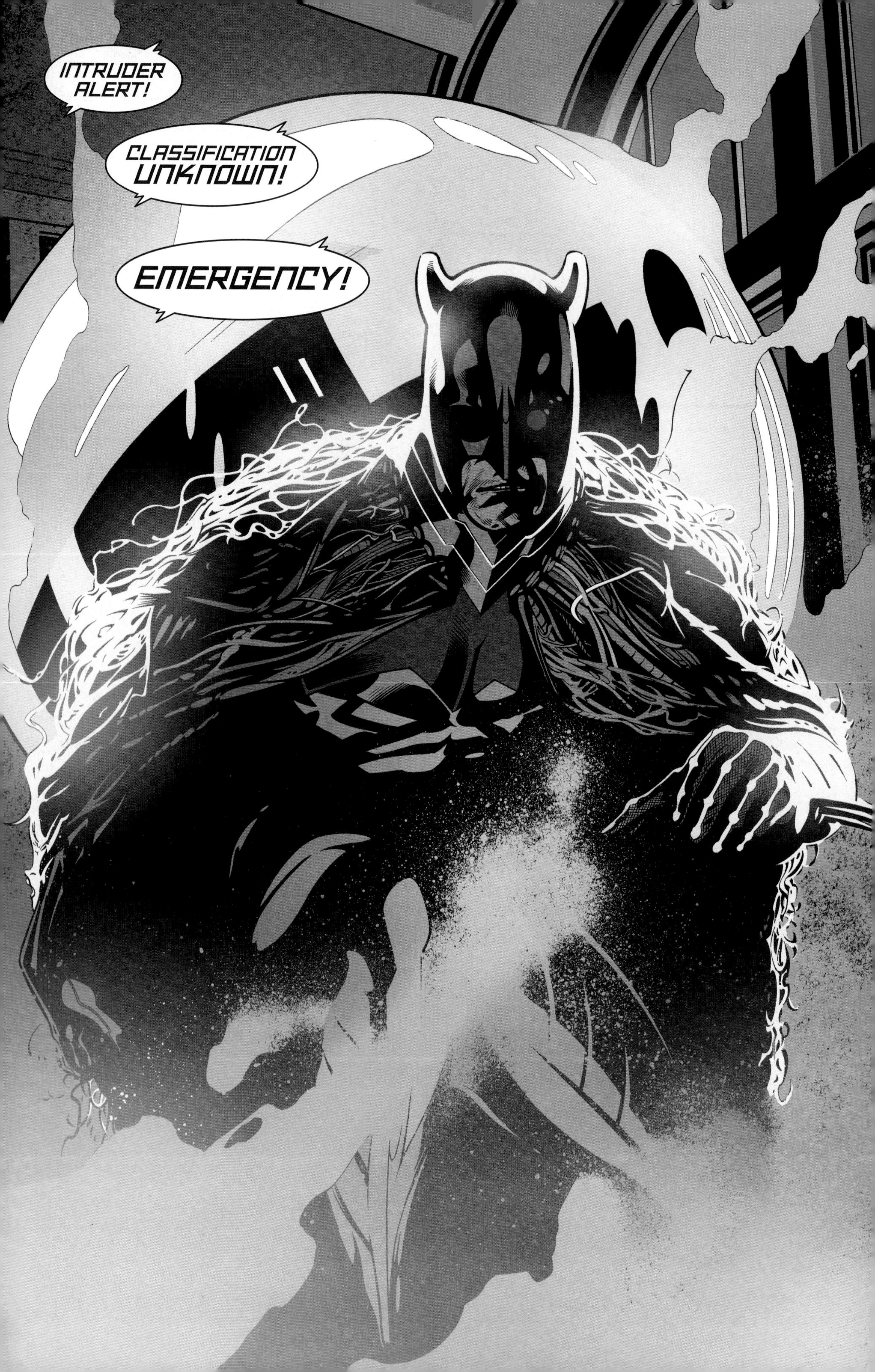
INTRUDER ALERT!
CLASSIFICATION UNKNOWN!
EMERGENCY!

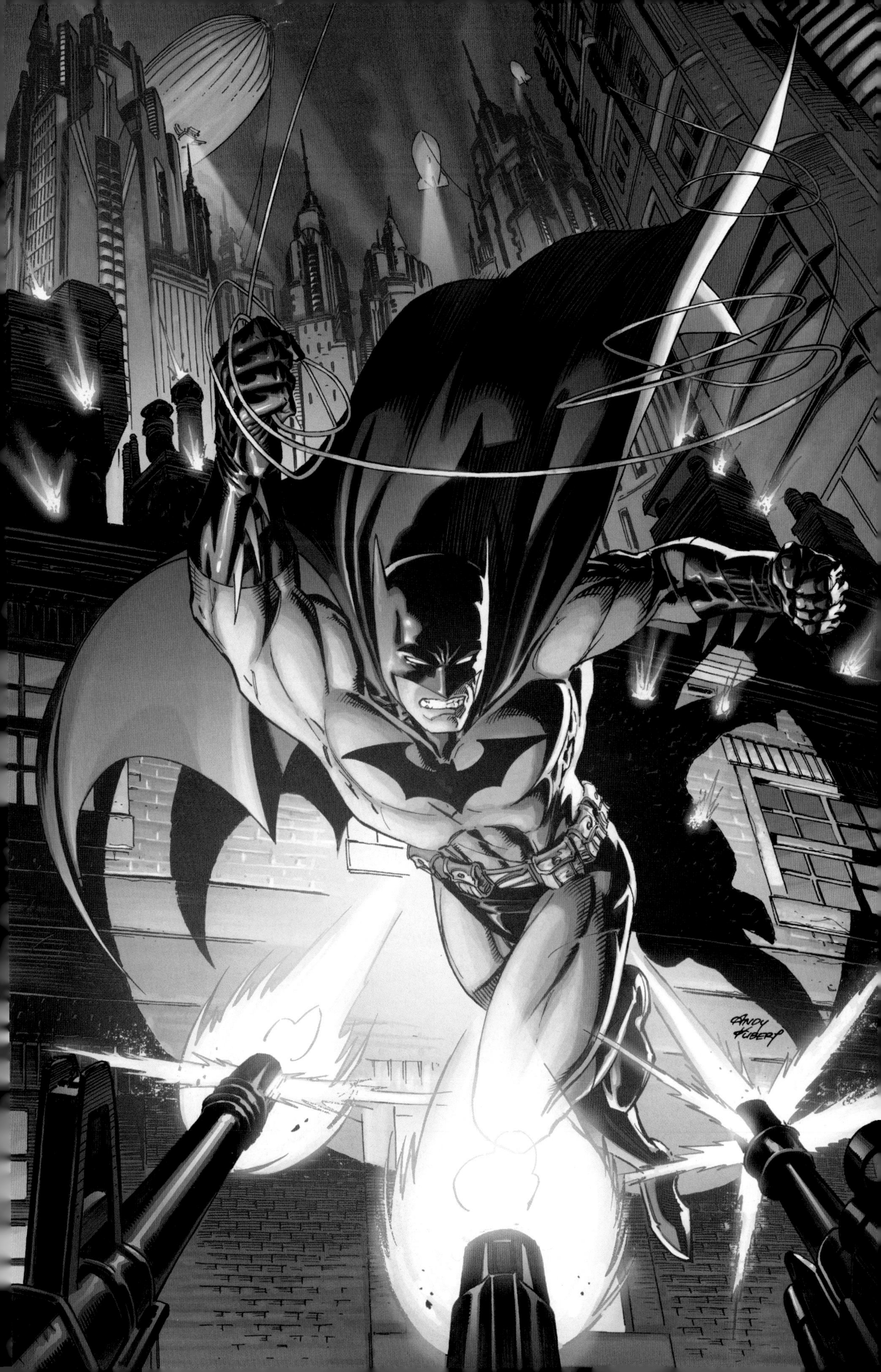
ANDY KUBERT

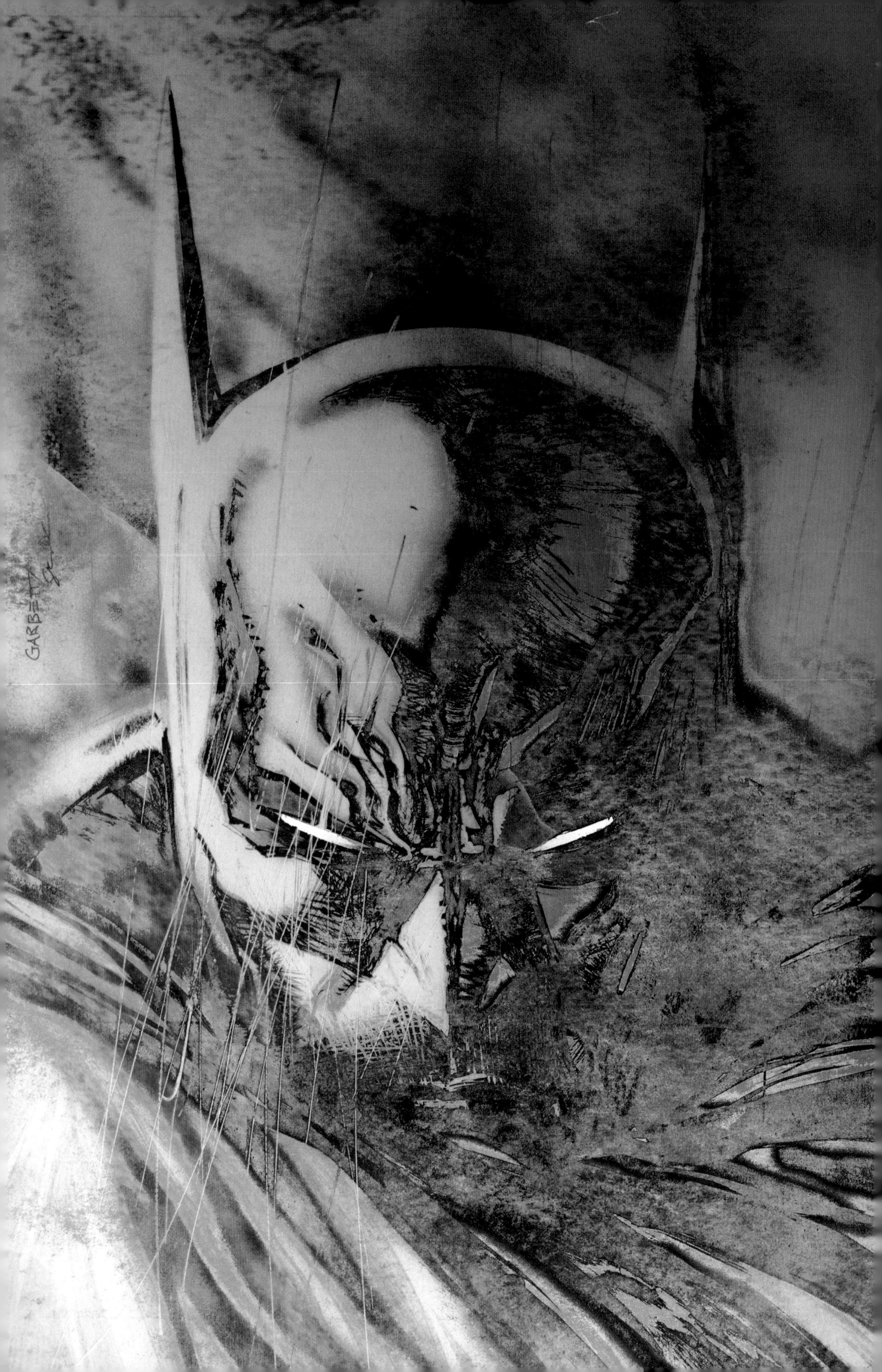

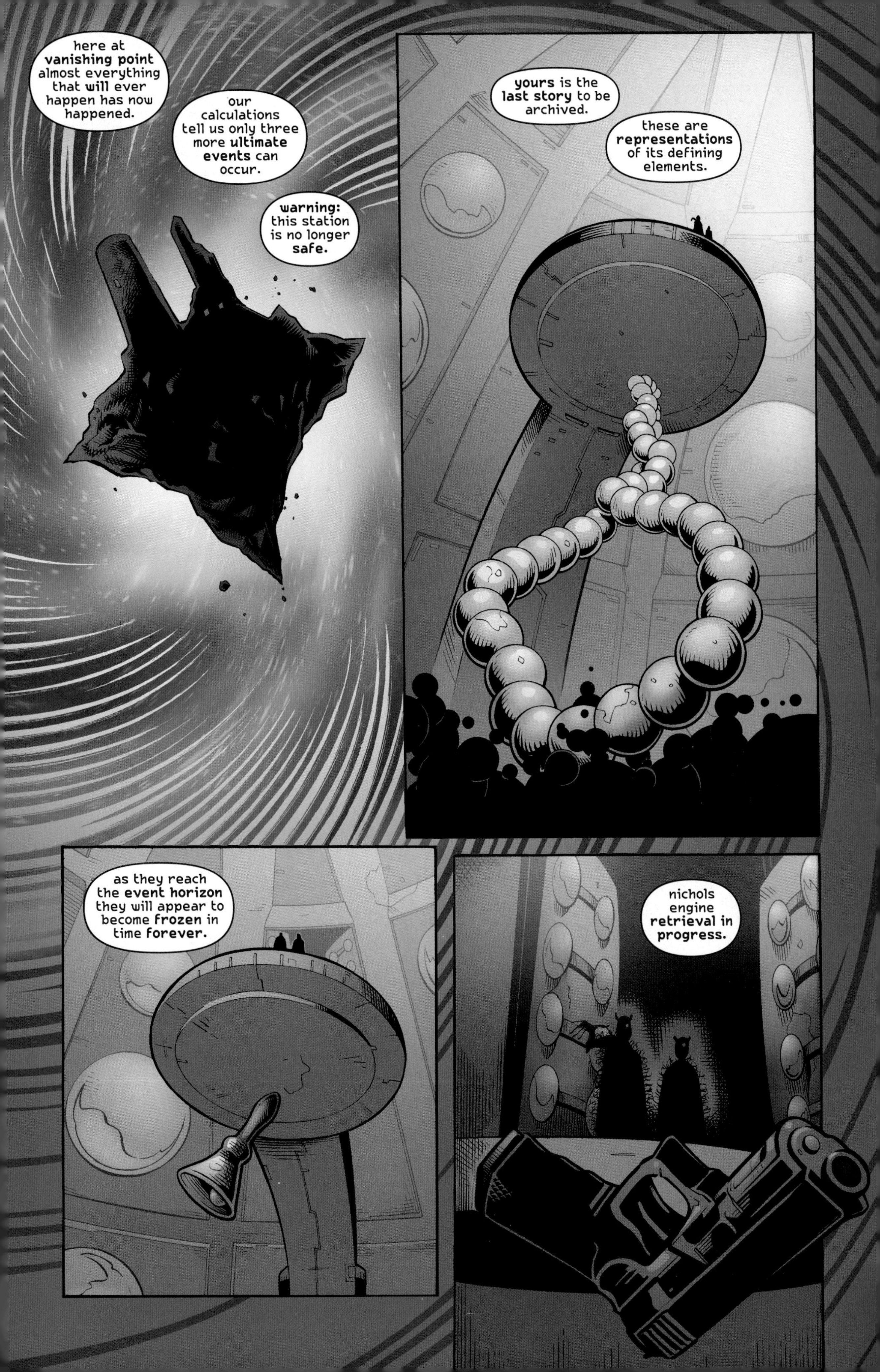
here at vanishing point almost everything that will ever happen has now happened.
our calculations tell us only three more ultimate events can occur.
warning: this station is no longer safe.
yours is the last story to be archived.
these are representations of its defining elements.
as they reach the event horizon they will appear to become frozen in time forever.
nichols engine retrieval in progress.

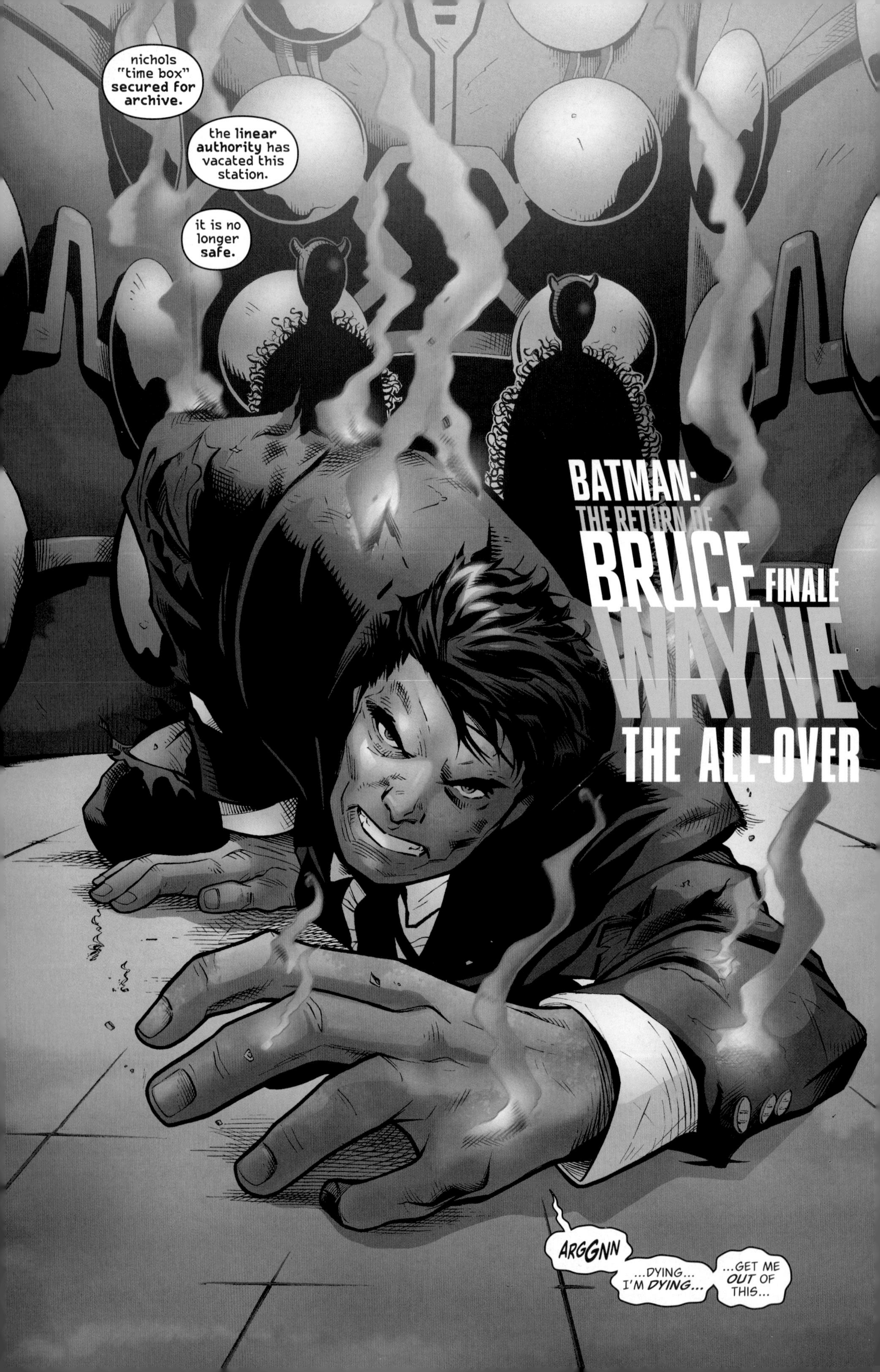
nichols "time box" secured for archive.
the linear authority has vacated this station.
it is no longer safe.
BATMAN: THE RETURN OF BRUCE WAYNE FINALE
THE ALL-OVER
ARGGNN
...DYING... I'M DYING...
...GET ME OUT OF THIS...

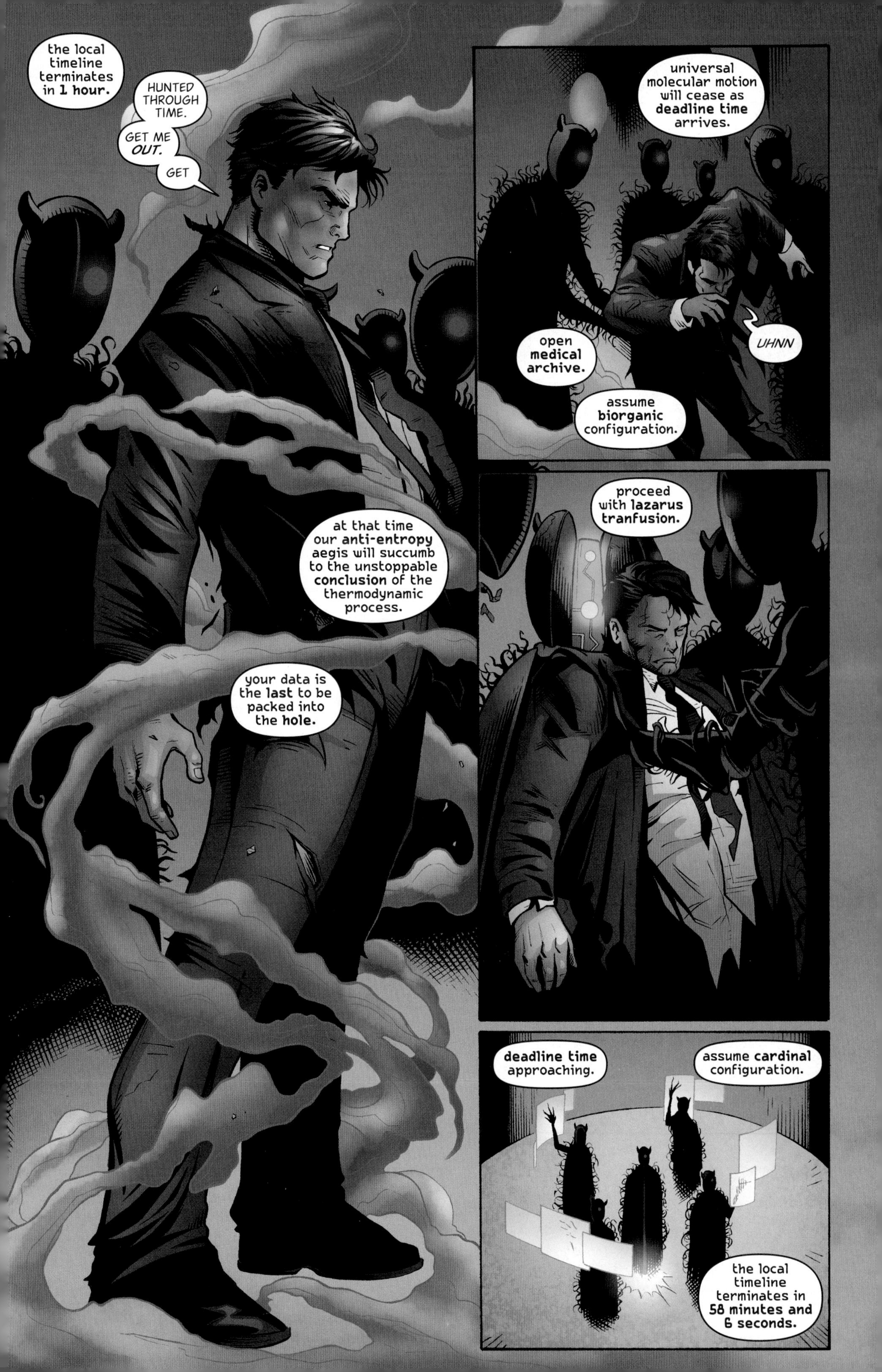
the local timeline terminates in **1 hour.**
HUNTED THROUGH TIME.
GET ME *OUT.*
GET
at that time our **anti-entropy** aegis will succumb to the unstoppable **conclusion** of the thermodynamic process.
your data is the **last** to be packed into the **hole.**
universal molecular motion will cease as **deadline time** arrives.
open **medical archive.**
UHNN
assume **biorganic** configuration.
proceed with **lazarus tranfusion.**
deadline time approaching.
assume **cardinal** configuration.
the local timeline terminates in **58 minutes and 6 seconds.**

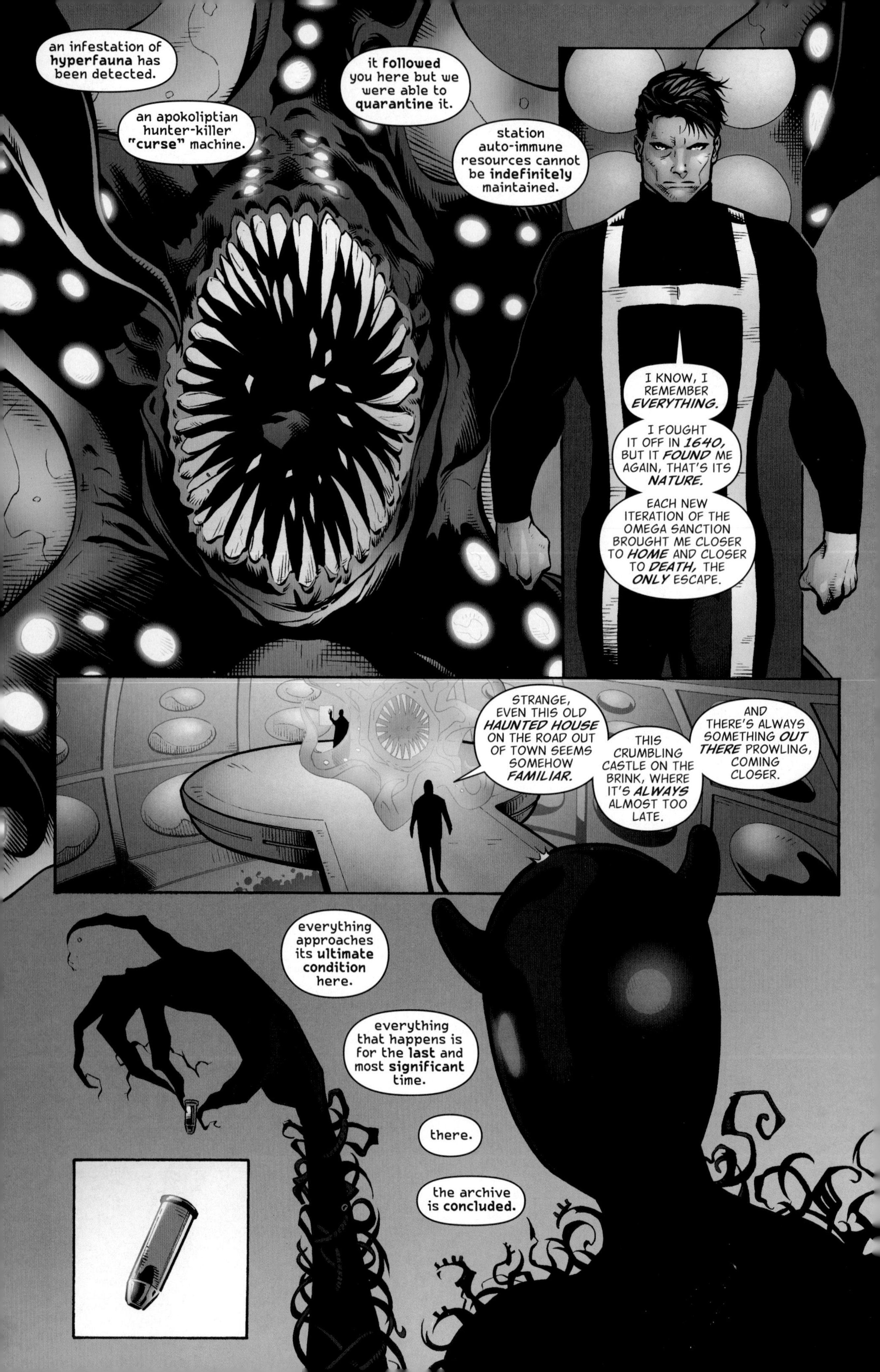
an infestation of hyperfauna has been detected.
an apokoliptian hunter-killer "curse" machine.
it followed you here but we were able to quarantine it.
station auto-immune resources cannot be indefinitely maintained.
I KNOW, I REMEMBER EVERYTHING.
I FOUGHT IT OFF IN 1640, BUT IT FOUND ME AGAIN, THAT'S ITS NATURE.
EACH NEW ITERATION OF THE OMEGA SANCTION BROUGHT ME CLOSER TO HOME AND CLOSER TO DEATH, THE ONLY ESCAPE.
STRANGE, EVEN THIS OLD HAUNTED HOUSE ON THE ROAD OUT OF TOWN SEEMS SOMEHOW FAMILIAR.
THIS CRUMBLING CASTLE ON THE BRINK, WHERE IT'S ALWAYS ALMOST TOO LATE.
AND THERE'S ALWAYS SOMETHING OUT THERE PROWLING, COMING CLOSER.
everything approaches its ultimate condition here.
everything that happens is for the last and most significant time.
there.
the archive is concluded.

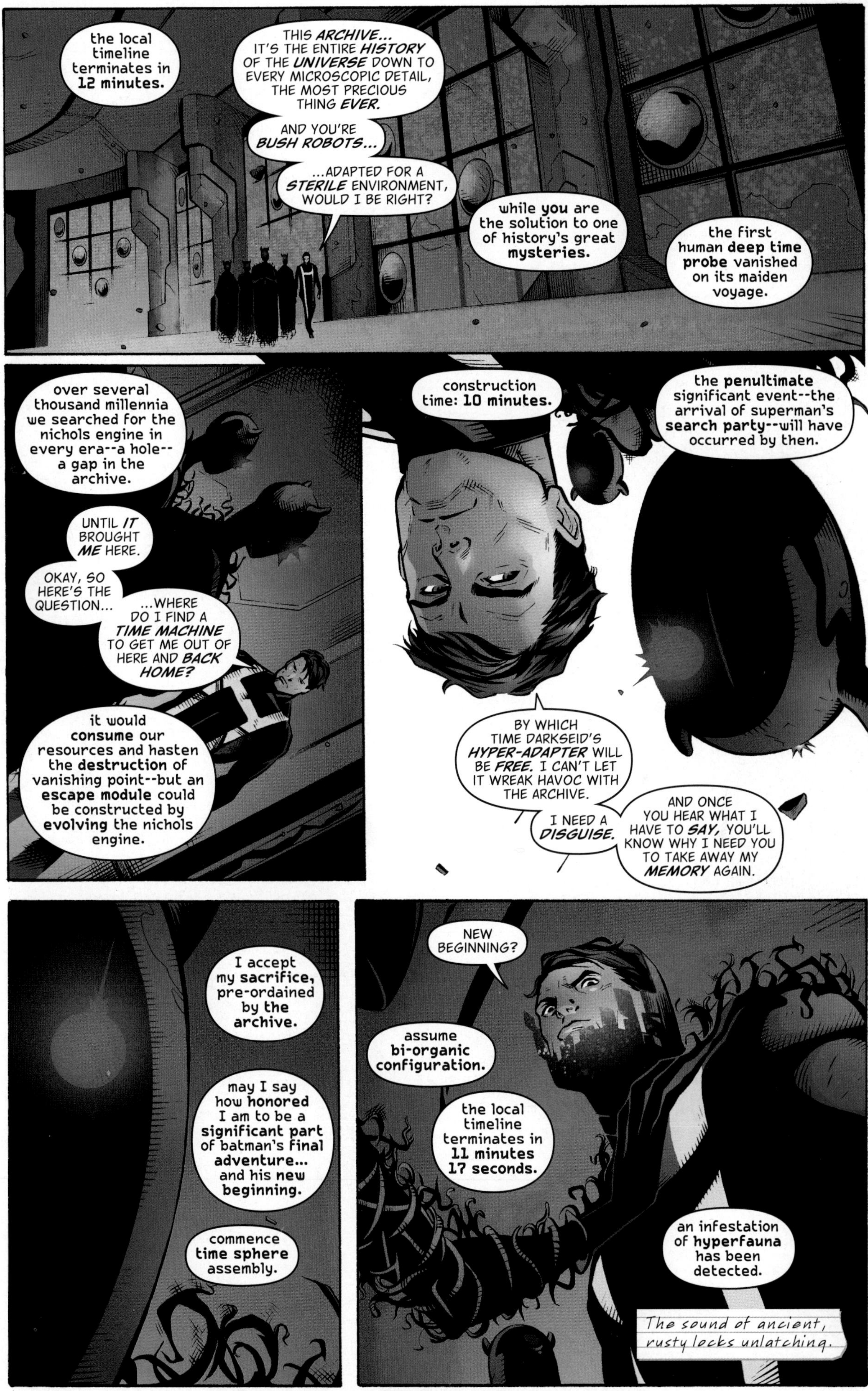
the local timeline terminates in 12 minutes.
THIS ARCHIVE... IT'S THE ENTIRE HISTORY OF THE UNIVERSE DOWN TO EVERY MICROSCOPIC DETAIL, THE MOST PRECIOUS THING EVER.
AND YOU'RE BUSH ROBOTS...
...ADAPTED FOR A STERILE ENVIRONMENT, WOULD I BE RIGHT?
while you are the solution to one of history's great mysteries.
the first human deep time probe vanished on its maiden voyage.
over several thousand millennia we searched for the nichols engine in every era--a hole--a gap in the archive.
UNTIL IT BROUGHT ME HERE.
OKAY, SO HERE'S THE QUESTION...
...WHERE DO I FIND A TIME MACHINE TO GET ME OUT OF HERE AND BACK HOME?
it would consume our resources and hasten the destruction of vanishing point--but an escape module could be constructed by evolving the nichols engine.
construction time: 10 minutes.
the penultimate significant event--the arrival of superman's search party--will have occurred by then.
BY WHICH TIME DARKSEID'S HYPER-ADAPTER WILL BE FREE. I CAN'T LET IT WREAK HAVOC WITH THE ARCHIVE.
I NEED A DISGUISE.
AND ONCE YOU HEAR WHAT I HAVE TO SAY, YOU'LL KNOW WHY I NEED YOU TO TAKE AWAY MY MEMORY AGAIN.
I accept my sacrifice, pre-ordained by the archive.
may I say how honored I am to be a significant part of batman's final adventure... and his new beginning.
commence time sphere assembly.
NEW BEGINNING?
assume bi-organic configuration.
the local timeline terminates in 11 minutes 17 seconds.
an infestation of hyperfauna has been detected.
The sound of ancient, rusty locks unlatching.

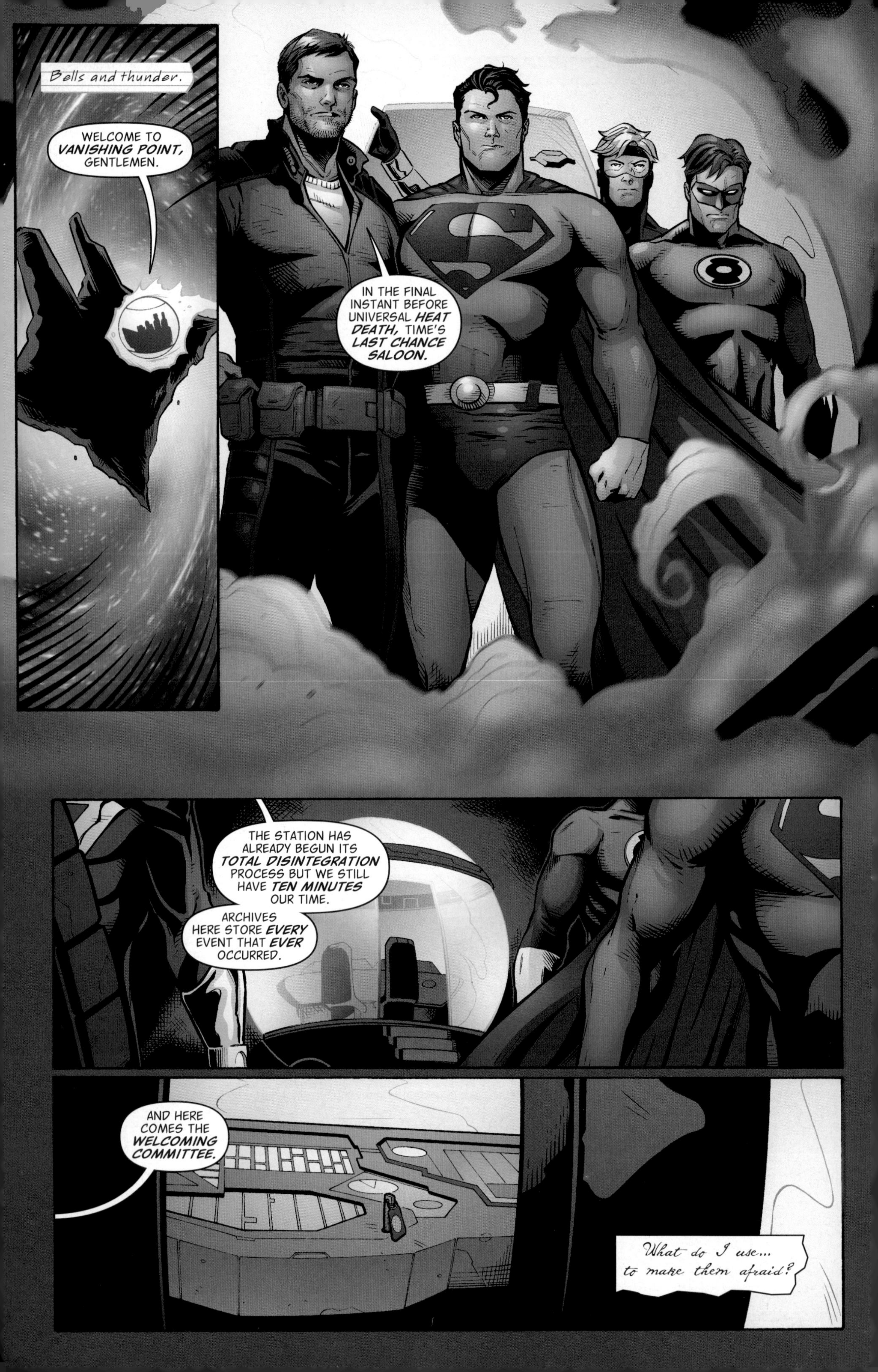

Bells and thunder.
WELCOME TO VANISHING POINT, GENTLEMEN.
IN THE FINAL INSTANT BEFORE UNIVERSAL HEAT DEATH, TIME'S LAST CHANCE SALOON.
THE STATION HAS ALREADY BEGUN ITS TOTAL DISINTEGRATION PROCESS BUT WE STILL HAVE TEN MINUTES OUR TIME.
ARCHIVES HERE STORE EVERY EVENT THAT EVER OCCURRED.
AND HERE COMES THE WELCOMING COMMITTEE.
What do I use... to make them afraid?

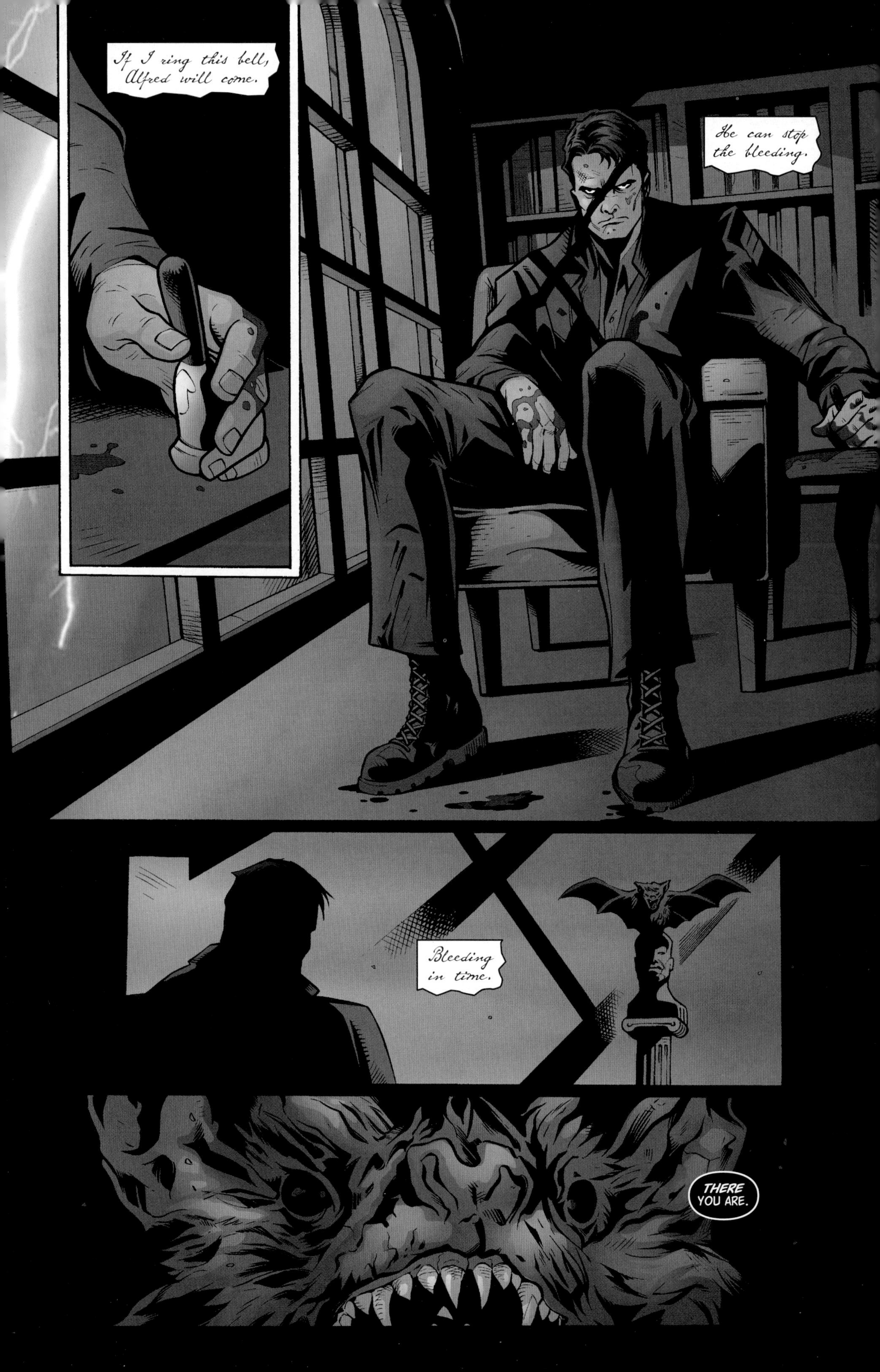
If I ring this bell, Alfred will come.
He can stop the bleeding.
Bleeding in time.
THERE YOU ARE.

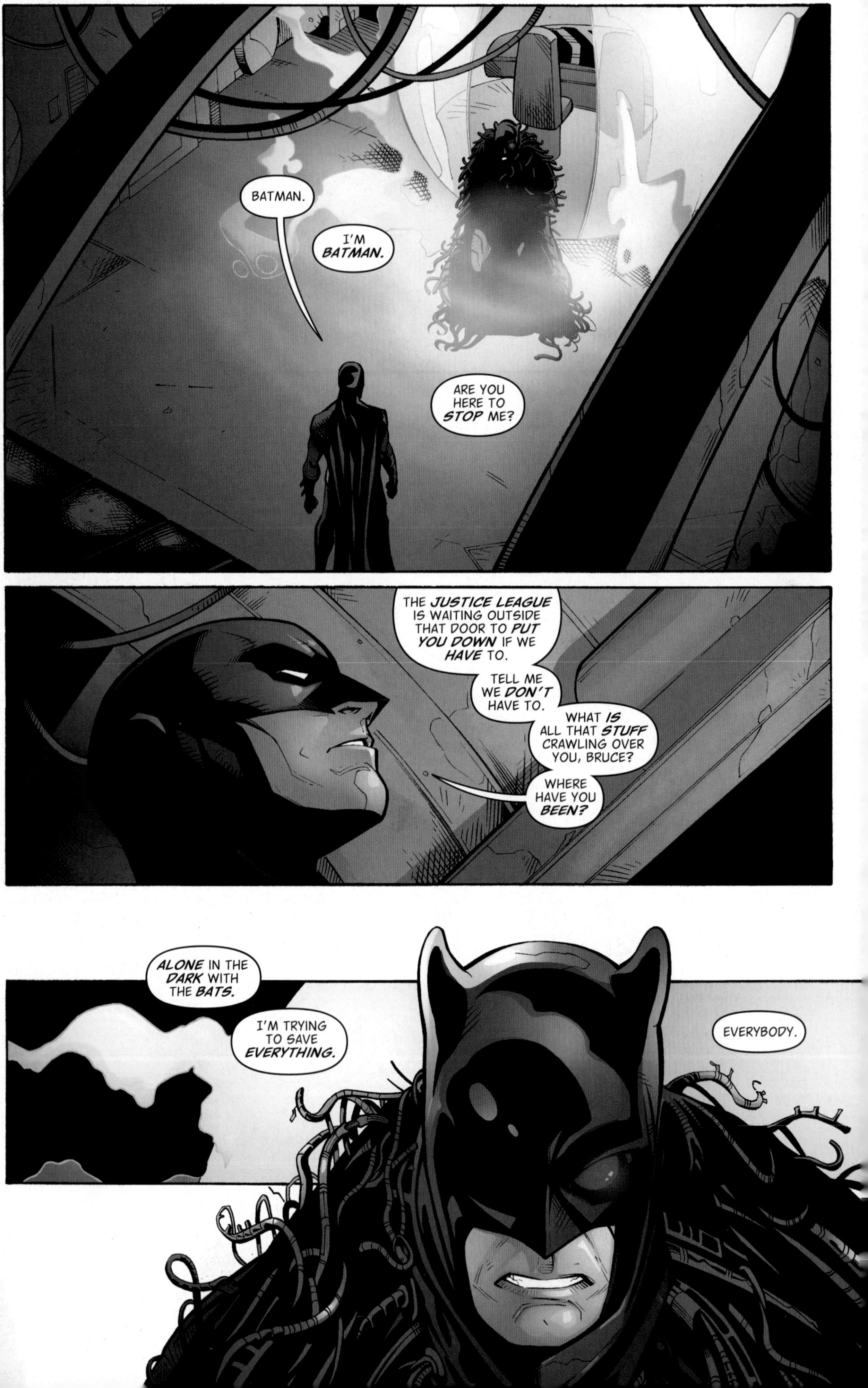
BATMAN.
I'M BATMAN.
ARE YOU HERE TO STOP ME?
THE JUSTICE LEAGUE IS WAITING OUTSIDE THAT DOOR TO PUT YOU DOWN IF WE HAVE TO.
TELL ME WE DON'T HAVE TO.
WHAT IS ALL THAT STUFF CRAWLING OVER YOU, BRUCE?
WHERE HAVE YOU BEEN?
ALONE IN THE DARK WITH THE BATS.
I'M TRYING TO SAVE EVERYTHING.
EVERYBODY.

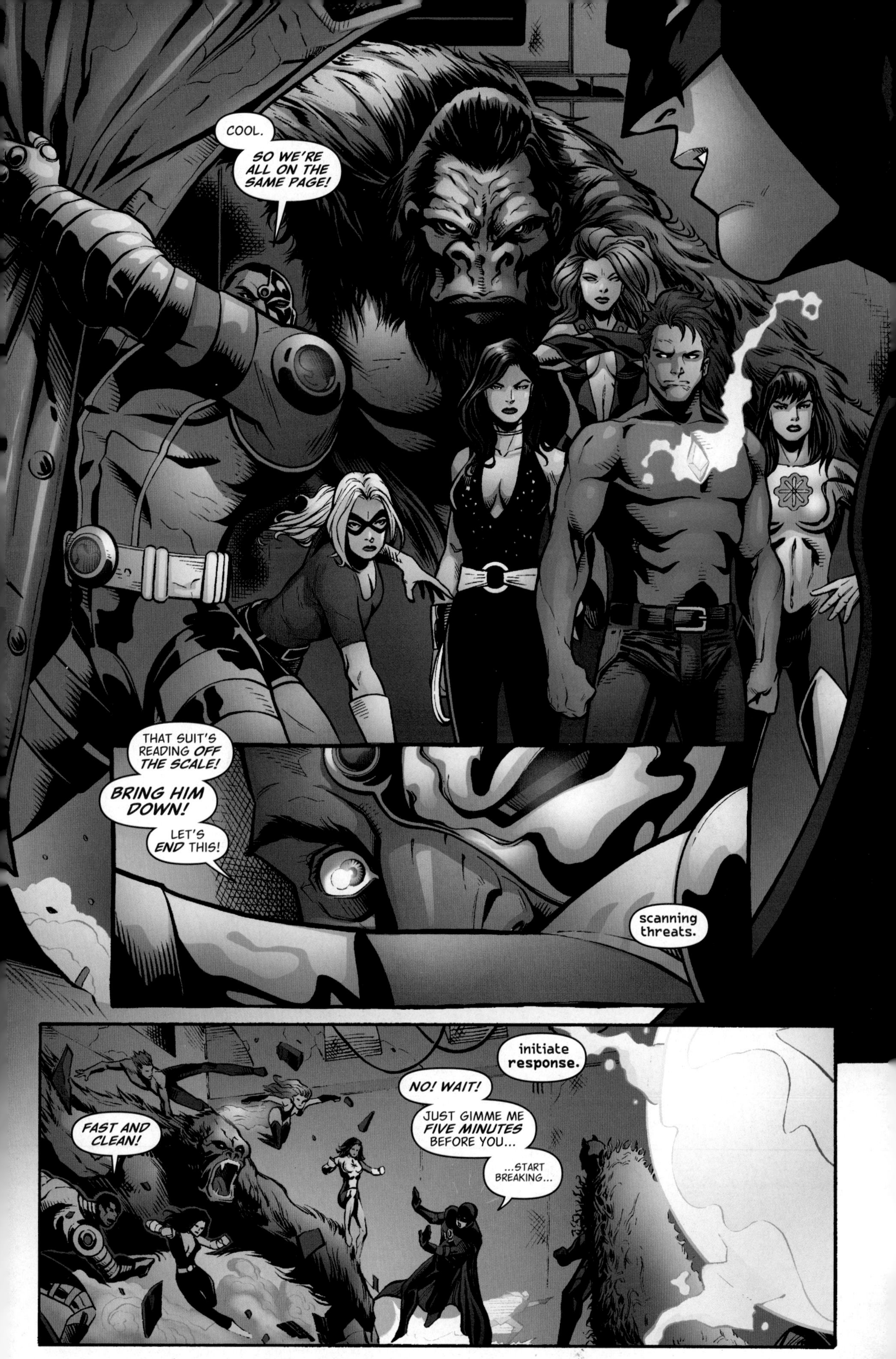
COOL.
SO WE'RE ALL ON THE SAME PAGE!
THAT SUIT'S READING OFF THE SCALE!
BRING HIM DOWN!
LET'S END THIS!
scanning threats.
initiate response.
NO! WAIT!
JUST GIMME ME FIVE MINUTES BEFORE YOU...
...START BREAKING...
FAST AND CLEAN!

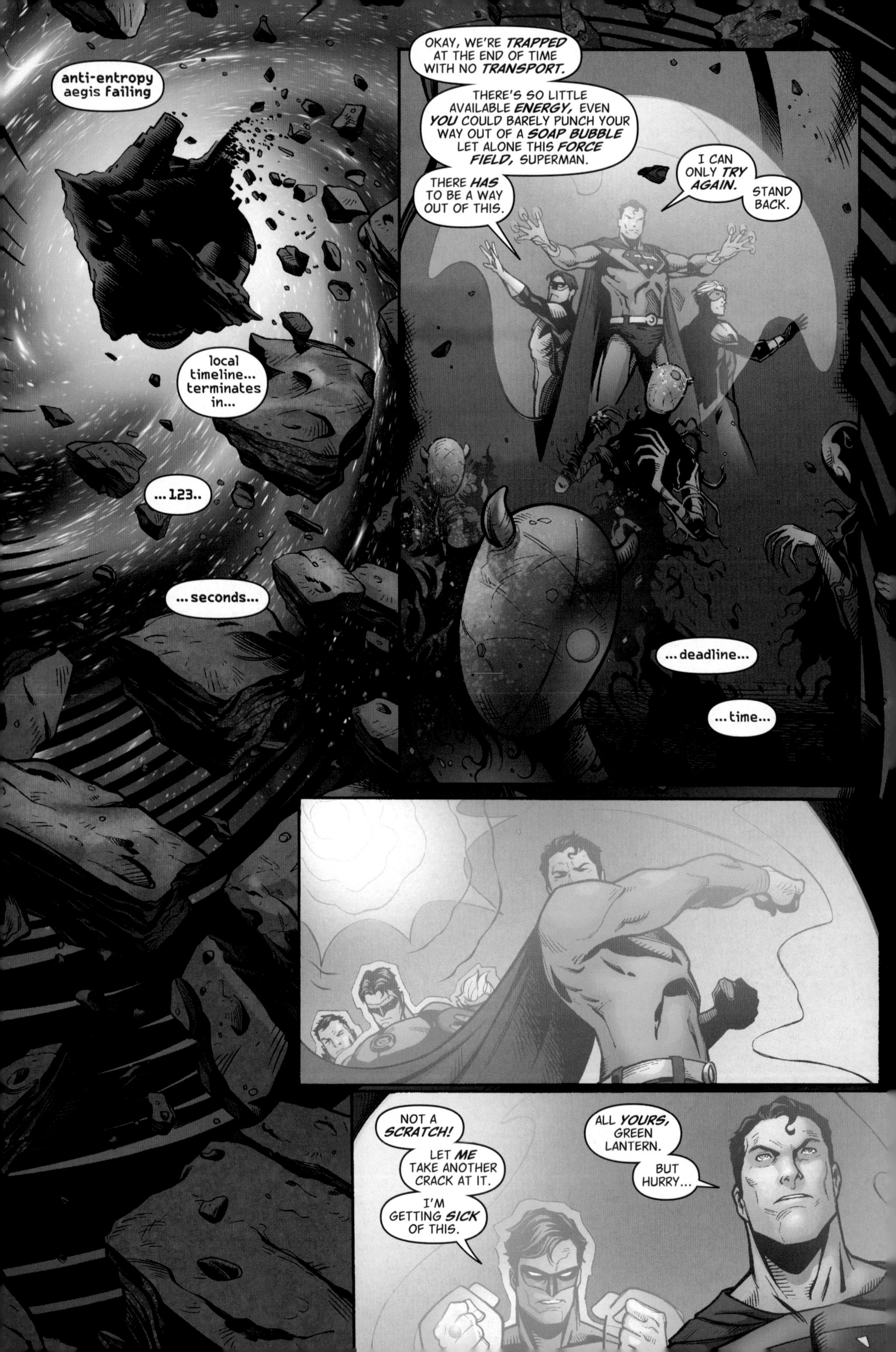
anti-entropy aegis failing
local timeline... terminates in...
...123..
...seconds...
OKAY, WE'RE TRAPPED AT THE END OF TIME WITH NO TRANSPORT.
THERE'S SO LITTLE AVAILABLE ENERGY, EVEN YOU COULD BARELY PUNCH YOUR WAY OUT OF A SOAP BUBBLE LET ALONE THIS FORCE FIELD, SUPERMAN.
THERE HAS TO BE A WAY OUT OF THIS.
I CAN ONLY TRY AGAIN.
STAND BACK.
...deadline...
...time...
NOT A SCRATCH!
LET ME TAKE ANOTHER CRACK AT IT.
I'M GETTING SICK OF THIS.
ALL YOURS, GREEN LANTERN.
BUT HURRY...

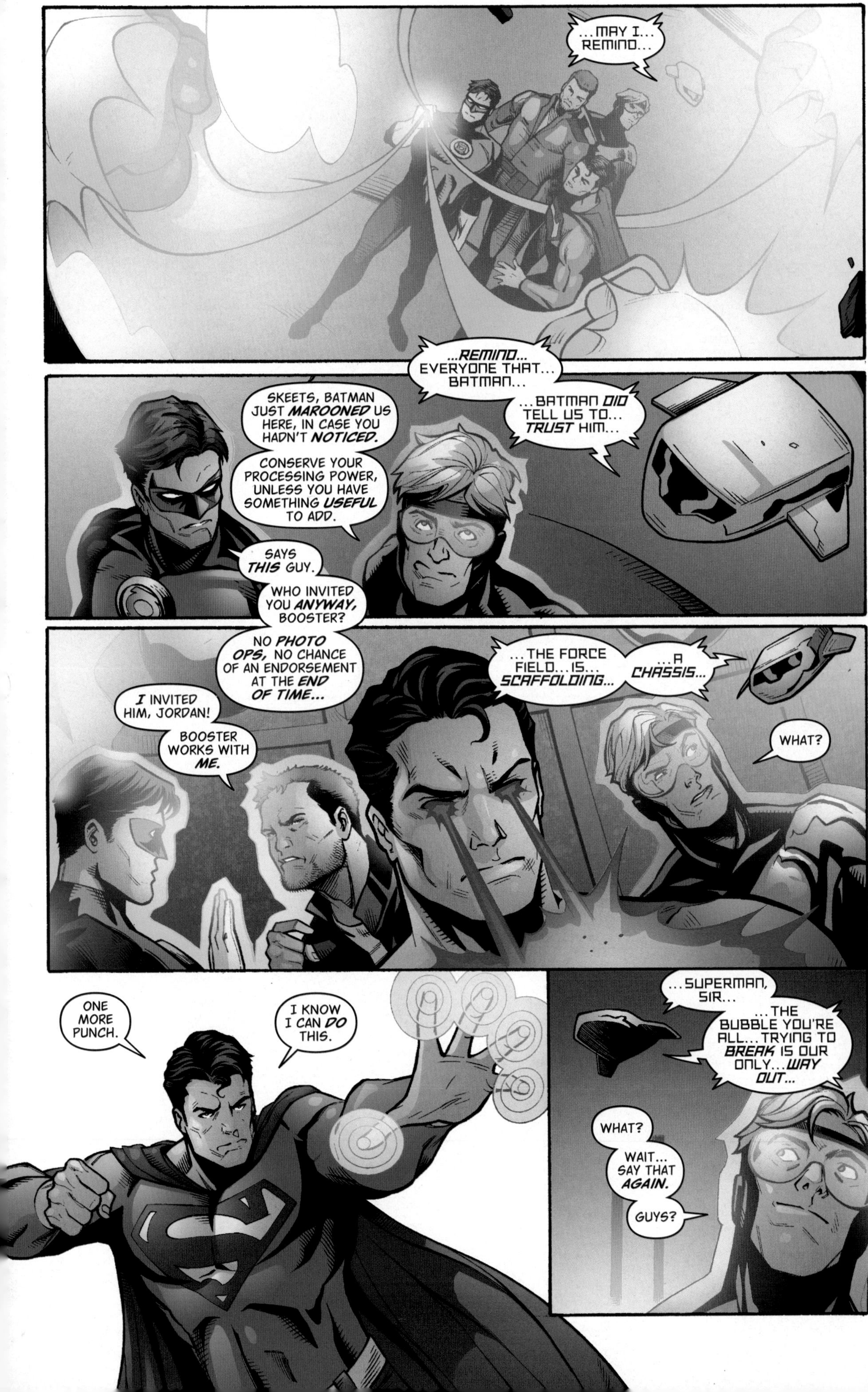

...MAY I... REMIND...
...REMIND... EVERYONE THAT... BATMAN...
SKEETS, BATMAN JUST MAROONED US HERE, IN CASE YOU HADN'T NOTICED.
...BATMAN DID TELL US TO... TRUST HIM...
CONSERVE YOUR PROCESSING POWER, UNLESS YOU HAVE SOMETHING USEFUL TO ADD.
SAYS THIS GUY.
WHO INVITED YOU ANYWAY, BOOSTER?
NO PHOTO OPS, NO CHANCE OF AN ENDORSEMENT AT THE END OF TIME...
...THE FORCE FIELD... IS... SCAFFOLDING...
...A CHASSIS...
I INVITED HIM, JORDAN!
BOOSTER WORKS WITH ME.
WHAT?
ONE MORE PUNCH.
I KNOW I CAN DO THIS.
...SUPERMAN, SIR...
...THE BUBBLE YOU'RE ALL... TRYING TO BREAK IS OUR ONLY... WAY OUT...
WHAT?
WAIT... SAY THAT AGAIN.
GUYS?

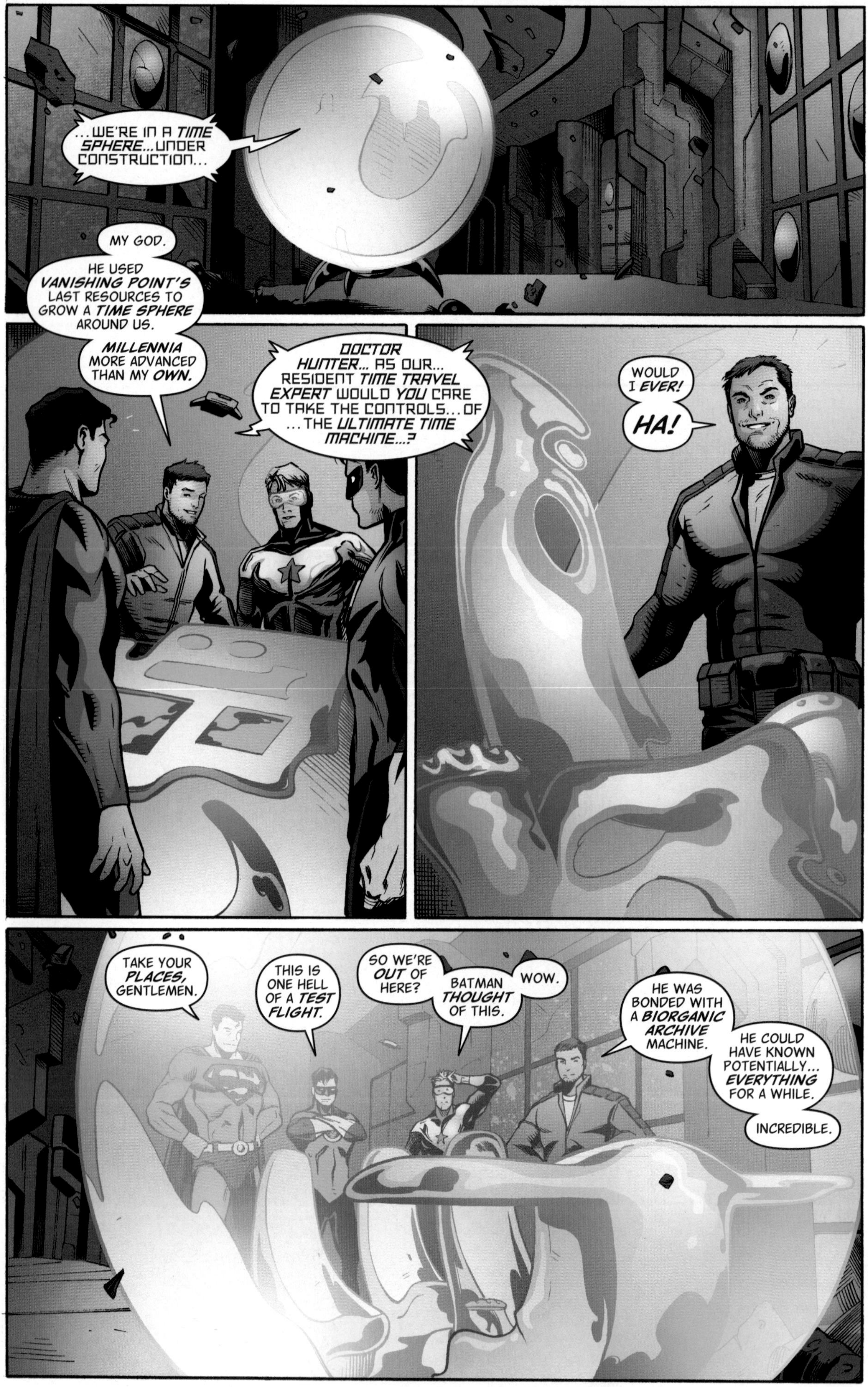
...WE'RE IN A TIME SPHERE...UNDER CONSTRUCTION...
MY GOD.
HE USED VANISHING POINT'S LAST RESOURCES TO GROW A TIME SPHERE AROUND US.
MILLENNIA MORE ADVANCED THAN MY OWN.
DOCTOR HUNTER... AS OUR... RESIDENT TIME TRAVEL EXPERT WOULD YOU CARE TO TAKE THE CONTROLS... OF ...THE ULTIMATE TIME MACHINE...?
WOULD I EVER!
HA!
TAKE YOUR PLACES, GENTLEMEN.
THIS IS ONE HELL OF A TEST FLIGHT.
SO WE'RE OUT OF HERE?
BATMAN THOUGHT OF THIS.
WOW.
HE WAS BONDED WITH A BIORGANIC ARCHIVE MACHINE.
HE COULD HAVE KNOWN POTENTIALLY... EVERYTHING FOR A WHILE.
INCREDIBLE.

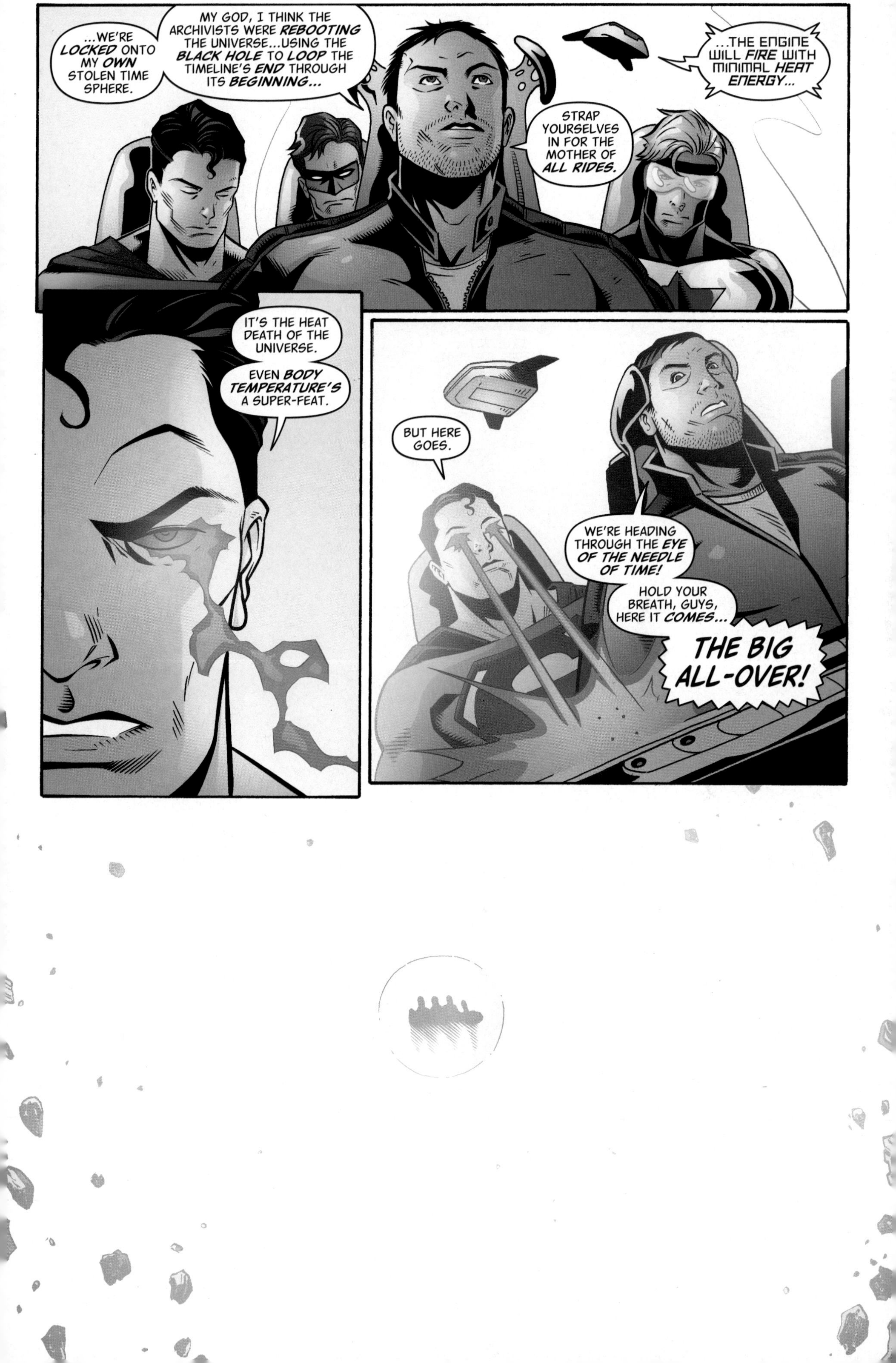
...WE'RE LOCKED ONTO MY OWN STOLEN TIME SPHERE.
MY GOD, I THINK THE ARCHIVISTS WERE REBOOTING THE UNIVERSE...USING THE BLACK HOLE TO LOOP THE TIMELINE'S END THROUGH ITS BEGINNING...
...THE ENGINE WILL FIRE WITH MINIMAL HEAT ENERGY...
STRAP YOURSELVES IN FOR THE MOTHER OF ALL RIDES.
IT'S THE HEAT DEATH OF THE UNIVERSE.
EVEN BODY TEMPERATURE'S A SUPER-FEAT.
BUT HERE GOES.
WE'RE HEADING THROUGH THE EYE OF THE NEEDLE OF TIME!
HOLD YOUR BREATH, GUYS, HERE IT COMES...
THE BIG ALL-OVER!

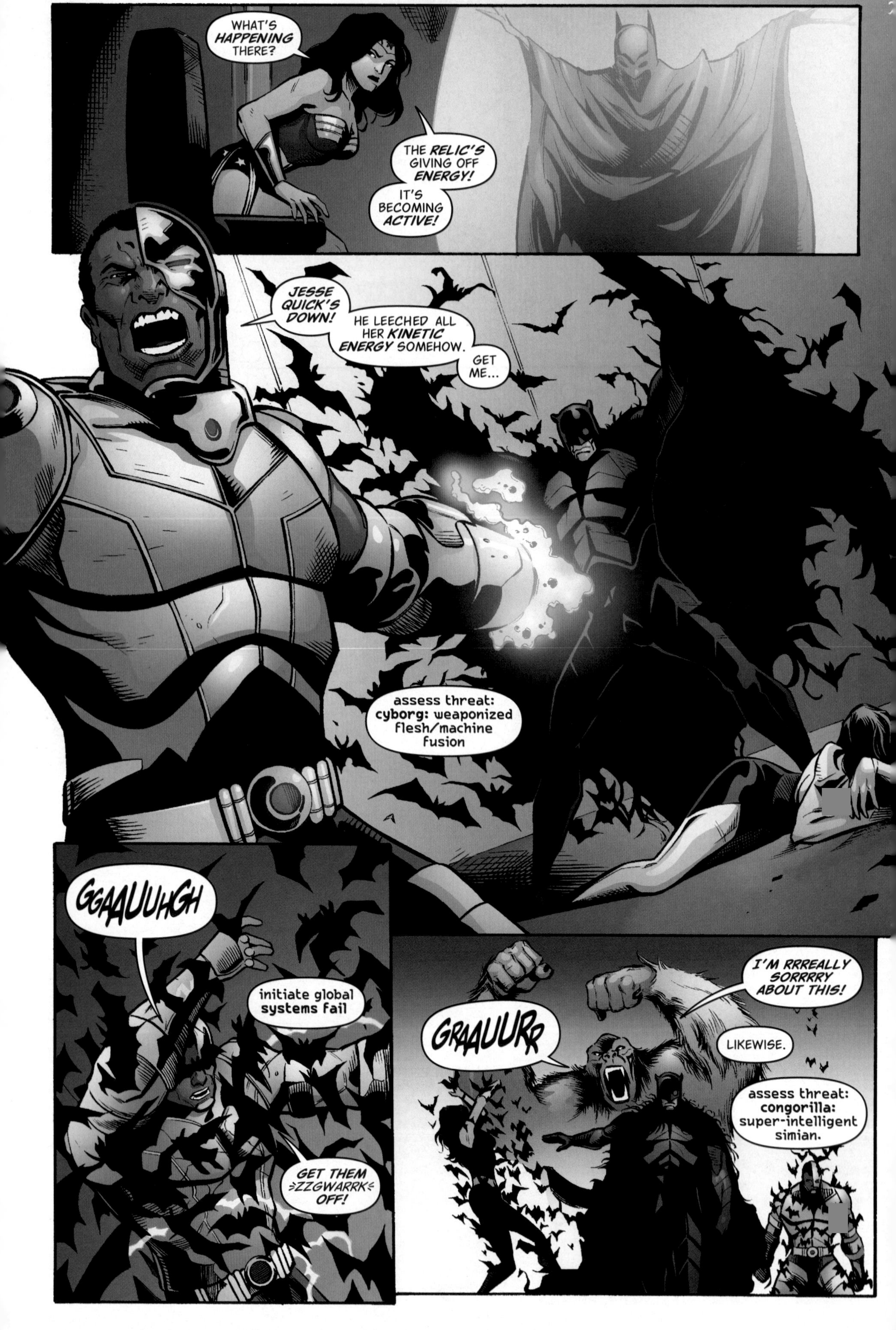
WHAT'S HAPPENING THERE?
THE RELIC'S GIVING OFF ENERGY!
IT'S BECOMING ACTIVE!
JESSE QUICK'S DOWN!
HE LEECHED ALL HER KINETIC ENERGY SOMEHOW.
GET ME...
assess threat: cyborg: weaponized flesh/machine fusion
GGAAUUHGH
initiate global systems fail
GET THEM ZZGWARRK OFF!
I'M RRREALLY SORRRRY ABOUT THIS!
GRAAUURR
LIKEWISE.
assess threat: congorilla: super-intelligent simian.

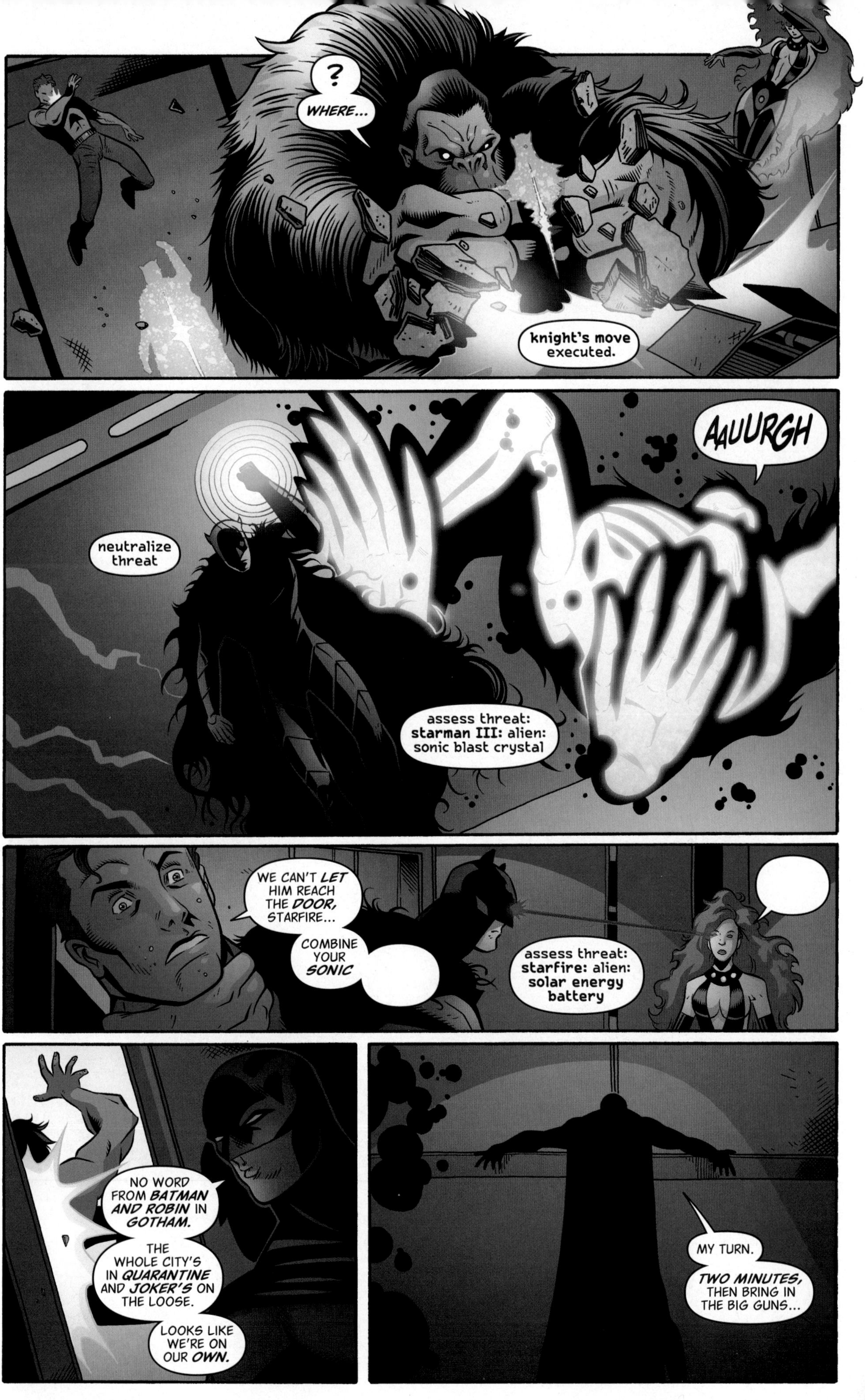
?
WHERE...
knight's move executed.
neutralize threat
AAUURGH
assess threat: starman III: alien: sonic blast crystal
WE CAN'T LET HIM REACH THE DOOR, STARFIRE...
COMBINE YOUR SONIC
assess threat: starfire: alien: solar energy battery
NO WORD FROM BATMAN AND ROBIN IN GOTHAM.
THE WHOLE CITY'S IN QUARANTINE AND JOKER'S ON THE LOOSE.
LOOKS LIKE WE'RE ON OUR OWN.
MY TURN.
TWO MINUTES, THEN BRING IN THE BIG GUNS...

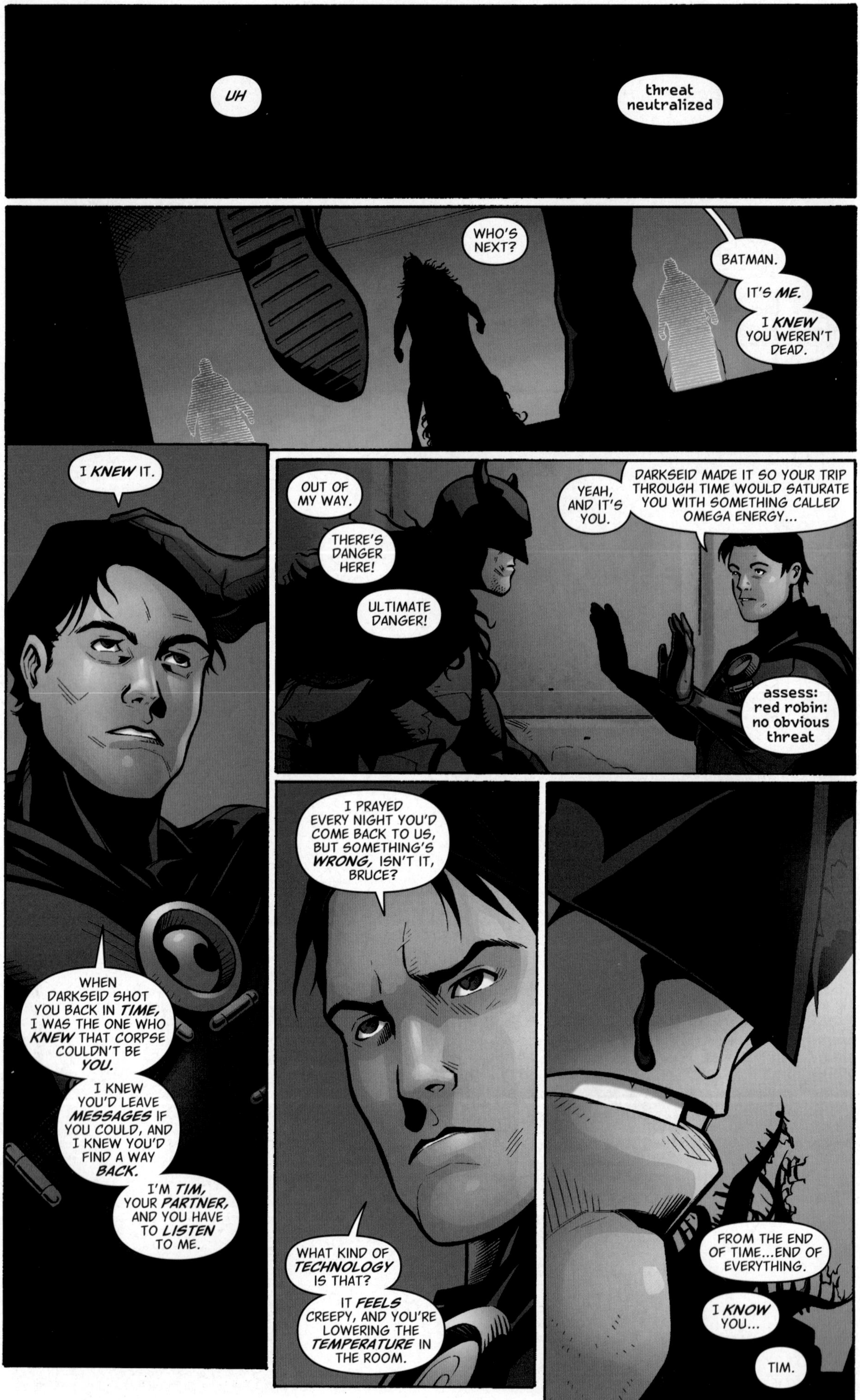
UH
threat neutralized
WHO'S NEXT?
BATMAN.
IT'S ME.
I KNEW YOU WEREN'T DEAD.
I KNEW IT.
OUT OF MY WAY.
THERE'S DANGER HERE!
ULTIMATE DANGER!
YEAH, AND IT'S YOU.
DARKSEID MADE IT SO YOUR TRIP THROUGH TIME WOULD SATURATE YOU WITH SOMETHING CALLED OMEGA ENERGY...
assess: red robin: no obvious threat
WHEN DARKSEID SHOT YOU BACK IN TIME, I WAS THE ONE WHO KNEW THAT CORPSE COULDN'T BE YOU.
I KNEW YOU'D LEAVE MESSAGES IF YOU COULD, AND I KNEW YOU'D FIND A WAY BACK.
I'M TIM, YOUR PARTNER, AND YOU HAVE TO LISTEN TO ME.
I PRAYED EVERY NIGHT YOU'D COME BACK TO US, BUT SOMETHING'S WRONG, ISN'T IT, BRUCE?
WHAT KIND OF TECHNOLOGY IS THAT?
IT FEELS CREEPY, AND YOU'RE LOWERING THE TEMPERATURE IN THE ROOM.
FROM THE END OF TIME...END OF EVERYTHING.
I KNOW YOU...
TIM.

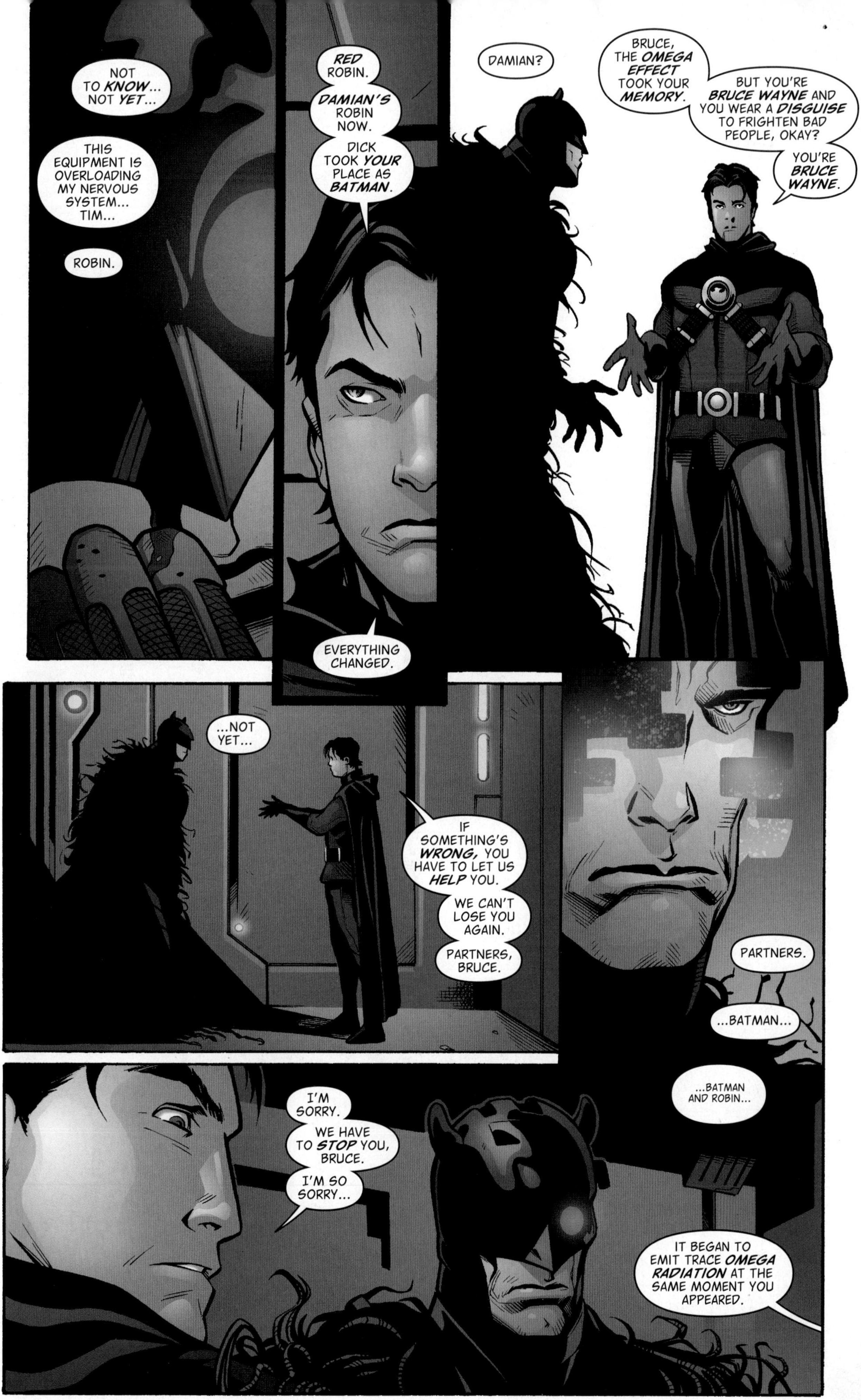

NOT TO *KNOW*... NOT *YET*...
THIS EQUIPMENT IS OVERLOADING MY NERVOUS SYSTEM... TIM...
ROBIN.
RED ROBIN.
DAMIAN'S ROBIN NOW.
DICK TOOK *YOUR* PLACE AS *BATMAN*.
EVERYTHING CHANGED.
DAMIAN?
BRUCE, THE *OMEGA EFFECT* TOOK YOUR *MEMORY*.
BUT YOU'RE *BRUCE WAYNE* AND YOU WEAR A *DISGUISE* TO FRIGHTEN BAD PEOPLE, OKAY?
YOU'RE *BRUCE WAYNE*.
...NOT YET...
IF SOMETHING'S *WRONG,* YOU HAVE TO LET US *HELP* YOU.
WE CAN'T LOSE YOU AGAIN.
PARTNERS, BRUCE.
PARTNERS.
...BATMAN...
...BATMAN AND ROBIN...
I'M SORRY.
WE HAVE TO *STOP* YOU, BRUCE.
I'M SO SORRY...
IT BEGAN TO EMIT TRACE *OMEGA RADIATION* AT THE SAME MOMENT YOU APPEARED.

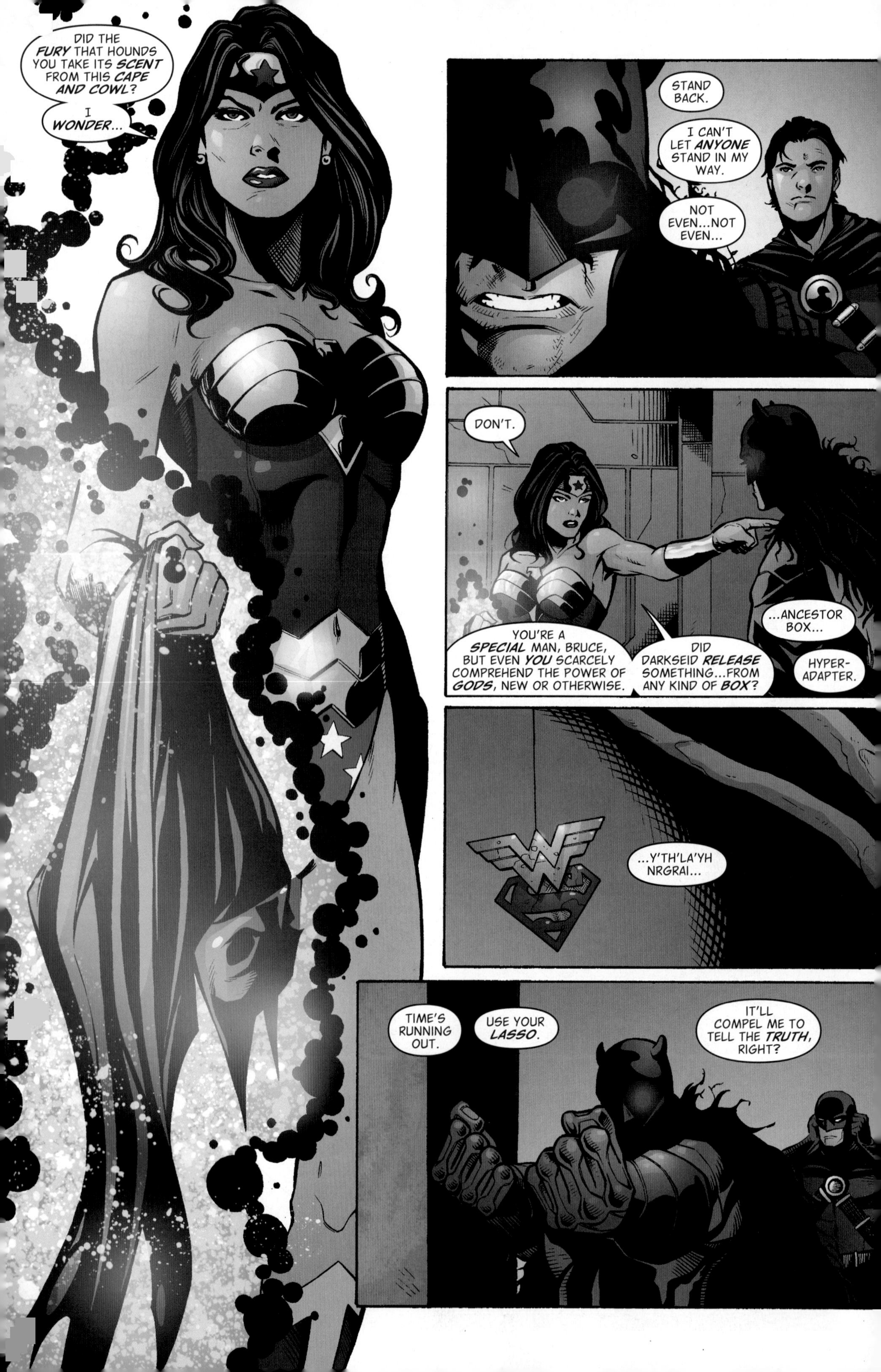
DID THE FURY THAT HOUNDS YOU TAKE ITS SCENT FROM THIS CAPE AND COWL?
I WONDER...
STAND BACK.
I CAN'T LET ANYONE STAND IN MY WAY.
NOT EVEN...NOT EVEN...
DON'T.
YOU'RE A SPECIAL MAN, BRUCE, BUT EVEN YOU SCARCELY COMPREHEND THE POWER OF GODS, NEW OR OTHERWISE.
DID DARKSEID RELEASE SOMETHING...FROM ANY KIND OF BOX?
...ANCESTOR BOX...
HYPER-ADAPTER.
...Y'TH'LA'YH NRGRAI...
TIME'S RUNNING OUT.
USE YOUR LASSO.
IT'LL COMPEL ME TO TELL THE TRUTH, RIGHT?

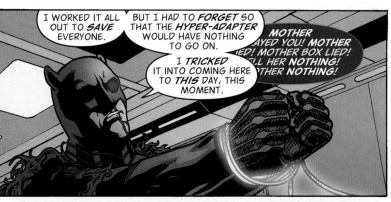

MAYBE I'LL FINALLY REMEMBER WHO I *AM*.

I WORKED IT ALL OUT TO *SAVE* EVERYONE.

BUT I HAD TO *FORGET* SO THAT THE *HYPER-ADAPTER* WOULD HAVE NOTHING TO GO ON.

I *TRICKED* IT INTO COMING HERE TO *THIS* DAY, THIS MOMENT.

MOTHER ...AYED YOU! MOTHER ...IED! MOTHER BOX LIED! ...ELL HER NOTHING! ...OTHER NOTHING!

THE POWER OF THE MAGIC LASSO CAN BE NEITHER *BROKEN* NOR *RESISTED*.

TELL ME HOW YOU CAME TO *BE* HERE, LIKE *THIS*...

NOTHING. I'M *BRUCE WAYNE*.

NOW IT *KNOWS*.

I NEED YOUR *HELP*, DIANA.

FATHER ...TED YOU! STAY ...ONELY! STAY DEAD FOREVER FATHER FEAR!

HE'S TELLING THE *TRUTH*.

BUT... THERE'S *MORE*.

THERE'S SOMETHING *ELSE*, ISN'T THERE?

WHAT *IS* IT?

WHAT'S THAT WEIRD DOUBLE ECHO?

I'M GETTING *HARDCORE* DEJÁ VU...

PROTECT YOURSELF, TIM.

GODS AND *NEW GODS* LIKE *DARKSEID* ARE SELF-AWARE *IDEAS*. THEY USE *CONCEPT-WEAPONS*, ANTI-LIFE *EQUATIONS*, HUNTER-KILLER *METAPHORS*.

I KNOW *YOU'RE* TELLING THE TRUTH, BRUCE...

...NOW LET THE *ARCHIVIST* SPEAK.

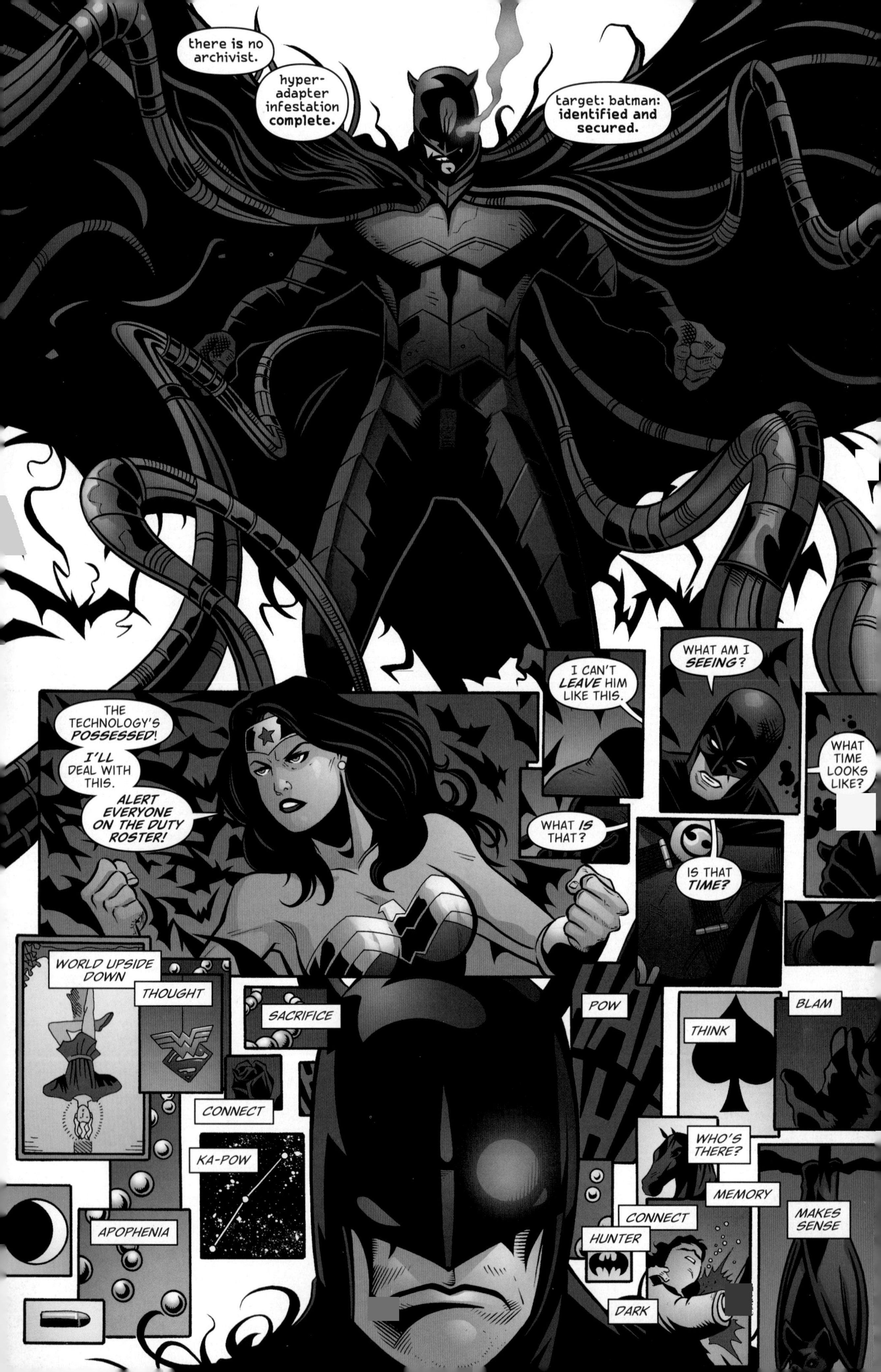
there is no archivist.
hyper-adapter infestation complete.
target: batman: identified and secured.
THE TECHNOLOGY'S POSSESSED!
I'LL DEAL WITH THIS.
ALERT EVERYONE ON THE DUTY ROSTER!
I CAN'T LEAVE HIM LIKE THIS.
WHAT IS THAT?
WHAT AM I SEEING?
IS THAT TIME?
WHAT TIME LOOKS LIKE?
WORLD UPSIDE DOWN
THOUGHT
SACRIFICE
CONNECT
KA-POW
APOPHENIA
POW
THINK
BLAM
WHO'S THERE?
MEMORY
CONNECT
HUNTER
MAKES SENSE
DARK

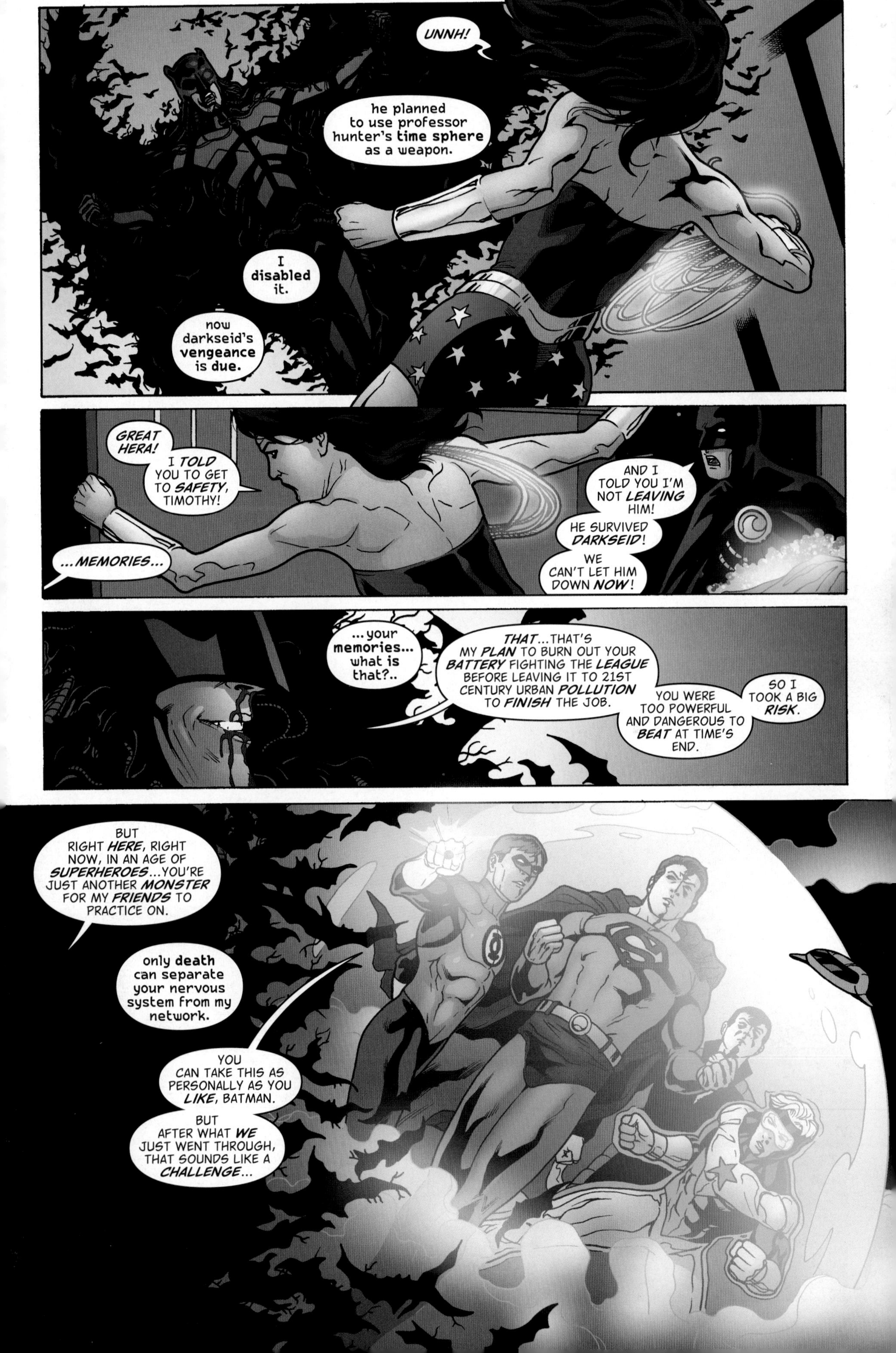
UNNH!
he planned to use professor hunter's time sphere as a weapon.
I disabled it.
now darkseid's vengeance is due.
GREAT HERA! I TOLD YOU TO GET TO SAFETY, TIMOTHY!
...MEMORIES...
AND I TOLD YOU I'M NOT LEAVING HIM!
HE SURVIVED DARKSEID!
WE CAN'T LET HIM DOWN NOW!
...your memories... what is that?..
THAT...THAT'S MY PLAN TO BURN OUT YOUR BATTERY FIGHTING THE LEAGUE BEFORE LEAVING IT TO 21ST CENTURY URBAN POLLUTION TO FINISH THE JOB.
YOU WERE TOO POWERFUL AND DANGEROUS TO BEAT AT TIME'S END.
SO I TOOK A BIG RISK.
BUT RIGHT HERE, RIGHT NOW, IN AN AGE OF SUPERHEROES...YOU'RE JUST ANOTHER MONSTER FOR MY FRIENDS TO PRACTICE ON.
only death can separate your nervous system from my network.
YOU CAN TAKE THIS AS PERSONALLY AS YOU LIKE, BATMAN.
BUT AFTER WHAT WE JUST WENT THROUGH, THAT SOUNDS LIKE A CHALLENGE...

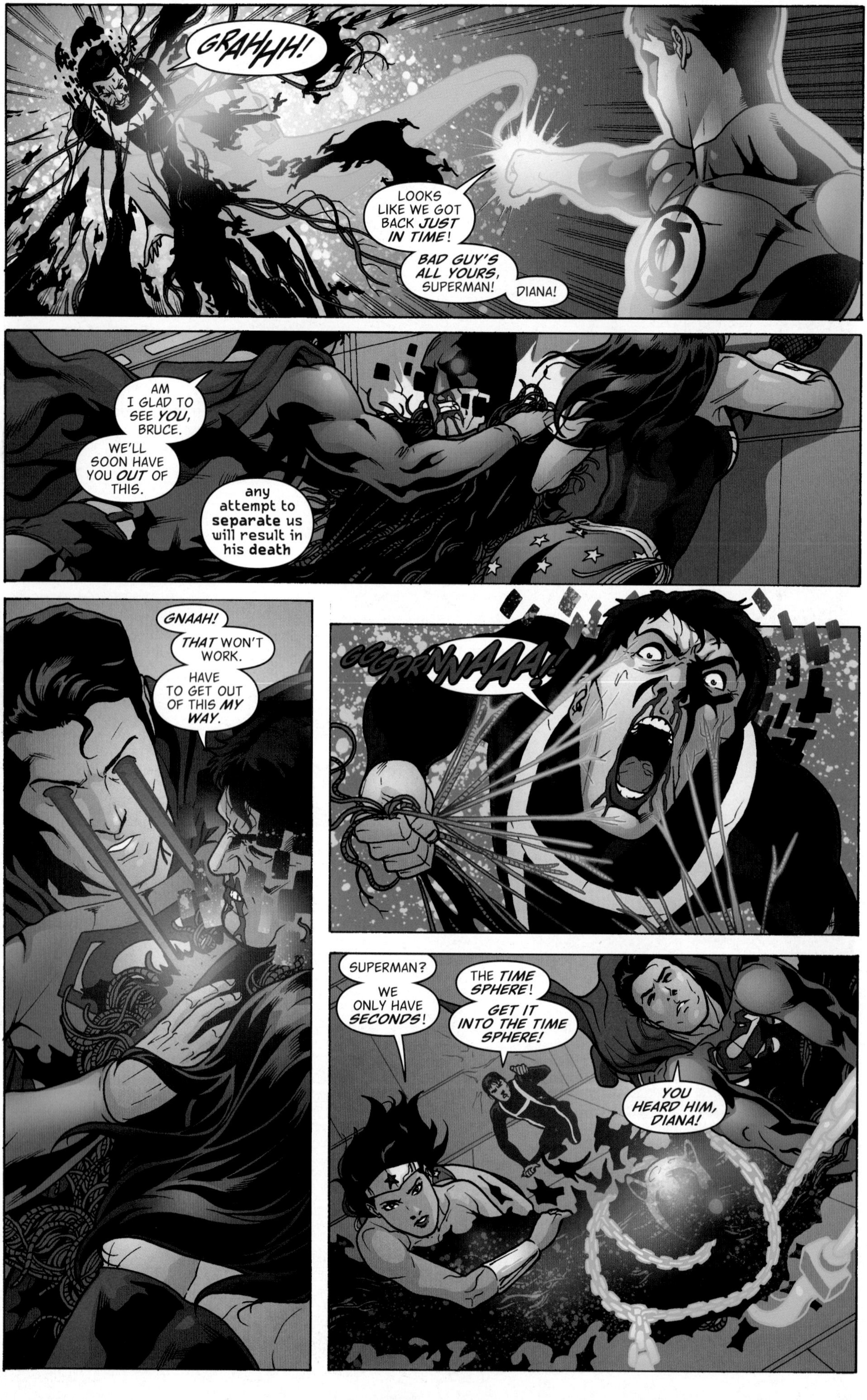
GRAHHH!
LOOKS LIKE WE GOT BACK JUST IN TIME!
BAD GUY'S ALL YOURS, SUPERMAN!
DIANA!
AM I GLAD TO SEE YOU, BRUCE.
WE'LL SOON HAVE YOU OUT OF THIS.
any attempt to separate us will result in his death
GNAAH!
THAT WON'T WORK.
HAVE TO GET OUT OF THIS MY WAY.
GGGRRNNAAAA!!
SUPERMAN?
WE ONLY HAVE SECONDS!
THE TIME SPHERE!
GET IT INTO THE TIME SPHERE!
YOU HEARD HIM, DIANA!

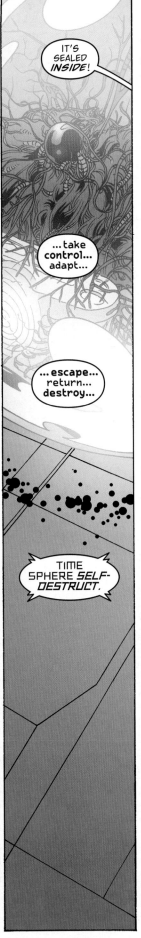

..."HYPER-ADAPTER"...

...HUNTER-KILLER...A LIVING *CURSE* MADE TO DESTROY *BATMAN* AND THE *WORLD*...

..."*DEATH-IDEA*" THAT NEVER TIRES, NEVER *STOPS*...

...BUT THE SPHERE'S RIGGED TO BLOW AND TURN IT *BACK* ON ITSELF.

IT'S SEALED *INSIDE*!

...take control... adapt...

...escape... return... destroy...

TIME SPHERE *SELF-DESTRUCT*.

ENGAGE.

Whatever they touch turns to myth.

♪♪

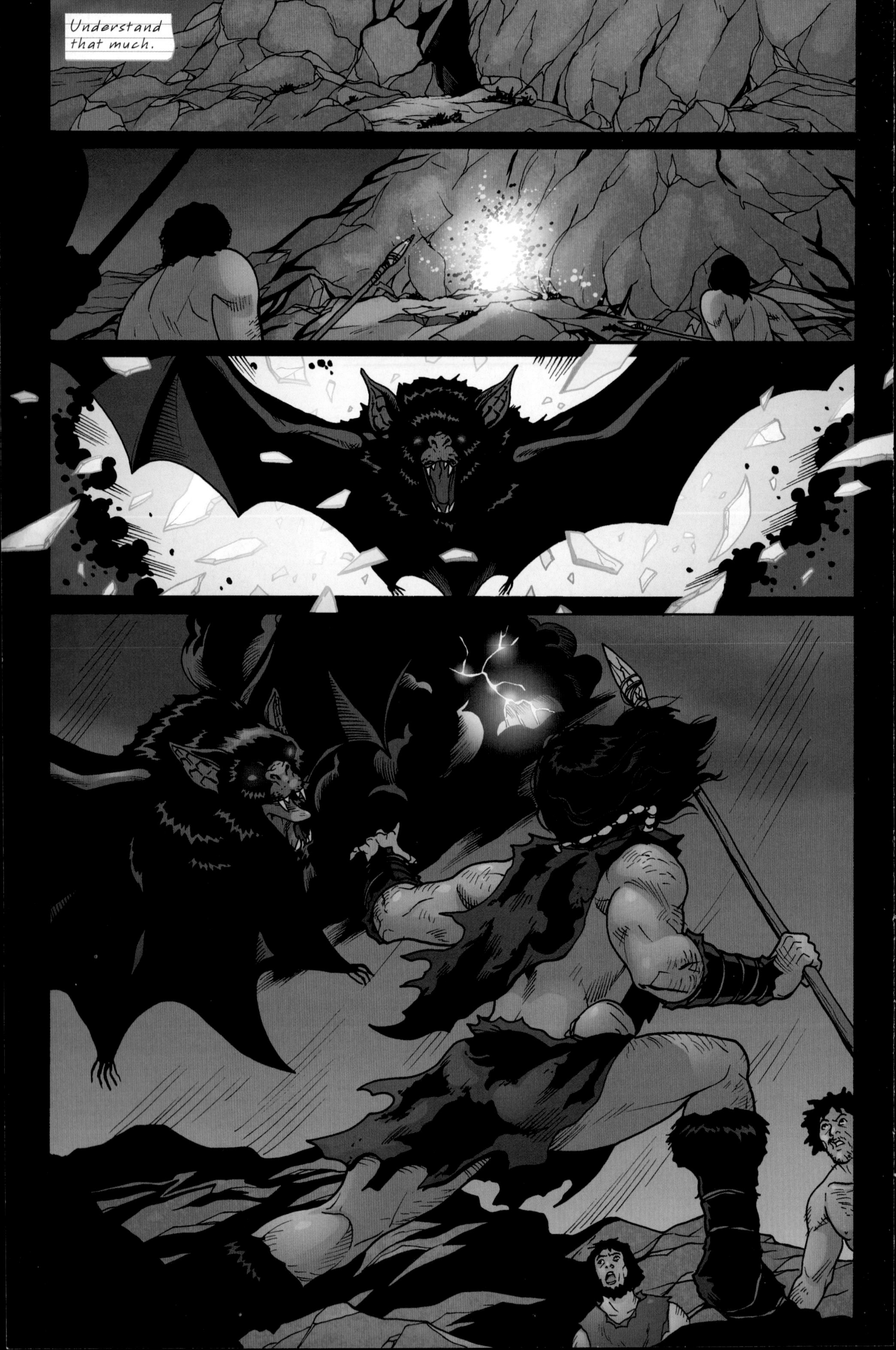
Understand that much.

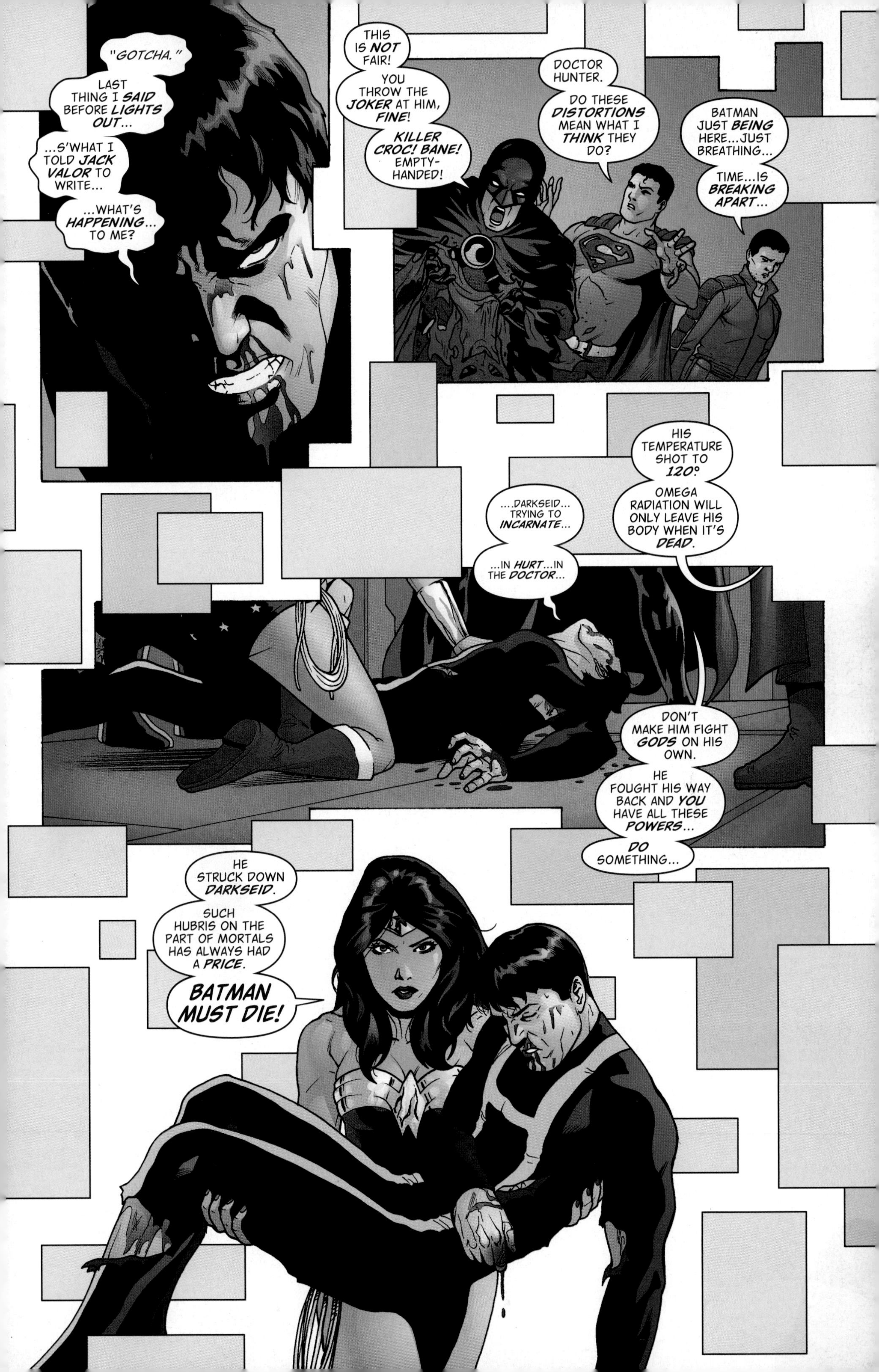
"GOTCHA."
LAST THING I SAID BEFORE LIGHTS OUT...
...S'WHAT I TOLD JACK VALOR TO WRITE...
...WHAT'S HAPPENING... TO ME?
THIS IS NOT FAIR!
YOU THROW THE JOKER AT HIM, FINE!
KILLER CROC! BANE! EMPTY-HANDED!
DOCTOR HUNTER.
DO THESE DISTORTIONS MEAN WHAT I THINK THEY DO?
BATMAN JUST BEING HERE...JUST BREATHING...
TIME...IS BREAKING APART...
....DARKSEID... TRYING TO INCARNATE...
...IN HURT...IN THE DOCTOR...
HIS TEMPERATURE SHOT TO 120°
OMEGA RADIATION WILL ONLY LEAVE HIS BODY WHEN IT'S DEAD.
DON'T MAKE HIM FIGHT GODS ON HIS OWN.
HE FOUGHT HIS WAY BACK AND YOU HAVE ALL THESE POWERS...
DO SOMETHING...
HE STRUCK DOWN DARKSEID.
SUCH HUBRIS ON THE PART OF MORTALS HAS ALWAYS HAD A PRICE.
BATMAN MUST DIE!

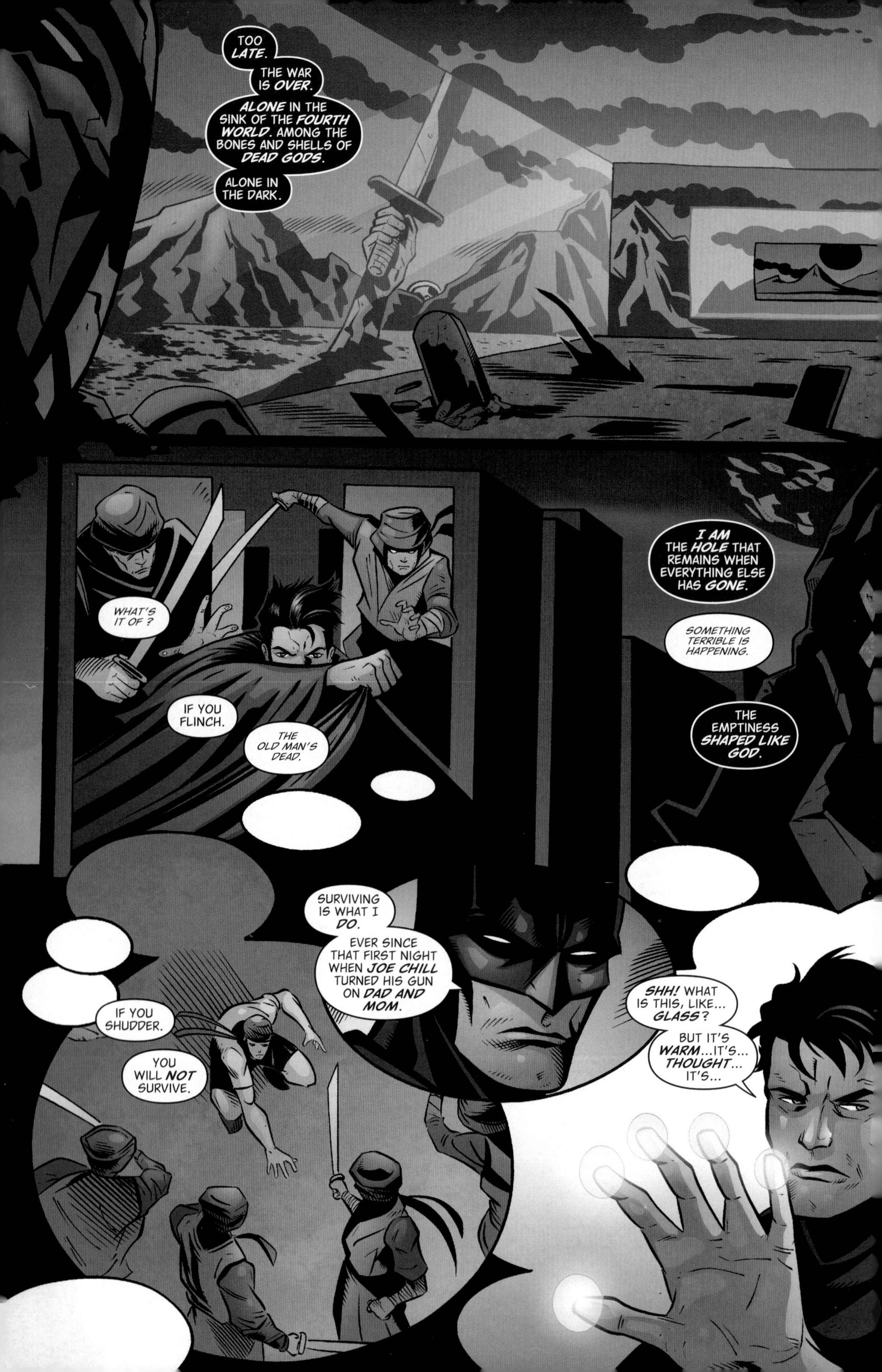
TOO LATE.
THE WAR IS OVER.
ALONE IN THE SINK OF THE FOURTH WORLD. AMONG THE BONES AND SHELLS OF DEAD GODS.
ALONE IN THE DARK.
WHAT'S IT OF?
IF YOU FLINCH.
THE OLD MAN'S DEAD.
I AM THE HOLE THAT REMAINS WHEN EVERYTHING ELSE HAS GONE.
SOMETHING TERRIBLE IS HAPPENING.
THE EMPTINESS SHAPED LIKE GOD.
SURVIVING IS WHAT I DO.
EVER SINCE THAT FIRST NIGHT WHEN JOE CHILL TURNED HIS GUN ON DAD AND MOM.
IF YOU SHUDDER.
YOU WILL NOT SURVIVE.
SHH! WHAT IS THIS, LIKE... GLASS?
BUT IT'S WARM...IT'S... THOUGHT... IT'S...

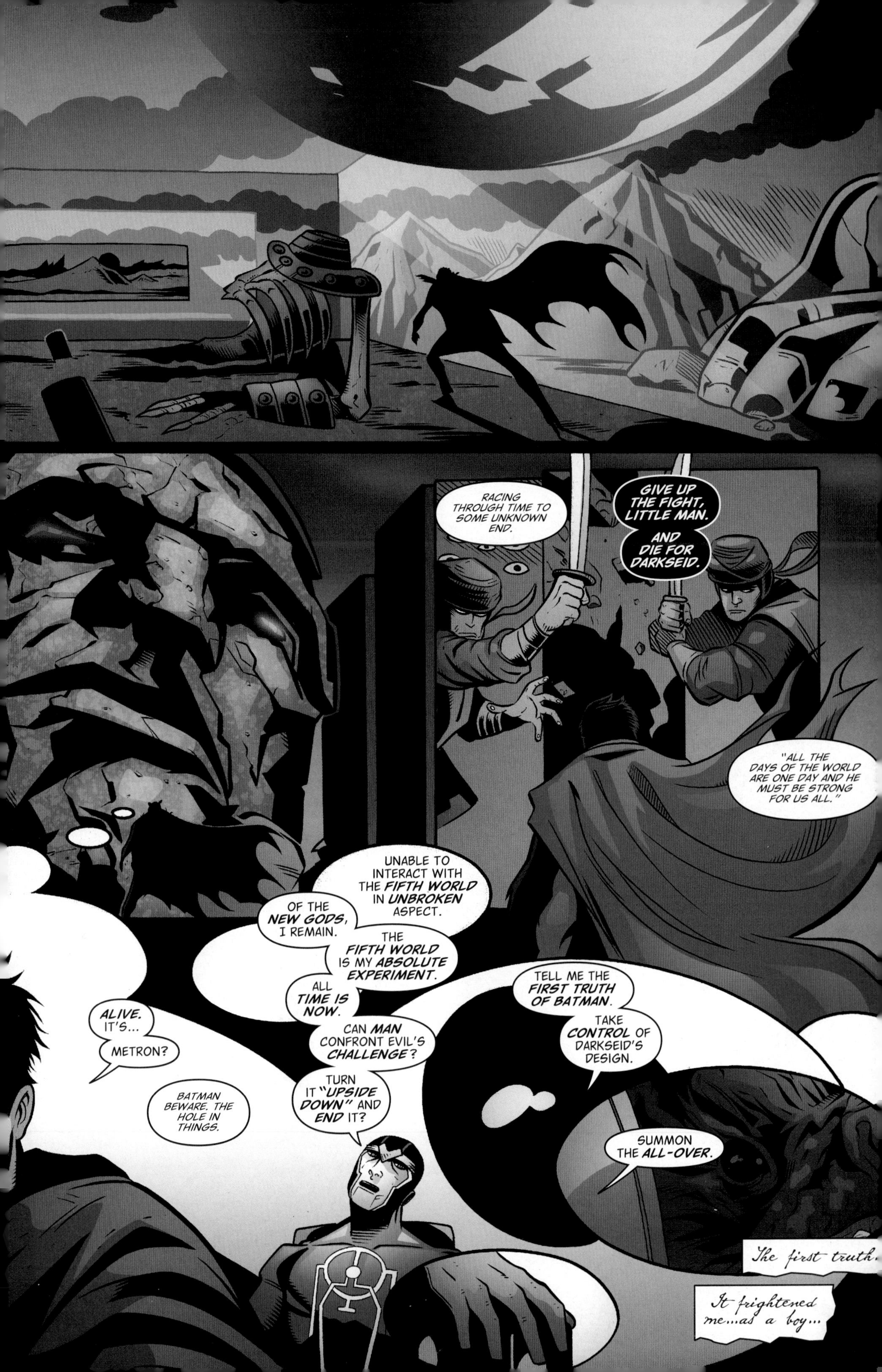
RACING THROUGH TIME TO SOME UNKNOWN END.
GIVE UP THE FIGHT, LITTLE MAN.
AND DIE FOR DARKSEID.
"ALL THE DAYS OF THE WORLD ARE ONE DAY AND HE MUST BE STRONG FOR US ALL."
UNABLE TO INTERACT WITH THE FIFTH WORLD IN UNBROKEN ASPECT.
OF THE NEW GODS, I REMAIN.
THE FIFTH WORLD IS MY ABSOLUTE EXPERIMENT.
ALL TIME IS NOW.
CAN MAN CONFRONT EVIL'S CHALLENGE?
TURN IT "UPSIDE DOWN" AND END IT?
ALIVE. IT'S...
METRON?
BATMAN BEWARE. THE HOLE IN THINGS.
TELL ME THE FIRST TRUTH OF BATMAN.
TAKE CONTROL OF DARKSEID'S DESIGN.
SUMMON THE ALL-OVER.
The first truth.
It frightened me...as a boy...

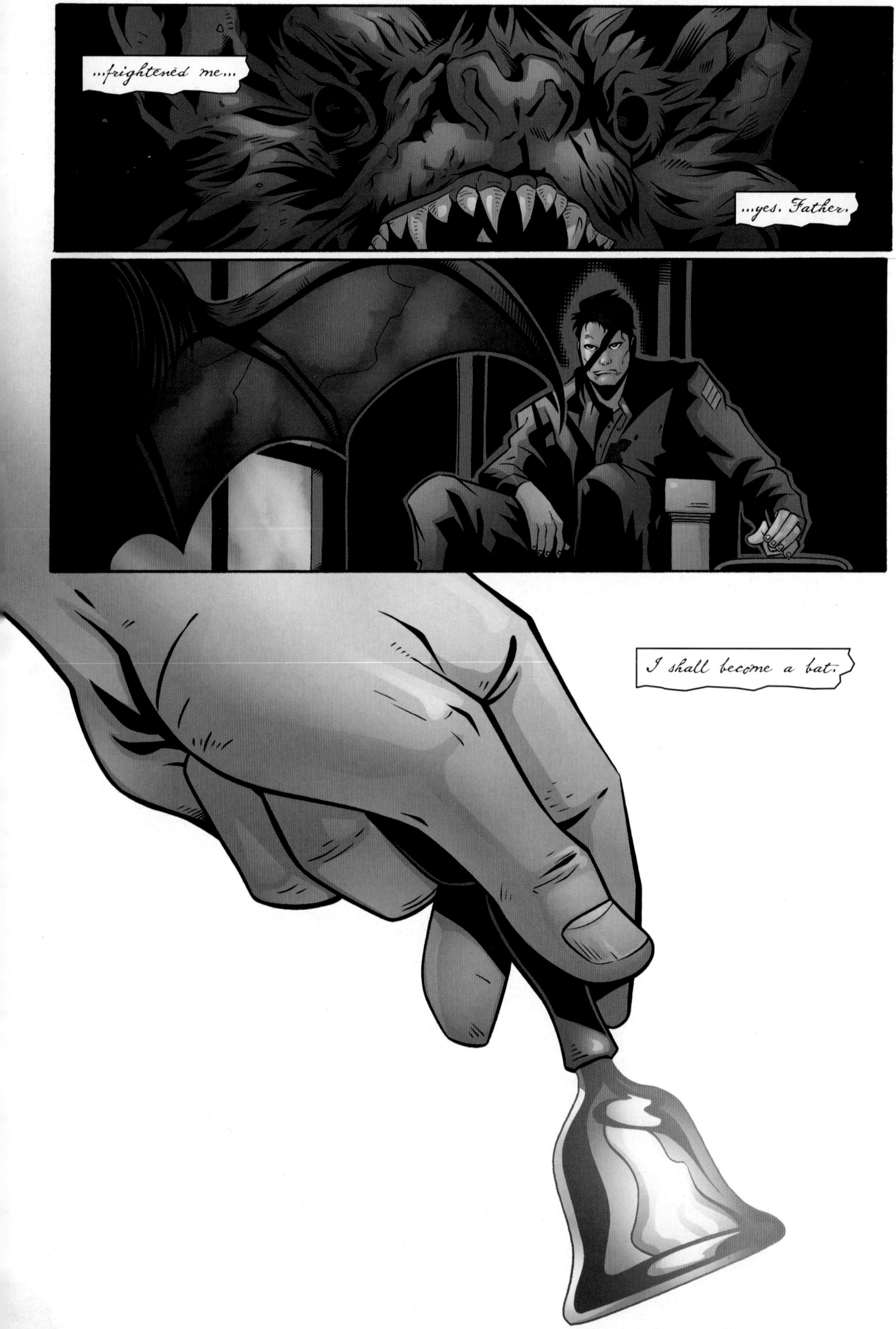
...frightened me...
...yes. Father.
I shall become a bat.

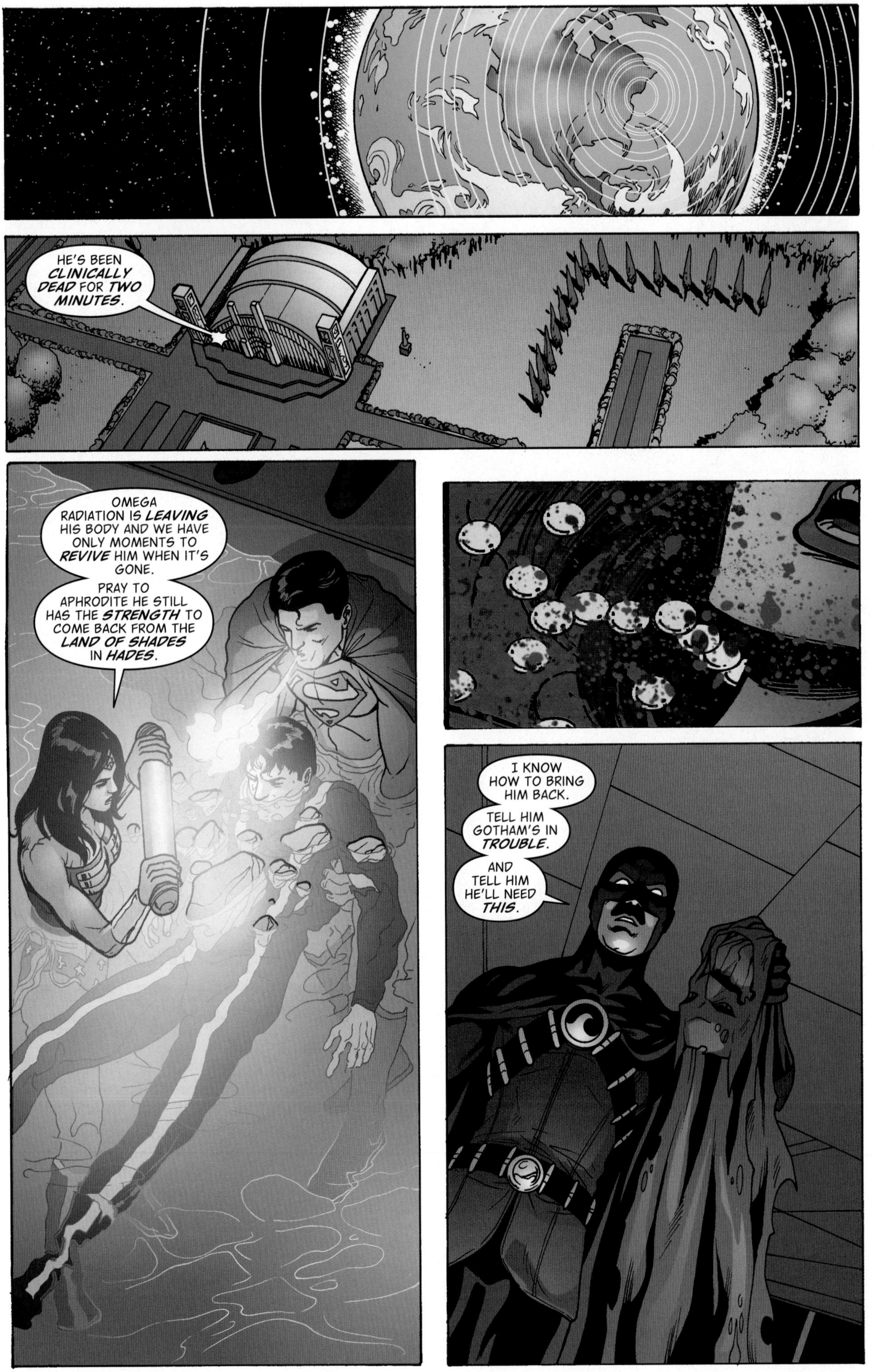
HE'S BEEN CLINICALLY DEAD FOR TWO MINUTES.
OMEGA RADIATION IS LEAVING HIS BODY AND WE HAVE ONLY MOMENTS TO REVIVE HIM WHEN IT'S GONE.
PRAY TO APHRODITE HE STILL HAS THE STRENGTH TO COME BACK FROM THE LAND OF SHADES IN HADES.
I KNOW HOW TO BRING HIM BACK.
TELL HIM GOTHAM'S IN TROUBLE.
AND TELL HIM HE'LL NEED THIS.

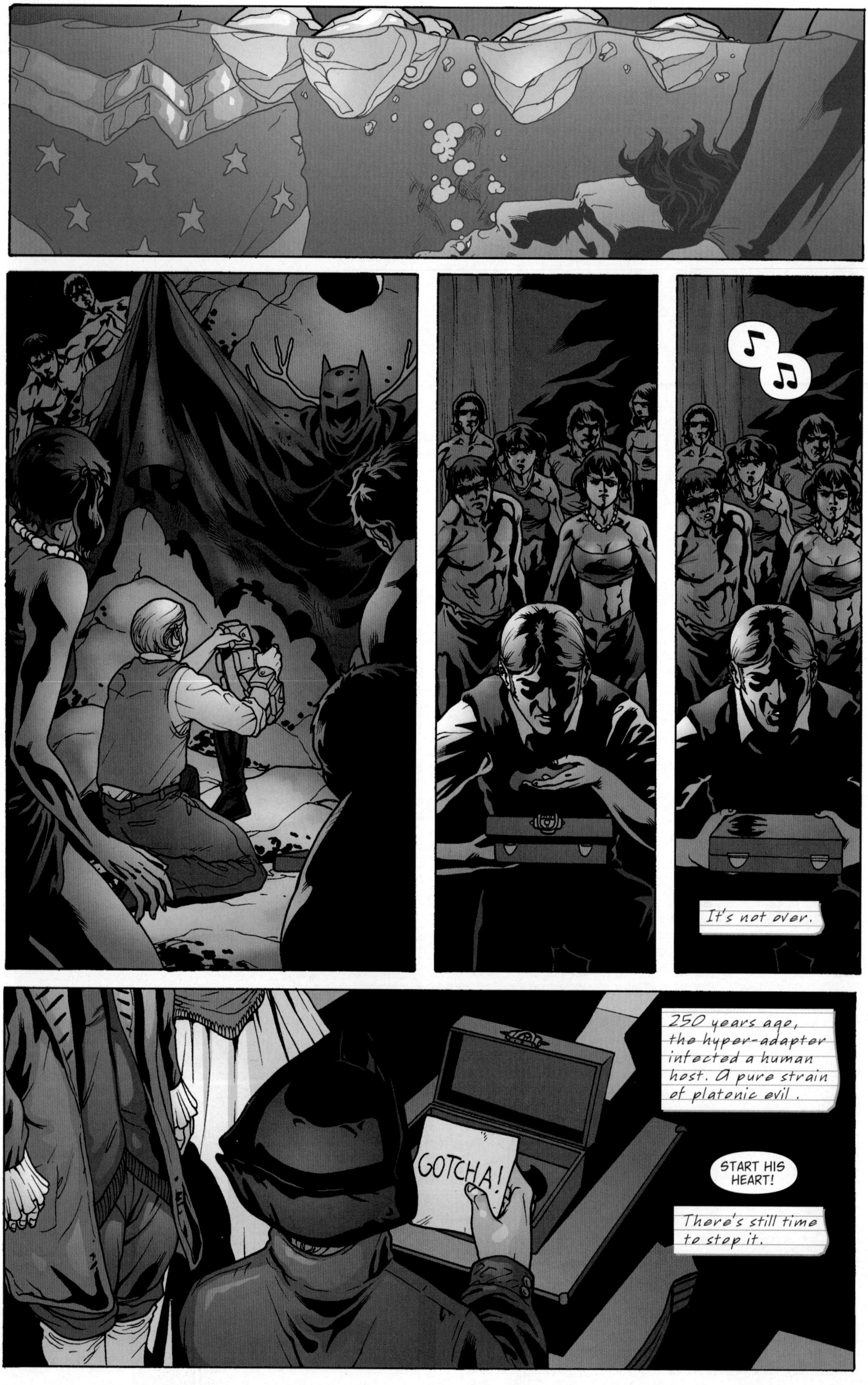
♪ ♫
It's not over.
GOTCHA!
250 years ago, the hyper-adapter infected a human host. A pure strain of platonic evil.
START HIS HEART!
There's still time to stop it.

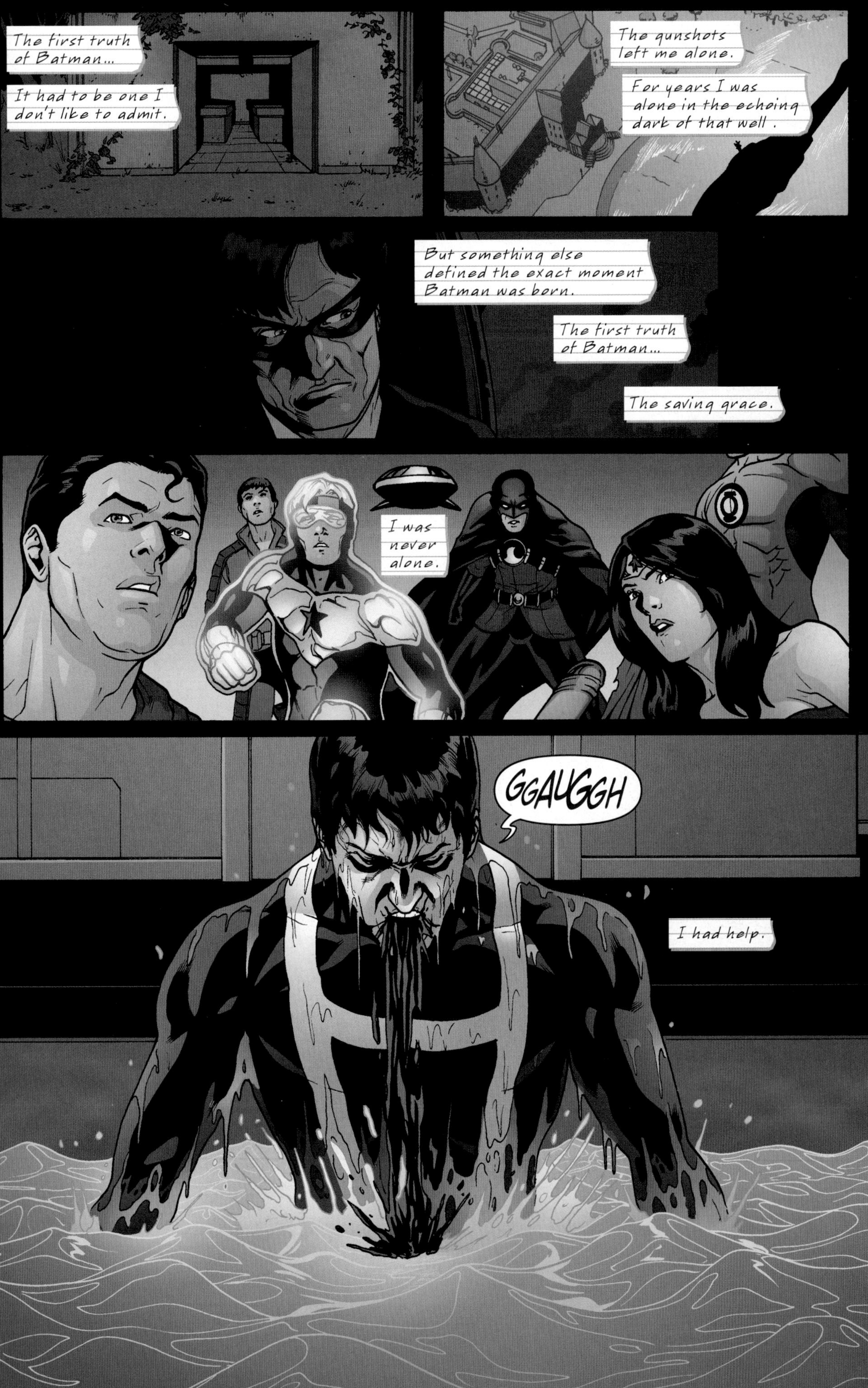

The first truth of Batman...
It had to be one I don't like to admit.
The gunshots left me alone.
For years I was alone in the echoing dark of that well.
But something else defined the exact moment Batman was born.
The first truth of Batman...
The saving grace.
I was never alone.
GGAUGGH
I had help.

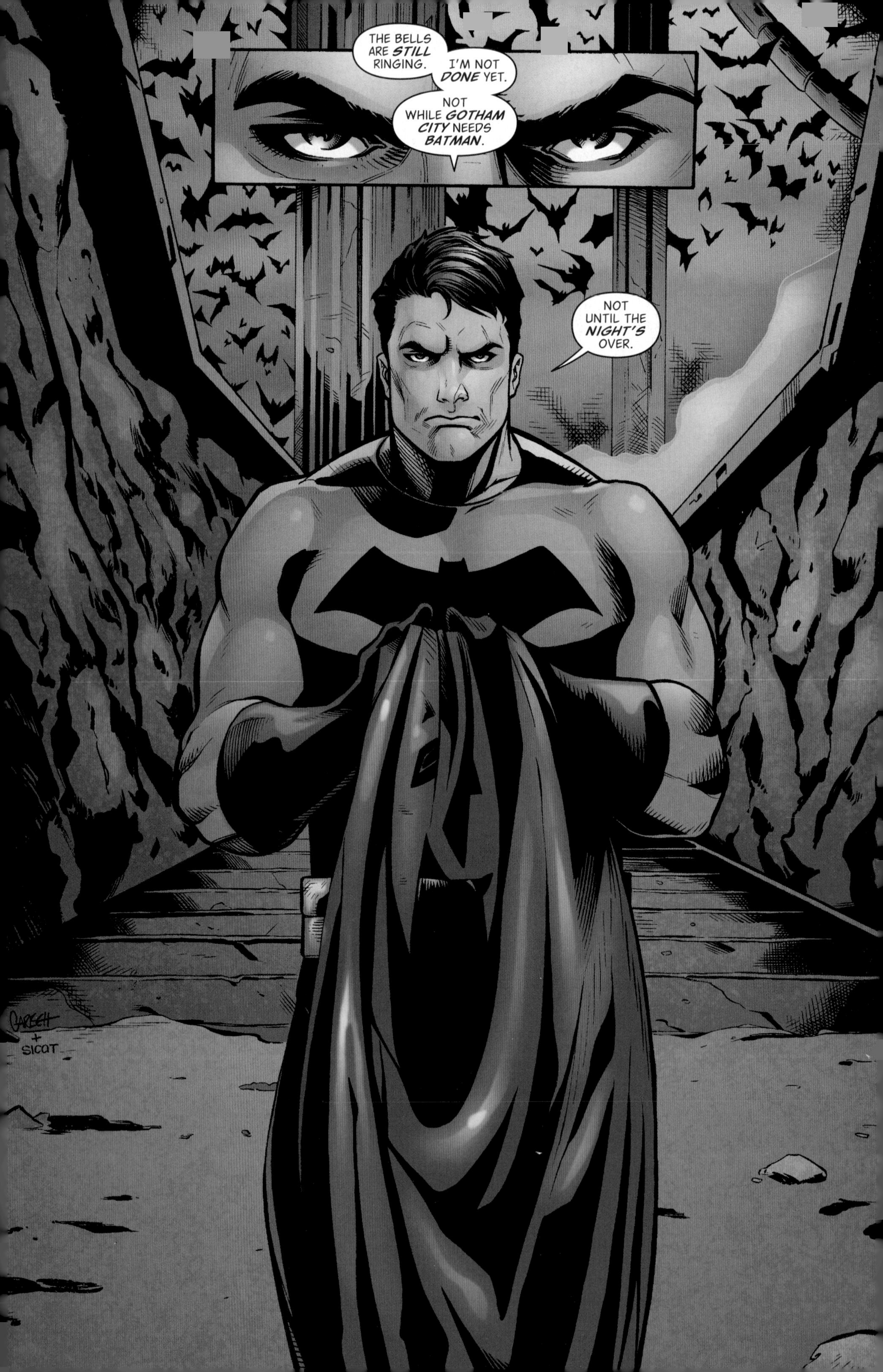
THE BELLS ARE STILL RINGING.
I'M NOT DONE YET.
NOT WHILE GOTHAM CITY NEEDS BATMAN.
NOT UNTIL THE NIGHT'S OVER.
GARBETT + SICAT

BACK iN TIME

THE RETURN OF BRUCE WAYNE SKETCHBOOK

Grant Morrison • Andy Kubert • Chris Sprouse

Frazer Irving • Yanick Paquette • Ryan Sook

RETURN OF BRUCE WAYNE #6

PAGE 20 frame ①

frame ②

— PANE EDGES TILT
AND BREAK LOOSE

frame ③

RETURN OF BRUCE WAYNE 6

PAGE ㉕

RED ROBIN
(skull Relic
in his hands
disintegrating

HUNTER

SKEETS

BOOSTER

GL

PANELS BREAK UP
LOOKING A LITTLE
LIKE THIS

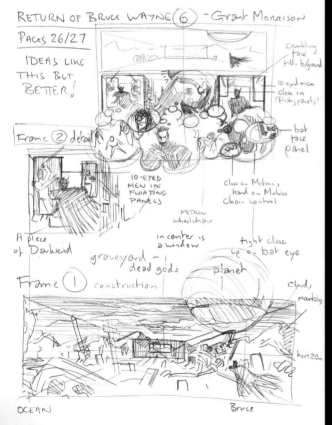

RETURN OF BRUCE WAYNE ⑥ — Grant Morrison

PAGES 26/27

IDEAS LIKE
THIS BUT
BETTER!

Crumbling
face tilts. b/ground

10-eyed men
close in (floating panels)

Frame ② detail

bat
face
panel

10-EYED
MEN IN
FLOATING
PANELS

Close on Metron's
hand on Mobius
Chair control

METRON
wheelchair

A piece
of Darkseid

in center is
a window

tight close
up on bat eye

graveyard —
dead gods

planet

Frame ① construction

Cloud
mountains

horizon

OCEAN

Bruce

This page: A sampling of thumbnail layouts by Grant Morrison for issue #6.

Opposite: Morrison's character design for the Archivist.

FAO FRAZER IRVING

ARCHIVIST - RETURN of BRUCE WAYNE ②

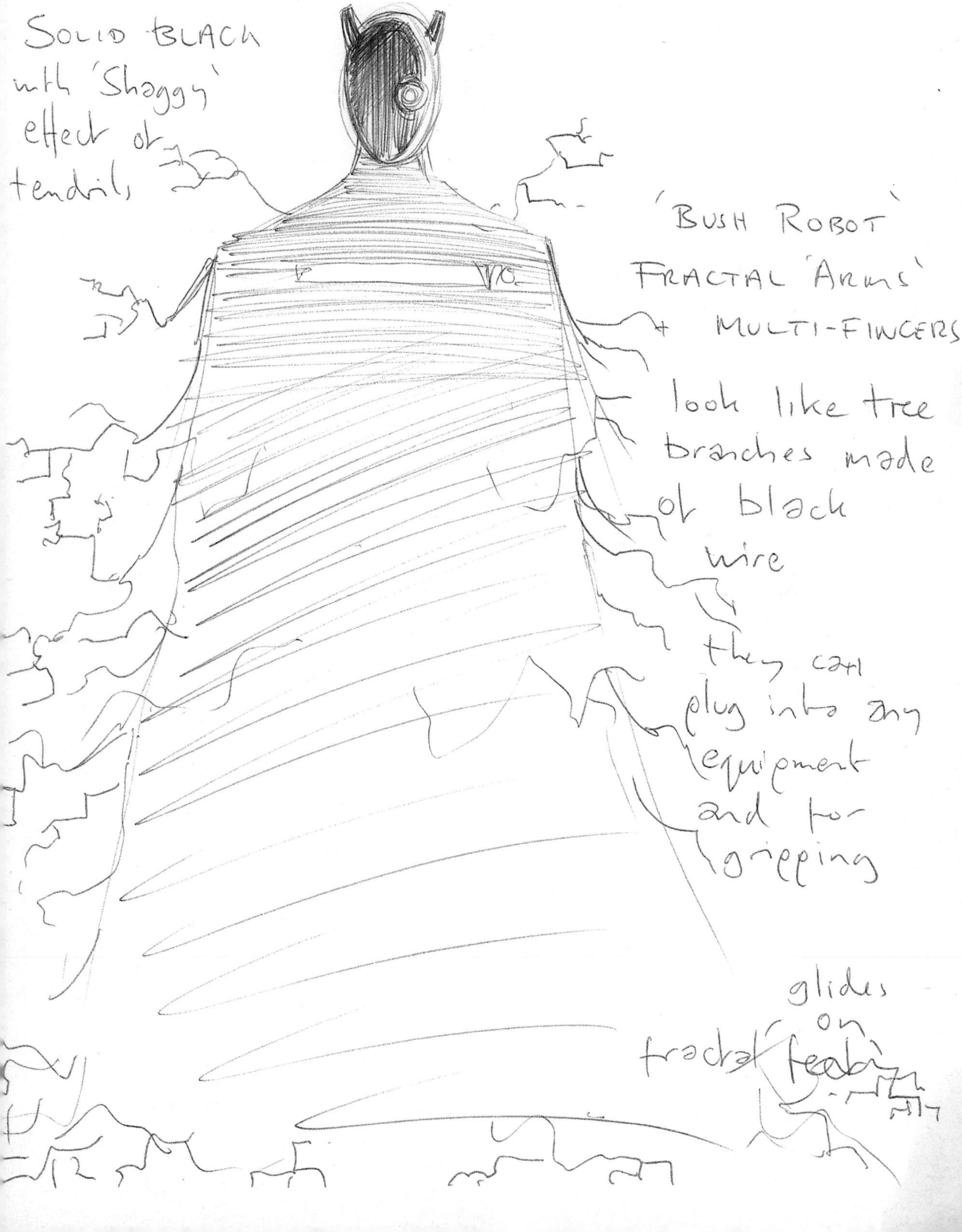
SOLID BLACK with 'Shaggy' effect of tendrils
'BUSH ROBOT' FRACTAL 'ARMS' + MULTI-FINGERS
look like tree branches made of black wire
they can plug into any equipment and for gripping
glides on fractal feet

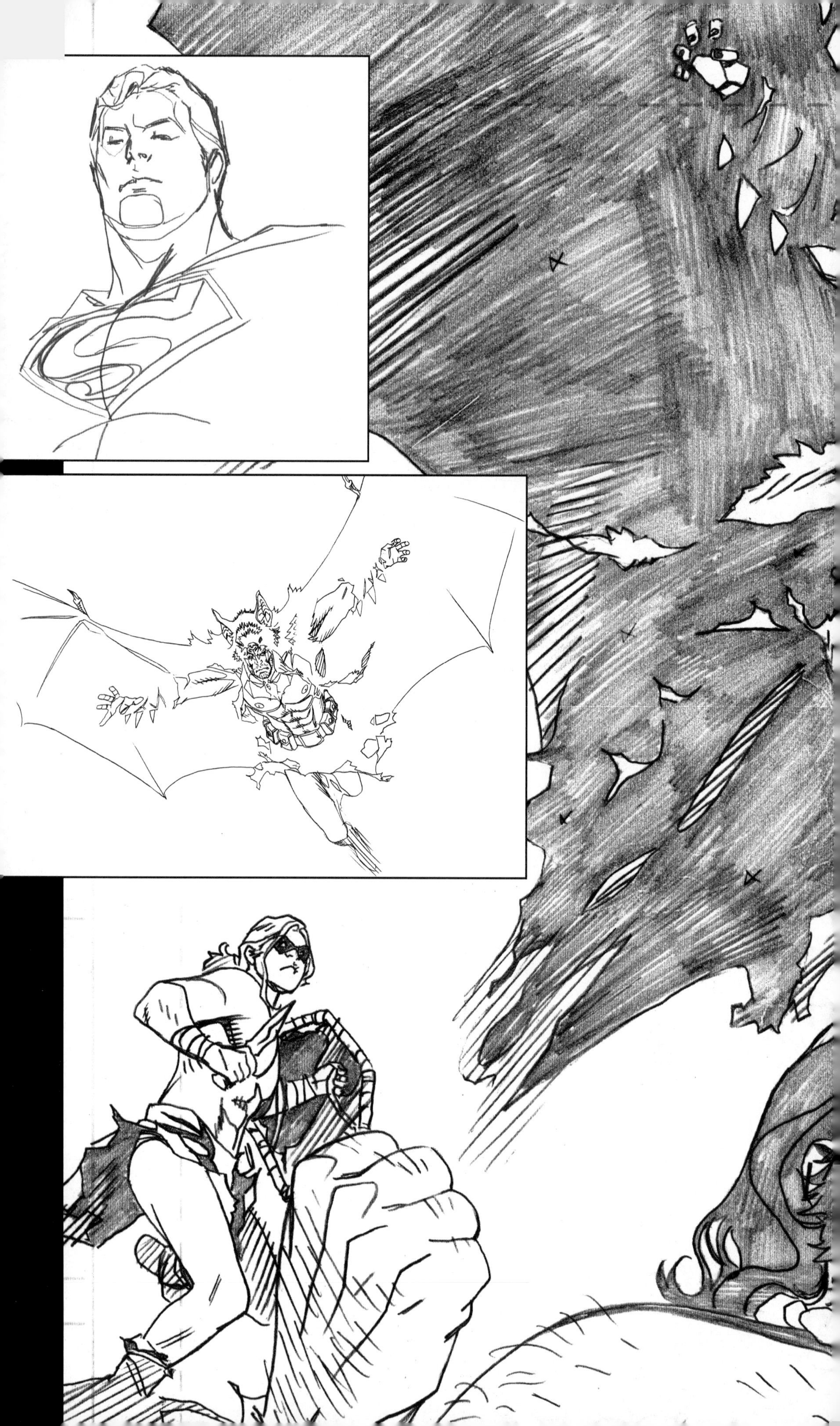

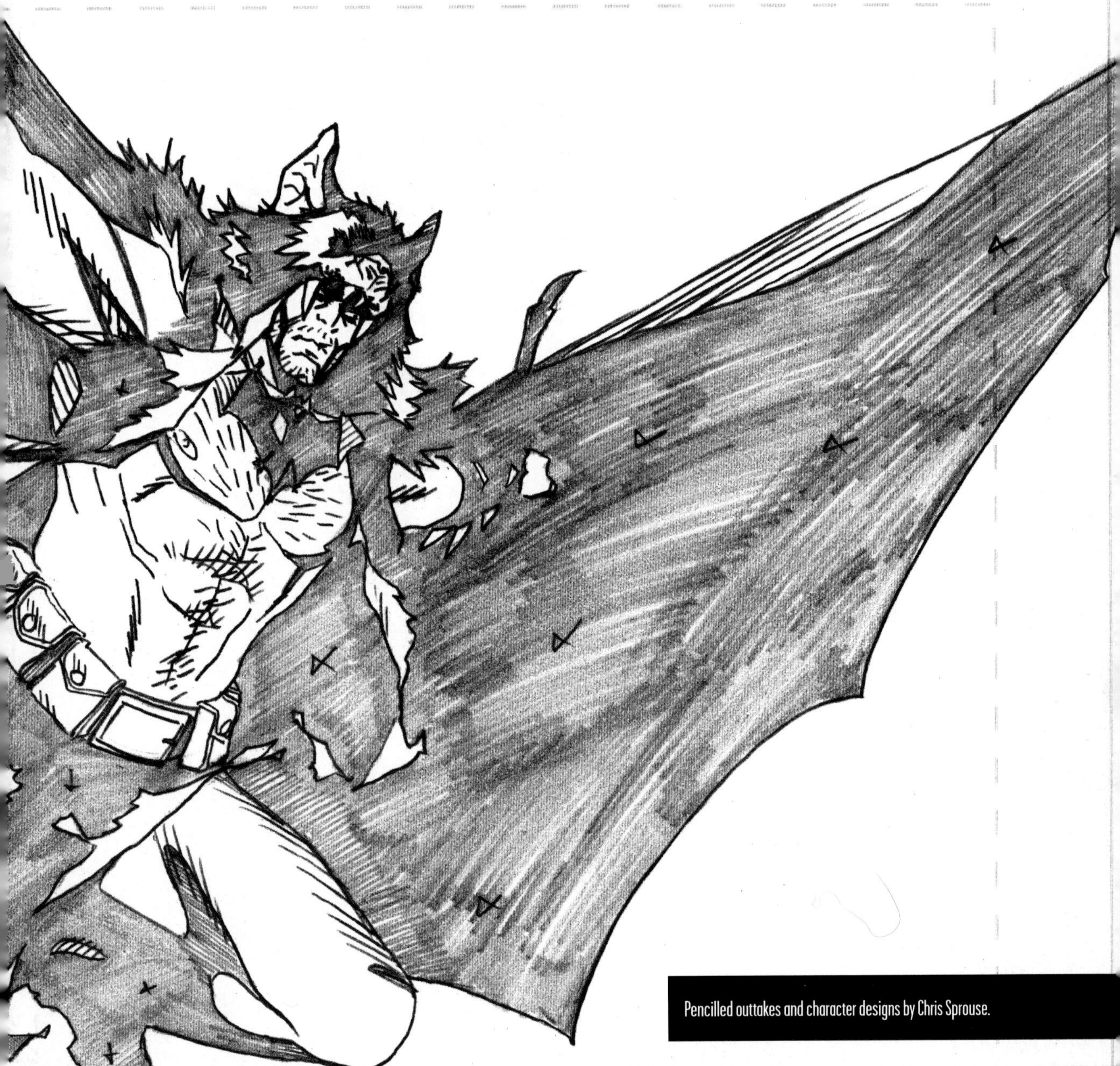

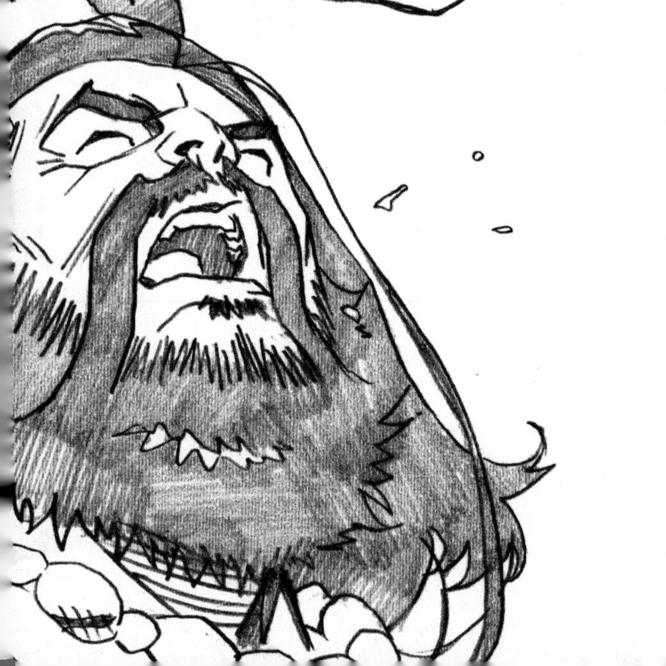

Pencilled outtakes and character designs by Chris Sprouse.

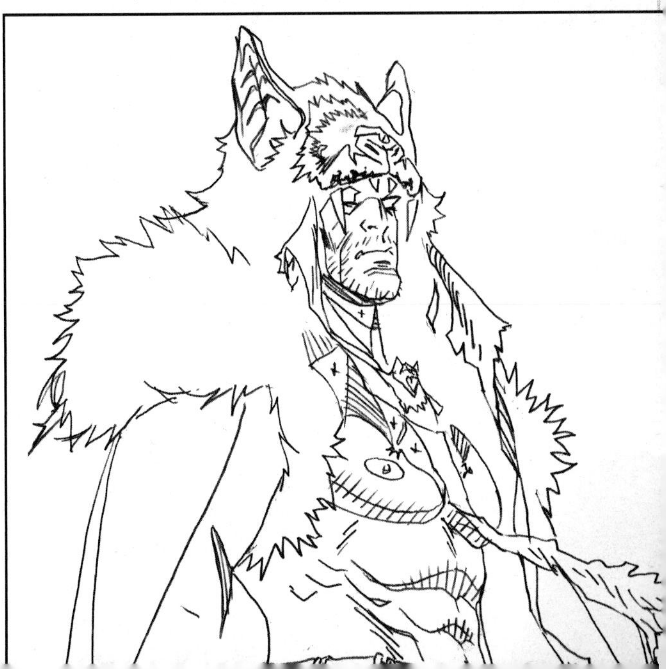

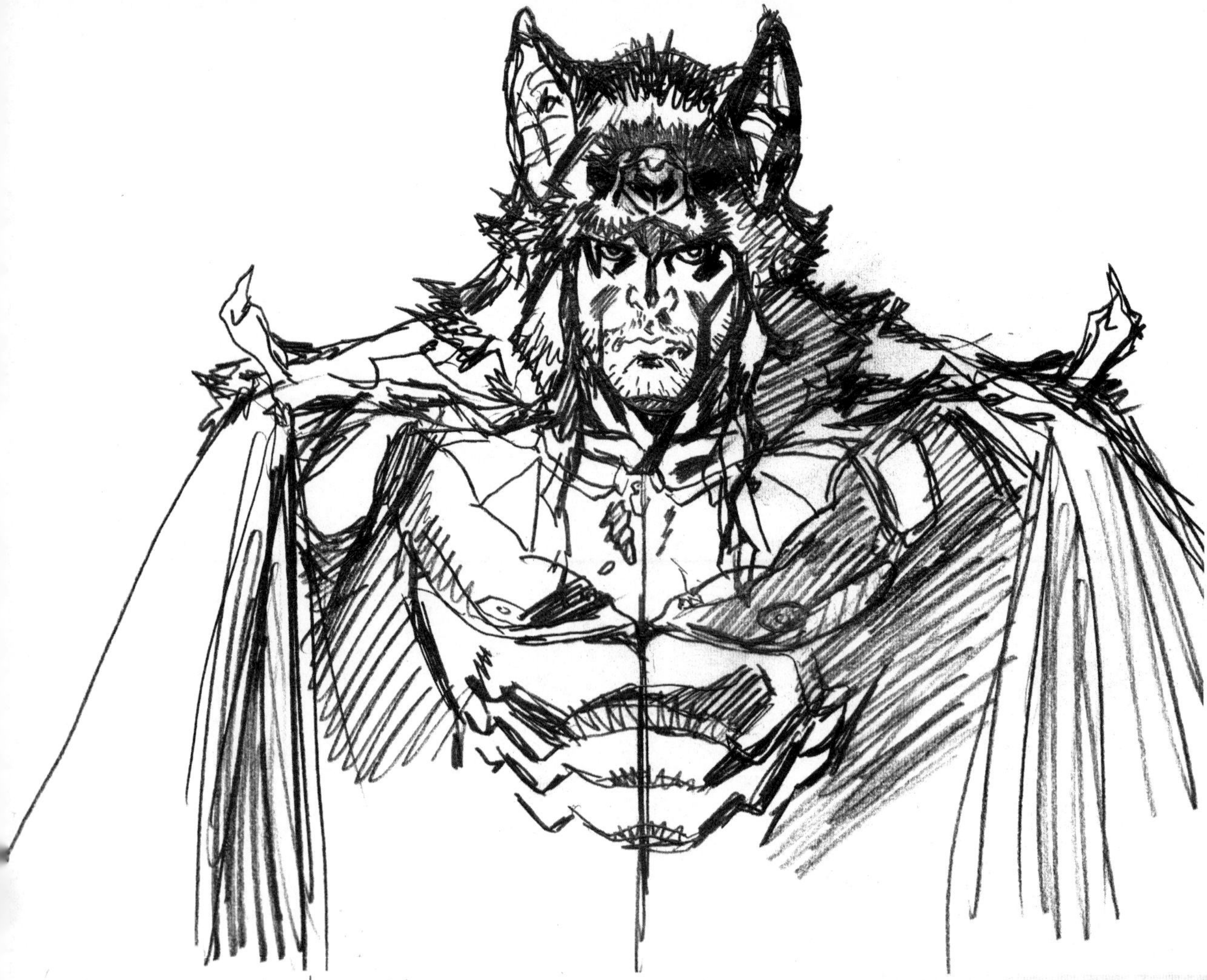

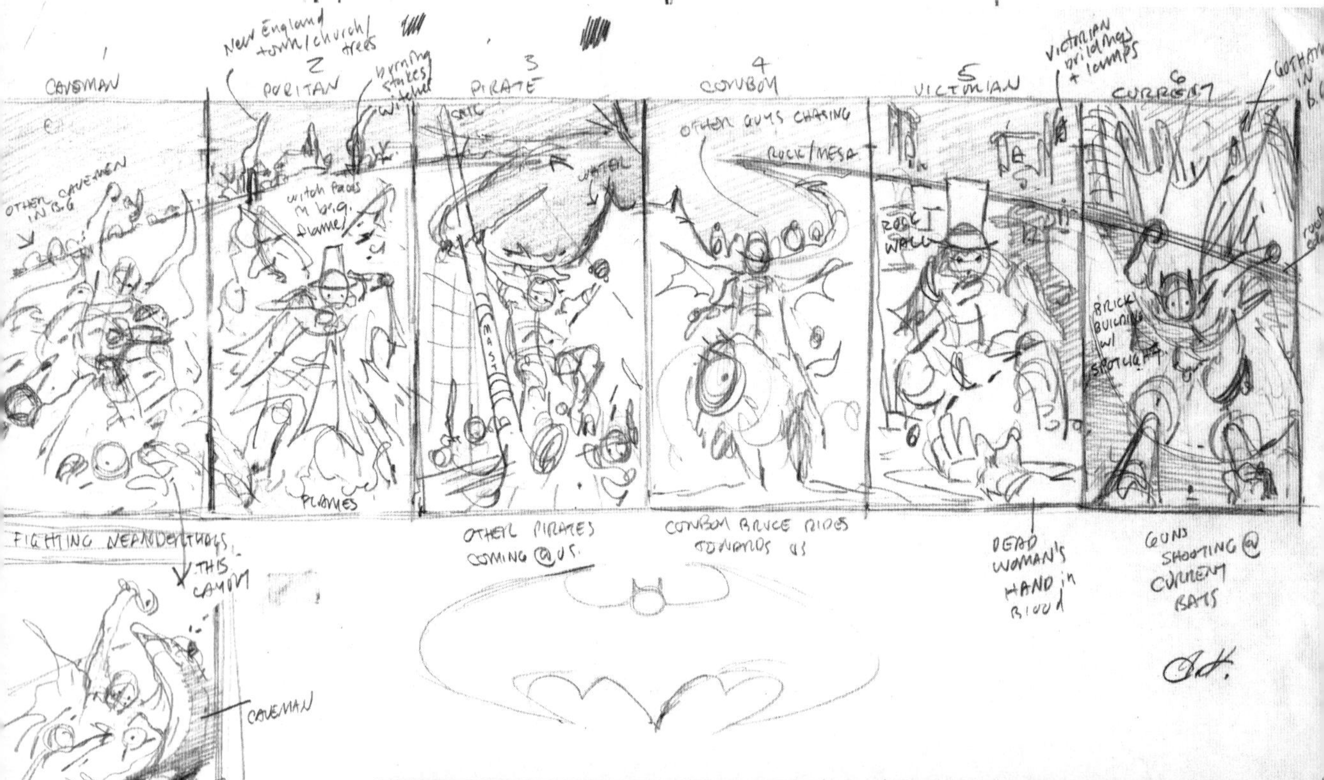

1 CAVEMAN
New England town/church/trees
2 PURITAN
burning stakes/
3 PIRATE
4 COWBOY
5 VICTORIAN
Victorian buildings + lamps
6 CURRENT
GOTHAM IN B.G.
OTHER CAVEMEN IN B.G.
witch faces in b.g. flames
WATER
MAST
OTHER GUYS CHASING
ROCK/MESA
ROCK WALL
BRICK BUILDING W/ SPOTLIGHT
FLAMES
FIGHTING NEANDERTHALS
OTHER PIRATES COMING @ US.
COWBOY BRUCE RIDES TOWARDS US
DEAD WOMAN'S HAND in BLOOD
GUNS SHOOTING @ CURRENT BATS

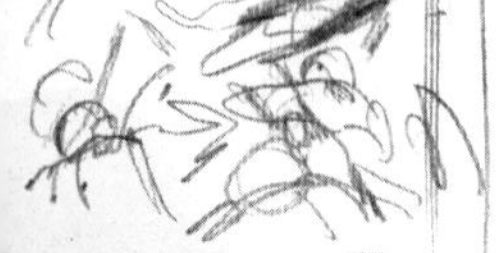

THIS CAVEMAN
CAVEMAN

Top: A variant cover art sketch by Chris Sprouse for issue #1.

Above: Andy Kubert's thumbnail roughs for the series' covers.

Opposite: Character designs by Andy Kubert for the cover art to issues #1-2

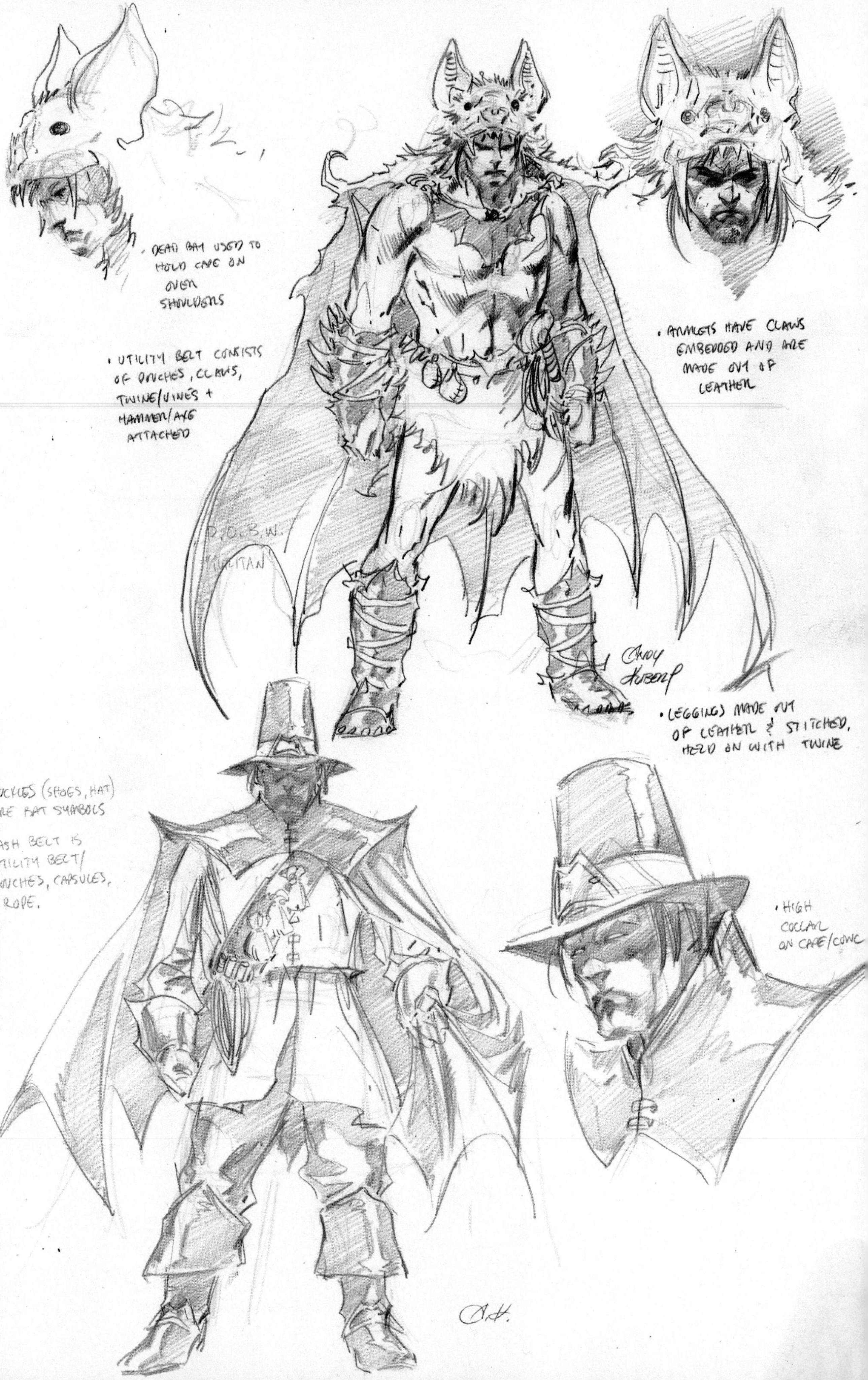
• DEAD BAT USED TO HOLD CAPE ON OVER SHOULDERS
• UTILITY BELT CONSISTS OF POUCHES, CLAWS, TWINE/VINES + HAMMER/AXE ATTACHED
• ARMLETS HAVE CLAWS EMBEDDED AND ARE MADE OUT OF LEATHER
R.O.B.W.
ANDY KUBERT
• LEGGINGS MADE OUT OF LEATHER & STITCHED, HELD ON WITH TWINE
• BUCKLES (SHOES, HAT) ARE BAT SYMBOLS
• SASH BELT IS UTILITY BELT/ POUCHES, CAPSULES, ROPE.
• HIGH COLLAR ON CAPE/COWL
A.K.

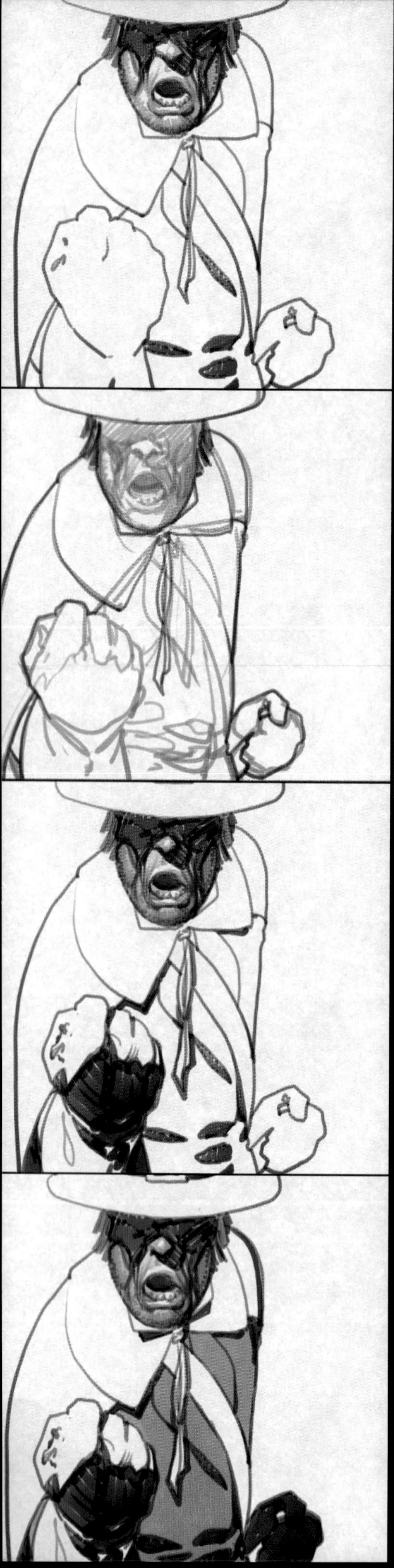

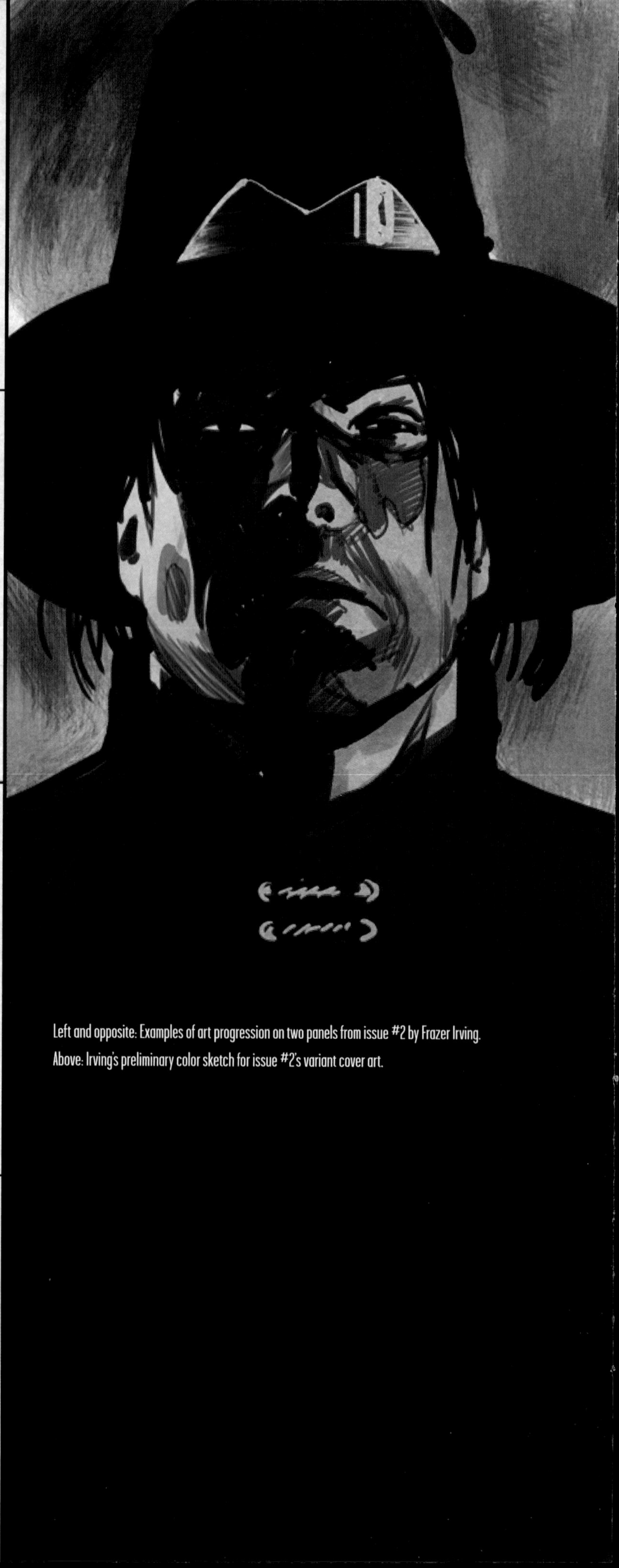

Left and opposite: Examples of art progression on two panels from issue #2 by Frazer Irving.
Above: Irving's preliminary color sketch for issue #2's variant cover art.

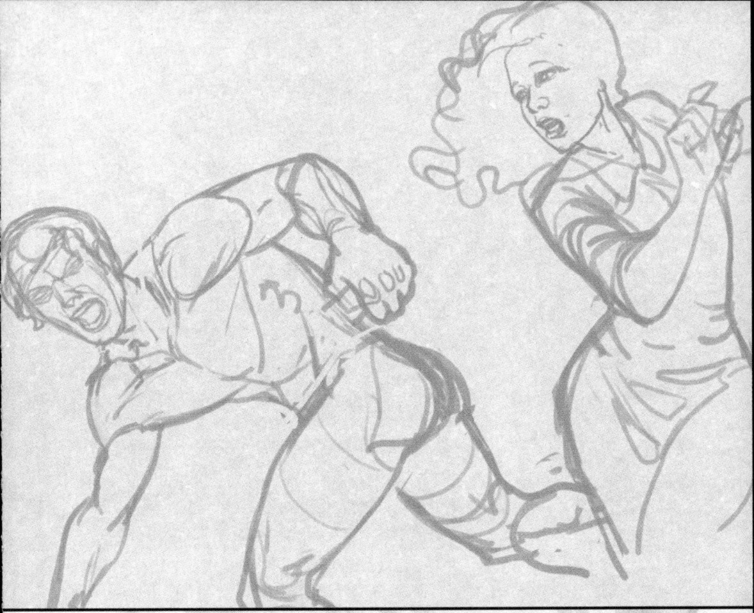

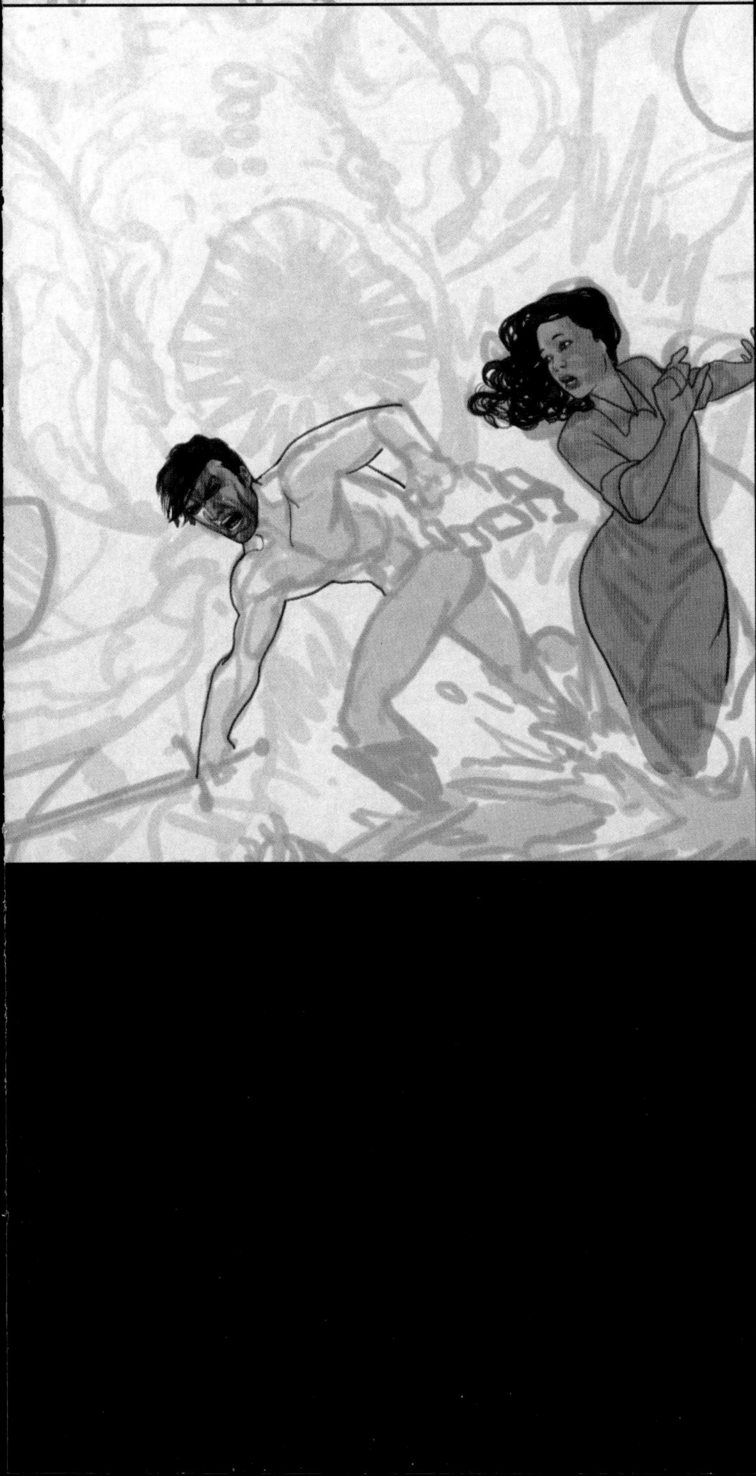

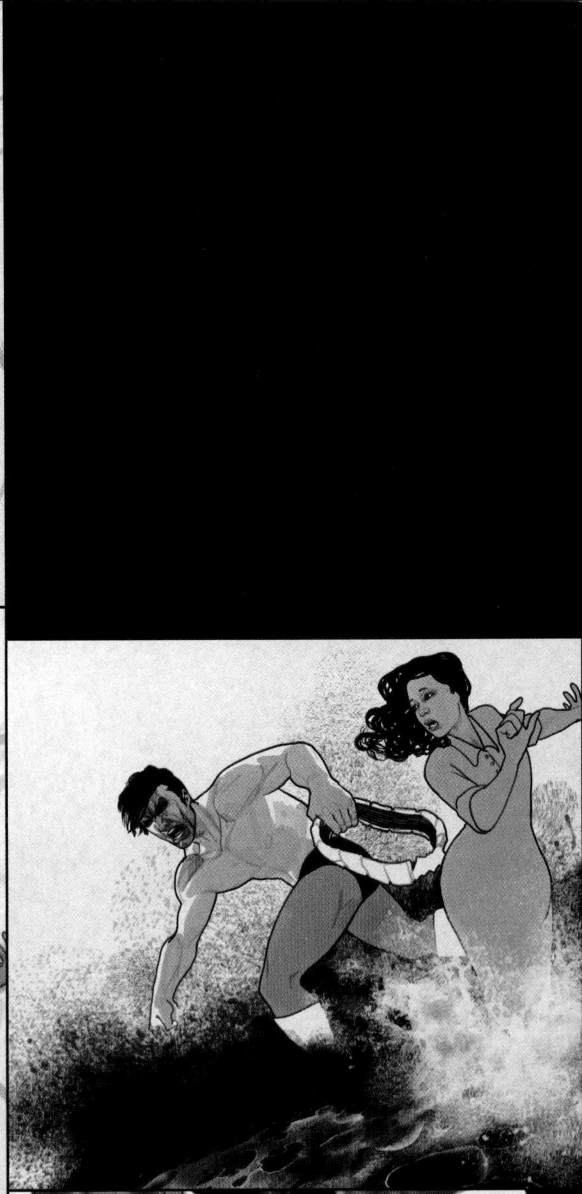

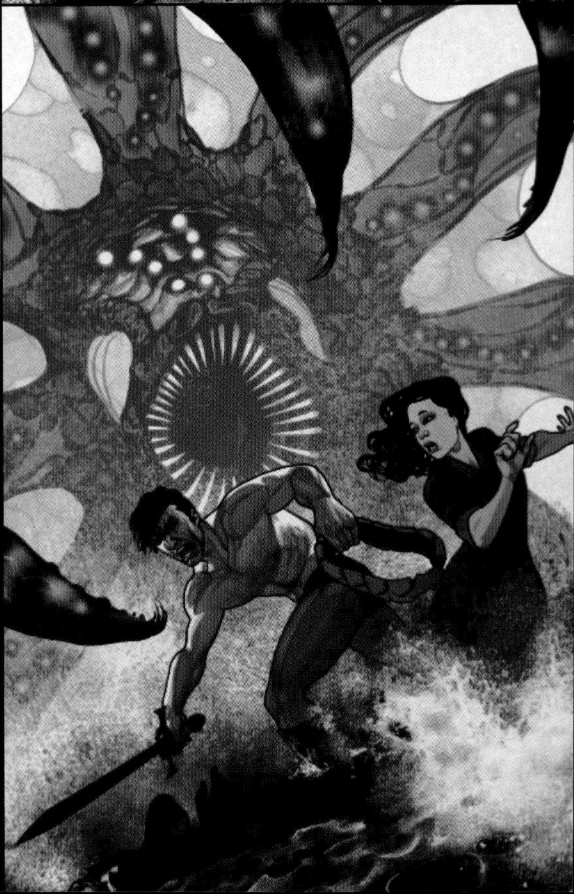

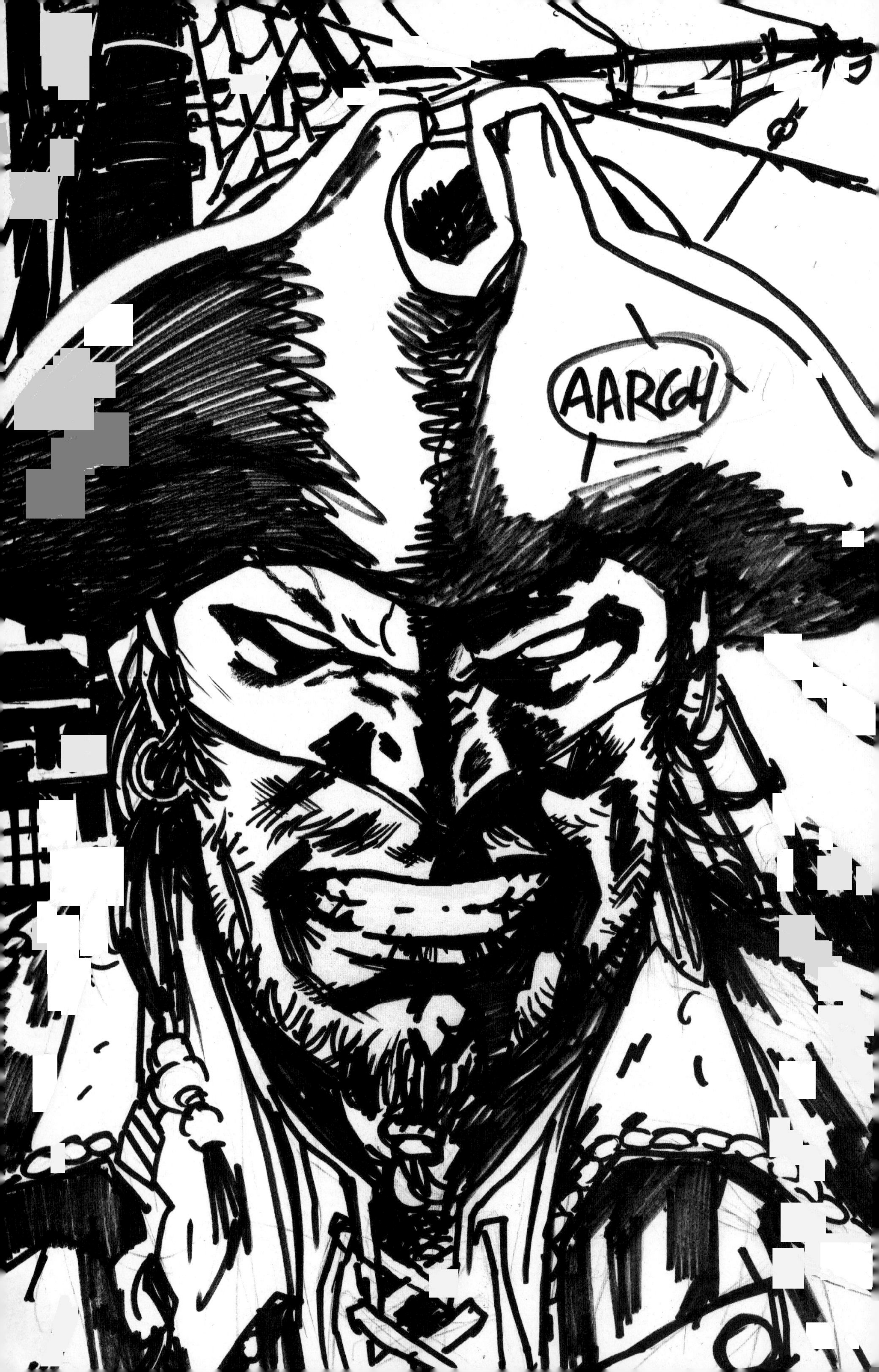
AARGH

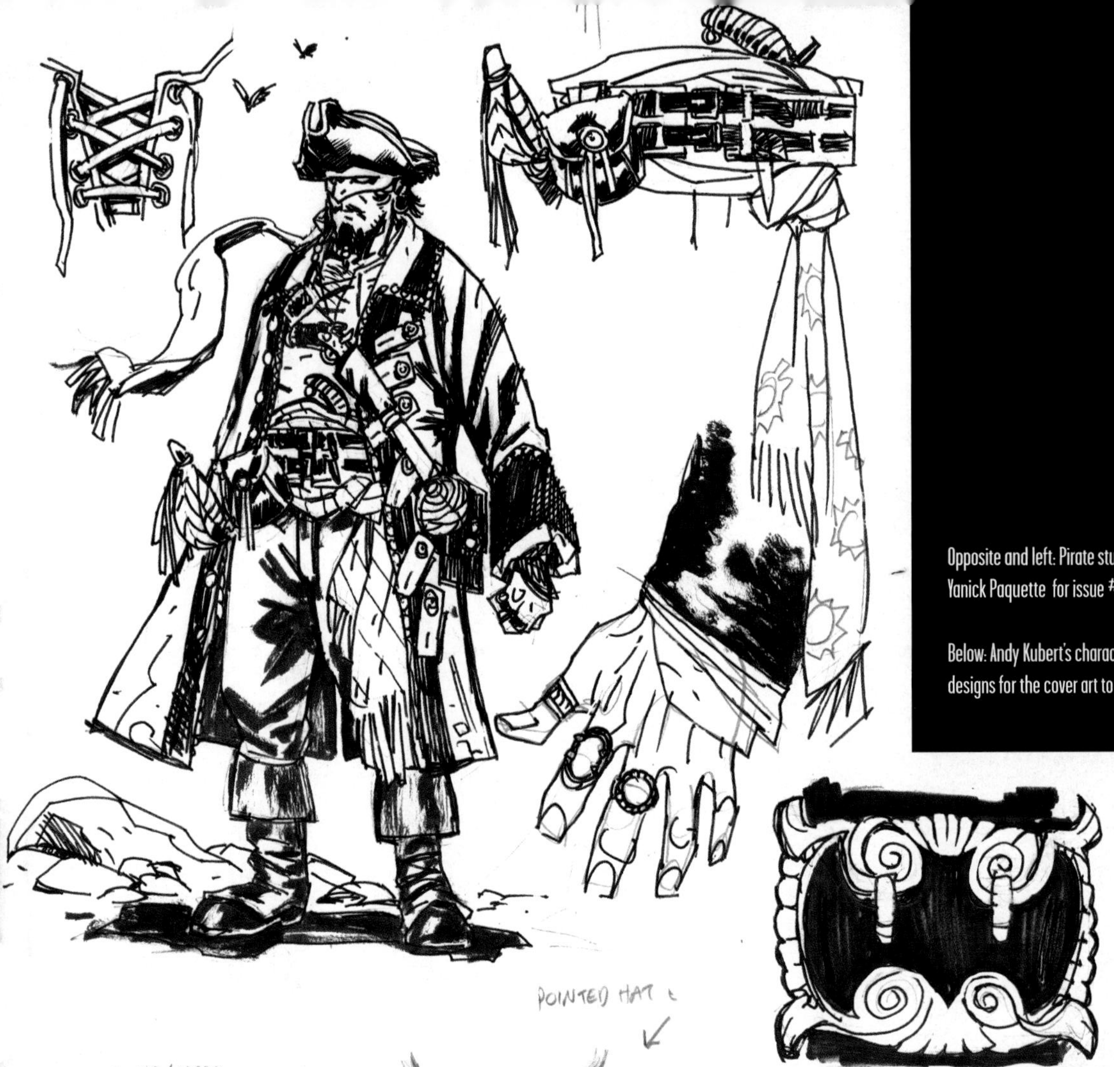

Opposite and left: Pirate studies by Yanick Paquette for issue #3.

Below: Andy Kubert's character designs for the cover art to issue #3.

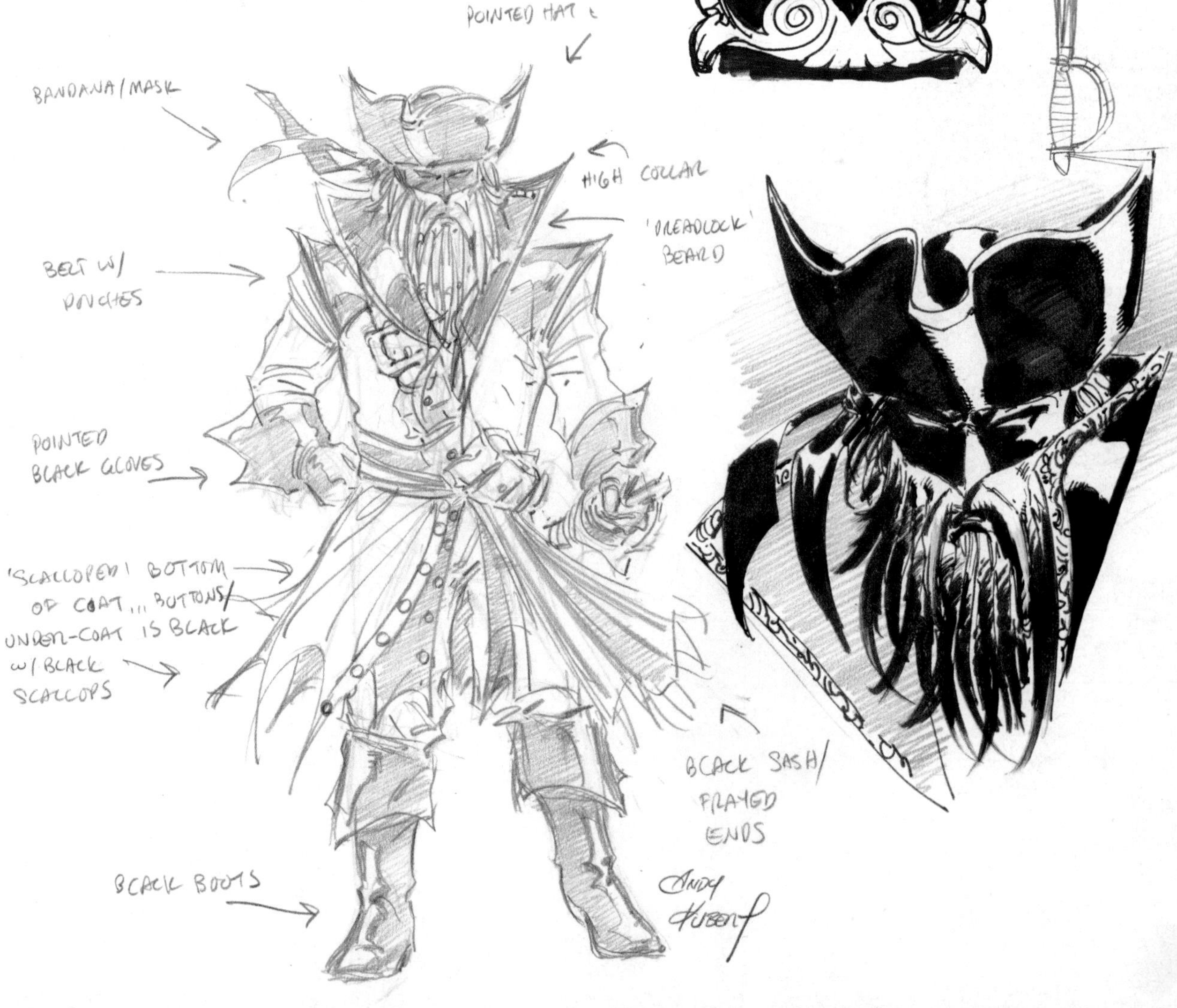
POINTED HAT
BANDANA/MASK
HIGH COLLAR
'DREADLOCK' BEARD
BELT W/ POUCHES
POINTED BLACK GLOVES
'SCALLOPED' BOTTOM OF COAT... BUTTONS/
UNDER-COAT IS BLACK W/ BLACK SCALLOPS
BLACK SASH/ FRAYED ENDS
BLACK BOOTS
ANDY KUBERT

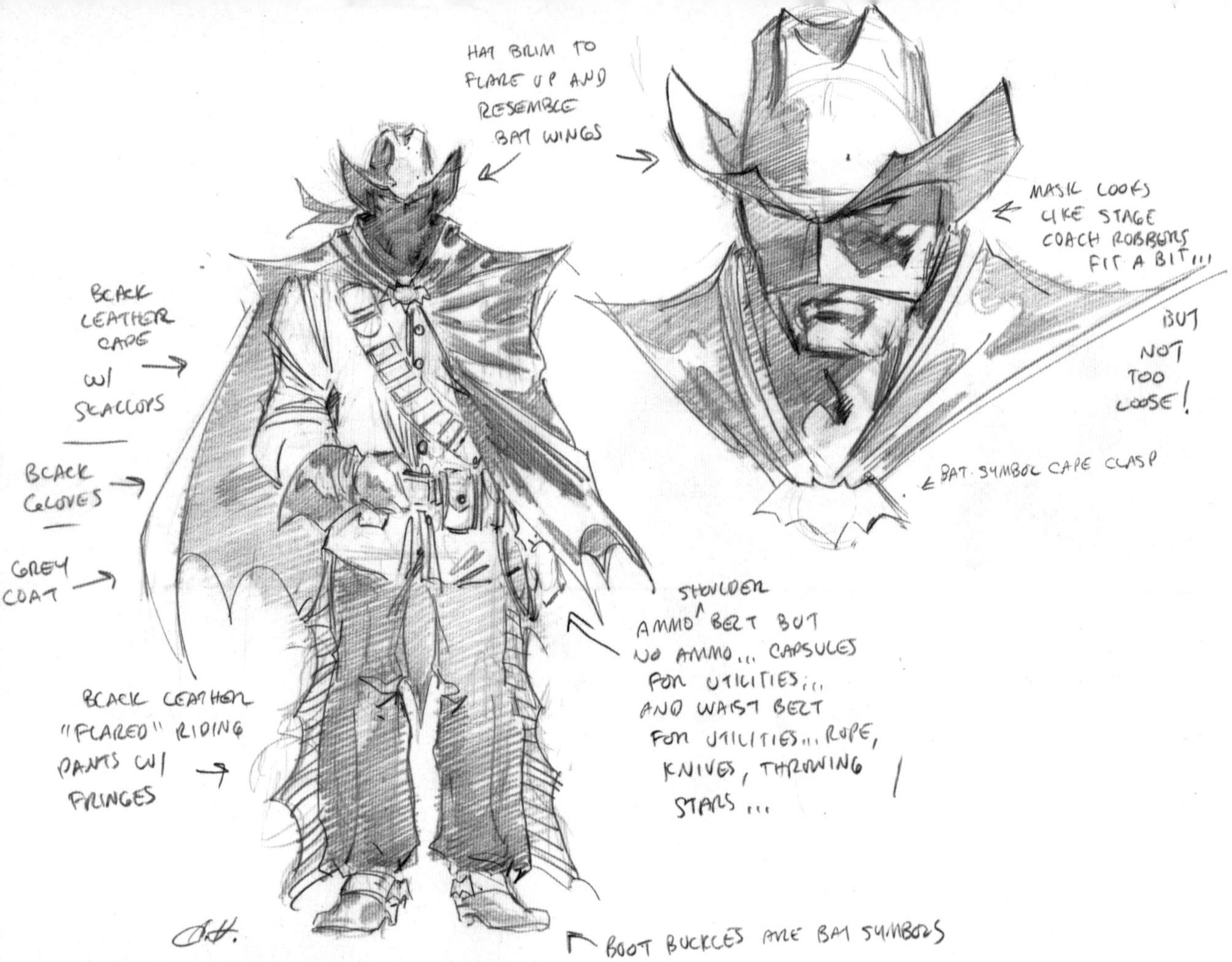
HAT BRIM TO FLARE UP AND RESEMBLE BAT WINGS
MASK LOOKS LIKE STAGE COACH ROBBERS FIT A BIT...
BUT NOT TOO LOOSE!
BAT SYMBOL CAPE CLASP
BLACK LEATHER CAPE W/ SCALLOPS
BLACK GLOVES
GREY COAT
SHOULDER AMMO BELT BUT NO AMMO... CAPSULES FOR UTILITIES... AND WAIST BELT FOR UTILITIES... ROPE, KNIVES, THROWING STARS...
BLACK LEATHER "FLARED" RIDING PANTS W/ FRINGES
BOOT BUCKLES ARE BAT SYMBOLS

Above and right: Character designs by Andy Kubert for issue #4's cover art.

Opposite top: An unused Victorian Batman design by Kubert.

Opposite bottom: Kubert's gangster Batman designs for the cover art to issue #5.

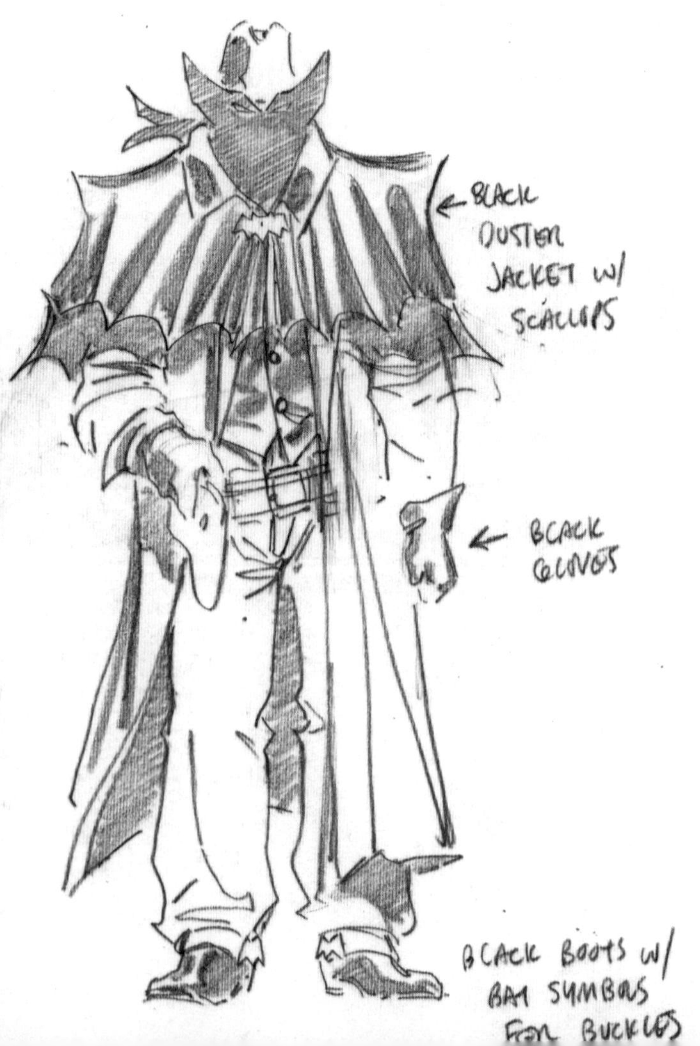
BLACK DUSTER JACKET W/ SCALLOPS
BLACK GLOVES
BLACK BOOTS W/ BAT SYMBOLS FOR BUCKLES

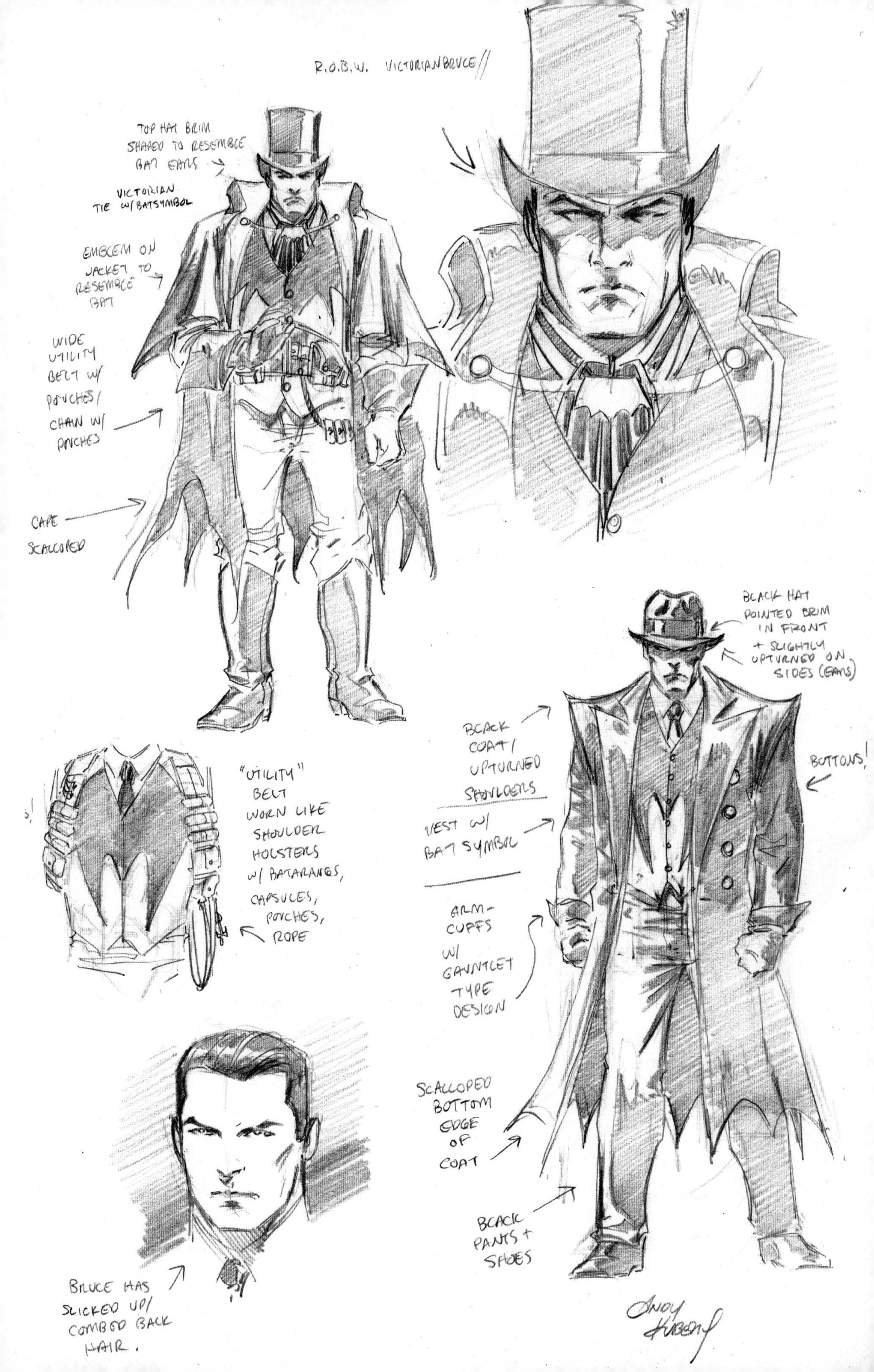
R.O.B.W. VICTORIANBRUCE//
TOP HAT BRIM SHAPED TO RESEMBLE BAT EARS
VICTORIAN TIE W/BATSYMBOL
EMBLEM ON JACKET TO RESEMBLE BAT
WIDE UTILITY BELT W/ POUCHES/ CHAIN W/ POUCHES
CAPE SCALLOPED
BLACK HAT POINTED BRIM IN FRONT + SLIGHTLY UPTURNED ON SIDES (EARS)
BLACK COAT/ UPTURNED SHOULDERS
BUTTONS!
VEST W/ BAT SYMBOL
ARM-CUFFS W/ GAUNTLET TYPE DESIGN
"UTILITY" BELT WORN LIKE SHOULDER HOLSTERS W/ BATARANGS, CAPSULES, POUCHES, ROPE
SCALLOPED BOTTOM EDGE OF COAT
BLACK PANTS + SHOES
BRUCE HAS SLICKED UP/ COMBED BACK HAIR.
Andy Kubert

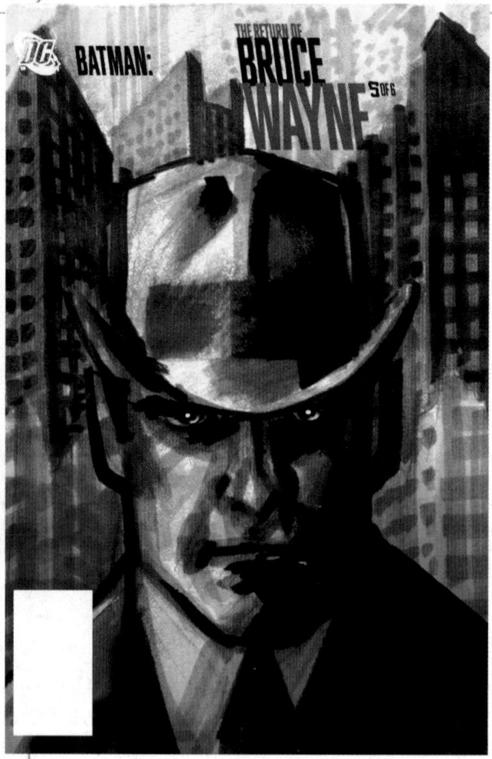
BATMAN:
THE RETURN OF
BRUCE
WAYNE
5 OF 6

Left: A color sketch by Ryan Sook for issue #5's variant cover art.

Below and following pages: Selected page layout thumbnails by Ryan Sook for issue #5.

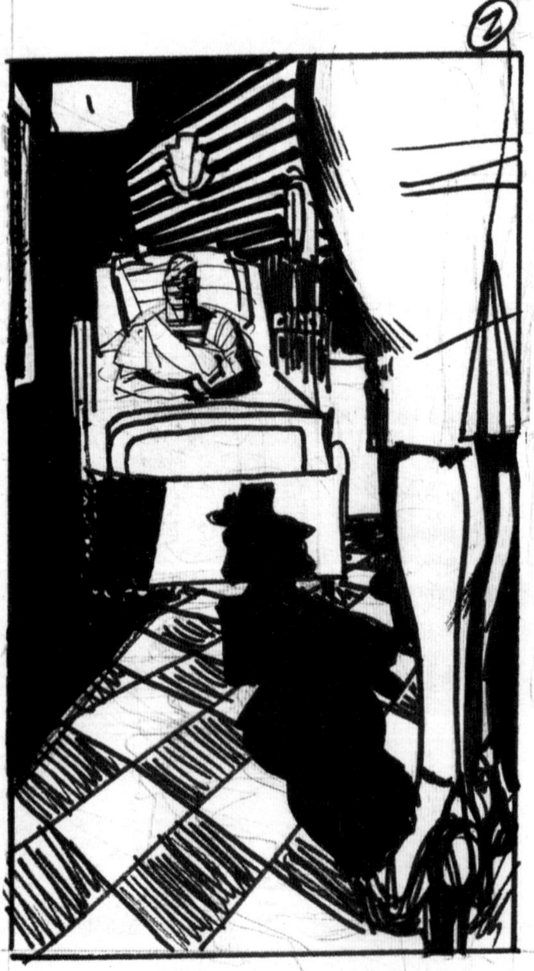
2
1

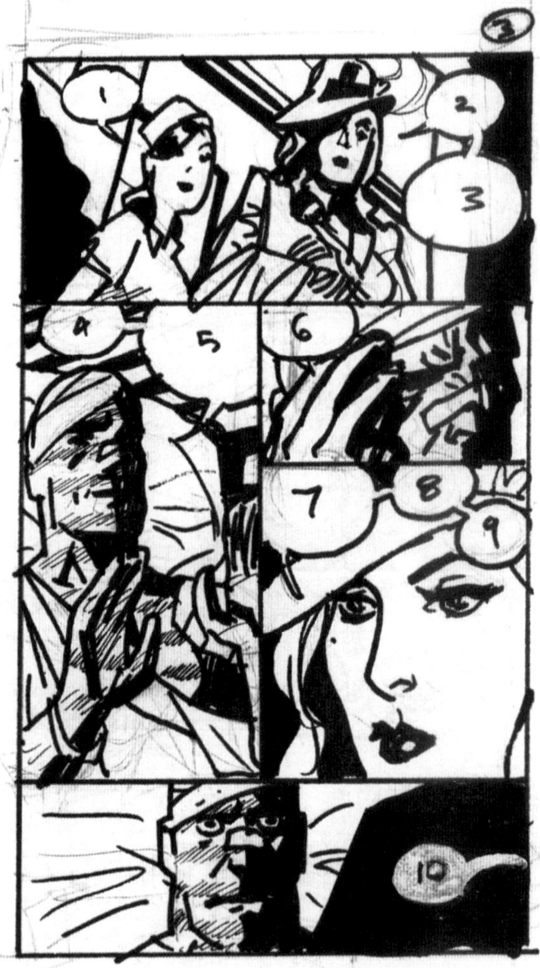
3
1
2
3
4
5
6
7
8
9
10

FULL BLEED

4

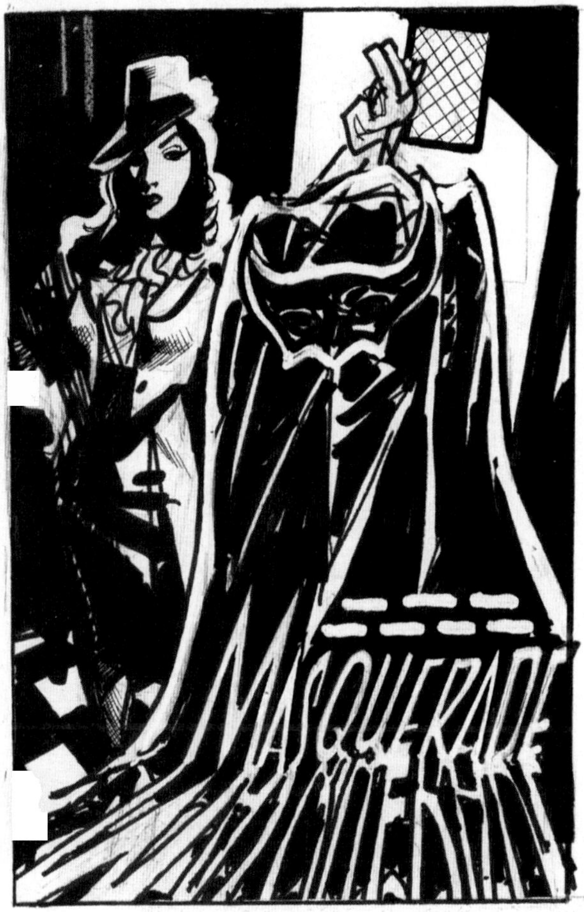
MASQUERADE

5

TURNS ON LAMP

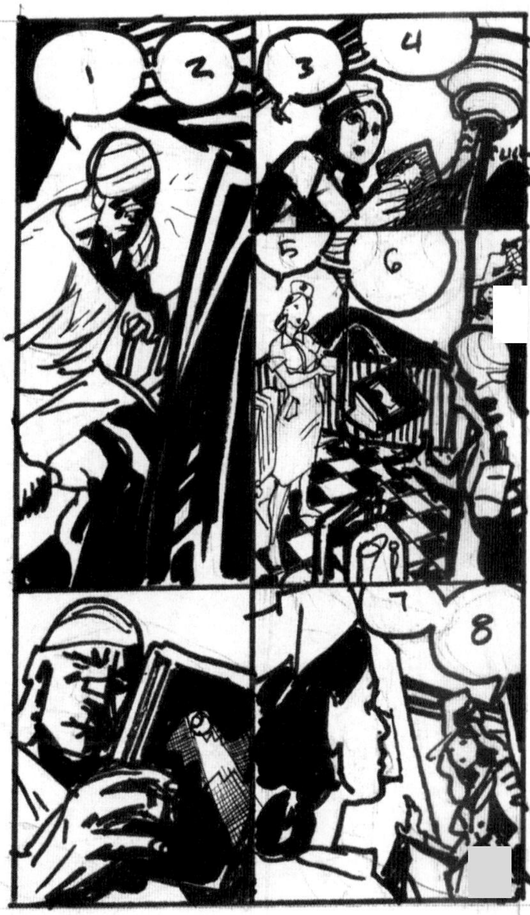
1
2
3
4
5
6
7
8

6

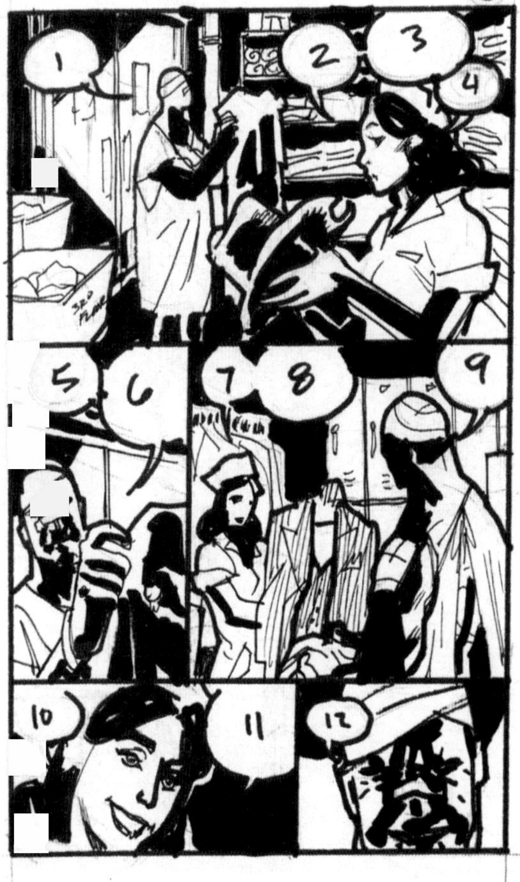
1
2
3
4
5
6
7
8
9
10
11
12

7

CAPTION BECOMES B.GROUND

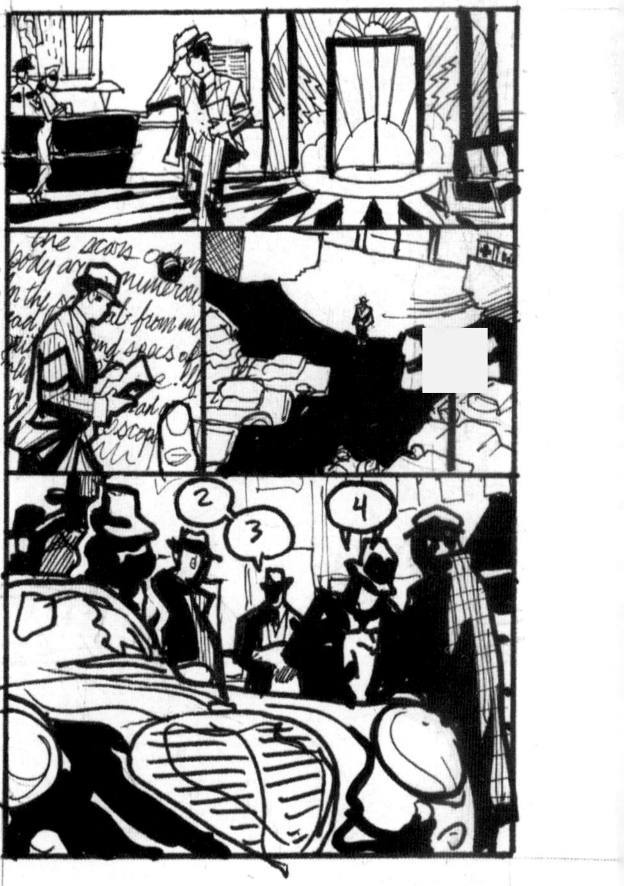
2
3
4

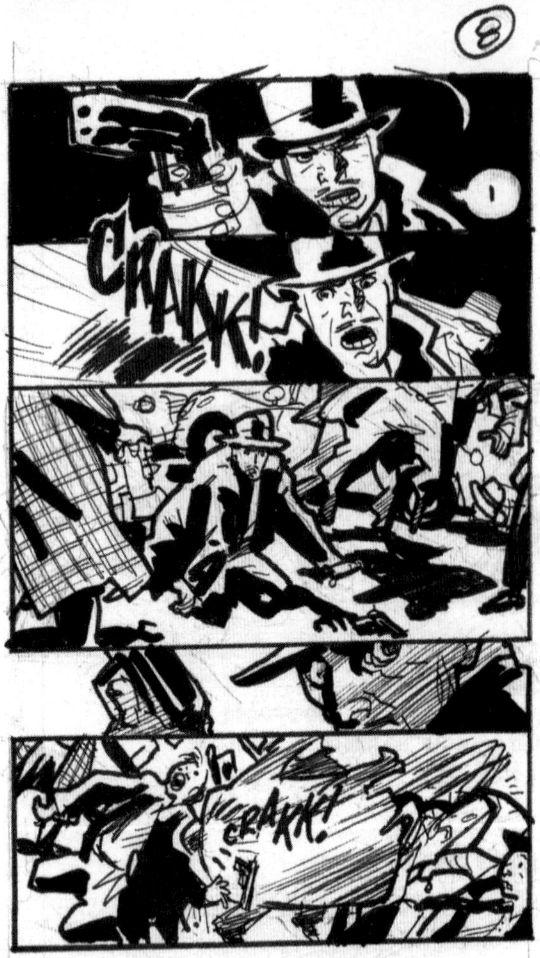
8
1
CRAKK!
CRAKK!

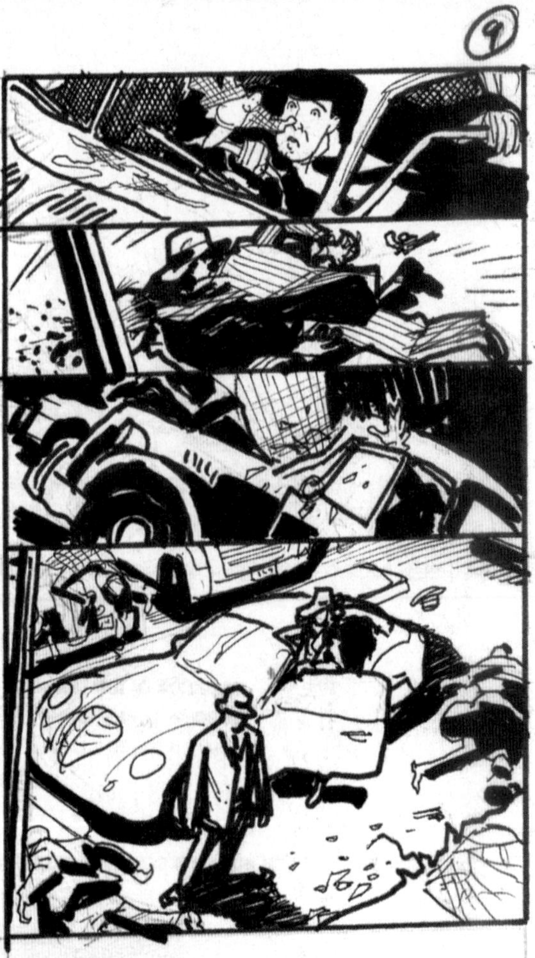
9

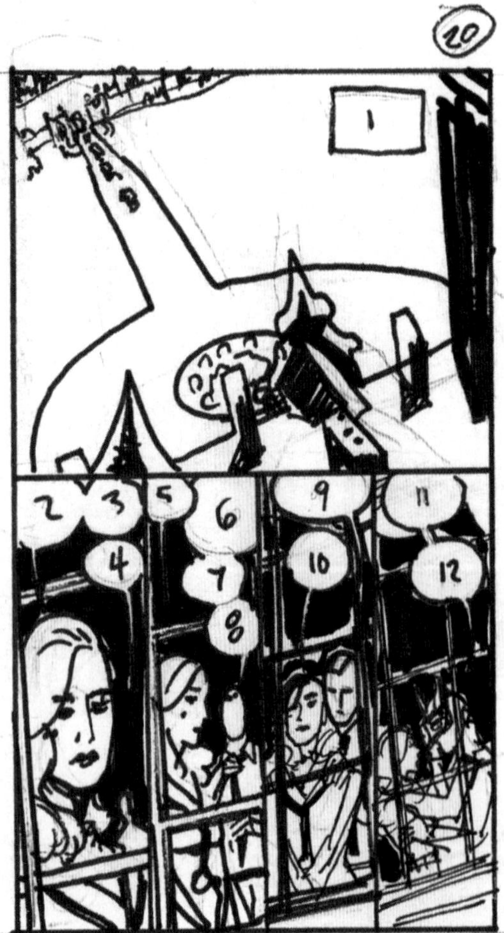
20
1
2
3
4
5
6
7
8
9
10
11
12

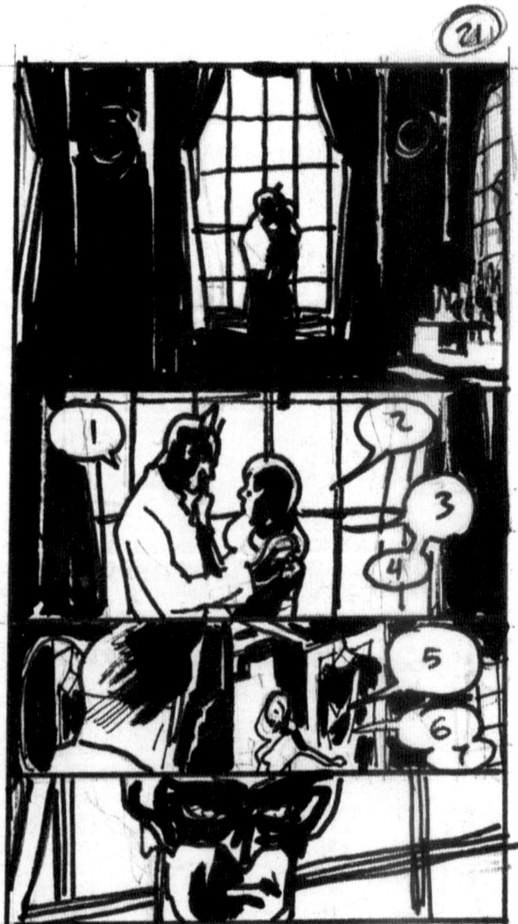
21
1
2
3
4
5
6